ASSOCIATED PRESS STYLEBOOK

2015

AND BRIEFING ON MEDIA LAW

AP

ASSOCIATED PRESS STYLEBOOK

2015

AND BRIEFING ON MEDIA LAW

EDITED BY

David Minthorn
Sally Jacobsen
Paula Froke

www.apstylebook.com

BASIC
BOOKS
A Member of the
Perseus Books Group
New York

Published by Basic Books,
A Member of the Perseus Books Group

Books published by Basic Books are available at special discounts for bulk purchases
in the United States by corporations, institutions, and other organizations.
For more information, please contact the Special Markets Department at the
Perseus Books Group, 2300 Chestnut Street, Suite 200, Philadelphia, PA 19103,
or call (800) 810-4145, ext. 5000, or e-mail special.markets@perseusbooks.com.

Design and content management by Satchmo Publishing Inc.

Library of Congress Control Number: 2015938607
ISBN: 978-0-465-06294-2

10 9 8 7 6 5 4 3 2 1

CONTENTS

FOREWORD

The first Associated Press Stylebook was 60 pages, bound together with staples, a basic guide for newswriting. It has evolved into a comprehensive reference manual that fills more than 500 pages and is published in Spanish as well as English across an array of digital platforms, encompassing the collective wisdom of its readers. Despite drastic changes in the media landscape, one constant remains: The AP Stylebook is a definitive resource for writers.

Today's Stylebook still outlines basic rules on grammar, punctuation, usage and journalistic style, but it also reflects changes in common language, offers guidance on media law, explains AP's news values and principles, and helps to navigate the ever-changing world of social media.

Input from a broad spectrum of readers and users has added nuance and authority.

A team of top AP editors meets throughout the year to make updates and improvements (our thanks and appreciation to Darrell Christian, who retired in 2014 after more than 40 years at the AP, including seven years as an editor of the Stylebook). Contributions come from the AP staff, AP's member news organizations and subscribers, journalism teachers and students, specialists in a host of fields and everyday readers. Indeed, some of the most talked-about changes have come at the suggestion of @APStylebook's Twitter followers.

A work constantly in progress, the Stylebook is updated every year but always with respect for language and commitment to the original goal: to be clear and concise and understandable around the globe, no matter what the news is or where it happens.

However you choose to access it — in print, online or via an app on your smartphone — The Associated Press Stylebook remains an essential tool in newsrooms, classrooms and boardrooms alike, the bible for journalists and anyone who cares about good writing.

GARY PRUITT
President and
Chief Executive Officer

WHAT'S NEW

In this edition of the AP Stylebook

Sports Guidelines have been updated with more than 60 new or revised entries, ranging over baseball playoffs, basketball's NCAA Tournament, O-line and D-line in football, horse racing, injuries, Olympic Games, race distances, soccer tactics, titles and winter sports.

New or updated terms include ACL for anterior cruciate ligament, day to day, double axel, free agent, hat trick, heatstroke, MCL for medial cruciate ligament, Olympian, shoestring catch, Sweet 16, "tiki-taka," Tommy John surgery, trifecta and zonal marking.

An 85-page index of Stylebook terms with page listings has been added to help quickly locate words and definitions. It replaces the Quick Reference Guide of recent years.

The Food chapter has been expanded with nearly three dozen new entries, ranging from amaretto for almond liqueur and BLT for a bacon, lettuce and tomato sandwich to meze for Middle Eastern appetizers, profiterole for a small cream puff and tsimmes, a Jewish sweet stew often made from carrots and dried fruit. New guidance calls for using craft brewery instead of microbrewery for a small, independent beer producer, and avoiding the term preheat and using heat instead: Heat the oven to 350 F.

More than a dozen new entries are in the Fashion chapter. They include Manolo Blahnik, dirndl, Tom Ford, Jean Paul Gaultier, guayabera, Christian Louboutin, neoprene and Alexander Wang. For describing garments, the spelling is short-sleeved with a hyphen.

A new entry covers suicide in news reports. The phrase "committed suicide" should be avoided except in direct quotations from authorities because it may imply an illegal act. Alternate phrases include killed himself, took her own life or died by suicide.

Global warming, which can be used interchangeably with climate change, is another new entry. Climate change is more accurate scientifically to describe the effects of greenhouse gases on the environment, including extreme weather and changes in rainfall patterns, ocean acidification and sea level. But global warming is used in common parlance and is widely accepted.

Other new or updated entries include abaya; Affordable Care Act; airsoft gun; animal welfare activist; Arab Spring; autism spectrum disorder; Crimea; dog walker; drop-down; drive-by; Ebola; execution-style; justify; Kathmandu; National Security Agency; obscenities, profanities and vulgarities; One World Trade Center; privacy; Schengen Area; Uber; and Ulaanbaatar. Entries on militant groups such as Boko Haram and Islamic State are also new this year.

Some terms that were previously in the Social Media Guidelines are now listed in the A-Z section. New entries include favorite, meme and Swarm.

Druze and Wicca are new to the Religion chapter.

The photo section includes our new style for caption signoffs on photos that are not taken by AP staff or freelance photographers, including handout photos and those shared by members. The chapter also updates our policy on handout photos with new byline titles and updated language in the instructions field.

STYLEBOOK KEY

This updated and revised version of The Associated Press Stylebook has been organized like a dictionary. Need the acronym for a government agency? Look under the agency's name. Should you capitalize a word? Check the word itself or the **capitalization** entry. What's the format for baseball boxes? See **baseball**.

Following is a key to the entries:

airport Capitalize as part of a proper name: *LaGuardia Airport, O'Hare International Airport.*

The first name of an individual and the word *international* may be deleted from a formal airport name while the remainder is capitalized: *John F. Kennedy International Airport, Kennedy International Airport* or *Kennedy Airport.* Use whichever is appropriate in the context.

Do not make up names, however. There is no *Boston Airport,* for example. The *Boston airport* (lowercase *airport*) would be acceptable if for some reason the proper name, *Logan International Airport,* were not used.

airstrike

airtight

air traffic controller No hyphen.

airways The system of routes that the federal government has established for airplane traffic.

See the **airline, airlines** entry for its use in carriers' names.

aka Abbreviation for *also known as.*

Alabama Abbreviate *Ala.* in datelines only; spell out in stories. Postal code: *AL*
See **state names**.

Entry words, in alphabetical order, are in **boldface**. They represent the accepted word forms unless otherwise indicated.

Text explains usage.

Examples of correct and incorrect usage are in italics. AP doesn't use italics in news stories.

Many entries simply give the correct spelling, hyphenation and/or capitalization.

Related topics are in **boldface**.

Abbreviate indicates the correct abbreviation of a word.

Other abbreviations used in the Stylebook:

n.: noun	**adj.:** adjective
v.: verb	**adv.:** adverb

a- The rules of **prefixes** apply, but in general no hyphen. Some examples:

achromatic   atonal

AAA Formerly the American Automobile Association.

Headquarters is in Heathrow, Florida.

a, an Use the article *a* before consonant sounds: *a historic event, a one-year term* (sounds as if it begins with a *w*), *a united stand* (sounds like *you*).

Use the article *an* before vowel sounds: *an energy crisis, an honorable man* (the *h* is silent), *an homage* (the *h* is silent), *an NBA record* (sounds like it begins with the letter *e*), *an 1890s celebration*.

A&P Acceptable in all references for *Great Atlantic & Pacific Tea Co. Inc.* Headquarters is in Montvale, New Jersey.

AARP Use only the initials for the organization formerly known as the American Association of Retired Persons.

abaya Robe-like outer garment worn by Muslim women.

abbreviations and acronyms

A few universally recognized abbreviations are required in some circumstances. Some others are acceptable depending on the context. But in general, avoid alphabet soup. Do not use abbreviations or acronyms that the reader would not quickly recognize.

Abbreviations and most acronyms should be avoided in headlines.

Guidance on how to use a particular abbreviation or acronym is provided in entries alphabetized according to the sequence of letters in the word or phrase.

An *acronym* is a word formed from the first letter or letters of a series of words: *laser* (light amplification by stimulated emission of radiation). An *abbreviation* is not an *acronym*.

Some general principles:

BEFORE A NAME: Abbreviate titles when used before a full name: *Dr., Gov., Lt. Gov., Mr., Mrs., Rep., the Rev., Sen.* and certain military designations listed in the **military titles** entry.

For guidelines on how to use titles, see **courtesy titles; legislative titles; military titles; religious titles;** and the entries for the most commonly used titles.

AFTER A NAME: Abbreviate *junior* or *senior* after an individual's name. Abbreviate *company, corporation, incorporated* and *limited* when used after the name of a corporate entity. See entries under these words and **company names.**

In some cases, an academic degree may be abbreviated after an individual's name. See **academic degrees**.

WITH DATES OR NUMERALS: Use the abbreviations *A.D., B.C., a.m., p.m., No.,* and abbreviate certain months when used with the day of the month.

Right: *In 450 B.C.; at 9:30 a.m.; in room No. 6; on Sept. 16.*

Wrong: *Early this a.m. he asked for the No. of your room.* The abbreviations are correct only with figures.

Right: *Early this morning he asked for the number of your room.*

See **months** and individual entries for these other terms:

IN NUMBERED ADDRESSES: Abbreviate *avenue, boulevard* and *street* in numbered addresses: *He lives on Pennsylvania Avenue. He lives at 1600 Pennsylvania Ave.*

See **addresses**.

STATES: The names of certain states and the *United States* are abbreviated with periods in some circumstances.

See **state names; datelines**; and individual entries.

ACCEPTABLE BUT NOT REQUIRED: Some organizations and government agencies are widely recognized by their initials: *CIA, FBI, GOP.*

If the entry for such an organization notes that an abbreviation is acceptable in all references or on second reference, that does not mean that its use should be automatic. Let the context determine, for example, whether to use *Federal Bureau of Investigation* or *FBI.*

See **second reference**.

AVOID AWKWARD CONSTRUCTIONS: Do not follow an organization's full name with an abbreviation or acronym in parentheses or set off by dashes. If an abbreviation or acronym would not be clear on second reference without this arrangement, do not use it.

Names not commonly before the public should not be reduced to acronyms solely to save a few words.

SPECIAL CASES: Many abbreviations are desirable in tabulations and certain types of technical writing. See individual entries.

CAPS, PERIODS: Use capital letters and periods according to the listings in this book. For words not in this book, use the first-listed abbreviation in Webster's New World College Dictionary. Generally, omit periods in acronyms unless the result would spell an unrelated word. But use periods in most two-letter abbreviations: *U.S., U.N., U.K., B.A., B.C. (AP,* a trademark, is an exception. Also, no periods in *GI, ID* and *EU.*) In headlines, do not use periods in abbreviations, unless required for clarity.

Use all caps, but no periods, in longer abbreviations when the individual letters are pronounced: *ABC, CIA, FBI.*

Use only an initial cap and then lowercase for abbreviations and acronyms of more than five letters, unless listed otherwise in this Stylebook or Webster's New World College Dictionary.

ABC Acceptable in all references for *American Broadcasting Cos.* (the plural is part of the corporate name). Owned by The Walt Disney Co.

ABCs

able-bodied

ABM, ABMs Acceptable in all references for *anti-ballistic missile(s),* but the term should be defined in the story. (The hyphen is an exception to Webster's New World College Dictionary.)

Avoid the redundant phrase *ABM missiles.*

Aborigine Capitalize when referring to Australian indigenous people. The adjective is *aboriginal*. *The aboriginal people.*

abortion Use *anti-abortion* instead of *pro-life* and *pro-abortion rights* instead of *pro-abortion* or *pro-choice*. Avoid *abortionist*, which connotes a person who performs clandestine abortions.

aboveboard

absent-minded

Abu Sayyaf Muslim separatist group based in the southern islands of the Philippines. The name is Arabic for *father of the bearer of the sword*.

academic degrees If mention of degrees is necessary to establish someone's credentials, the preferred form is to avoid an abbreviation and use instead a phrase such as: *John Jones, who has a doctorate in psychology.*

Use an apostrophe in *bachelor's degree, a master's*, etc., but there is no possessive in *Bachelor of Arts* or *Master of Science.*

Also: an *associate degree* (no possessive).

Use such abbreviations as *B.A., M.A., LL.D.* and *Ph.D.* only when the need to identify many individuals by degree on first reference would make the preferred form cumbersome. Use these abbreviations only after a full name — never after just a last name.

When used after a name, an academic abbreviation is set off by commas: *John Snow, Ph.D., spoke.*

Do not precede a name with a courtesy title for an academic degree and follow it with the abbreviation for the degree in the same reference.

See **doctor, Master of Arts, Master of Science, Master of Business Administration**.

academic departments Use lowercase except for words that are proper nouns or adjectives: *the department of history, the history department, the department of English, the English department*, or when *department* is part of the official and formal name: *University of Connecticut Department of Economics.*

academic titles Capitalize and spell out formal titles such as *chancellor, chairman*, etc., when they precede a name. Lowercase elsewhere.

Lowercase modifiers such as *department* in *department Chairman Jerome Wiesner.*

See **doctor** and **titles**.

academy See **military academies**.

Academy Awards Presented annually by the Academy of Motion Picture Arts and Sciences. Also known as the *Oscars*. (Both *Academy Awards* and *Oscars* are trademarks.)

Lowercase *the academy* and *the awards* whenever they stand alone.

accent marks Do not use any diacritical or accent marks because they cause garble for some users.

accept, except *Accept* means to receive.

Except means to exclude.

accommodate

accounts payable Current liabilities or debts of a business which must be paid within one year.

accounts receivable Amounts due to a company for merchandise or services sold on credit. These are short-term assets.

accused A person is *accused of*, not *with*, a crime.

To avoid any suggestion that an individual is being judged before a trial, do not use a phrase such as *accused slayer John Jones;* use *John Jones, accused of the slaying.*

For guidelines on related words, see **allege**; **arrest**; and **indict**.

Ace A trademark for a brand of elastic bandage. *Elastic bandage* is preferred in all references.

Achilles tendon No apostrophe for the tendon connecting the back of the heel to the calf muscles. But it's *Achilles' heel*, with an apostrophe, for a vulnerable spot.

acknowledgment

acquisition The process of buying or acquiring some asset. The term can refer to the purchase of a block of stock or, more often, to the acquisition of an entire company.

acre Equal to 43,560 square feet or 4,840 square yards. The metric equivalent is 0.4 (two-fifths) of a hectare or 4,047 square meters.

One square mile is 640 acres.

To convert to hectares, multiply by 0.4 (5 acres x 0.4 equals 2 hectares).

Use square miles to describe the size of wildfires.

See **wildfires** and **hectare**.

acronyms See **abbreviations and acronyms**.

act Capitalize when part of the name for pending or implemented legislation: *the Taft-Hartley Act.*

ACT Use only the initials in referring to the previously designated *American College Testing.*

acting Always lowercase, but capitalize any formal title that may follow before a name: *acting Mayor Peter Barry.*

See **titles**.

act numbers Use Arabic figures and capitalize *act*: *Act 1*; *Act 2, Scene 2*. But: *the first act, the second act.* See **numerals**.

actor (man) **actress** (woman) It is acceptable to use *actor* for a woman if she prefers it.

A.D. Acceptable in all references for *anno Domini*: in the year of the Lord.

Because the full phrase would read *in the year of the Lord 96*, the abbreviation A.D. goes before the figure for the year: *A.D. 96.*

Do not write: *The fourth century A.D. The fourth century* is sufficient. If *A.D.* is not specified with a year, the year is presumed to be A.D.

See **B.C.**

addresses Use the abbreviations *Ave., Blvd.* and *St.* only with a numbered address: *1600 Pennsylvania Ave.* Spell them out and capitalize when part of a formal street name without a number: *Pennsylvania Avenue.* Lowercase and spell out when used alone or with more than one street name: *Massachusetts and Pennsylvania avenues.*

All similar words (*alley, drive, road, terrace*, etc.) always are spelled out. Capitalize them when part of a formal name without a number; lowercase when used alone or with two or more names.

Always use figures for an address number: *9 Morningside Circle.*

Spell out and capitalize *First* through *Ninth* when used as street names; use figures for *10th* and above: *7 Fifth Ave., 100 21st St.*

Abbreviate compass points used to indicate directional ends of a street or quadrants of a city in a numbered address: *222 E. 42nd St., 562 W. 43rd St., 600 K St. NW*. Do not abbreviate if the number is omitted: *East 42nd Street, West 43rd Street, K Street Northwest*. No periods in quadrant abbreviations — NW, SE — unless customary locally.

See **highway designations**.

Use periods in the abbreviation *P.O.* for P.O. Box numbers.

See **numerals**.

adjectives The abbreviation *adj.* is used in this book to identify the spelling of the adjectival forms of words that frequently are misspelled.

The **comma** entry provides guidance on punctuating a series of adjectives.

The **hyphen** entry provides guidance on handling compound modifiers used before a noun.

adjustable-rate mortgage A mortgage that has a fixed interest rate for a short period of time and then resets, usually yearly, over the life of the loan, based on an index tied to changes in market interest rates. *ARM* should be used only in direct quotes.

ad-lib

administration Lowercase: *the administration, the president's administration, the governor's administration, the Obama administration*.

See **government, junta, regime, administration** for distinctions that apply in using these terms.

administrative law judge This is the federal title for the position formerly known as *hearing examiner*. Capitalize it when used as a formal title before a name.

To avoid the long title, seek a construction that sets the title off by commas: *The administrative law judge, John Williams, disagreed.*

administrator Never abbreviate. Capitalize when used as a formal title before a name.

See **titles**.

admiral See **military titles**.

admissible

admit, admitted These words may in some contexts give the erroneous connotation of wrongdoing.

A person who acknowledges that he is a recovering alcoholic, for example, is not *admitting* it. *Said* is usually sufficient.

ad nauseam

adopt, approve, enact, pass Amendments, ordinances, resolutions and rules are *adopted* or *approved*.

Bills are *passed*.

Laws are *enacted*.

adoption The adoptive status of a child or his or her parents should be mentioned only when its relevance is made clear in the story. If relevant, use the term *biological parents* to refer to the birth mother and father. Preferred phrasing: *A child is placed for adoption*, rather than *given up for adoption*.

Adrenalin A trademark for the synthetic or chemically extracted forms of epinephrine, a substance produced by the adrenal glands.

The nonproprietary terms are *epinephrine hydrochloride* or *adrenaline*.

adult A person who has reached 18. See **privacy**.

Advance Publications Inc. Privately held company whose holdings include Conde Nast Publications, Parade Publications and newspapers in more than 25 U.S. cities, including The Star-Ledger of Newark, New Jersey, and The Oregonian of Portland, Oregon. Headquarters is in New York.

adverbs The abbreviation *adv.* is used in this book to identify the spelling of adverbial forms of words frequently misspelled.

See the **hyphen** entry in the **Punctuation** chapter for guidelines on when an adverb should be followed by a hyphen in constructing a compound modifier.

adverse, averse *Adverse* means unfavorable: *He predicted adverse weather.*

Averse means reluctant, opposed: *She is averse to change.*

adviser Not *advisor.*

advisory

Aer Lingus Headquarters of this airline is in Dublin, Ireland.

Aeroflot Headquarters of this airline is in Moscow.

Aeromexico Headquarters of this airline is in Mexico City.

aesthetic

affect, effect *Affect*, as a verb, means to influence: *The game will affect the standings.*

Affect, as a noun, is best avoided. It occasionally is used in psychology to describe an emotion, but there is no need for it in everyday language.

Effect, as a verb, means to cause: *He will effect many changes in the company.*

Effect, as a noun, means result: *The effect was overwhelming. He miscalculated the effect of his actions. It was a law of little effect.*

Affordable Care Act Shorthand for the formal title of the health care overhaul that President Barack Obama signed into law in 2010. Its full name is Patient Protection and Affordable Care Act. Use *President Barack Obama's health care law* or the *health care law* on first reference. *"Obamacare"* in quotation marks is acceptable on second reference. *Affordable Care Act* can be used on subsequent references when necessary to refer to the law, but should be used sparingly. Polling indicates that not all Americans know the law by its formal name.

Afghan The term for the people and culture of Afghanistan. *Afghani* is the *Afghan* unit of currency.

AFL-CIO Acceptable in all references for the *American Federation of Labor and Congress of Industrial Organizations*. Headquarters is in Washington.

A-frame

African Of or pertaining to Africa, or any of its peoples or languages.

In some countries of Africa, *colored* is used to describe those of mixed white and black ancestry. In other societies *colored* is considered a derogatory word.

Because of the ambiguity, avoid the term in favor of a phrase such as *mixed racial ancestry*. If the word cannot be avoided, place it in quotation marks and provide its meaning.

See **colored**.

African-American Acceptable for an American black person of African descent. Also acceptable is *black.* The terms are not necessarily interchangeable. People from Caribbean nations, for example, generally refer to themselves as *Caribbean-American.* Follow a person's preference. See **nationalities and races** and **race**.

African Union The African Union, established in 2002 to succeed the Organization of African Unity, has the following members:

Algeria, Angola, Benin, Botswana, Burkina Faso, Burundi, Cameroon, Cape Verde, Central African Republic, Chad, Comoros, Congo, Djibouti, Egypt, Equatorial Guinea, Eritrea, Ethiopia, Gabon, Gambia, Ghana, Guinea-Bissau, Guinea, Ivory Coast, Kenya, Lesotho, Liberia, Libya, Madagascar, Malawi, Mali, Mauritania, Mauritius, Mozambique, Namibia, Niger, Nigeria, Republic of Congo, Rwanda, Sao Tome and Principe, Senegal, Seychelles, Sierra Leone, Somalia, South Africa, South Sudan, Sudan, Swaziland, Tanzania, Togo, Tunisia, Uganda, Western Sahara, Zambia, Zimbabwe.

after- No hyphen after this prefix when it is used to form a noun:

aftereffect   afterthought

Follow *after* with a hyphen when it is used to form compound modifiers:

after-dinner drink   after-theater snack

after-party

afterward Not *afterwards.*

Agence France-Presse A global news agency with headquarters in Paris. *AFP* acceptable on second reference.

agent Lowercase unless it is a formal title used before a name.

In the FBI, the formal title is *special agent.* In most cases, make it *agent William Smith* or *FBI agent William Smith.*

See **titles**.

ages Use when deemed relevant to the situation. If someone is quoted as saying, *I'm too old to get another job,* the age is relevant. Generally, use ages for profiles, obituaries, significant career milestones and achievements unusual for the age. Do not use ages for sources commenting or providing information in an official capacity. Appropriate background, such as a *parent of two young children* or a *World War II veteran,* may suffice instead of the actual age.

Always use figures. *The girl is 15 years old; the law is 8 years old; the 101-year-old house.* When the context does not require *years* or *years old,* the figure is presumed to be *years.*

Use hyphens for ages expressed as adjectives before a noun or as substitutes for a noun.

Examples: *A 5-year-old boy,* but *the boy is 5 years old. The boy, 7, has a sister, 10. The woman, 26, has a daughter 2 months old. The race is for 3-year-olds. The woman is in her 30s* (no apostrophe).

See also **boy**, **girl**, **infant**, **youth**, **numerals** and **elderly**.

See **comma** in punctuation guidelines.

aggregator A website or feed that amasses content from other sources and assembles it in a form digestible to its users.

agnostic, atheist An *agnostic* is a person who believes it is impossible to know whether there is a God.

An *atheist* is a person who believes there is no God.

A.H. Belo Corp. Owner of The Dallas Morning News and the

Denton Record-Chronicle in Texas. Headquarters is in Dallas.

aid, aide *Aid* is assistance.

An *aide* is a person who serves as an assistant.

aide-de-camp, aides-de-camp A military officer who serves as assistant and confidential secretary to a superior.

AIDS Acceptable in all references for *acquired immune deficiency syndrome*, sometimes called *acquired immunodeficiency syndrome*.

AIDS is a disease that weakens the immune system, gradually destroying the body's ability to fight infections and certain cancers. It is caused by *human immunodeficiency virus*, or *HIV*. (*HIV virus* is redundant.)

HIV is spread most often through sexual contact; contaminated needles or syringes shared by drug abusers; infected blood or blood products; and from infected women to their babies at birth or through breast-feeding.

Several types of tests are available for *HIV*. One is a blood test that looks for antibodies the body has made to defend against *HIV*. Other tests look for parts of the virus itself in blood. Avoid using *HIV/AIDS* construction. People can be infected with the virus and not have *AIDS*; they do not have *AIDS* until they develop serious symptoms. Many remain infected but apparently healthy for years.

ain't A dialectical or nonstandard contraction. Use it only in quoted matter or special contexts.

air bag Two words.

air base Two words. Follow the practice of the U.S. Air Force, which uses *air force base* as part of the proper name for its bases in the United States and *air base* for its installations abroad. Some bases have become joint bases with other services.

On second reference: *the Air Force base, the air base,* or *the base.*

Do not abbreviate, even in datelines:

LACKLAND AIR FORCE BASE, Texas (AP) —

JOINT BASE ANDREWS, Md. (AP) —

Air Canada Headquarters of this airline is in Saint-Laurent, Canada.

Air China Headquarters of this airline is in Beijing.

air-condition, air-conditioned (v. and adj.) The nouns are: *air conditioner, air conditioning.*

aircraft names Use a hyphen when changing from letters to figures; no hyphen when adding a letter after figures.

Some examples of aircraft: *B-1, C-5A, FH-227, F-15 Eagle, F-16 Falcon, MiG-29, Tu-154, Il-96, Boeing 737-800, 747, 747B. Airbus A380, A380F* (no hyphen) is an exception.

This hyphenation principle is the one used most frequently by manufacturers and users. Apply it in all cases for consistency. For other elements of a name, use the form adopted by the manufacturer or user. If in doubt, consult IHS Jane's All the World's Aircraft.

NO QUOTES: Do not use quotation marks for aircraft with names: *Air Force One, the Spirit of St. Louis.*

AVOID PROMOTIONAL NAMES: *Boeing 787*, not Dreamliner.

PLURALS: *747s.* But: *747B's.* (As noted in plurals, the apostrophe is used in forming the plural of a single letter.)

SEQUENCE: Use Arabic figures to establish the sequence of aircraft, spacecraft and missiles: *Apollo 10.* Do not use hyphens.

See **numerals**.

aircraft terms Use *engine*, not *motor*, for the units that propel aircraft: a *twin-engine* plane (not *twin engined*).

Use *jet plane* or *jetliner* to describe only those aircraft driven solely by jet engines. Use *turboprop* to describe an aircraft on which the jet engine is geared to a propeller. Turboprops sometimes are called *propjets*.

See **engine, motor**.

airfare One word.

air force Capitalize when referring to U.S. forces: *the U.S. Air Force, the Air Force, Air Force regulations.* Do not use the abbreviation *USAF*.

Congress established the Army Air Forces (note the *s*) in 1941. Prior to that, the air arm was known as the U.S. Army Air Corps. The U.S. Air Force (no *s*) was created as a separate service in 1947.

Use lowercase for the forces of other nations: *the Israeli air force.*

This approach has been adopted for consistency, because many foreign nations do not use *air force* as the proper name.

See **military academies** and **military titles**.

air force base See **air base**.

Air Force One The Air Force applies this name to any of its aircraft the president of the United States may be using.

In ordinary usage, however, *Air Force One* is the name of the Air Force plane normally reserved for the president's use.

Air France Corporate name is *Air France-KLM.* Headquarters of this airline is in Roissy, France.

Air India Headquarters of this airline is in Mumbai, India.

airline, airlines Capitalize *airlines, air lines* and *airways* when used as part of a proper airline name.

Companies that use *Airlines* in the title include American, Hawaiian, Japan, Southwest and United.

Companies that use *Airways* include British, JetBlue and Qantas.

Delta uses *Air Lines.*

Companies that use none of these include Aer Lingus, Aeromexico, Air Canada, Air France, Air India, Alitalia, Emirates and Iberia.

On second reference, use just the proper name (*Delta*), an abbreviation if applicable, or the airline. Acceptable abbreviations are *ANA* for *All Nippon Airways, BA* for *British Airways* and *JAL* for *Japan Airlines.* Use airlines when referring to more than one line.

Do not use *air line, air lines* or *airways* in generic references to an airline.

Major U.S. airlines, where they are headquartered, and their parent companies, where applicable:

Alaska Airlines, Seattle, owned by Alaska Air Group Inc.

Allegiant Air, Las Vegas, owned by Allegiant Travel Co.

American Airlines, Fort Worth, Texas, owned by American Airlines Group Inc. See **American Airlines**.

Delta Air Lines Inc., Atlanta

Hawaiian Airlines, Honolulu, owned by Hawaiian Holdings Inc.

JetBlue Airways Corp., New York

Mesa Air Group Inc., Phoenix

Republic Airways, Indianapolis, owned by Republic Airways Holdings Inc.

SkyWest Inc., St. George, Utah

Southwest Airlines Co., Dallas

Spirit Airlines Inc., Miramar, Fla.

United Airlines, Chicago, owned by United Continental Holdings Inc. See **United Airlines**.

US Airways, Fort Worth, Texas, owned by American Airlines Group Inc. See **US Airways Group**.

Virgin America Inc., Burlingame, Calif.

Major international airlines, where they are headquartered, and their parent companies, where applicable.

Air Canada, Saint-Laurent, Quebec

Air China Ltd., Beijing

Air France, Roissy, France, owned by Air France-KLM

Alitalia, Rome

All Nippon Airways Co. Ltd., Tokyo

Avianca Airlines, Bogota, Columbia, owned by Avianca Holdings S.A.

British Airways PLC, Hounslow, England, owned by International Consolidated Airlines Group S.A.

Cathay Pacific Airways Ltd., Hong Kong

China Eastern Airlines Corp., Shanghai

China Southern Airlines Co., Guangzhou, China

Copa Airlines, Panama City, Panama, owned by Copa Holdings, S.A.

Emirates, Dubai, United Arab Emirates, owned by The Emirates Group

Ethiad Airways, Abu Dhabi

Iberia, Madrid, owned by International Consolidated Airlines Group S.A.

Japan Airlines Corp., Tokyo

KLM Royal Dutch Airlines, Amstelveen, Netherlands, owned by Air France-KLM

Korean Airlines Co. Ltd., Seoul, South Korea

LAN Airlines, Santiago, Chile, part of the LATAM Airlines Group S.A.

Lufthansa, Cologne, Germany, owned by Deutsche Lufthansa AG

Malaysia Airlines, Subang, Malaysia, owned by Malaysia Airlines System Berhad

Qantas Airways Ltd., Mascot, Australia

Qatar Airways, Doha, Qatar, owned by Qatar Airways Company Q.C.S.C.

Ryanair Holdings PLC, Dublin

Singapore Airlines, Singapore

TAM Airlines, Santiago, Chile, part of the LATAM Airlines Group S.A.

Thai Airways International PLC, Bangkok

Turkish Airlines, Istanbul

Virgin Atlantic Airways Ltd., Crawley, England

airmail

airman See **military titles**.

Air National Guard

airport Capitalize as part of a proper name: *LaGuardia Airport,* *O'Hare International Airport.*

The first name of an individual and the word *international* may be deleted from a formal airport name while the remainder is capitalized: *John F. Kennedy International Airport, Kennedy International Airport,* or *Kennedy Airport.* Use whichever is appropriate in the context.

Do not make up names, however. There is no *Boston Airport,* for example. The *Boston airport* (lowercase *airport*) would be acceptable if for some reason the proper name, *Logan International Airport,* were not used.

airsoft gun A gun that commonly shoots plastic spheres, typically propelled by compressed air or springs. *Pellet gun* is acceptable on first reference.

airstrike

airtight

air traffic controller No hyphen.

airways The system of routes that the federal government has established for airplane traffic.
See the **airline, airlines** entry for its use in carriers' names.

aka Abbreviation for *also known as*.

Alabama Abbreviate *Ala.* in datelines only; spell out in stories. Postal code: *AL*
See **state names**.

Al-Aqsa The mosque completed in the eighth century atop the Haram al-Sharif, or *Noble Sanctuary*, in the Old City of Jerusalem; Arabs also use *Al-Aqsa* to refer to the whole area, which houses the Dome of the Rock shrine, too. To Jews the area is known as the *Temple Mount*, the site of the ancient Jewish temples.

Alaska Do not abbreviate in datelines or stories. Largest land area of the 50 states. Postal code: *AK*
See **state names**.

Alaska Air Group Inc. Headquarters of this airline is in Seattle. *Alaska Airlines* is subsidiary.

Alaska Native See **Indians**.

Alaska Standard Time The time zone used in all of Alaska, except the western Aleutian Islands and St. Lawrence Island, which are on *Hawaii-Aleutian Standard Time*.
There is also an *Alaska Daylight Time*.
See **time zones**.

Alberta A province of western Canada. Do not abbreviate.

See **datelines**.

albino, albinos

Alcoa Inc. Formerly named Aluminum Company of America. *Alcoa* also is a city in Tennessee.

alcoholic Use *recovering*, not *reformed*, in referring to those who have the disease of alcoholism.

Alcoholics Anonymous *AA* is acceptable on second reference.

alderman Do not abbreviate. See **legislative titles**.

alert See **weather terms**.

Alibaba Group Holding Ltd.
Chinese e-commerce site owner that raised a record $25 billion in an initial public offering of stock completed in September 2014. Its websites include Taobao, Tmall and Alibaba. Yahoo Inc. acquired a large stake in Alibaba for $1 billion in 2005. After selling some of its Alibaba stock in 2012 and 2014, Yahoo announced plans in January 2015 to spin off its remaining 15 percent stake into a newly created holding company.

A-list

Alitalia Airlines Headquarters of this airline is in Rome.

Al-Jazeera Pan-Arab satellite television news network based in Doha, Qatar. *Al-Jazeera America* is a sister network broadcast and based in the United States.

all- Use a hyphen:
all-around (not all-round)   all-out
all-clear   all-star
See **all right** and the **all time, all-time** entries.

Allah The Arabic word for God. The word *God* should be used, unless the Arabic name is used in a quote written or spoken in English.

Allahu akbar The Arabic phrase for *God is great.*

allege The word must be used with great care.

Some guidelines:

—Avoid any suggestion that the writer is making an allegation.

—Specify the source of an allegation. In a criminal case, it should be an arrest record, an indictment or the statement of a public official connected with the case.

—Use *alleged bribe* or similar phrase when necessary to make it clear that an unproved action is not being treated as fact. Be sure that the source of the charge is specified elsewhere in the story.

—Avoid, where possible, *alleged victim.* It is too easily construed as skepticism of a victim's account.

—Avoid redundant uses of *alleged.* It is proper to say: *The district attorney alleged that she took a bribe.* Or: *The district attorney accused her of taking a bribe.* But not: *The district attorney accused her of allegedly taking a bribe.*

—Do not use *alleged* to describe an event that is known to have occurred, when the dispute is over who participated in it. Do not say: *He attended the alleged meeting* when what you mean is: *He allegedly attended the meeting.*

—Do not use *alleged* as a routine qualifier. Instead, use a word such as *apparent, ostensible* or *reputed.*

For guidelines on related words, see **accused**; **arrest**; and **indict**.

Allegheny Mountains Or simply: *the Alleghenies.*

Allegiant Air Airline is owned by Allegiant Travel Co. Headquarters is in Las Vegas.

alley Do not abbreviate. See **addresses**.

allies, allied Capitalize *allies* or *allied* only when referring to the combination of the United States and its Allies during World War I or World War II: *The Allies defeated Germany. He was in the Allied invasion of France.*

All Nippon Airways Headquarters of this airline is in Tokyo.

all right Never *alright.* Hyphenate only if used colloquially as a compound modifier: *He is an all-right guy.*

all-terrain vehicle *ATV* is acceptable on second reference.

all time, all-time An *all-time high*, but *the greatest runner of all time.*

Avoid the redundant phrase *all-time record.*

allude, refer To *allude* to something is to speak of it without specifically mentioning it.

To *refer* is to mention it directly.

allusion, illusion *Allusion* means an indirect reference: *The allusion was to his opponent's war record.*

Illusion means an unreal or false impression: *The scenic director created the illusion of choppy seas.*

alma mater

al-Qaida Muslim militant group founded by Osama bin Laden that carried out the attacks in the United States on Sept. 11, 2001. Bin Laden was killed by U.S. forces in Pakistan in May 2011. Al-Qaida's current leader is Ayman al-Zawahri.

Affiliated groups include:

al-Qaida in the Arabian Peninsula, operating in Yemen and Saudi Arabia.

Nusra Front, operating in Syria.

al-Qaida in the Islamic Maghreb, operating in the Sahel region, a region along the Sahara Desert stretching across North Africa.

Khorasan group, an al-Qaida cell that the United States says operated in Syria to plot attacks on the U.S.

Al-Quds The Arabic name for Jerusalem; it means *the holy*.

al-Shabab The preferred spelling for the Somali militant group.

also-ran (n.)

altar, alter An *altar* is a tablelike platform used in a religious service. *To alter* is to change.

Altria Group Inc. Headquarters is in Richmond, Virginia.

alumnus, alumni, alumna, alumnae Use *alumnus* (*alumni* in the plural) when referring to a man who has attended a school.

Use *alumna* (*alumnae* in the plural) for similar references to a woman.

Use *alumni* when referring to a group of men and women.

Alzheimer's disease A progressive, irreversible neurological disorder and the most common form of dementia. Most victims are older than 65, but Alzheimer's can strike in the 40s or 50s.

Symptoms include gradual memory loss, impairment of judgment, disorientation, personality change, difficulty in learning and loss of language skills.

No cure is known.

AM Acceptable in all references to the *amplitude modulation* system of radio transmission.

ambassador Use for both men and women. Capitalize as a formal title before a name.

See **titles**.

Amber Alert A procedure for rapidly publicizing the disappearance of a child.

amendments to the Constitution Use *First Amendment*, *10th Amendment*, etc.

Colloquial references to the Fifth Amendment's protection against self-incrimination are best avoided, but where appropriate: *He took the Fifth seven times.*

American An acceptable description for a citizen of the United States.

American Airlines Headquarters is in Fort Worth, Texas. Parent company is American Airlines Group Inc. The company is the result of the 2013 merger of AMR Corp. and US Airways Group. The company plans to phase out the US Airways name and fly as American Airlines.

American Baptist Association See **Baptist churches** in **Religion** chapter.

American Baptist Churches in the U.S.A. See **Baptist churches** in **Religion** chapter.

American Bar Association *ABA* is acceptable on second reference. Also: *the bar association, the association.*

Headquarters is in Chicago.

American Broadcasting Cos.
See **ABC**.

American Civil Liberties Union *ACLU* is acceptable on second reference.
Headquarters is in New York.

American depositary receipt A negotiable certificate representing a foreign company's equity or debt. *ADR* is acceptable on second reference.

American depositary share A security issued by a foreign company representing an ownership interest in that company. It can represent a fixed number of securities on deposit, or a fraction of them. *ADS* is acceptable on second reference.

American Express Co. Headquarters is in New York.

American Federation of Government Employees Use this full name on first reference to prevent confusion with other unions that represent government workers. *AFGE* is acceptable on second reference.
Headquarters is in Washington.

American Federation of Labor and Congress of Industrial Organizations *AFL-CIO* is acceptable in all references.
Headquarters is in Washington.

American Federation of Musicians Use this full name on first reference.
The shortened form *Musicians' union* is acceptable on second reference.
Headquarters is in New York.

American Federation of State, County and Municipal Employees Use this full name on first reference to prevent confusion with other unions that represent government workers. *AFSCME* is acceptable on second reference.
Headquarters is in Washington.

American Federation of Teachers Use this full name on first reference to prevent confusion with other unions that represent teachers. *AFT* is acceptable on second reference.
Headquarters is in Washington.

American Hospital Association *AHA* is acceptable on second reference. Also: *the hospital association, the association.*
Headquarters is in Chicago.

American International Group Inc. *AIG* is acceptable on second reference. Headquarters is in New York.

Americanisms Words and phrases that have become part of the English language as spoken in the United States are listed with a star in Webster's New World College Dictionary.
Most Americanisms are acceptable in news stories, but let the context be the guide.

American Legion Capitalize also *the Legion* in second reference. Members are *Legionnaires,* just as members of the Lions Club are *Lions.*
Legion and *Legionnaires* are capitalized because they are not being used in their common noun sense. A *legion* (lowercase) is a large group of soldiers or, by derivation, a large number of items: *His friends are legion.* A *legionnaire* (lowercase) is a member of such a legion.
See **fraternal organizations and service clubs**.

American Medical Association *AMA* is acceptable on second reference. Also: *the medical association, the association.*

Headquarters is in Chicago.

American Newspaper Publishers Association See **Newspaper Association of America**.

American Petroleum Institute *API* is acceptable on second reference.

Headquarters is in Washington.

American Postal Workers Union This union represents clerks and similar employees who work inside post offices.

Use the full name on first reference to prevent confusion with the National Association of Letter Carriers. The shortened form *Postal Workers union* is acceptable on second reference.

Headquarters is in Washington.

American Press Institute *API* is acceptable on second reference.

Headquarters is in Arlington, Virginia.

American Society for the Prevention of Cruelty to Animals This organization is limited to the five boroughs of New York City and neighboring Suffolk County in providing animal adoption services, although it has offices elsewhere that offer legal advice and other services to other animal welfare organizations. *ASPCA* is acceptable on second reference.

See **Society for the Prevention of Cruelty to Animals**.

American Society of Composers, Authors and Publishers *ASCAP* is acceptable on second reference.

Headquarters is in New York.

AmeriCorps

amid Not *amidst.*

ammunition See **weapons**.

amnesty See **pardon, parole, probation**.

amok Not *amuck.*

among, between The maxim that *between* introduces two items and *among* introduces more than two covers most questions about how to use these words: *The funds were divided among Ford, Carter and McCarthy.*

However, *between* is the correct word when expressing the relationships of three or more items considered one pair at a time.

As with all prepositions, any pronouns that follow these words must be in the objective case: *among us, between him and her, between you and me.*

ampersand (&) Use the ampersand when it is part of a company's formal name or composition title: *House & Garden, Procter & Gamble, Wheeling & Lake Erie Railway.*

The ampersand should not otherwise be used in place of *and,* except for some accepted abbreviations: *B&B, R&B.*

amplitude modulation *AM* is acceptable in all references.

a.m., p.m. Lowercase, with periods. Avoid the redundant *10 a.m. this morning.*

Amsterdam The city in the Netherlands stands alone in datelines.

Amtrak This acronym, drawn from the words *American travel by* *track*, may be used in all references to the *National Railroad Passenger Corp*. Do not use *AMTRAK*.

The corporation was established by Congress in 1970 to take over intercity passenger operations from railroads that wanted to drop passenger service. Amtrak contracts with railroads for the use of their tracks and of certain other operating equipment and crews.

Amtrak is subsidized in part by federal funds appropriated yearly by Congress and administered through the Department of Transportation.

Amtrak headquarters is in Washington.

AMVETS Acceptable in all references for *American Veterans*, the organization formerly known as *American Veterans of World War II, Korea, and Vietnam*.

Headquarters is in Washington.

anchor, anchorman, anchorwoman, co-anchor

anemia, anemic

Android An operating system created by Google that's used in many smartphones and tablets.

Anglo- Always capitalized. No hyphen when the word that follows is in lowercase:

Anglomania	Anglophobe
Anglophile	

Use a hyphen when the word that follows is capitalized:

Anglo-American	Anglo-Indian
Anglo-Catholic	Anglo-Saxon

angry *At* someone or *with* someone.

animals Do not apply a personal pronoun to an animal unless its sex has been established or the animal has a name: *The dog was scared; it barked. Rover was scared; he barked. The cat, which was scared, ran to its*

basket. Susie the cat, who was scared, ran to her basket. The bull tosses his horns.

Capitalize the name of a specific animal, and use Roman numerals to show sequence: *Bowser, Whirlaway II*.

For breed names, follow the spelling and capitalization in Webster's New World College Dictionary. For breeds not listed in the dictionary, capitalize words derived from proper nouns; use lowercase elsewhere: *basset hound, Boston terrier*.

animal welfare activist Use instead of *animal rights activist*.

anniversary Avoid *first anniversary*, the redundant *one-year anniversary* and terms such as *six-month anniversary* (or other time spans less than a year). Similarly, avoid *first annual*.

anno Domini See **A.D.**

annual An event cannot be described as *annual* until it has been held in at least two successive years.

Do not use the term *first annual*. Instead, note that sponsors plan to hold an event annually.

annual meeting Lowercase in all uses.

anonymous sources Whenever possible, we pursue information on the record. When a source insists on background or off-the-record ground rules, we must adhere to a strict set of guidelines.

Under AP's rules, material from anonymous sources may be used only if:

—The material is information and not opinion or speculation, and is vital to the news report.

—The information is not available except under the conditions of anonymity imposed by the source.

—The source is reliable, and in a position to have accurate information.

Reporters who intend to use material from anonymous sources must get approval from their news managers.

Explain in the story why the source requested anonymity. And, when it's relevant, describe the source's motive for disclosing the information.

The story also must provide attribution that establishes the source's credibility; simply quoting *a source* is not allowed. Be as descriptive as possible about the source of information. If space is limited, use *source* as a last resort. *Official* or similar word will often suffice, including in headlines. See **source**.

Examples:

Speaking on customary condition of anonymity in line with government rules, the official said the two sides were engaged "in very fierce" battles near the border crossing, and that one woman was wounded by a stray bullet.

Incorrect: Granting anonymity "*on customary condition ... in line with government rules*" is insufficient. Readers need a plausible explanation of such a condition, and why we're accepting it. For instance, "*The rules of the official's job did not allow him to be quoted by name.*"

A security official, who requested anonymity because of the sensitivity of the case, said the suspect was monitoring and recording the movements of tourists before his arrest in July.

Incorrect: Explanation: First, we grant anonymity only to those who insist on it, not those who *request* it. Second, granting anonymity because of the *sensitivity of the case* is insufficient explanation. Did the official insist on anonymity because he was not allowed to speak with reporters? Because he was not authorized to release information in advance of a public announcement of details of the case?

Speaking privately, a senior Foreign Ministry official said any further increase in tension could strengthen "warlike" sentiment on both sides and make a resolution of the problem even more difficult.

Incorrect: *Speaking privately* isn't the same thing as insisting on anonymity, so we cannot use the *privately* explanation. Moreover, the official is speculating on something that might happen. We grant anonymity for factual information, not speculation or opinion.

Sometimes a government or corporation intentionally leaks information, but insists we publish it attributed to an anonymous official. If we cannot convince the government or company to go on the record, it's best to use a formulation that implies that the release of the information was official, even though anonymous. For instance: "... according to the official, who insisted on anonymity because he was not allowed to use his own name in releasing the findings."

For additional guidance, see **Statement of News Values**.

another *Another* is not a synonym for *additional*; it refers to an element that somehow duplicates a previously stated quantity.

Right: *Ten people took the test; another 10 refused.*

Wrong: *Ten people took the test; another 20 refused.*

Right: *Ten people took the test; 20 others refused.*

Antarctic, Antarctica, Antarctic Ocean

ante- The rules in **prefixes** apply, but in general, no hyphen. Some examples:

antebellum   antedate

anthems See **composition titles**. Lowercase the term *national anthem*.

anti- Hyphenate all except the following words, which have specific meanings of their own:

antibiotic	antipasto
antibody	antiperspirant
anticlimax	antiphon
antidepressant	antiphony
antidote	antipollution
antifreeze	antipsychotic
antigen	antiseptic
antihistamine	antiserum
antiknock	antithesis
antimatter	antitoxin
antimony	antitrust
antiparticle*	antitussive

*And similar terms in physics such as *antiproton*.

This approach has been adopted in the interests of readability and easily remembered consistency.

It's *anti-lock* in Webster's New World College Dictionary. But note these Stylebook exceptions to Webster's spellings:

anti-abortion	anti-social
anti-aircraft	anti-war
anti-labor	

See **Antichrist, anti-Christ** in **Religion** chapter.

anticipate, expect *Anticipate* means to expect and prepare for something; *expect* does not include the notion of preparation:

They expect a record crowd. They have anticipated it by adding more seats to the auditorium.

antitrust Any law or policy designed to encourage competition by curtailing monopolistic power and unfair business practices.

anti-virus, anti-spyware

anybody, any body, anyone, any one One word for an indefinite reference: *Anyone can do that.*

Two words when the emphasis is on singling out one element of a group: *Any one of them may speak up.*

AOL Acceptable for AOL Inc. In business stories about the company, *AOL Inc.* should be used in at least one reference. The Internet company was spun off from Time Warner Inc. in 2009. Headquarters is in New York. Do not use its former name, *America Online.*

AP Acceptable on second reference for *The Associated Press.*

On second reference, *AP* or *the AP* (no capital on *the*) may be used. See **Associated Press**.

API Abbreviation for *application programming interface*. A programming interface that a website or a piece of software uses to allow other websites or software to interact with it. For example, an eBay API lets auction listings appear on other sites.

apostolic delegate, papal nuncio An *apostolic delegate* is a Roman Catholic diplomat chosen by the pope to be his envoy to the church in a nation that does not have formal diplomatic relations with the Vatican.

A *papal nuncio* is the pope's envoy to a nation with which the Vatican has diplomatic relations.

apostrophe (') See entry in **Punctuation** section.

app Short for *application*. A program that runs inside another service. Many cellphones, tablets and Web browsers allow applications to be downloaded to give the user access to additional functions. *App* is acceptable on first reference.

Appalachia In the broadest sense, the word applies to the entire region along the Appalachian Mountains, which extend from Maine into northern Alabama.

In a sense that often suggests economic depression and poverty, the reference is to sections of eastern Tennessee, eastern Kentucky, southeastern Ohio and the western portion of West Virginia.

The Appalachian Regional Commission, established by federal law in 1965, has a mandate to foster development in 397 counties in 13 states — all of West Virginia and parts of Alabama, Georgia, Kentucky, Maryland, Mississippi, New York, North Carolina, Ohio, Pennsylvania, South Carolina, Tennessee and Virginia.

When the word *Appalachia* is used, specify the extent of the area in question.

Appalachian Mountains Or simply: *the Appalachians*.

appeals court See **U.S. Court of Appeals**.

Apple Inc. Headquarters is in Cupertino, California.

appreciation Increase in value of property, as opposed to *depreciation*.

approve See **adopt, approve, enact, pass**.

April Fools' Day

APTN, AP Radio Do not refer to these units of The Associated Press as if they were separate entities. Say *Alexander Barbosa told the AP [not APTN] in Rio de Janeiro; AP [not APTN] video journalist John*

Smith contributed to this report. See **Associated Press**.

Arab Spring Wave of pro-democratic protests, revolutions and civil wars that have swept some Arab nations since 2011.

Arabic names In general, use an English spelling that approximates the way a name sounds in Arabic.

If an individual has a preferred spelling in English, use that. If usage has established a particular spelling, use that.

Problems in transliteration of Arabic names often are traceable to pronunciations that vary from region to region. The *g*, for example, is pronounced like the *g* of *go* mainly in Egypt, and the *j* of *joy* in the rest of the Arab world. Thus it is *Gamal* in Egypt and *Jamal* in nations on the peninsula. Follow local practice in deciding which letter to use.

Arabs commonly are known by two names (*Hassan Nasrallah*), or by three (*Mohammed Mahdi Akef*). Follow the individual's preference on first reference. On second reference, use only the final name in the sequence.

The articles *al-* or *el-* may be used or dropped depending on the person's preference or established usage. (*Ayman al-Zawahri, al-Zawahri,* or *Moammar Gadhafi, Gadhafi*). The article *al-* or *el-* should not be capitalized.

The Arabic word for son (*ibn* or *bin*) is sometimes part of a name. On second reference, it is often dropped, using only the final name. In cases of personal preference or common usage, it should be retained. (*Osama bin Laden, bin Laden; Abdul-Aziz bin Baz, bin Baz*).

The word *abu* or *abou*, meaning *father of*, occasionally is used as a last name (*Abdel-Halim Abou*

Ghazala). Capitalize and repeat it on second reference: *Abou Ghazala.*

The word *abdul*, meaning "servant of (God)," generally does not stand alone as a name, except sometimes in South Asia and Afghanistan. It is used in combination with a second name (an Arabic word for an attribute of God). This combination should be hyphenated, unless the individual prefers otherwise, and capitalized (*Adil Abdul-Mahdi, Abdul-Mahdi*). In Egypt and some other countries, *Abdul* is often written *Abdel*, reflecting local pronunciation.

For royalty, the titles *king, emir, sheikh* and *imam* are used, but *prince* usually replaces *emir*. Some Arabs are known only by the title and a given name on first reference (*King Abdullah*). Others are known by a complete name (*Sheikh Mohammed bin Rashid Al Maktoum*). Follow the common usage on first reference. On second reference, drop the title and use only the first name (*Abdullah, Mohammed*). The full names of many Gulf royals include the word *Al*, which in their case should be capitalized without a hyphen since it means *family of*.

The *al* should be capitalized in front of most Muslim and Arab institutions, universities, newspapers and major mosques, as in *Al-Azhar*, the university in Cairo; *Al-Aqsa*, the Jerusalem mosque, the newspaper *Al-Ahram* and the satellite television news network *Al-Jazeera*.

Arabic numerals The numerical figures 0, 1, 2, 3, 4, 5, 6, 7, 8, 9.

In general, use Arabic forms unless denoting the sequence of wars or establishing a personal sequence for people or animals. See **Roman numerals**.

Separate entries list more details and examples. For a full list, see **numerals**.

arbitrage Buying currencies, commercial bills or securities in one market and selling them at the same time in another to make a profit on the price discrepancy.

arbitrate, mediate Both terms are used in reports about labor negotiations, but they should not be interchanged.

One who *arbitrates* hears evidence from all people concerned, then hands down a decision.

One who *mediates* listens to arguments of both parties and tries by the exercise of reason or persuasion to bring them to an agreement.

arch- No hyphen after this prefix unless it precedes a capitalized word:

archbishop	arch-Republican
archenemy	archrival

archaeology

arctic Lowercase for adjective meaning frigid; capitalize for region around the North Pole. **Arctic Circle, arctic fox, Arctic Ocean**

area codes See **telephone numbers**.

Argentine The preferred term for the people and culture of Argentina.

Arizona Abbreviate *Ariz.* in datelines only; spell out in stories. Postal code: *AZ*
See **state names**.

Arkansas Abbreviate *Ark.* in datelines only; spell out in stories. Postal code: *AR*
See **state names**.

army Capitalize when referring to U.S. forces: *the U.S. Army, the Army, Army regulations.* Do not use the abbreviation *USA*.

Use lowercase for the forces of other nations: *the French army*.

This approach has been adopted for consistency, because many foreign nations do not use *army* as the proper name.

See **military academies** and **military titles**.

arrest To avoid any suggestion that someone is being judged before a trial, do not use a phrase such as *arrested for killing*. Instead, use *arrested on a charge of killing*. If a charge hasn't been filed, *arrested on suspicion of*, or a similar phrase, should be used.

For guidelines on related words, see **accused**; **allege**; and **indict**.

arrive It requires the preposition *at*. Do not omit, as airline dispatchers often do in: *He will arrive LaGuardia*.

artifact

artillery See **weapons**.

artworks Lowercase impressionism, modernism and other art styles and movements unless used in formal titles of shows or exhibits with quotation marks. Exception: *Bauhaus* is capitalized as the name of a school. *Gothic*, *Renaissance* and other historical periods are capitalized for art and architecture from those ages. Titles of paintings are enclosed in quotes: *"Mona Lisa."* Sculptures are capitalized without quotes: *The Thinker, Michelangelo's Pieta*.

See **composition titles**.

as See **like, as**.

ASCII An acronym for *American Standard Code for Information Interchange*. A numeric code used to represent the letters of the Roman alphabet, numbers and punctuation

marks. Use of the acronym on first reference is acceptable if it is identified as a code.

ashtray

Asian-American A person of Asian birth or descent who lives in the U.S. When possible, refer to a person's country of origin. For example: *Filipino-American* or *Indian-American*. Follow the person's preference. See **nationalities and races** and **race**.

Asian, Asiatic Use *Asian* or *Asians* when referring to people.

Some Asians regard *Asiatic* as offensive when applied to people.

Asian subcontinent In popular usage the term applies to Bangladesh, Bhutan, India, Nepal, Pakistan, Sikkim and the island nation of Sri Lanka (formerly Ceylon) at the southeastern tip of India.

For definitions of the terms that apply to other parts of Asia, see **Far East**; **Middle East**; and **Southeast Asia**.

Asperger's syndrome After Hans Asperger, an Austrian pediatrician. A milder form of autism, once a separate diagnosis but now part of a broader term called "autism spectrum disorder." People with this condition can have high intelligence and narrow, sometimes obsessive interests but lack social skills.

assassin, killer, murderer An *assassin* is one who kills a politically important or prominent person.

A *killer* is anyone who kills with a motive of any kind.

A *murderer* is one who is convicted of murder in a court of law.

Preferred use: *Joe Smith was convicted of second-degree murder*.

See **execute** and the **homicide, murder, manslaughter** entry.

assassination Use the term
only if it involves the murder of a
politically important or prominent
individual by surprise attack.

assassination, date of A prominent person is shot one day and
dies the next. Which day was he as-
sassinated? The day he was attacked.

assault, battery *Assault* almost
always implies physical contact and
sudden, intense violence.

Legally, however, *assault* means
simply to threaten violence, as in
pointing a pistol at an individual
without firing it. *Assault and battery*
is the legal term when the victim
was touched by the assaulter or
something the assaulter put in motion.

assembly Capitalize when part
of the proper name for the lower
house of a legislature: *the California
Assembly*. Retain capitalization if the
state name is dropped but the reference is specific:
*SACRAMENTO, Calif. (AP) — The
state Assembly ...*

If a legislature is known as a
general assembly: *the Missouri General Assembly*, *the General Assembly*,
the assembly. *Legislature* also may be
used as the proper name, however.
See **legislature**.

Lowercase all plural uses: *the
California and New York assemblies*.

**assemblyman, assembly-
woman** Do not abbreviate. See **legislative titles**.

assets Everything a company or
an individual owns or is owed.

Assets may be broken down as:
Current assets: cash, investments,
money due to a corporation, unused
raw materials and inventories of finished but unsold products.

Fixed assets: buildings, machinery
and land.

Intangible assets: patents and
goodwill.
See **goodwill**.

asset-backed security A financial security backed by loans, leases,
credit-card debt, royalties, a company's accounts receivables, etc. *ABS*
should not be used in copy.

asset, fixed Plant, land, equipment, long-term investments that
cannot be readily liquefied without
disturbing the operation of the business.

assistant Do not abbreviate.
Capitalize only when part of a formal title before a name: *Assistant
Secretary of State Richard Boucher*.
Whenever practical, however, an ap-
positional construction should be
used: *Richard Boucher, assistant secretary of state*.
See **titles**.

associate Never abbreviate.
Apply the same capitalization norms
listed under **assistant**.

Associated Press, The The
newsgathering cooperative dating
from 1846.

Use *The Associated Press* on first
reference (the capitalized article is
part of the formal name).

On second reference, *AP* or *the
AP* (no capital on *the*) may be used.

Do not refer to APTN and AP
Radio, units of the AP, as if they
were separate entities. Say *Alexander
Barbosa told the AP* [*not APTN*] *in
Rio de Janeiro*; *AP* [*not APTN*] *video
journalist John Smith contributed to
this report.*

The address is 450 W. 33rd St.,
New York, NY 10001. The telephone
number is 212-621-1500.

Online: http://www.ap.org
See **AP**.

Association Do not abbreviate. Capitalize as part of a proper name: *American Medical Association.*

assure See **ensure, insure, assure**.

asterisk Do not use the symbol. It rarely translates and in many cases cannot be seen by AP computers or received by newspaper or other computers.

astronaut It is not a formal title. Do not capitalize when used before a name: *astronaut John Glenn.*

AT&T Inc. The full name of the business formerly known as American Telephone & Telegraph Co. AT&T was acquired in 2005 by its former subsidiary, SBC Communications Inc., which renamed itself AT&T. Headquarters is in Dallas.

atheist See **agnostic, atheist**.

athlete's foot

Atlanta The city in Georgia stands alone in datelines.

Atlantic Ocean

Atlantic Standard Time, Atlantic Daylight Time Used in the Maritime Provinces of Canada and in Puerto Rico.
See **time zones**.

at large Usually two words for an individual representing more than a single district: *councilman at large.*
But it is *ambassador-at-large* for an ambassador assigned to no particular country.

ATM Acceptable in all references for *automated teller machine.*
Do not use the redundant *ATM machine.*

attache It is not a formal title. Always lowercase.

attorney general, attorneys general Never abbreviate. Capitalize only when used as a title before a name: *Attorney General Eric Holder.*
See **titles**.

attorney, lawyer In common usage the words are interchangeable.
Technically, however, an *attorney* is someone (usually, but not necessarily, a lawyer) empowered to act for another. Such an individual occasionally is called an *attorney in fact.*
A *lawyer* is a person admitted to practice in a court system. Such an individual occasionally is called an *attorney at law.*
Do not abbreviate. Do not capitalize unless it is an officeholder's title: *defense attorney Perry Mason, attorney Perry Mason, District Attorney Hamilton Burger.*
Power of attorney is a written statement legally authorizing a person to act for another.
See **lawyer**.

attribution AP news reports must attribute facts not gathered or confirmed on our own, whether the pickup is from a newspaper, website, broadcaster or blog, U.S. or international, AP member or subscriber. AP reports must also credit other organizations when they break a story and AP matches or further develops it. News from a government, agency, organization, company or other recognized group may be attributed to that entity on first reference in the story: *the White House announced.* In a follow-up attribution, specify whether the information came from a spokesman or other named official or in a news release.

augur A transitive verb. Do not follow it with the preposition *for.*

Correct: *The tea leaves augur a time of success.*

"Auld Lang Syne" Sung to greet the New Year, poem by Robert Burns set to Scottish music.

autism spectrum disorder

An umbrella term for a group of developmental disorders that can involve varying degrees of language and social impairments, and repetitive behaviors. It encompasses mild autism and the more classic form. Acceptable to use the term *autism* in stories. See **Asperger's syndrome**.

author A noun used for both men and women. Do not use it as a verb.

automaker, automakers

automatic See **pistol** and **weapons**.

Auto Train Rail service that carries passengers and their cars. Owned and operated by Amtrak.

autoworker, autoworkers

One word when used generically.
But *United Auto Workers* when referring to the union.

autumn See **seasons**.

avatar A version of yourself that you put forward in an online or video game setting. Sometimes bears a strong resemblance to the user; at other times, it is used to highlight a company or organization's brand, make a political statement or act out fantasies of a wished-for identity.

avenue Abbreviate only with a numbered address. See **addresses**.

average, mean, median, norm
Average refers to the result obtained by dividing a sum by the number of quantities added together: *The average of 7, 9, 17 is 33 divided by 3, or 11.*

Mean, in its sense used in arithmetic and statistics, is an *average* and is determined by adding the series of numbers and dividing the sum by the number of cases: *The mean temperature of five days with temperatures of 67, 62, 68, 69, 64 is 66.*

Median is the middle number of points in a series arranged in order of size: *The median grade in the group of 50, 55, 85, 88, 92 is 85. The average is 74.*

Norm implies a standard of average performance for a given group: *The child was below the norm for his age in reading comprehension.*

average of The phrase takes a plural verb in a construction such as: *An average of 100 new jobs are created daily.*

averse See **adverse, averse**.

Avianca Headquarters of this airline is in Bogota, Colombia.

aviator Use for both men and women.

awards and decorations Capitalize them: *Bronze Star, Medal of Honor,* etc.
See **Nobel Prize** and **Pulitzer Prizes**.

awe-struck

awhile (adv.) **a while** *He plans to stay awhile* (adv.). *He plans to stay for a while* (n.).

AWOL Acceptable in all references for *absent without leave.*

ax Not *axe.*
The verb forms: *ax, axed, axing.*

Axis The alliance of Germany, Italy and Japan during World War II.

B

baby boom, baby boomer
Lowercase, no hyphen. But *baby-boom generation* for those born between 1946 and 1964.

baby-sit, baby-sitting, baby-sat, baby sitter

baccalaureate

Bachelor of Arts, Bachelor of Science *A bachelor's degree* or *bachelor's* is acceptable in any reference.
See **academic degrees** for guidelines on when the abbreviations *B.A.* or *B.S.* are acceptable.

backfire In wildfires, this term is for a fire set along the inner edge of a fireline to consume the fuel in the fire's path or change its direction.

backstage Part of the stage or theater behind the proscenium, particularly the wings and dressing rooms. Also can refer to the press area where award winners meet with the news media.

backup (n. and adj.) **back up** (v.)

backward Not backwards.

backyard One word in all uses.

bad, badly *Bad* should not be used as an adverb. It does not lose its status as an adjective, however, in a sentence such as *I feel bad*. Such a statement is the idiomatic equivalent of *I am in bad health*. An alternative, *I feel badly*, could be interpreted as meaning that your sense of touch was bad.
See **good, well**.

Baghdad The city in Iraq stands alone in datelines.

Bagram Air Field The preferred spelling for the U.S. base in Afghanistan.

Bahamas In datelines, give the name of the city or town followed by *Bahamas*:
NASSAU, Bahamas (AP) —
In stories, use *Bahamas, the Bahamas or the Bahama Islands* as the construction of a sentence dictates.
Identify a specific island in the text if relevant.

bail *Bail* is money or property that will be forfeited to the court if an accused individual fails to appear for trial. It may be posted as follows:
—The accused may deposit with the court the full amount or its equivalent in collateral such as a deed to property.
—A friend or relative may make such a deposit with the court.
—The accused may pay a professional bail bondsman a percentage of the total figure. The bondsman, in turn, guarantees the court that it will receive from him the full

amount in the event the individual fails to appear for trial.

It is correct in all cases to say that an accused *posted bail* or *posted a bail bond* (the money held by the court is a form of bond). When a distinction is desired, say that the individual *posted his own bail*, that *bail was posted by a friend or relative*, or that *bail was obtained through a bondsman*.

balance of payments, balance of trade

The *balance of payments* is the difference between the amount of money that leaves a nation and the amount that enters it during a period of time.

The *balance of payments* is determined by computing the amount of money a nation and its citizens send abroad for all purposes — including goods and services purchased, travel, loans, foreign aid, etc. — and subtracting from it the amount that foreign nations send into the nation for similar purposes.

The *balance of trade* is the difference between the monetary value of the goods a nation imports and the goods it exports.

An example illustrating the difference between the two:

The United States and its citizens might send $10 billion abroad — $5 billion for goods, $3 billion for loans and foreign aid, $1 billion for services and $1 billion for tourism and other purposes.

Other nations might send $9 billion into the United States — $6 billion for U.S. goods, $2 billion for services and $1 billion for tourism and other purposes.

The United States would have a *balance-of-payments* deficit of $1 billion but a *balance-of-trade* surplus of $1 billion.

balance sheet
A listing of assets, liabilities and net worth showing the financial position of a company at the specific time. A bank balance sheet is generally referred to as a statement of condition.

ballclub, ballpark, ballplayer, ballroom

balloon mortgage
A mortgage whose amortization schedule will not extinguish the debt by the end of the mortgage term, leaving a large payment (called balloon payment) of the remaining principal balance to be paid at that time.

ballpoint pen

baloney
Foolish or exaggerated talk.

The sausage or luncheon meat is *bologna*.

Baltimore
The city in Maryland stands alone in datelines.

Band-Aid
A trademark for a type of adhesive bandage.

Bangkok
The city in Thailand stands alone in datelines.

Bank of America Corp.
Headquarters is in Charlotte, North Carolina.

bankruptcy
Federal courts have exclusive jurisdiction over bankruptcy cases and each of the 94 federal judicial districts handles bankruptcy matters. The primary purposes of the federal bankruptcy laws are to give honest debtors a fresh start in life by relieving them of most debts, and to repay creditors in an orderly manner to the extent debtors have property available for payment. Bankruptcies can be voluntary or involuntary.

Chapter 7 of the Bankruptcy Code is available to both individual and business debtors. Its purpose is to achieve a fair distribution to creditors of the debtor's available non-exempt property. It provides a fresh financial start for individuals, although not all debt is wiped away; debts for certain taxes, fraudulently incurred credit card debt, family support obligations — including child support and alimony — and most student loans must still be repaid. The bankruptcy law that took effect in October 2005 limits Chapter 7 as an option for many Americans: Those deemed by a "means test" to have at least $100 a month left over after paying certain debts and expenses must file a five-year repayment plan under the more restrictive Chapter 13 instead. When a company files for Chapter 7, it usually leads to liquidation. But a company in Chapter 7 proceedings can continue to operate under the direction of a court trustee until the matter is settled, and if it can settle with creditors in the interim, it may not have to be liquidated.

Chapter 11 of the Bankruptcy Code is available for both business and consumer debtors. Its purpose is to rehabilitate a business as a going concern or reorganize an individual's finances through a court-approved reorganization plan. When referring to such a filing, say the company is seeking Chapter 11 protection. This action frees a company from the threat of creditors' lawsuits while it reorganizes its finances. The debtor's reorganization plan must be accepted by a majority of its creditors. Unless the court rules otherwise, the debtor remains in control of the business and its assets.

Chapter 12 of the Bankruptcy Code is designed to give special debt relief to a family farmer with regular income from farming.

Chapter 13 of the Bankruptcy Code is likely to be required for an increasing percentage of individuals seeking to wipe the slate clean. Those deemed by a "means test" to have at least $100 a month left over after paying certain debts and expenses will have to file a five-year repayment plan under Chapter 13 allowing unsecured creditors to recover part or all of what they are owed.

Chapter 15 was added to the Bankruptcy Code in 2005 and covers U.S. filings that are secondary to bankruptcy cases filed overseas. Courts can authorize trustees to act in a foreign country on behalf of a bankruptcy estate in a Chapter 15 proceeding. It represents the U.S. adoption of a model law on cross-border bankruptcy developed by the United Nations.

barbiturate

baron, baroness See **nobility**.

barrel A standard barrel in U.S. measure contains 31.5 gallons.

A standard barrel in British and Canadian measure contains 36 imperial gallons.

In international dealings with crude oil, a standard barrel contains 42 U.S. gallons or 35 imperial gallons.

See the **oil** entry for guidelines on computing the volume and weight of petroleum products.

barrel, barreled, barreling

barrister See **lawyer**.

barroom

bartender Preferred in all references. Do not use *bar maid*.

basis point One one-hundredth of one percentage point. Changes in interest rates are measured in basis points. If the Federal Reserve's target rate was 2 percent and it was cut by 50 basis points, the new rate would be 1.5 percent.

battalion Capitalize when used with a figure to form a name: *the 3rd Battalion, the 10th Battalion*.

battlefield Also: *battlefront, battleground, battleship*. But *battle station*.

battleground states States where candidates from both major political parties have a reasonable chance for victory in a statewide race or presidential vote.

bay Capitalize as an integral part of a proper name: *Hudson Bay, San Francisco Bay*.
Capitalize also *San Francisco Bay Area* or *the Bay Area* as the popular name for the nine-county region that has San Francisco as its focal point.

bazaar A fair. *Bizarre* means unusual.

B.C. Acceptable in all references to a calendar year in the period *before Christ*.
Because the full phrase would be *in the year 43 before Christ*, the abbreviation *B.C.* is placed after the figure for the year: *43 B.C.*
See **A.D.**

bear market A period of generally declining stock prices over a prolonged period, generally defined as a 20 percent or larger decline in broad stock indexes such as the Standard & Poor's 500.

bearer bond A bond for which the owner's name is not registered on the books of the issuing company. Interest and principal is thus payable to the bondholder.

bearer stock Stock certificates that are not registered in any name. They are negotiable without endorsement and transferable by delivery.

bed-and-breakfast *B&B* is acceptable on second reference.

bedbug

because, since Use *because* to denote a specific cause-effect relationship: *He went because he was told.*
Since is acceptable in a causal sense when the first event in a sequence led logically to the second but was not its direct cause: *They went to the game, since they had been given the tickets.*

before Christ See **B.C.**

Beijing The city in China stands alone in datelines.

Beirut The city in Lebanon stands alone in datelines.

bellwether

benefit, benefited, benefiting

Ben-Gurion International Airport Located at Lod, Israel, about 10 miles southeast of Tel Aviv.
See **airport**.

Berkshire Hathaway Inc. Headquarters is in Omaha, Nebraska.

Berlin The city in Germany stands alone in datelines.

Berlin Wall

Bermuda collar, Bermuda grass, Bermuda shorts

beside, besides *Beside* means at the side of.

Besides means in addition to.

besiege

best-seller Hyphenate in all uses.

betting odds Use figures and a hyphen: *The odds were 5-4, he won despite 3-2 odds against him.* See **numerals**.

bettor A person who bets.

between See **among, between**.

bi- The rules in **prefixes** apply, but in general, no hyphen. Some examples:

bifocal	bimonthly
bilateral	bipartisan
bilingual	

biannual, biennial *Biannual* means twice a year and is a synonym for the word *semiannual*.

Biennial means every two years.

Bible Capitalize, without quotation marks, when referring to the Scriptures in the Old Testament or the New Testament. Capitalize also related terms such as the *Gospels, Gospel of St. Mark, the Scriptures, the Holy Scriptures*.

Lowercase *biblical* in all uses.

Lowercase *bible* as a nonreligious term: *My dictionary is my bible.*

Do not abbreviate individual books of the Bible.

Old Testament is a Christian designation; Hebrew Bible or Jewish Bible is the appropriate term for stories dealing with Judaism alone.

The standard names and order of Old Testament books as they appear in Protestant Bibles are: Genesis, Exodus, Leviticus, Numbers, Deuteronomy, Joshua, Judges, Ruth, 1 Samuel, 2 Samuel, 1 Kings, 2 Kings, 1 Chronicles, 2 Chronicles, Ezra, Nehemiah, Esther, Job, Psalms, Proverbs, Ecclesiastes, Song of Solomon, Isaiah, Jeremiah, Lamentations, Ezekiel, Daniel, Hosea, Joel, Amos, Obadiah, Jonah, Micah, Nahum, Habakkuk, Zephaniah, Haggai, Zechariah, Malachi.

Jewish Bibles contain the same 39 books, in different order. Roman Catholic Bibles follow a different order, usually use some different names and include the seven Deuterocanonical books (called the Apocrypha by Protestants): Tobit, Judith, 1 Maccabees, 2 Maccabees, Wisdom, Sirach, Baruch.

The books of the New Testament, in order: Matthew, Mark, Luke, John, Acts, Romans, 1 Corinthians, 2 Corinthians, Galatians, Ephesians, Philippians, Colossians, 1 Thessalonians, 2 Thessalonians, 1 Timothy, 2 Timothy, Titus, Philemon, Hebrews, James, 1 Peter, 2 Peter, 1 John, 2 John, 3 John, Jude, Revelation.

Citation listing the number of chapter and verse(s) use this form: *Matthew 3:16, Luke 21:1-13, 1 Peter 2:1.*

Big Board Acceptable on second reference for the *New York Stock Exchange*.

big brother One's older brother is a *big brother. Big Brother* (capitalized) means under the watchful eye of big government, from George Orwell's "1984."

Capitalize also in reference to members of Big Brothers Big Sisters of America Inc. The organization has headquarters in Philadelphia.

Big Three automakers In the past, the Big Three referred to General Motors, Ford and Chrysler. Given that more companies now make and sell vehicles in the U.S., the term *Detroit Three* is preferred.

bigwig

billion A thousand million. For forms, see **millions, billions**.

Bill of Rights The first 10 amendments to the Constitution.

bimonthly Means every other month. *Semimonthly* means twice a month.

Bing Internet search engine owned by Microsoft Corp. that also powers Yahoo Inc.'s search service. Introduced in 2009, it replaced earlier Microsoft services known as Live Search and MSN Search.

bin Laden, Osama Use *bin Laden* on all references except at the start of a sentence. It is the family preference for the last name, which is an exception to the general rule on Arabic names. He founded al-Qaida and was killed by U.S. forces in Pakistan in May 2011.

bioterrorism

bird flu Preferred term for *avian influenza*, viruses that mostly infect poultry and other birds. Several types are known to infect humans and the deadliest form so far appears to be H5N1. Other strains that have infected people include H7N9, H9N2 and H6N1. The viruses mainly infect people who have direct contact with sick birds but human-to-human transmission occasionally occurs.

birthday Capitalize as part of the name for a holiday: *Washington's Birthday*. Lowercase in other uses.

bit Acceptable in all references as an abbreviation for *binary digit*. Actual data take the form of electrical impulses. These can be thought of as either on or off or 1 and 0. The pulses are bits.

bitcoin A digital currency created and exchanged independent of banks or governments. A maximum of 21 million bitcoins can be created, a limit that probably won't be reached for several more decades if the currency survives. Transactions typically are completed anonymously, making the currency popular among people who want to conceal their financial activity. The currency can be converted into cash when deposited into accounts at prices set in online trading. Lowercase in all uses except at the start of a sentence.

biweekly Means every other week. *Semiweekly* means twice a week.

bizarre Unusual. A fair is a *bazaar*.

black Acceptable for a person of the black race. *African-American* is acceptable for an American black person of African descent. (Use *Negro* only in names of organizations or in quotations.) Do not use *colored* as a synonym. See **African-American**, **colored**, **nationalities and races** and **race**.

BlackBerry, BlackBerrys A brand of smartphone manufactured by BlackBerry Ltd.

blackout, brownout A *blackout* is a total power failure over a large area or the concealing of lights that might be visible to enemy raiders.

The term *rolling blackout* is used by electric companies to describe a situation in which electric power to some sections temporarily is cut off on a rotating basis to assure that voltage will meet minimum standards in other sections.

A *brownout* is a small, temporary voltage reduction, usually from 2 percent to 8 percent, implemented to conserve electric power.

blastoff (n. and adj.) **blast off** (v.)

blind See **disabled, handicapped**.

blizzard See **weather terms**.

bloc, block A *bloc* is a coalition of people, groups or nations with the same purpose or goal.

Block has more than a dozen definitions, but a political alliance is not one of them.

blog A website where entries are usually (but not always) presented in reverse chronological order. Can be news, commentary, personal memoirs, photos, video or any combination of the above and other items. An update to a blog is a *blog post* or *blog entry*.

Blogs can also be distributed outside the website context via RSS feed, tweets and other types of social media posts.

For blog names, use the name as spelled by the writer, capitalizing the first letter and other main words. Don't enclose the name in quotation marks unless it's an unusual spelling that might otherwise be unclear.

blond, blonde Use *blond* as a noun for males and as an adjective for all applications: She has *blond* hair.

Use *blonde* as a noun for females.

blood alcohol content The concentration of alcohol in blood. It is usually measured as weight per volume. For example, 0.02 percent means 0.02 grams of alcohol per deciliter of an individual's blood. The legal limit for intoxication in most states is 0.08 percent. *The jury found he was driving with a blood al-cohol level above Florida's 0.08 percent limit.*

bloodbath One word, an exception to Webster's New World College Dictionary.

bloodhound

Bloomberg LP A provider of financial news and information. Its Bloomberg News service, which started in 1990, provides news to newspapers worldwide and to financial professionals. Bloomberg LP also owns the magazine Bloomberg Businessweek and has television and radio divisions. The company is privately owned and has its headquarters in New York.

blue chip stock Stock in a company known for its long-established record of making money and paying dividends.

Bluetooth A standard for short-range wireless transmissions, such as in headsets, that enable hands-free use of cellphones and other devices.

Blu-ray Disc A successor to the DVD, *Blu-ray Disc* is a standard used to deliver high-definition video and other digital content.

board Capitalize only when an integral part of a proper name. See **capitalization**.

board of aldermen See **city council**.

board of directors, board of trustees Always lowercase. See **organizations and institutions**.

board of supervisors See **city council**.

boats, ships A *boat* is a water-craft of any size but generally is used to indicate a small craft. A *ship* is a large, seagoing vessel.

The word *boat* is used, however, in some words that apply to large craft: *ferryboat, PT boat.*

Use *it*, not the pronoun *she*, in references to boats and ships.

Use Arabic or Roman numerals in the names of boats and ships: *the Queen Elizabeth 2* or *QE2; Titan I, Titan II.*

The reference for military ships is IHS Jane's Fighting Ships; for nonmilitary ships, IHS Fairplay Register of Ships.

See **numerals**.

bobblehead

body mass index A measurement calculated from weight and height. *BMI* is acceptable on second reference. To calculate: multiply weight in pounds by 703, divide by height in inches, divide again by height in inches. An easy-to-use Web calculator: http://www.nhlbi.nih.gov/health/educational/lose_wt/BMI/bmicalc.htm

Boeing Co. Headquarters is in Chicago.

Bogota The city in Colombia carries the country name in datelines.

Boko Haram Muslim militant group in northeast Nigeria.

bona fide

bondholder

bond ratings Standard & Poor's, Moody's Investors Service and Fitch Ratings sell information — mainly to institutional investors — about what they view as the relative risk of various issues of debt. They also charge companies, municipalities and even foreign governments that wish to sell debt and have it rated. The ratings are a fundamental way for investors to form an opinion on whether they are likely to be repaid, and then decide whether the interest rate is high enough to compensate for the risk that they may get back none or only a portion of their investment (in the case of a bankruptcy or some other adverse event). The ratings also effectively set benchmarks for how much interest companies will have to pay to sell bonds, commercial paper, preferred stock and for bank loans they obtain. The higher the grade, the lower the interest rate a borrower must pay.

Standard & Poor's bond ratings, for example, include 10 categories that are referred to as investment-grade, from AAA to BBB-, given to borrowers with the strongest ability to repay. Another six categories, from BB+ to CCC-, are assigned to more speculative securities that are commonly referred to as *junk* or *high-yield debt*. The lowest category, D, is for securities that are in payment default.

A reduction in the rating of a company's debt to non-investment-grade can force some mutual funds and pension funds to sell those bonds because they are prohibited from holding junk debt.

book publishers Major U.S. publishers are:

Hachette Book Group USA, (formerly Time Warner Books), a division of French media company Lagardere SCA

HarperCollins Publishers, owned by News Corp.

Houghton Mifflin Harcourt

Hyperion Books, some titles released through The Walt Disney Co.

and some through Hachette Book Group.

Macmillan (formerly Holtzbrinck), including Farrar, Straus & Giroux, St. Martin's Press, Henry Holt and Picador

Penguin Random House, comprising Penguin Group (USA), including Penguin Press, G.P. Putnam's Sons, Blue Rider Press, Riverhead books and Viking, owned by Pearson PLC; and Random House Inc., including the Crown Publishing Group, the Knopf Doubleday Publishing Group and the Random House Publishing Group

Perseus Book Group

Scholastic Books, owned by Scholastic Corp.

Simon & Schuster Inc., owned by CBS Corp.

W.W. Norton and Co.

John Wiley & Sons Inc.

Books on Tape A trademark for a brand of audiobooks. Use a generic term such as *audiotape* or *audiocassette*.

book titles See **composition titles**.

book value The difference between a company's assets and liabilities.

The *book value per share* of common stock is the *book value* divided by the number of common shares outstanding.

Bosnia-Herzegovina The country has been divided into a Bosnian Serb republic and a Muslim-Croat federation since 1995. Both have wide autonomy but share a common presidency, parliament and government. In datelines: *SARAJEVO, Bosnia-Herzegovina*. The people are *Bosnians*.

Bosporus, the Not the Bosporus Strait.

Boston The capital of Massachusetts stands alone in datelines.

Boston terrier

boulevard Abbreviated only with a numbered address: *43 Park Blvd.* See **addresses**.

bowlegged

Boxing Day Post-Christmas holiday Dec. 26 in British Commonwealth countries. Term came from practice of giving gift boxes to employees and others.

box office (n.) **box-office** (adj.)

boy Applicable until 18th birthday is reached. Use *man* or *young man* afterward. See **children**.

boycott, embargo A *boycott* is an organized refusal to buy a particular product or service, or to deal with a particular merchant or group of merchants.

An *embargo* is a legal restriction against trade. It usually prohibits goods from entering or leaving a country. The plural is *embargoes*.

boyfriend, girlfriend

Boy Scouts The full name of the national organization is *Boy Scouts of America*. Headquarters is in Irving, Texas.

Cub Scouting is for boys 7 through 10. Members are *Cub Scouts* or *Cubs*.

Boy Scouting is for boys 11 through 17. Members are *Boy Scouts* or *Scouts*. As a rank or formal leadership title, capped before a full name: *Troop 6 Scoutmaster John Smith*. In other uses, lowercase: *John Smith, scoutmaster of Troop 1.*

Exploring is a separate program open to boys and girls from high school age through 20. Members are *Explorers,* not *Explorer Scouts.* Members of units that stress nautical programs are *Sea Explorers.*

Venturing, originally part of the *Exploring* division, is for young adults, 14 through 20.

See **Girl Scouts**.

BP PLC Formerly British Petroleum. *BP* is acceptable in all references.

Headquarters is in London.

brackets See entry in **Punctuation** chapter.

Brahman, Brahmin *Brahman* applies to the priestly Hindu caste and a breed of cattle.

Brahmin applies to aristocracy in general: *Boston Brahmin.*

See **Hindu, Hinduism** in **Religion** chapter.

brain-dead (adj.) **brain death** Complete absence of brain function based on a series of tests. Used as a legal definition of death. In the U.S., most organ transplants are done after the donor has been declared brain-dead. See **clinically dead, clinical death**.

brand names When they are used, capitalize them.

Brand names normally should be used only if they are essential to a story.

Sometimes, however, the use of a brand name may not be essential but is acceptable because it lends an air of reality to a story: *He fished a Camel from his shirt pocket* may be preferable to the less specific *cigarette.*

When a company sponsors a sports or other event identified only by the company's name, use the name on first reference: Example: *Buick Open.*

However, when an event is clearly identifiable without the company's name, drop the name on first reference and include the sponsor name elsewhere in the story or at the bottom as an Editor's Note. Example: *FedEx Orange Bowl* would be identified in the story only as *Orange Bowl.*

Also use a separate paragraph to provide the name of a sponsor when the brand name is not part of the formal title.

See **trademark** entry.

brand-new (adj.)

break-in (n. and adj.) **break in** (v.)

breakup (n. and adj.) **break up** (v.)

breast-feed, breast-feeding, breast-fed

Breathalyzer Trademarked name for a device to test blood-alcohol level.

bride, bridegroom, bridesmaid *Bride* is appropriate in wedding stories, but use *wife* or *spouse* in other circumstances.

brigadier See **military titles**.

Britain Acceptable in all references for *Great Britain,* which consists of England, Scotland and Wales.

See **United Kingdom**.

British Airways PLC Headquarters of this airline is in Hounslow, England. Owned by Consolidated Airlines Group S.A.

British, Briton(s) The people of Great Britain: the English, the Scottish, the Welsh. *Brits* is slang.

British Broadcasting Corp. *BBC* is acceptable in all references.

British Columbia The Canadian province bounded on the west by the Pacific Ocean. Do not abbreviate.

See **datelines**.

British Commonwealth See **Commonwealth, the**.

British thermal unit The amount of heat required to increase the temperature of a pound of water 1 degree Fahrenheit. *Btu* (the same for singular and plural) is acceptable on second reference.

British ton See **ton**.

British Virgin Islands Use with a community name in datelines on stories from these islands. Do not abbreviate.

Specify an individual island in the text if relevant.

See **datelines**.

broadcast The past tense also is *broadcast*, not *broadcasted*.

broadcast networks Major U.S. networks are:

ABC, owned by The Walt Disney Co.

CBS, owned by CBS Corp.

NBC, part of NBCUniversal, which is controlled by Comcast Corp.

Fox, owned by News Corp.

PBS, a private, nonprofit organization owned and operated by public television stations

The CW, a joint venture between Time Warner Inc.'s Warner Bros. unit and CBS Corp.

Telemundo, part of NBCUniversal

Univision Communications Inc.

Broadway, off-Broadway, off-off-Broadway When applied to stage productions, these terms refer to distinctions made by union contracts, not to location of a theater.

Actors' Equity Association and unions representing craft workers have one set of pay scales for *Broadway* productions (generally those in New York City theaters of 500 or more seats) and a lower scale for smaller theaters, classified as *off-Broadway* houses.

The term *off-off-Broadway* refers to workshop productions that may use Equity members for a limited time at substandard pay. Other unions maintain a hands-off policy, agreeing with the Equity attitude that actors should have an opportunity to develop their talents in offbeat roles without losing their Equity memberships.

Bronze Age The age characterized by the development of bronze tools and weapons, from 3500 to 1000 B.C. Regarded as coming between the Stone Age and the Iron Age.

Brothers Generally abbreviate as *Bros.* in formal company names: *Warner Bros.*, but follow the spelling preferred by the company.

For possessives: *Warner Bros.' profits*.

brownout See **blackout, brownout**.

brunette Use *brunette* as a noun for females. Use *brown-haired* for males.

Brussels The city in Belgium stands alone in datelines.

Btu The same in singular and plural. See **British thermal unit**.

Bubble Wrap A registered trademark. Unless the trademark name is important to the story, use *cushioning* or *packaging material*.

Budapest The capital of Hungary. In datelines, follow it with *Hungary*.

Bufferin A trademark for buffered aspirin.

bug, tap A concealed listening device designed to pick up sounds in a room, an automobile, or such is a *bug*.

A *tap* is a device attached to a telephone circuit to pick up conversations on the line.

building Never abbreviate. Capitalize the proper names of buildings, including the word *building* if it is an integral part of the proper name: *the Empire State Building*.

buildup (n. and adj.) **build up** (v.)

bull's-eye

bullet See **weapons**.

bullfight, bullfighter, bullfighting

bullion Unminted precious metals of standards suitable for coining.

bullpen One word, for the place where baseball pitchers warm up, and for a pen that holds cattle.

bull market A period of generally rising stock prices over a prolonged period, generally defined as a 20 percent or larger increase in broad stock indexes such as the Standard & Poor's 500.

bureau Capitalize when part of the formal name for an organization or agency: *the Bureau of Labor Statistics*.

Lowercase when used alone or to designate a corporate subdivision: *the Washington bureau of The Associated Press*.

Bureau of Alcohol, Tobacco, Firearms and Explosives *ATF* is acceptable in subsequent references to this agency of the Department of Justice. (Note the *Explosives* part of the name.)

burglary, larceny, robbery, theft Legal definitions of *burglary* vary, but in general a *burglary* involves entering a building (not necessarily by breaking in) and remaining unlawfully with the intention of committing a crime.

Larceny is the legal term for the wrongful taking of property. Its nonlegal equivalents are *stealing* or *theft*.

Robbery in the legal sense involves the use of violence or threat in committing larceny. In a wider sense it means to plunder or rifle, and may thus be used even if a person was not present: *His house was robbed while he was away*.

Theft describes a larceny that did not involve threat, violence or plundering.

USAGE NOTE: You *rob* a person, bank, house, etc., but you *steal* the money or the jewels.

Burlington Northern Santa Fe LLC The freight railroad, with headquarters in Fort Worth, Texas, is now owned by Berkshire Hathaway Inc.

burn To copy data, audio or video to optical media (such as a CD, a DVD or a Blu-ray Disc) with a laser.

burqa The all-covering dress worn by some Muslim women.

bus, buses Transportation vehicles. The verb forms: *bus, bused, busing.*

In a restaurant, to clear dishes from a table: *The busboy buses tables.* See **buss, busses**.

bushel A unit of dry measure equal to 4 pecks or 32 dry quarts. The metric equivalent is approximately 35.2 liters.

To convert to liters, multiply by 35.2 (5 bushels x 35.2 equals 176 liters).

See **liter**.

business editor Capitalize when used as a formal title before a name. See **titles**.

business names See **company names**.

buss, busses Kisses. The verb forms: *buss, bussed, bussing.* See **bus, buses**.

by- The rules in **prefixes** apply, but in general, no hyphen. Some examples:

byline	byproduct
bypass	bystreet

By-election is an exception. See the next entry.

by-election A special election held between regularly scheduled elections. The term most often is associated with special elections to the British House of Commons.

bylaw

bylines Our standard byline consists of *By*, followed by the name, in the byline field, and *Associated Press* as the bytitle. The bytitle can also be a special designation, like *AP Sports Writer.*

Use a byline only if the reporter was in the datelined community to gather the information reported.

Nicknames should not be used unless they specifically are requested by the writer.

In the case of a double byline, at least one of the bylined reporters must have reported in the datelined community. If the other reported from elsewhere, note that location in a tag line at the bottom of the story: *Smith reported from Washington.*

For materials or columns contributed by people like politicians or celebrities — cases in which we want to stress that the writer is not working for AP — use the bytitle *For The Associated Press.*

byte The digital basis for quantifying the amount of storage in computers and mobile devices. A byte consists of characters known as bits. The definition of larger storage amounts depend on whether they are counted under binary or decimal measurements. For instance, a kilobyte translates into 1,024 bytes under the binary method compared with 1,000 bytes in decimal terms. The disk storage on most devices is determined under the decimal system, which defines a megabyte as 1,000 kilobytes (or 1 million bytes), a gigabyte as 1,000 megabytes (or 1 billion bytes) and a terabyte as 1,000 gigabytes (or 1 trillion bytes). Abbreviate *GB* for *gigabyte, KB* for *kilobyte, MB* for *megabyte* and *TB* for *terabyte.*

cabinet Capitalize references to a specific body of advisers heading executive departments for a president, king, governor, etc.: *The president-elect said he has not made his Cabinet selections.*

See **department** for a listing of all the U.S. Cabinet departments.

cable networks Major U.S. cable networks are:

A&E, owned by A&E Television Networks, a joint venture of Hearst Corp. and The Walt Disney Co.

AMC (also We tv, IFC and Sundance Channel) owned by AMC Networks Inc.

Animal Planet, owned by Discovery Communications Inc.

BET, owned by Viacom Inc.

Bravo, owned by Comcast Corp.'s NBCUniversal

Cartoon Network, owned by Time Warner Inc.

CNBC, owned by Comcast Corp.'s NBCUniversal

CNN, owned by Time Warner Inc.

Comedy Central, owned by Viacom Inc.

Discovery Channel, owned by Discovery Communications Inc.

Disney Channel and Disney XD, owned by The Walt Disney Co.

Epix, owned by Viacom Inc., Metro-Goldwyn-Mayer Inc. and Lions Gate Entertainment Corp.

E! Entertainment Television, owned by Comcast Corp.'s NBCUniversal

ESPN, 80 percent owned by The Walt Disney Co. and 20 percent owned by Hearst Corp.

Esquire Network, owned by Comcast Corp.'s NBCUniversal

Fox News Channel, owned by Twenty-First Century Fox Inc.

FX, owned by Twenty-First Century Fox Inc.

Golf Channel, owned by Comcast Corp.'s NBCUniversal

HBO, owned by Time Warner Inc.

History, owned by A&E Television Networks, a joint venture of Hearst Corp. and The Walt Disney Co.

Lifetime, owned by A&E Television Networks, a joint venture of Hearst Corp. and The Walt Disney Co.

MSNBC, owned by Comcast Corp.'s NBCUniversal

MTV, owned by Viacom Inc.

NBC Sports Network, owned by Comcast Corp.'s NBCUniversal

NFL Network, owned by the National Football League

Nickelodeon, owned by Viacom Inc.

OWN: The Oprah Winfrey Network, a joint venture of Discovery Communications Inc. and Oprah Winfrey's Harpo Productions

Oxygen, owned by Comcast Corp.'s NBCUniversal

Showtime, owned by CBS Corp.

Sprout, owned by Comcast Corp.'s NBCUniversal

Starz, owned by Starz

Syfy, owned by Comcast Corp.'s NBCUniversal

TNT, TBS and Turner Classic Movies, owned by Time Warner Inc.

Travel Channel, 65 percent owned by Scripps Networks Interactive Inc. and 35 percent owned by Cox Communications Inc.

TV One, a joint venture between Radio One Inc. and Comcast Corp.'s NBCUniversal

USA Network, owned by Comcast Corp.'s NBCUniversal

VH1, owned by Viacom Inc.

The Weather Channel, owned by Comcast Corp.'s NBCUniversal, Bain Capital LLC and The Blackstone Group

cactus, cactuses

cadet See **military academies**.

Cairo The city in Egypt stands alone in datelines.

caliber The form: *.38-caliber pistol.*

See **weapons**.

California Abbreviate *Calif.* in datelines only; spell out in stories. Postal code: *CA*

See **state names**.

call letters Use all caps. Use hyphens to separate the type of station from the base call letters: *WBZ-AM, WBZ-FM, WBZ-TV.*

Citizens band operators, since 1983, are not required to be licensed by the Federal Communications Commission. Identification of such stations, either by the call sign previously assigned or made up by the operator, including the letter *K*, the operator's initials and the operator's ZIP code, is optional.

Amateur radio stations, which operate with greater power than citizens band stations and on different frequencies, typically mix letters and figures: *K2LRX.*

See **channel**; **citizens band**; **radio station**; and **television station**.

call-up (n. and adj.) **call up** (v.)

Cameroon See **geographic names**.

campaign manager Do not treat as a formal title. Always lowercase.

See **titles**.

Canada Montreal, Quebec City and Toronto stand alone in datelines. For all other datelines, use the city name and the name of the province or territory spelled out.

The 10 provinces of Canada are Alberta, British Columbia, Manitoba, New Brunswick, Newfoundland and Labrador (but usually known as just Newfoundland), Nova Scotia, Ontario, Prince Edward Island, Quebec and Saskatchewan.

The three territories are the Yukon, the Northwest Territories, and Nunavut (created April 1, 1999).

The provinces have substantial autonomy from the federal government.

The territories are administered by the federal government, although residents of the territories do elect their own legislators and representatives to Parliament.

See **datelines**.

Canada goose

Canadian Broadcasting Corp. *CBC* is acceptable in all references within contexts such as a television column. Otherwise, do not use *CBC* until second reference.

Canadian Press, The Canada's multimedia news agency. Its Francophone counterpart is La Presse Canadienne. Do not abbreviate *CP*.

canal Capitalize as an integral part of a proper name: *the Suez Canal.*

Canal Zone Do not abbreviate. No longer used except when referring to the Panama Canal area during the time it was controlled by the United States, exclusively or jointly with Panama, 1904-1999.

cancel, canceled, canceling, cancellation

cannon, canon A *cannon* is a weapon; plural is *cannons.* See **weapons**.

A *canon* is a law or rule, particularly of a church, or a musical composition.

cannot

cant The distinctive stock words and phrases used by a particular sect or class.

See **dialect**.

Canuck This reference to a Canadian is sometimes considered derogatory. It should be avoided except when in quoted matter or in terms used in Canada, such as references to the hockey team, the *Vancouver Canucks.*

canvas, canvass *Canvas* is heavy cloth.

Canvass is a noun and a verb denoting a survey.

cape Capitalize as part of a proper name: *Cape Cod, Cape Hatteras.* Lowercase when standing alone.

Although local practice may call for capitalizing *the Cape* when the rest of the name is clearly understood, always use the full name on first reference.

Cape Canaveral, Florida Formerly Cape Kennedy. See **John F. Kennedy Space Center**.

capital The city where a seat of government is located. Do not capitalize.

When used in a financial sense, *capital* describes money, equipment or property used in a business by a person or corporation.

See **Capitol**.

capital gain, capital loss The difference between what a *capital* asset cost and the price it brought when sold.

capitalization In general, avoid unnecessary capitals. Use a capital letter only if you can justify it by one of the principles listed here.

Many words and phrases, including special cases, are listed separately in this book. Entries that are capitalized without further comment should be capitalized in all uses.

If there is no relevant listing in this book for a particular word or phrase, consult Webster's New World College Dictionary. Use lowercase if the dictionary lists it as an acceptable form for the sense in which the word is being used.

As used in this book, *capitalize* means to use uppercase for the first letter of a word. If additional capital letters are needed, they are called for by an example or a phrase such as *use all caps.*

Some basic principles:

PROPER NOUNS: Capitalize nouns that constitute the unique identification for a specific person, place, or thing: *John, Mary, America, Boston, England.*

Some words, such as the examples just given, are always proper nouns. Some common nouns receive proper noun status when they are used as the name of a particular entity: *General Electric, Gulf Oil.*

PROPER NAMES: Capitalize common nouns such as *party, river, street* and *west* when they are an integral part of the full name for a person, place or thing: *Democratic Party, Mississippi River, Fleet Street, West Virginia.*

Lowercase these common nouns when they stand alone in subsequent references: *the party, the river, the street.*

Lowercase the common noun elements of names in plural uses: *the Democratic and Republican parties, Main and State streets, lakes Erie and Ontario.* Exception: plurals of formal titles with full names are capitalized: *Presidents Jimmy Carter and Gerald R. Ford.*

Among entries that provide additional guidelines are:

animals	**legislature**
brand names	**months**
building	**monuments**
committee	**nationalities**
Congress	**and races**
datelines	**nicknames**
days of the week	**organizations**
directions and	**and institutions**
regions	**planets**
family names	**plants**
food	**police department**
geographic names	**religious references**
governmental bodies	**trademarks**
heavenly bodies	**seasons**
historical periods	**trademarks**
and events	**unions**
holidays and	
holy days	

POPULAR NAMES: Some places and events lack officially designated proper names but have popular names that are the effective equivalent: *the Combat Zone* (a section of downtown Boston), *the Main Line* (a group of Philadelphia suburbs), *the South Side* (of Chicago), *the Badlands* (of South Dakota), *the Street* (the financial community in the Wall Street area of New York).

The principle applies also to shortened versions of the proper names of one-of-a-kind events: *the Series* (for the World Series), *the Derby* (for the Kentucky Derby). This practice should not, however, be interpreted as a license to ignore the general practice of lowercasing the common noun elements of a name when they stand alone.

DERIVATIVES: Capitalize words that are derived from a proper noun and still depend on it for their meaning: *American, Christian, Christianity, English, French, Marxism, Shakespearean.*

Lowercase words that are derived from a proper noun but no longer depend on it for their meaning: *french fries, herculean, malapropism, pasteurize, quixotic, venetian blind.*

SENTENCES: Capitalize the first word in a statement that stands as a sentence. See **sentences** and **parentheses**.

In poetry, capital letters are used for the first words of some phrases that would not be capitalized in prose. See **poetry**.

COMPOSITIONS: Capitalize the principal words in the names of books, movies, plays, poems, operas, songs, radio and television programs, works of art, etc. See **composition titles**, **magazine names** and **newspaper names**.

TITLES: Capitalize formal titles when used immediately before a name. Lowercase formal titles when used alone or in constructions that set them off from a name by commas.

Use lowercase at all times for terms that are job descriptions rather than formal titles.

See **academic titles**, **courtesy titles**, **legislative titles**, **military titles**, **nobility**, **religious titles** and **titles**.

ABBREVIATIONS: Capital letters apply in some cases. See **abbreviations and acronyms**.

Capitol Capitalize *U.S. Capitol* and *the Capitol* when referring to the building in Washington: *The meeting was held on Capitol Hill in the west wing of the Capitol.*

Follow the same practice when referring to state capitols: *The Virginia Capitol is in Richmond. Thomas Jefferson designed the Capitol of Virginia.*

See **capital**.

captain See **military titles** for military and police usage.

Lowercase and spell out in such uses as *team captain Carl Yastrzemski.*

carat, caret, karat The weight of precious stones, especially diamonds, is expressed in *carats*. A carat is equal to 200 milligrams or about 3 grains.

A *caret* is a writer's and a proofreader's mark.

The proportion of pure gold used with an alloy is expressed in *karats*.

carbine See **weapons**.

cardholder, credit card holder

cardinal numbers See **numerals**.

CARE CARE USA has its headquarters in Atlanta. CARE International is based in Geneva. They refer to themselves simply as *CARE.*

carefree

caretaker

Caribbean See **Western Hemisphere**.

carmaker, carmakers

Carnival Capitalize when referring specifically to the revelry in many Roman Catholic countries preceding Lent. Otherwise, a *carnival* is lowercase. See **Mardi Gras**.

car pool (n.) **carpool** (v. and adj.)

carry-on

carry-over (n. and adj.)

cash or collect on delivery The abbreviation *c.o.d.* is preferred in all references. This is an exception to Webster's New World College Dictionary.

caster, castor *Caster* is a roller. *Castor* is the spelling for the oil and the bean from which it is derived.

catalog, cataloged, cataloger, cataloging, catalogist

Caterpillar A trademark for a brand of crawler tractor. The formal name of the company is *Caterpillar Inc.* Headquarters is in Peoria, Illinois.

Use lowercase for the wormlike larva of various insects.

Cathay Pacific Airways Ltd. Headquarters of this airline is in Hong Kong.

Catholic, Catholicism Use *Roman Catholic Church, Roman Catholic* or *Roman Catholicism* in the first references to those who believe that the pope, as bishop of Rome, has the ultimate authority in administering an earthly organization founded by Jesus Christ.

Most subsequent references may be condensed to *Catholic Church, Catholic* or *Catholicism. Roman Catholic* should continue to be used, however, if the context requires a distinction between Roman Catholics and members of other denominations who often describe themselves as Catholic. They include some high church Episcopalians (who often call themselves *Anglo-Catholics*), members of Eastern Orthodox churches, and members of some national Catholic churches that have broken with Rome. Included in this last category is the Polish National Catholic Church.

Lowercase *catholic* where used in its generic sense of general or universal, meanings derived from a similar word in Greek.

Those who use *Catholic* in a religious sense are indicating their belief that they are members of a universal church that Jesus Christ left on Earth.

See **Roman Catholic Church**.

cats See **animals**.

CAT scan See **CT scan**.

cattle See **animals**.

Caucasian

Caucasus Mountains

cave-in (n. and adj.) **cave in** (v.)

CB See **citizens band radio**.

CBS The formal name is CBS Corp., which was created in December 2005 when Viacom Inc. split into two companies. Owner of *Simon & Schuster* book publishing and the *Showtime* cable network, besides TV and radio properties. Headquarters is in New York.

CD See **compact disc**.

CD-ROM Acronym for *compact disc* acting as *read-only memory*. *CD-ROM disc* is redundant.

cease-fire, cease-fires (n. and adj.) The verb form is *cease fire*.

cellophane Formerly a trademark, now a generic term.

cellphone

Celsius Use this term rather than *centigrade* for the temperature scale that is part of the metric system.

The Celsius scale is named for Anders Celsius, a Swedish astronomer who designed it. In it, zero represents the freezing point of water, and 100 degrees is the boiling point at sea level.

To convert to Fahrenheit, multiply a Celsius temperature by 9, divide by 5 and add 32 (25 x 9 equals 225, divided by 5 equals 45, plus 32 equals 77 degrees Fahrenheit).

To convert a temperature difference from Celsius to Fahrenheit, multiply by 9 and divide by 5. A difference of 5 degrees C is a 9-degree F difference.

When giving a Celsius temperature, use these forms: *40 degrees Celsius* or *40 C* (note the space and no period after the capital *C*) if degrees and Celsius are clear from the context.

See **Fahrenheit** and **metric system**.

cement *Cement* is the powder mixed with water and sand or gravel to make *concrete*. The proper term is *concrete* (not *cement*) *pavement*, *blocks*, *driveways*, etc.

censer, censor, censure A *censer* is a container in which incense is burned.

To *censor* is to prohibit or restrict the use of something.

To *censure* is to condemn.

census Capitalize only in specific references to the *U.S. Census Bureau.* Lowercase in other uses: *the census data was released Tuesday.*

Centers for Disease Control and Prevention
Located in Atlanta, the Centers for Disease Control and Prevention is part of the U.S. Department of Health and Human Services and works to control and prevent infectious and chronic diseases and promote good health. The centers also work with state and local health officials to provide specialized services.

On first reference, use *Centers for Disease Control and Prevention.* Precede with *national, federal* or *U.S.* if needed for clarity. *CDC* is acceptable on second reference and takes a singular verb.

Online: http://www.cdc.gov

centi- A prefix denoting one-hundredth of a unit. Move a decimal point two places to the left in converting to the basic unit: *155.6 centimeters equals 1.556 meters.*

centigrade See **Celsius**.

centimeter One-hundredth of a meter.

There are 10 millimeters in a centimeter.

To convert to inches, multiply by 0.4 (5 centimeters x 0.4 equals 2 inches).

See **meter**; **metric system**; and **inch**.

Central America
See **Western Hemisphere**.

Central Asia
The region includes Kyrgyzstan, Kazakhstan, Turkmenistan, Tajikistan and Uzbekistan.

central bank A bank having responsibility for controlling a country's monetary policy.

Central Intelligence Agency
CIA is acceptable in all references.

The formal title for the individual who heads the agency is *director of central intelligence.* On first reference: *Director Richard Helms of the CIA* or *CIA Director Richard Helms.*

Central Standard Time (CST), Central Daylight Time (CDT)
See **time zones**.

cents Spell out the word *cents* and lowercase, using numerals for amounts less than a dollar: *5 cents, 12 cents.* Use the *$* sign and decimal system for larger amounts: *$1.01, $2.50.* See **numerals**.

century Lowercase, spelling out numbers less than 10: *the first century, the 21st century.*

For proper names, follow the organization's practice: *21st Century Fox, Twentieth Century Limited.*

CEO, CFO, COO
Leading executives of a company.

CEO is acceptable in all references for *chief executive officer,* who typically has the primary decision-making authority. This role is separate from *chief financial officer* and *chief operating officer,* but an individual may hold more than one of these positions at a time.

Use *chief financial officer* on first reference and *CFO* thereafter. Typically handles major financial responsibilities, such as record keeping and financial planning.

Use *chief operating officer* on first reference and *COO* thereafter. Often responsible for a company's day-to-day operations.

Spell out other "C-level" positions, such as *chief administrative officer, chief information officer* or *chief risk officer*.

cesarean section *C-section* is acceptable on second reference.

Ceylon It is now *Sri Lanka*, which should be used in datelines and other references to the nation.

The people may be referred to as *Ceylonese* (n. or adj.) or *Sri Lankans*. The language is *Sinhalese*.

cha-cha

chain saw

chairman, chairwoman
Capitalize as a formal title before a name: *company Chairman Henry Ford, committee Chairwoman Margaret Chase Smith*.

Do not capitalize as a casual, temporary position: *meeting chairman Robert Jones*.

Do not use *chairperson, chair* or *co-chair* unless it is an organization's formal title for an office.

See **titles**.

chamber of deputies See **legislative bodies**.

chancellor The translation to English for the first minister in the governments of Germany and Austria. Capitalize when used before a name.

See **premier, prime minister** and **titles**.

changeable

changeover

change-up (n. and adj.) change up (v.)

channel Capitalize when used with a figure; lowercase elsewhere:

She turned to Channel 3. No channel will broadcast the game.

Also: *the English Channel*, but the channel on second reference.

chapters Capitalize *chapter* when used with a numeral in reference to a section of a book or legal code. Always use Arabic figures: *Chapter 1, Chapter 20.*

Lowercase when standing alone. See **numerals**.

character, reputation *Character* refers to moral qualities.

Reputation refers to the way a person is regarded by others.

charge off A loan that no longer is expected to be repaid and is written off as a bad debt.

Charleston, Charlestown, Charles Town *Charleston* is the name of the capital of West Virginia and a port city in South Carolina.

Charlestown is a section of Boston.

Charles Town is the name of a small city in West Virginia.

chauffeur

chauvinism, chauvinist The words mean unreasoning devotion to one's race, sex, country, etc., with contempt for other races, sexes, countries, etc.

The terms come from Nicolas Chauvin, a soldier of Napoleon I, who was famous for his devotion to the lost cause.

check-in (n. and adj.) check in (v.) When using a social network with location-based services, such as Facebook or Swarm, the act of sharing a location via a mobile device.

checkout (n. and adj.) check out (v.)

checkup (n.) **check up** (v.)

Chemical Mace A trademark, usually shortened to *Mace*, for a brand of tear gas that is packaged in an aerosol canister and temporarily stuns its victims.

Chennai Indian city formerly known as Madras.

Chevron Corp. Headquarters is in San Ramon, California.

Chevy Not *Chevie* or *Chevvy*. This nickname for the *Chevrolet* should be used only in automobile features or in quoted matter.

Chicago The city in Illinois stands alone in datelines.

Chicago Board of Trade Commodity trading market where contracts are traded for Treasury bonds, corn, soybeans, wheat, gold, silver, etc. Owned by CME Group Inc. See **CME Group Inc.**

Chicago Board Options Exchange Originally set up by the Chicago Board of Trade, the CBOE is the world's largest options exchange. Not part of CME Group Inc., parent company of the Chicago Board of Trade.

Chicano Sometimes used by Mexican-Americans in the Southwest. Not interchangeable with *Mexican-American*. Use only if a person's preference. See **Hispanic**, **Latino**, **nationalities and races**, and **race**.

chickenpox

chief Capitalize as a formal title before a name: *She spoke to police Chief Michael Codd. He spoke to Chief Michael Codd of the New York police.*

Lowercase when it is not a formal title: *union chief Walter Reuther*. See **titles**.

chief justice Capitalize only as a formal title before a name: *Chief Justice John Roberts*. The officeholder is the chief justice of the United States, not of the Supreme Court. See **judge**.

child care Two words, no hyphen, in all cases.

children In general, call children 15 or younger by their first name on second reference. Use the last name, however, if the seriousness of the story calls for it, as in a murder case, for example. For ages 16 and 17, use judgment, but generally go with the surname unless it's a light story. Use the surname for those 18 and older. See **privacy**.

Chile The nation.

chili, chillies See **Food Guidelines**.

China When used alone, it refers to the nation that includes the mainland, Hong Kong and Macau. Use China in mainland datelines; Hong Kong and Macau stand alone in datelines.

Use *People's Republic of China*, *Communist China* and *mainland China* only in direct quotations or when needed to distinguish the mainland and its government from Taiwan. Use *Red China* only in direct quotes.

For datelines on stories from the island of Taiwan, use the name of a community and *Taiwan*. In the body of a story, use *Taiwan* for references to the government based on the island. Use the formal name of the government, the *Republic of China*, when required for legal precision.

China Eastern Airlines Corp.
Headquarters is in Shanghai.

China Southern Airlines Headquarters is in Guangzhou, China.

Chinese names
A variety of systems are used for spelling Chinese names. For personal and place names from China, use the official Chinese spelling system known as *Pinyin: Senior leader Deng Xiaoping, Beijing*, or *Zhejiang province*.

In personal names, Chinese generally place surnames first and then given names, *Deng Xiaoping*. Second reference should be the family name, *Deng* in this case.

Some Chinese have Westernized their names, putting their given names or the initials for them first or sometimes using both an English name and a Chinese name: *P.Y. Chen, Jack Wang, Frank Hsieh Chang-ting.* In general, follow an individual's preferred spelling.

Normally Chinese women do not take their husbands' surnames. Use the courtesy titles *Mrs., Miss*, or *Ms.* only when specifically requested.

The Pinyin spelling system eliminates the hyphen or apostrophe previously used in many given names. Use the new spelling for *Mao Zedong* and *Zhou Enlai*, but keep the traditional American spelling for such historical figures as *Sun Yat-sen* and *Chiang Kai-shek*.

If the new Pinyin spelling of a proper noun is so radically different from the traditional American spelling that a reader might be confused, provide the Pinyin spelling followed by the traditional spelling in parentheses. For example, the city of *Fuzhou (Foochow).* Or use a descriptive sentence: *Fuzhou, long known in the West as Foochow, is the capital of Fujian province, on China's eastern coast.*

Use the traditional American spellings for these place names: *China, Inner Mongolia, Shanghai, Tibet.*

Follow local spellings in stories dealing with Hong Kong and Taiwan.

Capitalize the animal names for years in the Chinese lunar calendar: *Year of the Sheep, Year of the Dog.*

chip
In electronics, a sliver of semiconducting material (usually but not always silicon) on which an integrated circuit is fabricated. Chips perform a variety of functions, including processing information (microprocessors) and storing information (memory chips).

chipmaker (n.) chipmaking
(adj.)

Christmas, Christmas Day
Dec. 25. The federal legal holiday is observed on Friday if Dec. 25 falls on a Saturday, on Monday if it falls on a Sunday.

Never abbreviate *Christmas* to *Xmas* or any other form.

Christmastime
One word.

Christmas tree
Lowercase *tree* and other seasonal terms with *Christmas: card, wreath, carol*, etc. Exception: *National Christmas Tree.*

church
Capitalize as part of the formal name of a building, a congregation or a denomination; lowercase in other uses: *St. Mary's Church, the Roman Catholic Church, the Catholic and Episcopal churches, a Roman Catholic church, a church.*

Lowercase in phrases where the church is used in an institutional sense: *She believes in the separation of church and state. The pope said the church opposes abortion.*

See **religious titles** and the entry for the denomination in question in the **Religion** chapter.

CIA *CIA* is acceptable in all references.

The formal title for the individual who heads the agency is *director of central intelligence*. On first reference: *Director Richard Helms of the CIA* or *CIA Director Richard Helms*.

cigarette

Cincinnati The city in Ohio stands alone in datelines.

circles The central organizing principle of Google Plus. Users group each other into circles so they can control, on a case-by-case basis, who can see their posts.

Cisco Systems Inc. Headquarters is in San Jose, California.

cities and towns See **datelines** for guidelines on when they should be followed by a state or a country name.

Capitalize official names, including separate political entities such as *East St. Louis, Illinois*, or *West Palm Beach, Florida*.

The preferred form for the section of a city is lowercase: *the west end*, *northern Los Angeles*. But capitalize widely recognized names for the sections of a city: *South Side* (Chicago), *Lower East Side* (New York). See **city**.

Citigroup Inc. Formed from the combination of Travelers Group and Citicorp in 1998. *Citibank* is its banking unit. Headquarters is in New York.

citizen, resident, subject, national, native A *citizen* is a person who has acquired the full civil rights of a nation either by birth or naturalization. Cities and states in the United States do not confer citizenship. To avoid confusion, use *resident*, not *citizen*, in referring to inhabitants of states and cities.

Citizen is also acceptable for those in the United Kingdom, or other monarchies where the term *subject* is often used.

National is applied to a person residing away from the nation of which he or she is a citizen, or to a person under the protection of a specified nation.

Native is the term denoting that an individual was born in a given location.

citizens band Without an apostrophe after the *s*, based on widespread practice.

CB is acceptable on second reference.

The term describes a group of radio frequencies set aside by the Federal Communications Commission for local use at low power by individuals or businesses.

city Capitalize *city* if part of a proper name, an integral part of an official name, or a regularly used nickname: *Kansas City, New York City, Windy City, City of Light, Fun City*.

Lowercase elsewhere: *a Texas city*; *the city government*; *the city Board of Education*; and all *city of* phrases: *the city of Boston*.

Capitalize when part of a formal title before a name: *City Manager Francis McGrath*. Lowercase when not part of the formal title: *city Health Commissioner Frank Smith*.

See **city council** and **governmental bodies**.

city commission See the next entry.

city council Capitalize when part of a proper name: *the Boston City Council*.

Retain capitalization if the reference is to a specific council but the context does not require the city name:

BOSTON (AP) — The City Council ...

Lowercase in other uses: *the council, the Boston and New York city councils, a city council.*

Use the proper name if the body is not known as a city council: *the Miami City Commission, the City Commission, the commission; the Louisville Board of Aldermen, the Board of Aldermen, the board.*

Use *city council* in a generic sense for plural references: *the Boston, Louisville and Miami city councils.*

city editor Capitalize as a formal title before a name. See **titles**.

city hall Capitalize with the name of a city, or without the name of a city if the reference is specific: *Boston City Hall, City Hall.*

Lowercase plural uses: *the Boston and New York city halls.*

Lowercase generic uses, including: *You can't fight city hall.*

citywide

civil cases, criminal cases
A *civil case* is one in which an individual, business or agency of government seeks damages or relief from another individual, business or agency of government. Civil actions generally involve a charge that a contract has been breached or that someone has been wronged or injured.

A *criminal case* is one that the state or the federal government brings against an individual charged with committing a crime.

Civil War

cleanup (n. and adj.) **clean up** (v.)

clear-cut (adj.)

clerical titles See **religious titles**.

Cleveland The city in Ohio stands alone in datelines.

click-thrus A way of measuring how many people click a link online to see its destination site. Click-thrus are often used to set advertising rates.

clientele

climate change See **global warming**.

clinically dead, clinical death Avoid these terms and seek explanation if used by a medical professional. There is no standard definition, though generally means the heart and breathing have stopped. It's possible in some cases to resuscitate a person, such as a victim of sudden cardiac arrest. See **brain-dead, brain death**.

cloak-and-dagger

Clorox A trademark for a brand of bleach.

closed shop A *closed shop* is an agreement between a union and an employer that requires workers to be members of a union before they may be employed.

A *union shop* requires workers to join a union within a specified period after they are employed.

An *agency shop* requires that the workers who do not want to join the union pay the union a fee instead of union dues.

A *guild shop*, a term often used when the union is The Newspaper Guild, is the same as a *union shop*.

See the **right-to-work** entry for an explanation of how some states prohibit contracts that require workers to join unions.

closely held corporation A corporation in which stock shares and voting control are concentrated in the hands of a small number of investors, but for which some shares are available and traded on the market.

close-up (n. and adj.)

cloture Not *closure*, for the parliamentary procedure for closing debate.

Whenever practical, use a phrase such as closing debate or ending debate instead of the technical term.

cloud Remote servers that can be accessed online for the storage of data and the use of related computing services.

CME Group Inc. Parent of the Chicago Board of Trade, the Chicago Mercantile Exchange, the New York Mercantile Exchange and COMEX, which operates the CME Globex electronic trading platform and live trading floors in Chicago and New York. Its products include futures and options based on interest rates, equity indexes, foreign exchange, agricultural commodities, energy, metals, and alternative investment products, such as weather and real estate. It also clears over-the-counter derivatives. Headquarters is in Chicago.

CNN Acceptable in all references for the *Cable News Network*. Owned by Time Warner Inc.

co- Retain the hyphen when forming nouns, adjectives and verbs that indicate occupation or status:

co-author	co-pilot
co-chairman	co-respondent
	(in a divorce suit)
co-defendant	co-signer
co-host	co-sponsor
co-owner	co-star
co-partner	co-worker

(Several are exceptions to Webster's New World College Dictionary in the interests of consistency.)

Use no hyphen in other combinations:

coed	cooperate
coeducation	cooperative
coequal	coordinate
coexist	coordination
coexistence	copay

Cooperate, coordinate and related words are exceptions to the rule that a hyphen is used if a prefix ends in a vowel and the word that follows begins with the same vowel.

Co. See **company, companies**.

coast Lowercase when referring to the physical shoreline: *Atlantic coast, Pacific coast, east coast.*

Capitalize when referring to regions of the United States lying along such shorelines: *the Atlantic Coast states, a Gulf Coast city, the West Coast, the East Coast.*

Do not capitalize when referring to smaller regions: *the Virginia coast.*

Capitalize *the Coast* when standing alone only if the reference is to the West Coast.

coastal waters See **weather terms**.

Coast Guard Capitalize when referring to this branch of the U.S. armed forces, a part of the Department of Homeland Security: *the U.S. Coast Guard, the Coast Guard, Coast Guard policy.* Do not use the abbreviation *USCG*, except in quotes.

Use lowercase for similar forces of other nations.

This approach has been adopted for consistency, because many foreign nations do not use *coast guard* as the proper name.

See **military academies**.

Coast Guardsman Capitalize as a proper noun when referring to an individual in a U.S. Coast Guard unit: *He is a Coast Guardsman.*

Lowercase *guardsman* when it stands alone.

See **military titles**.

coastline

coattails

cocaine The slang term *coke* should appear only in quoted matter.

Crack is a refined cocaine in crystalline rock form.

c.o.d. Preferred in all references for *cash on delivery* or *collect on delivery.* This is an exception to Webster's New World College Dictionary.

coed The preferred term as a noun is *female student*, but *coed* is acceptable as an adjective to describe coeducational institutions. No hyphen.

Cold War Capitalize when referring specifically to the post-World War II rivalry between the United States and the former Soviet Union. Use only in the historic sense.

collateral Stock or other property that a borrower is obliged to turn over to a lender if unable to repay a loan.

See **loan terminology**.

collateralized debt obligations Debt, including bonds or mortgages, that is pooled, sliced up and resold to investors.

collectibles

collective nouns Nouns that denote a unit take singular verbs and pronouns: *class, committee, crowd, family, group, herd, jury, orchestra, team.*

Some usage examples: *The committee is meeting to set its agenda. The jury reached its verdict. A herd of cattle was sold.*

Team names and musical group names that are plural take plural verbs. *The Yankees are in first place. The Jonas Brothers are popular.*

Team or group names with no plural forms also take plural verbs: *The Miami Heat are battling for third place.* Other examples: *Orlando Magic, Oklahoma City Thunder, Utah Jazz.*

Many singular names take singular verbs: *Coldplay is on tour. Boston is favored in the playoffs. Stanford is in the NCAA Tournament.*

But some proper names that are plural in form take a singular verb: *Brooks Brothers is holding a sale.*

PLURAL IN FORM: Some words that are plural in form become collective nouns and take singular verbs when the group or quantity is regarded as a unit.

Right: *A thousand bushels is a good yield.* (A unit.)

Right: *A thousand bushels were created.* (Individual items.)

Right: *The data is sound.* (A unit.)

Right: *The data have been carefully collected.* (Individual items.)

collectors' item

college Capitalize when part of a proper name: *Dartmouth College.*

See **organizations and institutions**.

collide, collision Two objects must be in motion before they can *collide.* A moving train cannot *collide* with a stopped train.

colloquialisms The word describes the informal use of a language. It is not local or regional in nature, as dialect is.

Webster's New World College Dictionary identifies many words as colloquial with the label *Informal*.

Many colloquial words and phrases characteristic of informal writing and conversation are acceptable in some contexts but out of place in others.

Other colloquial words normally should be avoided because they are pejorative. Webster's New World College Dictionary notes, for example, that *ain't* is informal, a "dialectal or nonstandard usage," although "widely used informally by educated speakers." Many still consider it illiterate and it should not be used in news stories unless needed to illustrate nonstandard speech in writing.

See **dialect**.

colon See entry in **Punctuation** chapter.

colonel See **military titles**.

colonial Capitalize *Colonial* as a proper adjective in all references to the *Colonies*. (See the next entry.)

colonies Capitalize only for the British dependencies that declared their independence in 1776, now known as the United States.

Colorado Abbreviate *Colo.* in datelines only; spell out in stories. Postal code: *CO*
See **state names**.

colorblind

colored In some societies, including the United States, the word is considered derogatory and should not be used.

In some countries of Africa, it is used to denote individuals of mixed racial ancestry. Whenever the word is used, place it in quotation marks and provide an explanation of its meaning.

Columbus Day Oct. 12. The federal legal holiday is the second Monday in October.

coma A state of unconsciousness in which the eyes are closed and the patient can't be aroused as if simply asleep. There is no sign of a sleep-wake cycle, or of any awareness of self or environment. The patient cannot communicate or hear, and shows no emotion. Any movement is purely reflex. This is the first stage after a severe brain injury; the patient may recover partially or completely, die, or progress to a vegetative or minimally conscious state.

See **minimally conscious state** and **vegetative state**.

combat, combated, combating

combustible

Comcast Corp. Nation's largest operator of cable TV and residential Internet services. Owns *NBCUniversal*, which includes the NBC television network and such cable channels as *MSNBC, CNBC, Bravo* and *Syfy, Universal Pictures* movie studio and theme parks. Headquarters is in Philadelphia.

comedian Use for both men and women.

comma See entry in **Punctuation** chapter.

commander See **military titles**.

commander in chief Capitalize only if used as a formal title before a name.
See **titles**.

commercial paper Short-term loans, issued primarily by corporations, to finance their daily needs, such as making payroll. Historically, a lower cost alternative to bank loans.

commissioner Do not abbreviate. Capitalize when used as a formal title.
See **titles**.

commitment

committee Do not abbreviate. Capitalize when part of a formal name: *the House Appropriations Committee*.
Do not capitalize committee in shortened versions of long committee names: *The Senate Banking, Housing and Urban Affairs Committee*, for example, became *the Senate banking committee*.
See **subcommittee**.

commodities futures contract A contract to purchase or sell a specific amount of a given commodity at a specified future date.

commodity The products of mining or agriculture before they have undergone extensive processing.

common stock, preferred stock An ownership interest in a corporation.
If other classes of stock are outstanding, the holders of common stock are the last to receive dividends and the last to receive payments if a corporation is dissolved. The company may raise or lower

common stock dividends as its earnings rise or fall.
When preferred stock is outstanding and company earnings are sufficient, a fixed dividend is paid. If a company is liquidated, holders of preferred stock receive payments up to a set amount before any money is distributed to holders of common stock.

commonwealth A group of people united by their common interests.
See **state**.

Commonwealth of Independent States Founded Dec. 8, 1991, the organization is made up of 11 of the former republics of the USSR, or Soviet Union. Russia is the largest and richest. Three other former republics — Latvia, Lithuania and Estonia — became independent nations earlier in 1991. (The Soviet Union was formally dissolved in December 1991. Its last leader, Mikhail Gorbachev, resigned on Dec. 25, 1991.)
The republics (with adjective form in parentheses):
Armenia (Armenian); Azerbaijan (Azerbaijani); Belarus (Belarusian); Kazakhstan (Kazakh); Kyrgyzstan (Kyrgyz); Moldova (Moldovan); Russia (Russian); Tajikistan (Tajik); Turkmenistan (Turkmen); Ukraine (no *the*) (Ukrainian); Uzbekistan (Uzbek). Georgia (Georgian) quit CIS in 2008.
DATELINES: MOSCOW stands alone. Follow all other datelines with the name of the state. *ALMATY, Kazakhstan.*

Commonwealth, the Formerly the British Commonwealth. The members of this free association of sovereign states recognize the British sovereign as head of the Commonwealth. Some also recognize the sovereign as head of their state; others do not.

The members are: Antigua and Barbuda, Australia, Bahamas, Bangladesh, Barbados, Belize, Botswana, Brunei, Cameroon, Canada, Cyprus, Dominica, Fiji, Gambia, Ghana, Grenada, Guyana, India, Jamaica, Kenya, Kiribati, Lesotho, Malawi, Malaysia, Maldives, Malta, Mauritius, Mozambique, Namibia, Nauru, New Zealand, Nigeria, Pakistan (suspended after the 1999 military coup; suspension lifted 2004), Papua New Guinea, St. Kitts and Nevis, St. Lucia, St. Vincent and the Grenadines, Samoa, Seychelles, Sierra Leone, Singapore, Solomon Islands, South Africa, Sri Lanka, Swaziland, Tanzania, Tonga, Trinidad and Tobago, Tuvalu, Uganda, United Kingdom, Vanuatu and Zambia. (Zimbabwe withdrew in 2003.)

Communications Workers of America *CWA* is acceptable on second reference.

Headquarters is in Washington.

communism, communist See **political parties and philosophies**.

commutation A legal term for a change of sentence or punishment to one that is less severe.

See **pardon, parole, probations**.

compact disc *CD* is acceptable in all references.

company, companies Use *Co.* or *Cos.* when a business uses either word at the end of its proper name: *Ford Motor Co., American Broadcasting Cos.*

If *company* or *companies* appears alone in second reference, spell the word out.

The forms for possessives: *Ford Motor Co.'s profits, American Broadcasting Cos.' profits.*

company (military) Capitalize only when part of a name: *Company B.* Do not abbreviate.

company names For a company's formal name, consult the national stock exchanges: the New York Stock Exchange, www.nyse.com, or Nasdaq, www.nasdaq.com or filings with the Securities and Exchange Commission.

Do not use a comma before *Inc.* or *Ltd.*, even if it is included in the formal name.

You must include the full company name somewhere in the story. This ensures the story will be among the search results on major websites.

The formal name need not be used on first reference — for example, *Costco* is acceptable for *Costco Wholesale Corp.* — but it should be contained in the body of any story in which the subject matter could affect a company's business. For example, include the corporate name in a story on an earnings report, or in a story on a plane crash that could affect the airline's stock price. However, the corporate name might be irrelevant in a story about a political candidate's appearance at a local retail store.

If "The" is part of the formal company name it should be included. For example: *The Walt Disney Co.*

Generally, follow the spelling preferred by the company, but capitalize the first letter of company names in all uses: e.g., *Adidas, Lululemon.* Exceptions include company names such as *eBay*, which have a capital letter elsewhere in the name. However, company names should always be capitalized at the beginning of a sentence. For corporate news, AP may use the legal name from the Securities and Exchange Commission filing rather than a company's preference: *Wal-Mart*, not *Walmart*;

Twenty-First Century Fox, not *21st Century Fox*.

Do not use all-capital-letter names unless the letters are individually pronounced: *BMW*. Others should be uppercase and lowercase. *Ikea*, not *IKEA*; *USA Today*, not *USA TODAY*.

Do not use symbols such as exclamation points, plus signs or asterisks that form contrived spellings that might distract or confuse a reader. Use *Yahoo*, not *Yahoo!*; *Toys R Us*, not *Toys "R" Us*; *E-Trade*, not *E*Trade*.

Use an ampersand only if it is part of the company's formal name, but not otherwise in place of *and*.

Use *the* lowercase unless it is part of the company's formal name.

Here are 125 major U.S. companies, listed alphabetically with ticker symbols and headquarters:

3M Co. (MMM) St. Paul, Minn.

Abbott Laboratories (ABT) Abbott Park, Ill.

Aetna Inc. (AET) Hartford, Conn.

Alcoa Inc. (AA) New York

The Allstate Corp. (ALL) Northbrook, Ill.

Altria Group Inc. (MO) Richmond, Va.

Amazon.com Inc. (AMZN) Seattle

American Express Co. (AXP) New York

American International Group Inc. (AIG) New York

Amgen Inc. (AMGN) Thousand Oaks, Calif.

Anadarko Petroleum Corp. (APC) The Woodlands, Texas

Anthem Inc. (ANTM) Indianapolis (previously WellPoint Inc.)

Apple Inc. (AAPL) Cupertino, Calif.

AT&T Inc. (T) Dallas

Bank of America Corp. (BAC) Charlotte, N.C.

Berkshire Hathaway Inc. (BRK.B) Omaha, Neb.

Best Buy Co. (BBY) Richfield, Minn.

Biogen Idec Inc. (BIIB) Cambridge, Mass.

Boeing Co. (BA) Chicago

Bristol-Myers Squibb Co. (BMY) New York

Carnival Corp. (CCL) Miami

Caterpillar Inc. (CAT) Peoria, Ill.

CBS Corp. (CBS) New York

Chevron Corp. (CVX) San Ramon, Calif.

Cisco Systems Inc. (CSCO) San Jose, Calif.

Citigroup Inc. (C) New York

The Coca-Cola Co. (KO) Atlanta

Colgate-Palmolive Co. (CL) New York

Comcast Corp. (CMCSA) Philadelphia

ConAgra Foods Inc. (CAG) Omaha, Neb.

ConocoPhillips (COP) Houston

Costco Wholesale Corp. (COST) Issaquah, Wash.

CVS Health Corp. (CVS) Woonsocket, R.I.

Deere & Co. (DE) Moline, Ill.

Delta Air Lines Inc. (DAL) Atlanta

DirecTV (DTV) El Segundo, Calif.

Dow Chemical Co. (DOW) Midland, Mich.

Duke Energy Corp. (DUK) Charlotte, N.C.

DuPont Co. (DD) Wilmington, Del.

eBay Inc. (EBAY) San Jose, Calif.

Eli Lilly and Co. (LLY) Indianapolis

Exelon Corp. (EXC) Chicago

Express Scripts Holding Co. (ESRX) St. Louis

Exxon Mobil Corp. (XOM) Irving, Texas

Facebook Inc. (FB) Menlo Park, Calif.

FedEx Corp. (FDX) Memphis, Tenn.

Ford Motor Co. (F) Dearborn, Mich.

The Gap Inc. (GPS) San Francisco

General Dynamics Corp. (GD) Falls Church, Va.

General Electric Co. (GE) Fairfield, Conn.

General Mills Inc. (GIS) Minneapolis

General Motors Co. (GM) Detroit

The Goldman Sachs Group Inc. (GS) New York

Google Inc. (GOOG) Mountain View, Calif.

Halliburton Co. (HAL) Houston

Hewlett-Packard Co. (HPQ) Palo Alto, Calif.

The Home Depot Inc. (HD) Atlanta

Honeywell International Inc. (HON) Morris Township, N.J.

Intel Corp. (INTC) Santa Clara, Calif.

International Business Machines Corp. (IBM) Armonk, N.Y.

J.C. Penney Co. (JCP) Plano, Texas

Johnson & Johnson (JNJ) New Brunswick, N.J.

JPMorgan Chase & Co. (JPM) New York

Kellogg Co. (K) Battle Creek, Mich.

Kimberly-Clark Corp. (KMB) Irving, Texas

Kraft Foods Group Inc. (KRFT) Northfield, Ill.

The Kroger Co. (KR) Cincinnati, Ohio

Lockheed Martin Corp. (LMT) Bethesda, Md.

Lowe's Cos. (LOW) Mooresville, N.C.

Macy's Inc. (M) corporate offices in New York and Cincinnati

Marathon Oil Corp. (MRO) Houston

MasterCard Inc. (MA) Purchase, N.Y.

McDonald's Corp. (MCD) Oak Brook, Ill.

McKesson Corp. (MCK) San Francisco

Medtronic Inc. (MDT) Minneapolis

Merck & Co. (MRK) Whitehouse Station, N.J.

MetLife Inc. (MET) New York

Microsoft Corp. (MSFT) Redmond, Wash.

Mondelez International Inc. (MDLZ) Deerfield, Ill.

Monsanto Co. (MON) St. Louis

Morgan Stanley (MS) New York

News Corp. (NWSA) New York

Nike Inc. (NKE) Beaverton, Ore.

Norfolk Southern Corp. (NSC) Norfolk, Va.

Northrop Grumman Corp. (NOC) Falls Church, Va.

Occidental Petroleum Corp. (OXY) Houston

Oracle Corp. (ORCL) Redwood City, Calif.

PepsiCo Inc. (PEP) Purchase, N.Y.

Pfizer Inc. (PFE) New York

Phillips 66 (PSX) Houston

PNC Financial Services Group Inc. (PNC) Pittsburgh

The Procter & Gamble Co. (PG) Cincinnati

Prudential Financial Inc. (PRU) Newark, N.J.

Qualcomm Inc. (QCOM) San Diego

Raytheon Co. (RTN) Waltham, Mass.

Schlumberger Ltd. (SLB) Houston

Sears Holdings Corp. (SHLD) Hoffman Estates, Ill.

Simon Property Group Inc. (SPG) Indianapolis

Southwest Airlines Co. (LUV) Dallas

Sprint Corp. (S) Overland Park, Kan.

Starbucks Corp. (SBUX) Seattle
Staples Inc. (SPLS) Framingham, Mass.
Target Corp. (TGT) Minneapolis
Texas Instruments Inc. (TXN) Dallas
Time Warner Inc. (TWX) New York
Travelers Cos. (TRV) St. Paul, Minn.
Twitter Inc. (TWTR) San Francisco
Tyson Foods Inc. (TSN) Springdale, Ark.
Union Pacific Corp. (UNP) Omaha, Neb.
United Continental Holdings Inc. (UAL) Chicago
UnitedHealth Group Inc. (UNH) Minnetonka, Minn.
United Parcel Service Inc. (UPS) Atlanta
United States Steel Corp. (X) Pittsburgh
United Technologies Corp. (UTX) Hartford, Conn.
U.S. Bancorp (USB) Minneapolis
Verizon Communications Inc. (VZ) New York
Viacom Inc. (VIA) New York
Visa Inc. (V) Foster City, Calif.
Walgreen Co. (WAG) Deerfield, Ill.
Wal-Mart Stores Inc. (WMT) Bentonville, Ark.
The Walt Disney Co. (DIS) Burbank, Calif.
WellPoint Inc. (WLP) Indianapolis
Wells Fargo & Co. (WFC) San Francisco
Whole Foods Market Inc. (WFM) Austin, Texas
Xerox Corp. (XRX) Norwalk, Conn.
Yahoo Inc. (YHOO) Sunnyvale, Calif.

Here are 75 major non-U.S. companies, listed alphabetically with headquarters:

Airbus Group, Leiden, Netherlands
Allianz SE, Munich
America Movil SAB de CV, Mexico City
Anheuser-Busch InBev SA, Leuven, Belgium
ArcelorMittal, Luxembourg
AstraZeneca PLC, London
Baidu Inc., Beijing
Banco Santander SA, Madrid
Bank of China Ltd., Beijing
Barclays PLC, London
Barrick Gold Corp., Toronto
Bayer AG, Leverkusen, Germany
BHP Billiton Ltd., Melbourne, Australia
BMW Group, Munich
BNP Paribas SA, Paris
BP PLC, London
Carrefour SA, Boulogne-Billancort, France
China Construction Bank Corp., Beijing
China Mobile Ltd., Hong Kong
China Petroleum & Chemical Corp. or Sinopec, Beijing
CNOOC Ltd., Beijing
Credit Suisse Group AG, Zurich
Daimler AG, Stuttgart, Germany
Deutsche Bank AG, Frankfurt, Germany
Deutsche Telekom AG, Bonn, Germany
Diageo PLC, London
Electricite de France SA, Paris
Eni SpA, Rome
E.ON SE, Dusseldorf, Germany
Fiat Automobiles SpA, Turin, Italy
Gazprom OAO, Moscow
GlaxoSmithKline PLC, London
Glencore PLC, Baar, Switzerland
H&M Hennes & Mauritz AB, Stockholm
Honda Motor Co., Tokyo
HSBC Holdings PLC, London
Industrial and Commercial Bank of China Ltd., Beijing
ING Groep NV, Amsterdam
L'Oreal SA, Paris

LVMH Moet Hennessy Louis Vuitton SA, Paris

Mitsubishi UFJ Financial Group Inc., Tokyo

Nestle SA, Vevey, Switzerland

Nintendo Co., Kyoto, Japan

Nippon Telegraph & Telephone Corp., Tokyo

Nissan Motor Co., Yokohama, Japan

Nokia Corp., Espoo, Finland

Novartis AG, Basel, Switzerland

Novo Nordisk A/S, Bagsværd, Denmark

PetroChina Co., Beijing

Petroleo Brasileiro SA, Rio de Janeiro

Ranbaxy Laboratories Ltd., Gurgaon, India

Reliance Industries Ltd., Mumbai, India

Rio Tinto PLC, London

Roche Holding AG, Basel, Switzerland

Royal Dutch Shell PLC, The Hague, Netherlands

SABMiller PLC, London

Samsung Electronics Co., Suwon, South Korea

Sanofi SA, Paris

SAP SE, Walldorf, Germany

Siemens AG, Munich

Societe Generale SA, Paris

Sony Corp., Tokyo

Tata Group, Mumbai, India

Telefonica SA, Madrid

Tesco PLC, Hertfordshire, England

Teva Pharmaceutical Industries Ltd., Petach Tikvah, Israel

ThyssenKrupp AG, Essen, Germany

Total SA, Paris

Toyota Motor Corp., Toyota City, Japan

UBS AG, Zurich

Unilever NV, London and Rotterdam, Netherlands

Vale SA, Rio de Janeiro

Vivendi SA, Paris

Vodafone Group PLC, Newbury, England

Volkswagen AG, Wolfsburg, Germany

compared to, compared with

Use *compared to* when the intent is to assert, without the need for elaboration, that two or more items are similar: *She compared her work for women's rights to Susan B. Anthony's campaign for women's suffrage.*

Use *compared with* when juxtaposing two or more items to illustrate similarities and/or differences: *His time was 2:11:10, compared with 2:14 for his closest competitor.*

compatible

complacent, complaisant

Complacent means self-satisfied.

Complaisant means eager to please.

complement, compliment

Complement is a noun and a verb denoting completeness or the process of supplementing something: *The ship has a complement of 200 sailors and 20 officers. The tie complements his suit.*

Compliment is a noun or a verb that denotes praise or the expression of courtesy: *The captain complimented the sailors. She was flattered by the compliments on her project.*

complementary, complimentary
The husband and wife have complementary careers.

They received complimentary tickets to the show.

compose, comprise, constitute
Compose means to create or put together. It commonly is used in both the active and passive voices: *She composed a song. The United States is composed of 50 states. The zoo is composed of many animals.*

Comprise means to contain, to include all or embrace. It is best used only in the active voice, followed by a direct object: *The United States comprises 50 states. The jury comprises five men and seven women. The zoo comprises many animals.*

Constitute, in the sense of form or make up, may be the best word if neither *compose* nor *comprise* seems to fit: *Fifty states constitute the United States. Five men and seven women constitute the jury. A collection of animals can constitute a zoo.*

Use *include* when what follows is only part of the total: *The price includes breakfast. The zoo includes lions and tigers.*

composition titles Apply the guidelines listed here to book titles, computer game titles, movie titles, opera titles, play titles, poem titles, album and song titles, radio and television program titles, and the titles of lectures, speeches and works of art.

The guidelines, followed by a block of examples:

—Capitalize the principal words, including prepositions and conjunctions of four or more letters.

—Capitalize an article — *the, a, an* — or words of fewer than four letters if it is the first or last word in a title.

—Put quotation marks around the names of all such works except the Bible and books that are primarily catalogs of reference material. In addition to catalogs, this category includes almanacs, directories, dictionaries, encyclopedias, gazetteers, handbooks and similar publications. Do not use quotation marks around such software titles as WordPerfect or Windows.

—Translate a foreign title into English unless a work is generally known by its foreign name. An exception to this is reviews of musical performances. In those instances, generally refer to the work in the language it was sung in, so as to differentiate for the reader. However, musical compositions in Slavic languages are always referred to in their English translations.

EXAMPLES: *"The Star-Spangled Banner," "The Rise and Fall of the Third Reich," "Gone With the Wind," "Of Mice and Men," "For Whom the Bell Tolls," "Time After Time,"* the NBC-TV *"Today"* program, the *"CBS Evening News," "The Mary Tyler Moore Show."* See television program names for further guidelines and examples.

Reference works: *IHS Jane's All the World's Aircraft; Encyclopaedia Britannica; Webster's New World Dictionary of the American Language, Second Edition.*

Names of most websites and apps are capitalized without quotes: *Facebook, Foursquare.*

Exception: *"FarmVille"* and similar computer game apps are in quotes.

Foreign works: *Rousseau's "War,"* not *Rousseau's "La Guerre."* But: *Leonardo da Vinci's "Mona Lisa."* Mozart's *"The Marriage of Figaro"* if sung in English but *"Le Nozze di Figaro"* if sung in Italian. Mozart's *"The Magic Flute"* if sung in English but *"Die Zauberfloete"* if sung in German. *"Die Walkuere"* and *"Goetterdaemmerung"* from Wagner's *"Der Ring des Nibelungen"* if sung in German but *"The Valkyrie"* and *"The Twilight of the Gods"* from *"The Ring of the Nibelung"* if sung in English. Janacek's *"From the House of the Dead,"* not Janacek's *"Z Mrtveho Domu."*

— For other classical music titles, use quotation marks around the composition's nicknames but not compositions identified by its sequence.

EXAMPLES: *Dvorak's "New World Symphony." Dvorak's Symphony No. 9.*

compound adjectives See **hyphen** entry in **Punctuation** chapter.

comptroller, controller *Comptroller* generally is the accurate word for government financial officers.

The U.S. comptroller of the currency is an appointed official in the Treasury Department who is responsible for the chartering, supervising and liquidation of banks organized under the federal government's National Bank Act.

Controller generally is the proper word for financial officers of businesses and for other positions such as *air traffic controller*.

Capitalize *comptroller* and *controller* when used as the formal titles for financial officers. Use lowercase for *air traffic controller* and similar occupational applications of the word.

See **titles**.

concentration camps For World War II camps in countries occupied by Nazi Germany, do not use phrases like *Polish death camps* that confuse the location and the perpetrators. Use instead, for example, *death camps in Nazi-occupied Poland.*

conclave A private or secret meeting. In the Roman Catholic Church it describes the private meeting of cardinals to elect a pope.

concrete See **cement**.

Confederate States of America The formal name of the states that seceded during the Civil War. The shortened form *the Confederacy* is acceptable in all references.

Conference Board, The The capitalized article is part of the formal name of the business organization.

confess, confessed In some contexts the words may be erroneous.

See **admit**.

confidant, confidante (n.) A male friend to whom one confides secrets. The female spelling is *confidante*.

conglomerate A corporation that has diversified its operations, usually by acquiring enterprises in widely varied industries.

Congo Note the two countries in Africa: the Democratic Republic of Congo whose capital is Kinshasa, and the Republic of Congo whose capital is Brazzaville.

In datelines:
KINSHASA, Congo (AP) —
BRAZZAVILLE, Republic of Congo (AP) —

Use Congo when referring to the Democratic Republic of Congo. If referring to the country whose capital is Brazzaville, the full name — *Republic of Congo* — should be used.

Congress Capitalize *U.S. Congress* and *Congress* when referring to the U.S. Senate and House of Representatives. Although *Congress* sometimes is used as a substitute for the House, it properly is reserved for reference to both the Senate and House.

Capitalize *Congress* also if referring to a foreign body that uses the term, or its equivalent in a foreign language, as part of its formal name: *the Argentine Congress, the Congress.*

Lowercase when used as a synonym for *convention* or in second reference to an organization that uses the word as part of its formal name: *the Congress of Racial Equality, the congress.*

congressional Lowercase unless part of a proper name: *congressional salaries, the Congressional Quarterly, the Congressional Record.*

Congressional Directory Use this as the reference source for questions about the federal government that are not covered by this stylebook.

congressional districts Use figures and capitalize district when joined with a figure: *the 1st Congressional District, the 1st District.*

Lowercase *district* whenever it stands alone.

See **numerals**.

Congressional Record A daily publication of the proceedings of Congress including a complete stenographic report of all remarks and debates.

congressman, congresswoman Use only in reference to members of the U.S. House of Representatives. *Rep.* and *U.S. Rep.* are the preferred first-reference forms when a formal title is used before the name of a U.S. House member. The words *congressman* or *congresswoman,* in lowercase, may be used in subsequent references that do not use an individual's name, just as *senator* is used in references to members of the Senate.

Congressman and *congresswoman* should appear as capitalized formal titles before a name only in direct quotation.

See **legislative titles**.

Congress of Racial Equality *CORE* is acceptable on second reference.

Headquarters is in New York.

Connecticut Abbreviate *Conn.* in datelines only; spell out in stories. Postal code: *CT*

See **state names**.

connote, denote *Connote* means to suggest or imply something beyond the explicit meaning: *To some people, the word "marriage" connotes too much restriction.*

Denote means to be explicit about the meaning: *The word "demolish" denotes destruction.*

ConocoPhillips Headquarters is in Houston.

consensus

conservative See **political parties and philosophies**.

constable Capitalize when used as a formal title before a name.

See **titles**.

constitute See **compose, comprise, constitute**.

constitution Capitalize references to the U.S. Constitution, with or without the *U.S.* modifier: *The president said he supports the Constitution.*

When referring to constitutions of other nations or of states, capitalize only with the name of a nation or a state: *the French Constitution, the Massachusetts Constitution, the nation's constitution, the state constitution, the constitution.*

Lowercase in other uses: *the organization's constitution.*

Lowercase *constitutional* in all uses.

consulate A *consulate* is the residence of a consul in a foreign city. It handles the commercial affairs and personal needs of citizens of the appointing country.

Capitalize with the name of a nation; lowercase without it: *the French Consulate, the U.S. Consulate, the consulate.*

See **embassy** for the distinction between a consulate and an embassy.

consul, consul general, consuls general Capitalize when used as a formal title before a noun.
See **titles**.

consumer credit Loans extended to individuals or small businesses usually on an unsecured basis, and providing for monthly repayment. Also referred to as installment credit or personal loans.

Consumer Financial Protection Bureau Created by Congress under the 2010 financial overhaul to oversee mortgages, payday loans and other consumer borrowing. It aimed to close regulatory gaps exposed by the 2008 financial crisis. *CFPB* is acceptable on second reference.

consumer price index A measurement of changes in the retail prices of a constant marketbasket of goods and services. It is computed by comparing the cost of the marketbasket at a fixed time with its cost at subsequent or prior intervals.

It is issued monthly by the Bureau of Labor Statistics, an agency of the Labor Department. It should not be referred to as a *cost-of-living index*, because it does not include the impact of income taxes and Social Security taxes on the cost of living, nor does it reflect changes in buying patterns that result from inflation. It is, however, the basis for computing cost-of-living raises in many union contracts.

The preferred form for second reference is *the index*. Confine *CPI* to quoted material.

The *chained consumer price index* is a version of the CPI used by the government to account for substitutions consumers typically make in their purchases when prices of certain goods change. Some consider it a more accurate gauge of consumer prices than the conventional CPI. Avoid using the term *chained CPI* in stories.

Consumer Product Safety Commission *CPSC* is acceptable on second reference. Headquarters is in Bethesda, Maryland.

contagious

contemptible

continent The seven continents, in order of their land size: Asia, Africa, North America, South America, Europe, Antarctica and Australia.

Capitalize *the Continent* and *Continental* only when used as synonyms for Europe or European. Lowercase in other uses such as: *the continent of Europe, the European continent, the African and Asian continents.*

Continental Divide The ridge along the Rocky Mountains that separates rivers flowing east from those that flow west.

continental shelf, continental slope Lowercase. The *shelf* is the part of a continent that is submerged in relatively shallow sea at gradually increasing depths, generally up to about 600 feet below sea level.

The *continental slope* begins at the point where the descent to the ocean bottom becomes very steep.

continual, continuous *Continual* means a steady repetition, over and over again: *The merger has been the source of continual litigation.*

Continuous means uninterrupted, steady, unbroken: *All she saw ahead of her was a continuous stretch of desert.*

Contra, Contras Uppercase when used to describe former Nicaraguan rebel groups.

contractions Contractions reflect informal speech and writing. Webster's New World College Dictionary includes many entries for contractions: *aren't* for *are not*, for example.

Avoid excessive use of contractions. Contractions listed in the dictionary are acceptable, however, in informal contexts where they reflect the way a phrase commonly appears in speech or writing.

See **colloquialisms** and **quotations in the news**.

contrasted to, contrasted with Use *contrasted to* when the intent is to assert, without the need for elaboration, that two items have opposite characteristics: *He contrasted the appearance of the house today to its ramshackle look last year.*

Use *contrasted with* when juxtaposing two or more items to illustrate similarities and/or differences: *He contrasted the Republican platform with the Democratic platform.*

control, controlled, controlling

controller See **comptroller, controller**.

controversial An overused word; avoid it.

convention Capitalize as part of the name for a specific national or state political convention: *the Democratic National Convention, the Republican State Convention.*

Lowercase in other uses: *the national convention, the state convention, the convention, the annual convention of the American Medical Association.*

convertible bond See **loan terminology**.

convict (v.) Follow with preposition *of*, not *for*: *He was convicted of murder.*

convince, persuade You may be *convinced that* something or *of* something. You must be *persuaded* to *do* something.

Example: *John convinced Marsha of his good intentions. John persuaded Marsha to marry him.*

cookie, cookies A file many websites place on computers to save identifying information.

cooperate, cooperative But *co-op* as a short term of *cooperative*, to distinguish it from *coop*, a cage for animals.

Cooperative for Assistance and Relief Everywhere See **CARE**.

coordinate, coordination

cop Be careful in the use of this colloquial term for *police officer*. It may be used in lighter stories and in casual, informal descriptions, but often is a derogatory term out of place in serious police stories.

Copenhagen The city in Denmark carries the country name in datelines.

copter Acceptable shortening of *helicopter*. But use it only as a noun or adjective. It is not a verb.

copy editor Seldom a formal title. Also: *copy editing, copy edit*. See **titles**.

copyright (n., v. and adj.) *A copyright story.*

Use *copyrighted* only as the past tense of the verb: *He copyrighted the article.*

See **Copyright Infringement** in **Briefing on Media Law** section.

co-respondent In a divorce suit.

Corn Belt The region in the north-central Midwest where much corn and corn-fed livestock are raised. It extends from western Ohio to eastern Nebraska and northeastern Kansas.

Corp. See **corporation**.

corporal See **military titles**.

corporate names See **company names**.

corporation An entity that is treated as a person in the eyes of the law. It is able to own property, incur debts, sue and be sued.

Abbreviate *corporation* as *Corp.* when a company or government agency uses the word at the end of its name: *the Federal Deposit Insurance Corp.*

Spell out *corporation* when it occurs elsewhere in a name: *the Corporation for Public Broadcasting.*

Spell out and lowercase *corporation* whenever it stands alone.

The form for possessives: *Chevron Corp.'s profits.*

corps Capitalize when used with a word or a figure to form a proper name: *the Marine Corps, the Signal Corps, the 9th Corps, the Army Corps of Engineers.*

Capitalize when standing alone only if it is a shortened reference to *U.S. Marine Corps* or *Army Corps of Engineers.*

The possessive form is *corps'* for both singular and plural: *one corps' location, two corps' assignments.*

corral, corralled, corralling

correctional facility, correctional institution See **prison, jail**.

Corsica Use instead of *France* in datelines on stories from communities on this island.

Cortes The Spanish parliament. See **legislative bodies**.

cosmonaut A Russian or Soviet astronaut.

cost of living The amount of money needed to pay taxes and to buy the goods and services deemed necessary to make up a given standard of living, taking into account changes that may occur in tastes and buying patterns.

The term often is treated incorrectly as a synonym for the *U.S. Consumer Price Index*, which does not take taxes into account and measures only price changes, keeping the quantities constant over time.

Hyphenate when used as a compound modifier: *The cost of living went up, but he did not receive a cost-of-living raise.*

See **consumer price index** and **inflation**.

cost-plus

Cotton Belt The region in the South and Southwestern sections of the United States where much cotton is grown.

council, councilor, councilman, councilwoman A deliberative body and those who are members of it.

See **counsel** and **legislative titles**.

Council of Economic Advisers

A group of advisers who help the U.S. president prepare his annual economic report to Congress and recommend economic measures to him throughout the year.

counsel, counseled, counseling, counselor, counselor at law

To *counsel* is to advise. A *counselor* is one who advises.

A *counselor at law* (no hyphens for consistency with *attorney at law*) is a lawyer. See **lawyer**.

count, countess See **nobility**.

counter- The rules in **prefixes**

apply, but in general, no hyphen. Some examples:

counteract	counterproposal
countercharge	counterspy
counterfoil	

countryside

county Capitalize when an

integral part of a proper name: *Dade County, Nassau County, Suffolk County.*

Capitalize the full names of county governmental units: *the Dade County Commission, the Orange County Department of Social Services, the Suffolk County Legislature.*

Retain capitalization for the name of a county body if the proper noun is not needed in the context; lowercase the word *county* if it is used to distinguish an agency from state or federal counterparts: *the Board of Supervisors, the county Board of Supervisors; the Department of Social Services, the county Department of Social Services.* Lowercase *the board, the department,* etc. whenever they stand alone.

Capitalize *county* if it is an integral part of a specific body's name even without the proper noun: *the County Commission, the County Legislature.* Lowercase *the commission, the legislature,* etc. when not preceded by the word *county.*

Capitalize as part of a formal title before a name: *County Manager John Smith.* Lowercase when it is not part of the formal title: *county Health Commissioner Frank Jones.*

Avoid *county of* phrases where possible, but when necessary, always lowercase: *the county of Westchester.*

Lowercase plural combinations: *Westchester and Rockland counties.*

Apply the same rules to similar terms such as *parish.*

See **governmental bodies**.

county court In some states, it

is not a court but the administrative body of a county. In most cases, the *court* is presided over by a *county judge,* who is not a judge in the traditional sense but the chief administrative officer of the county.

The terms should be explained if they are not clear in the context.

Capitalize all references to a specific *county court,* and capitalize *county judge* when used as a formal title before a name. Do not use *judge* alone before a name except in direct quotations.

Examples:

SEVIERVILLE, Tenn. (AP) — A reluctant County Court approved a school budget today that calls for a 10 percent tax increase for property owners.

The county had been given an ultimatum by the state: Approve the budget or shut down the schools.

The chief administrative officer, County Judge Ray Reagan, said ...

coup d'etat The word *coup* usually is sufficient.

couple When used in the sense

of two people, the word takes plural verbs and pronouns: *The couple were married Saturday and left Sunday on their honeymoon. They will return in two weeks.*

In the sense of a single unit, use a singular verb: *Each couple was asked to give $10.*

couple of The *of* is necessary. Never use *a couple tomatoes* or a similar phrase.

The phrase takes a plural verb in constructions such as: *A couple of tomatoes were stolen.*

coupon See **loan terminology** for its meaning in a financial sense.

course numbers Use Arabic numerals and capitalize the subject when used with a numeral: *History 6, Philosophy 209.* Otherwise, lowercase: *calculus, world history.*

court decisions Use figures and a hyphen: *The Supreme Court ruled 5-4, a 5-4 decision.* The word *to* is not needed, but use hyphens if it appears in quoted matter: *The court ruled 5-to-4, the 5-to-4 decision.*

court districts See **court names**.

courtesy titles Refer to both men and women by first and last name, without courtesy titles, on first reference: *Susan Smith* or *Robert Smith.* Refer to both men and women by last name, without courtesy titles, in subsequent references. Use the courtesy titles *Mr., Miss, Ms.* or *Mrs.* only in direct quotations or after first reference when a woman specifically requests it: for example, where a woman prefers to be known as *Mrs. Smith* or *Ms. Smith.*

When it is necessary to distinguish between two people who use the same last name, as in married couples or brothers and sisters, use the first and last name, without courtesy title.

In cases where a person's gender is not clear from the first name or from the story's context, indicate the gender by using *he* or *she* in subsequent reference.

courthouse Capitalize with the name of a jurisdiction: *the Cook County Courthouse, the U.S. Courthouse.* Lowercase in other uses: *the county courthouse, the courthouse, the federal courthouse.*

Court House (two words) is used in the proper names of some communities: *Appomattox Court House, Virginia.*

court-martial, court-martialed, courts-martial

court names Capitalize the full proper names of courts at all levels.

Retain capitalization if *U.S.* or a state name is dropped: *the U.S. Supreme Court, the Supreme Court, the state Superior Court, the Superior Court, Superior Court.*

For courts identified by a numeral: *2nd District Court, 8th U.S. Circuit Court of Appeals.*

For additional details on federal courts, see **judicial branch** and separate listings under **U.S.** and the court name.

See **judge** for guidelines on titles before the names of judges.

Court of St. James's Note the *'s.* The formal name for the royal court of the British sovereign. Derived from St. James's Palace, the former scene of royal receptions.

courtroom

cover-up (n. and adj.) **cover up** (v.)

Cox Enterprises Inc. Privately held communications company with headquarters in Atlanta. It operates cable TV, newspapers, TV and radio. It also owns Valpak, the direct-marketing service.

CPR Acceptable in all references for *cardiopulmonary resuscitation*.

crackup (n. and adj.) **crack up** (v.)

crawfish Not *crayfish*. An exception to Webster's New World College Dictionary based on the dominant spelling in Louisiana, where it is a popular delicacy.

credit default swaps A form of insurance that promises payment to investors in mortgage securities and other bonds if borrowers default.

Creutzfeldt-Jakob disease A rare degenerative brain disorder. Another form, *variant Creutzfeldt-Jakob disease*, is related to mad cow disease. The word *"variant"* is needed to distinguish it from the classic *Creutzfeldt-Jakob disease*, which is not related to mad cow disease. See **mad cow disease**.

Crimea A Black Sea peninsula seized from Ukraine by Russia and annexed in March 2014. The international community has refused to recognize the Russian annexation, while tacitly acknowledging that Ukraine has lost control over Crimea for the foreseeable future. The capital is Simferopol. In stories, the dateline should be Crimea, without reference to Ukraine or Russia: *SIMFEROPOL, Crimea*.

criminal cases See **civil cases, criminal cases** and **privacy**.

cripple See **disabled, handicapped**.

crisis, crises

crisscross

criterion, criteria

cross-examination (n.) **cross-examine** (v.)

crossfire

crossover (n. and adj.)

cross rate The rate of exchange between two currencies calculated by referring to the rates between each and a third currency.

cross section (n.) **cross-section** (v.)

crosstown

crowdsourcing The practice of asking a large collection of individuals online to help gather information or produce ideas. Social networks are commonly used for crowdsourcing. A blogger or journalist might crowdsource ideas for his or her writing, or a company might crowdsource a commercial from amateur video submissions.

CSX Corp. Freight railroad, with headquarters in Jacksonville, Florida.

CT scan *Computerized tomography*, a method of making multiple X-ray images of the body or parts of the body and using a computer to construct, from those images, cross-sectional views. (Formerly known as *CAT scan*.)

Cub Scouts See **Boy Scouts**.

cup Equal to 8 fluid ounces. The approximate metric equivalents are 240 milliliters or 0.24 of a liter.
To convert to liters, multiply by 0.24 (14 cups x 0.24 = 3.36 liters, or 3,360 milliliters).
See **liter**.

curate To find, select, package and present hand-picked content to the public online, in contrast to the distribution of material through automated news feeds. Often used in conjunction with social media.

cure-all

currency conversions Currency conversions are necessary in stories that use foreign currency to make clear for readers how a number translates into dollars. But conversions should be used sparingly and preferably not in the lead unless it's a significant part of a story. A conversion is generally needed only the first time a currency is mentioned. The reader can make the necessary conversions after that.

Do not convert amounts that are not current because exchange rates change over time.

If necessary for clarity in the story, specify that the conversion is at current exchange rates.

Examples:

AMSTERDAM (AP) — Anheuser-Busch InBev, the world's largest brewer, says its third-quarter profits rose as the takeover of new brands and higher selling prices offset the impact of lower sales volumes.

The company, based in Leuven, Belgium, said Thursday that net profit was up 31 percent to $2.37 billion (1.73 billion euros), from $1.81 billion in the same period a year earlier.

The gain largely reflects the company's $20 billion purchase in June of the 50 percent of Mexico's Grupo Modelo it didn't already own.

PARIS (AP) — French cosmetics giant L'Oreal says sales of its Maybelline makeup, Garnier shampoo and other beauty aids helped lift earnings to a new record in 2013.

The company behind Lancome cosmetics and the Body Shop retail chain reported net profit of 2.96 billion euros

($4 billion) last year, up 3.2 percent from 2.87 billion in 2012.

For all other currencies, following the amount, spell out the name of the currency followed in parentheses by the equivalent in U.S. dollars. *Japan approved a 1.8 trillion yen ($18 billion) extra budget to partially finance an economic stimulus package.*

When dealing with a dollar currency of a country other than the United States, use the following abbreviations before the amount on second and subsequent references:

AU$ Australian dollars
CA$ Canadian dollars
SG$ Singapore dollars
NZ$ New Zealand dollars
HK$ Hong Kong dollars
NT$ New Taiwan dollars
ZW$ Zimbabwe dollars

Treasurer Wayne Swan approved a 16 billion Australian dollar ($10.74 billion) deal. Swan said AU$8 billion would be reserved for capital expenditure.

currency depreciation, currency devaluation A nation's money *depreciates* when its value falls in relation to the currency of other nations or in relation to its own prior value.

A nation's money is *devalued* when its value is reduced in relation to the currency of other nations, either deliberately by the government or through market forces.

When a nation devalues its currency, the goods it imports tend to become more expensive. Its exports tend to become less expensive in other nations and thus more competitive.

See **devaluations**.

curtain raiser

Customs Capitalize in U.S. Immigration and Customs Enforcement and in U.S. Customs and Border Protection, both agencies of the Department of Homeland Security.

Lowercase elsewhere: *a customs official, a customs ruling, she went through customs.*

cutback (n. and adj.) **cut back** (v.)

cutoff (n. and adj.) **cut off** (v.)

The CW U.S. television network jointly owned by CBS Corp. and Time Warner Inc.'s Warner Bros. division. Formed through merger of the WB and UPN networks.

cyber-, cyberspace, cyber Follow the general rule for prefixes and do not use a hyphen: *cyberattack, cyberbullying, cybercafe, cybersecurity.* Exceptions: *Cyber Monday* (n.) and *cyber* (adj.) as a separate modifier: e.g., *cyber shopping, cyber liability insurance.*

cyclone See **weather terms**.

Cyclone A trademark for a brand of chain-link fence.

cynic, skeptic A *skeptic* is a doubter.

A *cynic* is a disbeliever.

czar Not *tsar*. It was a formal title only for the ruler of Russia and some other Slavic nations.

Lowercase in all other uses.

D

dad Uppercase only when the noun substitutes for a name as a term of address: *Hi, Dad!*

Daimler AG German luxury automaker. Divested its *Chrysler* unit in August 2007. Brands are *Mercedes-Benz, smart* and *Maybach*. Based in Stuttgart, Germany.

Dallas The city in Texas stands alone in datelines.

dam Capitalize when part of a proper name: *Hoover Dam.*

damage, damages *Damage* is destruction: *Authorities said damage from the storm would total more than $1 billion.*

Damages are awarded by a court as compensation for injury, loss, etc.: *The woman received $25,000 in damages.*

dame See **nobility**.

damn it Use instead of *dammit*, but like other profanity it should be avoided unless there is a compelling reason.

See **obscenities, profanities, vulgarities**.

dangling modifiers Avoid modifiers that do not refer clearly and logically to some word in the sentence.

Dangling: *Taking our seats, the game started.* (*Taking* does not refer to the subject, *game,* nor to any other word in the sentence.)

Correct: *Taking our seats, we watched the opening of the game.* (*Taking* refers to *we,* the subject of the sentence.)

Dardanelles, the Not *the Dardanelles Strait.*

Dark Ages The period beginning with the fall of Rome in 476 and ending about the 10th century. The term is derived from the idea that this period in Europe was characterized by intellectual stagnation, widespread ignorance and poverty.

dark horse

dash See entry in **Punctuation** chapter.

data A plural noun, it normally takes plural verbs and pronouns.

See the **collective nouns** entry, however, for an example of when *data* may take singular verbs and pronouns.

Use *databank* and *database,* but *data processing* (n. and adj.) and *data center.*

date line Two words for the imaginary line that separates one day from another.

See the **international date line** entry.

datelines Datelines on stories should contain a city name, entirely in capital letters, followed in most cases by the name of the state, county or territory where the city is located.

DOMESTIC DATELINES: A list of domestic cities that stand alone in datelines:

ATLANTA	MILWAUKEE
BALTIMORE	MINNEAPOLIS
BOSTON	NEW ORLEANS
CHICAGO	NEW YORK
CINCINNATI	OKLAHOMA CITY
CLEVELAND	PHILADELPHIA
DALLAS	PHOENIX
DENVER	PITTSBURGH
DETROIT	ST. LOUIS
HONOLULU	SALT LAKE CITY
HOUSTON	SAN ANTONIO
INDIANAPOLIS	SAN DIEGO
LAS VEGAS	SAN FRANCISCO
LOS ANGELES	SEATTLE
MIAMI	WASHINGTON

Stories from all other U.S. cities should have both the city and state name in the dateline, including *KANSAS CITY, Mo.*, and *KANSAS CITY, Kan.*

Spell out *Alaska, Hawaii, Idaho, Iowa, Maine, Ohio, Texas* and *Utah.* Abbreviate others as listed in this book under the full name of each state.

Use *Hawaii* on all cities outside Honolulu. Specify the island in the text if needed.

Follow the same practice for communities on islands within the boundaries of other states: *EDGARTOWN, Mass.*, for example, not *EDGARTOWN, Martha's Vineyard.*

Use *BEVERLY HILLS, Calif.* It's an incorporated city and the dateline for the Golden Globes movie awards, sponsored by the Hollywood Foreign Press Association and held at the Beverly Hilton Hotel.

STATE SERVICES: Additional cities in a state or region may stand alone.

U.S. POSSESSIONS: Apply the guidelines listed below in the IS-LAND NATIONS AND TERRITORIES section and the OVERSEAS TERRITORIES section.

INTERNATIONAL DATELINES: These international locations stand alone in datelines:

AMSTERDAM	MEXICO CITY
BAGHDAD	MILAN
BANGKOK	MONACO
BEIJING	MONTREAL
BEIRUT	MOSCOW
BERLIN	MUNICH
BRUSSELS	NEW DELHI
CAIRO	PANAMA CITY
DJIBOUTI	PARIS
DUBLIN	PRAGUE
GENEVA	QUEBEC CITY
GIBRALTAR	RIO DE JANEIRO
GUATEMALA CITY	ROME
HAVANA	SAN MARINO
HELSINKI	SAO PAULO
HONG KONG	SHANGHAI
ISLAMABAD	SINGAPORE
ISTANBUL	STOCKHOLM
JERUSALEM	SYDNEY
JOHANNESBURG	TOKYO
KUWAIT CITY	TORONTO
LONDON	VATICAN CITY
LUXEMBOURG	VIENNA
MACAU	ZURICH
MADRID	

In addition, use *UNITED NATIONS* alone, without a *N.Y.* designation, in stories from *U.N.* headquarters.

BALKANS: With the independence of Montenegro from Serbia-Montenegro formalized in 2006, use a Montenegro-only dateline, such as *PODGORICA, Montenegro.* Stories originating in Serbia carry a Serbia-only dateline: *BELGRADE, Serbia.* With the independence of Kosovo in 2008, use Kosovo in the dateline, such as *PRISTINA, Kosovo.*

CANADIAN DATELINES: Datelines on stories from Canadian cities other than Montreal, Quebec City and Toronto should contain the name of the city in capital letters followed by the name of the province. Do not abbreviate any province or territory name.

COMMONWEALTH OF INDEPENDENT STATES: For cities in the former Soviet Union, datelines include city and republic name: *ALMATY, Kazakhstan.*

OTHER NATIONS: Stories from other international cities that do not stand alone in datelines should contain the name of the country or territory (see the next section) spelled out.

SPELLING AND CHOICE OF NAMES: In most cases, the name of the nation in a dateline is the conventionally accepted short form of its official name: *Argentina,* for example, rather than *Republic of Argentina.* (If in doubt, look for an entry in this book. If none is found, follow Webster's New World College Dictionary.)

Note these special cases:

–Instead of *United Kingdom,* use *England, Northern Ireland, Scotland* or *Wales.*

–For divided nations, use the commonly accepted names based on geographic distinctions: *North Korea, South Korea.*

–Use an article only with *El Salvador.* For all others, use just a country name – *Gambia, Netherlands, Philippines,* etc.

See *geographic names* for guidelines on spelling the names of international cities and nations not listed here or in separate entries.

ISLAND NATIONS AND TERRITORIES: When reporting from nations and territories that are made up primarily of islands but commonly are linked under one name, use the city name and the general name in the dateline. Identify an individual island, if needed, in the text:

Examples:

British Virgin Islands
Netherlands Antilles
Indonesia   Philippines

OVERSEAS TERRITORIES: Some overseas territories, colonies and other areas that are not independent nations commonly have accepted separate identities based on their geographic character or special status under treaties. In these cases, use the commonly accepted territory name after a city name in a dateline.

Examples:

Bermuda	Martinique
Corsica	Puerto Rico
Crimea	Sardinia
Faeroe Islands	Sicily
Greenland	Sikkim
Guadeloupe	Tibet
Guam	

WITHIN STORIES: In citing other cities within the body of a story:

—No further information is necessary if a city is in the same state as the datelined city. Make an exception only if confusion would result.

—Follow the city name with further identification in most cases where it is not in the same state or nation as the dateline city. The additional identification may be omitted, however, if no confusion would result. There is no need, for example, to refer to *Boston, Mass.,* in a story datelined *NEW YORK.*

—Provide a state or nation identification for the city if the story has no dateline. However, cities that stand alone in datelines may be used alone in those stories if no confusion would result.

dateline selection A dateline should tell the reader that the AP obtained the basic information for the story in the datelined city.

Do not, for example, use a Washington dateline on a story written primarily from information that a newspaper reported under a Washington dateline. Use the home city of the newspaper instead.

This rule does not preclude the use of a story with a dateline different from the home city of a newspaper if it is from the general area served by the newspaper.

Use an international dateline only if the basic information in a story was obtained by a full- or part-time correspondent physically present in the datelined community.

If a radio broadcast monitored in another city was the source of information, use the dateline of the city where the monitoring took place and mention the fact in the story.

When a story has been assembled from sources in widely separated areas, use no dateline.

dates Always use Arabic figures, without *st, nd, rd* or *th*. See **months** for examples and **punctuation** guidelines.

daughter-in-law, daughters-in-law

Daughters of the American Revolution *DAR* is acceptable on second reference.

Headquarters is in Washington.

day care Two words, no hyphen, in all uses.

daylight saving time Not *savings*. No hyphen.

When linking the term with the name of a time zone, use only the word *daylight*: *Eastern Daylight Time, Pacific Daylight Time*, etc.

Lowercase *daylight saving time* in all uses and *daylight time* whenever it stands alone.

A federal law specifies that daylight time applies from 2 a.m. on the second Sunday of March until 2 a.m. on the first Sunday of November in areas that do not specifically exempt themselves.

See **time zones**.

daylong, dayslong

Day One Capitalize and spell out as a chronological device for summarizing multiday events such as Day One, Day Two. Lowercase in casual or conversational references.

days of the week Capitalize them. Do not abbreviate, except when needed in a tabular format: *Sun, Mon, Tue, Wed, Thu, Fri, Sat* (three letters, without periods, to facilitate tabular composition).

See **time element**.

daytime

day to day, day-to-day Hyphenate when used as a compound modifier: *They have extended the contract on a day-to-day basis.*

D.C. See **District of Columbia**.

D-Day June 6, 1944, the day the Allies invaded Western Europe in World War II.

DDT Preferred in all references for the insecticide *dichlorodiphenyltrichloroethane*.

dead center

dead end (n.) **dead-end** (adj.)

Dead Sea Scrolls

deaf See **disabled, handicapped**.

deaf-mute Avoid the term. The preferred form is to say that an individual cannot hear or speak. A *mute* person may be deaf or may be able to hear.

Do not use *deaf and dumb*.

dean Capitalize when used as a formal title before a name: *Dean John Jones, Deans John Jones and Susan Smith.*

Lowercase in other uses: *John Jones, dean of the college; the dean.*

dean's list Lowercase in all uses: *He is on the dean's list. She is a dean's list student.*

deathbed (n. and adj.)

death, die Don't use euphemisms like *passed on* or *passed away* except in a direct quote.

death row

debt The money a company or individual owes a creditor.

debt service The outlay necessary to meet all interest and principal payments during a given period.

decades Use Arabic figures to indicate decades of history. Use an apostrophe to indicate numerals that are left out; show plural by adding the letter *s*: *the 1890s, the '90s, the Gay '90s, the 1920s, the mid-1930s.*
See **historical periods and events**.

deci- A prefix denoting one-tenth of a unit. Move the decimal point one place to the left in converting to the basic unit: 15.5 decigrams = 1.55 grams.

decimal units Use a period and numerals to indicate decimal amounts. Decimalization should not exceed two places in textual material unless there are special circumstances.
For amounts less than 1, use the numeral zero before the decimal point: 0.03.
See **fractions** and **numerals**.

Declaration of Independence Lowercase *the declaration* whenever it stands alone.

decorations See **awards and decorations**.

deep-sea (adj.)

Deep South Capitalize both words when referring to the region that consists of Alabama, Georgia, Louisiana, Mississippi and South Carolina.

deep water (n.) **deep-water** (adj.)

default The failure to meet a financial obligation, the failure to make payment either of principal or interest when due or a breach or nonperformance of the terms of a note or mortgage.

defendant

defense Do not use it as a verb.

defense attorney Always lowercase, never abbreviate.
See **attorney** and **titles**.

defense spending *Military spending* usually is the more precise term.

definitely Overused as a vague intensifier. Avoid it.

deflation A decrease in the general price level, which results from a decrease in total spending relative to the supply of available goods on the market. Deflation's immediate effect is to increase purchasing power.

degree-day See **weather terms**.

degrees See **academic degrees**.

dek- (before a vowel), **deka-** (before a consonant) A prefix denoting 10 units of a measure. Move the decimal point one place to the right to convert to the basic unit: 15.6 dekameters = 156 meters.

Delaware Abbreviate *Del.* in datelines only; spell out in stories. Postal code: *DE*
See **state names**.

delegate The formal title for members of the lower houses of legislatures in states including Delaware, Maryland, Virginia and West Virginia. Capitalize only before their names. Abbreviate as a formal title before names, as local usage allows.

Always lowercase in other uses: *convention delegate Richard Henry Lee.*

Delta Air Lines Inc. Headquarters is in Atlanta.

demagogue, demagoguery

democrat, democratic, Democratic Party See the **political parties and philosophies** entry.

Democratic Governors Association No apostrophe.

Democratic National Committee On the second reference: *the national committee, the committee* or *the DNC.*

Similarly: *Democratic State Committee, Democratic County Committee, Democratic City Committee, the state committee, the city committee, the committee.*

demolish, destroy Both mean to do away with something completely. Something cannot be partially *demolished* or *destroyed*. It is redundant to say *totally demolished* or *totally destroyed*.

denote See **connote, denote**.

Denver The city in Colorado stands alone in datelines.

depart Follow it with a preposition: *He will depart from LaGuardia. She will depart at 11:30 a.m.*

department The following are the U.S. Cabinet departments: *Department of Agriculture (USDA* acceptable on second reference); *Department of Commerce; Department of Defense (DOD* or *Pentagon* acceptable on second reference); *Department of Education; Department of Energy (DOE* acceptable on second reference); *Department of Health and Human Services (HHS* acceptable on second reference); *Department of Homeland Security (DHS* acceptable on second reference); *Department of Housing and Urban Development (HUD* acceptable on second reference); *Department of the Interior; Department of Justice (DOJ* acceptable on second reference); *Department of Labor; Department of State; Department of Transportation (DOT* acceptable on second reference); *Department of the Treasury,* and *Department of Veterans Affairs (VA* acceptable on second reference).

It is preferable to list the subject first in stories, such as the *Agriculture Department* and *Commerce Department*. Exceptions are *Department of Health and Human Services, Department of Homeland Security, Department of Housing and Urban Development* and *Department of Veterans Affairs*.

Avoid acronyms when possible. A phrase such as *the department* is preferable on second reference because it is more readable and avoids alphabet soup.

Lowercase *department* in plural uses, but capitalize the proper name element: *the departments of Labor and Justice*.

A shorthand reference to the proper name element also is capitalized: *Kissinger said, "State and Justice must resolve their differences."* But: *Henry Kissinger, the secretary of state.*

Lowercase *the department* whenever it stands alone.

Do not abbreviate *department* in any usage.

TITLES: In stories with U.S. datelines, do not include U.S. before the titles of Secretary of State or other government officials, except where necessary for clarity. Examples: *Secretary of State John Kerry, Attorney General Eric Holder.*

In stories with international datelines, include U.S. before the titles: *U.S. Secretary of State John Kerry, U.S. Attorney General Eric Holder.* Exceptions: *President Barack Obama, Vice President Joe Biden.*

See **academic departments**.

dependent (n. and adj.)

depreciation The reduction in the value of capital goods due to wear and tear or obsolescence.

Estimated depreciation may be deducted from income each year as one of the costs of doing business.

depression Capitalize *Depression* and *the Great Depression* when referring to the worldwide economic hard times generally regarded as having begun with the stock market collapse of Oct. 28-29, 1929.

Lowercase in other uses: *the depression of the 1970s.*

depths See **dimensions**.

deputy Capitalize as a formal title before a name. See **titles**.

derivative A contract whose value depends on the financial performance of its underlying assets, such as mortgages, stock or traded commodities. Credit default swaps are one form of derivative.

derogatory terms Do not use a derogatory term except in extremely rare circumstances — when it is crucial to the story or the understanding of a news event. Flag the contents in an editor's note.

See **obscenities, profanities, vulgarities**.

-designate Hyphenate: *chairman-designate.* Capitalize only the first word if used as a formal title before a name.

See **titles**.

destroy See **demolish, destroy**.

detective Do not abbreviate. Capitalize before a name only if it is a formal rank: *police Detective Frank Serpico, private detective Richard Diamond.*

See **titles**.

detente

detention center See **prison, jail**.

Detroit The city in Michigan stands alone in datelines.

Deutsche Lufthansa AG The headquarters of this airline is in Cologne, Germany. *Lufthansa* is acceptable on first reference.

devaluations Devaluations occur when the value of a country's currency goes down in its relation to another currency. This may happen by government decree, or through market forces. Devaluations are expressed in percentages, but the normal method of figuring a percentage change won't work. Use the following rules:

Say currency A is quoted in a set of units to currency B. When currency A is devalued, 1) take the new exchange rate and subtract the old exchange rate, 2) divide the answer by the new exchange rate and 3) multiply the answer by 100 to get the percentage devaluation.

Example:

9.5 (new rate) minus 6.3 (old rate) = 3.2

3.2 divided by 9.5 = 0.3368

0.3368 times 100 = 33.68421 (or 34 percent).

The ruble has been devalued against the dollar by 34 percent.

devil But capitalize *Satan*.

diabetes There are two main forms of this disease: Type 1, formerly called juvenile diabetes, and Type 2, the most common kind, formerly called adult-onset diabetes.

dialect The form of language peculiar to a region or a group, usually in matters of pronunciation or syntax. Dialect should be avoided, even in quoted matter, unless it is clearly pertinent to a story.

There are some words and phrases in everyone's vocabulary that are typical of a particular region or group. Quoting dialect, unless used carefully, implies substandard or illiterate usage.

When there is a compelling reason to use dialect, words or phrases are spelled phonetically, and apostrophes show missing letters and sounds: *"Din't ya yoosta live at Toidy-Toid Street and Sekun' Amya? Across from da moom pitchers?"*

See **colloquialisms** and **quotes in the news**.

dialogue (n.)

diarrhea

dictionaries For spelling, style and usage questions not covered in this stylebook, consult Webster's New World College Dictionary, Fifth Edition, Houghton Mifflin Harcourt, Boston and New York, 2014.

Use the first spelling listed in Webster's New World College Dictionary unless a specific exception is listed in this book.

If Webster's New World College Dictionary provides different spellings in separate entries (*tee shirt* and *T-shirt*, for example), use the spelling that is followed by a full definition (*T-shirt*).

If Webster's New World College Dictionary provides definitions under two spellings for the same sense of a word, either use is acceptable.

Webster's New World College Dictionary is also the first reference for geographic names not covered in this stylebook. See **geographic names**.

die-hard (n. and adj.)

Diet The Japanese parliament. See **legislative bodies**.

dietitian

different Takes the preposition *from*, not *than*.

differ from, differ with To *differ from* means to be unlike.

To *differ with* means to disagree.

Digital First Media New York-based media company created when MediaNews Group Inc. and the former Journal Register Co. combined in December 2013. It owns dailies including *The Denver Post, San Jose Mercury News* and *The Detroit News*.

dilemma It means more than a problem. It implies a choice between two unattractive alternatives.

dimensions Use figures and spell out *inches, feet, yards*, etc., to indicate depth, height, length and width. Hyphenate adjectival forms before nouns.

EXAMPLES: *He is 5 feet 6 inches tall, the 5-foot-6-inch man, the 5-foot man, the basketball team signed a 7-footer.*

The car is 17 feet long, 6 feet wide and 5 feet high. The rug is 9 feet by 12 feet, the 9-by-12 rug.

The storm left 5 inches of snow.

The building has 6,000 square feet of floor space.

Use an apostrophe to indicate feet and quote marks to indicate inches (5'6") only in very technical contexts.

Diners Club No apostrophe, in keeping with the practice the company has adopted for its public identity. Only its incorporation papers still read Diners' Club. Parent company Citigroup Inc. sold Diners Club to Discover Financial Services in 2008.

directions and regions In general, lowercase *north, south, northeast, northern,* etc., when they indicate compass direction; capitalize these words when they designate regions.

Some examples:

COMPASS DIRECTIONS: *He drove west. The cold front is moving east.*

REGIONS: *A storm system that developed in the Midwest is spreading eastward. It will bring showers to the East Coast by morning and to the entire Northeast by late in the day. Showers and thunderstorms were forecast in the Texas Panhandle. High temperatures will prevail throughout the Western states.*

The North was victorious. The South will rise again. Settlers from the East went to the West in search of new lives. The customs of the East are different from those of the West. The Northeast depends on the Midwest for its food supply.

She has a Southern accent. He is a Northerner. Asian nations are opening doors to Western businessmen. The candidate developed a Southern strategy.

The storm developed in the South Pacific. European leaders met to talk about supplies of oil from Southeast Asia.

WITH NAMES OF NATIONS: Lowercase unless they are part of a proper name or are used to designate a politically divided nation: *northern France, eastern Canada, the western United States.*

But: *Northern Ireland, South Korea.*

WITH STATES AND CITIES: The preferred form is to lowercase directional or area descriptions when referring to a section of a state or city: *western Montana, southern Atlanta.*

But capitalize compass points:

—When part of a proper name: *North Dakota, West Virginia.*

—When used in denoting widely known sections: *Southern California, West Texas, the South Side of Chicago, the Lower East Side of New York.* If in doubt, use lowercase.

IN FORMING PROPER NAMES: When combining with another common noun to form the name for a region or location: *the North Woods, the South Pole, the Far East, the Middle East, the West Coast* (the entire region, not the coastline itself — see **coast**), *the Eastern Shore* (see separate entry), *the Western Hemisphere.*

direct message A personal message sent via Twitter to one of your followers. DMs differ from mentions and @ replies in that they can only be seen by the sender and recipient. A DM exchange can only take place between users who follow each other.

dis- The rules in **prefixes** apply, but in general, no hyphen. Some examples:

dismember   disservice
dissemble   dissuade

dis, dissing, dissed

disabled, handicapped In general, do not describe an individual as disabled or handicapped unless it is clearly pertinent to a story. If a description must be used, try to be specific. *An ad featuring actor Michael J. Fox swaying noticeably from the effects of Parkinson's disease drew nationwide attention.*

Avoid descriptions that connote pity, such as *afflicted with* or *suffers from multiple sclerosis*. Rather, *has multiple sclerosis*.

Some terms include:

blind Describes a person with complete loss of sight. For others, use terms such as *visually impaired* or *person with low vision*.

cripple Considered offensive when used to describe a person who is disabled.

deaf Describes a person with total hearing loss. For others, use *partial hearing loss* or *partially deaf*. Avoid using *deaf-mute*. Do not use *deaf and dumb*.

disabled A general term used for a physical, mental, developmental or intellectual disability. Do not use *mentally retarded*.

handicap It should be avoided in describing a disability.

mute Describes a person who cannot speak. Others with speaking difficulties are *speech impaired*.

wheelchair user People use wheelchairs for independent mobility. Do not use *confined to a wheelchair*, or *wheelchair-bound*. If a wheelchair is needed, say why.

See **mental illness**.

disc jockey *DJ* is acceptable on second reference.

discount Interest withheld when a note, draft or bill is purchased.

discount rate The rate of interest charged by the Federal Reserve on loans it makes to member banks. This rate has an influence on the rates banks then charge their customers.

discreet, discrete *Discreet* means prudent, circumspect: *"I'm afraid I was not very discreet," she wrote.*

Discrete means detached, separate: *There are four discrete sounds from a quadraphonic system.*

diseases Do not capitalize *arthritis, emphysema, leukemia, pneumonia*, etc.

When a disease is known by the name of a person or geographical area identified with it, capitalize only the proper noun element: *Alzheimer's disease, Parkinson's disease, Ebola virus*, etc.

Avoid such expressions as: *He is battling cancer. She is a stroke victim.* Use neutral, precise descriptions: *He has stomach cancer. She is a stroke patient.*

See **disabled, handicapped**.

disinterested, uninterested *Disinterested* means *impartial*, which is usually the better word to convey the thought.

Uninterested means that someone lacks interest.

disk, disc Use *disk* for computer-related references (*diskette*) and medical references, such as a *slipped disk*. Use the *disc* spelling for optical and laser-based devices (a *Blu-ray Disc, CD, DVD*) and for *disc brake*.

dispel, dispelled, dispelling

disposable personal income
The income that a person retains after deductions for income taxes, Social Security taxes, property taxes and for other payments such as fines and penalties to various levels of government.

Disposall A trademark for a type of mechanical garbage disposer.

dissociate Not *disassociate*.

distances Always use figures: *He walked 4 miles*. See **numerals**.

district Always spell it out. Use a figure and capitalize *district* when forming a proper name: *the 2nd District*.

district attorney Capitalize when used as a formal title before a name: *District Attorney Hamilton Burger*.
DA acceptable on second reference.
See **titles**.

district court See **court names** and **U.S. District Court**.

District of Columbia In datelines Washington doesn't take *D.C.* Use *District of Columbia* within a story only to avoid confusion with Washington state or other localities of that name. Postal code: *DC*.
On second reference, *the District* is acceptable.
See **state names**.

dive, dived or **dove, diving**

divided nations See **datelines** and entries under the names of these nations.

dividend In a financial sense, the word describes the payment per share that a corporation distributes to its stockholders as their return on the money they have invested in its stock.
See **profit terminology**.

division See **organizations and institutions; military units;** and **political divisions**.

divorce Use the same standards for men and women in deciding whether to mention marital status in a story. Avoid describing a woman as a *divorcee*, or a man as a *divorce*, unless used in an essential quote. When the news isn't about a marital breakup, but marital status is relevant, say in the body of the story that the woman or man is divorced.

Dixie cup A trademark for a paper drinking cup.

Djibouti Stands alone in datelines for the East African country and capital.

DNA Acceptable for all reference to deoxyribonucleic acid, which carries genetic information in the cell.

DNS Abbreviation for the *Domain Name System*, an international network of Internet domain servers, names and addresses. Spell out on first reference.

doctor Use *Dr.* in first reference as a formal title before the name of an individual who holds a doctor of dental surgery, doctor of medicine, doctor of optometry, doctor of osteopathic medicine, doctor of podiatric medicine, or doctor of veterinary medicine: *Dr. Jonas Salk*.
The form *Dr.*, or *Drs.*, in a plural construction, applies to all first-ref-

erence uses before a name, including direct quotations.

If appropriate in the context, *Dr.* also may be used on first reference before the names of individuals who hold other types of doctoral degrees. However, because the public frequently identifies *Dr.* only with physicians, care should be taken to ensure that the individual's specialty is stated in first or second reference. The only exception would be a story in which the context left no doubt that the person was a dentist, psychologist, chemist, historian, etc.

In some instances it also is necessary to specify that an individual identified as *Dr.* is a physician. One frequent case is a story reporting on joint research by physicians, biologists, etc.

Do not use *Dr.* before the names of individuals who hold only honorary doctorates.

Do not continue the use of *Dr.* in subsequent references.

See **academic degrees; courtesy titles**; and **religious titles**.

Doctors Without Borders Use English translation in copy for the French group Medecins Sans Frontieres.

dog walker Two words.

dogs See **animals**.

dollars Always lowercase. Use figures and the *$* sign in all except casual references or amounts without a figure: *The book cost $4. Dad, please give me a dollar. Dollars are flowing overseas.*

For specified amounts, the word takes a singular verb: *He said $500,000 is what they want.*

For amounts of more than $1 million, use up to two decimal places. Do not link the numerals and the word by a hyphen: *He is worth*

$4.35 million. He proposed a $300 billion budget.

The form for amounts less than $1 million: *$4, $25, $500, $1,000, $650,000.*

See **cents**.

domain names The address used to locate a particular website or reach an email system. In email addresses, it is the portion to the right of the @ sign. It includes a suffix defining the type of entity, such as ".com" (for commerce, the most common suffix); ".net" initially for network service providers, but often used when ".com" is unavailable; ".org" (organizations); ".edu" (educational institutions); ".gov" (U.S. government) and ".mil" (U.S. military). There are also country-code suffixes (such as ".fr" for France, ".us" for the United States), along with many other types of available domain names.

domino, dominoes

"don't ask, don't tell" The law barring gays from serving in the U.S. military if they acknowledged their sexual orientation. The 1993 law was repealed by Congress in 2010, effective in 2011. Gays now may serve openly.

door to door, door-to-door Hyphenate when used as a compound modifier: *He is a door-to-door salesman.*

But: *He went from door to door.*

do's and don'ts

dot-com An informal description of companies that do business mainly on the Internet.

double-click

double-faced

doughnut

Dow Jones & Co. The company, a subsidiary of News Corp., publishes *The Wall Street Journal* and *Barron's* magazine. It also operates the Dow Jones News Service.

For stock market watchers, it provides the Dow Jones industrial average, the Dow Jones transportation average, the Dow Jones utility average, and the Dow Jones composite average.

Headquarters is in New York.

Dow Jones industrial average The market indicator comprises 30 leading U.S. stocks. Executives of Dow Jones Indexes choose the companies in the average. Always use the full name on first reference in stories. On subsequent references, use *the Dow*.

-down Follow Webster's New World College Dictionary. Some examples, all nouns and/or adjectives:

breakdown	rundown
countdown	sit-down

All are two words when used as verbs.

down- The rules in **prefixes** apply, but in general, no hyphen. Some examples:

downgrade	downtown

Down East Use only in reference to Maine.

down payment

downside risk The probability that the price of an investment will fall.

downstage

downstate Lowercase unless part of a proper name: *downstate Illinois*. But: *the Downstate Medical Center*.

Down syndrome Not *Down's*, for the genetic, chromosomal disorder first reported in 1866 by Dr. J. Langdon Down.

Down Under Australia, New Zealand and environs.

dpa *Deutsche Presse-Agentur GmbH* is an international news agency with headquarters in Hamburg, Germany, owned by a cooperative of German newspaper publishers and radio and television stations. It was founded in 1949. Lowercase *dpa* is acceptable in all references, though it's *Dpa* to start a sentence.

Dr. See **doctor**.

drama See **composition titles**.

Dramamine A trademark for a brand of motion sickness remedy.

dreidel Toy spinning top used in games played during Hanukkah.

dressing room

drive See **addresses**.

drive-by (adj.) *A drive-by shooting.*

drive-in (n.)

driver's license(s)

drive-thru (n. and adj.)

drop-down (adj.)

dropout (n.) **drop out** (v.)

drought

drowned, was drowned If a person suffocates in water or other fluid, the proper statement is that the individual *drowned*. To say that someone *was drowned* implies that another person caused the death by holding the victim's head under the water.

Drug Enforcement Administration *DEA* on second reference.

drugmaker

drugs Because the word *drugs* has come to be used as a synonym for narcotics in recent years, *medicine* is frequently the better word to specify that an individual is taking medication.

drugstore

drunk, drunken *Drunk* is the spelling of the adjective used after a form of the verb *to be*: *He was drunk.*

Drunken is the spelling of the adjective used before nouns: *a drunken driver, drunken driving.*

DUI, driving under the influence; *DWI, driving while intoxicated*; follow official state usage.

drunkenness

DSL Abbreviation acceptable in all references for *digital subscriber line*, for high-speed access to the Internet over a telephone network.

Dublin The city in Ireland stands alone in datelines.

duel A contest between two people. Three people cannot duel.

duffel

DUI, DWI Abbreviations for *driving under the influence* or *driving while intoxicated*. Acceptable in all references. See **drunk, drunken**.

duke, duchess See **nobility**.

dumping The selling of a product in a foreign market at a price lower than the domestic price. It is usually done by a monopoly when it has such a large output that selling entirely in the domestic market would substantially reduce the price.

dumpster A large metal trash bin.

Dunkirk Use this spelling rather than *Dunkerque*, in keeping with widespread practice.

du Pont, E.I. Note the spelling of the name of the U.S. industrialist born in France. Use *du Pont* on second reference.

The company named after him is *E.I. du Pont de Nemours & Co.* of Wilmington, Delaware. Capitalize the shortened form *DuPont* (no space, capital P) in keeping with company practice. The shortened form is acceptable in all references. See **foreign names**.

durable goods Long-lasting goods such as appliances that are bought by consumers.

dust storm See **weather terms**.

Dutch auction A bidding process where the price is lowered until the lowest price at which all securities will sell becomes the set price. Used on Treasury auctions and in risk arbitrage.

DVD Abbreviation for *digital video disc* (or *digital versatile disc*), similar to CD-ROMs, but able to hold more music, video or data.

The abbreviation is acceptable in all references.

DVR Acceptable on second reference for *digital video recorder*. TiVo is the trademark for one type of *DVR*. Do not use *TiVo* to describe

the generic *DVRs* offered by many
cable systems.

dwarf The preferred term for
people with a medical or genetic
condition resulting in short stature.
Plural is *dwarfs*.

dyed-in-the-wool (adj.)

dyeing, dying *Dyeing* refers to
changing colors.
Dying refers to death.

each Takes a singular verb.

each other, one another Two people look at *each other*.

More than two look at *one another*.

Either phrase may be used when the number is indefinite: *We help each other. We help one another.*

earl, countess See **nobility**.

earmark

earth Generally lowercase; capitalize when used as the proper name of the planet. *She is down-to-earth. How does the pattern apply to Mars, Jupiter, Earth, the sun and the moon? The astronauts returned to Earth. He hopes to move heaven and earth.*

See **planets**.

earthquakes Over a million earthquakes occur in the world each year. Most strike remote regions or are so small they cannot be felt.

The best source for information on major earthquakes is the National Earthquake Information Center, operated by the U.S. Geological Survey, in Golden, Colorado.

Online sources:

http://earthquake.usgs.gov

http://earthquake.usgs.gov/regional/neic/

http://earthquake.usgs.gov/earthquakes/pager/

http://earthquake.usgs.gov/earthquakes/shakemap/

Earthquake magnitudes are measures of earthquake size calculated from ground motion recorded on seismographs. The Richter scale, named for Dr. Charles F. Richter, is no longer widely used.

Magnitudes are usually reported simply as *magnitude 6.7*, for example. Hyphenate as a compound modifier: *magnitude-6.7 quake.*

In the first hours after a quake, earthquake size should be reported as a *preliminary magnitude of 6.7.* Early estimates are often revised, and it can be several days before seismologists calculate a final figure.

The most commonly used measure is the *moment magnitude*, related to the area of the fault on which an earthquake occurs, and the amount the ground slips.

The magnitude scale being used should be specified only when necessary. An example would be when two centers are reporting different magnitudes because they are using different scales. The various scales usually differ only slightly.

With each scale, every increase of one number, say from 5.5 to 6.5, means that the quake's magnitude is 10 times as great. Theoretically, there is no upper limit to the scales.

A quake of magnitude 2.5 to 3 is the smallest generally felt by people.

—Magnitude 4: The quake can cause moderate damage.

—Magnitude 5: The quake can cause considerable damage.

—Magnitude 6: The quake can cause severe damage.

—Magnitude 7: A major earthquake, capable of widespread, heavy damage.

—Magnitude 8: An earthquake capable of tremendous damage.

Depth is a key factor in determining how damaging an earthquake will be. The closer to the surface an earthquake starts, the more ground shaking and potential damage it will cause, particularly in places without strict building codes. The strength of the earth shaking decreases the farther a quake gets from its source, so a deeper quake weakens as it gets closer to the surface.

Quakes are divided into three categories: shallow, intermediate and deep. Shallow quakes are at depths of less than 70 km (43 miles) and are the ones that have broader damage. Intermediate quakes are between 70 km and 300 km in depth (43 miles to 186 miles) and deep are deeper than 300 km (186 miles).

To show the importance of depth in two similarly sized earthquakes: In 1994 in the Los Angeles neighborhood of Northridge, a 6.7-magnitude quake struck at a depth of 12 miles (19 km), caused tens of billions of dollars' worth of damage and killed several dozen people. In 2001, a 6.8-magnitude quake struck Seattle at a depth of 33 miles (51 km); the damage was only in the millions and only a few people were killed.

The magnitude and depth of an earthquake can change as scientists get more information from seismic stations and should be reported as *preliminary magnitude* and *preliminary depth*.

The deadliest quake on record occurred in Shaanxi province of China, Jan. 23, 1556. It killed 830,000 people, the largest number of fatalities on record from an earthquake.

A series of major quakes struck the region around New Madrid, Missouri, in the winter of 1811-1812. The shock was felt over a wide area from St. Louis, Missouri, to Memphis, Tennessee. The area was sparsely populated at the time and there were no instruments to measure the power of the quakes, but the land was raised as much as 30 feet in some areas, and subsidence elsewhere created Reelfoot Lake in western Tennessee.

NOTABLE QUAKES since 1900, according to the U.S. Geological Survey's list, based on magnitude or amount of damage and arranged by number of fatalities:

—July 27, 1976, Tangshan, China, magnitude 7.5. Official casualty figure is 255,000 deaths. Estimated death toll as high as 655,000, 799,000 injured and extensive damage in the area. This is probably the greatest death toll from an earthquake in the last four centuries, and the second greatest in recorded history.

—Jan. 12, 2010, Haiti, 7.0. More than 300,000 people were killed, 300,000 injured, 1.3 million displaced, about 105,000 homes destroyed and 208,000 damaged in the Port-au-Prince area and much of southern Haiti, according to government estimates.

—Dec. 26, 2004, Sumatra, 9.1. This is the third-largest earthquake in the world since 1900 and the largest since the 1964 Prince William Sound, Alaska, earthquake. In total, 228,000 people were killed or were missing and presumed dead in 14 countries due to the quake and ensuing tsunami.

—Dec. 16, 1920, Haiyuan, Ningxia, China, 7.8. Total destruction in the Lijunbu-Haiyuan-Ganyanchi area. Estimated death toll of 200,000.

—Sept. 1, 1923, Kanto, Japan, 7.9. Extreme destruction in the Tokyo-Yokohama area from the earthquake and subsequent firestorms, 143,000 dead.

—Oct. 5, 1948, Ashgabat, Turkmenistan, 7.3, 110,000 killed.

—May 12, 2008, Eastern Sichuan, China, 7.9, 87,600.

—Oct. 8, 2005, Pakistan, 7.6, 86,000.

—Dec. 28, 1908, Messina, Italy, 7.2, 72,000.

—May 31, 1970, Chimbote, Peru, 7.4, 70,000.

—June 20, 1990, Western Iran, 7.4, 40,000 to 50,000.

—May 22, 1927, Gulang, China, 7.6, 40,900.

—Dec. 26, 1939, Erzincan, Turkey, 7.8, 32,700.

—Jan. 13, 1915, Avezzano, Italy, 7.0, 32,610.

—Dec. 26, 2003, Southeastern Iran, 6.6, 31,000.

—May 30, 1935, Quetta, Pakistan, 7.6, 30,000.

—Jan. 25, 1939, Chillan, Chile, 7.8, 28,000.

—Dec. 7, 1988, Spitak, Armenia, 6.8, 25,000.

—Feb. 4, 1976, Guatemala, 7.5, 23,000.

—Jan. 26, 2001, Gujarat, India, 7.6, 20,000.

—March 11, 2011, Japan, 9.0, quake and tsunami killed more than 18,000, displaced 450,000 and caused radiation leaks from damaged reactors at a nuclear power plant.

OTHER NOTABLE QUAKES SINCE 1900:

–April 18, 1906, San Francisco, 7.8, death toll varies, but recent estimates put it at more than 3,000.

–May 22, 1960, Valdivia, Chile, 9.5, most powerful earthquake recorded in the world killed 1,655 and injured 3,000.

–March 27, 1964, Prince William Sound, Alaska, 9.2, quake and tsunami killed 128.

–Dec. 23, 1972, Nicaragua, 6.2, 5,000 killed.

–Sept. 19, 1985, Mexico City, 8.0, at least 9,500 killed.

–Oct. 17, 1989, near Santa Cruz, Calif. (the Loma Prieta earthquake), 6.9, 63 killed and 3,757 injured.

–Jan. 17, 1994, Los Angeles (the Northridge earthquake), 6.7. At least 57 people killed and more than 9,000 injured, according to the state. A 1995 study put the death toll at 72, including heart attacks.

–Jan. 17, 1995, Kobe, Japan, 6.9, 5,500 killed.

–Feb. 22, 2011, near Christchurch, New Zealand, 6.3, at least 166 killed.

OTHER TERMS: The word *temblor* (not *tremblor*) is a synonym for *earthquake*.

The word *epicenter* refers to the point on Earth's surface above the underground center, or focus, of an earthquake.

east, eastern See **directions and regions.**

Easter Christian holy day commemorating the resurrection of Jesus Christ. Christians believe Jesus was raised from the dead three days after his crucifixion.

Western Christian churches and most Orthodox Christian churches follow different calendars and observe Easter on different dates.

Eastern Europe No longer a separate political unit, but can be used in specific references to the region. Use only in historic sense. (Also *Western Europe*.)

Eastern Hemisphere The half of the Earth made up primarily of Africa, Asia, Australia and Europe.

Eastern Orthodox churches

The term applies to a group of churches that have roots in the earliest days of Christianity and do not recognize papal authority over their activities.

Churches in this tradition were part of the undivided Christendom that existed until the Great Schism of 1054. At that time, many of the churches in the western half of the old Roman Empire accorded the bishop of Rome supremacy over other bishops. The result was a split between eastern and western churches.

The autonomous churches that constitute Eastern Orthodoxy are organized along mostly national lines. They recognize the patriarch of Constantinople (modern-day Istanbul) as their leader. He convenes councils, but his authority is otherwise that of a "first among equals."

Eastern orthodox churches include the Greek Orthodox Church and the Russian Orthodox Church.

In the United States, organizational lines are rooted in the national backgrounds of various ethnic groups, such as the Greek Orthodox Archdiocese of America, and the Orthodox Church in America, which includes people of Bulgarian, Romanian, Russian and Syrian descent.

The churches have their own disciplines on matters such as married clergy — a married man may be ordained, but a priest may not marry after ordination.

Some of these churches call the archbishop who leads them a *metropolitan*; others use the term *patriarch*. He normally heads the principal archdiocese within a nation. Working with him are other archbishops, bishops, priests and deacons.

Archbishops and bishops frequently follow a monastic tradition in which they are known only by a first name. When no last name is used, repeat the title before the sole name in subsequent references.

Some forms: *Metropolitan Tikhon, archbishop of Washington and metropolitan of America and Canada.* On second reference: *Metropolitan Tikhon. Archbishop* may be replaced by *the Most Rev.* on first reference. *Bishop* may be replaced by *the Rt. Rev.* on first reference.

Use *the Rev.* before the name of a priest on first reference.

See **religious titles**.

Eastern Seaboard Synonym for *East Coast*.

Eastern Shore A region on the east side of Chesapeake Bay, including parts of Maryland and Virginia.

Eastern Shore is not a synonym for *East Coast*.

Eastern Standard Time (EST), Eastern Daylight Time (EDT) See **time zones**.

easygoing

eBay Inc. The online auctioneer is based in San Jose, California. Lowercase *"e"* unless it's the start of a sentence.

Ebola A virus that causes a severe and often fatal illness. It is named for a river in the Democratic Republic of Congo in Africa where one of the first outbreaks of the disease occurred in 1976. About two dozen outbreaks have occurred in Africa since then. The one that began in early 2014 is by far the largest.

Ebola virus comes from wild animals and then spreads person-to-person through direct contact with an infected person or contaminated materials. Symptoms can include sudden fever, muscle pain, headache, sore throat, vomiting, diarrhea, rash, kidney or liver problems and bleeding. People are not infectious until they develop symptoms, and the incubation period is two to 21 days.

No specific drugs or vaccines are approved to treat Ebola but some experimental ones are being tested. Early supportive care, such as intravenous fluids, can improve survival odds.

e-book The electronic, nonpaper version of a book or publication, sold digitally and commonly consumed on an *e-book reader* or *e-reader*, such as Amazon's Kindle, or on an e-reader app on a smartphone, tablet or PC.

E. coli Acceptable in all references for *Escherichia coli O157:H7 bacteria*.

ecology The study of the relationship between organisms and their surroundings. It is not synonymous with *environment*.
Right: *The laboratory is studying the ecology of man and the desert.*
Wrong: *Even so simple an undertaking as maintaining a lawn affects ecology.* (Use *environment* instead.)

ecosystem

ecotourism

Ecstasy Capitalize (no quote marks) this and other synthetic drug names.

Ecuadorean The term for the people and culture of Ecuador.

editor Capitalize *editor* before a name only when it is an official

corporate or organizational title. Do not capitalize as a job description.
See **titles**.

editor-in-chief Use hyphens and capitalize when used as a formal title before a name: *Editor-in-Chief Horace Greeley*. The hyphens, reflecting industry usage, are an exception to Webster's New World College Dictionary.
See **titles**.

eerie

EFE An international news agency with headquarters in Madrid, Spain. It was founded in 1939.

effect See **affect, effect**.

e.g. Meaning *for example*, it is always followed by a comma.

Eglin Air Force Base, Florida

Eid al-Adha Meaning "Feast of Sacrifice," this most important Islamic holiday marks the willingness of the Prophet Ibrahim (Abraham to Christians and Jews) to sacrifice his son. During the holiday, which in most places lasts four days, Muslims slaughter sheep or cattle, distribute part of the meat to the poor and eat the rest. The holiday begins on the 10th day of the Islamic lunar month of Dhul-Hijja, during the annual hajj pilgrimage to Mecca.

Eid al-Fitr A three-day holiday marking the end of Ramadan, Islam's holy month of fasting.

either Use it to mean one or the other, not both.
Right: *She said to use either door.*
Wrong: *There were lions on either side of the door.*
Right: *There were lions on each side of the door. There were lions on both sides of the door.*

either ... or, neither ... nor The nouns that follow these words do not constitute a compound subject; they are alternate subjects and require a verb that agrees with the nearer subject:
Neither they nor he is going. Neither he nor they are going.

El Al Israel Airlines. An *El Al airliner* is acceptable in any reference. Headquarters in Tel Aviv.

elderly Use this word carefully and sparingly. Do not refer to a person as *elderly* unless it is clearly relevant to the story.
It is appropriate in generic phrases that do not refer to specific individuals: *concern for the elderly*, *a home for the elderly*, etc.
If the intent is to show that an individual's faculties have deteriorated, cite a graphic example and give attribution for it. Use age when available and appropriate.
Apply the same principle to terms such as *senior citizen*.

-elect Always hyphenate and lowercase: *President-elect Barack Obama.*

Election Day, election night The first Tuesday after the first Monday in November.

election returns Use figures, with commas every three digits starting at the right and counting left. Use the word *to* (not a hyphen) in separating different totals listed together: *Jimmy Carter outpolled Gerald Ford 40,827,292 to 39,146,157 in 1976.*
Use the word *votes* if there is any possibility that the figures could be confused with a ratio: *Nixon outpolled McGovern 16 votes to 3 votes in Dixville Notch.*

Do not attempt to create adjectival forms such as *the 40,827,292-39,146,157 vote.*
See **vote tabulations**.

Electoral College But *electoral vote(s).*

electrocardiogram *EKG* is acceptable on second reference.

eleventh Spell out only in the phrase *the eleventh hour*, meaning at the last moment; otherwise use the numeral.

ellipsis See entry in **Punctuation** chapter.

El Salvador The use of the article in the name of the nation helps to distinguish it from its capital, *San Salvador.*
Use *Salvadoran(s)* in references to citizens of the nation.

email Acceptable in all references for *electronic mail.* Many *email* or Internet addresses use symbols such as the *at* symbol (@), or the *tilde* (~) that cannot be transmitted correctly by some computers. When needed, spell them out and provide an explanatory editor's note. Use a hyphen with other *e-* terms: *e-book, e-business, e-commerce.*

embargo See **boycott, embargo**.

embargo times See **Hold-for-Release Stories** in the **Sending Text Stories** chapter.

embarrass, embarrassing, embarrassed, embarrassment

embassy An *embassy* is the official office of an ambassador in a foreign country and the office that handles the political relations of one nation with another.

A *consulate*, the office of a consul in a foreign city, handles the commercial affairs and personal needs of citizens of the appointing country.

Capitalize with the name of a nation; lowercase without it: *the French Embassy, the U.S. Embassy, the embassy.*

embryo In human development, the first seven weeks after conception. See **fetus**.

emcee, emceed, emceeing A phrase such as: *He was the master of ceremonies* is preferred.

emergency room *ER* is acceptable on second reference.

emeritus This word often is added to formal titles to denote that individuals who have retired retain their rank or title.

When used, place *emeritus* after the formal title, in keeping with the general practice of academic institutions: *Professor Emeritus Samuel Eliot Morison, Dean Emeritus Courtney C. Brown, Publisher Emeritus Barnard L. Colby.*

Or: *Samuel Eliot Morison, professor emeritus of history; Courtney C. Brown, dean emeritus of the faculty of business; Barnard L. Colby, publisher emeritus.*

emigrate, immigrate One who leaves a country *emigrates* from it.

One who comes into a country *immigrates*.

The same principle holds for *emigrant* and *immigrant*.

Emirates The airline's headquarters is in Dubai, United Arab Emirates.

Emmy, Emmys The annual awards by the Academy of Television Arts & Sciences (for prime-time programming; based in Los Angeles) and the National Academy of Television Arts and Sciences (for daytime, news and sports; based in New York).

emoji Symbols including cartoon faces, hand gestures, food and animals, often used on mobile devices such as smartphones. They can be used instead of words or as illustrations in text messages and in social media posts. Plural: *emojis*. See **emoticon**.

emoticon A typographical cartoon or symbol generally used to indicate mood or appearance, as :-) and often looked at sideways. See **emoji**.

employee

empty-handed

enact See **adopt, approve, enact, pass**.

encyclopedia But follow the spelling of formal names: *Encyclopaedia Britannica.*

end user (n.) **end-user** (adj.) A phrase commonly referred to by technology developers when imagining the audience for software or hardware. *End-user experience.*

enforce But *reinforce.*

engine, motor An *engine* develops its own power, usually through internal combustion or the pressure of air, steam or water passing over vanes attached to a wheel: *an airplane engine, an automobile engine, a jet engine, a missile engine, a steam engine, a turbine engine.*

A *motor* receives power from an outside source: *an electric motor, a hydraulic motor.*

England London stands alone in datelines. Use *England* after the names of other English communities in datelines.

See **datelines** and **United Kingdom**.

enroll, enrolled, enrolling

en route Always two words.

ensign See **military titles**.

ensure, insure, assure Use *ensure* to mean guarantee: *Steps were taken to ensure accuracy.*

Use *insure* for references to insurance: *The policy insures his life.*

Use *assure* to mean to make sure or give confidence: *She assured us the statement was accurate.*

entitled Use it to mean a right to do or have something. Do not use it to mean titled.

Right: *She was entitled to the promotion.*

Right: *The book was titled "Gone With the Wind."*

enumerations See examples in **dash** and **periods** entries in **Punctuation** chapter.

envelop (v.) Other verb forms: *enveloping, enveloped.* But: *envelope* (n.)

environment See **ecology**.

Environmental Protection Agency *EPA* is acceptable on second reference.

envoy Not a formal title. Lowercase.

See **titles**.

epicenter The point on the Earth's surface above the underground center, or focus, of an earthquake.

See **earthquakes**.

epidemic, pandemic An *epidemic* is the rapid spreading of disease in a certain population or region; a *pandemic* is an *epidemic* that has spread worldwide. Use sparingly; follow declarations of public health officials.

epidemiology

epoch See **historical periods and events**.

equal An adjective without comparative forms.

When people speak of a *more equal* distribution of wealth, what is meant is *more equitable.*

Equal Employment Opportunity Commission *EEOC* is acceptable on second reference.

equal, equaled, equaling

equally as Do not use the words together; one is sufficient.

Omit the *equally* shown here in parentheses: *She was (equally) as wise as Marilyn.*

Omit the *as* shown here in parentheses: *She and Marilyn were equally (as) wise.*

equal time *Equal time* applies to the Federal Communications Commission regulation that requires a radio or television station to provide a candidate for political office with air time equal to any time that an opponent receives beyond the coverage of news events.

equator Always lowercase.

equitable See **equal**.

equity When used in a financial sense, *equity* means the value of property beyond the amount that is owed on it.

A *stockholder's equity* in a corporation is the value of the shares he holds.

A *homeowner's equity* is the difference between the value of the house and the amount of the unpaid mortgage.

ERA Acceptable in all references to baseball's *earned run average*.

eras See **historical periods and events**.

e-reader Or *e-book reader*. Devices used to display electronic books and other digital publications. Other devices have e-reader software that can perform similar functions.

escalator Formerly a trademark, now a generic term.

escalator clause A clause in a contract providing for increases or decreases in wages, prices, etc., based on fluctuations in the cost of living, production, expenses, etc.

Eskimo, Eskimos Some, especially in northern Canada, use the term *Inuit* for these native peoples of northern North America. Follow the preference of those involved in the story.

ESOP Acronym for *employee stock ownership plan*. Spell out on first reference.

essential clauses, nonessential clauses These terms are used in this book instead of *restrictive clause* and *nonrestrictive clause* to convey the distinction between the two in a more easily remembered manner.

Both types of clauses provide additional information about a word or phrase in the sentence.

The difference between them is that the *essential clause* cannot be eliminated without changing the meaning of the sentence — it so *restricts* the meaning of the word or phrase that its absence would lead to a substantially different interpretation of what the author meant.

The *nonessential clause*, however, can be eliminated without altering the basic meaning of the sentence — it does not *restrict* the meaning so significantly that its absence would radically alter the author's thought.

PUNCTUATION: An essential clause must not be set off from the rest of a sentence by commas. A nonessential clause must be set off by commas.

The presence or absence of commas provides the reader with critical information about the writer's intended meaning. Note the following examples:

—*Reporters who do not read the Stylebook should not criticize their editors.* (The writer is saying that only one class of reporters, those who do not read the Stylebook, should not criticize their editors. If the *who ... Stylebook* phrase were deleted, the meaning of the sentence would be changed substantially.)

—*Reporters, who do not read the Stylebook, should not criticize their editors.* (The writer is saying that all reporters should not criticize their editors. If the *who ... Stylebook* phrase were deleted, this meaning would not be changed.)

USE OF WHO, WHOM, THAT, WHICH. See separate entries on **that (conjunction); that, which (pronouns); who, whom**.

That is the preferred pronoun to introduce essential clauses that refer to an inanimate object or an animal without a name. *Which* is the only acceptable pronoun to introduce a nonessential clause that refers to an inanimate object or an animal without a name.

The pronoun *which* occasionally may be substituted for *that* in the introduction of an essential clause that refers to an inanimate object or an animal without a name. In general, this use of *which* should appear only when *that* is used as a conjunction to introduce another clause in the same sentence: *He said Monday that the part of the army which suffered severe casualties needs reinforcement.*

See **that (conjunction)** for guidelines on the use of *that* as a conjunction.

essential phrases, nonessential phrases These terms are used in this book instead of *restrictive phrase* and *nonrestrictive phrase* to convey the distinction between the two in a more easily remembered manner.

The underlying concept is the one that also applies to clauses:

An *essential phrase* is a word or group of words critical to the reader's understanding of what the author had in mind.

A *nonessential phrase* provides more information about something. Although the information may be helpful to the reader's comprehension, the reader would not be misled if the information were not there.

PUNCTUATION: Do not set an essential phrase off from the rest of a sentence by commas:

We saw the award-winning movie "One Flew Over the Cuckoo's Nest." (No comma, because many movies have won awards, and without the name of the movie the reader would not know which movie was meant.)

They ate dinner with their daughter Julie. (Because they have more than one daughter, the inclusion of Julie's name is critical if the reader is to know which daughter is meant.)

Set off nonessential phrases by commas:

We saw the 1975 winner of the Academy Award competition for best picture, "One Flew Over the Cuckoo's Nest." (Only one movie won the award. The name is informative, but even without the name no other movie could be meant.)

They ate dinner with their daughter Julie and her husband, David. (Julie has only one husband. If the phrase read *and her husband David*, it would suggest that she had more than one husband.)

The company chairman, Henry Ford II, spoke. (In the context, only one person could be meant.)

Indian corn, or maize, was harvested. (*Maize* provides the reader with the name of the corn, but its absence would not change the meaning of the sentence.)

DESCRIPTIVE WORDS: Do not confuse punctuation rules for nonessential clauses with the correct punctuation when a nonessential word is used as a descriptive adjective. The distinguishing clue often is the lack of an article or pronoun:

Right: *Julie and husband Jeff went shopping. Julie and her husband, Jeff, went shopping.*

Right: *Company Chairman Henry Ford II made the announcement. The company chairman, Henry Ford II, made the announcement.*

ETF Abbreviation for *exchange-traded fund*. A security that tracks a benchmark much as a mutual fund does, but trades throughout market days like a stock on the exchange. Spell out on first reference.

ethanol Fuel additive distilled from mashed and fermented grain. Gasoline blends are written as a percentage of *ethanol*, e.g., E85 for 85

*percent ethanol and 15 percent gaso-
line.*

ethnic cleansing Euphemism
for a campaign to force a population from a region by expulsions
and other violence often including
killings and rapes. The term came
to prominence in former Yugosla-
via during the 1990s to whitewash
atrocities of warring ethnic groups,
then usage spread to other conflicts.
AP does not use "ethnic cleansing"
on its own. It must be enclosed in
quotes, attributed and explained.
Don't use the term as a keyword
(slug) or in headlines.

euro The common currency
of 19 of the 28 members of the
European Union, known as the
eurozone: Austria, Belgium, Cyprus,
Estonia, Finland, France, Germany,
Greece, Ireland, Italy, Latvia,
Lithuania, Luxembourg, Malta,
Netherlands, Portugal, Slovakia,
Slovenia and Spain. Some smaller
countries and territories also use the
euro, either through agreement with
the EU or as a de facto currency.
   Plural is *euros*. Write euro
amounts in the form *100 euros*. Do
not use the "€" sign. See **currency
conversions**.

eurodollar A U.S. dollar on deposit in a European bank, including
foreign branches of U.S. banks.

European Union *EU* (no periods). The 28-nation European
Union, based in Brussels, was created by the Treaty on European
Union, which was signed in February
1992 and took effect Nov. 1, 1993. Its
executive body is the 28-member
European Commission, which runs
the EU's day-to-day affairs, drafts
European laws and, after their adoption by governments, ensures their
enforcement across the bloc. It also
represents the EU in international
trade negotiations and conducts
antitrust investigations. The EU
created the positions of president
and foreign minister in 2010 in
an effort to give the bloc greater
prominence in world affairs. It
also gave the European Parliament
more powers in making EU laws.
The EU is an outgrowth of the 1958
European Economic Community,
which itself was formed out of the
1952 European Coal and Steel Community. The six founding members
are: France, Germany, Italy, Netherlands, Belgium and Luxembourg.
Other members are: Austria, Britain,
Bulgaria, Croatia, Cyprus, Czech Republic, Denmark, Estonia, Finland,
Greece, Hungary, Ireland, Latvia,
Lithuania, Malta, Poland, Portugal,
Romania, Slovakia, Slovenia, Spain
and Sweden.

eurozone See **euro**.

Eve Capitalize when used with
New Year's Eve, Christmas Eve.

every day (adv.) **everyday**
(adj.)

every one, everyone Two
words when it means each individual item: *Every one of the clues was
worthless.*
   One word when used as a pronoun meaning all persons: *Everyone
wants his life to be happy.* (Note that
everyone takes singular verbs and
pronouns.)

ex- Use no hyphen for words
that use *ex-* in the sense of *out of*:
   excommunicate   expropriate

   Hyphenate when using *ex-* in the
sense of *former*:
   ex-convict   ex-president
   Do not capitalize *ex-* when attached to a formal title before a
name: *ex-President Richard Nixon.*
The prefix modifies the entire term:

ex-New York Gov. Mario Cuomo; not *New York ex-Gov.*
Usually *former* is better.

exaggerate

except See **accept, except**.

exclamation point See entry in **Punctuation** chapter.

execute To *execute* a person is to kill him in compliance with a military order or judicial decision.
See **assassin, killer, murderer** and **homicide, murder, manslaughter**.

execution-style Avoid use of this term to describe how people are killed, since it means different things to different people. Be specific as to how the person was killed, if that information is necessary.

executive branch Always lowercase.

executive director Capitalize before a name only if it is a formal corporate or organizational title.
See **titles**.

Executive Mansion Capitalize only in references to the White House.

executor Use for both men and women.
Not a formal title. Always lowercase.
See **titles**.

expel, expelled, expelling

Explorers See **Boy Scouts**.

Export-Import Bank of the United States *Export-Import Bank* is acceptable in all references; *Ex-Im Bank* is acceptable on second reference.
Headquarters is in Washington.

extol, extolled, extolling

extra- Do not use a hyphen when *extra* means *outside of* unless the prefix is followed by a word beginning with *a* or a capitalized word:

extralegal	extraterrestrial
extramarital	extraterritorial

Follow *extra-* with a hyphen when it is part of a compound modifier describing a condition beyond the usual size, extent or degree:

extra-base hit	extra-large book
extra-dry drink	extra-mild taste

extraordinary loss, extraordinary income See **profit terminology**.

extrasensory perception *ESP* is acceptable on second reference.

extreme unction See **sacraments**.

Exxon Mobil Corp. Headquarters is in Irving, Texas, with exploration, production and chemical operations based in Houston. *Exxon Mobil* is acceptable on second reference.

eye, eyed, eyeing

eyestrain

eye to eye, eye-to-eye Hyphenate when used as a compound modifier: *an eye-to-eye confrontation*.

eyewitness

Facebook The world's most popular social network. Users share content in the form of text, photos, video clips and links to websites. They also use the service to communicate with one another privately, form groups around topics of interest, play games and promote businesses and organizations.

face-lift

face to face When a story says two people meet for discussions, talks or debate, it is unnecessary to say they met *face to face*.

fact-finding (adj.)

factor A financial organization whose primary business is purchasing the accounts receivable of other firms, at a discount, and taking the risk and responsibilities of making collection.

Faeroe Islands Use in datelines after a community name in stories from this group of Danish islands in the northern Atlantic Ocean between Iceland and the Shetland Islands.

Fahrenheit The temperature scale commonly used in the United States.

The scale is named for Gabriel Daniel Fahrenheit, a German physicist who designed it. In it, the freezing point of water is 32 degrees and the boiling point is 212 degrees.

To convert to Celsius, subtract 32 from Fahrenheit figure, multiply by 5 and divide by 9 (77 - 32 = 45, times 5 = 225, divided by 9 = 25 degrees Celsius.)

To convert a temperature difference from Fahrenheit to Celsius, multiply by 5 and divide by 9. A difference of 18 degrees F is a 10-degree C difference.

In cases that require mention of the scale, use these forms: *86 degrees Fahrenheit* or *86 F* (note the space and no period after the *F*) if degrees and Fahrenheit are clear from the context.

See **Celsius** and **Kelvin scale**.

For guidelines on when Celsius temperatures should be used, see **metric system** entry.

TEMPERATURE CONVERSIONS

Following is a temperature conversion table. Celsius temperatures have been rounded to the nearest whole number.

F	C	F	C	F	C
-26	-32	19	-7	64	18
-24	-31	21	-6	66	19
-22	-30	23	-5	68	20
-20	-29	25	-4	70	21
-18	-28	27	-3	72	22
-17	-27	28	-2	73	23
-15	-26	30	-1	75	24
-13	-25	32	0	77	25
-11	-24	34	1	79	26
-9	-23	36	2	81	27
-8	-22	37	3	82	28

F	C	F	C	F	C
-6	-21	39	4	84	29
-4	-20	41	5	86	30
-2	-19	43	6	88	31
0	-18	45	7	90	32
1	-17	46	8	91	33
3	-16	48	9	93	34
5	-15	50	10	95	35
7	-14	52	11	97	36
9	-13	54	12	99	37
10	-12	55	13	100	38
12	-11	57	14	102	39
14	-10	59	15	104	40
16	-9	61	16	106	41
18	-8	63	17	108	42

fall See **seasons**.

fallout (n.)

family names Capitalize words denoting family relationships only when they precede the name of a person or when they stand unmodified as a substitute for a person's name: *I wrote to Grandfather Smith. I wrote Mother a letter. I wrote my mother a letter.*

Fannie Mae A government-controlled company that helps provide money for the U.S. housing market by buying residential mortgages and packaging pools of those loans for sale to investors. The company, whose name is short for *Federal National Mortgage Association*, was seized by the government in September 2008 and is overseen by the Federal Housing Finance Agency.

FAQ Acceptable in all uses for *frequently asked questions*.

Far East The easternmost portions of the continent of Asia: China, Japan, North and South Korea, Taiwan, Hong Kong and the eastern portions of Russia.
Confine *Far East* to this restricted sense. Use the *Far East and South-east Asia* when referring to a wider portion of eastern Asia.
See **Asian subcontinent** and **Southeast Asia**.

far-flung (adj.)

farmworker

far-off (adj.)

far-ranging (adj.)

farsighted When used in a medical sense, it means that a person can see objects at a distance but has difficulty seeing materials at close range.

farther, further Farther refers to physical distance: *He walked farther into the woods.*
Further refers to an extension of time or degree: *She will look further into the mystery.*

Far West For the U.S. region, generally west of the Rocky Mountains.

FASB Abbreviation for *Financial Accounting Standards Board*. Spell out on first reference.

fascism, fascist See **political parties and philosophies**.

Fatah A secular Palestinian party and former guerrilla movement founded by Yasser Arafat. Do not use with the prefix *al-*.

father Use *the Rev.* in first reference before the names of Episcopal, Orthodox and Roman Catholic priests. Use *Father* before a name only in direct quotations.
See **religious titles**.

Father's Day The third Sunday in June.

father-in-law, fathers-in-law

Father Time

favorite A button that a Twitter user can click to express approval for a tweet and/or to bookmark that tweet, and any associated links, for later consumption. Also, the act of clicking on this button.

faze, phase *Faze* means to embarrass or disturb: *The snub did not faze her.*
Phase denotes an aspect or stage: *They will phase in a new system.*

FBI Acceptable in all references for *Federal Bureau of Investigation.*

featherbedding The practice of requiring an employer to hire more workers than needed to handle a job.

features They are not exempt from normal style rules. See **special contexts** for guidelines on some limited exceptions.

federal Use a capital letter for the architectural style and for corporate or governmental bodies that use the word as part of their formal names: *the Federal Trade Commission.* (See separate entries for governmental agencies.)
Lowercase when used as an adjective to distinguish something from state, county, city, town or private entities: *federal assistance, federal court, the federal government, a federal judge.*
Also: *federal court* (but *U.S. District Court* is preferred) and *federal Judge Ann Aldrich* (but *U.S. District Judge Ann Aldrich* is preferred).

Federal Aviation Administration *FAA* is acceptable on second reference.

Federal Bureau of Investigation *FBI* is acceptable in all references. To avoid alphabet soup, however, use *the bureau* in some references.

Federal Communications Commission *FCC* is acceptable on second reference.

federal court Always lowercase. The preferred form for first reference is to use the proper name of the court. See entries under **U.S.** and the court name.
Do not create nonexistent entities such as *Manhattan Federal Court.* Instead, use *a federal court in Manhattan.*
See **judicial branch**.

Federal Crop Insurance Corp. Do not abbreviate.

Federal Deposit Insurance Corp. The government agency that insures deposits in banks and thrifts. *FDIC* is acceptable on second reference.

Federal Emergency Management Agency *FEMA* is acceptable on second reference.

Federal Energy Regulatory Commission The government agency that regulates interstate natural gas and electricity transactions.
FERC is acceptable on second reference, but *the agency* or *the commission* is preferred.

Federal Farm Credit Board Do not abbreviate.

Federal Farm Credit System The federally chartered cooperative banking system that provides most of the nation's agricultural loans. The system is cooperatively

owned by its farm borrowers and is made up of the regional banks that issue operating and mortgage loans through local land bank associations and production credit associations.

federal funds, federal funds rate Money in excess of what the Federal Reserve says a bank must have on hand to back up deposits. The excess can be lent overnight to banks that need more cash on hand to meet their reserve requirements. The interest rate of these loans is the *federal funds rate*. Its target rate is set by the Federal Reserve's policymaking panel, the Federal Open Market Committee. See **Federal Reserve**.

Federal Highway Administration Reserve the *FHA* abbreviation for the *Federal Housing Administration*.

Federal Home Loan Bank Board Do not abbreviate.

Federal Home Loan Mortgage Corp. See **Freddie Mac**.

Federal Housing Administration *FHA* is acceptable on second reference.

federal legal holidays See **holidays and holy days**.

Federal Mediation and Conciliation Service Do not abbreviate. Use *the mediation service* on second reference.

Federal National Mortgage Association See **Fannie Mae**.

Federal Register This publication, issued every workday, is the legal medium for recording and communicating the rules and regulations established by the executive branch of the federal government.

Individuals or corporations cannot be held legally responsible for compliance with a regulation unless it has been published in the Register.

In addition, executive agencies are required to publish in advance some types of proposed regulations.

Federal Reserve The central bank of the United States. It comprises the Federal Open Market Committee, which sets interest rates; the Federal Reserve Board, the regulatory body made up of Fed governors in Washington; and the Federal Reserve System, which includes the Fed in Washington and 12 regional Fed banks. Use *Federal Reserve* on first reference, *the Fed* on second reference. Use *Federal Reserve Board Chair Janet Yellen*, her preference.

Federal Trade Commission *FTC* is acceptable on second reference.

FedEx Use this official brand name for the delivery service company. The formal name of the parent company is FedEx Corp. Headquarters is in Memphis, Tennessee.

feed A stream of constantly updated material.

felony, misdemeanor A *felony* is a serious crime. A *misdemeanor* is a minor offense against the law.

A fuller definition of what constitutes a felony or misdemeanor depends on the governmental jurisdiction involved.

At the federal level, a *misdemeanor* is a crime that carries a potential penalty of no more than a year in jail. A *felony* is a crime that carries a potential penalty of more than a year in prison. Often, however, a statute gives a judge options such as imposing a fine or probation in addition to or instead of a jail or prison sentence.

A *felon* is a person who has been convicted of a *felony*, regardless of whether the individual actually spends time in confinement or is given probation or a fine instead.

Convicted felon is redundant.

See **prison, jail**.

female Use *female* as an adjective, not *woman*. *She is the first female governor of North Carolina.*

Ferris wheel

ferryboat

fertility rate As calculated by the federal government, it is the number of live births per 1,000 females age 15 through 44 years.

fetus In human development, from the eighth week to birth. See **embryo**.

fewer, less In general, use *fewer* for individual items, *less* for bulk or quantity.

Wrong: *The trend is toward more machines and less people.* (People in this sense refers to individuals.)

Wrong: *She was fewer than 60 years old.* (Years in this sense refers to a period of time, not individual years.)

Right: *Fewer than 10 applicants called.* (Individuals.)

Right: *I had less than $50 in my pocket.* (An amount.) But: *I had fewer than 50 $1 bills in my pocket.* (Individual items.)

Fez The preferred spelling for the city in Morocco.

fiance (man) **fiancee** (woman)

Fiberglas Note the single *s*. A trademark for fiberglass or glass fiber.

field house

figuratively, literally *Figuratively* means in an analogous sense, but not in the exact sense. *He bled them white.*

Literally means in an exact sense; do not use it figuratively.

Wrong: *He literally bled them white.* (Unless the blood was drained from their bodies.)

figure The symbol for a number: *the figure 5.*

See **numerals**.

filibuster To *filibuster* is to make long speeches to obstruct the passage of legislation.

A legislator who used such methods also is a *filibuster*, not a *filibusterer*.

Filipinos The people of the Philippines. *Filipina* is acceptable as the feminine form.

film noir

filmgoer

filmmaker

film ratings See **movie ratings**.

financial editor Capitalize only as a formal title before a name.
See **titles**.

financial institutions Here are 10 major U.S.-based financial institutions and their headquarters.

JPMorgan Chase & Co., New York

Bank of America Corp., Charlotte, N.C.

Citigroup Inc., New York

Wells Fargo & Co., San Francisco

Goldman Sachs Group Inc., New York

MetLife Inc., New York

Morgan Stanley, New York
U.S. Bancorp, Minneapolis
American Express Co., New York
Bank of New York Mellon Corp.,
New York
HSBC North America Holdings
Inc., New York
Travelers Cos., New York

Finland A Nordic state, not part
of Scandinavia.

firearms See **weapons**.

fire department See the **governmental bodies** entry for the basic
rules on capitalization.
See **titles** and **military titles** for
guidelines on titles.

firefight

firefighter, fireman The preferred term to describe a person
who fights fire is *firefighter*.
One meaning of *fireman* is a
person who tends fires in a furnace.
Fireman is also an acceptable synonym for *firefighter*.

firewall A device or software
designed to stop malicious or unauthorized Internet traffic from
reaching a computer or local data
network. Some firewalls also inspect
outgoing traffic.

firm A business partnership is
correctly referred to as a *firm*: *He
joined a law firm.*
Do not use *firm* in references
to an incorporated business entity.
Use *the company* or *the corporation*
instead.

first aid (n.) **first-aid** (adj.)

first class, first-class Hyphenate as a modifier before a noun. *The
restaurant was first class. It was a
first-class restaurant.*

first degree, first-degree Hyphenate when used as a compound
modifier: *It was murder in the first
degree. He was convicted of first-degree
murder.*

first family Always lowercase.

firsthand (adj. and adv.)

first lady Not a formal title.
Do not capitalize, even when used
before the name of a chief of state's
wife.
See **titles**.

first quarter, first-quarter Hyphenate when used as a compound
modifier: *He scored in the first quarter. The team took the lead on his first-quarter goal.*

fiscal, monetary *Fiscal* applies
to budgetary matters.
Monetary applies to money supply.

fiscal year The 12-month period
that a corporation or governmental
body uses for bookkeeping purposes.
The federal government's fiscal
year starts three months ahead of
the calendar year — fiscal 2007, for
example, ran from Oct. 1, 2006, to
Sept. 30, 2007.

fitful It means restless, not a
condition of being fit.

fjord

flack, flak *Flack* is slang for *press
agent*. Avoid using in copy.
Flak is a type of anti-aircraft fire,
hence figuratively a barrage of criticism.

flagpole, flagship

flail, flay To *flail* is to swing the arms widely.

To flay is, literally, to strip off the skin by whipping. Figuratively, *to flay* means to tongue-lash a person.

flair, flare *Flair* is conspicuous talent or style.

Flare is a verb meaning to blaze with sudden, bright light or to burst out in anger. It is also a noun meaning a flame.

flak See **flack, flak**.

flare-up (n.) **flare up** (v.) See **flair, flare**.

flash flood See **weather terms**.

flash mob A gathering of people performing an action in a public place designated by a text message, email, social media post or other notification sent to the participants. Organizers of flash mobs are often aiming to get the attention of passers-by by performing spontaneous actions en masse.

flat-panel TV, flat-screen TV A flat-panel television set contains no cathode-ray tube or optical path, which means it can be thinner than a tube-based TV set. The two most popular technologies are plasma displays and liquid-crystal displays, or LCDs. Flat-screen TVs have a flat front glass surface, as opposed to the convex surfaces of older CRT sets. The term can apply to CRT sets and rear-projection sets that are not flat panels.

flaunt, flout To *flaunt* is to make an ostentatious or defiant display: *She flaunted her intelligence.*

To flout is to show contempt for: *He flouts the law.*

fleet Use figures and capitalize *fleet* when forming a proper name: *the 6th Fleet.*

Lowercase *fleet* whenever it stands alone.

Flickr A photo- and video-storing and -sharing service owned by Yahoo Inc.

flier, flyer *Flier* is the preferred term for an aviator or a handbill. *Flyer* is the proper name of some trains and buses: *The Western Flyer.*

flip-flop (n. and v.)

float Money that has been committed but not yet credited to an account, like a check that has been written but has not yet cleared.

flood plain

floods, flood stage See **weather terms**.

floodwaters

floor leader Treat it as a job description, lowercased, rather than a formal title: *Republican floor leader John Smith.*

Do not use when a formal title such as *majority leader*, *minority leader* or *whip* would be the accurate description.

See **legislative titles** and **titles**.

Florida Abbreviate *Fla.* in datelines only; spell out in stories. Postal code: *FL*

See **state names**.

Florida Keys A chain of small islands extending southwest from the southern tip of mainland Florida.

Cities, or the islands themselves, are followed by *Fla.* in datelines: *KEY WEST, Fla. (AP) —*

flounder, founder A *flounder* is a fish; to *flounder* is to move clumsily or jerkily, to flop about: *The fish floundered on land.*

To *founder* is to bog down, become disabled or sink: *The ship floundered in the heavy seas for hours, then foundered.*

flout See **flaunt, flout**.

flowers See **plants**.

fluid ounce Equal to 1.8 cubic inches, 2 tablespoons or 6 teaspoons. The metric equivalent is approximately 30 milliliters.

To convert to milliliters, multiply by 30 (3 ounces x 30 equals 90 milliliters).

See **liter**.

flu-like

fluorescent

flush To become red in the face. See **livid**.

flyer See **flier, flyer**.

FM Acceptable in all references for the *frequency modulation* system of radio transmission.

f.o.b. Acceptable on first reference for *free on board*, meaning a seller agrees to put a commodity on a truck, ship, etc., at no charge, but transportation costs must be paid by the buyer.

-fold No hyphen: *twofold, fourfold* and *hundredfold*.

folk singer, folk song

following The word usually is a noun, verb or adjective: *He has a large following. He is following his conscience. The following statement was made.*

Although Webster's New World College Dictionary records its use as a preposition, the preferred word is *after*: *He spoke after dinner.* Not: *He spoke following dinner.*

follow-up (n. and adj.) Use two words (no hyphen) in verb form.

food Most food names are lowercase: *apples, cheese, peanut butter.*

Capitalize brand names and trademarks: *Roquefort cheese, Tabasco sauce.*

Most proper nouns or adjectives are capitalized when they occur in a food name: *Boston brown bread, Russian dressing, Swiss cheese, Waldorf salad.*

Lowercase is used, however, when the food does not depend on the proper noun or adjective for its meaning: *french fries.*

If a question arises, check the separate section on **Food Guidelines**. If there is no entry, follow Webster's New World College Dictionary. Use lowercase if the dictionary lists it as an acceptable form for the sense in which the word is used.

The same principles apply to foreign names for foods: *mousse de saumon* (salmon mousse), *pomme de terre* (literally, "apple of the earth" — for potato), *salade Russe* (Russian salad).

Food and Agriculture Organization Not *Agricultural*. FAO is acceptable on second reference to this U.N. agency.

Food and Drug Administration *FDA* is acceptable on second reference.

foodborne (adj.)

foot The basic unit of length in the measuring system used in the United States. Its origin was a calculation that this was the length of the average human foot.

The metric equivalent is exactly 30.48 centimeters, which may be rounded to 30 centimeters for most comparisons.

For most conversions to centimeters, it is adequate to multiply 30 (5 feet x 30 equals 150 centimeters). For more exact figures, multiply by 30.48 (5 feet x 30.48 equals 152.4 centimeters).

To convert to meters, multiply by 0.3 (5 feet x 0.3 equals 1.5 meters).

See **centimeter**; **meter**; and **dimensions**.

foot-and-mouth disease Not *hoof-and-mouth disease*.

forbear, forebear *To forbear* is to avoid or shun.

A *forebear* is an ancestor.

forbid, forbade, forbidding

force majeure A condition permitting a company to depart from the strict terms of a contract because of an event or effect that can't be reasonably controlled.

forcible rape A redundancy that usually should be avoided. It may be used, however, in stories dealing with both rape and statutory rape, which does not necessarily involve the use of force.

Ford Motor Co. Use *Ford* on second reference.

Headquarters is in Dearborn, Michigan.

fore- The rules in **prefixes** apply, but in general, no hyphen. Some examples:

forebrain	foregoing
forefather	foretooth

There are three nautical exceptions, based on long-standing practice:

fore-topgallant	fore-topsail
fore-topmast	

forecast Use *forecast* also for the past tense, not *forecasted*.

See **weather terms**.

foreclosure The process by which a lender seizes property from a mortgage holder who has failed to make payments and is in default.

forego, forgo *To forego* means to go before, as in *foregone conclusion*.

To forgo means to abstain from, as in: *He decided to forgo his senior year of eligibility*.

foreign names For foreign place names, use the primary spelling in Webster's New World College Dictionary. If it has no entry, follow the National Geographic Atlas of the World.

For personal names, follow the individual's preference for an English spelling if it can be determined. Otherwise:

—Use the nearest phonetic equivalent in English if one exists: *Alexander Solzhenitsyn*, for example, rather than *Aleksandr*, the spelling that would result from a transliteration of the Russian letters into the English alphabet.

If a name has no close phonetic equivalent in English, express it with an English spelling that approximates the sound in the original language: *Anwar Sadat*.

In general, lowercase particles such as *de, der, la, le*, and *van, von* when part of a given name: *Charles de Gaulle, Baron Manfred von Richthofen*. But follow individual preferences, as in *bin Laden*, or Dutch names such as *Van Gogh* or *Van der Graaf*. Capitalize the particles when the last names start a sentence: *De Gaulle spoke to von Richthofen*.

For additional guidelines, see **Arabic names**; **Chinese names**; **Portu-**

guese names; Russian names; Spanish names.

foreign words Some foreign words and abbreviations have been accepted universally into the English language: *bon voyage*; *versus, vs.*; *et cetera, etc.*

Many foreign words and their abbreviations are not understood universally, although they may be used in special applications such as medical or legal terminology. If such a word or phrase is needed in a story, place it in quotation marks and provide an explanation: *"ad astra per aspera," a Latin phrase meaning "to the stars through difficulty."*

foreman, forewoman Seldom a formal title. Never use foreperson.

formal titles See **titles**.

former Always lowercase. But retain capitalization for a formal title used immediately before a name: *former President Bill Clinton*.

Formica A trademark for a brand of laminated plastic.

formula, formulas Use figures in writing formulas. See **metric system**.

forsake, forsook, forsaken

fort Do not abbreviate for cities or for military installations.
In datelines for cities:
FORT LAUDERDALE, Fla. (AP)
—
In datelines for military installations:
FORT BRAGG, N.C. (AP) —

fortuneteller, fortunetelling

forward Not *forwards*.

foul, fowl *Foul* means offensive, out of line.
A *fowl* is a bird, especially the larger domestic birds used as food: chickens, ducks, turkeys.

founder See **flounder, founder**.

Founding Fathers Capitalize when referring to the creators of the U.S. Constitution.

Four-H Club *4-H Club* is preferred. Members are *4-H'ers*.

Foursquare A location-based app that aims to connect users with establishments that they might enjoy based on previous check-ins at similar locations as well as reviews by other users. The check-ins used to take place on Foursquare, but that functionality has been moved to the separate Swarm app. See **Swarm**.

four-star general

Fourth Estate Capitalize when used as a collective name for journalism and journalists.
The description is attributed to Edmund Burke, who is reported to have called the reporters' gallery in Parliament a "Fourth Estate."
The three estates of early English society were the Lords Spiritual (the clergy), the Lords Temporal (the nobility) and the Commons (the bourgeoisie).

Fourth of July, July Fourth Also *Independence Day*. The federal legal holiday is observed on Friday if July 4 falls on a Saturday, on Monday if it falls on a Sunday.

4x4 *Four-wheel drive* is preferred, unless *4x4* is part of the car model's proper name.

401(k) (no space)

Fox U.S. television network owned by Twenty-First Century Fox Inc. See **News Corp.** and **Twenty-First Century Fox Inc.**

fracking Acceptable with brief explanation. The energy industry uses the technique to extract oil and gas from rock by injecting high-pressure mixtures of water, sand or gravel and chemicals. See **hydraulic fracturing**.

fractions Spell out amounts less than 1 in stories, using hyphens between the words: *two-thirds, four-fifths, seven-sixteenths*, etc.

Use figures for precise amounts larger than 1, converting to decimals whenever practical.

When using fractional characters, remember that most newspaper type fonts can set only 1/8, 1/4, 3/8, 1/2, 5/8, 3/4 and 7/8 as one unit; for mixed numbers, use 1 1/2, 2 5/8, etc. with a full space between the whole number and the fraction. Other fractions require a hyphen and individual figures, with a space between the whole number and the fraction: 1 3-16, 2 1-3, 5 9-10.

In tabular material, use figures exclusively, converting to decimals if the amounts involve extensive use of fractions that cannot be expressed as a single character. See **numerals** and **percent**.

fragment, fragmentary *Fragment* describes a piece or pieces broken from the whole: *She sang a fragment of the song.*

Fragmentary describes disconnected and incomplete parts: *Early returns were fragmentary.*

frame-up (n.) **frame up** (v.)

Frankfurt The city in Germany carries the name of the country in datelines.

fraternal organizations and service clubs Capitalize the proper names: *American Legion, Lions Club, Independent Order of Odd Fellows, Rotary Club.*

Capitalize also words describing membership: *He is a Legionnaire, a Lion, an Odd Fellow, an Optimist and a Rotarian.* See **American Legion** for the rationale on *Legionnaire*.

Capitalize the formal titles of officeholders when used before a name.

See **titles**.

Freddie Mac A government-controlled company that helps provide money for the U.S. housing market by buying residential mortgages and packaging pools of those loans for sale to investors. The company, whose name is short for *Federal Home Loan Mortgage Corp.*, was seized by the government in September 2008 and is overseen by the Federal Housing Finance Agency.

free-for-all (n. and adj.)

freelancer (n.) **freelance** (v. and adj.)

freely floating Describes an exchange rate that is allowed to fluctuate in response to supply and demand in the foreign markets.

free on board See **f.o.b.**

Free Syrian Army Armed opposition group in Syria. Active in the Syrian civil war that began in March 2011.

freewheeling

freeze-dry, freeze-dried, freeze-drying

freezing drizzle, freezing rain See **weather terms**.

French Canadian, French Canadians A Canadian whose native language is French. Spelled without a hyphen, an exception to the usual practice for dual ethnic heritage.

French Foreign Legion Retain capitalization if shortened to the Foreign Legion.

Lowercase *the legion* and *legionnaires*. Unlike the situation with the American Legion, the French Foreign Legion is a group of active soldiers.

frequency modulation *FM* is acceptable in all references.

frequent flier

friend, follow, like Acceptable as both nouns and verbs. Actions by which users connect to other users on social networks. Friend and like are typically used on Facebook, while Twitter, Pinterest, Tumblr and Instagram users follow and have followers. Facebook users who enable public access to profiles can also give fellow users the option to "follow" their public updates without being their friends.

Frigidaire A trademark for a brand of kitchen and laundry appliances.

Frisbee A trademark for a plastic disc thrown as a toy. Use *Frisbee disc* for the trademarked version and *flying disc* for other generic versions.

Frontier Airlines Holdings Inc. Headquarters is in Denver.

front line (n.) **front-line** (adj.)

frontman

front page (n.) **front-page** (adj.)

front-runner

frost See **weather terms**.

fruits See **food**.

FTP The abbreviation stands for *File Transfer Protocol*, a common procedure for transferring files on the *Internet*. The abbreviation is acceptable in all uses.

fulfill, fulfilled, fulfilling

full- Hyphenate when used to form compound modifiers:

full-dress	full-page
full-fledged	full-scale
full-length	

See the listings that follow and Webster's New World College Dictionary for the spelling of other combinations.

full-body scanner

full faith and credit bond See **loan terminology**.

full house Three of a kind and a pair in poker.

full time, full-time Hyphenate when used as a compound modifier: *He works full time. She has a full-time job.*

fulsome It means disgustingly excessive. Do not use it to mean lavish or profuse.

fundraising, fundraiser One word in all cases.

funnel cloud See **weather terms**.

furlough

further See **farther, further**.

fuselage

fusillade

futures *Futures* contracts are agreements to deliver a quantity of goods, generally commodities, at a specified price at a certain time in the future. *Options*, which also are widely traded on the nation's commodities exchanges, give buyers the right but not the obligation to buy or sell something at a certain price within a specified period.

The purpose of the futures exchanges is to transfer the risk of price fluctuations from people who don't want the risk, such as farmers or metals processors, to speculators who are willing to take a gamble on making big profits.

Major U.S. commodities markets are the Chicago Board Options Exchange, Chicago Board of Trade, Chicago Mercantile Exchange, New York Mercantile Exchange, the New York Cotton Exchange, and the Coffee, Sugar and Cocoa Exchange.

F-word See **obscenities, profanities, vulgarities**.

G

GAAP The acronym stands for *generally accepted accounting principles*. Spell out on first reference.

gage, gauge A *gage* is a security or a pledge.

A *gauge* is a measuring device.

Gauge is also a term used to designate the size of shotguns. See **weapons**.

gaiety

gale See **weather terms**.

gallon Equal to 128 fluid ounces. The metric equivalent is approximately 3.8 liters. There are 42 gallons in a barrel of oil.

To convert to liters, multiply by 3.8 (3 gallons x 3.8 = 11.4 liters).

See **imperial gallon**; **liter**; and **metric system**.

Gallup Poll Prepared by the Gallup Organization, Princeton, New Jersey.

gambling Preferred term for playing games of chance. Avoid use of the term *gaming* except in quotations or proper names or when referring to video games.

game plan

gaming See **gambling**.

gamut, gantlet, gauntlet A *gamut* is a scale of notes or any complete range or extent.

A *gantlet* is a flogging ordeal, literally or figuratively.

A *gauntlet* is a glove. *To throw down the gauntlet* means to issue a challenge. To *take up the gauntlet* means to accept a challenge.

Gannett Co. The largest owner of U.S. newspapers, including USA Today. Also owns television stations. In August 2014 the company said it plans to spin off its print and broadcast units as separate entities. Gannett's publishing arm will retain the Gannett name and include USA Today, 81 local U.S. daily publications and Newsquest, a regional community news provider in the U.K. Gannett's broadcasting and digital arm, which has yet to be named, will operate the company's 46 television stations and websites such as CareerBuilder. It will also include Cars.com. Both units will be headquartered in McLean, Virginia. The spinoff is expected to be completed in 2015.

garnish (v. and n.) **garnishee** (n.) *Garnish* means to adorn or decorate. The noun *garnish* is a decoration or ornament. In a legal context, *garnish* means to attach property or wages as a result of a legal action. A *garnishee* is an individual whose property was attached, or garnished.

gauge See **gage, gauge**.

gay Used to describe men and women attracted to the same sex, though *lesbian* is the more common term for women. Preferred over *homosexual* except in clinical contexts or references to sexual activity.

Include sexual orientation only when it is pertinent to a story, and avoid references to "sexual preference" or to a gay or alternative "lifestyle." See **LGBT** and **phobia**.

Gazprom Russia's state-controlled gas monopoly. Corporate name is *OAO Gazprom*. Headquarters is in Moscow.

GED A trademark abbreviation for *General Educational Development* tests, a battery of five exams designed by the American Council on Education to measure high school equivalency. *GED* should be used as an adjective, not as a noun. Those passing the tests earn a *GED diploma* or *certificate*, not a *GED*.

G-8 See **G-7**.

general assembly See **legislature** for its treatment as the name of a state's legislative body.

Capitalize when it is the formal name for the ruling or consultative body of an organization: *the General Assembly of the World Council of Churches*.

General Assembly (U.N.) *General Assembly* may be used on the first reference in a story under a United Nations dateline.

Use *U.N. General Assembly* in other first references, *the General Assembly* or *the assembly* in subsequent references.

general court Part of the official proper name for the legislatures in Massachusetts and New Hampshire. Capitalize specific references with or without the state name: *the Massachusetts General Court, the General Court*.

In keeping with the accepted practice, however, *Legislature* may be used instead and treated as a proper name. See **legislature**.

Lowercase *legislature* in a generic use such as: *The General Court is the legislature in Massachusetts*.

General Dynamics Corp. Headquarters is in Falls Church, Virginia.

General Electric Co. *GE* is acceptable on second reference.

Headquarters is in Fairfield, Connecticut.

general, general of the Air Force, general of the Army See **military titles**.

general manager Capitalize only as a formal title before a name: corporate *General Manager Jim Smith*. Lowercase as a job description for sports teams: *Giants general manager Jerry Reese*.

See **titles**.

General Motors Co. *GM* is acceptable on second reference.

Headquarters is in Detroit.

general obligation bond See **loan terminology**.

General Services Administration *GSA* is acceptable on second reference.

Geneva The city in Switzerland stands alone in datelines.

Geneva Conventions Note the final *s*.

gentile Generally, any person not Jewish; often, specifically a Christian. But to Mormons it is anyone not a Mormon.

gentleman Do not use as a synonym for *man*. See **lady**.

genus, species In scientific or biological names, capitalize the first, or generic, Latin name for the class of plant or animal and lowercase the species that follows: *Homo sapiens, Tyrannosaurus rex.*

In second references, use the abbreviated form: *P. borealis, T. rex.*

geographic names The basic guidelines:

DOMESTIC: Do not use the postal abbreviations for state names. For acceptable abbreviations, see entries in this book under each state's name. See **state names** for rules on when the abbreviations may be used.

Abbreviate *Saint* as *St.* (But abbreviate *Sault Sainte Marie* as *Sault Ste. Marie.*)

FOREIGN: The first source for the spelling of all foreign place names is Webster's New World College Dictionary as follows:

—Use the first-listed spelling if an entry gives more than one.

—If the dictionary provides different spellings in separate entries, use the spelling that is followed by a full description of the location.

If the dictionary does not have an entry, use the first-listed spelling in the National Geographic Atlas of the World.

Online:
http://www.nationalgeographic.com

NEW NAMES: Follow the styles adopted by the United Nations and the U.S. Board on Geographic Names for new cities, new independent nations and nations that change their names.

DATELINES: See the **datelines** entry.

CAPITALIZATION: Capitalize common nouns when they form an integral part of a proper name, but lowercase them when they stand alone: *Pennsylvania Avenue, the avenue; the Philippine Islands, the islands; the Mississippi River, the river.*

Lowercase common nouns that are not a part of a specific name: *the Pacific islands, the Swiss mountains, Zhejiang province.*

For additional guidelines, see **addresses**; **capitalization**; **directions and regions**; and **island**.

geolocation The association of your virtual location with your physical location. Many social networks (like Facebook) have enabled geolocation features, and some are built completely around geolocation (like Foursquare).

Georgia Abbreviate *Ga.* in datelines only; spell out in stories. Postal code: *GA*
See **state names**.

geotagging The act of adding geographical metadata to pieces of media or social media updates. A *geotagged* tweet, post, photo or video would also indicate latitude and longitude of the location the photo was taken, or possibly the name of the city and/or country.

German measles Also known as *rubella.*

Germany *East Germany* and *West Germany* were reunited as of Oct. 3, 1990. *Berlin* stands alone in datelines.

getaway (n.)

get-together (n.)

ghetto, ghettos Do not use indiscriminately as a synonym for the sections of cities inhabited by minorities or the poor. *Ghetto* has a connotation that government decree has forced people to live in a certain area.

In most cases, *section, district, slum area* or *quarter* is the more accurate word.

gibe, jibe *To gibe* means to taunt or sneer: *They gibed him about his mistakes.*

Jibe means to shift direction or, colloquially, to agree: *They jibed their ship across the wind. Their stories didn't jibe.*

Gibraltar, Strait of Not *Straits*. The entrance to the Mediterranean from the Atlantic Ocean. The British colony on the peninsula that juts into the strait stands alone in datelines as *GIBRALTAR*.

GIF Acronym for *Graphics Interchange Format*, a compression format for images. *GIF* is acceptable in copy but should be explained in the story. Use lowercase in a file name.

giga- A prefix denoting 1 billion units of a measure. Move a decimal point nine places to the right, adding zeros if necessary, to convert to the basic unit: 5.5 gigatons = 5,500,000,000 tons.

gigabyte See **byte**.

GI, GIs Believed to have originated as an abbreviation for *government issue* supplies, it describes military personnel in general, but normally is used for the Army. (No periods is an exception to the general rule for two-letter abbreviations.)

Soldier is preferred unless the story contains the term in quoted matter or involves a subject such as the *GI Bill of Rights*.

Ginnie Mae Commonly used for *Government National Mortgage Association*.

girl Applicable until 18th birthday is reached. Use *woman* or *young woman* afterward.

girlfriend, boyfriend

Girl Scouts The full name of the national organization is *Girl Scouts of the United States of America*. Headquarters is in New York. Note that *Girl Scout Cookies* is a trademark name.

Girls 6 through 8 are *Brownie Girl Scouts* or *Brownies*. Girls 9 through 11 are *Junior Girl Scouts* or *Juniors*. Girls 12 through 14 are *Cadette Girl Scouts* or *Cadettes*. Girls 15 through 17 are *Senior Girl Scouts* or *Seniors*.

See **Boy Scouts**.

glamour One of the few *our* endings still used in American writing. But the adjective is *glamorous*.

GlaxoSmithKline PLC Headquarters is in London.

Global Positioning System See **GPS**.

global warming The terms global warming and climate change can be used interchangeably. Climate change is more accurate scientifically to describe the various effects of greenhouse gases on the world because it includes extreme weather, storms and changes in rainfall patterns, ocean acidification and sea level. But global warming as a term is more common and understandable to the public.

Though some public officials and laymen and only a few climate scientists disagree, the world's scientific organizations say that the world's climate is changing because of the buildup of heat-trapping gases, especially carbon dioxide, from the burning of coal, oil and gas. This is supported by more than 90 percent of the peer-reviewed scientific literature.

In a joint publication in 2014, the U.S. National Academy of Sciences and the Royal Society of the United Kingdom stated: "Human activities — especially the burning of fossil fuels since the start of the Industrial Revolution — have increased atmospheric carbon dioxide concentrations by about 40 percent, with more than half the increase occurring since 1970. Since 1900, the global average surface temperature has increased by about 0.8 degrees Celsius (1.4 degrees Fahrenheit). This has been accompanied by warming of the ocean, a rise in sea level, a strong decline in Arctic sea ice, and many other associated climate effects. Much of this warming has occurred in the last four decades."

globe-trotter, globe-trotting But the proper name of the basketball team is the *Harlem Globetrotters*.

GMT For *Greenwich Mean Time*. Also referred to as *Coordinated Universal Time* or *UTC*. See **time zones** and **meridians**.

gobbledygook

go-between (n.)

godchild, goddaughter Also: *godfather, godliness, godmother, godsend* and *godson*. Always lowercase.

gods and goddesses Capitalize *God* in references to the deity of all monotheistic religions. Capitalize all noun references to the deity: *God the Father, Holy Ghost, Holy Spirit, Allah,* etc. Lowercase personal pronouns: *he, him, thee, thou.*

Lowercase *gods* and *goddesses* in references to the deities of polytheistic religions.

Lowercase *god, gods* and *goddesses* in references to false gods: *He made money his god.*

See **religious references**.

Godspeed

-goer One word. Examples: *concertgoer, moviegoer, partygoer, theatergoer.*

go-go

Goldman Sachs Group Inc. Headquarters is in New York.

goodbye

Good Conduct Medal Military service medal.

Good Friday The Friday before Easter.

good Samaritan But uppercase when used in a title: *Good Samaritan Hospital.*

good, well *Good* is an adjective that means something is as it should be or is better than average.

When used as an adjective, *well* means suitable, proper, healthy. When used as an adverb, *well* means in a satisfactory manner or skillfully.

Good should not be used as an adverb. It does not lose its status as an adjective in a sentence such as *I feel good.* Such a statement is the idiomatic equivalent of *I am in good health.* An alternative, *I feel well,* could be interpreted as meaning that your sense of touch is good.

See **bad, badly** and **well**.

goodwill One word in all uses.

Google Internet company that runs a search engine and digital advertising network. *Google, Googling* and *Googled* are used informally as a verb for performing an Internet search. Google has built several other digital products, including Android software for mobile devices, the Chrome Web browser, the Gmail email service and the YouTube video site. Headquarters is in Mountain View, California.

Google Hangout A function within Google Plus that allows users to have live, face-to-face, multi-person video chats with chosen participants, or make phone calls. Google Hangouts On Air are Hangouts in which the video stream displays publicly on the Google Plus profile page of the user who launched the chat. They can also be displayed on the user's YouTube channel or website.

Google Plus A social network owned by Google in which users can share text updates, videos, photos or other content, and organize fellow users into circles based on relationships or other factors. One popular feature of Google Plus is Hangouts, where users can chat with others using webcams.

GOP Grand Old Party. *GOP* is acceptable on second reference for *Republican Party*.

Gospel(s), gospel Capitalize when referring to any or all of the first four books of the New Testament: *the Gospel of St. John, the Gospels.*

Lowercase in other references: *She is a famous gospel singer.*

government Always lowercase, never abbreviate: *the federal govern-ment, the state government, the U.S. government.*

Government Accountability Office The *Government Accountability Office* is a nonpartisan congressional agency that audits federal programs. (Formerly the General Accounting Office.)

GAO is acceptable on second reference.

governmental bodies Follow these guidelines:

FULL NAME: Capitalize the full proper names of governmental agencies, departments and offices: *The U.S. Department of State, the Georgia Department of Human Resources, the Boston City Council, the Chicago Fire Department.*

WITHOUT JURISDICTION: Retain capitalization in referring to a specific body if the dateline or context makes the name of the nation, state, county, city, etc. unnecessary: *The Department of State* (in a story from Washington), *the Department of Human Resources* or *the state Department of Human Resources* (in a story from Georgia), *the City Council* (in a story from Boston), *the Fire Department* or *the city Fire Department* (in a story from Chicago).

Lowercase further condensations of the name: *the department, the council,* etc.

For additional guidance see **assembly; city council; committee; Congress; legislature; House of Representatives; Senate; Supreme Court of the United States**; and **supreme courts of the states**.

FLIP-FLOPPED NAMES: Retain capital names for the name of a governmental body if its formal name is flopped to delete the word *of: the State Department, the Human Resources Department.*

GENERIC EQUIVALENTS: If a generic term has become the equivalent of a proper name in popular use, treat it as a proper name: *Walpole State Prison*, for example, even though the proper name is the *Massachusetts Correctional Institute-Walpole*.

For additional examples, see **legislature**; **police department**; and **prison, jail**.

PLURALS, NONSPECIFIC REFERENCES: All words that are capitalized when part of a proper name should be lowercased when they are used in the plural or do not refer to a specific, existing body. Some examples:

All states except Nebraska have a state senate. The town does not have a fire department. The bill requires city councils to provide matching funds. The president will address the lower houses of the New York and New Jersey legislatures.

NON-U.S. BODIES: The same principles apply.

Capitalize the names of the specific governmental agencies and departments, either with the name of the nation or without it if clear in the context: *French Foreign Ministry, the Foreign Ministry.*

Lowercase *the ministry* or a similar term when standing alone.

government, junta, regime, administration A *government* is an established system of political administration: *the U.S. government.*

A *junta* is a group or council that often rules after a coup: *A military junta controls the nation.* A *junta* becomes a government after it establishes a system of political administration.

A *regime* is a form of political system, generally an oppressive or undemocratic one: *an authoritarian regime, a communist regime.* The word regime should be used only in general terms. Do not use in references to a specific country or leader: *the North Korean regime, Assad's regime.*

An *administration* consists of officials who make up the executive branch of a government: *the Reagan administration.*

governor Capitalize and abbreviate as *Gov.* or *Govs.* when used as a formal title before one or more names.

See the next entry and **titles**.

governor general, governors general The formal title for the British sovereign's representatives in Canada and some other countries of the Commonwealth.

Do not abbreviate in any use.

GPA Acceptable in all references for *grade-point average.*

GPS Acceptable in all references to *Global Positioning System.* If a descriptive word is used following, use it in lowercase: *The GPS satellite.*

grade, grader Hyphenate in combining forms: *a fourth-grade pupil, a 12th-grade student, first-grader, 10th-grader.*

graduate (v.) *Graduate* is correctly used in the active voice: *She graduated from the university.*

It is correct, but unnecessary, to use the passive voice: *He was graduated from the university.*

Do not, however, drop *from: John Adams graduated from Harvard.* Not: *John Adams graduated Harvard.*

Graham Holdings Co. Formerly known as The Washington Post Co. The company changed its name in November 2013 after selling off *The Washington Post* and other newspapers to Amazon.com Inc. founder Jeff Bezos. The company's remaining media properties include *Slate* magazine, cable TV operator *Cable*

One and several television stations. It also owns Kaplan, an education, test-preparation, language instruction and professional training business. Headquarters is in Arlington, Virginia.

grain The smallest unit in the system of weights that has been used in the United States. It originally was defined as the weight of 1 grain of wheat.

It takes 437.5 grains to make an ounce. There are 7,000 grains to a pound.

See **ounce (weight)** and **pound**.

gram The basic unit of mass in the metric system. It is equal to approximately one-twenty-eighth of an ounce. To convert to ounces, multiply by .035 (86 grams x .035 equals 3 ounces).

See **metric system**.

grammar

granddad, granddaughter Also: *grandfather, grandmother, grandson*.

grand jury Always lowercase: *a Los Angeles County grand jury, the grand jury*.

This style has been adopted because, unlike the case with city council and similar governmental units, a jurisdiction frequently has more than one grand jury session.

grant-in-aid, grants-in-aid

gray Not *grey*. But: *greyhound*.

great- Hyphenate *great-grandfather, great-great-grandmother*, etc.

Use *great grandfather* only if the intended meaning is that the grandfather was a great man.

Great Atlantic & Pacific Tea Co. Inc. *A&P* is acceptable in all references.

Headquarters is in Montvale, New Jersey.

Great Britain It consists of England, Scotland and Wales, but not Northern Ireland.

Britain is acceptable in all references.

See **United Kingdom**.

Great Depression See **Depression**.

greater Capitalize when used to define a community and its surrounding region: *Greater Boston*.

Great Lakes The five, from the largest to the smallest: Lake Superior, Lake Huron, Lake Michigan, Lake Erie, Lake Ontario.

Great Plains Capitalize *Great Plains* or *the Plains* when referring to the U.S. prairie lands that extend from North Dakota to Texas and from the Rocky Mountains east to the Mississippi River valley. Use *northern Plains, southwestern Plains*, etc., when referring to a portion of the region.

Great Recession The recession that began in December 2007 and became the longest and deepest since the Great Depression of the 1930s. It occurred after losses on subprime mortgages battered the U.S. housing market. The National Bureau of Economic Research said it officially ended in June 2009, having lasted 18 months.

Green Berets See **special forces**.

gringo A derogatory term for a foreigner, especially an American, in parts of Latin America. Use only in direct quotes when essential to the story. See **nationalities and races**.

grisly, grizzly *Grisly* is horrifying, repugnant.

Grizzly means grayish or is a short form for *grizzly bear*.

gross domestic product The sum of all goods and services produced within a nation's borders. In the U.S., it is calculated quarterly by the Commerce Department.

Lowercase in all uses, but *GDP* is acceptable in later references.

Groundhog Day Feb. 2.

groundskeeper

groundswell

ground zero

group Takes singular verbs and pronouns: *The group is reviewing its position.*

grown-up (n. and adj.)

G-7 Use a hyphen in the abbreviated form for the Group of Seven, made up of representatives of the major industrial nations, Britain, Canada, France, Germany, Italy, Japan and the United States. Russia was suspended from the Group of Eight in March 2014. A general description rather than the full name is preferred on first reference: *Leading industrial nations*. See **G-20**.

G-string

G-20 Use a hyphen in the abbreviated form for the *Group of 20*, made up of representatives of industrial and emerging-market nations. A general description rather than the full name is preferred on first reference: *Leading rich and developing nations*. Members are the European Union and the following 19 countries: Argentina, Australia, Brazil, Britain, Canada, China, France, Germany, India, Indonesia, Italy, Japan, Mexico, Russia, Saudi Arabia, South Africa, South Korea, Turkey and the United States.

Guadalupe (Mexico)

Guadeloupe (West Indies)

Guam Use in datelines after the name of a community. See **datelines**.

Guangzhou City in China formerly known as Canton.

guarantee Preferred to *guaranty*, except in proper names.

guard Usually a job description, not a formal title. See **titles**.

guardsman See **National Guard** and **Coast Guardsman**.

Guatemala City Stands alone in datelines.

gubernatorial

guerrilla Unorthodox soldiers and their tactics.

guest Do not use as a verb except in quoted matter.

Guinness World Records The book is published by Guinness World Records Ltd.

Gulf, Gulf Coast Capitalize when referring to the region of the United States lying along the Gulf of Mexico. Also: *Mexico's Gulf Coast* or *Gulf Coast of Mexico*.

See **coast**.

Gulf Stream But the racetrack is *Gulfstream Park*.

gunbattle, gunboat, gunfight, gunfire, gunpoint, gunpowder

gung-ho A colloquialism to be used sparingly.

guns See **weapons**.

guru

gyp (n. and v.) Fraud or swindle or to cheat someone. Avoid use. Offensive to Gypsies, also known as Roma.

Gypsy, Gypsies Capitalize references to the nomadic ethnic group also known as *Roma*. Either is acceptable. In Europe, where most Gypsies live, they are widely referred to as *Roma*. The word should be explained: *Gypsies, also known as Roma*. Lowercase otherwise: *gypsy cab, gypsy-cab driver, gypsy moth*. See **Roma**.

gypsy moth

habeas corpus A writ ordering a person in custody to be brought before a court. It places the burden of proof on those detaining the person to justify the detention.

When *habeas corpus* is used in a story, define it.

hacker The term is commonly used to describe someone who unlawfully penetrates proprietary computer systems, but it has also evolved to mean anyone who tinkers with technology to explore new uses.

Hades But lowercase *hell*.

Hague, The In datelines:
THE HAGUE, *Netherlands* (AP) —
In text: *The Hague*.

hajj The pilgrimage to Mecca required of every Muslim who can afford it and is physically able to make it. The person making the *hajj* is a *hajji*.

half It is not necessary to use the preposition *of*: *half the time* is correct, but *half of the time* is not wrong.

half- Follow Webster's New World College Dictionary. Hyphenate if not listed there.

Some frequently used words without a hyphen:

halfback	halftone
halfhearted	halftrack

Also: *halftime*, in keeping with widespread practice in sports copy.

Some frequently used combinations that are two words without a hyphen:

half brother	half size
half dollar	

Some frequently used combinations that include a hyphen:

half-baked	half-life
half-blood	half-moon
half-cocked	half-truth
half-hour	

half day (n.) **half-day** (adj.)

half-mast, half-staff On ships and at naval stations ashore, flags are flown at *half-mast*.

Elsewhere ashore, flags are flown at *half-staff*.

hallelujah Lowercase the biblical praise to God, but capitalize in composition titles: Handel's "Hallelujah" chorus.

Halley's comet After Edmund Halley, an English astronomer who predicted the comet's appearance once every 75 years. It was last seen in 1985-86.

Halliburton Co. Headquarters is in Houston.

Halloween

halo, halos

Hamas A Palestinian Islamic political party, which has an armed wing of the same name. The word is an acronym for the Arabic words for *Islamic Resistance Movement.*

Hamburg The city in Germany carries the country name in datelines.

handheld (n.) **hand-held** (adj.)

handicapped See **disabled, handicapped.**

handle A self-selected, public-facing username on a social network, particularly Twitter. May be used interchangeably with *username.*

handmade

hand-picked

hands-free

hands off, hands-off Hyphenate when used as a compound modifier: *He kept his hands off the matter. He follows a hands-off policy.*

hand to hand, hand-to-hand, hand to mouth, hand-to-mouth Hyphenate when used as compound modifiers: *The cup was passed from hand to hand. They live a hand-to-mouth existence.*

hand-washing

hangar, hanger A *hangar* is a building.
A *hanger* is used for clothes.

hang, hanged, hung One *hangs* a picture, a criminal or oneself.
For past tense or the passive, use *hanged* when referring to executions or suicides, *hung* for other actions.

hangover

hang-up (n.) **hang up** (v.)

Hanukkah The Jewish Festival of Lights, an eight-day commemoration of rededication of the Temple by the Maccabees after their victory over the Syrians.
Usually occurs in December but sometimes falls in late November.

happy holidays, merry Christmas, season's greetings Such phrases are generally spelled lowercase, though *Christmas* is always capitalized.

Haqqani network Militant Islamic group based in Pakistan that seeks to establish Islamic law in Afghanistan.

harass, harassment

harelip Avoid. *Cleft lip* is preferred.

hard line (n.) **hard-liner** (n.) **hard-line** (adj.)

Harper's Magazine Not to be confused with Harper's Bazaar.

Harris Poll Prepared by Harris Interactive of New York.

Hartford Financial Services Group Inc. Headquarters is in Hartford, Connecticut.

hashtag The use of a number sign (#) in a social network post to convey the subject a user is writing about so that it can be indexed and accessed in other users' feeds. If someone is writing about the Super Bowl, for example, the use of *#superbowl* could be an appropriate hashtag. No space is used between the number sign and the accompanying search term. Hashtags were popularized on Twitter but are now also common on a variety of social networks, such as Instagram and Facebook.

Havana The city in Cuba stands alone in datelines.

Hawaii Do not abbreviate the state name in datelines or stories. Postal code: *HI*

Hawaiians are members of an ethnic group indigenous to the Hawaiian Islands and are also called *Native Hawaiians*. Use *Hawaii resident* for anyone living in the state.

The state comprises 132 islands about 2,400 miles southwest of San Francisco. Collectively, they are the *Hawaiian Islands*.

The largest island in land area is Hawaii. Honolulu and Pearl Harbor are on Oahu, where more than 80 percent of the state's residents live.

Honolulu stands alone in datelines. Use *Hawaii* after all other cities in datelines, specifying the island in the text, if needed.

See **datelines** and **state names**.

Hawaiian Airlines Headquarters is in Honolulu.

Hawaii Standard Time The time zone used in Hawaii. There is no daylight saving time in Hawaii.

headlines All AP stories need a short headline and a long headline. Only the first word and proper nouns are capitalized. Exception: First word after colon is always uppercase in headlines.

Use numerals for all numbers except in casual uses: "hundreds" instead of "100s." Use single quotes for quotation marks. Exception: use *US*, *UK* and *UN* (no periods) in all headlines.

Label opinion pieces. Short and long headlines for news analyses must begin with *"Analysis:"* followed

by a colon. Likewise, reviews must begin with *"Review:"*

Attribute carefully. Attribution is as important in headlines as in stories.

Use locators when necessary. They should be spelled out whenever possible; limit the use of abbreviations. If an abbreviation is essential because of space constraints, don't use periods for U.S. states abbreviated with two capital letters: NY, NJ, NH, NM, NC, SC, ND, SD and RI. Also DC. Other states retain periods: Ga., Ky., Mont., Conn. Do not use postal abbreviations.

headlong

head-on (adj. and adv.)

headquarters May take a singular or a plural verb.

headscarf, headscarves

health care

hearing examiner See **administrative law judge**.

hearsay

heart attack, heart failure, cardiac arrest A *heart attack* (myocardial infarction) occurs when one or more arteries supplying blood to the heart become blocked. *Heart failure* is a chronic condition that occurs when a weakened heart can no longer effectively pump blood. *Cardiac arrest*, or *sudden cardiac arrest*, occurs when the heart suddenly stops beating. It can be due to a *heart attack*, a heart rhythm problem, or as a result of trauma.

heaven

heavenly bodies Capitalize the proper names of planets, stars, constellations, etc.: *Mars, Arcturus, the Big Dipper, Aries*. See **earth**.

Lowercase *red planet* when referring to Mars.

For comets, capitalize only the proper noun element of the name: *Halley's comet*.

Lowercase *sun* and *moon*, but capitalize them if their Greek or Latin names are used: *Helios, Luna*.

Capitalize nouns and adjectives derived from the proper names of planets: *Martian, Venusian*, but lowercase adjectives derived from other heavenly bodies: *solar, lunar*.

hect- (before a vowel), **hecto-** (before a consonant) A prefix denoting 100 units of a measure. Move a decimal point two places to the right, adding zeros if necessary, to convert to the basic unit: 5.5 hectometers = 550 meters.

hectare A unit of surface measure in the metric system equal to 100 ares or 10,000 square meters.

A hectare is equal to 2.47 acres, 107,639.1 square feet or 11,959.9 square yards.

To convert to acres, multiply by 2.47 (5 hectares x 2.47 = 12.35 acres). See **acre** and **metric system**.

hedge fund Unregulated funds that pool money from wealthy investors and trade in everything from commodities to real estate to complex derivative investments. The private investment funds use sophisticated techniques to try to achieve higher returns than the stock market.

hedging A method of selling for future delivery whereby a dealer protects himself from falling prices between the time he buys a product and the time he resells or processes it. A miller, for example, who buys wheat to convert to flour will sell a similar quantity of wheat he doesn't own at near the price at which he bought his own. He will agree to deliver it at the same time his flour is ready for market. If at that time the price of wheat and therefore flour has fallen, he will lose on the flour but can buy the wheat at a low price and deliver it at a profit. If prices have risen, he will make an extra profit on his flour which he will have to sacrifice to buy the wheat for delivery. But either way he has protected his profit.

he, him, his, thee, thou Personal pronouns referring to the deity are lowercase.

See **deity**.

heights See **dimensions**.

heliport

hell But capitalize *Hades*.

Hells Angels

Helsinki The city in Finland stands alone in datelines.

helter-skelter

hemisphere Capitalize *Northern Hemisphere, Western Hemisphere*, etc.

Lowercase *hemisphere* in other uses: *the Eastern and Western hemispheres, the hemisphere*.

hemorrhage The word *bleed* can be used instead in most cases.

hemorrhoid

her Do not use this pronoun in reference to nations, ships or storms, except in quoted matter.

Use *it* instead.

here The word is frequently redundant, particularly in the lead of a datelined story. Use only if there is some specific need to stress that the event being reported took place in the community.

If the location must be stressed in the body of the story, repeat the name of the datelined community, both for the reader's convenience and to avoid problems if the story is topped with a different dateline.

Her Majesty Capitalize when it appears in quotations or is appropriate before a name as the long form of a formal title.

For other purposes, use the woman's name or *the queen*.

See **nobility**.

heroin The narcotic, originally a trademark.

heroes

hertz This term, the same in singular or plural, has been adopted as the international unit of frequency equal to one cycle per second.

In contexts where it would not be understood by most readers, it should be followed by a parenthetical explanation: *15,400 hertz (cycles per second)*.

Do not abbreviate.

Hewlett-Packard Co. *HP* (no hyphen) is acceptable on second reference. Headquarters is in Palo Alto, California.

Hezbollah The Lebanese Shiite Muslim political party, which has an armed wing of the same name. The word means *party of God* in Arabic.

hideaway

hideout

high blood pressure Preferred term. Avoid using *hypertension*.

high definition (n.) **high-definition** (adj.) The term refers to moving-image hardware and content that produces at least 720 lines of vertical resolution. *HD* is acceptable on second reference. *HDTV* is acceptable on second reference for a high-definition television set. A U.S. DVD or analog TV broadcast has 480 lines of vertical resolution — neither is HD.

high-five (n.) **high-fived** (v.)

high-rise (n. and adj.)

high-tech

highway designations Use these forms, as appropriate in the context, for highways identified by number: *U.S. Highway 1, U.S. Route 1, U.S. 1, state Route 34, Route 34, Interstate Highway 495, Interstate 495*. On second reference only for *Interstate*: *I-495*.

When a letter is appended to a number, capitalize it but do not use a hyphen: *Route 1A*.

See **addresses** and **numerals**.

highway patrol Capitalize if used in the formal name of a police agency: *the Kansas Highway Patrol, the Highway Patrol*. Lowercase *highway patrolman* in all uses.

See **state police**.

hijab The headscarf worn by some Muslim women.

hike Acceptable as a verb for increasing or raising prices sharply.

hillbilly Usually a derogatory term for an Appalachian backwoods or mountain person. Avoid unless in direct quotes or special context.

hip-hop

Hiroshima On Aug. 6, 1945, this Japanese city and military base were the targets of the first atomic bomb dropped as a weapon. The explosion had the force of 20,000 tons (20 kilotons) of TNT. It destroyed more than four square miles and killed or injured 140,000 people, according to an official count taken between August and December 1945. Hiroshima city officials say the toll may be 220,000 if including those who died after December 1945 of non-acute injuries or radiation.

his, her Do not presume maleness in constructing a sentence, but use the pronoun *his* when an indefinite antecedent may be male or female: *A reporter tries to protect his sources.* (Not *his or her* sources, but note the use of the word *reporter* rather than *newsman.*)

Frequently, however, the best choice is a slight revision of the sentence: *Reporters try to protect their sources.*

His Majesty Capitalize when it appears in quotations or is appropriate before a name as the long form of a formal title.

For other purposes, use the man's name or *king.*

See **nobility**.

Hispanic A person from — or whose ancestors were from — a Spanish-speaking land or culture. *Latino* and *Latina* are sometimes preferred. Follow the person's preference. Use a more specific identification when possible, such as *Cuban, Puerto Rican* or *Mexican-American.* See **Latino, nationalities and races**, and **race**.

Hispaniola The island shared by the Dominican Republic and Haiti. See **Western Hemisphere**.

historical periods and events Capitalize the names of widely recognized epochs in anthropology, archaeology, geology and history: *the Bronze Age, the Dark Ages, the Middle Ages, the Pliocene Epoch.*

Capitalize also widely recognized popular names for the periods and events: *the Atomic Age, the Boston Tea Party, the Civil War, the Exodus* (of the Israelites from Egypt), *the Great Depression, Prohibition.*

Lowercase *century*: *the 18th century.*

Capitalize only the proper nouns or adjectives in general descriptions of a period: *ancient Greece, classical Rome, the Victorian era, the fall of Rome.*

For additional guidance, see separate entries in this book for other epochs, events and historical periods. If this book has no entry, follow the capitalization in Webster's New World College Dictionary, using lowercase if the dictionary lists it as an acceptable form for the sense in which the word is used.

historic, historical A *historic* event is an important occurrence, one that stands out in history.

Any occurrence in the past is a *historical* event.

history Avoid the redundant *past history.*

hit-and-run (n. and adj.) **hit and run** (v.) *The coach told him to hit and run. He scored on a hit-and-run.*

hitchhike, hitchhiker

Hitler, Adolf Not *Adolph.*

HIV See **AIDS**.

H.J. Heinz Co. Headquarters is in Pittsburgh.

hocus-pocus

hodgepodge

Hodgkin lymphoma After Dr. Thomas Hodgkin, the English physician who first described the disease of the lymph nodes. Formerly called *Hodgkin's disease*.

Non-Hodgkin lymphoma, spelled without a possessive, is the more common type and spreads rapidly, especially among older people and those with HIV infections.

ho-hum

holding company A company whose principal assets are the securities it owns in companies that actually provide goods or services.

The usual reason for forming a holding company is to enable one corporation and its directors to control several companies by holding a majority of their stock.

holdup (n. and adj.) **hold up** (v.)

holidays and holy days Capitalize them: *New Year's Eve, New Year's Day, Groundhog Day, Easter, Hanukkah*, etc.

The federal legal holidays are New Year's, Martin Luther King Jr. Day, Washington's Birthday, Memorial Day, Independence Day, Labor Day, Columbus Day, Veterans Day, Thanksgiving and Christmas. See individual entries for the official dates and when they are observed if they fall on a weekend.

The designation of a day as a federal legal holiday means that federal employees receive the day off or are paid overtime if they must work. Other requirements that may apply to holidays generally are left to the states. Many follow the federal lead in designating a holiday, but they are not required to do so.

Hollywood District of the city of Los Angeles where the film industry used to be centered and where film studios and other production facilities, as well as landmark theaters, are still located. It is not a dateline and is most commonly used to describe Southern California's entertainment industry.

Holy Land Capitalize the biblical region.

Holy See The headquarters of the Roman Catholic Church in Vatican City.

Holy Week The week before Easter.

homebuilder

homebuyer, homeowner

Home Depot Inc. Headquarters is in Atlanta.

home equity line of credit (HELOC) A line of credit secured by a home. Borrowers can draw on it for a fixed period set by the lender, usually five to 10 years.

homefront

homemade

home page Two words. The "front" page of a particular website.

home schooling (n.) **homeschooler** (n.) **home-school** (v.) **home-schooled** (adj.)

hometown Use a comma to set off an individual's hometown when it is placed in apposition to a name, whether *of* is used or not: *Tim John-*

son, of Vermillion, South Dakota; Mary Richards, Minneapolis.

homicide, murder, manslaughter
Homicide is a legal term for slaying or killing.

Murder is malicious, premeditated homicide. Some states define certain homicides as murder if the killing occurs in the course of armed robbery, rape, etc.

Generally speaking, *manslaughter* is homicide without malice or premeditation.

A *homicide* should not be described as murder unless a person has been convicted of that charge.

Do not say that a victim was *murdered* until someone has been convicted in court. Instead, say that a victim *was killed* or *slain*. Do not write that X was charged with *murdering* Y. Use the formal charge — *murder* — and, if not already in the story, specify the nature of the killing – shooting, stabbing, beating, poisoning, drowning, etc.: *Jones was charged with murder in the shooting of his girlfriend.*

Examples:

An officer pulled over 29-year-old John White, who was arrested and charged with murder, according to Andrew Johnson, the county sheriff's spokesman.

The 66-year-old amateur photographer has pleaded not guilty to four counts of first-degree murder in the slaying of four women.

The killings occurred between 1977 and 1979. Prosecutors say Adams raped, tortured and robbed some of them before killing them.

Cook County Sheriff James Jones says a shooting that left a man and a woman dead appears to be a murder-suicide.

See **execute** and **assassin, killer, murderer**.

Hong Kong
Stands alone in datelines.

Honolulu
The city in Hawaii stands alone in datelines. It is on the island of Oahu.

See **Hawaii**.

honorary degrees
All references to honorary degrees should specify that the degree was honorary.

Do not use *Dr.* before the name of an individual whose only doctorate is honorary.

honorary titles
See **nobility**.

hoof-and-mouth disease
Use *foot-and-mouth disease*.

hooky

hopefully
The traditional meaning is *in a hopeful manner*. Also acceptable is the modern usage: *it's hoped, we hope*.

Correct: *"You're leaving soon?" she asked hopefully.*

Correct: *Hopefully, we'll be home before dark.*

horse meat

horsepower

horse races
Capitalize their formal names: *Kentucky Derby, Preakness, Belmont Stakes*, etc.

horses' names
Capitalize. See **animals**.

hotel
Capitalize as part of the proper name for a specific hotel: *the Waldorf-Astoria Hotel.*

Lowercase when standing alone or used in an indefinite reference to one hotel in a chain: *The city has a Sheraton hotel.*

hotline A telephone line for use in an emergency or a crisis, especially between government leaders.

hot spot Two words, for descriptions of the area where computers can connect wirelessly, or for global trouble spots, or areas of intense heat in general.

hourlong, hourslong

household, housing unit

In the sense used by the Census Bureau, a *household* is made up of all occupants of a *housing unit*. A *household* may contain more than one family or may be used by one person.

A *housing unit*, as defined by the bureau, is a group of rooms or single room occupied by people who do not live and eat with any other person in the structure. It must have either direct access from the outside or through a common hall, or have a kitchen or cooking equipment for the exclusive use of the occupants.

House of Commons, House of Lords The two houses of the British Parliament.

On second reference: *Commons* or *the Commons, Lords* or *the Lords*.

House of Representatives

Capitalize when referring to a specific governmental body: *the U.S. House of Representatives, the Massachusetts House of Representatives*.

Capitalize shortened references that delete the words *of Representatives*: *the U.S. House, the Massachusetts House*.

Retain capitalization if *U.S.* or the name of a state is dropped but the reference is to a specific body.

BOSTON (AP) — The House has adjourned for the year.

Lowercase plural uses: *the Massachusetts and Rhode Island houses*.

Apply the same principle to similar legislative bodies such as *the Virginia House of Delegates*.

See **organizations and institutions** for guidelines on how to handle the term when it is used by a nongovernmental body.

Houston The city in Texas stands alone in datelines.

howitzer See **weapons**.

HPV Acceptable on first reference for *human papillomavirus*, which can cause cervical and other types of cancer. *HPV virus* is redundant. Short-term HPV infections are very common, especially in sexually active young people, and usually clear on their own. Infection must persist for several years to pose a cancer risk. The U.S. Centers for Disease Control has recommended HPV vaccines for all boys and girls ages 11 or 12.

HTML For *HyperText Markup Language.* (Lowercase in Web addresses.) In stories, describe as *the Web programming language known as HTML*.

HTTP For *Hypertext Transfer Protocol.* (Lowercase in Web addresses.) In stories, describe as *the start of all Web addresses*.

The Huffington Post *The Huffington Post* news website is affiliated with AOL. It's *HuffPost* in shortened form. Headquarters is in New York.

human, human being *Human* is preferred, but either is acceptable.

Humane Society of the United States An animal protection agency headquartered in Washington. It operates 10 regional offices across the country, but has no formal affiliation with the many local organizations that use the name *Humane Society*.

Humvee A trademark for a four-wheeled military vehicle, built by AM General and used by U.S. and allied forces. *Hummer* is the sport utility vehicle.

hurricane Capitalize hurricane when it is part of the name that weather forecasters assign to a storm: *Hurricane Hazel*.
But use *it* and *its* — not *she, her* or *hers* or *he, him* or *his* — in pronoun references.
See **weather terms**.

husband, wife Regardless of sexual orientation, *husband* for a man or *wife* for a woman is acceptable in all references to individuals in any legally recognized marriage. *Spouse* or *partner* may be used if requested.

hush-hush

hybrid A vehicle that can be powered by more than one energy source, for example, a car with a gasoline engine and an electric motor. See **engine, motor**.

hydraulic fracturing A technique used by the energy industry to extract oil and gas from rock by injecting high-pressure mixtures of water, sand or gravel and chemicals. The short form is *fracking*. Although the industry considers the short form pejorative, AP accepts *fracking* with a brief definition. See **fracking**.

hydro- The rules in **prefixes** apply, but in general, no hyphen. Some examples:
hydroelectric   hydrophobia

hyper- The rules in **prefixes** apply, but in general, no hyphen. Some examples:
hyperactive   hypercritical

hyperlink A link from one part of a Web page to another page, such as a restaurant home page with a link to its menu.

hypertension Preferred term is *high blood pressure*.

hypertext A system of linking electronic documents.

hyphen See entry in **Punctuation** chapter.

I

Iberia Airlines Headquarters is in Madrid.

IBM Acceptable as first reference for *International Business Machines Corp.*

Headquarters is in Armonk, New York.

ICBM, ICBMs Abbreviation for *intercontinental ballistic missile(s)*. *ICBM* is acceptable on second reference. Avoid the redundant *ICBM missiles*.

ice age Lowercase, because it denotes not a single period but any of a series of cold periods marked by glaciation alternating with periods of relative warmth.

Capitalize the proper nouns in the names of individual ice ages, such as the *Wisconsin ice age*.

The most recent series of ice ages happened during the *Pleistocene epoch*, which began about 1.6 million years ago. During that time, glaciers sometimes covered much of North America and northwestern Europe.

The present epoch, the *Holocene* or *Recent*, began about 10,000 years ago, when the continental glaciers had retreated to Antarctica and Greenland.

ice storm See **weather terms**.

ID Acceptable abbreviation for *identification*, including *ID card*. The spelling without periods is an excep-

tion to guidance on most two-letter abbreviations. However, spell out verb forms such as *identified*. See **abbreviations and acronyms**.

Idaho Do not abbreviate in datelines or stories. Postal code: *ID* See **state names**.

i.e. Abbreviation for the Latin *id est* or *that is (to say)* and is always followed by a comma.

IED Abbreviation for *improvised explosive device*. *IED* is acceptable on second reference. *Roadside bomb* is preferable.

IHS Jane's All the World's Aircraft, IHS Jane's Fighting Ships The reference sources for questions about aircraft and military ships not covered in this book.

The reference for nonmilitary ships is IHS Fairplay Register of Ships.

illegal Use *illegal* only to mean a violation of the law. Be especially careful in labor-management disputes, where one side often calls an action by the other side illegal. Usually it is a charge that a contract or rule, not a law, has been violated.

illegal immigration Entering or residing in a country in violation of civil or criminal law. Except in direct quotes essential to the story, use *illegal* only to refer to an action, not a person: *illegal immigration*, but not *illegal immigrant*. Acceptable variations include *living in* or *entering a country illegally* or *without legal permission*.

Except in direct quotations, do not use the terms *illegal alien, an illegal, illegals* or *undocumented*.

Do not describe people as violating immigration laws without attribution.

Specify wherever possible how someone entered the country illegally and from where. Crossed the border? Overstayed a visa? What nationality?

People who were brought into the country as children should not be described as having immigrated illegally. For people staying in the U.S. under the Deferred Action for Childhood Arrivals program, specify in the story that they are protected from deportation for two years and allowed to work. Add details on the DACA program lower in the story.

illegitimate Do not refer to the child of unmarried parents as *illegitimate*. If it is pertinent to the story at all, use an expression such as *whose parents were not married*.

Illinois Abbreviate *Ill.* in datelines only; spell out in stories. Postal code: *IL*
See **state names**.

illusion See **allusion, illusion**.

IM Abbreviation for *instant message*; sometimes used as a verb: *IMing, IMed*. Acceptable on second reference for *instant messaging*. See **text messaging/instant messaging**.

Imax Corp. Headquarters is in Mississauga, Ontario.

immigrate See **emigrate, immigrate**.

impassable, impassible, impassive *Impassable* means that passage is impossible: *The bridge was impassable*.

Impassible and *impassive* describe lack of sensitivity to pain or suffering. Webster's New World College Dictionary notes, however, that *impassible* suggests an inability to be affected, while *impassive* implies only that no reaction was noticeable: *She was impassive throughout the ordeal*.

impeachment The constitutional process accusing an elected official of a crime in an attempt to remove the official from office. Do not use as a synonym for *conviction* or *removal from office*.

impel, impelled, impelling

imperial gallon The standard British gallon, equal to 277.42 cubic inches or about 1.2 U.S. gallons.

The metric equivalent is approximately 4.5 liters.
See **liter**.

imperial quart One-fourth of an imperial gallon.

implausible

imply, infer Writers or speakers *imply* in the words they use.

A listener or reader *infers* something from the words.

impostor

impromptu It means without preparation or advance thought.

improvised explosive device *IED* is acceptable on second reference. *Roadside bomb* is preferable.

in, into *In* indicates location: *He was in the room*.

Into indicates motion: *She walked into the room.*

-in Precede with a hyphen:

break-in	walk-in
cave-in	write-in

in- No hyphen when it means *not*:

inaccurate	insufferable

Other uses without a hyphen:

inbound	infighting
indoor	inpatient (n., adj.)
infield	

A few combinations take a hyphen, however:

in-depth	in-house
in-group	in-law

Follow Webster's New World College Dictionary when in doubt.

"in" When employed to indicate that something is in vogue, use quotation marks only if followed by a noun: *It was the "in" thing to do. Raccoon coats are in again.*

inasmuch as

Inauguration Day Capitalize only when referring to the total collection of events that include inauguration of a U.S. president; lowercase in other uses: *Inauguration Day is Jan. 20. The inauguration day for the change has not been set.*

inbox

Inc. See **incorporated**.

inch Equal to one-twelfth of a foot.

The metric equivalent is exactly 2.54 centimeters.

To convert to centimeters, multiply by 2.54 (6 inches x 2.54 equals 15.24 centimeters).

See **centimeter; foot;** and **dimensions**.

include Use *include* to introduce a series when the items that follow are only part of the total: *The price includes breakfast. The zoo includes lions and tigers.*

Use *comprise* when the full list of individual elements is given: *The zoo comprises 100 types of animals, including lions and tigers.*

See **compose, comprise, constitute**.

income See **profit terminology**.

incorporated Abbreviate and capitalize as *Inc.* when used as a part of a corporate name. Do not set off with commas: *Time Warner Inc. announced ...*

See **company names**.

incorporator Do not capitalize when used before a name.

See **titles**.

incredible, incredulous *Incredible* means unbelievable.

Incredulous means skeptical.

incur, incurred, incurring

Independence Day *July Fourth* or *Fourth of July* also are acceptable.

The federal legal holiday is observed on Friday if July 4 falls on a Saturday, on Monday if it falls on a Sunday.

index, indexes

Index of Leading Economic Indicators A composite of 10 economic measurements developed to help forecast shifts in the direction of the U.S. economy.

It is compiled by the Conference Board, a private business-sponsored research group, which took it over from the Commerce Department in 1995.

India Country in South Asia. Use *Indian* to describe its peoples and cultures.

Indiana Abbreviate *Ind.* in datelines only; spell out in stories. Postal code: *IN*

See **state names**.

Indianapolis The city in Indiana stands alone in datelines.

Indian Ocean See **ocean**.

Indians *American Indian* or *Native American* is acceptable for those in the U.S. Follow the person's preference. Where possible, be precise and use the name of the tribe: *He is a Navajo commissioner.* Such words as *wampum, warpath, powwow, teepee, brave, squaw,* etc., can be disparaging and offensive. In Alaska, the indigenous groups include Aleuts, Eskimos and Indians, collectively known as *Alaska Natives.*

First Nation is the preferred term for native tribes in Canada.

Indian is also used to describe the peoples and cultures of the South Asian nation of India.

See **Native American, nationalities and races**, **race** and **tribe, tribal**.

indict Use *indict* only in connection with the legal process of bringing charges against an individual or corporation.

To avoid any suggestion that someone is being judged before a trial, do not use phrases such as *indicted for killing* or *indicted for bribery.* Instead, use *indicted on a charge of killing* or *indicted on a bribery charge.*

For guidelines on related words, see **accused; allege;** and **arrest.**

indie Short for *independent film* or *recorded music*, meaning that it was originally made without the support of a major studio or company.

indigenous A term used to refer to original inhabitants of a place.

Aboriginal leaders welcomed a new era of indigenous relations in Australia. Bolivia's indigenous peoples represent some 62 percent of the population. See **nationalities and races**, and **race**.

indiscreet, indiscrete *Indiscreet* means lacking prudence. Its noun form is *indiscretion.*

Indiscrete means not separated into distinct parts. Its noun form is *indiscreteness.*

indiscriminate, indiscriminately

individual retirement account *IRA* is acceptable on second reference.

indispensable

indo- Usually hyphenated and capitalized:

Indo-Aryan	Indo-Hittite
Indo-German	Indo-Iranian
But: *Indochina.*	

Indonesia Use after the name of a community in datelines on stories from this nation.

Specify an individual island, if needed, in the text.

indoor (adj.) **indoors** (adv.)

infant Applicable to children through 12 months old.

infantile paralysis The preferred term is *polio.*

inflation A sustained increase in prices. The result is a decrease in the purchasing power of money.

There are two basic types of inflation:

—*Cost-push inflation* occurs when increases in the price of specific items, such as oil or food, are big enough to drive up prices overall.

—*Demand-pull inflation* occurs when the amount of money available exceeds the amount of goods and services available for sale.

infra- The rules in **prefixes** apply, but in general, no hyphen. Some examples:

infrared   infrastructure

infrastructure An economy's capital in the form of roads, railways, water supplies, educational facilities, health services, etc., without which investment in factories can't be fully productive.

initial public offering *IPO* acceptable on second reference.

initials Use periods and no space when an individual uses initials instead of a first name: *H.L. Mencken.*

Do not give a name with a single initial (*J. Jones*) unless it is the individual's preference or a first name cannot be learned.

See **middle initials**.

injuries They are *suffered*, not *sustained* or *received*.

in-law

innocent, not guilty In court cases, plea situations and trials, *not guilty* is preferable to *innocent*, because it is more precise legally. (However, special care must be taken to prevent omission of the word *not*.) When possible, say a defendant was *acquitted* of criminal charges.

innocuous

innuendo

inoculate

input Do not use as a verb in describing the introduction of data into a computer.

inquire, inquiry Not *enquire*, *enquiry*.

insignia Same form for singular and plural.

insofar as

in spite of *Despite* means the same thing and is shorter.

Instagram A social network in which users share photos or short videos they've taken, usually on a phone, with people who have chosen to follow them. Some users apply filters to Instagram images to make them appear old or otherwise stylized, and hashtags are sometimes used to help users find photos related to particular topic. Instagram photos are frequently shared onto other social networks. Facebook bought Instagram in 2012.

Institute for Supply Management Produces monthly reports on manufacturing and service sectors. *ISM* acceptable on second reference.

insure See **ensure, insure, assure**.

Intel Corp. Headquarters is in Santa Clara, California.

inter- The rules in **prefixes** apply, but in general, no hyphen. Some examples:

inter-American   interstate
interracial

intercontinental ballistic missile See **ICBM, ICBMs**.

Internal Revenue Service *IRS* is acceptable in all references.

Capitalize also *Internal Revenue Service*, but lowercase *the revenue service*.

International Bank for Reconstruction and Development *World Bank* is acceptable in all references.

Headquarters is in Washington.

International Brotherhood of Teamsters, Chauffeurs, Warehousemen and Helpers of America *Teamsters* union is acceptable in all references. See **Teamsters union**.

International Court of Justice

The principal judicial organ of the United Nations, established at The Hague in 1945.

The court is not open to individuals. It has jurisdiction over all matters specifically provided for either in the U.N. charter or in treaties and conventions in force. It also has jurisdiction over cases referred to it by U.N. members and by nonmembers such as Switzerland that subscribe to the court statute.

The court serves as the successor to the Permanent Court of International Justice of the League of Nations, which also was known as the World Court.

On second reference use *international court* or *world court* in lowercase. Do not abbreviate.

International Criminal Police Organization *Interpol* is acceptable in all references.

Headquarters is in Lyon, France.

international date line The imaginary line drawn north and south through the Pacific Ocean, largely along the 180th meridian.

By international agreement, when it is 12:01 a.m. Sunday just west of the line, it is 12:01 a.m. Saturday just east of it.

See **time zones**.

International Energy Agency

Paris-based energy adviser for developed nations. *IEA* acceptable on second reference.

International Labor Organization *ILO* is acceptable on second reference.

Headquarters is in Geneva.

International Monetary Fund

IMF is acceptable on second reference. Headquarters is in Washington.

A supply of money supported by subscriptions of member nations, for the purpose of stabilizing international exchange and promoting orderly and balanced trade. Member nations may obtain foreign currency needed, making it possible to correct temporary maladjustments in their balance of payments without currency depreciation.

International Space Station

International Telecommunications Satellite Organization

ITSO is acceptable on first reference, but the body of the story should identify it as the shortened form of the full name.

(The original name was International Telecommunications Satellite Consortium.)

Headquarters is in Washington.

Internet A decentralized, worldwide network of computers that can communicate with each other.

The World Wide Web, like email, is a subset of the Internet. They are not synonymous and should not be used interchangeably in stories.

USE IN STORIES: Be acutely aware of the potential dangers of using information from Internet and email sources. Email headers are easily forged, and websites may be set up by fraudulent groups. Be sure of the authenticity and correctness before using the information.

All such information, from computer disk data to email to material posted on the Internet, falls into the "tangible form" category that is subject to copyright protection as well as libel guidelines.

INTERNET ADDRESSES: The current Internet address system based on domain names — such as "ap.org" — was developed in the 1980s. See **domain names**.

Website addresses are also known as Uniform Resource Locators, or URLs. Follow the spelling and capitalization of the website owner. In stories, try to use the name of the website rather than the Web address, the way you'd refer to *the Empire State Building* in the physical world and not *350 Fifth Avenue*. So it's *Facebook*, not *Facebook.com*. Use ".com" only if it's part of the legal name, as in *Amazon.com Inc.*

If an Internet address falls at the end of a sentence, use a period. If an address breaks between lines, split it directly after a slash or a dot that is part of the address, without an inserted hyphen. Use the *http://* protocol at the start of the Web address, as well as other starts, such as *ftp://*.

When a story prominently mentions a specific website or Web service, include within the text the full Internet address with *http://* and set it off with commas. Add other addresses to the end of a story when they provide additional information, even when they aren't specifically referred to in a story.

An example:

CHICAGO (AP) — Harmless lung cancer? A provocative study found that nearly 1 in 5 lung tumors detected on CT scans are probably so slow-growing that they would never cause problems.

The analysis suggests the world's No. 1 cause of cancer deaths isn't as lethal as doctors once thought.

In the study, these were not false-positives — suspicious results that turn out upon further testing not to be cancer. These were indeed cancerous tumors, but ones that caused no symptoms and were unlikely ever to become deadly, the researchers said. ...

Online:

JAMA Internal Medicine: http://jamainternalmedicine.com

American Cancer Society: http://bit.ly/1cwqhfX

Avoid URLs that are particularly lengthy and complicated, unless essential to guide the reader to a particular document. Consider a URL abbreviation service such as bit.ly.

Some symbols in Internet addresses, such as the "at" sign, the equal sign, the underscore and the tilde, result in garbles in some newspaper computers. This is the case when referring to specific videos on YouTube or specific documents at other sites. Spell them out instead and provide an explanatory note, or use a URL abbreviation service.

See separate listings for some commonly used Internet, computer and telecommunications terms.

OPERATIONS: No single individual, organization or government runs the Internet, and anyone may connect to the network by following the TCP/IP protocols.

However, the U.S. government has tremendous influence over the Internet by controlling the Domain Name System. The government has delegated the policy-making authority to the Internet Corporation for Assigned Names and Numbers, but it retains veto power over the Marina del Rey, California, nonprofit group also known as ICANN. The U.S. government in 2014 proposed ending its oversight of ICANN by the time its governing agreement expires in September 2015.

———

Caution:

Do not mistake the Internet for an encyclopedia, and the search engine for a table of contents. The Internet is a sprawling information repository. Anything you find should be assessed and vetted with the same care that you use for everything else. Even what may look like an official press release issued by a company can be doctored or fabricated. Be especially leery of press releases posted on sites other than prnewswire.com, businesswire.com and globenewswire.com.

Be especially careful about websites and social networks that allow anyone to contribute text, photos and other information. The stated name on an account may not actually reflect an individual or group's real identity.

Some points to consider:

• Who is sponsoring a Web page? Is the author's identity verifiable, or is that person pretending to be someone else? You should avoid anonymous pages just as you would avoid a source whose identity you could not verify.

• Is there contact information in case you want to follow up? One way to check who owns a page is through a "Whois" query at a website such as http://www.networksolutions.com/whois/index.jsp. Keep in mind, however, that data is self-reported and could be incorrect.

• The source for the information on the page should be clearly stated, whether original or borrowed. Is it a primary or secondary source? Can it be checked somewhere else?

• Does the website accept user contributions? If so, is there a vetting process? Wikipedia, for instance, allows individuals to contribute to encyclopedia entries regardless of expertise. It may provide a good starting point for research, but you should follow the footnotes for the source material and look for additional sources of information.

• Based on what you know, how accurate does the information seem? If there's something on the site that you know is incorrect, there may be other errors.

• Are there any obvious signs of bias? One possible clue: the type of sites linked to.

• Is the page current? If it hasn't been updated lately, the information may be outdated.

• For social networks such as Facebook, Twitter and YouTube, are you sure that the account actually belongs to the individual or group it says it belongs to? Keep in mind that a password to an account could be compromised, and someone may have temporarily taken over a legitimate account. One way to check authenticity is to verify it directly with the individual or group, using contact information independently obtained.

• Be wary of information in email because the sender's address can be easily forged. Again, it is best to verify information directly with the person you believe is the sender.

• Don't believe everything you see. Software such as Photoshop makes it easy to manufacture photographs that look real to the untrained eye.

• Use common sense. Just as you wouldn't necessarily trust an anonymous flier you pick up on the street, be wary of websites you stumble across. Do not assume that a site belongs to a particular company or group just because its name is in the Web address.

See **Web**.

Internet radio The broadcasting of audio content over the Internet, offering programming to listeners through websites, desktop apps and mobile apps. Some Internet radio services, such as Spotify and Pandora, feature social sharing options.

Internet TV A television set that can be connected directly to the Internet to display Web content without going through a computer.

Interpol Acceptable in all references for *International Criminal Police Organization*.

intifada An Arabic term for the Palestinian uprising against Israel.

intra- Within, inside. The rules in **prefixes** apply, but in general, no hyphen. Some examples:
intracity   intraparty

intranet A private network inside a company or organization, only for internal use.

in vitro fertilization Creating embryos by mixing eggs and sperm in a lab dish. Do not hyphenate; *IVF* acceptable on second reference. Use *test-tube babies* sparingly.

IOU, IOUs

Iowa Do not abbreviate in datelines or stories. Postal code: *IA*
See **state names**.

IP address *Internet Protocol address*, a numeric address given to a computer connected to the Internet. Most users type in domain names as stand-ins for IP addresses, and domain name servers help with the translation in the background. Traditional IP addresses take the form of four numbers from 0 to 255 connected by dots, as in xx.xx.xx.xx. See **domain names**.

iPad A touch-screen tablet computer sold by Apple Inc. that is much like an iPhone but with a larger screen. Use *IPad* when the word starts a sentence or headline.

iPhone Apple Inc.'s smartphone. Use *IPhone* when the word starts a sentence or headline.

iPod A digital media player sold by Apple Inc. Use *IPod* when the word starts a sentence or headline.

IQ Acceptable in all references for intelligence quotient.

Iran The nation formerly called Persia. It is not an Arab country.
The official name of the country is the *Islamic Republic of Iran*.
Uppercase *Islamic Revolution* when referring to the 1979 event.
The people are *Iranians*, not *Persians* or *Irani*.
The official language is *Persian*, also known as *Farsi*.

Iraq The Arab nation coinciding roughly with ancient Mesopotamia.
Its people are *Iraqis*. The dialect of Arabic is *Iraqi*.

Ireland Acceptable in most references to the independent nation known formally as the Irish Republic.
Use *Irish Republic* when a distinction must be made between this nation and *Northern Ireland*, a part of the United Kingdom.

Irish Republican Army An outlawed paramilitary group committed to overthrowing Northern Ireland and its links with Britain. Its formal name is Provisional IRA. It was founded in 1969 with the aim of abolishing Northern Ireland as a predominantly British Protestant state. Its members claim direct lineage to the old IRA, which wrested the predominantly Catholic rest of Ireland from British control following a 1919-21 rebellion.

IRA is acceptable, but *Irish Republican Army* should be spelled out somewhere in the story.

Sinn Fein (pronounced "shin fane") is a legal political party that is linked with the *IRA*, but not technically a wing of it.

irregardless A double negative. *Regardless* is correct.

IRS Acceptable in all references for *Internal Revenue Service*. Capitalize *Internal Revenue Service*, but lowercase *the revenue service*.

Islam Followers are called Muslims. Their holy book is the Quran, which according to Islamic belief was revealed by Allah (God) to the Prophet Muhammad in the seventh century in Mecca and Medina. The place of worship is a mosque. The weekly holy day is Friday.

It is the religion of more than 1 billion people in the world, making it the world's second-largest faith, after Christianity. Although Arabic is the language of the Quran and Muslim prayers, not all Arabs are Muslims and not all Muslims are Arabs. Most of the world's Muslims live in a wide belt that stretches halfway around the world: across West Africa and North Africa, through the Arab countries of the Middle East and on to Turkey, Iran, Afghanistan, Pakistan and other Asian countries, parts of the former Soviet Union and western China, to Indonesia and the southern Philippines.

There are two major divisions in Islam:

—*Sunni* The biggest single sect in Islam, comprising about 85 percent of all Muslims. Nations with Sunni majorities include Egypt, Saudi Arabia and most other Arab nations, as well as non-Arab Turkey and Afghanistan. Most Palestinian Muslims and most West African Muslims are Sunnis.

The Saudis sometimes are referred to as Wahhabi Muslims. This is a subgroup within the Sunni branch of Islam.

—*Shiite* The second-largest sect. Iran is the only nation with an overwhelming Shiite majority. Iraq, Lebanon and Bahrain have large Shiite communities, in proportion to their overall populations.

(The schism between Sunni and Shiite stems from the early days of Islam and arguments over Muhammad's successors as caliph, the spiritual and temporal leader of Muslims during that period. The Shiites wanted the caliphate to descend through Ali, Muhammad's son-in-law. Ali eventually became the fourth caliph, but he was murdered; Ali's son al-Hussein was massacred with his fighters at Karbala, in what is now Iraq. Shiites considered the later caliphs to be usurpers. The Sunnis no longer have a caliph.)

Titles for the clergy vary from sect to sect and from country to country, but these are the most common:

Grand Mufti — The highest authority in Quranic law and interpretation, a title used mostly by Sunnis.

Sheikh — Used by most clergymen in the same manner that the Rev. is used as a Christian clerical title, especially common among Sunnis. (Not all sheikhs are clergymen. *Sheikh* can also be a secular title of respect or nobility.)

Ayatollah — Used by Shiites, especially in Iran, to denote senior clergymen, such as *Ayatollah Ruhollah Khomeini*.

Hojatoleslam — A rank below ayatollah.

Mullah — Lower-level clergy.

Imam — Used by some sects as a title for the prayer leader at a mosque. Among the Shiites, it usually has a more exalted connotation.

The adjective is *Islamic. Islamist* is an advocate of political Islam, the philosophy that the Quran should rule all aspects of life — religious, political and personal. *Islamic fundamentalist* should not be used as a synonym for *Islamic militant* or *radical.*

Islamabad The city in Pakistan stands alone in datelines.

Islamic State group Islamic militant organization that broke with the al-Qaida network and took control of large parts of Iraq and Syria, where it declared a caliphate, a traditional form of Islamic rule. It is largely made up of Sunni militants from Iraq and Syria but has drawn jihadi fighters from across the Muslim world and Europe.

Islamist An advocate or supporter of a political movement that favors reordering government and society in accordance with laws prescribed by Islam. Do not use as a synonym for *Islamic fighters, militants, extremists* or *radicals,* who may or may not be Islamists. Where possible, be specific and use the name of militant affiliations: *al-Qaida-linked, Hezbollah, Taliban,* etc. Those who view the Quran as a political model encompass a wide range of Muslims, from mainstream politicians to militants known as jihadis.

island Capitalize *island* or *islands* as part of a proper name: *Prince Edward Island, the Hawaiian Islands.*

Lowercase *island* and *islands* when they stand alone or when the reference is to the islands in a given area: *the Pacific islands.*

Lowercase all *island of* constructions: *the island of Nantucket.*

U.S. DATELINES: For communities on islands within the boundaries of the United States, use the community name and the state name:

EDGARTOWN, *Mass.* (AP) —

Honolulu stands alone, however.

DATELINES ABROAD: If an island has an identity of its own (*Bermuda, Prince Edward Island, Puerto Rico, Sardinia, Taiwan,* etc.) use the community name and the island name:

HAMILTON, *Bermuda* (AP) —

Havana, Hong Kong, Macau and *Singapore* stand alone, however.

If the island is part of a chain, use the community name and the name of the chain:

MANILA, *Philippines* (AP) —

Identify the name of the island in the text if relevant: *Manila is on the island of Luzon.*

For additional guidelines, see **datelines.**

Istanbul The city in Turkey stands alone in datelines.

IT Abbreviation for *information technology*; *IT* is acceptable on second reference.

italics AP does not italicize words in news stories. Italics are used in Stylebook entries to highlight examples of correct and incorrect usage.

it's, its *It's* is a contraction for *it is* or *it has: It's up to you. It's been a long time.*

Its is the possessive form of the neuter pronoun: *The company lost its assets.*

IUD Acceptable on second reference for *intrauterine device.*

IV Acceptable in all references for *intravenous*.

Ivy League Brown University, Columbia University, Cornell University, Dartmouth College, Harvard University, Princeton University, the University of Pennsylvania and Yale University.

jack-o'-lantern

Jacuzzi Trademark for a brand of whirlpool products. Generic terms are whirlpool bath or whirlpool spa.

jail Not interchangeable with *prison*. See **prison, jail**.

Japan Airlines Corp. *JAL* is acceptable on second reference. Headquarters is in Tokyo.

Japan Current A warm current flowing from the Philippine Sea east of Taiwan and northeast past Japan.

jargon The special vocabulary and idioms of a particular class or occupational group.

In general, avoid jargon. When it is appropriate in a special context, include an explanation of any words likely to be unfamiliar to most readers.

See **dialect**.

Java A trademark of Oracle Corp. for a computer programming language that can be run on some computer systems and inside Web browsers.

Jaws of Life Trademark name for the tool used to pry open parts of a vehicle to free those trapped inside.

Jaycees Members of the U.S. Junior Chamber of Commerce, affiliated with the worldwide body, Junior Chamber International.

See **fraternal organizations and service clubs** and **Junior Chamber of Commerce**.

J.C. Penney Co. Headquarters is in Plano, Texas.

jeep, Jeep Lowercase the military vehicle. Capitalize if referring to the civilian vehicle, formerly a brand of Chrysler Group, now known as FCA US LLC, a unit of Fiat Chrysler Automobiles NV.

Jemaah Islamiyah Southeast Asian Islamic radical group. The words are Arabic for *Islamic congregation*, or *Islamic group*.

Jerusalem The city in Israel stands alone in datelines.

Jesus The central figure of Christianity, he also may be called *Jesus Christ* or *Christ*.

Personal pronouns referring to him are lowercase as is *savior*.

JetBlue Airways Corp. Headquarters is in New York.

jet, jetliner, jet plane See **aircraft terms**.

Jet Ski A registered trademark of Kawasaki for a type of personal watercraft.

jibe See **gibe, jibe**.

Jiddah, Saudi Arabia

jihad Arabic noun used to refer to the Islamic concept of the struggle to do good. In particular situations, that can include holy war, the meaning extremist Muslims commonly use. Use *jihadi* and *jihadis*. Do not use *jihadist*.

job descriptions Always lowercase. See **titles**.

Johannesburg The city in South Africa stands alone in datelines.

John F. Kennedy Space Center

Located in Cape Canaveral, Florida, the National Aeronautics and Space Administration's principal launch site in years past, and in years to come, for manned spacecraft.

Kennedy Space Center is acceptable in all references.

For datelines on launch stories:
CAPE CANAVERAL, Fla. (AP) —
See **Lyndon B. Johnson Space Center**.

Johns Hopkins University No apostrophes.

Johnson & Johnson Headquarters is in New Brunswick, New Jersey.

Joint Chiefs of Staff Also: *the Joint Chiefs*. But lowercase *the chiefs* or *the chiefs of staff*.

Journal Media Group In July 2014 Scripps agreed with Journal Communications to combine broadcasting operations and spin off newspaper holdings into a separate public entity. The deal is expected to be finalized in 2015. Newspaper components of both companies will be operated by Journal Media Group. It will be headquartered in Milwaukee and operate Journal Communications' Milwaukee Journal Sentinel, community publications and digital products as well as Scripps' daily newspapers, including the Memphis (Tennessee) Commercial Appeal, plus community and digital products.

JPEG, JPG Acronyms for *Joint Photographic Experts Group*, a common image format used on the World Wide Web. Acronyms acceptable in all references.

JPMorgan Chase & Co. Formed from the 2000 merger of J.P. Morgan & Co. with Chase Manhattan Corp. and the 2004 merger with Bank One Corp. Acquired Bear Stearns Cos. and Washington Mutual Inc. in 2008. Headquarters is in New York.

Jr. See **junior, senior**.

judge Capitalize before a name when it is the formal title for an individual who presides in a court of law. Do not continue to use the title in second reference.

Do not use *court* as part of the title unless confusion would result without it:

—No *court* in the title: *U.S. District Judge John Bates, District Judge John Bates, federal Judge John Bates, Judge John Bates, U.S. Circuit Judge Priscilla Owen, appellate Judge Priscilla Owen.*

—*Court* needed in the title: *Juvenile Court Judge John Jones, Criminal Court Judge John Jones, Superior Court Judge Robert Harrison, state Supreme Court Judge William Cushing.*

When the formal title *chief judge* is relevant, put the court name after the judge's name: *Chief Judge Royce Lamberth of the U.S. District Court in Washington, D.C.*; *Chief Judge Karen J. Williams of the 4th U.S. Circuit Court of Appeals.*

Do not pile up long court names before the name of a judge. Make it *Judge John Smith of Allegheny County Common Pleas Court.* Not: *Allegheny County Common Pleas Court Judge John Smith.*

Lowercase *judge* as an occupational designation in phrases such as *contest judge Simon Cowell.*

See **administrative law judge**; **court names**; **judicial branch**; **justice**; and **magistrate**.

judge advocate The plural: *judge advocates.* Also: *judge advocate general, judge advocates general.*

Capitalize as a formal title before a name.

See **titles**.

judgment

judicial branch Always lowercase.

The federal court system that exists today as the outgrowth of Article 3 of the Constitution is composed of the Supreme Court of the United States, the U.S. Court of Appeals, U.S. District Courts and the U.S. Customs Court. There are also four district judges for U.S. territories.

U.S. bankruptcy and magistrate judges are fixed-term judges serving in U.S. District Courts. Magistrate judges are generalist judges who preside in cases referred from U.S. district judges. Bankruptcy judges are specialized judges whose authority is restricted to bankruptcy issues.

The U.S. Tax Court and the U.S. Court of Military Appeals for the Armed Forces are not part of the judicial branch as such.

For more detail on all federal courts, see separate entries under the names listed here.

Judicial Conference of the United States This policymaking body for the courts of the judicial branch meets twice a year. Its 27 members are the chief justice of the United States, the chief judges of the 12 regional circuit courts of appeals, the chief judge of the Federal Circuit Court of Appeals, a district judge from each of the regional circuits, and the chief judge of the Court of International Trade.

Day-to-day functions are handled by the Administrative Office of U.S. Courts.

jukebox

jumbo jet Any very large jet plane, including the Airbus A380 and Boeing 747.

jumbo loan A home loan that exceeds $417,000 in much of the country, except in high-cost areas where the limit can go as high as $625,500 for 2015.

Junior Chamber of Commerce A volunteer organization of young men and women involved in civic service and leadership training.

Members are called *Jaycees.*

U.S. headquarters is in Tulsa, Oklahoma; international headquarters in Coral Gables, Florida.

See **Jaycees**.

junior, senior Abbreviate as *Jr.* and *Sr.* only with full names of persons. Do not precede by a comma: *Martin Luther King Jr.*

The notation *II* or *2nd* may be used if it is the individual's preference. Note, however, that *II* and *2nd* are not necessarily the equivalent of *junior* — they often are used by a grandson or nephew.

If necessary to distinguish between father and son in second reference, use the *elder Smith* or the *younger Smith*.

See **names**.

junk bonds Also known as non-investment-grade bonds, these corporate debt securities provide high yields to investors to compensate for their higher-than-normal credit risk. They are typically issued by companies with a lot of debt to repay loans, fund takeovers or buy out stockholders.

junta See **government, junta, regime, administration**.

jury The word takes singular verbs and pronouns: *The jury has been sequestered until it reaches a verdict.*

Include racial and gender breakdown only if relevant.

Do not capitalize: *a U.S. District Court jury, a federal jury, a Massachusetts Superior Court jury, a Los Angeles County grand jury.*

See **grand jury**.

justice Capitalize before a name when it is the formal title. It is the formal title for members of the U.S. Supreme Court and for jurists on some state courts. In such cases, do not use *judge* in first or subsequent references.

See **judge**; **Supreme Court of the United States**; and **titles**.

justice of the peace Capitalize as a formal title before a name. Do not abbreviate.

See **titles**.

justify *Smith justified his actions* means Smith demonstrated that his actions were right. If the actions are still controversial, say *Smith sought to justify his actions*.

juvenile delinquent Juveniles may be declared delinquents in many states for anti-social behavior or for breaking the law. In some states, laws prohibit publishing or broadcasting the names of juvenile delinquents.

Follow the local law unless there is a compelling reason to the contrary. Consult with regional editors if you believe such an exception is warranted.

See **privacy**.

juveniles See **privacy**.

K Use *K* in references to modem transmission speeds, in keeping with standard usage: *a 56K modem* (no space after numeral).

The *K* abbreviation is now acceptable in headline and statistical references to kilometers, such as *a 10K race*; in baseball for strikeouts: *pitcher records 12 K's*; and monetary amounts in thousands: *employee earns $80K*

Kabul The city in Afghanistan carries the name of the country in datelines.

kaffiyeh The men's headdress in Arab countries.

Kansas Abbreviate *Kan.* in datelines only; spell out in stories. Postal code: *KS*
See **state names**.

Kansas City Use *KANSAS CITY, Kan.*, or *KANSAS CITY, Mo.*, in datelines to avoid confusion between the two.

Kansas City Southern Freight railroad, with headquarters in Kansas City, Missouri. It is the parent of Kansas City Southern Railway Co. and Kansas City Southern de Mexico SA and it holds a 50 percent stake in Panama Canal Railway Co.

karat See **carat, caret, karat**.

Kathmandu Preferred spelling for the capital of Nepal.

Kelvin scale A scale of temperature based on, but different from, the Celsius scale. It is used primarily in science to record very high and very low temperatures. The Kelvin scale starts at zero and indicates the total absence of heat (absolute zero).

Zero on the Kelvin scale is equal to minus 273.16 degrees Celsius and minus 459.67 degrees Fahrenheit.

The freezing point of water is 273.16 kelvins. The boiling point of water is 373.16 kelvins. (Note temperatures on the Kelvin scale are called *kelvins*, not *degrees*. The symbol, a capital K, stands alone with no degree symbol.)

To convert from Celsius to Kelvin, add 273.16 to the Celsius temperature.

See **Celsius** and **Fahrenheit**.

Kennedy Space Center See **John F. Kennedy Space Center**.

Kentucky Abbreviate *Ky.* in datelines only; spell out in stories. Postal code: *KY*
See **state names**.

kerosene Formerly a trademark, now a generic term.

keynote address Also: *keynote speech*.

keywords Terms used to define an online search or embedded in a file so that it becomes searchable.

KGB Acceptable on first reference, but the story should contain a phrase identifying it as the former Russian secret police and intelligence agency.

The initials stand for the Russian words meaning *Committee for State Security*.

kibbutz An Israeli collective settlement.

The plural is *kibbutzim*.

kidnap, kidnapped, kidnapping, kidnapper

killer See **assassin, killer, murderer**.

kilo- A prefix denoting 1,000 units of a measure. Move a decimal point three places to the right, adding zeros if necessary, to convert to the basic unit: 10.5 kilograms equals 10,500 grams.

kilobyte See **byte**.

kilocycles The new term is *kilohertz*.

kilogram The metric term for 1,000 grams.

A kilogram is equal to approximately 2.2 pounds or 35 ounces.

To convert to pounds, multiply by 2.2 (9 kilograms x 2.2 equals 19.8 pounds).

See **gram**; **metric system**; and **pound**.

kilohertz Equals 1,000 hertz (1,000 cycles per second), replacing *kilocycles* as the correct term in applications such as broadcast frequencies. Spell out on first reference. Abbreviate *kHz*.

kilometer The metric term for 1,000 meters. Abbreviate *km*.

A kilometer is equal to approximately 3,281 feet, or five-eighths (0.62) of a mile.

To convert to miles, multiply by 0.62 (5 kilometers x 0.62 equals 3.1 miles).

See **meter**; **metric system**; and **miles**.

kilometers per hour The abbreviation *kph* is acceptable in all references.

kiloton, kilotonnage A unit used to measure the power of nuclear explosions. One kiloton has the explosive force of 1,000 tons of TNT.

The atomic bomb dropped Aug. 6, 1945, on Hiroshima, Japan, in the first use of the bomb as a weapon had an explosive force of 20 kilotons.

A *megaton* has the force of a million tons of TNT. A *gigaton* has the force of a billion tons of TNT.

kilowatt-hour The amount of electrical energy consumed when 1,000 watts are used for one hour.

The abbreviation *kwh* is acceptable on second reference.

kindergarten, kindergartners But *pre-K, K-12*.

king Capitalize only when used before the name of royalty: *King George VI*. Continue in subsequent references that use the king's given name: *King George*, not *George*.

Lowercase *king* when it stands alone.

Capitalize in plural uses before names: *Kings George and Edward*.

Lowercase in phrases such as *strikeout king Nolan Ryan*.

See **nobility** and **titles**.

Kitty Litter A brand of absorbent material used in cat litter boxes. Use a generic term such as *cat litter*.

Kleenex A trademark for a brand of facial tissue.

Kmart No hyphen, no space, lowercase *m*.
See **Sears Holdings Corp**.

Knesset The Israeli parliament.

knight See **nobility**.

K-9

knot A knot is 1 nautical mile (6,076.10 feet) per hour. It is redundant to say *knots per hour*.
To convert knots into approximate statute miles per hour, multiply knots by 1.15.
Always use figures: *Winds were at 7 to 9 knots*; *a 10-knot wind*.
See **nautical mile**.

know-how

Kolkata Indian city formerly known as Calcutta.

Koran Use *Quran* in all references except when preferred by an organization or in a specific title or name. See **Quran**.

Korea The Korean Peninsula remains in a technical state of war, divided by the *Demilitarized Zone* into *North Korea*, officially the *Democratic People's Republic of Korea*, and *South Korea*, officially the *Republic of Korea*. On follow-ups, the *North* and the *South* are acceptable. The abbreviations *NKorea* and *SKorea* are used only in headlines. *DMZ* is acceptable on second reference.

Korean Airlines Co. Ltd. Headquarters of this airline is in Seoul, Korea.

Korean names The style and spelling of names in North Korea and South Korea follow each government's standard policy for transliterations unless the subject has a personal preference.
North Korean names are written as three separate words, each starting with a capital letter: *Kim Jong Il*. Use *Kim* on second reference.
South Korean names are written as two names, with the given name hyphenated and a lowercase letter after the hyphen: *Lee Myung-bak*. Use *Lee* on second reference.
For South Korean place names, use the revised Romanized spellings introduced by the South Korean government in 2000: *Incheon* (formerly Inchon), *Busan* (formerly Pusan).
In both Koreas, the family name comes first.

Korean War But lowercase *Korean conflict*.

kosher Always lowercase.

Kosovo The capital is Pristina.

kowtow

K2 world's second-tallest mountain. No hyphen.

Kriss Kringle Not *Kris*. Derived from the German word, *Christkindl*, or baby Jesus.

kudos It means credit or praise for an achievement.
The word is singular and takes singular verbs.

Ku Klux Klan A secretive society organized in the South after the

Civil War to assert white supremacy, often using violence. The organization splintered, and not all successor groups use the full name. But each may be referred to as *Ku Klux Klan*, and *KKK* may be used on second reference.

Kuomintang The Chinese Nationalist political party. Do not follow with the word *party*. *Tang* means party.

Kuril Islands Use in datelines after a community name in stories from these islands. Name an individual island, if needed, in the text.

Explain in the text that a small portion of the archipelago is claimed by Japan but most are part of Russia.

Kuwait City The capital city of Kuwait stands alone in datelines.

Kyodo News The nonprofit international news agency is based in Tokyo. It was founded in 1945. *Kyodo* is acceptable on second reference.

Labor Day The first Monday in September.

Labrador The mainland portion of the Canadian province of Newfoundland and Labrador.
Use *Newfoundland* in datelines after the name of a community. Specify in the text that it is in Labrador.

lady Do not use as a synonym for *woman*. *Lady* may be used when it is a courtesy title or when a specific reference to fine manners is appropriate without patronizing overtones.
See **nobility.**

lake Capitalize as part of a proper name: *Lake Erie, Canandaigua Lake, the Finger Lakes.*
Lowercase in plural uses: *lakes Erie and Ontario; Canandaigua and Seneca lakes.*

lame duck (n.) **lame-duck** (adj.)

landline

Land Rover No hyphen. A trademark for a brand of all-terrain vehicle. Parent company Ford Motor Co. sold Land Rover and its Jaguar vehicle group to India's Tata Motors Ltd. in 2008.

languages Capitalize the proper names of languages and dialects: *Ar-amaic, Cajun, English, Gullah, Persian, Serbo-Croatian, Yiddish.*

laptop

larceny See **burglary, larceny, robbery, theft.**

last Avoid the use of *last* as a synonym for *latest* if it might imply finality. *The last time it rained, I forgot my umbrella*, is acceptable. But: *The last announcement was made at noon* may leave the reader wondering whether the announcement was the final announcement, or whether others are to follow.
The word *last* is not necessary to convey the notion of most recent when the name of a month or day is used:
Preferred: *It happened Wednesday. It happened in April.* Correct, but redundant: *It happened last Wednesday.*
But: *It happened last week. It happened last month.*

Las Vegas The city in Nevada stands alone in datelines.

late Do not use it to describe someone's actions while alive.
Wrong: *Only the late senator opposed this bill.* (The senator was not dead at that time.)

latex A resin-based substance used in making elastic materials and paints.

Latin America See **Western Hemisphere**.

Latino Often the preferred term for a person from — or whose ancestors were from — a Spanish-speaking land or culture or from Latin America. *Latina* is the feminine form. Follow the person's preference. Use a more specific identification when possible, such as *Cuban, Puerto Rican, Brazilian* or *Mexican-American*. See **Hispanic, nationalities and races**, and **race**.

latitude and longitude *Latitude,* the distance north or south of the equator, is designated by parallels. *Longitude,* the distance east or west of Greenwich, England, is designated by meridians.

Use these forms to express degrees of latitude and longitude: *New York City lies at 40 degrees 45 minutes north latitude and 74 degrees 0 minutes west longitude; New York City lies south of the 41st parallel north and along the 74th meridian west.*

laws Capitalize legislative acts but not bills: *the Taft-Hartley Act, the Kennedy bill.*

lawsuit *Civil lawsuit* is redundant.

lawyer A generic term for all members of the bar.

An *attorney* is someone legally appointed or empowered to act for another, usually, but not always, a lawyer. An *attorney at law* is a lawyer.

A *barrister* is an English lawyer who is specially trained and appears exclusively as a trial lawyer in higher courts. He is retained by a solicitor, not directly by the client. There is no equivalent term in the United States.

Counselor, when used in a legal sense, means a person who conducts a case in court, usually, but not always, a lawyer. A *counselor at law* is a lawyer. *Counsel* frequently is used collectively for a group of counselors.

A *solicitor* in England is a lawyer who performs legal services for the public. A solicitor appears in lower courts but does not have the right to appear in higher courts, which are reserved to barristers.

A *solicitor* in the United States is a lawyer employed by a governmental body. *Solicitor* is generally a job description, but in some agencies it is a formal title.

Solicitor general is the formal title for a chief law officer (where there is no attorney general) or for the chief assistant to the law officer (when there is an attorney general). Capitalize when used before a name.

Do not use *lawyer* as a formal title.

See **attorney, lawyer** and **titles**.

lay, lie The action word is *lay.* It takes a direct object. *Laid* is the form for its past tense and its past participle. Its present participle is *laying.*

Lie indicates a state of reclining along a horizontal plane. It does not take a direct object. Its past tense is *lay.* Its past participle is *lain.* Its present participle is *lying.*

When *lie* means to make an untrue statement, the verb forms are *lie, lied, lying.*

Some examples:

PRESENT OR FUTURE TENSES:

Right: *I will lay the book on the table. The prosecutor tried to lay the blame on him.*

Wrong: *He lays on the beach all day. I will lay down.*

Right: *He lies on the beach all day. I will lie down.*

IN THE PAST TENSE:

Right: *I laid the book on the table. The prosecutor has laid the blame on him.*

Right: *He lay on the beach all day. He has lain on the beach all day. I lay down. I have lain down.*

WITH THE PRESENT PARTICIPLE:

Right: *I am laying the book on the table. The prosecutor is laying the blame on him.*

Right: *He is lying on the beach. I am lying down.*

layoff (n.) **lay off** (v.)

Leaning Tower of Pisa

leatherneck Lowercase this nickname for a member of the U.S. Marine Corps. It is derived from the leather lining that was formerly part of the collar on the Marine uniform.

lectern, podium, pulpit, rostrum A speaker stands *behind a lectern, on a podium* or *rostrum*, or *in the pulpit*.

lectures Capitalize and use quotation marks for their formal titles, as described in **composition titles**.

left hand (n.) **left-hander** (n.) **left-handed** (adj.)

leftist, ultra-leftist In general, avoid these terms in favor of a more precise description of an individual's political philosophy.

Ultra-leftist suggests an individual who subscribes to a communist view or one holding that liberal or socialist change cannot come within the present form of government.

See **radical** and **rightist, ultra-rightist**.

left wing (n.) **left-winger** (n.) **left-wing** (adj.) Generally try to avoid in describing political leanings.

legal holiday See **holidays and holy days**.

legion, legionnaire See **American Legion** and **French Foreign legion**.

Legionnaires' disease The disease takes its name from an outbreak at the Pennsylvania American Legion convention held at the Bellevue-Stratford Hotel in Philadelphia in July 1976. The bacterium believed to be responsible is found in soil and grows in water, such as air-conditioning ducts, storage tanks and rivers.

legislative bodies In general, capitalize the proper name of a specific legislative body abroad: *the Knesset, the Diet*.

The most frequent names in use are *Congress, National Assembly* and *Parliament*.

GENERIC USES: Lowercase *parliament* or a similar term only when used generically to describe a body for which the formal name is being given: *the Diet, Japan's parliament*.

PLURALS: Lowercase *parliament* and similar terms in plural constructions: *the parliaments of England and France, the English and French parliaments*.

INDIVIDUAL HOUSES: The principle applies also to individual houses of the nation's legislature, just as *Senate* and *House* are capitalized in the United States:

ROME (AP) — New leaders have taken control in the Chamber of Deputies.

Lowercase *assembly* when used as a shortened reference to *national assembly*.

In many countries, *national assembly* is the name of a unicameral legislative body. In some, such as France, it is the name for the lower house of a legislative body known by some other name such as *parliament*.

legislative titles FIRST-REFERENCE FORM: Use *Rep., Reps., Sen.* and *Sens.* as formal titles before one or more names. Spell out and lowercase *representative* and *senator* in other uses.

Spell out other legislative titles in all uses. Capitalize formal titles such as *assemblyman, assemblywoman, city councilor, delegate,* etc., when they are used before a name. Lowercase in other uses.

Add *U.S.* or *state* before a title only if necessary to avoid confusion: *Former state attorney general Dan Sullivan, a Republican, defeated U.S. Sen. Mark Begich, a Democrat from Alaska, during the 2014 general election.*

In stories with international datelines, include *U.S.* before legislative titles.

FIRST-REFERENCE PRACTICE: The use of a title such as *Rep.* or *Sen.* in first reference is normal in most stories. It is not mandatory, however, provided an individual's title is given later in the story.

Deletion of the title on first reference is frequently appropriate, for example, when an individual has become well known: *Barack Obama declared Americans were ready to "cast aside cynicism" as he looked for a convincing win in the Democratic contest. The Illinois senator was leading in the polls.*

SECOND REFERENCE: Do not use legislative titles before a name on second reference unless they are part of a direct quotation.

CONGRESSMAN, CONGRESSWOMAN: *Rep.* and *U.S. Rep.* are the preferred first-reference forms when a formal title is used before the name of a U.S. House member. The words *congressman* or *congresswoman*, in lowercase, may be used in subsequent references that do not use an individual's name, just as *senator* is used in references to members of the Senate.

Congressman and *congresswoman* should appear as capitalized formal titles before a name only in direct quotation.

ORGANIZATIONAL TITLES: Capitalize titles for formal, organizational offices within a legislative body when they are used before a name: *House Speaker John Boehner, Senate Majority Leader Mitch McConnell, House Minority Leader Nancy Pelosi, Senate Majority Whip John Cornyn, President Pro Tem Orrin Hatch, Senate Judiciary Committee Chairman Charles Grassley.*

See **party affiliation** and **titles**.

legislature Capitalize when preceded by the name of a state: *the Kansas Legislature.*

Retain capitalization when the state name is dropped but the reference is specifically to that state's legislature:

TOPEKA, Kan. (AP) — Both houses of the Legislature adjourned today.

Capitalize *legislature* in subsequent specific references and in such constructions as: *the 100th Legislature, the state Legislature.*

If a given context or local practice calls for the use of a formal name such as *Missouri General Assembly*, retain the capital letters if the name of the state can be dropped, but lowercase the word *assembly* if it stands alone. Lowercase *legislature* if a story uses it in a subsequent reference to a body identified as a general assembly.

Lowercase *legislature* when used generically: *No legislature has approved the amendment.*

Use *legislature* in lowercase for all plural references: *The Arkansas and Colorado legislatures are considering the amendment.*

In 49 states the separate bodies are a *senate* and a *house* or *assembly.* The *Nebraska Legislature* is a unicameral body. All members are *senators.*

See **assembly**; **general assembly**; **governmental bodies**; **House of Representatives**; and **Senate**.

lesbian See **gay**.

-less No hyphen before this suffix:

childless   waterless
tailless

less See **fewer, less**.

letup (n. and adj.) **let up** (v.)

leverage The use of debt to enhance returns. The expectation is that the cost of the debt will be lower than the earnings generated.

leveraged buyout A corporate acquisition in which the bulk of the purchase price is paid with borrowed money. The debt then is repaid with the acquired company's earnings, money raised by the sale of some of its assets or by the later sale of the entire company.

Levi's A trademark for a brand of jeans.

LGBT Acceptable on first reference for *lesbian, gay, bisexual and transgender.* Should be spelled out in body of the story.

liabilities When used in a financial sense, the word means all the claims against a corporation.

They include accounts payable, wages and salaries due but not paid, dividends declared payable, taxes payable, and fixed or long-term obligations such as bonds, debentures and bank loans.

See **assets**.

liaison

liberal, liberalism See **political parties and philosophies**.

Libor The rate that international banks charge for short-term loans to each other. Libor, an acronym for the London Interbank Offered Rate, is calculated every business day.

lie See **lay, lie**.

lie in state Only people who are entitled to a state funeral may formally lie in state. In the United States, this occurs in the rotunda in the Capitol.

Those entitled to a state funeral are a president, a former president, a president-elect or any other person designated by the president.

Members of Congress may lie in state, and a number have done so. The decision is either house's to make, although the formal process normally begins with a request from the president.

Those entitled to an official funeral, but not to lie in state, are the vice president, the chief justice, Cabinet members and other government officials when designated by the president.

lieutenant See **military titles**.

lieutenant governor Capitalize and abbreviate as *Lt. Gov.* or *Lt. Govs.* when used as a formal title before one or more names both inside and outside quotations. Lowercase and spell out in all other uses.

See **titles**.

life-size

life span

lifestyle

lifetime

liftoff (n. and adj.) **lift off** (v.)

light, lighted, lighting *Lit* is acceptable as the past tense form.

lightning The electrical discharge.

light-year The distance that light travels in one year at the rate of 186,282 miles per second. It works out to about 5.88 trillion miles (5,878,612,800,000 miles).

likable

-like Do not precede this suffix by a hyphen unless the letter l would be tripled or the main element is a proper noun:

bill-like	Norwalk-like
businesslike	shell-like

An exception is *flu-like*.

like- Follow with a hyphen when used as a prefix meaning similar to:

like-minded	like-natured

No hyphen in words that have meanings of their own:

likelihood	likewise
likeness	

like, as Use *like* as a preposition to compare nouns and pronouns. It requires an object: *Jim blocks like a pro.*

The conjunction *as* is the correct word to introduce clauses: *Jim blocks the linebacker as he should.*

limousine

linage, lineage *Linage* is the number of lines.

Lineage is ancestry or descent.

Lincoln's Birthday Capitalize *birthday* in references to the holiday.

Lincoln was born Feb. 12. His birthday is not a federal legal holiday.

line numbers Use figures and lowercase the word line in naming individual lines of a text: *line 1, line 9*. But: *the first line, the 10th line*. See **numerals**.

LinkedIn A social media site used mainly for professional networking. Users create contact networks for information exchanges, job searches and business opportunities.

link shortener A tool that allows users to shorten a longer URL to make it easier to share. Some link shorteners also allow users to track statistics related to clicks on those links, and they may allow "vanity" addresses that carry a brand's name. (For example: apne.ws.) Bit.ly and Ow.ly are two link shorteners.

linoleum Formerly a trademark, now a generic term.

lion's share The term comes from an Aesop fable in which the lion took all the spoils of a joint hunt.

Use it to mean the whole of something, or the best and biggest portion.

Do not use it to mean majority.

liquefied natural gas Natural gas that has been cooled to minus 260 degrees Fahrenheit, making it liquid. The process reduces the volume of the gas, making it easier to transport. *LNG* is acceptable on second reference.

liquefy

liquidation When used in a financial sense, the word means the process of converting stock or other assets into cash.

When a company is liquidated, the cash obtained is first used to pay debts and obligations to holders of bonds and preferred stock. Whatever cash remains is distributed on a per-share basis to the holders of common stock.

liquidity The ease with which assets can be converted to cash without loss in value. The faster it can be sold, the more liquid it is.

Listserv A trademark for a software program for setting up and maintaining discussion groups through email.

liter The basic unit of volume in the metric system. It is defined as the volume occupied by 1 kilogram of distilled water at 4 degrees Celsius. It works out to a total of 1,000 cubic centimeters (1 cubic decimeter).

It takes 1,000 milliliters to make a liter.

A liter is equal to approximately 34 fluid ounces or 1.06 liquid quarts. A liter equals 0.91 of a dry quart. The metric system makes no distinction between dry volume and liquid volume.

To convert to liquid quarts, multiply by 1.06 (4 liters x 1.06 equals 4.24 liquid quarts).

To convert to dry quarts, multiply by 0.91 (4 liters x 0.91 equals 3.64 dry quarts).

To convert to liquid gallons, multiply by 0.26 (8 liters x 0.26 equals 2.08 gallons).

See **gallon; kilogram; metric system; quart (dry);** and **quart (liquid)**.

literally See **figuratively, literally**.

literature See **composition titles**.

Little League, Little League Baseball The official name of the worldwide youth baseball and softball organization and its affiliated local leagues.

livable

live-blog Snippets of information about a particular event that are posted online in real time, usually in reverse chronological order, with the newest entry first. Can be used as a noun or verb.

livid It is not a synonym for *fiery, bright, crimson, red* or *flaming*. If a person turns *livid* with rage, his face becomes ashen or pale. It can mean *blue, bluish gray, gray, dull white, dull purple* or *grayish black*.

Lloyds Bank International Ltd. A prominent bank with headquarters in London.

Lloyd's of London A self-regulating market of insurance. Founded in Britain in 1680, it relies on individual investors worldwide, known as Names, along with several hundred companies, to provide the money for underwriting insurance.

loan terminology Note the meanings of these terms in describing loans by governments and corporations:

bond A certificate issued by a corporation or government stating the amount of a loan, the interest to be paid, the time for repayment and the collateral pledged if payment cannot be made. Repayment generally is not due for a long period, usually seven years or more.

collateral Stock or other property that a borrower is obligated to turn over to a lender if unable to repay a loan.

convertible bond A bond carrying the stipulation that it may be exchanged for a specific amount of stock in the company that issued it.

coupon The interest rate stated on a bond and paid to a bondholder, usually semiannually.

debenture A certificate stating the amount of a loan, the interest to be paid and the time for repayment, but not providing collateral. It is backed only by the corporation's reputation and promise to pay.

default A person, corporation or government is in default if it fails to meet the terms for repayment.

full faith and credit bond An alternate term for general obligation bond, often used to contrast such a bond with a moral obligation bond.

general obligation bond A bond that has had the formal approval of either the voters or their legislature. The government's promise to repay the principal and pay the interest is constitutionally guaranteed on the strength of its ability to tax the population.

maturity The date on which a bond, debenture or note must be repaid.

moral obligation bond A government bond that has not had the formal approval of either the voters or their legislature. It is backed only by the government's "moral obligation" to repay the principal and interest on time.

municipal bond A general obligation bond issued by a state, country, city, town, village, possession or territory, or a bond issued by an agency or authority set up by one of these governmental units. In general, interest paid on municipal bonds is exempt from federal income taxes. It also usually is exempt from state and local taxes if held by someone living within the state of issue.

note A certificate issued by a corporation or government stating the amount of a loan, the interest to be paid and the collateral pledged in the event payment cannot be made. The date for repayment is generally more than a year after issue but not more than seven or eight years later. The shorter interval for repayment is the principal difference between a note and a bond.

revenue bond A bond backed only by the revenue of the airport, turnpike or other facility that was built with the money it raised.

Treasury borrowing A *Treasury bill* is a certificate representing a loan to the federal government that matures in three, six or 12 months. A *Treasury note* may mature in one to 10 years or more. A *Treasury bond* matures in more than 10 years. Because Treasurys carry the full backing of the government, they are viewed as the safest investment.

loan (n.) **lend** (v.) The preferred usage.

loath (adj.) **loathe** (v.) Note the difference. She is *loath* to leave. He *loathes* bureaucracy.

local Avoid the irrelevant use of the word.

Irrelevant: *The injured were taken to a local hospital.*

Better: *The injured were taken to a hospital.*

local of a union Always use a figure and capitalize *local* when giving the name of a union subdivision: *Local 123 of the United Auto Workers.*

Lowercase *local* standing alone in plural uses: *The local will vote Tuesday. He spoke to locals 2, 4 and 10.*

See **union names**.

Lockheed Martin Corp. Headquarters is in Bethesda, Maryland.

lodges See **fraternal organizations and service clubs**.

login, logon, logoff (n.) But use as two words in verb form: *I log in to my computer.*

London The city in England stands alone in datelines.

long distance, long-distance (adj.) *We traveled a long distance. She's a long-distance runner.*

longitude See **latitude and longitude**.

longshoreman Capitalize *longshoreman* only if the intended meaning is that the individual is a member of the International Longshore and Warehouse Union or the International Longshoremen's Association.

long term, long-term Hyphenate when used as a compound modifier: *We will win in the long term. He has a long-term assignment.*

long time, longtime *They have known each other a long time. They are longtime partners.*

long ton Also known as a *British ton.* Equal to 2,240 pounds. See **ton**.

Los Angeles The city in California stands alone in datelines. *LA* is acceptable on second reference. *Hollywood* is a district of the city of Los Angeles where the film industry used to be centered and where film studios and other production facilities, as well as landmark theaters, are still located. It is not a dateline and is most commonly used to describe Southern California's entertainment industry. *Beverly Hills* is an incorporated city and the dateline for the Golden Globes movie awards.

Louisiana Abbreviate *La.* in datelines only; spell out in stories. Postal code: *LA*
See **state names**.

lowercase One word (n., v., adj.) when referring to the absence of capital letters. Originally from printers' practice.

LSD Acceptable in all references for *lysergic acid diethylamide*.

Lt. Gov. See **lieutenant governor**.

Lucite A trademark for an acrylic plastic.

Luxembourg Stands alone in datelines.

-ly Do not use a hyphen between adverbs ending in *-ly* and adjectives they modify: *an easily remembered rule, a badly damaged island, a fully informed woman.*
See the compound modifiers section of the **hyphen** entry.

Lycra Unless referring to the trademark fiber or fabric, use a generic term such as *spandex* or *elastic* or *stretch fabric*.

Lyme disease

Lyndon B. Johnson Space Center Located in Houston, the National Aeronautics and Space Administration's principal control and training center for manned spaceflight.
Johnson Space Center is acceptable in all references.
In datelines:
HOUSTON (AP) —
See **John F. Kennedy Space Center**.

Macau Stands alone in datelines. Spelling is an exception to Webster's New World College Dictionary.

Mace A trademark, shortened from *Chemical Mace*, for a brand of tear gas that is packaged in an aerosol canister and temporarily stuns its victims.

machine gun (n.) **machine-gun** (v. and adj.) **machine-gunner**, **machine-gun fire**
See **weapons**.

Mach number Named for Ernst Mach, an Austrian physicist, the figure represents the ratio of the speed of an object to the speed of sound in the surrounding medium, such as air, through which the object is moving.
A rule of thumb for speed of sound is approximately 750 mph at sea level and approximately 660 mph at 30,000 feet above sea level.
A body traveling at *Mach 1* would be traveling at the speed of sound. *Mach 2* would equal twice the speed of sound.

mad cow disease Acceptable for bovine spongiform encephalopathy, a progressive neurological disease that afflicts cattle. The disorder caused in humans by eating meat from diseased cattle is called *variant Creutzfeldt-Jakob disease.* See **Creutzfeldt-Jakob disease**.

Madrid The city in Spain stands alone in datelines.

Mafia Secret criminal organization operating mainly in the U.S. and Italy and engaged in illegal activities such as gambling, drug-dealing and prostitution. Lowercase as a synonym for organized crime.

magazine names Capitalize the initial letters of the name but do not place it in quotes. Lowercase *magazine* unless it is part of the publication's formal title: *Harper's Magazine, Newsweek magazine, Time magazine.*
Check the masthead if in doubt.

Magi Wise men who brought gifts to the infant Jesus at Epiphany, celebrated Jan. 6.

magistrate Capitalize when used as a formal title before a name. Use *magistrate judge* when referring to the fixed-term judge who presides in U.S. District Court and handles cases referred by U.S. district judges. See **titles**.

mahjong

mailman *Mail* or *letter carrier* is preferable.

Maine Do not abbreviate *Maine* in datelines or stories. Postal code: *ME*
See **state names**.

mainland China See **China**.

major See **military titles**.

majority leader Capitalize when used as a formal title before a name: *Majority Leader John Boehner.* Lowercase elsewhere.
See **legislative titles** and **titles**.

majority, plurality *Majority* means more than half of an amount.
Plurality means more than the next highest number.
COMPUTING MAJORITY: To describe how large a majority is, take the figure that is more than half and subtract everything else from it: If 100,000 votes were cast in an election and one candidate received 60,000 while opponents received 40,000, the winner would have a *majority* of 20,000 votes.
COMPUTING PLURALITY: To describe how large a plurality is, take the highest number and subtract from it the next highest number: If, in the election example above, the second-place finisher had 25,000 votes, the winner's *plurality* would be 35,000 votes.
Suppose, however, that no candidate in this example had a majority. If the first-place finisher had 40,000 votes and the second-place finisher had 30,000, for example, the leader's *plurality* would be 10,000 votes.
USAGE: When *majority* and *plurality* are used alone, they take singular verbs and pronouns: *The majority has made its decision.*
If a plural word follows an *of* construction, the decision on whether to use a singular or plural verb depends on the sense of the sentence: *A majority of two votes is not adequate to control the committee. The majority of the houses on the block were destroyed.*

-maker Follow Webster's New World College Dictionary. For words not in this book, if the word combination is not listed, use two words for the verb form and hyphenate any noun or adjective forms. Exceptions: *chipmaker, drugmaker, policymaker, coffee maker.*

makeup (n. and adj.) **make up** (v.)

Malaysia Airlines Headquarters of this airline is in Subang, Malaysia.

Maldives Use this official name with a community name in a dateline: *MALE, Maldives.* Refer to the country in the body of the story as *the Maldives: The president won a referendum on the Maldives' future form of government.*

Mallorca Use instead of Spain in datelines on stories from communities on this island.

manageable

manager Capitalize when used as a formal title before a name: *City Manager Dick O'Connell.*
Do not capitalize in job descriptions, including sports teams: *Mets manager Terry Collins.*
See **titles**.

managing editor Capitalize when used as a formal title before a name.
See **titles**.

Manitoba A province of central Canada. Do not abbreviate.
See **datelines**.

man-made

man, mankind Either may be used when both men and women are involved and no other term is convenient. In these cases, do not use duplicate phrases such as *a man or a woman* or *mankind and womankind.*

Frequently the best choice is a substitute such as *humanity, a person* or *an individual.*

See **women**.

manslaughter See **homicide, murder, manslaughter**.

mantel, mantle A *mantel* is a shelf. A *mantle* is a cloak.

Manual de Estilo Online de la AP The Associated Press' Spanish-language Online Stylebook. The website is: http://manualdeestiloap.com.

Maoism (Maoist) The communist philosophy and policies of Mao Zedong. See **political parties and philosophies**.

Marcellus Shale Capitalize major geologic formations.

Mardi Gras Literally *fat Tuesday*, the term describes a day of merrymaking on the Tuesday before Ash Wednesday, the first day of Lent.

In New Orleans and many Roman Catholic countries, the Tuesday celebration is preceded by a week or more of parades and parties. See **Carnival**.

margin The practice of purchasing securities in part with borrowed money, using the purchased securities as collateral in anticipation of an advance in the market price. If the advance occurs, the purchaser may be able to repay the loan and make a profit. If the price declines, the stock may have to be sold to settle the loan. The margin is the difference between the amount of the loan and the value of the securities used as collateral.

marijuana

Marines Capitalize when referring to U.S. forces: *the U.S. Marines, the Marines, the Marine Corps, Marine regulations.* Do not use the abbreviation *USMC.*

Capitalize *Marine* when referring to an individual in a Marine Corps unit: *He is a Marine.*

Do not describe *Marines* as soldiers, which is generally associated with the Army. Use *troops* if a generic term is needed.

Maritime Provinces The Canadian provinces of Nova Scotia, New Brunswick and Prince Edward Island.

marketbasket, marketplace

mark to market An accounting requirement that securities must be valued at their current price, rather than the purchase price or the price they might fetch later. Also called "fair value."

marquess, marchioness, marquis, marquise See **nobility**.

Marseille Preferred spelling for the French city.

Marshall Islands Named for John Marshall, a British explorer.

In datelines, give the name of a city and *Marshall Islands.* List the name of an individual island in the text.

marshal, marshaled, marshaling, Marshall *Marshal* is the spelling for both the verb and the noun: *Marilyn will marshal her forces. Erwin Rommel was a field marshal.*

Marshall is used in proper names: *George C. Marshall, John Marshall, the Marshall Islands.*

Martin Luther King Jr. Day
Federal holiday honoring Martin
Luther King Jr., who was born Jan.
15, 1929, is on the third Monday in
January. It was first celebrated in
1986.

Marxism (Marxist) The system
of thought developed by Karl Marx
and Friedrich Engels. See **political
parties and philosophies**.

Maryland Abbreviate *Md.* in
datelines only; spell out in stories.
Postal code: *MD*
   See **state names**.

mashup A combination of two
or more pieces of content, such
as photos or video, used to create something new. For example, a
video that blends audio from a song
with footage from several movies to
build a new storyline.

Mason-Dixon Line The bound-
ary line between Pennsylvania and
Maryland, generally regarded as sep-
arating the North from the South.
(Named for 18th-century surveyors
Charles Mason and Jeremiah Dixon,
the line later was extended to West
Virginia.)

Massachusetts Abbreviate
Mass. in datelines only; spell out in
stories. Postal code: *MA*
   See **state names**.

**Master of Arts, Master of Sci-
ence, Master of Business Administration** Abbreviated *M.A., M.S.* but
MBA. A *master's degree* or a *master's*
is acceptable in any reference.
   See **academic degrees**.

matrimony See **sacraments** in
Religion Guidelines.

maturity In a financial sense,
the date on which a bond, debenture

or note must be repaid. See **loan
terminology**.

May Day, mayday *May Day* is
May 1, often observed as a festive or
political holiday.
   Mayday is the international
distress signal, from the French
m'aider, meaning "help me."

McClatchy Co. U.S. newspaper
publisher with headquarters in Sacramento, California. Owns dailies
including *The Miami Herald* and *The
Sacramento Bee*.

McDonald's Corp. Headquarters is in Oak Brook, Illinois.

M.D. A word such as *physician* or
surgeon is preferred. The periods in
the abbreviation are an exception to
Webster's New World College Dictionary.
   See **doctor** and **academic titles**.

meager

mean See **average, mean, median, norm**.

mecca Lowercase in the meta-
phorical sense; capitalize the city in
Saudi Arabia.

Medal of Freedom It is now
the *Presidential Medal of Freedom*. See
entry under that name.

Medal of Honor The nation's
highest military honor, awarded by
Congress for risk of life in combat
beyond the call of duty. Use *Medal
of Honor recipient* or a synonym, but
not *winner*.
   There is no *Congressional Medal
of Honor*.

medevac Acceptable abbreviation for *medical evacuation*, especially
in referring to aircraft used to transport wounded military personnel.

Medfly Mediterranean fruit fly. The capital *M* is an exception to Webster's New World College Dictionary.

media In the sense of mass communication, such as magazines, newspapers, the news services, radio, television and online, the word is plural: *The news media are resisting attempts to limit their freedom.*

median See **average, mean, median, norm**.

mediate See **arbitrate, mediate**.

Medicaid A federal-state program that helps pay for health care for the needy, aged, blind and disabled, and for low-income families with children.

A state determines eligibility and which health services are covered. The federal government reimburses a percentage of the state's expenditures.

Medicare The federal health care insurance program for people aged 65 and over, and for the disabled. Eligibility is based mainly on eligibility for Social Security.

Medicare helps pay charges for hospitalization, for stays in skilled nursing facilities, for physician's charges and for some associated health costs. There are limitations on the length of stay and type of care.

In Canada, *Medicare* refers to the nation's national health insurance program.

medicine See **drugs, medicine**.

medieval

mega- A prefix denoting 1 million units of a measure. Move the decimal point six places to the right, adding zeros if necessary, to convert to the basic unit: 5.5 megatons = 5,500,000 tons.

megabyte See **byte**.

megahertz A measure of radio frequency or the speed of a computer processor, equal to a million hertz, or cycles per second. Spell out on first reference. Abbreviate *MHz*.

melee

meme A piece of information, such as a cultural practice or idea, that's shared verbally or transmitted widely, often in social media.

memento, mementos

memo, memos

memorandum, memorandums

Memorial Day Formerly May 30. The federal legal holiday is the last Monday in May.

menswear Not *men's wear*.

mental illness Do not describe an individual as mentally ill unless it is clearly pertinent to a story and the diagnosis is properly sourced.

When used, identify the source for the diagnosis. Seek firsthand knowledge; ask how the source knows. Don't rely on hearsay or speculate on a diagnosis. Specify the time frame for the diagnosis and ask about treatment. A person's condition can change over time, so a diagnosis of mental illness might not apply anymore. Avoid anonymous sources. On-the-record sources may be family members, mental health professionals, medical authorities, law enforcement officials or court records. Be sure they have accurate information to make the diagnosis. Provide examples of symptoms.

Mental illness is a general term. Specific conditions are disorders and should be used whenever possible: *He was diagnosed with schizophrenia, according to court documents. She was diagnosed with anorexia, according to her parents. He was treated for depression.*

Some common mental disorders, according to the National Institute of Mental Health (they are lowercase):

— Autism spectrum disorder. Many experts consider autism a developmental disorder, not a mental illness.

— Bipolar disorder (manic-depressive illness)

— Depression

— Obsessive-compulsive disorder (OCD)

— Post-traumatic stress disorder (PTSD)

— Schizophrenia

Here is a link from the NIMH that can be used as a reference: http://www.nimh.nih.gov/
Do not use derogatory terms, such as *insane, crazy/crazed, nuts* or *deranged*, unless they are part of a quotation that is essential to the story.

Do not assume that mental illness is a factor in a violent crime, and avoid unsubstantiated statements by witnesses or first responders attributing violence to mental illness.

Studies have shown that the vast majority of people with mental illness are not violent, and experts say most people who are violent are not mentally ill.

Nevertheless, a first responder often is quoted as saying, without direct knowledge, that a crime was committed by a person with a "history of mental illness." If used, such comments must be attributed to law enforcement authorities, medical professionals, family members or others who have knowledge of the history and can authoritatively

speak to its relevance. In the absence of definitive information, there should be a disclaimer that a link had yet to be established.

Avoid descriptions that connote pity, such as *afflicted with, suffers from* or *victim of*. Rather, *he has obsessive-compulsive disorder*.

Double-check specific symptoms and diagnoses. Avoid interpreting behavior common to many people as symptoms of mental illness. Sadness, anger, exuberance and the occasional desire to be alone are normal emotions experienced by people who have mental illness as well as those who don't.

When practical, let people with mental disorders talk about their own diagnoses.

Avoid using mental health terms to describe non-health issues. Don't say that an awards show, for example, was schizophrenic.

Use the term *mental* or *psychiatric hospital*, not *asylum*.

See **disabled, handicapped**; **phobia**; **post-traumatic stress disorder**.

mentally disabled, intellectually disabled, developmentally disabled The preferred terms, not *mentally retarded*. See **disabled, handicapped**.

mention The inclusion of a username in a social media post created by another user. The user who's been mentioned will generally be notified that this has happened, so a mention can be used as a way to get someone's attention. Example from Twitter: *I refer to the @APStylebook as I edit stories.*

Mercedes-Benz Note hyphen in this division of Daimler AG.

merchant marine Lowercase in referring to the ships of a nation used in commerce. Capitalize only in references to the organization the Merchant Marine or the U.S. Merchant Marine Academy. Members are *merchant mariners* or *merchant crewmen*, but not marines.

Merck & Co. Headquarters is in Whitehouse Station, New Jersey.

merger Few business combinations are truly a merger of equals, so be precise and sparing in the use of the word *merger*. It is not a synonym for acquisition or takeover, which should be the preferred descriptives in most stories. Use the following rules for deciding whether it's a merger or acquisition, and as a guide in concluding who is the acquirer and the company being taken over:

—Is one of the companies' stock being used as the currency? If the answer is yes, that's usually a good sign that company is the acquirer and it is not a merger.

—What is the message from the exchange ratio in stock transactions? Typically when shareholders of Company A are offered new shares in a combined company at a 1-for-1 ratio, and Company B shares are exchanged at something less or more (i.e., each Company B will be exchanged for 0.47 percent of a share of the new company), it's an indication that Company A's stock is being used as the basis for the transaction. But it also could be a sign that the companies' boards have agreed to a merger that uses a formula to compensate for the differing market value (total number of shares multiplied by the closing stock price the day before the announcement) of the two companies to come up with an exchange ratio for stock in the new company.

—What is the message from the stock movements after the announcement? Shares of companies being acquired typically rise and shares of the acquirer often fall after the announcement. Not always, of course, but that's usually the case because most bidders pay a premium, or an above-market price, for the shares of the company being acquired, and investors often are worried about the amount of debt the acquirer is taking on to complete the transaction.

—Whose cash is being used to fund the cash portion of a transaction? If the announcement says Company A's cash will be used or that its existing lines of credit will be tapped to pay for Company B's shares, that's a strong indication that Company A is the acquirer.

—Which company's executives are filling most of the top management roles? The key distinction usually is who gets the CEO slot. But if one of the two CEOs is named to head the company for a limited period (say two years or less) before his fellow CEO takes over, that's a good sign of a political compromise to paper over the fact that the second CEO's company is going to be in charge long term.

—Which company will end up with the majority of the seats on the new board of directors? This is often a key tie breaker. When Company A and Company B insist it's a merger of equals and other checklist items are inconclusive, if one ends up with 60 percent of the board seats and the other gets 40 percent, that's a good indication of which is going to be in charge. Also, make sure you get not only the short-term makeup of the board of the combined company, but also whether there were any deals cut for some members to retire in short order.

—Where will the company be headquartered? Since CEOs typically do the negotiating and they typically aren't anxious to move, this can be an informative tell.

meridians Use numerals and lowercase to identify the imaginary locater lines that ring the globe from north to south through the poles. They are measured in units of 0 to 180 degrees east and west of the *prime meridian*, which runs through Greenwich, England.

Examples: *33rd meridian* (if location east or west of Greenwich is obvious), *1st meridian west, 100th meridian*.

See **latitude and longitude**.

merry Christmas See **happy holidays, merry Christmas, season's greetings**.

merry-go-round

MERS Middle East respiratory syndrome. *MERS* is acceptable on second reference. Previously known as a novel coronavirus, MERS is related to SARS but do not describe as SARS-like. It was first identified in the Middle East and can cause symptoms including fever, breathing problems, pneumonia and kidney failure. Scientists are not sure how humans are being infected but suspect animals such as camels or bats may be passing on the virus. Human-to-human transmission has also been known to happen occasionally.

Mesa Air Group Inc. Headquarters of this airline is in Phoenix.

messiah Capitalize in religious uses, such as references to the promised deliverer of the Jews or to Jesus in Christianity. Lowercase when referring to the liberator of a people or country.

metadata Behind-the-scenes data that provide important information about a piece of content. Examples of metadata include descriptors indicating when information was created, by whom and in what format. Do not use in a story without an explanation of what information is being revealed in a given set of metadata: *Investigators determined that Johnson wrote the document by analyzing its metadata, which indicated that it had been saved on his computer.*

meter The basic unit of length in the metric system.

It is equal to approximately 39.37 inches, which may be rounded off to 39.5 inches in most comparisons.

It takes 100 centimeters to make a meter.

It takes 1,000 meters to make a kilometer.

To convert to inches, multiply by 39.37 (5 meters x 39.37 = 196.85 inches).

To convert to yards, multiply by 1.1 (5 meters x 1.1 = 5.5 yards).

See **inch**; **metric system**; and **yard**.

metric system For U.S. members, use metric terms only in situations where they are universally accepted forms of measurement (*16 mm film*) or where the metric distance is an important number in itself: *He vowed to walk 100 kilometers (62 miles) in a week.*

Normally, the equivalent should be in parentheses after the metric figure. A general statement, however, such as *A kilometer equals about five-eighths of a mile*, would be acceptable to avoid repeated use of parenthetical equivalents in a story that uses *kilometers* many times.

A conversion is generally needed only the first time a metric number is mentioned. The reader can make the necessary conversions after that.

To avoid the need for long strings of figures, prefixes are added to the metric units to denote fractional elements or large multiples. The prefixes are: *pico-* (one-trillionth), *nano-* (one-billionth), *micro-* (one-millionth), *milli-* (one-thousandth), *centi-* (one-hundredth), *deci-* (one-tenth), *deka-* (10 units), *hecto-* (100 units), *kilo-* (1,000 units), *mega-* (1 million units), *giga-* (1 billion units), *tera-* (1 trillion units). Entries for each prefix show how to convert a unit preceded by the prefix to the basic unit.

In addition, separate entries for **gram**, **meter**, **liter**, **Celsius** and other frequently used metric units define them and give examples of how to convert them to equivalents in the terminology that has been used in the United States.

Similarly, entries for **pound**, **inch**, **quart**, **Fahrenheit**, etc., contain examples of how to convert these terms to metric forms.

Online:
http://www.megaconverter.com/ mega2/

ABBREVIATIONS: The abbreviation *mm* for millimeter is acceptable in references to film widths (*8 mm film*) and weapons (*a 105 mm cannon*). (Note space between numeral and abbreviation.)

METRIC CONVERSION CHART

INTO METRIC			OUT OF METRIC		
multiply	*by this number*	*to get*	*multiply*	*by this number*	*to get*
LENGTH					
inches	2.54	centimeters	millimeters	0.04	inches
feet	0.3	meters	centimeters	0.39	inches
yards	0.91	meters	meters	3.28	feet
miles	1.61	kilometers	kilometers	0.62	miles
AREA					
sq. inches	6.45	sq. centimeters	sq. centimeters	0.16	sq. inches
sq. feet	0.09	sq. meters	sq. meters	0.2	sq. yards
sq. yards	0.84	sq. meters	sq. kilometers	0.39	sq. miles
sq. miles	2.59	sq. kilometers	hectares	2.47	acres
acres	0.39	hectares			
MASS (weight)					
ounces	28	grams	grams	0.035	ounces
pounds	0.45	kilograms	kilograms	2.2	pounds
short ton	0.91	metric ton	metric ton	1.1	short tons
VOLUME					
teaspoons	5	milliliters	milliliters	0.03	fluid ounces
tablespoons	15	milliliters	liters	2.1	pints
fluid ounces	30	milliliters	liters	1.06	quarts
cups	0.24	liters	liters	0.26	gallons
pints	0.47	liters	cubic meters	35	cubic feet
quarts	0.95	liters	cubic meters	1.3	cubic yards
gallons	3.79	liters			
cubic feet	0.03	cubic meters			
cubic yards	0.76	cubic meters			

The principal abbreviations, for reference in the event they are used by a source, are: *g* (gram), *kg* (kilogram), *t* (metric ton), *m* (meter), *cm* (centimeter), *km* (kilometer), *mm* (millimeter), *L* (liter, capital *L* to avoid confusion with the figure 1) and *mL* (milliliter).

metric ton Equal to approximately 2,204.62 pounds. See **ton**.

Metro-Goldwyn-Mayer Inc.
MGM is acceptable in all references.
Headquarters is in Santa Monica, California.

Mexico There are 31 states and Mexico City, the capital and an independent federal district run by a city government. The states are Aguascalientes, Baja California, Baja California Sur, Campeche, Chiapas, Chihuahua, Coahuila, Colima, Durango, Guanajuato, Guerrero, Hidalgo, Jalisco, Mexico, Michoacan, Morelos, Nayarit, Nuevo Leon, Oaxaca, Puebla, Queretaro, Quintana Roo, San Luis Potosi, Sinaloa, Sonora, Tabasco, Tamaulipas, Tlaxcala, Veracruz, Yucatan and Zacatecas.
Mexican states elect their own governor and legislators. Congress is made up of two houses: the lower House of Deputies, with 500 members, and the Senate, with 128 members.
In datelines, use only the city and country.

Mexico City The city in Mexico stands alone in datelines.

Miami The city in Florida stands alone in datelines.

mic (n.) Informal form of *microphone*.

Michigan Abbreviate *Mich.* in datelines only; spell out in stories. Postal code: *MI*

See **state names**.

micro- A prefix denoting one-millionth of a unit.
Move the decimal point six places to the left in converting to the basic unit: 2,999,888.5 microseconds = 2.9998885 seconds.

microsite A tightly focused group of Web pages typically dedicated to a single topic, product or service.

Microsoft Corp. Headquarters is in Redmond, Washington.

mid- No hyphen unless a capitalized word follows: *midair, midAmerica, mid-Atlantic, midsemester* and *midterm*.
But use a hyphen when *mid-* precedes a figure: *mid-30s*.

Middle Ages A.D. 476 to approximately A.D. 1450.

Middle Atlantic States As defined by the U.S. Census Bureau, they are New Jersey, New York and Pennsylvania.
Less formal references often consider Delaware part of the group. See **Northeast region**.

middle class (n.) **middle-class** (adj.)

Middle East The term applies to southwest Asia west of Pakistan and Afghanistan (Iran, Iraq, Israel, Kuwait, Jordan, Lebanon, Oman, Bahrain, Qatar, Saudi Arabia, Syria, the eastern part of Turkey known also as Asia Minor, United Arab Emirates and Yemen), and northeastern Africa (Egypt and Sudan).
Popular usage once distinguished between the *Near East* (the westerly nations in the listing) and the *Middle East* (the easterly nations), but the two terms now overlap, with cur-

rent practice favoring *Middle East* for both areas.

Use *Middle East* unless *Near East* is used by a source in a story.

Mideast is also acceptable, but *Middle East* is preferred.

middle initials Use according to a person's preference.

Include middle initials in stories where they help identify a specific individual. Examples include casualty lists and stories naming the accused in a crime. A middle initial may be dropped if a person does not use one or is publicly known without it: *Mickey Mantle* (not *Mickey C.*), *the Rev. Billy Graham* (not *Billy F.*).

See **names**.

middleman

middle names Use them only with people who are publicly known that way (*James Earl Jones*), or to prevent confusion with people of the same name.

See **middle initials; names**.

Middle West Definitions vary, but the term generally applies to the 12 states that the U.S. Census Bureau includes in the *Midwest* region. See **Midwest region**.

The shortened form *Midwest* is acceptable in all references.

The forms for adjectives are *Middle Western, Midwestern*.

See **directions and regions**.

midget Considered offensive when used to describe a person of short stature. *Dwarf* is the preferred term for people with that medical or genetic condition. See **dwarf**.

midnight Do not put a 12 in front of it. It is part of the day that is ending, not the one that is beginning.

midshipman See **military academies**.

Midwest region As defined by the U.S. Census Bureau, the region (previously designated the North Central region) is broken into two divisions.

The East North Central states are Indiana, Illinois, Michigan, Ohio and Wisconsin.

The West North Central states are Iowa, Kansas, Minnesota, Missouri, Nebraska, North Dakota and South Dakota.

See **Northeast region; South;** and **West** for the bureau's other regional breakdowns.

MiG The *i* in this designation for a type of Russian fighter jet is lowercase because it is the Russian word for *and*. The initials are from the last names of the designers, Arten Mikoyan and Mikhail Gurevich.

The forms: *MiG-19, MiG-21s*.

See **aircraft names**.

Milan The city in Italy stands alone in datelines.

mile Also called a statute mile, it equals 5,280 feet.

The metric equivalent is approximately 1.6 kilometers.

To convert to kilometers, multiply by 1.6 (5 miles x 1.6 equals 8 kilometers).

Use figures in all references: *The farm measures 5 miles by 4 miles. The car slowed to 7 mph. The new model gets 4 miles more per gallon. He walked 3 miles.*

See **foot; kilometer; knot; nautical mile** and **numerals**.

miles per gallon The abbreviation *mpg* is acceptable in all references.

miles per hour The abbreviation *mph* is acceptable in all references. No hyphen when used with a figure: *60 mph.*

military academies Capitalize *U.S. Air Force Academy, U.S. Coast Guard Academy, U.S. Merchant Marine Academy, U.S. Military Academy, U.S. Naval Academy.* Retain capitalization if the *U.S.* is dropped: *the Air Force Academy,* etc.

Lowercase *academy* whenever it stands alone.

Cadet is the proper title on first reference for men and women enrolled at the Army, Air Force, Coast Guard and Merchant Marine academies. *Midshipman* is the proper title for men and women enrolled at the Naval Academy.

Use the appropriate title on first reference. On second reference, use only the last name.

military titles Capitalize a military rank when used as a formal title before an individual's name.

See the lists that follow to determine whether the title should be spelled out or abbreviated in regular text.

On first reference, use the appropriate title before the full name of a member of the military.

In subsequent references, do not continue using the title before a name. Use only the last name.

Spell out and lowercase a title when it is substituted for a name: *Gen. John Jones is the top U.S. commander in Afghanistan. The general endorsed the idea.*

In some cases, it may be necessary to explain the significance of a title: *Army Sgt. Maj. John Jones described the attack. Jones, who holds the Army's highest rank for enlistees, said it was unprovoked.*

In addition to the ranks listed on the next page, each service has ratings such as *machinist, radarman, torpedoman,* etc., that are job descriptions. Do not use any of these designations as a title on first reference. If one is used before a name in a subsequent reference, do not capitalize or abbreviate it.

Moreover, each service branch has its own systems of abbreviating officer and enlisted ranks — e.g., COL for colonel in the Army, CMDR for Navy commander — that vary widely from AP style. However, the Department of Defense uses AP's military titles in news releases because the abbreviations are easily understood.

ABBREVIATIONS: The abbreviations, with the highest ranks listed first:

MILITARY TITLES

Rank	Usage before a name

ARMY

Commissioned Officers

general	Gen.
lieutenant general	Lt. Gen.
major general	Maj. Gen.
brigadier general	Brig. Gen.
colonel	Col.
lieutenant colonel	Lt. Col.
major	Maj.
captain	Capt.
first lieutenant	1st Lt.
second lieutenant	2nd Lt.

Warrant Officers

chief warrant officer five (CW5)	Chief Warrant Officer 5
chief warrant officer four (CW4)	Chief Warrant Officer 4
chief warrant officer three (CW3)	Chief Warrant Officer 3
chief warrant officer two (CW2)	Chief Warrant Officer 2
warrant officer (WO1)	Warrant Officer

Enlisted Personnel

sergeant major of the Army	Sgt. Maj. of the Army
command sergeant major	Command Sgt. Maj.
sergeant major	Sgt. Maj.
first sergeant	1st Sgt.

master sergeant	Master Sgt.
sergeant first class	Sgt. 1st Class
staff sergeant	Staff Sgt.
sergeant	Sgt.
corporal	Cpl.
specialist	Spc.
private first class	Pfc.
private	Pvt.

NAVY, COAST GUARD

Commissioned Officers

admiral	Adm.
vice admiral	Vice Adm.
rear admiral upper half	Rear Adm.
rear admiral lower half	Rear Adm.
captain	Capt.
commander	Cmdr.
lieutenant commander	Lt. Cmdr.
lieutenant	Lt.
lieutenant junior grade	Lt. j.g.
ensign	Ensign

Warrant Officers

| chief warrant officer | Chief Warrant Officer |

Enlisted Personnel

master chief petty officer of the Navy	Master Chief Petty Officer of of the Navy
master chief petty officer	Master Chief Petty Officer
senior chief petty officer	Senior Chief Petty Officer
chief petty officer	Chief Petty Officer
petty officer first class	Petty Officer 1st Class
petty officer second class	Petty Officer 2nd Class
petty officer third class	Petty Officer 3rd Class
seaman	Seaman
seaman apprentice	Seaman Apprentice
seaman recruit	Seaman Recruit

MARINE CORPS

Ranks and abbreviations for commissioned officers are the same as those in the Army. Warrant officer ratings follow the same system used in the Navy. There are no specialist ratings.

Others

sergeant major of the Marine Corps	Sgt. Maj. of the Marine Corps
sergeant major	Sgt. Maj.
master gunnery sergeant	Master Gunnery Sgt.
first sergeant	1st Sgt.
master sergeant	Master Sgt.
gunnery sergeant	Gunnery Sgt.
staff sergeant	Staff Sgt.
sergeant	Sgt.
corporal	Cpl.
lance corporal	Lance Cpl.
private first class	Pfc.
private	Pvt.

AIR FORCE

Ranks and abbreviations for commissioned officers are the same as those in the Army.

Enlisted Designations

chief master sergeant of the Air Force	Chief Master Sgt. of the Air Force
chief master sergeant	Chief Master Sgt.
senior master sergeant	Senior Master Sgt.
master sergeant	Master Sgt.
technical sergeant	Tech. Sgt.
staff sergeant	Staff Sgt.
senior airman	Senior Airman
airman first class	Airman 1st Class
airman	Airman
airman basic	Airman

PLURALS: Add *s* to the principal element in the title: *Majs. John Jones and Robert Smith; Maj. Gens. John Jones and Robert Smith; Spcs. John Jones and Robert Smith.*

RETIRED OFFICERS: A military rank may be used in first reference before the name of an officer who has retired if it is relevant to a story. Do not, however, use the military abbreviation *Ret.*

Instead, use *retired* just as *former* would be used before the title of a civilian: *They invited retired Army Gen. John Smith.*

FIREFIGHTERS, POLICE OFFICERS: Use the abbreviations listed here when a military-style title is used before the name of a firefighter or police officer outside a direct quotation. Add *police* or *fire* before the title if needed for clarity: *police Sgt. William Smith, fire Capt. David Jones.*

Spell out titles such as *detective* that are not used in the armed forces.

military units Use Arabic figures and capitalize the key words when linked with the figures: *1st Infantry Division (or the 1st Division), 5th Battalion, 395th Field Artillery, 7th Fleet.*

But: *the division, the battalion, the artillery, the fleet.*

See **numerals**.

millennium

milli- A prefix denoting one-thousandth of a unit. Move the decimal three places to the left in converting to the basic unit: 1,567.5 millimeters equals 1.5675 meters.

milligram One-thousandth of a gram.

Equal to approximately one-twenty-eight-thousandth of an ounce.

To convert to ounces, multiply by 0.000035 (140 milligrams x 0.000035 equals 0.0049 ounce).

See **metric system**.

milliliter One-thousandth of a liter.

Equal to approximately one-fifth of a teaspoon.

Thirty milliliters equals 1 fluid ounce.

To convert to teaspoons, multiply by 0.2 (5 milliliters x 0.2 equals 1 teaspoon).

See **liter** and **metric system**.

millimeter One-thousandth of a meter.

It takes 10 millimeters to make a centimeter.

To convert to inches, multiply by 0.04 (5 millimeters x 0.04 is 0.2 of an inch).

May be abbreviated as *mm* when used with a numeral in first or subsequent references to film or weapons: *35 mm film, 105 mm artillery piece.* (Note space after numeral.)

See **meter**; **metric system**; and **inch**.

millions, billions, trillions Use figures with *million, billion* or *trillion* in all except casual uses: *I'd like to make a billion dollars.* But: *The nation has 1 million citizens. I need $7 billion. The government ran a deficit of more than $1 trillion.*

Do not go beyond two decimal places. *7.51 million people, $256 billion, 7,542,500 people, $2,565,750,000.* Decimals are preferred where practical: *1.5 million.* Not: *1 1/2 million.*

Do not mix *millions* and *billions* in the same figure: *2.6 billion.* Not: *2 billion 600 million.*

Do not drop the word *million* or *billion* in the first figure of a range: *He is worth from $2 million to $4 million.* Not: *$2 to $4 million,* unless you really mean $2.

Note that a hyphen is not used to join the figures and the word *million* or *billion,* even in this type of phrase: *The president submitted a $300 billion budget.*

In headlines, abbreviate only *millions, billions: $5M lawsuit, $17.4B trade deficit*

See **numerals**.

Milwaukee The city in Wisconsin stands alone in datelines.

mindset

mini- The rules in **prefixes** apply, but in general, no hyphen. Some examples:

miniseries	miniskirt
minivan	

minimally conscious state In this condition, the eyes are open, but the patient shows only minimal and intermittent signs of awareness of self and environment and responds only inconsistently when asked to gesture, move or speak. At times, the patient may be able to reach for objects, indicate yes or no and follow objects with the eyes, but a given patient may not be able to do all these things.

See **coma** and **vegetative state**.

minister It is not a formal title in most religions, with exceptions such as the Nation of Islam, and is not capitalized. Where it is a formal title, it should be capitalized before the name: *Minister John Jones*.

See **religious titles** and the entry for an individual's denomination in the **Religion** chapter.

ministry See **governmental bodies**.

Minneapolis The city in Minnesota stands alone in datelines.

Minnesota Abbreviate *Minn.* in datelines only; spell out in stories. Postal code: *MN*
See **state names**.

minority leader Treat the same as *majority leader*. See that entry and **legislative titles**.

minuscule Not miniscule.

minus sign Use a hyphen, not a dash, but use the word *minus* if there is any danger of confusion.

Use a word, not a minus sign, to indicate temperatures below zero: *minus 10* or *5 below zero*.

MIRV, MIRVs Acceptable on first reference for *multiple independently targetable re-entry vehicle(s)*.

Explain in the text that a *MIRV* is an intercontinental ballistic missile with several warheads, each of which can be directed to a different target.

misdemeanor See **felony, misdemeanor**.

mishap A minor misfortune. People are not killed in *mishaps*.

Miss See **courtesy titles**.

missile names Use Arabic figures and capitalize the proper name but not the word *missile*: *Pershing 2 missile*.

See **ABM; ICBM; MIRV;** and **SAM**.

Mississippi Abbreviate *Miss.* in datelines only; spell out in stories. Postal code: *MS*
See **state names**.

Missouri Abbreviate *Mo.* in datelines only; spell out in stories. Postal code: *MO*
See **state names**.

mix-up (n. and adj.) **mix up** (v.)

mock-up (n.)

model numbers See **serial numbers**.

modem Acceptable in all references for the acronym formed from *modulator* and *demodulator*.

modified tweet A tweet amended before sharing with one's own followers uses the abbreviation *MT*.

mom Uppercase only when the noun substitutes for a name as a term of address: *Hi, Mom!*

Monaco After the Vatican, the world's smallest state.

The *Monaco* section stands alone in datelines. The other two sections, *La Condamine* and *Monte Carlo*, are followed by *Monaco*:
MONTE CARLO, Monaco (AP) —

monetary See the **fiscal, monetary** entry.

monetary units See **cents**; **dollars**; and **pounds**.

moneymaker

Montana Abbreviate *Mont.* in datelines only; spell out in stories. Postal code: *MT*
See **state names**.

Montessori method After Maria Montessori, a system of training young children. It emphasizes training of the senses and guidance to encourage self-education.

monthlong, monthslong

months Capitalize the names of months in all uses. When a month is used with a specific date, abbreviate only *Jan., Feb., Aug., Sept., Oct., Nov.* and *Dec.* Spell out when using alone, or with a year alone.
When a phrase lists only a month and a year, do not separate the year with commas. When a phrase refers to a month, day and year, set off the year with commas.
EXAMPLES: *January 1972 was a cold month. Jan. 2 was the coldest day of the month. His birthday is May 8. Feb. 14, 1987, was the target date. She testified that it was Friday, Dec. 3, when the accident occurred.*
In tabular material, use these three-letter forms without a period: *Jan, Feb, Mar, Apr, May, Jun, Jul, Aug, Sep, Oct, Nov, Dec.*
See **dates** and **years**.

Montreal The city in Canada stands alone in datelines.

monuments Capitalize the popular names of monuments and similar public attractions: *Lincoln Memorial, Statue of Liberty, Washington Monument, Leaning Tower of Pisa,* etc.

moon Lowercase. See **heavenly bodies**.

moped

mop-up (n. and adj.) **mop up** (v.)

moral obligation bond See **loan terminology**.

more than, over Acceptable in all uses to indicate greater numerical value. *Salaries went up more than $20 a week. Salaries went up over $20 a week.* See **over**.

Morgan Stanley Headquarters is in New York.

Mormon church Acceptable in references to *The Church of Jesus Christ of Latter-day Saints*, but the official name is preferred in first reference in a story dealing primarily with church activities.
See **Church of Jesus Christ of Latter-day Saints, The** in the **Religion** chapter.

mortgage A loan secured by property. The contract between the borrower and the lender gives the lender the right to take possession and resell the property if the borrower defaults. See **adjustable-rate mortgage** and **balloon mortgage**.

mortgage-backed security A bond backed by home or commercial mortgage payments. These provide income from payments of the underlying mortgages.

Moscow The city in Russia stands alone in datelines.

mosquito, mosquitoes

Mother's Day The second Sunday in May.

mother-in-law, mothers-in-law

Mother Nature

motor See the **engine, motor** entry.

mount Spell out in all uses, including the names of communities and of mountains: *Mount Clemens, Mich.*; *Mount Everest.*

mountains Capitalize as part of a proper name: *Appalachian Mountains, Ozark Mountains, Rocky Mountains.*
Or simply: *the Appalachians, the Ozarks, the Rockies.*

Mountain Standard Time (MST), Mountain Daylight Time (MDT) See **time zones**.

Mountain States As defined by the U.S. Census Bureau, the eight are Arizona, Colorado, Idaho, Montana, Nevada, New Mexico, Utah and Wyoming.

mouse, mice Use *mice* as the plural form of hand-held computer-input devices.

moviegoer

movie ratings The ratings used by the Motion Picture Association of America are:
G — General audiences. All ages admitted.
PG — Parental guidance suggested. Some material may not be suitable for children.
PG-13 — Special *parental guidance* strongly suggested for children under 13. Some material may be inappropriate for young children.
R — Restricted. Under 17 requires accompanying parent or adult guardian.
NC-17 — No one under 17 admitted.
When the ratings are used in news stories or reviews, use these forms as appropriate: *the movie has an R rating, an R-rated movie, the movie is R-rated.*

movie studios Major U.S. movie studios and production companies are:
Columbia Pictures, owned by Sony Corp.
Dimension Films, owned by The Weinstein Co.
Disney, owned by The Walt Disney Co.
DreamWorks SKG Inc., owned by Steven Spielberg, Stacey Snider and Reliance Big Entertainment
DreamWorks Animation SKG Inc.
Focus Features, a unit of Universal Pictures, part of Comcast Corp.'s NBCUniversal
Fox Searchlight, owned by Twenty-First Century Fox Inc.
IFC Films, owned by AMC Networks Inc.
Lionsgate, owned by Lions Gate Entertainment Corp. (the brand Lionsgate is one word, the corporate name is two)
Lucasfilm, owned by The Walt Disney Co.
Marvel Entertainment, owned by The Walt Disney Co.
Metro-Goldwyn-Mayer and United Artists, owned by MGM Holdings Inc., which is owned by a group of former creditors including Highland Capital, Anchorage Advisors.
Miramax, owned by Filmyard Holdings LLC, whose investors

include Ron Tutor, Colony Capital LLC, Tom Barrack and Qatar Holding LLC.

New Line Cinema, a brand of Time Warner Inc.'s Warner Bros.

Paramount Pictures, owned by Viacom Inc.

Pixar Animation Studios, owned by The Walt Disney Co.

Relativity Media LLC

Rogue Pictures, a unit of Relativity Media LLC

Screen Gems, owned by Sony Corp.

Sony Pictures Classics, owned by Sony Corp.

Summit Entertainment LLC, owned by Lions Gate Entertainment Corp.

Touchstone, owned by The Walt Disney Co.

TriStar Pictures, owned by Sony Corp.

Twentieth Century Fox, owned by Twenty-First Century Fox Inc.

Universal Pictures, owned by Comcast Corp.'s NBCUniversal

Warner Bros., owned by Time Warner Inc.

The Weinstein Co.

movie titles See **composition titles**.

MPEG-2 An international standard for digital video compression and decompression. *MPEG* is an acronym for *Moving Picture Experts Group*.

mpg Acceptable in all references for *miles per gallon*.

mph Acceptable in all references for *miles per hour* or *miles an hour*.

MP3 A popular audio compression format on the Internet.

MRI Magnetic resonance imaging, a noninvasive diagnostic procedure used to render images of the inside of an object. It is primarily used in medical imaging to demonstrate pathological or other physiological alterations of living tissues. *MRI* is acceptable on first reference and in all uses.

Mr., Mrs. See **courtesy titles**.

MRSA Abbreviation for *methicillin-resistant Staphylococcus aureus*. *MRSA* is acceptable on first reference but include full name in story.

Ms. This is the spelling and punctuation for all uses of the courtesy title, including direct quotations.

There is no plural. If several women who prefer *Ms.* must be listed in a series, repeat *Ms.* before each name.

See **courtesy titles** for guidelines on when to use *Ms.*

Muhammad The chief prophet and central figure of the Islamic religion, *the Prophet Muhammad*. Use other spellings only if preferred by a specific person for his own name or in a title or the name of an organization. Capitalize *Prophet* before a name.

mujahedeen Lowercase when using the Arabic for *holy warriors*; uppercase if it is part of the name of a group. The Iranian opposition group is *Mujahedeen-e-Khalq*. The singular for *holy warrior* is *mujahed*.

mullah An Islamic leader or teacher, often a general title of respect for a learned man.

multi- The rules in prefixes apply, but in general, no hyphen. Some examples:

multicolored	multimillion
multilateral	multimillionaire

Mumbai India's largest city, formerly known as Bombay.

Munich The city in Germany stands alone in datelines.

municipal bond See **loan terminology**.

murder See **homicide, murder, manslaughter**.

murderer See **assassin, killer, murderer**.

Murphy's law The law is: *If something can go wrong, it will.*

music Capitalize, but do not use quotation marks, on descriptive titles for orchestral works: *Bach's Suite No. 1 for Orchestra; Beethoven's Serenade for Flute, Violin and Viola.* If the instrumentation is not part of the title but is added for explanatory purposes, the names of the instruments are lowercased: *Mozart's Sinfonia Concertante in E flat major* (the common title) *for violin and viola.* If in doubt, lowercase the names of the instruments.

Use quotation marks for nonmusical terms in a title: *Beethoven's "Eroica" Symphony.* If the work has a special full title, all of it is quoted: *"Symphonie Fantastique," "Rhapsody in Blue."*

In subsequent references, lowercase *symphony, concerto,* etc.

See **composition titles**.

music companies Major U.S. music companies:

Astralwerks, owned by Universal Music Group, a subsidiary of Vivendi SA

Atlantic Records Group, which includes Atlantic Records, Atlantic Nashville, Elektra and Roadrunner Records, owned by Warner Music Group Corp.

Blue Note, owned by Universal Music Group, a subsidiary of Vivendi SA

Capitol Music Group, which includes Capitol Records, Virgin Records, Astralwerks and others, owned by Universal Music Group, a subsidiary of Vivendi SA

Columbia Records, Columbia Nashville and Sony Music Nashville, owned by Sony Music Entertainment Inc., a Sony Corp. subsidiary

Decca Records and Decca Classics, owned by Universal Music Group, a subsidiary of Vivendi SA

EMI, bought by Universal Music Group, a subsidiary of Vivendi SA, in 2012. Parts of it were sold off.

Elektra Records, owned by Warner Music Group

Epic Records, owned by Sony Music Entertainment Inc., a Sony Corp. subsidiary

Interscope Geffen A&M, which includes Interscope Records, Geffen Records and A&M Records. Owned by Universal Music Group, a subsidiary of Vivendi SA

Island Records, owned by Universal Music Group, a subsidiary of Vivendi SA

LaFace Records, owned by Sony Music Entertainment Inc., a Sony Corp. subsidiary

Legacy Recordings, owned by Sony Music Entertainment Inc., a Sony Corp. subsidiary

Lost Highway Records, owned by Universal Music Group, a subsidiary of Vivendi SA

Machete Music, owned by Universal Music Group, a subsidiary of Vivendi SA

Manhattan Records, owned by Universal Music Group, a subsidiary of Vivendi SA

Maverick Records, owned by Warner Music Group Corp.

Mercury Records, owned by Universal Music Group, a subsidiary of Vivendi SA

Motown Records, including Universal Motown and Classic Motown, owned by Universal Music Group, a subsidiary of Vivendi SA

Mute Records, an independent record label formerly owned by Universal Music Group

Nonesuch Records, owned by Warner Music Group Corp.

Parlophone, owned by Warner Music Group

Provident Label Group, owned by Sony Music Entertainment Inc., a Sony Corp. subsidiary

RCA Records and RCA Records Label Nashville, owned by Sony Music Entertainment Inc., a Sony Corp. subsidiary

RCA Inspiration Music Group (formerly Verity Gospel Music Group), owned by Sony Music Entertainment Inc., a Sony Corp. subsidiary

Reprise Records, owned by Warner Music Group Corp.

Rhino Entertainment, which includes Rhino Records, owned by Warner Music Group Corp.

Roc Nation, a joint venture between rapper Jay-Z and Live Nation Entertainment Inc.

Show Dog/Universal Music, owned by Universal Music Group, a subsidiary of Vivendi SA

Sire Records, owned by Warner Music Group Corp.

Sony Masterworks, owned by Sony Music Entertainment Inc., a Sony Corp. subsidiary

Sony Music Latin, owned by Sony Music Entertainment Inc., a Sony Corp. subsidiary

Universal Music Group Nashville, which includes MCA Nashville Records, Mercury Nashville Records and Lost Highway Records, owned by Universal Music Group, a subsidiary of Vivendi SA

Universal Motown Records Group, which includes Universal Motown Records and Universal Republic Records. Owned by Universal Music Group, a subsidiary of Vivendi SA

Universal Music Classical, owned by Universal Music Group, a subsidiary of Vivendi SA

Universal Music Enterprises, which includes UMe Records and Verve Records. Owned by Universal Music Group, a subsidiary of Vivendi SA

Universal Music Latin Entertainment, owned by Universal Music Group, a subsidiary of Vivendi SA

Universal Republic Records, owned by Universal Music Group, a subsidiary of Vivendi SA

Virgin Records, owned by Universal Music Group, a subsidiary of Vivendi SA

Warner Bros. Records, owned by Warner Music Group Corp.

Warner Nashville, owned by Warner Music Group Corp.

musket See **weapons**.

Muslim Brotherhood Pan-Arab Islamist political movement.

Muzak A trademark for a type of recorded background music.

Myanmar Use this name for the country (formerly *Burma*). Use *Myanmar's people* or *people of Myanmar* for the inhabitants. Use *Myanmar* for the country's dominant language.

myriad (adj.) Note word is not followed by *of*: *The myriad books in the library.*

NAACP Acceptable in all references for the *National Association for the Advancement of Colored People.* Define as the nation's oldest civil rights organization. Headquarters is in Baltimore.

naive

names In general, use only last names on second reference, unless an individual requests otherwise for a legitimate reason. For example, a public name rather than a real name may be used for a political dissident, or a *nom de guerre* for a rebel leader, if the person's safety is an issue. See **Arabic names, Chinese names, Korean names, Russian names** and **Spanish names**.

When it is necessary to distinguish between two people who use the same last name, as in married couples or brothers and sisters, generally use the first and last name. See **courtesy titles**.

In stories involving juveniles, generally refer to them on second reference by surname if they are 16 or older and by first name if they are 15 or younger. Exceptions would be if they are involved in serious crimes or are athletes or entertainers.

nano- A prefix denoting one-billionth of a unit. Move the decimal point nine places to the left in converting to the basic unit: 2,999,888,777.5 nanoseconds equals 2.9998887775 seconds.

narrow-minded

Nasdaq The nation's largest all-electronic stock market and a direct competitor to the New York Stock Exchange. Formerly an acronym, it is now a proper name. Parent company is Nasdaq OMX Group, Inc.

national See **citizen, resident, subject, national, native**.

National Aeronautics and Space Administration *NASA* is acceptable in all references.

national anthem Lowercase. But: *"The Star-Spangled Banner."*

National Broadcasting Co. See **NBC**.

National Education Association *NEA* is acceptable on second reference.
Headquarters is in Washington.

National FFA Organization Formerly the Future Farmers of America. *FFA* is acceptable on second reference.
Headquarters is in Alexandria, Virginia.

National Governors Association Represents the governors of the 50 states and five territories.
Its office is in Washington.

National Guard Capitalize when referring to U.S. or state-level forces, or foreign forces when that is the formal name: *the National Guard, the Guard, the Iowa National Guard, Iowa's National Guard, National Guard troops, the Iraqi National Guard*. On second reference, *the guard*.

When referring to an individual in a National Guard unit, use National Guardsman: *He is a National Guardsman*.

Lowercase *guardsman* when it stands alone.

See **military titles**.

National Hurricane Center
See **weather terms**.

National Institutes of Health
This agency within the Department of Health and Human Services is the principal biomedical research arm of the federal government.

Its institutes are: National Cancer Institute; National Eye Institute; National Heart, Lung and Blood Institute; National Human Genome Research Institute; National Institute on Aging; National Institute on Alcohol Abuse and Alcoholism; National Institute of Allergy and Infectious Diseases; National Institute of Arthritis and Musculoskeletal and Skin Diseases; National Institute of Biomedical Imaging and Bioengineering; Eunice Kennedy Shriver National Institute of Child Health and Human Development; National Institute on Drug Abuse; National Institute on Deafness and Other Communication Disorders; National Institute of Diabetes and Digestive and Kidney Diseases; National Institute of Dental and Craniofacial Research; National Institute of Environmental Health Sciences; National Institute of General Medical Sciences; National Institute of Mental Health; National Institute of Minor-

ity Health and Health Disparities; National Institute of Neurological Disorders and Stroke; and National Institute of Nursing Research; and National Library of Medicine.

Its centers are: Center for Information Technology; Center for Scientific Review; Fogarty International Center; National Center for Complementary and Integrative Health; National Center for Advancing Translational Sciences; and NIH Clinical Center.

All are in Bethesda, Maryland, except the National Institute of Environmental Health Sciences, which is in Research Triangle Park, North Carolina.

nationalist Lowercase when referring to a partisan of a country. Capitalize only when referring to alignment with a political party for which this is the proper name.

See **political parties and philosophies**.

Nationalist China See **China**.

nationalities and races Capitalize the proper names of nationalities, peoples, races, tribes, etc.: *Arab, Arabic, African, American, Caucasian, Cherokee, Chinese* (both singular and plural), *Eskimo* (plural *Eskimos*) or *Inuit, French Canadian, Japanese* (singular and plural), *Jew, Jewish, Nordic, Sioux, Swede*, etc.

See **race** for guidelines on when racial identification is pertinent in a story.

Do not use a derogatory term except in extremely rare circumstances — when it is crucial to the story or the understanding of a news event. Flag the contents in an editor's note.

National Labor Relations Board *NLRB* is acceptable on second reference.

National League of Cities Its members include the governments of about 2,000 U.S. cities and 48 state municipal leagues.

It is separate from the U.S. Conference of Mayors, whose membership is limited to mayors of cities with 30,000 or more residents.

The office is in Washington.

National Newspaper Association A newspaper association representing community newspapers and their owners, publishers and editors. *NNA* is acceptable on second reference.

Headquarters is at the Missouri School of Journalism, Columbia, Missouri.

National Organization for Women Not *of*. *NOW* is acceptable on second reference.

Headquarters is in Washington.

National Park Service A bureau of the Interior Department, it manages the 391 units of the National Park System, which includes 58 national parks as well as monuments, battlefields, historic sites and seashores, and the White House. It was created in 1916, although the first national park, Yellowstone, was established much earlier in 1872. The National Park Service also helps administer dozens of affiliated sites, the National Register of Historic Places, National Heritage Areas, National Wild and Scenic Rivers, National Historic Landmarks, and National Trails. On second reference, *Park Service*.

National Rifle Association *NRA* is acceptable on second reference.

Headquarters is in Washington.

National Security Agency A U.S. intelligence agency that collects and analyzes signals from foreign and domestic sources for the purpose of intelligence and counterintelligence. It also defends U.S. government signals and codes from intrusion. The NSA is based in Fort Meade, Maryland. *NSA* is acceptable on second reference.

National Weather Service Use *National Weather Service* on first reference and *weather service* on subsequent references.

See **weather terms**.

nationwide

native See **citizen, resident, subject, national, native**.

Native American Acceptable for those in the U.S. Follow the person's preference. Where possible, be precise and use the name of the tribe: *He is a Navajo commissioner.* Such words or terms as *wampum, warpath, powwow, teepee, brave, squaw,* etc., can be disparaging and offensive.

First Nation is the preferred term for native tribes in Canada.

See **Indians, nationalities and races, race** and **tribe, tribal**.

Nativity scene Only the first word is capitalized.

NATO Acceptable in all references for the *North Atlantic Treaty Organization*.

Naugahyde A trademark for a brand of simulated leather.

nautical mile It equals 1 minute of arc of a great circle of the Earth or 6,076.11549 feet, or 1,852 meters. To convert to approximate statute miles (5,280 feet), multiply the number of nautical miles by 1.15.

See **knot**.

naval, navel Use *naval* in copy pertaining to a navy.

A *navel* is a bellybutton.

A *navel orange* is a seedless orange, so named because it has a small depression, like a navel.

naval station Capitalize only as part of a proper name: *Norfolk Naval Station*.

navy Capitalize when referring to U.S. forces: *the U.S. Navy, the Navy, Navy policy*. Do not use the abbreviation *USN*.

Lowercase when referring to the naval forces of other nations: *the British navy*.

This approach has been adopted for consistency, because many foreign nations do not use *navy* as the proper name.

See **military academies** and **military titles**.

Nazi, Nazism Derived from the German for the National Socialist German Workers' Party, the fascist political party founded in 1919 and abolished in 1945. Under Adolf Hitler, it seized control of Germany in 1933.

See **political parties and philosophies**.

NBC Acceptable in all references to the *National Broadcasting Co.* NBC is part of NBCUniversal, which is controlled by Comcast Corp.

nearsighted When used in a medical sense, it means an individual can see well at close range but has difficulty seeing objects at a distance.

Nebraska Abbreviate *Neb.* in datelines only; spell out in stories. Postal code: *NE*

See **state names**.

negligee

neither ... nor See **either ... or, neither ... nor**.

Nestle Headquarters is in Vevey, Switzerland.

Netherlands In datelines, give the name of the community followed by *Netherlands*:

MAASTRICHT, *Netherlands* (AP) —

In stories: *the Netherlands* or *Netherlands* as the construction of a sentence dictates.

Netherlands Antilles In datelines, give the name of the community followed by *Netherlands Antilles*. Do not abbreviate.

Identify an individual island, if needed, in the text.

net income, net profit See **profit terminology**.

net neutrality The idea that everyone with an Internet connection should have equal access to video, music, email, photos, social networks, maps and other content, with some exceptions that allow Internet service providers to block spam and child pornography. U.S. Internet service providers typically oppose net neutrality, arguing it will discourage them from investing in network upgrades. They want the ability to charge Netflix and other content providers to access a fast lane to reach consumers.

Nevada Abbreviate *Nev.* in datelines only; spell out in stories. Postal code: *NV*

See **state names**.

never-ending

New Brunswick One of the three Maritime Provinces of Canada. Do not abbreviate.
See **datelines**.

New Delhi The city in India stands alone in datelines.

New England Connecticut, Maine, Massachusetts, New Hampshire, Rhode Island and Vermont.

Newfoundland This Canadian province, officially renamed Newfoundland and Labrador in 2001, comprises the island of Newfoundland and the mainland section of Labrador. Do not abbreviate.

In datelines, use Newfoundland after the names of all cities and towns. Specify in the text whether the community is on the island or in Labrador.
See **datelines**.

New Hampshire Abbreviate *N.H.* in datelines only; spell out in stories. Postal code: *NH*
See **state names**.

New Jersey Abbreviate *N.J.* in datelines only; spell out in stories. Postal code: *NJ*
See **state names**.

New Mexico Abbreviate *N.M.* in datelines only; spell out in stories. Postal code: *NM*
See **state names**.

New Orleans The city in Louisiana stands alone in datelines.

News Corp. Publishing conglomerate controlled by Rupert Murdoch. The company includes newspapers, book publishing and information services located primarily in the United States, United Kingdom and Australia that remained after the company split off its enter-

tainment businesses into a separate company called Twenty-First Century Fox Inc. in June 2013. Properties include the *New York Post*; *Dow Jones & Co.*, publisher of *The Wall Street Journal* and *Barron's* magazine. The company also operates information service Dow Jones Newswires and owns book publisher *HarperCollins*. For stock market watchers, it provides the Dow Jones industrial average, the Dow Jones transportation average, the Dow Jones utility average, and the Dow Jones composite average. Headquarters is in New York.

Newspaper Association of America Formerly the American Newspaper Publishers Association. *NAA* is acceptable in second reference. Also *the newspaper association, the association*.

Headquarters is in Arlington, Virginia.

Newspaper Guild-Communications Workers of America, The Formerly the American Newspaper Guild, it is a union for newspaper and news service employees, generally those in the news and business departments.

On second reference: *the Guild.* Headquarters is in Washington.

The News Media Guild, formerly the Wire Service Guild, is the local representing employees of The Associated Press.

newspaper names Capitalize *the* in a newspaper's name if that is the way the publication prefers to be known. Do not place name in quotes.

Lowercase *the* before newspaper names if a story mentions several papers, some of which use *the* as part of the name and some of which do not.

Where location is needed but is not part of the official name, use parentheses: *The Huntsville (Alabama) Times*.

newspapers Some prominent U.S. newspapers, with owners, in alphabetical order. Note some capitalize *The* in their names.

Chicago Sun-Times, Sun-Times Media LLC

Chicago Tribune, Tribune Publishing Co.

Daily News, New York, real estate billionaire Mortimer B. Zuckerman

The Dallas Morning News, A.H. Belo Corp.

The Denver Post, Digital First Media

Houston Chronicle, Hearst Corp.

Los Angeles Times, Tribune Publishing Co.

New York Post, News Corp.

The New York Times, The New York Times Co.

Newsday, Long Island, N.Y., Cablevision Systems Corp.

The Orange County (Calif.) Register, Freedom Communications Inc.

The Philadelphia Inquirer, Interstate General Media

The Plain Dealer, Cleveland, Advance Publications Inc.

San Jose (Calif.) Mercury News, Digital First Media

Star Tribune, Minneapolis, The Star Tribune Media Co.

The Star-Ledger, Newark, N.J., Advance Publications Inc.

Tampa Bay (Fla.) Times, The Poynter Institute for Media Studies

USA Today, Gannett Co.

The Wall Street Journal, Dow Jones & Co., part of News Corp.

The Washington Post, owned by Jeff Bezos' WP Express Publications LLC, a division of Nash Holdings LLC

It is unnecessary to provide state identification for a newspaper cited in the body of a story if the newspaper is in the same state as the dateline. For example, a story datelined Newport, R.I., would reference the *Providence Journal*, not the *Providence (R.I.) Journal*.

However, the state should be included and spelled out in the body of undated stories or stories datelined in other states: Tampa (Florida) Tribune in a story with a Georgia dateline.

newsstand

New Testament See **Bible**.

New World The Western Hemisphere.

New Year's, New Year's Day, New Year's Eve But: *What will the new year bring?*

The federal legal holiday is observed on Friday if Jan. 1 falls on a Saturday, on Monday if it falls on a Sunday.

New York Abbreviate *N.Y.* in datelines only; spell out in stories. Postal code: *NY*

See **state names**.

New York City Use *NEW YORK* in datelines, not the name of an individual community or borough such as *Flushing* or *Queens*.

Identify the borough in the body of the story if pertinent.

New York Stock Exchange *NYSE* is acceptable on second reference. It is operated by NYSE Euronext, a subsidiary of IntercontinentalExchange Group Inc. IntercontinentalExchange, a publicly traded company, is headquartered in Atlanta. It acquired NYSE Euronext in 2013.

The New York Times Co. Owner of *The New York Times*. In

October 2013, the company sold off *The Boston Globe* and rebranded the *International Herald Tribune* as the *International New York Times.* Headquarters is in New York.

NGO *Nongovernmental organization.* Usually refers to a nonprofit, humanitarian organization. Use *NGO* sparingly and only on second reference.

nicknames A nickname should be used in place of a person's given name in stories only when it is the way the individual prefers to be known: *Jimmy Carter, Bill Clinton, Babe Ruth, Tiger Woods, Magic Johnson.*

When a nickname is inserted into the identification of an individual, use quotation marks: Sen. Henry M. "Scoop" Jackson, Paul "Bear" Bryant.

Capitalize without quotation marks such terms as *Sunshine State, the Old Dominion, Motown, the Magic City, Old Hickory, Old Glory, Galloping Ghost.* See **names**.

nightclub

nighttime

9/11 Acceptable in all references to describe the attacks in the United States on Sept. 11, 2001.

911 Acceptable for the U.S. emergency call number.

nitpicking

nitty-gritty

No. Use as the abbreviation for *number* in conjunction with a figure to indicate position or rank: *No. 1 man, No. 3 choice.*

Do not use in street addresses, with this exception: *No. 10 Downing St.,* the residence of Britain's prime minister.

Do not use in the names of schools: *Public School 19.*

See **numerals**.

Nobel Prize, Nobel Prizes
The five established under terms of the will of Alfred Nobel are: Nobel Peace Prize, Nobel Prize in chemistry, Nobel Prize in literature, Nobel Prize in physics, Nobel Prize in physiology or medicine. (Note the capitalization styles.)

The Nobel Memorial Prize in Economic Sciences (officially it is the cumbersome Bank of Sweden Prize in Economic Sciences in Memory of Alfred Nobel) is not a Nobel Prize in the same sense. The Central Bank of Sweden established it in 1968 as a memorial to Alfred Nobel. References to this prize should include the word *Memorial* to help make this distinction. Explain the status of the prize in the story when appropriate.

Nobel Prize award ceremonies are held on Dec. 10, the anniversary of Alfred Nobel's death in 1896. The award ceremony for peace is in Oslo and the other ceremonies are in Stockholm.

Capitalize *prize* in references that do not mention the category: *He is a Nobel Prize winner. She is a Nobel Prize-winning scientist.*

Lowercase *prize* when not linked with the word *Nobel: The peace prize was awarded Monday.*

nobility References to members of the nobility in nations that have a system of rank present special problems because nobles frequently are known by their titles rather than their given or family names. Their titles, in effect, become their names.

The guidelines here relate to Britain's nobility. Adapt them as appropriate to members of nobility in other nations.

Orders of rank among British nobility begin with the royal family. The term *royalty* is reserved for the families of living and deceased sovereigns.

Next, in descending order, are dukes, marquesses (also called marquises), earls, viscounts and barons. There are also life peers who are appointed to serve in the House of Lords and hold their titles only for their own lifetimes. On first reference to a life peer, use the person's ordinary name, e.g., *Margaret Thatcher* or *Jeffrey Archer*. Elsewhere, if relevant, explain that the person has been appointed to the House of Lords.

Occasionally the sovereign raises an individual to the nobility and makes the title inheritable by the person's heirs, but the practice is increasingly rare.

Sovereigns also confer honorary titles, which do not make an individual a member of the nobility. The principal designations, in descending order, are *baronet* and *knight*.

In general, the guidelines in **courtesy titles** and **titles** apply. However, honorary titles and titles of nobility are capitalized when they serve as an alternate name.

Some guidelines and examples:

ROYALTY: Capitalize *king, queen, prince* and *princess* when they are used directly before one or more names; lowercase when they stand alone:

Queen Elizabeth II, Queen Elizabeth II of the United Kingdom of Great Britain and Northern Ireland, the queen. Kings George and Edward. Queen Mother Elizabeth, the queen mother.

Also capitalize a longer form of the sovereign's title when its use is appropriate in a story or it is being quoted: *Her Majesty Queen Elizabeth.*

Use *Prince* or *Princess* before the names of a sovereign's children: *Princess Anne, the princess; Prince Charles.*

In references to the queen's husband, first reference should be *Prince Philip* (not *Duke of Edinburgh,* commonly used in Britain).

The male heir to the throne normally is designated *Prince of Wales,* and the title becomes, in common usage, an alternate name. Capitalize when used: *The queen invested her eldest son as Prince of Wales. Prince Charles is now the Prince of Wales. The prince is married. His wife, Camilla, is called the Duchess of Cornwall.*

Prince Charles' eldest son is Prince William. Prince William's wife, the former Kate Middleton, is the Duchess of Cambridge. Their son is Prince George.

DUKE: The full title — *Duke of Wellington,* for example — is an alternate name, capitalized in all uses. Lowercase *duke* when it stands alone.

The designation *Arthur, Duke of Wellington,* is appropriate in some cases, but never *Duke Arthur* or *Lord Arthur.*

The wife of a duke is a *duchess: the Duchess of Wellington, the duchess,* but never *Duchess Diana* or *Lady Diana.*

A duke normally also has a lesser title. It is commonly used for his eldest son if he has one. Use the courtesy titles *Lord* or *Lady* before the first names of a duke's children.

Some examples:

Lady Jane Wellesley, only daughter of the eighth Duke of Wellington, has been linked romantically with Prince Charles, heir to the British throne. The eldest of Lady Jane's four brothers is Arthur Charles, the Marquess Douro. The Wellingtons, whose family name is Wellesley, are not of royal blood. However, they rank among the nation's most famous aristocrats thanks to the first duke, the victor at Waterloo.

MARQUESS, MARQUIS, EARL, VISCOUNT, BARON: The full titles serve as alternate names and should be capitalized. Frequently, however, the holder of such a title is identified as a lord: *The Marquess of Bath*, for example, more commonly is known as *Lord Bath*.

Use *Lady* before the name of a woman married to a man who holds one of these titles. The wife of a marquess is a marchioness, the wife of a marquis is a marquise, the wife of an earl is a countess (earl is the British equivalent of count), the wife of a viscount is a viscountess and the wife of a baron is a baroness.

Use *Lord* or *Lady* before the first names of the children of a marquess.

Use *Lady* before the first name of an earl's daughter. *The Honorable* often appears before the names of sons of earls, viscounts and barons who do not have titles. Their names should stand alone in news stories, however.

The Honorable also appears frequently before the names of unmarried daughters of viscounts and barons. In news stories, however, use a full name on first reference.

Some examples:

Queen Elizabeth gave her sister's husband, Antony Armstrong-Jones, the title Earl of Snowdon. Their son, David, is the Viscount Linley. They also have a daughter, Lady Sarah Armstrong-Jones. Lord Snowdon, a photographer, was known as Antony Armstrong-Jones before he received his title.

BARONET, KNIGHT: *Sir John Smith* on first reference and *Smith* on second.

Do not use both an honorary title and a title of military rank or authority, such as *prime minister*, before a name.

Use *Lady* before the name of the wife of a baronet or knight.

For a woman who has received an honor in her own right, use *Dame* before her name: *Dame Margot Fonteyn* on first reference, *Fonteyn* on second.

noisome, noisy *Noisome* means offensive, noxious.

Noisy means clamorous.

Nokia Corp. Headquarters is in Espoo, Finland.

nolo contendere The literal meaning is, "I do not wish to contend." Terms such as *no contest* or *no-contest plea* are acceptable in all references.

When a defendant in a criminal case enters this plea, it means that he is not admitting guilt but is stating that he will offer no defense. The person is then subject to being judged guilty and punished as if he had pleaded guilty or had been convicted. The principal difference is that the defendant retains the option of denying the same charge in another legal proceeding.

no man's land

non- The rules of **prefixes** apply, but in general no hyphen when forming a compound that does not have special meaning and can be understood if *not* is used before the base word. Use a hyphen, however, before proper nouns or in awkward combinations, such as *non-nuclear*.

nonaligned nations A political rather than economic or geographic term used primarily during the Cold War. Although nonaligned nations do not belong to Western or Eastern military alliances or blocs, they may take positions on international issues. Hyphenate in formal name *Non-Aligned Movement*, a political group representing more than 120 developing nations.

Do not confuse *nonaligned* with *developing nations*, which refers to the economic developing nations of Africa, Asia and Latin America. Avoid use of the term Third World.

noncombat, noncombatant

none When used to mean *no one*, *not one* or *no amount of it*, none takes singular verbs and pronouns: *None of us is perfect. None of the seats was in its right place. None of the coffee was poured.*

When the sense is *none of them*, use plural verbs and pronouns: *None of the consultants agree on the same approach. None of the horses were in their stalls. None of the taxes have been paid.*

nonprofit

nonrestrictive clauses See essential clauses, nonessential clauses.

noon Do not put a 12 in front of it.

See **midnight** and **times**.

no one

Norfolk Southern Corp.
Freight railroad, with headquarters in Norfolk, Virginia.

norm See **average, mean, median, norm**.

North America See Western Hemisphere.

North Atlantic Treaty Organization *NATO* is acceptable in all references.

North Carolina Abbreviate *N.C.* in datelines only; spell out in stories. Postal code: *NC*
See **state names**.

North Dakota Abbreviate *N.D.* in datelines only; spell out in stories. Postal code: *ND*
See **state names**.

Northeast region As defined by the U.S. Census Bureau, the nine-state region is broken into two divisions — the *New England* states and the *Middle Atlantic* states.

Connecticut, Maine, Massachusetts, New Hampshire, Rhode Island and Vermont are the *New England* states.

New Jersey, New York and Pennsylvania are classified as the *Middle Atlantic* states.

See **Midwest region; South**; and **West** for the bureau's other regional breakdowns.

Northern Ireland Use *Northern Ireland* after the names of all communities in datelines.
See **datelines** and **United Kingdom**.

north, northern, northeast, northwest See **directions and regions**.

Northrop Grumman Corp.
Headquarters is in Falls Church, Virginia.

North Slope The portion of Alaska north of Brooks Range, a string of mountains extending across the northern part of the state.

North Warning System A system of long-range radar stations along the 70th parallel in North America. Previous system, known as the Distant Early Warning (DEW) line, was deactivated in 1985.

Northwest Territories A territorial section of Canada. Do not abbreviate. Use in datelines after the

names of all cities and towns in the territory.

See **Canada**.

note For use in a financial sense, see **loan terminology**.

nouns The abbreviation *n.* is used in this book to identify the spelling of the noun forms of words frequently misspelled.

Novartis AG Headquarters is in Basel, Switzerland.

Nova Scotia One of the three Maritime Provinces of Canada. Do not abbreviate.

See **datelines**.

Novocain A trademark for a drug used as a local anesthetic.

nowadays

NPR Acceptable in all references to National Public Radio. Producer and distributor of noncommercial news, talk and entertainment programming. Headquarters is in Washington, D.C.

Nuclear Non-Proliferation Treaty Global agreement intended to limit the spread of nuclear weapons. It provides civilian nuclear trade in exchange for a pledge from nations not to pursue nuclear weapons and for the United States and other nuclear weapons states to negotiate their nuclear disarmament.

Nuclear Regulatory Commission *NRC* is acceptable on second reference, but *the agency* or *the commission* is preferred.

nuclear terminology In reporting on nuclear energy, include the definitions of appropriate terms, especially those related to radiation.

core The part of a nuclear reactor that contains its fissionable fuel. In a reactor core, atoms of fuel, such as uranium, are split. This releases energy in the form of heat which, in turn, is used to boil water for steam. The steam powers a turbine, and the turbine drives a generator to produce electricity.

fission The splitting of the nucleus of an atom, releasing energy.

gray (Gy) The standard measure of radiation a material has absorbed. It has largely replaced the *rad*. One gray equals 100 rads. This measure does not consider biological effect of the radiation.

meltdown The worst possible nuclear accident in which the reactor core overheats to such a degree that the fuel melts. If the fuel penetrates its protective housing, radioactive materials will be released into the environment.

rad See **gray**.

radiation Invisible particles or waves given off by radioactive material, such as uranium. Radiation can damage or kill body cells, resulting in latent cancers, genetic damage or death.

rem See **sievert**.

roentgen The standard measure of X-ray exposure.

sievert (Sv) The standard measure of radiation absorbed in living tissue, adjusted for different kinds of radiation so that a single sievert of any kind of radiation produces the same biological effect. The sievert has largely replaced the rem. One *Sv* equals 100 rem. A *millisievert* (mSv) is a thousandth of a sievert; a millirem is a thousandth of a rem. On average, a resident of United States receives about 3 mSv, or 300 mrem, every year from natural sources.

uranium A metallic, radioactive element used as fuel in nuclear reactors.

numerals In general, spell out one through nine: *The Yankees finished second. He had nine months to go.*

Use figures for 10 or above and whenever preceding a unit of measure or referring to ages of people, animals, events or things. Also in all tabular matter, and in statistical and sequential forms.

Use figures for:

— Academic course numbers: *History 6, Philosophy 209.*

— Addresses: *210 Main St.* Spell out numbered streets nine and under: *5 Sixth Ave.; 3012 50th St.; No. 10 Downing St.* Use the abbreviations *Ave., Blvd.* and *St.* only with a numbered address: *1600 Pennsylvania Ave.* Spell them out and capitalize without a number: *Pennsylvania Avenue.*

See **addresses**.

— Ages: *a 6-year-old girl; an 8-year-old law; the 7-year-old house.* Use hyphens for ages expressed as adjectives before a noun or as substitutes for a noun. *A 5-year-old boy,* but *the boy is 5 years old. The boy, 5, has a sister, 10. The race is for 3-year-olds. The woman is in her 30s. 30-something,* but *Thirty-something* to start a sentence.

See **ages**.

— Planes, ships and spacecraft designations: *B-2 bomber, Queen Elizabeth 2, QE2, Apollo 9, Viking 2.* An exception: *Air Force One,* the president's plane. Use Roman numerals if they are part of the official designation: *Titan I, Titan II.*

See **aircraft names; boats, ships; spacecraft designations**.

— Centuries. Use figures for numbers 10 or higher: *21st century.* Spell out for numbers nine and lower: *fifth century.* (Note lowercase.) For proper names, follow the organization's usage: *20th Century Fox, Twentieth Century Fund.*

— Court decisions: *The Supreme Court ruled 5-4, a 5-4 decision.* The word *to* is not needed, except in quotations: *"The court ruled 5 to 4."*

— Court districts: *5th U.S. Circuit Court of Appeals.*

— Dates, years and decades: *Feb. 8, 2007, Class of '66, the 1950s.* For the Sept. 11, 2001, terrorist attacks, *9/11* is acceptable in all references. (Note comma to set off the year when the phrase refers to a month, date and year.)

— Decimals, percentages and fractions with numbers larger than 1: *7.2 magnitude quake, 3 1/2 laps, 3.7 percent interest, 4 percentage points.* Decimalization should not exceed two places in most text material. Exceptions: blood alcohol content, expressed in three decimals: as in *0.056,* and batting averages in baseball, as in *.324.* For amounts less than 1, precede the decimal with a zero: *The cost of living rose 0.03 percent.* Spell out fractions less than 1, using hyphens between the words: *two-thirds, four-fifths.* In quotations, use figures for fractions: *"He was 2 1/2 laps behind with four to go."*

See **decimal units; fractions; percent**.

— Dimensions, to indicate depth, height, length and width. Examples: *He is 5 feet 6 inches tall, the 5-foot-6 man* ("inch" is understood), *the 5-foot man, the basketball team signed a 7-footer. The car is 17 feet long, 6 feet wide and 5 feet high. The rug is 9 feet by 12 feet, the 9-by-12 rug. A 9-inch snowfall.* Exception: *two-by-four.* Spell out the noun, which refers to any length of untrimmed lumber approximately 2 inches thick by 4 inches wide.

See **dimensions**.

— Distances: *He walked 4 miles. He missed a 3-foot putt.*

— Golf clubs: *3-wood, 7-iron, 3-hybrid* (note hyphen).

— Highway designations: *Interstate 5, U.S. Highway 1, state Route 1A.* (Do not abbreviate *Route.* No hyphen between highway designation and number.)

See **highway designations**.

— Mathematical usage: *Multiply by 4, divide by 6. He added 2 and 2 but got 5.*

— Military ranks, used as titles with names, military terms and weapons: *Petty Officer 2nd Class Alan Markow, Spc. Alice Moreno, 1st Sgt. David Triplett, M16 rifle, 9 mm* (note space) *pistol, 6th Fleet.* In military ranks, spell out the figure when it is used after the name or without a name: *Smith was a second lieutenant. The goal is to make first sergeant.*

See **military units**.

— Millions, billions, trillions: Use a figure-word combination. *1 million people; $2 billion,* NOT *one million/two billion.* (Also note no hyphen linking numerals and the word million, billion or trillion.)

See **millions, billions, trillions**; **dollars**.

— Monetary units: *5 cents, $5 bill, 8 euros, 4 pounds.*

See **cents**.

— Odds, proportions and ratios: *9-1 longshot; 3 parts cement to 1 part water; a 1-4 chance,* but *one chance in three.*

See **betting odds**; **proportions**; **ratios**.

— Rank: *He was my No. 1 choice.* (Note abbreviation for "Number"). *Kentucky was ranked No. 3. The band had five Top 40 hits.*

— School grades. Use figures for grades 10 and above: *10th grade.* Spell out for first through ninth grades: *fourth grade, fifth-grader* (note hyphen).

— Sequential designations: *Page 1, Page 20A. They were out of sizes 4 and 5; magnitude 6 earthquake; Rooms 3 and 4; Chapter 2; line 1* but *first line; Act 3, Scene 4,* but *third act, fourth scene; Game 1,* but *best of seven.*

See **act numbers**; **chapters**; **earthquakes**; **line numbers**; **page numbers**; **scene numbers**.

— Political districts: *Ward 9, 9th Precinct, 3rd Congressional District.*

See **congressional districts**; **political divisions**.

— Recipes: *2 tablespoons of sugar to 1 cup of milk.*

See **recipes**.

— Speeds: *7 mph, winds of 5 to 10 mph, winds of 7 to 9 knots.*

— Sports scores, standings and standards: *The Dodgers defeated the Phillies 10-3* (No comma between the team and the score); in golf, *3 up,* but *a 3-up lead; led 3-2; a 6-1-2 record* (six wins, one loss, two ties); *par 3; 5 handicap, 5-under-par 67* but *he was 5 under par* (or *5 under,* with "par" understood). In narrative, spell out nine and under except for yard lines in football and individual and team statistical performances: *The ball was on the 5-yard line. Seventh hole.* In basketball, *3-point play* and *3-point shot.* In statistical performances, hyphenate as a modifier: *He completed 8 of 12 passes. He made 5 of 6* (shots is understood). *He was 5-for-12 passing. He had a 3-for-5 day. He was 3-for-5. He went 3-for-5* (batting, shooting, etc., is understood).

— Temperatures: Use figures, except zero. *It was 8 degrees below zero* or *minus 8. The temperature dropped from 38 to 8 in two hours.*

See **temperatures**.

— Times: Use figures for time of day except for noon and midnight: *1 p.m., 10:30 a.m., 5 o'clock, 8 hours, 30 minutes, 20 seconds, a winning time of 2:17:3* (2 hours, 17 minutes, 3 seconds). Spell out numbers less than 10 standing alone and in modifiers: *I'll be there in five minutes. He scored with two seconds left. An eight-hour day. The two-minute warning.*

See **times**; **time sequences**.

— Votes: *The bill was defeated by a vote of 6 to 4,* but *by a two-vote margin.*

Spell out:

— At the start of a sentence: *Forty years was a long time to wait.*

Fifteen to 20 cars were involved in the accident. The only exception is years: *1992 was a very good year.*

See **years**.

— In indefinite and casual uses: *Thanks a million. He walked a quarter of a mile. One at a time; a thousand clowns; one day we will know; an eleventh-hour decision; dollar store; a hundred dollars.*

— In fanciful usage or proper names: *Chicago Seven, Fab Four, Big Three automakers, Final Four, the Four Tops.*

— In formal language, rhetorical quotations and figures of speech: *"Fourscore and seven years ago ..." Twelve Apostles, Ten Commandments, high-five, Day One.*

— In fractions less than one that are not used as modifiers: *reduced by one-third, he made three-fourths of his shots.*

Roman Numerals

They may be used for wars and to establish personal sequence for people and animals: *World War I, Native Dancer II, King George V.* Also for certain legislative acts (*Title IX*). Otherwise, use sparingly. Except in formal reference, pro football Super Bowls should be identified by the year, rather than the Roman numerals: *1969 Super Bowl,* not *Super Bowl III.*

Ordinals

Numbers used to indicate order (first, second, 10th, 25th, etc.) are called ordinal numbers. Spell out first through ninth: *fourth grade, first base, the First Amendment, he was first in line.* Use figures starting with 10th.

Cardinal Numbers

Numbers used in counting or showing how many (2, 40, 627, etc.) are called cardinal numbers. The following separate entries provide additional guidance for cardinal numbers:

amendments to the Constitution
channel
court names
decades
election returns
fleet
formula
latitude and longitude
mile
parallels
proportions
serial numbers
telephone numbers
weights

Some other punctuation and usage examples:

— *3 ounces*

— *4-foot-long*

— *4-foot fence*

— *"The president's speech lasted 28 1/2 minutes,"* she said.

— *DC-10* but *747B*

— *the 1980s, the '80s*

— *the House voted 230-205* (fewer than 1,000 votes)

— *Jimmy Carter outpolled Gerald Ford 40,827,292 to 39,146,157* (more than 1,000 votes)

— *Carter outpolled Ford 10 votes to 2 votes in Little Junction* (to avoid confusion with ratio)

— *No. 3 choice,* but *Public School 3*

— *a pay increase of 12-15 percent.* Or: *a pay increase of between 12 and 15 percent*

But: *from $12 million to $14 million*

— *a ratio of 2-to-1, a 2-1 ratio*

— *1 in 4 voters*

— *seven houses 7 miles apart*

— *He walked 4 miles.*

— *minus 10, zero, 60 degrees* (spell out minus)

OTHER USES. For uses not covered by these listings, spell out whole numbers below 10, and use figures for 10 and above: *They had three sons and two daughters. They had a fleet of 10 station wagons and two buses.*

IN A SERIES. Apply the standard guidelines: *They had 10 dogs, six cats and 97 hamsters. They had four four-room houses, 10 three-room houses and 12 10-room houses.*

nuns See **sister**.

Nuremberg Use this spelling for the city in Germany, instead of Nuernberg, in keeping with widespread practice.

N-word Do not use this term or the racial slur it refers to, except in extremely rare circumstances — when it is crucial to the story or the understanding of a news event. Flag the contents in an editor's note. See **obscenities, profanities, vulgarities** and **race**.

nylon Not a trademark.

O

oasis, oases

OB-GYN Acceptable in all references for obstetrics and gynecology, a medical specialty.

obscenities, profanities, vulgarities Do not use them in stories unless they are part of direct quotations and there is a compelling reason for them.

Try to find a way to give the reader a sense of what was said without using the specific word or phrase. For example, an anti-gay or sexist slur.

If a profanity, obscenity or vulgarity must be used, flag the story at the top for editors, being specific about what the issue is:

Eds: Note use of vulgarity "f---" [or "s---"] However, online readers receiving direct feeds of the stories will not see that warning, so consider whether the word in question truly needs to be in the story at all.

When possible, confine the offending language, in quotation marks, to a separate paragraph that can be deleted easily by editors.

In reporting profanity that normally would use the words *damn* or *god*, lowercase *god* and use the following forms: *damn, damn it, goddamn it.*

If the obscenity involved is particularly offensive but the story requires making clear what the word was, replace the letters of the offensive word with hyphens, using only an initial letter: *f---, s---.*

Commonly used abbreviations or acronyms that contain an obscenity may be used if necessary to convey a meaning or mood: *WTF, snafu.* They should not appear in headlines unless the story turns on the use of such a term.

In some stories or scripts, it may be better to replace the offensive word with a generic descriptive in parentheses, e.g., *(vulgarity)* or *(obscenity).*

When the subject matter of a story may be considered offensive or disturbing, but the story does not contain quoted profanity, obscenities or vulgarities, flag the story at the top:

Eds: Graphic details of the killings could be offensive or disturbing to some readers.

For guidelines on racial or ethnic slurs, see **nationalities and races**.

Occupational Safety and Health Administration *OSHA* is acceptable on second reference.

occupational titles They are always lowercase. See **titles**.

occur, occurred, occurring Also: *occurrence.*

ocean The five, from the largest to the smallest: Pacific Ocean, Atlantic Ocean, Indian Ocean, Antarctic Ocean, Arctic Ocean.

Lowercase *ocean* standing alone or in plural uses: *the ocean, the Atlantic and Pacific oceans.*

oceangoing

odd-
Follow with a hyphen:
odd-looking   odd-numbered
See **betting odds**.

oddsmaker

off-Broadway, off-off-Broadway
See **Broadway, off-Broadway, off-off-Broadway**.

offering
The issue or sale of a company stock or bond. A company usually will sell financial securities to the public to raise capital.

office
Capitalize *office* when it is part of an agency's formal name: *Office of Management and Budget.*
Lowercase all other uses, including phrases such as: *the office of the attorney general, the U.S. attorney's office.*
See **Oval Office**.

officeholder

Office of Thrift Supervision
U.S. Treasury Department bureau that regulates the nation's savings and loan industry. *OTS* is acceptable on second reference.

offline
No hyphen is an exception to Webster's New World College Dictionary.

off of
The *of* is unnecessary: *He fell off the bed.* Not: *He fell off of the bed.*

off-, -off
Follow Webster's New World College Dictionary. Hyphenate if not listed there.
Some commonly used combinations with a hyphen:
off-color   off-white
off-peak   send-off

Some combinations without a hyphen:
cutoff   offside
liftoff   offstage
offhand   playoff
offset   standoff
offshore   takeoff

off-site
Hyphenated. Also: *on-site.*

Ohio
Do not abbreviate in datelines or stories. Postal code: *OH*
See **state names**.

oil
In shipping, oil and oil products normally are measured by the ton. For news stories, convert these tonnage figures to gallons.
There are 42 gallons to each barrel of oil. The number of barrels per ton varies, depending on the type of oil product.
To convert tonnage to gallons:
—Determine the type of oil.
—Consult the table on the following page to find out how many barrels per ton for that type of oil.
—Multiply the number of tons by the number of barrels per ton. The result is the number of barrels in the shipment.
—Multiply the number of barrels by 42. The result is the number of gallons.
EXAMPLE: A tanker spills 20,000 metric tons of foreign crude petroleum. The table shows 6.998 barrels of foreign crude petroleum per metric ton. Multiply 6.998 x 20,000 equals 139,960 barrels. Multiply 139,960 x 42 is 5,878,320 gallons.
TABLE: The table on the following page is based on figures supplied by the American Petroleum Institute.

oil and gas companies
Here are 10 major global oil and gas companies that list stock publicly, with their headquarters:
Gazprom OAO, Moscow

Exxon Mobil Corp., Irving, Texas
PetroChina, Beijing
Royal Dutch Shell PLC, The Hague, Netherlands
Chevron Corp., San Ramon, Calif.
BP PLC, London
Total SA, Courbevoie, France
Petrobras SA, Rio de Janeiro
Rosneft OAO, Moscow
Lukoil OAO, Moscow

OK, OK'd, OK'ing, OKs Do not use *okay*.

Oklahoma Abbreviate *Okla.* in datelines only; spell out in stories. Postal code: *OK*
   See **state names**.

Oklahoma City The city in Oklahoma stands alone in datelines.

Old City of Jerusalem The walled part of the city.

Old South The South before the Civil War.

Old Testament See **Bible**.

Old West The American West as it was being settled in the 19th century.

Old World The Eastern Hemisphere: Asia, Europe, Africa. The term also may be an allusion to European culture and customs.

Olympic Airways Headquarters is in Athens, Greece.

Olympics Capitalize all references to the international athletic contests: *the Olympics, the Winter Olympics, the Olympic Games, an Olympic-size pool, an Olympian*, but lowercase *the games* when used alone.
   An Olympic-size pool is 50 meters long by 25 meters wide.

on Do not use *on* before a date or day of the week when its absence would not lead to confusion, except at the beginning of a sentence: *The meeting will be held Monday. He will be inaugurated Jan. 20. On Sept. 3, the committee will meet to discuss the issue.*

OIL EQUIVALENCY TABLE

Type of Product	Barrels Per Short Ton (2,000 lbs.)	Barrels Per Metric Ton (2,204.6 lbs.)	Barrels Per Long Ton (2,240 lbs.)
crude oil, foreign	6.349	6.998	7.111
crude oil, domestic	6.770	7.463	7.582
gasoline and naphtha	7.721	8.511	8.648
kerosene	7.053	7.775	7.900
distillate fuel oil	6.580	7.253	7.369
residual fuel oil	6.041	6.660	6.766
lubricating oil	6.349	6.998	7.111
lubricating grease	6.665	7.346	7.464
wax	7.134	7.864	7.990
asphalt	5.540	6.106	6.205
coke	4.990	5.500	5.589
road oil	5.900	6.503	6.608
jelly and petrolatum	6.665	7.346	7.464
liquefied pet. gas	10.526	11.603	11.789
Gilsonite	5.515	6.080	6.177

Use *on* to avoid an awkward juxtaposition of a date and a proper name: *John met Mary on Monday. He told Reagan on Thursday that the bill was doomed.*

Use *on* also to avoid any suggestion that a date is the object of a transitive verb: *The House killed on Tuesday a bid to raise taxes. The Senate postponed on Wednesday its consideration of a bill to reduce import duties.*

onboard One word as a modifier: *There was onboard entertainment.* But: *he jumped on board the boat.*

one- Hyphenate when used in writing fractions:

one-half   one-third

Use phrases such as *a half* or *a third* if precision is not intended.

See **fractions**.

one another See **each other, one another**.

one person, one vote The adjective form: *one-person, one-vote. He supports the principle of one person, one vote. The one-man, one-vote rule.*

Supreme Court rulings all use the phrase *one person, one vote*, not *one man, one vote.*

one-sided

onetime, one-time, one time *He is the onetime (former) heavyweight champion. She is the one-time (once) winner in 2003. He did it one time.*

One World Trade Center Skyscraper opened in 2014 on the site of the Twin Towers destroyed in the 9/11 attacks. Spell out *One* as used by the Port Authority of New York and New Jersey, which owns both the building and the 16-acre World Trade Center site. Other buildings in the complex are named with numerals 2, 3, etc., as designated by the company that leased them.

online One word in all cases for the computer connection term.

online trading Buying or selling financial securities and/or currencies through a brokerage's Internet-based proprietary trading platforms.

onstage

Ontario This Canadian province is the nation's first in total population and second to Quebec in area. Do not abbreviate.

See **datelines**.

OPEC Acceptable in all references for the Organization of the Petroleum Exporting Countries.

Founded in 1960, OPEC has 12 members: Algeria, Angola, Ecuador, Iran, Iraq, Kuwait, Libya, Nigeria, Qatar, Saudi Arabia, United Arab Emirates and Venezuela.

Headquarters is in Vienna, Austria.

operas See **composition titles**.

opinion polls See **polls and surveys**.

opossum The only North American marsupial. No apostrophe is needed to indicate missing letters in a phrase such as *playing possum.*

option In the financial world, it is a contract that gives an investor the right, but not the obligation, to buy (call) or sell (put) a security or other financial asset at an agreed-upon price (strike price) during a certain period of time or on a specific date (exercise date).

Oracle Corp. Headquarters is in Redwood City, California.

oral, verbal, written Use *oral* to refer to spoken words: *He gave an oral promise.*

Use *written* to refer to words committed to paper: *We had a written agreement.*

Use *verbal* to compare words with some other form of communication: *His tears revealed the sentiments that his poor verbal skills could not express.*

ordinal numbers See **numerals**.

Oregon Abbreviate *Ore.* in datelines only; spell out in stories. Postal code: *OR*
See **state names**.

Organization of American States *OAS* is acceptable on second reference. Headquarters is in Washington.

organizations and institutions Capitalize the full names of organizations and institutions: *the American Medical Association; First Presbyterian Church; General Motors Corp.; Harvard University, Harvard University Medical School; the Procrastinators Club; the Society of Professional Journalists.*

Retain capitalization if *Co., Corp.* or a similar word is deleted from the full proper name: *General Motors.* See **company, companies; corporation**; and **incorporated**.

SUBSIDIARIES: Capitalize the names of major subdivisions: *the Pontiac Motor Division of General Motors.*

INTERNAL ELEMENTS: Use lowercase for internal elements of an organization when they have names that are widely used generic terms: *the board of directors of General Motors, the board of trustees of Columbia University, the history department of Harvard University, the*

sports department of the Daily Citizen-Leader.

Capitalize internal elements of an organization when they have names that are not widely used generic terms: *the General Assembly of the World Council of Churches, the House of Delegates of the American Medical Association, the House of Bishops and House of Deputies of the Episcopal Church.*

FLIP-FLOPPED NAMES: Retain capital letters when commonly accepted practice flops a name to delete the word of: *Harvard School of Dental Medicine, Harvard Dental School.*

Do not, however, flop formal names that are known to the public with the word of: *Massachusetts Institute of Technology*, for example, not *Massachusetts Technology Institute.*

ABBREVIATIONS AND ACRONYMS: Some organizations and institutions are widely recognized by their abbreviations: *Alcoa, GOP, NAACP, NATO.* For guidelines on when such abbreviations may be used, see the individual listings and the entries under **abbreviations and acronyms** and **second reference**.

Orient, Oriental Do not use when referring to East Asian nations and their peoples. *Asian* is the acceptable term for an inhabitant of those regions. See **nationalities and races** and **race**.

original equipment manufacturer A company that builds components or systems that are used in production of another company's systems or products. *OEM* is acceptable on second reference.

Oscar, Oscars See **Academy Awards**.

Oslo The city in Norway carries the country name in datelines.

Ottawa The capital of Canada carries Ontario, the province name, in datelines.

Ouija A trademark for a board used in seances.

ounce (dry) Units of dry volume are not customarily carried to this level.
See **pint (dry)**.

ounce (liquid) See **fluid ounce**.

ounce (weight) It is defined as 437.5 grains.
The metric equivalent is approximately 28 grams.
To convert to grams, multiply by 28 (5 ounces x 28 = 140 grams).
See **grain** and **gram**.

-out Follow Webster's New World College Dictionary. Hyphenate nouns and adjectives not listed there.
Some frequently used words (all nouns):

cop-out	hideout
fade-out	pullout
fallout	walkout
flameout	washout

Two words for verbs:

fade out	walk out
hide out	wash out
pull out	

out- Follow Webster's New World College Dictionary. Hyphenate if not listed there.
Some frequently used words:

outargue	outpost
outbox	output
outdated	outscore
outfield	outstrip
outfox	outtalk
outpatient (n., adj.)	

outbreak For disease references, reserve for larger numbers of an illness, not a few cases.

Outer Banks The barrier islands along the North Carolina coast.

out of bounds But as a modifier: *out-of-bounds. The ball went out of bounds. He took an out-of-bounds pass.*

out of court, out-of-court *They settled out of court. He accepted an out-of-court settlement.*

outperform

outsourcing A business practice used by companies to reduce costs by transferring work previously performed in-house to outside suppliers.

outstanding shares Stock held by shareholders of a company.

Oval Office The White House office of the president.

-over Follow Webster's New World College Dictionary. Hyphenate if not listed there.
Some frequently used words (all are nouns, some also are used as adjectives):

carry-over	stopover
holdover	walkover
takeover	

Use two words when any of these occurs as a verb.
See **suffixes**.

over Acceptable in all uses to indicate greater numerical value. *The crop was valued at over $5 billion.* See **more than, over**.

over- Follow Webster's New World College Dictionary. A hyphen seldom is used. Some frequently used words:

overbuy	overrate
overexert	override

See the **overall** entry.

overall A single word in adjectival and adverbial use: *Overall, the Democrats succeeded. Overall policy.*

The word for the garment is *overalls.*

over-the-counter stock A stock that isn't listed and traded on an organized exchange. OTC stocks are traditionally those of smaller companies that don't meet the listing requirements of the New York Stock Exchange or Nasdaq Stock Market. *OTC* is acceptable on second reference. See **Pink Sheets**.

owner Not a formal title. Always lowercase: *Dallas Cowboys owner Jerry Jones.*

Oyez Not *oyes.* The cry of court and public officials to command silence. *"Oyez! Oyez!"*

Ozark Mountains Or simply: *the Ozarks.*

P

PAC Acronym for *political action committee*. Raises money and makes contributions to campaigns of political candidates or parties. At the federal level, contribution amounts are limited by law and may not come from corporations or labor unions. Enforcement overseen by the Federal Election Commission. *PAC* acceptable on first reference; spell out in body of story. A *super PAC* is a political action committee that may raise and spend unlimited amounts of money, including from corporations and unions, to campaign independently for candidates for federal office. Its activities must be reported to the FEC, but are not otherwise regulated if not coordinated with the candidate or campaign.

pacemaker Formerly a trademark, now a generic term for a device that electronically helps a person's heart maintain a steady beat.

Pacific Ocean See **ocean**.

Pacific Standard Time (PST), Pacific Daylight Time (PDT) See **time zones**.

page numbers Use figures and capitalize *page* when used with a figure. When a letter is appended to the figure, capitalize it but do not use a hyphen: *Page 1, Page 10, Page 20A.* See **numerals**.

paintings See **composition titles**.

palate, palette, pallet *Palate* is the roof of the mouth.
   A *palette* is an artist's paint board.
   A *pallet* is a low platform. Also a small bed or pad filled with straw and used directly on the floor.

Palestine Liberation Organization Not *Palestinian*. *PLO* is acceptable in all references.

pan- Prefix meaning "all" takes no hyphen when combined with a common noun:
   panchromatic   pantheism
   Most combinations with *pan-* are proper nouns, however, and both *pan-* and the proper name it is combined with are capitalized:
   Pan-African   Pan-Asiatic
   Pan-American

Panama City The city in Panama stands alone in datelines.

pantsuit

pantyhose

Pap test (or **smear**) After George Papanicolaou, the U.S. anatomist who developed this test for cervical cancer.

paparazzi (plural), **paparazzo** (singular) A photographer, often a freelancer, who takes candid shots, often in an intrusive manner, of celebrities.

parallel, paralleled, paralleling

parallels Use figures and low-ercase to identify the imaginary locater lines that ring the globe from east to west. They are measured in units of 0 to 90 degrees north or south of the equator.

Examples: *4th parallel north*, *89th parallel south*, or, if location north or south of the equator is obvious: *19th parallel*.

See **latitude and longitude**.

pardon, parole, probation The terms often are confused, but each has a specific meaning. Do not use them interchangeably.

A *pardon* forgives and releases a person from further punishment. It is granted by a chief of state or a governor. By itself, it does not expunge a record of conviction, if one exists, and it does not by itself restore civil rights.

A *general pardon*, usually for political offenses, is called *amnesty*.

Parole is the release of a prisoner before the sentence has expired, on condition of good behavior. It is granted by a parole board, part of the executive branch of government, and can be revoked only by the board.

Probation is the suspension of sentence for a person convicted, but not yet imprisoned, on condition of good behavior. It is imposed and revoked only by a judge.

parentheses See entry in **Punctuation** chapter.

Parent Teacher Association

PTA is acceptable in all references.

Paris The city in France stands alone in datelines.

parish Capitalize as part of the formal name for a church congregation or a governmental jurisdiction: *St. John's Parish, Jefferson Parish*.

Lowercase standing alone or in plural combinations: *the parish, St. John's and St. Mary's parishes, Jefferson and Plaquemines parishes*.

See **county** for additional guidelines on governmental jurisdictions.

Parkinson's disease After James Parkinson, the English physician who described this degenerative disease of later life.

Parkinson's law After C. Northcote Parkinson, the British economist who came to the satirical conclusion that work expands to fill the time allotted to it.

parliament, Parliament Uppercase when referring to the legislative body in Great Britain or other countries.

parliamentary Lowercase unless part of a proper name.

parole See **pardon, parole, probation**.

partial quotes See **quotation marks** in the **Punctuation** chapter.

particles See **foreign names** entry.

part time, part-time Hyphenate when used as a compound modifier: *She works part time. She has a part-time job.*

party See **political parties and philosophies**.

party affiliation Let relevance be the guide in determining whether to include a political figure's party affiliation in a story.

Party affiliation is pointless in some stories, such as an account of a governor accepting a button from a poster child.

It will occur naturally in many political stories.

For stories between these extremes, include party affiliation if readers need it for understanding or are likely to be curious about what it is.

GENERAL FORMS: When party designation is given, use any of these approaches as logical in constructing a story:

—*Republican Sen. Tim Scott of South Carolina said ...*

—*Sen. Tim Scott, R-S.C., said ...*

—*Sen. Tim Scott also spoke. The South Carolina Republican said ...*

—*Rep. Frank Lucas of Oklahoma, the senior Republican on the House Agriculture Committee, said he supports the amendment.*

In stories about party meetings, such as a report on the Republican National Convention, no specific reference to party affiliation is necessary unless an individual is not a member of the party in question.

SHORT-FORM PUNCTUATION: Set short forms such as *R-S.C.* off from a name by commas, as illustrated above.

Use *R-* for Republicans, *D-* for Democrats, and *I-* for independents: *Sen. Joseph Lieberman, I-Conn., spoke with Sen. Bernie Sanders, I-Vt.*

FORM FOR U.S. HOUSE MEMBERS: The normal practice for U.S. House members is to identify them by party and state. In contexts where state affiliation is clear and home city is relevant, such as a state election roundup, identify representatives by party and city: *U.S. Reps. Ander Crenshaw, R-Jacksonville, and Frederica Wilson, D-Miami.* If this option is used, be consistent throughout the story.

FORM FOR STATE LEGISLATORS: Short-form listings showing party and home city are appropriate in state stories. For national stories, the normal practice is to say that the individual is a *Republican* or *Democrat*. Use a short-form listing only if the legislator's home city is relevant.

See **legislative titles**.

pass See **adopt, approve, enact, pass**.

passenger mile One passenger carried one mile, or its equivalent, such as two passengers carried one-half mile.

passer-by, passers-by

pasteurize

pat-down (n. and adj.)

patrolman, patrolwoman Capitalize before a name only if the word is a formal title. In some cities, the formal title is *police officer*.

See **titles**.

patrol, patrolled, patrolling

payload

PDF Abbreviation for *Portable Document Format*. A file format that allows a document to be shared among several types of computers without losing its formatting. Abbreviation is acceptable in all references.

peacekeeping

peacemaker, peacemaking

peace offering

peacetime

peacock It applies only to the male. The female is a *peahen*. Both are *peafowl*.

peasant Avoid the term, which is often derogatory, in referring to farm laborers (except in quotes or an organization name).

peck A unit of dry measure equal to 8 dry quarts or one-fourth of a bushel.

The metric equivalent is approximately 8.8 liters.

To convert to liters, multiply by 8.8 (5 pecks x 8.8 = 44 liters).

See **liter**.

pedal, peddle When riding a bicycle or similar vehicle, you *pedal* it.

When selling something, you may *peddle* it.

peddler

peninsula Capitalize as part of a proper name: *the Florida Peninsula, the Upper Peninsula of Michigan, the Korean Peninsula, the Indochina Peninsula, the Crimean Peninsula.*

penitentiary See **prison, jail**.

Pennsylvania Abbreviate *Pa.* in datelines only; spell out in stories. Postal code: *PA*

See **state names**.

Pennsylvania Dutch The individuals are of German descent. The word *Dutch* is a corruption of *Deutsch*, the German word for "German."

people's Use this possessive form when the word occurs in the formal name of a nation: *the People's Republic of China.*

Use this form also in such phrases as *the people's desire for freedom.*

people, persons Use *person* when speaking of an individual: *One person waited for the bus.*

The word *people* is preferred to *persons* in all plural uses. For example: *Thousands of people attended the fair. What will people say? There were 17 people in the room.*

Persons should be used only when it is in a direct quote or part of a title as in *Bureau of Missing Persons.*

People also is a collective noun that takes a plural verb when used to refer to a single race or nation: *The American people are united.*

PepsiCo Inc. Headquarters is in Purchase, New York.

percent One word. It takes a singular verb when standing alone or when a singular word follows an *of* construction: *The teacher said 60 percent was a failing grade. He said 50 percent of the membership was there.*

It takes a plural verb when a plural word follows an *of* construction: *He said 50 percent of the members were there.*

Use figures for percent and percentages: *1 percent, 2.5 percent* (use decimals, not fractions), *10 percent, 4 percentage points.*

For a range, *12 to 15 percent,* or *between 12 and 15 percent.*

For amounts less than 1 percent, precede the decimal with a zero: *The cost of living rose 0.6 percent.*

See **numerals**.

periods See entry in the **Punctuation** chapter.

perk A shortened form of *perquisite* often used to describe fringe benefits.

permissible

per-share earnings Also earnings per share.

Persian Gulf Use this long-established name for the body of water off the southern coast of Iran.

Some Arab nations call it the *Arabian Gulf.* Use *Arabian Gulf* only in direct quotations and explain in the text that the body of water is more commonly known as the *Persian Gulf.*

personifications Capitalize them: *Grim Reaper, Father Time, Mother Nature, Old Man Winter, Sol,* etc.

-persons Do not use coined words such as *chairperson* or *spokesperson* in regular text.

Instead, use *chairman* or *spokesman* if referring to a man or the office in general. Use *chairwoman* or *spokeswoman* if referring to a woman. Or, if applicable, use a neutral word such as *leader* or *representative.*

Use *chairperson* or similar coinage only in direct quotations or when it is the formal description for an office.

persons See **people, persons.**

persuade See **convince, persuade.**

Petroleo Brasileiro Headquarters is in Rio de Janeiro.

petty officer See **military titles.**

Pfizer Inc. Headquarters is in New York.

phase See **faze, phase.**

Ph.D., Ph.D.s The preferred form is to say a person *holds a doctorate* and name the individual's area of specialty.

See **academic degrees** and **doctor.**

phenomenon, phenomena

Philadelphia The city in Pennsylvania stands alone in datelines.

Philippines In datelines, give the name of a city or town followed by *Philippines*:
MANILA, *Philippines* (AP) —
In stories: *the Philippines.*
The people are *Filipinos. Filipina* is acceptable as the feminine form. The language is *Filipino,* an offshoot of Tagalog. *Philippine* is the adjective.

phishing A form of Internet fraud that aims to steal personal information such as credit card numbers, Social Security numbers, user IDs and passwords.

phobia An irrational, uncontrollable fear, often a form of mental illness. Examples: *acrophobia,* a fear of heights, and *claustrophobia,* a fear of being in small, enclosed spaces. Do not use in political or social contexts: *homophobia, Islamophobia.* See **mental illness.**

Phoenix The city in Arizona stands alone in datelines.

Photoshop Trademark for a brand of photo-editing software.

physician assistant No apostrophe in this medical profession title.

picket, pickets, picketed, picket line *Picket* is both the verb and the noun. Do not use *picketer.*

pickup (n. and adj.) **pick up** (v.)

picnic, picnicked, picnicking, picnicker

pico- A prefix denoting one-trillionth of a unit. Move the decimal point 12 places to the left in converting to the basic unit: 2,999,888,777,666.5 picoseconds equals 2.9998887776665 seconds.

pigeon

pigeonhole (n. and v.)

Pikes Peak No apostrophe. After Zebulon Montgomery Pike, a U.S. general and explorer. The 14,115-foot peak is in the Rockies of central Colorado.

pileup (n. and adj.) **pile up** (v.)

pill Do not capitalize in references to oral contraceptives. Use *birth control pill* on first reference if necessary for clarity.

pilot Not a formal title. Do not capitalize before a name.
See **titles**.

pingpong A synonym for *table tennis*.
The trademark name is *Ping-Pong*.

Pink Sheets A daily publication compiled by the National Quotation Bureau with bid and ask prices of over-the-counter stocks. See **over-the-counter stock**.

pint (dry) Equal to 33.6 cubic inches, or one-half of a dry quart.
The metric equivalent is approximately 0.55 of a liter.
To convert to liters, multiply by 0.55 (5 dry pints x 0.55 is 2.75 liters).
See **liter** and **quart (dry)**.

pint (liquid) Equal to 16 fluid ounces, or two cups.
The approximate metric equivalents are 470 milliliters or 0.47 of a liter.
To convert to liters, multiply by 0.47 (4 pints x 0.47 is 1.88 liters).
See **liter**.

Pinterest A social network in which users collect and share images from the Web in theme-based collections, also known as *pinboards* or simply *boards*. Images that are shared on Pinterest — or pinned — are sometimes referred to as *pins*.

Pinyin The official Chinese spelling system.
See **Chinese names**.

pipeline

Pittsburgh The city in Pennsylvania stands alone in datelines.
The spelling is *Pittsburg* (no *h*) for communities in California, Illinois, Kansas, New Hampshire, Oklahoma and Texas.

plains See **Great Plains**.

planets Capitalize the proper names of planets: *Jupiter, Mars, Mercury, Neptune, Saturn, Uranus, Venus*. (*Pluto* was redefined as a dwarf planet by the International Astronomical Union in 2006.)
Capitalize *Earth* when used as the proper name of our planet: *The astronauts returned to Earth*.
Capitalize nouns and adjectives derived from the proper names of planets: *Martian, Venusian*. But lowercase adjectives derived from other heavenly bodies: *solar, lunar*.
See **earth** and **heavenly bodies**.

planning Avoid the redundant *future planning*.

plants In general, lowercase the names of plants, but capitalize proper nouns or adjectives that occur in a name.
Some examples: *tree, fir, white fir, Douglas fir; Scotch pine; clover, white clover, white Dutch clover*.
If a botanical name is used, capitalize the first word; lowercase

others: *pine tree (Pinus), red cedar (Juniperus virginiana), blue azalea (Callicarpa americana), Kentucky coffee tree (Gymnocladus dioica).*

play titles See **composition titles**.

plead, pleaded, pleading Do not use the colloquial past tense form, *pled*.

Pledge of Allegiance

Plexiglas Note the single *s*. A trademark for plastic glass.

plow

plurality See **majority, plurality**.

plurals Follow these guidelines in forming and using plural words:

MOST WORDS: Add *s*: *boys, girls, ships, villages.*

WORDS ENDING IN CH, S, SH, SS, X and Z: Add *es*: *churches, lenses, parishes, glasses, boxes, buzzes.* (*Monarchs* is an exception.)

WORDS ENDING IN IS: Change *is* to *es*: *oases, parentheses, theses.*

WORDS ENDING IN Y: If *y* is preceded by a consonant or *qu*, change *y* to *i* and add *es*: *armies, cities, navies, soliloquies.* (See PROPER NAMES below for an exception.)

Otherwise add *s*: *donkeys, monkeys.*

WORDS ENDING IN O: If *o* is preceded by a consonant, most plurals require *es*: *buffaloes, dominoes, echoes, heroes, potatoes.* But there are exceptions: *pianos.* See individual entries in this book for many of these exceptions.

WORDS ENDINGS IN F: In general, change *f* to *v* and add *es*: *leaves, selves.* (*Roof, roofs* is an exception.)

LATIN ENDINGS: Latin-root words ending in *us* change *us* to *i*: *alumnus, alumni.* (Words that have taken on English endings by common usage are exceptions: *prospectuses, syllabuses.*)

Most ending in *a* change to *ae*: *alumna, alumnae* (*formula, formulas* is an exception).

Most ending in *um* add *s*: *memorandums, referendums, stadiums.* Among those that still use the Latin ending: *addenda, curricula, media.*

Use the plural that Webster's New World College Dictionary lists as most common for a particular sense of word.

FORM CHANGE: *man, men; child, children; foot, feet; mouse, mice;* etc.

Caution: When *s* is used with any of these words it indicates possession and must be preceded by an apostrophe: *men's, children's,* etc.

WORDS THE SAME IN SINGULAR AND PLURAL: *corps, chassis, deer, moose, sheep,* etc.

The sense in a particular sentence is conveyed by the use of a singular or plural verb.

WORDS PLURAL IN FORM, SINGULAR IN MEANING: Some take singular verbs: *measles, mumps, news.*

Others take plural verbs: *grits, scissors.*

COMPOUND WORDS: Those written solid add *s* at the end: *cupfuls, handfuls, tablespoonfuls.*

For those that involve separate words or words linked by a hyphen, make the most significant word plural:

—Significant word first: *adjutants general, aides-de-camp, attorneys general, courts-martial, daughters-in-law, passers-by, postmasters general, presidents-elect, secretaries-general, sergeants major.*

—Significant word in the middle: *assistant attorneys general, deputy chiefs of staff.*

—Significant word last: *assistant attorneys, assistant corporation coun-*

sels, deputy sheriffs, lieutenant colonels, major generals.

WORDS AS WORDS: Do not use *'s*: *His speech had too many "ifs," "ands" and "buts."*

PROPER NAMES: Most ending in *es* or *s* or *z* add *es*: *Charleses, Joneses, Gonzalezes.*

Most ending in *y* add *s* even if preceded by a consonant: *the Duffys, the Kennedys, the two Kansas Citys.* Exceptions include *Alleghenies* and *Rockies.*

For others, add *s*: *the Carters, the McCoys, the Mondales.*

FIGURES: Add *s*: *The custom began in the 1920s. The airline has two 727s. Temperatures will be in the low 20s. There were five size 7s.*

(No apostrophes, an exception to Webster's New World College Dictionary guideline under "apostrophe.")

SINGLE LETTERS: Use *'s*: *Mind your p's and q's. He learned the three R's and brought home a report card with four A's and two B's. The Oakland A's won the pennant.*

MULTIPLE LETTERS: Add *s*: *She knows her ABCs. I gave him five IOUs. Four VIPs were there.*

PROBLEMS, DOUBTS: Separate entries in this book give plurals for troublesome words and guidance on whether certain words should be used with singular or plural verbs and pronouns. See also **collective nouns** and **possessives**.

For questions not covered by this book, use the plural that Webster's New World College Dictionary lists as most common for a particular sense of a word.

p.m., a.m. Lowercase, with periods. Avoid the redundant *10 p.m. tonight.*

pocket veto Occurs only when Congress has adjourned. If Congress is in session, a bill that remains on the president's desk for 10 days becomes law without his signature. If Congress adjourns, however, a bill that fails to get his signature within 10 days is vetoed.

Many states have similar procedures, but the precise requirements vary.

podcast A digital media program, in audio or video form, that can be downloaded or streamed to a computer, smartphone or portable media device.

podium See **lectern, podium, pulpit, rostrum**.

poetry See **composition titles** for guidelines on the names of poems.

Capitalize the first word in a line of poetry unless the author deliberately has used lowercase for a special effect. Do not, however, capitalize the first word on indented lines that must be created simply because the writer's line is too long for the available printing width.

poinsettia Note the *ia.*

point Do not abbreviate. Capitalize as part of a proper name: *Point Pleasant.*

point-blank

poison pill In the financial world, any defensive measure to prevent the takeover of a corporation by making its acquisition prohibitively expensive for the party attempting the takeover.

police department In communities where this is the formal name, capitalize *police department* with or without the name of the community: *the Los Angeles Police Department, the Police Department.*

If a police agency has some other formal name such as *Division of Po-*

lice, use that name if it is the way the department is known to the public. If the story uses *police department* as a generic term for such an agency, put *police department* in lowercase.

If a police agency with an unusual formal name is known to the public as a *police department*, treat *police department* as the name, capitalizing it with or without the name of the community. Use the formal name only if there is a special reason in the story.

If the proper name cannot be determined for some reason, such as the need to write about a police agency from a distance, treat *police department* as the proper name, capitalizing it with or without the name of the community.

Lowercase *police department* in plural uses: *the Los Angeles and San Francisco police departments*.

Lowercase *the department* whenever it stands alone.

police titles See **military titles** and **titles**.

policymaker, policymaking

polio The preferred term for *poliomyelitis* and *infantile paralysis*.

Politburo Acceptable in all references for the *Political Bureau of the Communist Party*.

political divisions Use Arabic figures and capitalize the accompanying word when used with the figures: *1st Ward, 10th Ward, 3rd Precinct, 22nd Precinct, the ward, the precinct*. See **numerals**.

political parties and philosophies Capitalize both the name of the party and the word *party* if it is customarily used as part of the organization's proper name: *the Democratic Party, the Republican Party*.

Include the political affiliation of any elected officeholder.

Capitalize *Communist, Conservative, Democrat, Liberal, Republican, Socialist*, etc., when they refer to a specific party or its members. Lowercase these words when they refer to political philosophy (see examples below).

Lowercase the name of a philosophy in noun and adjective forms unless it is the derivative of a proper name: *communism, communist; fascism, fascist*. But: *Marxism, Marxist; Nazism, Nazi*.

EXAMPLES: *John Adams was a Federalist, but a man who subscribed to his philosophy today would be described as a federalist. The liberal Republican senator and his Conservative Party colleague said they believe that democracy and communism are incompatible. The Communist said he is basically a socialist who has reservations about Marxism.*

See **convention** and **party affiliation**.

politicking

politics Usually it takes a plural verb: *My politics are my own business.*

As a study or science, it takes a singular verb: *Politics is a demanding profession.*

polls and surveys Stories based on public opinion polls must include basic information that allows the reader to evaluate the results. Carefully word such stories to avoid exaggerating the meaning of poll results.

Every story based on a poll should include answers to these questions:

1. Who did the poll and who paid for it? Start with the polling firm, media outlet or other organization that conducted the poll. Be wary of polls paid for by candidates or

interest groups; their release of poll results may be done selectively and is often a campaign tactic or publicity ploy. Any reporting of such polls must highlight the poll's sponsor, so readers can be aware of potential bias from such sponsorship.

2. How many people were interviewed? The larger a poll's sample size, the more precise its results. Surveys with 500 respondents or more are preferable. How were they selected? Only a poll based on a scientific, random sample of a population — in which every member of the population has a known probability of inclusion — can be considered a valid and reliable measure of that population's opinions. Among surveys that do not meet this criterion:

• Samples drawn from panels of people who volunteer for online polls. These cannot be considered representative of larger populations because panel members are self-selected — often including "professional respondents" who sign up for numerous surveys to earn money or win prizes — and exclude people without Internet access. (Online panels recruited randomly from the entire population, with Internet access provided to those who don't already have it, are valid.)

• Balloting via websites, cell-phone text messaging or calls to 900 numbers. These too are self-selected samples, and results are subject to manipulation via blog and email campaigns and other methods. If such unscientific pseudo-polls are reported for entertainment value, they must never be portrayed as accurately reflecting public opinion and their failings must be highlighted.

3. Who was interviewed? A valid poll reflects only the opinions of the population that was sampled. A poll conducted only in urban areas

of a country cannot be considered nationally representative; people in rural areas often have different opinions from those in cities. Many political polls are based on interviews with registered voters, since registration is usually required for voting. Polls may be based on "likely voters" closer to an election; if so, ask the pollster how that group was identified and what percentage of the voting population it totaled. Are there far more "likely voters" in the poll than turnout in comparable past elections would suggest? Polls that screen for likely voters at the sample level by only attempting to interview those who have a history of voting leave out some potential voters and ought to be avoided.

4. How was the poll conducted — by telephone or some other way? Avoid polls in which computers conduct telephone interviews using a recorded voice (sometimes referred to as IVR polling). Among the problems of these surveys are that they do not randomly select respondents within a household, and they cannot exclude children from adult samples

5. When was the poll taken? Opinion can change quickly, especially in response to events.

6. What are the sampling error margins for the poll and for subgroups mentioned in the story? The polling organization should provide sampling error margins, which are expressed as "plus or minus X percentage points," not "percent." The margin varies inversely with sample size: the fewer people interviewed, the larger the sampling error. If the opinions of a subgroup — women, for example — are important to the story, the sampling error for that subgroup should be noted. (Some pollsters release survey results to the first decimal place, which implies a greater degree of precision than is possible from a sampling.

Round poll results to whole numbers. However, the sampling error margin — a statistical calculation — may be reported to the first decimal place.)

7. How were the questions worded and in what order were they asked? Small differences in question wording can cause big differences in results, and the results for one question may be affected by the preceding questions. The exact question wording need not be in a poll story unless it is crucial or controversial.

If a pollster or sponsor of research refuses to provide the information we need to answer these questions, we should not cover the poll.

When writing and editing poll stories, here are areas for close attention:

—Do not exaggerate poll results. In particular, with pre-election polls, these are the rules for deciding when to write that the poll finds one candidate is leading another:

• If the difference between the candidates is more than twice the sampling error margin, then the poll says one candidate is leading.

• If the difference is less than the sampling error margin, the poll says that the race is close, that the candidates are "about even." (Do not use the term "statistical dead heat," which is inaccurate if there is any difference between the candidates; if the poll finds the candidates are tied, say they're tied.)

• If the difference is at least equal to the sampling error but no more than twice the sampling error, then one candidate can be said to be "apparently leading" or "slightly ahead" in the race.

—A poll's existence is not enough to make it news. More often than not, they are better used as supporting material with other stories. Do not feel obligated to write

about a poll simply because it meets AP's standards.

—Comparisons with other polls are often newsworthy. Earlier poll results can show changes in public opinion. Be careful comparing polls from different polling organizations. Different poll techniques can cause differing results.

—Sampling error is not the only source of error in a poll, but it is one that can be quantified. Question wording and order, interviewer skill and refusal to participate by respondents randomly selected for a sample are among potential sources of error in surveys.

—No matter how good the poll, no matter how wide the margin, the poll does not say one candidate will win an election. Polls can be wrong and the voters can change their minds before they cast their ballots.

Ponzi scheme A fraudulent investing technique that promises high rates of return with little risk to investors. In the scheme, money provided by new investors is used to pay seeming high returns to early-stage investors to suggest the enterprise is prosperous. The scheme collapses when required redemptions exceed new investments. Named for Charles Ponzi, who set up such an illegal pyramid scheme in the 1920s as a way for investors to make money through international currency transactions. The largest fraud in U.S. history was perpetrated by Bernard Madoff, a New York financier who was sentenced to 150 years in prison after admitting to bilking investors of an estimated $20 billion.

pooh-pooh

pope Capitalize when used as a formal title before a name; lower-case in all other uses: *Pope Francis spoke to the crowd. At the close of his* *address, the pope gave his blessing. Pope Emeritus Benedict XVI* or *Benedict XVI, the pope emeritus. Benedict* alone on second reference.

Use *St. John Paul II* and *St. John XXIII* on first reference for the canonized popes. On second reference *John Paul* and *John.* Make clear in the body of a story they were popes.

See **Roman Catholic Church** and **religious titles**.

popular names See **capitalization**.

populist Supports the rights and power of the common people; advocates unorthodox solutions; often critical of establishment politicians and political parties.

pore, pour The verb *pore* means to gaze intently or steadily: *She pored over her books.*

The verb *pour* means to flow in a continuous stream: *It poured rain. He poured the coffee.*

port, starboard Nautical for left and right (when facing the bow, or forward). Port is left. Starboard is right. Change to *left* or *right* unless in direct quotes.

Portuguese names The family names of both the father and mother usually are considered part of a person's full name. In everyday use, customs sometimes vary with individuals and countries.

The normal sequence is given name, mother's family name, father's family name: *Maria Santos Ferreira.*

On second reference, use only the father's family name (*Ferreira*), unless the individual prefers or is widely known by a multiple last name (*Ferreira Castro*).

Some Portuguese use an *e* (for *and*) between the two names: *Joao Canto e Castro.* This would not be split on second reference, but would be *Canto e Castro.*

When a surname is preceded by *da, do, dos,* or *das,* include it in the second reference. *Jorge da Costa,* for example, would be *da Costa* on second reference.

A married woman adds her husband's surname to the end of hers. If *Maria Santos Ferreira* married *Joao Costa da Silva,* her full name would be *Maria Ferreira da Silva.*

Occasionally, a woman may choose not to take her husband's surname for personal reasons or because the mother's family has an aristocratic or famous surname. Use both surnames if the individual's choice is not known.

possessives Follow these guidelines:

PLURAL NOUNS NOT ENDING IN S: Add *'s: the alumni's contributions, women's rights.*

PLURAL NOUNS ENDING IN S: Add only an apostrophe: *the churches' needs, the girls' toys, the horses' food, the ships' wake, states' rights, the VIPs' entrance.*

NOUNS PLURAL IN FORM, SINGULAR IN MEANING: Add only an apostrophe: *mathematics' rules, measles' effects.* (But see INANIMATE OBJECTS below.)

Apply the same principle when a plural word occurs in the formal name of a singular entity: *General Motors' profits, the United States' wealth.*

NOUNS THE SAME IN SINGULAR AND PLURAL: Treat them the same as plurals, even if the meaning is singular: *one corps' location, the two deer's tracks, the lone moose's antlers.*

SINGULAR NOUNS NOT ENDING IN S: Add *'s: the church's needs, the girl's toys, the horse's food, the ship's route, the VIP's seat.*

Some style guides say that singular nouns ending in *s* sounds such as *ce*, *x*, and *z* may take either the apostrophe alone or *'s*. See SPECIAL EXPRESSIONS, but otherwise, for consistency and ease in remembering a rule, always use *'s* if the word does not end in the letter *s*: *Butz's policies, the fox's den, the justice's verdict, Marx's theories, the prince's life, Xerox's profits.*

SINGULAR COMMON NOUNS ENDING IN S: Add *'s* unless the next word begins with *s*: *the hostess's invitation, the hostess' seat; the witness's answer, the witness' story.*

SINGULAR PROPER NAMES ENDING IN S: Use only an apostrophe: *Achilles' heel, Agnes' book, Ceres' rites, Descartes' theories, Dickens' novels, Euripides' dramas, Hercules' labors, Jesus' life, Jules' seat, Kansas' schools, Moses' law, Socrates' life, Tennessee Williams' plays, Xerxes' armies.*

SPECIAL EXPRESSIONS: The following exceptions to the general rule for words not ending in *s* apply to words that end in an *s* sound and are followed by a word that begins with *s*: *for appearance' sake, for conscience' sake, for goodness' sake.* Use *'s* otherwise: *the appearance's cost, my conscience's voice.*

PRONOUNS: Personal interrogative and relative pronouns have separate forms for the possessive. None involve an apostrophe: *mine, ours, your, yours, his, hers, its, theirs, whose.*

Caution: If you are using an apostrophe with a pronoun, always double-check to be sure that the meaning calls for a contraction: *you're, it's, there's, who's.*

Follow the rules listed above in forming the possessives of other pronouns: *another's idea, others' plans, someone's guess.*

COMPOUND WORDS: Applying the rules above, add an apostrophe or *'s* to the word closest to the object possessed: *the major general's decision, the major generals' decisions, the attorney general's request, the attorneys general's request.* See the **plurals** entry for guidelines on forming the plurals of these words.

Also: *anyone else's attitude, John Adams Jr.'s father, Benjamin Franklin of Pennsylvania's motion.* Whenever practical, however, recast the phrase to avoid ambiguity: *the motion by Benjamin Franklin of Pennsylvania.*

JOINT POSSESSION, INDIVIDUAL POSSESSION: Use a possessive form after only the last word if ownership is joint: *Fred and Sylvia's apartment, Fred and Sylvia's stocks.*

Use a possessive form after both words if the objects are individually owned: *Fred's and Sylvia's books.*

DESCRIPTIVE PHRASES: Do not add an apostrophe to a word ending in *s* when it is used primarily in a descriptive sense: *citizens band radio, a Cincinnati Reds infielder, a teachers college, a Teamsters request, a writers guide.*

Memory aid: The apostrophe usually is not used if *for* or *by* rather than *of* would be appropriate in the longer form: *a radio band for citizens, a college for teachers, a guide for writers, a request by the Teamsters.*

An *'s* is required, however, when a term involves a plural word that does not end in *s*: *a children's hospital, a people's republic, the Young Men's Christian Association.*

DESCRIPTIVE NAMES: Some governmental, corporate and institutional organizations with a descriptive word in their names use an apostrophe; some do not. Follow the user's practice: *Actors' Equity, Diners Club, Ladies' Home Journal, the National Governors Association.*

QUASI POSSESSIVES: Follow the rules above in composing the possessive form of words that occur in such phrases as *a day's pay, two weeks' vacation, three days' work, your money's worth.*

Frequently, however, a hyphenated form is clearer: *a two-week vacation, a three-day job.*

DOUBLE POSSESSIVE: Two conditions must apply for a double possessive — a phrase such as *a friend of John's* — to occur: 1. The word after *of* must refer to an animate object, and 2. The word before *of* must involve only a portion of the animate object's possessions.

Otherwise, do not use the possessive form of the word after *of*: *The friends of John Adams mourned his death.* (All the friends were involved.) *He is a friend of the college.* (Not *college's*, because *college* is inanimate.)

Memory aid: This construction occurs most often, and quite naturally, with the possessive forms of personal pronouns: *He is a friend of mine.*

INANIMATE OBJECTS: There is no blanket rule against creating a possessive form for an inanimate object, particularly if the object is treated in a personified sense. See some of the earlier examples, and note these: *death's call, the wind's murmur.*

In general, however, avoid excessive personalization of inanimate objects, and give preference to an *of* construction when it fits the make-up of the sentence. For example, the earlier references to *mathematics' rules* and *measles' effects* would better be phrased: *the rules of mathematics, the effects of measles.*

post- Follow Webster's New World College Dictionary. Hyphenate if not listed there.

Some words without a hyphen:

postdate	postnuptial
postdoctoral	postoperative
postelection	postscript
postgame	postwar
postgraduate	

Some words that use a hyphen:

post-bellum	post-mortem
post-convention	

Post-it A trademark for small pieces of paper with an adhesive strip on the back that can be attached to documents.

post office It may be used but it is no longer capitalized because the agency is now the *U.S. Postal Service.*

Use lowercase in referring to an individual office: *I went to the post office.*

post-traumatic stress disorder *PTSD* is acceptable on second reference. See **mental illness**.

pothole

pound (monetary) The English pound sign is not used. Convert the figures to dollars in most cases. Use a figure and spell out *pounds* if the actual figure is relevant.

pound (weight) Equal to 16 ounces. The metric equivalent is approximately 454 grams, or 0.45 kilograms.

To convert to kilograms, multiply the number of pounds by 0.45 (20 pounds x 0.45 equals 9 kilograms). See **gram** and **kilogram**.

pour See **pore, pour**.

poverty level An income level judged inadequate to provide a family or individual with the essentials of life. The figure for the United States is adjusted regularly to reflect changes in the Consumer Price Index.

Prague The city in the Czech Republic stands alone in datelines.

pre- The rules in **prefixes** apply. The following examples of exceptions to first-listed spellings in Webster's New World College Dictionary are based on the general rule that a hyphen is used if a prefix ends in a vowel and the word that follows begins with the same vowel:

pre-election	pre-establish
pre-eminent	pre-exist
pre-empt	

Otherwise, follow Webster's New World College Dictionary, hyphenating if not listed there. Some examples:

prearrange	prehistoric
precondition	preignition
precook	prejudge
predate	premarital
predecease	prenatal
predispose	prenuptial
preflight	pretax
pregame	pretest
preheat	prewar

Some hyphenated coinage, not listed in the dictionary:

pre-convention	pre-noon

precincts See **political divisions**.

preferred stock An ownership in a company that has no voting rights but pays a fixed dividend and has a higher claim on the company's assets and earnings than common stock.

prefixes See separate listings for commonly used prefixes.

Generally do not hyphenate when using a prefix with a word starting with a consonant.

Three rules are constant:

—Except for *cooperate* and *coordinate*, use a hyphen if the prefix ends in a vowel and the word that follows begins with the same vowel.

—Use a hyphen if the word that follows is capitalized.

—Use a hyphen to join doubled prefixes: *sub-subparagraph*.

premiere A first performance.

premier, prime minister These two titles often are used interchangeably in translating to English the title of an individual who is the first minister in a national government that has a council of ministers.

Prime minister is the correct title throughout the Commonwealth, formerly the British Commonwealth. See **Commonwealth** for a list of members.

Prime minister is the best or traditional translation from most other languages. For consistency, use it throughout the rest of the world with these exceptions:

—Use *chancellor* in Austria and Germany.

—Follow the practice of a nation if there is a specific preference that varies from this general practice. For example, use *premier* in China.

Premier is also the correct title for the individuals who lead the provincial governments in Canada and Australia.

See **titles**.

presently Use it to mean *in a little while* or *shortly*, but not to mean *now*.

presidency Always lowercase.

president Capitalize *president* only as a formal title before one or more names: *President Barack Obama, Presidents Gerald R. Ford and Jimmy Carter*.

Lowercase in all other uses: *The president said Monday he will look into the matter. He is running for president. Lincoln was president during the Civil War.*

See **titles**.

FULL NAMES: Use the first and family name on first reference to a current or former U.S. president or the president-elect: *former President Jimmy Carter, President Barack Obama, President-elect Barack Obama.*

On subsequent references, use only the last name.

For presidents of other nations and of organizations and institutions, capitalize president as a formal title before a full name: *President Francois Hollande of France, President John Smith of Acme Corp.*

On second reference, use only the last name.

presidential Lowercase unless part of a proper name.

Presidential Medal of Freedom This is the nation's highest civilian honor. It is given by the president, on the recommendation of the Distinguished Civilian Service Board, for "exceptionally meritorious contribution to the security of the United States or other significant public or private endeavors."

Until 1963 it was known as the Medal of Freedom.

Presidents Day No apostrophe is an exception to Webster's New World College Dictionary. Not adopted by the federal government as the official name of the Washington's Birthday holiday. However, some federal agencies, states and local governments use the term.

presiding officer Always lowercase.

press conference *News conference* is preferred.

press secretary Seldom a formal title. For consistency, always use lowercase, even when used before an individual's name.

(The formal title for the person who serves a U.S. president in this capacity is *assistant to the president for press relations*.)

See **titles**.

pretax

pretense, pretext A *pretext* is something that is put forward to conceal a truth: *He was discharged for tardiness, but the reason given was only a pretext for general incompetence.*

A *pretense* is a false show, a more overt act intended to conceal personal feelings: *My profuse compliments were all pretense.*

preventive

price-earnings ratio The price of a share of stock divided by earnings per share for a 12-month period. Ratios in AP stock tables reflect earnings for the most recent 12 months.

For example, a stock selling for $60 per share and earning $6 per share would be selling at a price-earnings ratio of 10-to-1. *P/E* is acceptable on second reference.

See **profit terminology**.

PricewaterhouseCoopers

priest A vocational description, not a formal title. Do not capitalize.

See **religious titles** and the entries for the **Roman Catholic Church** and **Episcopal Church** in the **Religion** chapter.

prima-facie (adj.)

primary Do not capitalize: *the New Hampshire primary, the Democratic primary, the primary.*

primary day Use lowercase for any of the days set aside for balloting in a primary.

prime meridian See **meridians**.

prime minister See **premier, prime minister**.

prime rate A benchmark rate used by banks to set interest charges on a variety of corporate and consumer loans, including some adjustable home mortgages, revolving credit cards and business loans extended to their most creditworthy customers. Banks almost always raise or lower their rates by a similar amount on the same day Federal Reserve policymakers change their target for overnight loans between banks, known as the *federal funds rate*.

prime time (n.) **prime-time** (adj.)

Prince Edward Island One of the three Maritime Provinces of Canada. Do not abbreviate.
See **datelines**.

prince, princess Capitalize when used as a royal title before a name; lowercase when used alone: *Prince Charles, the prince*.
See **nobility**.

principal, principle *Principal* is a noun and adjective meaning someone or something first in rank, authority, importance or degree: *She is the school principal. He was the principal player in the trade. Money is the principal problem.*

Principle is a noun that means a fundamental truth, law, doctrine or motivating force: *They fought for the principle of self-determination.*

In a business context, *principal* refers to the amount of money that is borrowed in a loan, as distinct from interest that is paid.

prior to *Before* is less stilted for most uses. *Prior to* is appropriate, however, when a notion of requirement is involved: *The fee must be paid prior to the examination.*

prison, jail Do not use the two words interchangeably.

DEFINITIONS: *Prison* is a generic term that may be applied to the maximum security institutions often known as *penitentiaries* and to the medium security facilities often called *correctional institutions* or *reformatories*. All such facilities usually confine people serving sentences for felonies.

A *jail* is normally used to confine people serving sentences for misdemeanors, people awaiting trial or sentencing on either felony or misdemeanor charges, and people confined for civil matters such as failure to pay alimony and other types of contempt of court.
See **felony, misdemeanor**.

The guidelines for capitalization:

PRISONS: Many states have given elaborate formal names to their prisons. They should be capitalized when used, but commonly accepted substitutes should also be capitalized as if they were proper names. For example, use either *Massachusetts Correctional Institution-Walpole* or *Walpole State Prison* for the maximum security institution in Massachusetts.

Do not, however, construct a substitute when the formal name is commonly accepted: It is the *Colorado State Penitentiary*, for example, not *Colorado State Prison*.

On second reference, any of the following may be used, all in lowercase: *the state prison, the prison, the state penitentiary, the penitentiary*.

Use lowercase for all plural constructions: *the Colorado and Kansas state penitentiaries*.

JAILS: Capitalize *jail* when linked with the name of the jurisdiction: *Los Angeles County Jail*. Lowercase *county jail, city jail* and *jail* when they stand alone.

FEDERAL INSTITUTIONS: Maximum security institutions are known as *penitentiaries*: *the U.S. Penitentiary at Lewisburg* or *Lewisburg*

Penitentiary on first reference; *the federal penitentiary* or *the penitentiary* on second reference.

Medium security institutions include the word *federal* as part of their formal names: *the Federal Correctional Institution at Danbury, Connecticut.* On second reference: *the correctional institution, the federal prison, the prison.*

Most federal facilities used to house people awaiting trial or serving sentences of a year or less have the proper name *Federal Detention Center.* The term *Metropolitan Correctional Center* is being adopted for some new installations. On second reference: *the detention center, the correctional center.*

prisoner(s) of war *POW(s)* is acceptable on second reference.

Hyphenate when used as a compound modifier: *a prisoner-of-war trial.*

privacy Special care should be taken with regard to publishing the names of juveniles involved in crimes, or of people who may have been the victims of sexual assault or other abuse.

Generally, we do not identify juveniles (under 18) who are accused of crimes or transmit images that would reveal their identity. However, a regional editor or his/her designate may authorize exceptions to this practice.

Considerations in granting exceptions may include the severity of the alleged crime; whether police have formally released the juvenile's name; and whether the juvenile has been formally charged as an adult. Other considerations might include public safety, such as when the youth is the subject of a manhunt; or widespread publication of the juvenile suspect's name, making the identity de facto public knowledge.

In some situations, state or national laws may determine whether the person's name can be published.

We normally do not identify, in text or through images, juveniles who are witnesses to crimes.

We also do not identify, in text or through images, persons who may have been sexually assaulted (unless they have come forward and voluntarily identified themselves). We should also use discretion in naming victims of other extremely severe abuse.

Sometimes a person may be identified by AP in an abduction or manhunt situation, and it develops later that — because of a sexual assault or other reason — the name should not be used. In such cases we have sometimes refrained from using the identification in future coverage.

private See **military titles**.

privatization The process of transferring a government-owned enterprise to private ownership.

privilege, privileged

pro- Use a hyphen when coining words that denote support for something. Some examples:

pro-labor   pro-business
pro-peace   pro-war

No hyphen when *pro* is used in other senses: *produce, profile, pronoun, proactive,* etc.

probation See **pardon, parole, probation**.

problem-solving

Procter & Gamble Co. *P&G* is acceptable on second reference. Headquarters is in Cincinnati.

producer price index An index of changes in wholesale prices, produced by the Bureau of Labor Statistics, U.S. Department of Labor, and used as a gauge of inflation. Spell the index name lowercase.

profanity See **obscenities, profanities, vulgarities**.

professor Never abbreviate. Lowercase before a name, but capitalize Professor Emeritus as a conferred title before a name: *Professor Emeritus Susan Johnson*. Do not continue in second reference unless part of a quotation.

See **academic titles**, **emeritus** and **titles**.

profit-sharing (n. and adj.) The hyphen for the noun is an exception to Webster's New World College Dictionary.

profit-sharing plan A plan that gives employees a share in the profits of the company. Each employee receives a percentage of those profits based on the company's earnings.

profit-taking (n. and adj.) Avoid this term. It means selling a security after a recent rapid rise in price. It is inaccurate if the seller bought the security at a higher price, watched it fall, then sold it after a recent rise but for less than he bought it. In that case, he would be cutting his losses, not taking his profit.

profit terminology Note the meanings of the following terms in reporting a company's financial status. Always be careful to specify whether the figures given apply to quarterly or annual results.

The terms, listed in the order in which they might occur in analyzing a company's financial condition:

dividend The amount paid per share per year to holders of common stock. Payments generally are made in quarterly installments.

If a company shows no profit during a given period, it may be able to use earnings retained from profitable periods to pay its dividend on schedule.

earnings per share (or **loss per share**, for companies posting a net loss) The figure obtained by dividing the number of outstanding shares of common stock into the amount left after dividends have been paid on any preferred stock.

extraordinary loss, extraordinary income An expense or source of income that does not occur on a regular basis, such as a loss due to a major fire or the revenue from the sale of a subsidiary. Extraordinary items should be identified in any report on the company's financial status to avoid creating the false impression that its overall profit trend has suddenly plunged or soared.

gross profit The difference between the sales price of an item or service and the expenses directly attributed to it, such as the cost of raw materials, labor and overhead linked to the production effort.

income before taxes Gross profits minus companywide expenses not directly attributed to specific products or services. These expenses typically include interest costs, advertising and sales costs, and general administrative overhead.

net income, profit, earnings The amount left after taxes and preferred dividends have been paid.

Some of what remains may be paid in dividends to holders of common stock. The rest may be invested to obtain interest revenue or spent to acquire new buildings or equipment to increase the company's ability to make further profits.

To avoid confusion, do not use the word *income* alone — always specify whether the figure is *income before taxes* or *net income*.

The terms *profit* and *earnings* commonly are interpreted as meaning the amount left after taxes. The terms *net profit* and *net earnings* are acceptable synonyms.

return on investment A percentage figure obtained by dividing the company's assets into its net income.

revenue The amount of money a company took in, including interest earned and receipts from sales, services provided, rents and royalties.

The figure also may include excise taxes and sales taxes collected for the government. If it does, the fact should be noted in any report on revenue. The singular form is preferable in most uses.

sales The money a company received for the goods and services it sold.

In some cases the figure includes receipts from rents and royalties. In others, particularly when rentals and royalties make up a large portion of a company's income, figures for these activities are listed separately.

pro forma In the financial world, it describes a method of calculating a company's sales and earnings as if changes in circumstances existed throughout an entire period covered by a financial report. Pro forma figures are often given for companies that have been involved in a merger or acquisition, gone public or emerged from bankruptcy reorganization. Unlike earnings based on generally accepted accounting principles, pro forma earnings do not comply with any standardized rules or regulations.

Prohibition Capitalize when referring to the period that began when the 18th Amendment to the Constitution prohibited the manufacture, sale or transportation of alcoholic liquors.

The amendment was declared ratified Jan. 29, 1919, and took effect Jan. 16, 1920. It was repealed by the 21st Amendment, which took effect Dec. 5, 1933, the day it was declared ratified.

pronouncers When necessary to use a pronouncer, put it in parentheses immediately following the word or name. The syllable to be stressed should be in caps with an apostrophe: *acetaminophen* (*a-see-tuh-MIHN'-oh-fen*).

Here are the basic sounds represented by AP phonetic symbols:

Vowels	Consonants
a — apple, bat	g — got, beg
ah — father, hot	j — gem, job
ahr — part, car	k — cap, keep
aw — law, long	ch — chair
ay — ace, fate	s — see
eh — bed	sh — shut
ehr — merry	y — yes
ee — see, tea	z — zoom
ih — pin, middle	zh — mirage
oh — go, oval	kh — guttural "k"
oo — food, two	
or — for, torn	
ow — cow	
oy — boy	
u — foot, put	
uh — puff	
ur — burden, curl	
y, eye — ice, time	

propeller

proper nouns See **capitalization**.

prophecy (n.) **prophesy** (v.)

proportions Always use figures: *2 parts powder to 6 parts water*.

proposition Do not abbreviate unless in quotations. Capitalize when used with a figure in describing a ballot question: *He is uncom-mitted on Proposition 15.*

prosecutor Capitalize before a name when it is the formal title. In most cases, however, the formal title is a term such as *attorney general, state's attorney* or *U.S. attorney.* If so, use the formal title on first reference.

Lowercase *prosecutor* if used before a name on a subsequent reference, generally to help the reader distinguish between prosecutor and defense attorney without having to look back to the start of the story.

See **titles**.

prostate gland A gland that surrounds the urethra at the base of the bladder in males. Prostate cancer is among the most common cancers in older men in developed countries. Blood tests to measure *PSA,* or *prostate specific antigen,* are sometimes used for screening but do not indicate the presence of cancer — just the possible need for more definitive tests. *PSA* can be high for reasons other than cancer.

protective tariff A duty high enough to assure domestic producers against any effective competition from foreign producers.

protester

prove, proved, proving Use *proven* only as an adjective: *a proven remedy.*

provinces Names of provinces are set off from community names by commas, just as the names of U.S. states are set off from city names: *They went to Halifax, Nova Scotia, on their vacation.*

Do not capitalize *province: They visited the province of Nova Scotia. The earthquake struck Shensi province.*

See **datelines**.

proviso, provisos

provost marshal The plural: *provost marshals.*

proxy An authorization for someone else to vote on behalf of a shareholder at a company's annual shareholder meeting. *Proxy fight* is a strategy used by an acquiring company or investor group in its attempt to gain control of a target company; the acquirer tries to convince other shareholders that the management of the target company should be replaced or a specific corporate action be taken. *Proxy statement* is a document that disclosed important information about issues to be discussed at an annual meeting. It includes the qualifications of management and board directors, serves as a ballot for elections to the board of directors and provides detailed information about executive compensation.

PTA Acceptable in all references for *Parent Teacher Association.*

PT boat Acceptable in all references for *patrol torpedo boat,* a small, fast attack vessel used by the U.S. Navy in World War II.

Public Broadcasting Service An association of public television stations organized to buy and distribute programs selected by a vote of the members.

PBS is acceptable on first reference only within contexts such as a television column. Otherwise, do not use *PBS* until second reference.

public schools Use figures and capitalize *public school* when used with a figure: *Public School 3, Public School 10.*

If a school has a commemorative name, capitalize the name: *Benjamin Franklin School.*

publisher Capitalize when used as a formal title before an individual's name: *Publisher Isaiah Thomas of the Massachusetts Spy.*
See **titles**.

Puerto Rico Do not abbreviate. See **datelines**.

Pulitzer Prizes These yearly awards for outstanding work in journalism and the arts were endowed by the late Joseph Pulitzer, publisher of the old New York World, and first given in 1917. They are awarded by the trustees of Columbia University on recommendation of an advisory board.
Capitalize *Pulitzer Prize*, but lowercase the categories: *Pulitzer Prize for public service, Pulitzer Prize for fiction*, etc.
Also: *She is a Pulitzer Prize winner. He is a Pulitzer Prize-winning author.*

pullback (n.) **pull back** (v.)

pullout (n.) **pull out** (v.)

pullup (n.) **pull up** (v.)

pulpit See **lectern, podium, pulpit, rostrum**.

punctuation The punctuation entries in this book refer to guidelines rather than rules. Guidelines should not be treated casually, however.
See **Punctuation** chapter for separate entries under: **apostrophe; brackets; colon; comma; dash; ellipsis; exclamation point; hyphen; parentheses; periods; question mark; quotation marks;** and **semicolon**.

push-button (n. and adj.)

pushup (n. and adj.) **push up** (v.)

putout (n.) **put out** (v.)

pygmy Capitalize only when referring specifically to any of several races of unusually small African or Asian peoples.

Q&A format Use *Q&A* within the body of a story. See **question mark** in **Punctuation** chapter.

Qantas Airways Ltd. Headquarters of this airline is in Mascot, Australia.

QE2 Acceptable on second reference for the ocean liner Queen Elizabeth 2.

(But use a Roman numeral for the monarch: *Queen Elizabeth II.*)

Q-tips A trademark for a brand of cotton swabs.

quakes See **earthquakes**.

quart (dry) Equal in volume to 67.2 cubic inches. The metric equivalent is approximately 1.1 liters.

To convert to liters, multiply by 1.1 (5 dry quarts x 1.1 is 5.5 liters). See **liter**.

quart (liquid) Equal in volume to 57.75 cubic inches. Also equal to 32 fluid ounces.

The approximate metric equivalents are 950 milliliters or 0.95 of a liter.

To convert to liters, multiply by 0.95 (4 quarts x 0.95 is 3.8 liters). See **liter**.

quasar Acceptable in all references for a *quasi-stellar astronomical object*, often a source of radio waves.

Quebec Use *Quebec City* without the name of the province in datelines.

Do not abbreviate any reference to the province of *Quebec*, Canada's largest in area and second largest in population.

The people are *Quebecois*.
See **datelines**.

queen Capitalize only when used before the name of royalty: *Queen Elizabeth II*. Continue in second references that use the queen's given name: *Queen Elizabeth*.

Lowercase *queen* when it stands alone.

Capitalize in plural uses: *Queens Elizabeth and Victoria*.
See **nobility** and **titles**.

queen mother A widowed queen who is mother of the reigning monarch. See **nobility**.

question mark See entry in **Punctuation** chapter.

questionnaire

quick-witted

quiet period Avoid using this term. In the investing world, it is commonly thought to be the period following a company's initial public offering or just before earnings are reported in which it is subject to possible sanctions by the U.S. Securities and Exchange Commission for making public disclosures. But since SEC rules only prohibit disclosures that go beyond what the company has stated in SEC filings, the term *quiet period* is a misnomer.

quotation marks See entry in **Punctuation** chapter.

quotations in the news Never alter quotations even to correct minor grammatical errors or word usage. Casual minor tongue slips may be removed by using ellipses but even that should be done with extreme caution.

Use *sic*, the Latin word meaning *thus* or *so*, to show that quoted material or person's words include a misspelling, incorrect grammar or peculiar usage. Place *(sic)* in the text directly after the problem to show that the passage is precisely reproduced. To call attention to *(sic)* in wire versions of the story, use an editor's note atop the story.

If there is a question about a quote, either don't use it or ask the speaker to clarify.

If a person is unavailable for comment, detail attempts to reach that person. (*Smith was out of the country on business; Jones did not return phone messages left at the office.*)

Do not use substandard spellings such as *gonna* or *wanna* in attempts to convey regional dialects or informal pronunciations, except to help a desired touch or to convey an emphasis by the speaker.

Follow basic writing style and use abbreviations where appropriate, as in *No. 1, St., Gov., Sen.* and *$3*.

FULL vs. PARTIAL QUOTES: In general, avoid fragmentary quotes. If a speaker's words are clear and concise, favor the full quote. If cumbersome language can be paraphrased fairly, use an indirect construction, reserving quotation marks for sensitive or controversial passages that must be identified specifically as coming from the speaker.

CONTEXT: Remember that you can misquote someone by giving a startling remark without its modifying passage or qualifiers. The manner of delivery sometimes is part of the context. Reporting a smile or a deprecatory gesture may be as important as conveying the words themselves.

OFFENSIVE LANGUAGE: See the **obscenities, profanities, vulgarities** entry.

PUNCTUATION: See the **quotation marks** entry in the **Punctuation** chapter.

PROBLEMATIC QUOTES: See the **(sic)** entry.

Quran The preferred spelling for the Muslim holy book. Use the spelling *Koran* only if preferred by a specific organization or in a specific title or name.

R

race Identification by race or ethnicity is pertinent:

—In biographical and announcement stories that involve significant, groundbreaking or historic events, such as being elected U.S. president, being named to the U.S. Supreme Court or other notable occurrences. *Barack Obama is the first black U.S. president. Sonia Sotomayor is the first Hispanic justice of the U.S. Supreme Court. Jeremy Lin is the first American-born NBA player of Chinese or Taiwanese descent.*

—For suspects sought by the police or missing person cases using police or other credible, detailed descriptions. Such descriptions apply for all races. The racial reference should be removed when the individual is apprehended or found.

—When reporting a demonstration or disturbance involving race or such issues as civil rights or slavery.

In other situations with racial overtones, use news judgment.

Do not use a derogatory term except in extremely rare circumstances — when it is crucial to the story or the understanding of a news event. Flag the contents in an editor's note.

See **obscenities, profanities, vulgarities** and **nationalities and races**.

racket Not *racquet,* for the light bat used in tennis and badminton.

rack, wrack The noun *rack* applies to various types of framework; the verb *rack* means to arrange on a rack, to torture, trouble or torment: *He was placed on the rack. She racked her brain.*

The noun *wrack* means ruin or destruction, as in *wrack and ruin* and *wracked with pain.* Also *nerve-wracking.*

The verb *wrack* has substantially the same meaning as the verb *rack,* the latter being preferred.

radar A lowercase acronym for *radio detection and ranging.* Radar acceptable in all references.

radical In general, avoid this description in favor of a more precise definition of an individual's political views.

When used, it suggests that an individual believes change must be made by tearing up the roots or foundation of the present order.

Although *radical* often is applied to individuals who hold strong socialist or communist views, it also is applied at times to individuals who believe an existing form of government must be replaced by a more authoritarian or militaristic one.

See **leftist, ultra-leftist** and **rightist, ultra-rightist**.

radio Capitalize and use before a name to indicate an official or state-funded broadcast voice: *Radio Free Europe, Radio France International.*

Lowercase and place after the name when indicating only that the information was obtained from broadcasts in a city. *Mexico City radio*, for example, is the form used in referring to reports that are broadcast on various stations in the Mexican capital.

radio station Use lowercase: *radio station WHEC*.
See **call letters**.

railroads Railroads can be characterized as either freight carriers or passenger railroads. Freight carriers with North American operations:
BNSF Railway, a unit of Warren Buffett's Berkshire Hathaway Inc.
Canadian National Railway Co., parent of the Illinois Central and Wisconsin Central Ltd.
Canadian Pacific Railway Ltd., parent of the SOO Line, Delaware & Hudson, and the Dakota, Minnesota & Eastern railroads.
CSX Corp.
Ferromex, a Mexican railroad owned by the Grupo Mexico consortium.
Kansas City Southern
Norfolk Southern Corp.
Union Pacific Corp.
Genesee & Wyoming Inc. owns more than 100 short line and regional freight railroads in the United States, Canada, Australia, the Netherlands and Belgium.

rainstorm See **weather terms**.

raised, reared Only humans may be *reared*.
All living things, including humans, may be *raised*.

RAM Acronym for *random access memory*, the "working memory" of a computer into which programs can be introduced and then executed. *RAM* is acceptable in all uses.

Ramadan The Muslim holy month, marked by daily fasting from dawn to sunset, ending with the Islamic holiday of Eid al-Fitr. Avoid using *holiday* on second reference.

ranges The form: *$12 million to $14 million*. Not: *$12 to $14 million*. Also: *A pay increase of 12-15 percent*. Or: *A pay increase of between 12 and 15 percent*.

rank and file (n.) **rank-and-file** (adj.)

rape See **privacy**.

rarely It means seldom. *Rarely ever* is redundant, but *rarely if ever* often is the appropriate phrase.

ratings agency A company that measures the creditworthiness of companies, municipalities and countries. A ratings agency gauges an entity's ability to repay its debt and assigns a rating based on that assessment. The better the rating, the lower the cost for an entity to borrow money. The three main international ratings agencies are Standard & Poor's, a unit of McGraw Hill Financial Inc.; Moody's Investors Service, a unit of Moody's Corp.; and Fitch Ratings, which is jointly owned by Fimalac SA of Paris and Hearst Corp. of New York.

ratios Use figures and hyphens: *the ratio was 2-to-1, a ratio of 2-to-1, a 2-1 ratio, 1 in 4 voters*. As illustrated, the word *to* should be omitted when the numbers precede the word *ratio*.
Always use the word *ratio* or a phrase such as *a 2-1 majority* to avoid confusion with actual figures.
See **numerals**.

ravage, ravish To *ravage* is to wreak great destruction or devastation: *Union troops ravaged Atlanta*.
To *ravish* is to abduct, rape or carry away with emotion: *Soldiers ravished the women*.

Although both words connote an element of violence, they are not interchangeable. Buildings and towns cannot be *ravished*.

re- The rules in **prefixes** apply. The following examples of exceptions to first-listed spellings in Webster's New World College Dictionary are based on the general rule that a hyphen is used if a prefix ends in a vowel and the word that follows begins with the same vowel:

re-elect	re-enlist
re-election	re-enter
re-emerge	re-entry
re-employ	re-equip
re-enact	re-establish
re-engage	re-examine

For many other words, the sense is the governing factor:

recover (regain)	re-cover (cover again)
reform (improve)	re-form (form again)
resign (quit)	re-sign (sign again)

Otherwise, follow Webster's New World College Dictionary. Use a hyphen for words not listed there unless the hyphen would distort the sense.

Realtor The term *real estate agent* is preferred. Use *Realtor* only if there is a reason to indicate that the individual is a member of the National Association of Realtors.

reared See **raised, reared**.

rebut, refute *Rebut* means to argue to the contrary: *He rebutted his opponent's statement.*

Refute connotes success in argument and almost always implies an editorial judgment. Instead, use *deny, dispute, rebut* or *respond to*.

receivership A legal action in which a court appoints a *receiver* to manage a business while the court tries to resolve problems that could ruin the business, such as insolvency. *Receivership* is often used in federal bankruptcy court proceedings.

But it also can be used for nonfinancial troubles such as an ownership dispute.

In bankruptcy proceedings, the court appoints a trustee called a *receiver* who attempts to settle the financial difficulties of the company while under protection from creditors.

recession A falling-off of economic activity that may be a temporary phenomenon or could continue into a depression.

recession-proof

recipes Always use figures. See **fractions** and **numerals**.

Do not use abbreviations. Spell out *teaspoon, tablespoon*, etc.

See the **food** entry for guidelines on when to capitalize the names of foods.

reconnaissance

Reconstruction The process of reorganizing the Southern states after the Civil War.

record Avoid the redundant *new record*.

recur, recurred, recurring Not *reoccur*.

Red Capitalize when used as a political, geographic or military term: *the Red Army*.

red carpet The ceremonial gantlet where guests arriving at award shows strut their finery, greet fans and give media interviews. Red carpets can be green, as they are for the Grammy Awards, as well as other colors.

reddit A social network that features message board-style posts, organized into topic-based pages called *subreddits*, where users share content and converse about it. Users can vote up or down individual conversation threads and comments, determining which ones are most prominently displayed on the site.

red-haired, redhead, redheaded All are acceptable for a person with red hair.

Redhead also is used colloquially to describe a type of North American diving duck.

red-handed (adj. and adv.)

red-hot

redneck From the characteristic sunburned neck acquired in the fields by farm laborers. It refers to poor, white rural residents of the South and often is a derogatory term.

re-elect, re-election

refer See **allude, refer**.

referable

reference works Capitalize their proper names.

Do not use quotation marks around the names of books that are primarily catalogs of reference material. In addition to catalogs, this category includes almanacs, directories, dictionaries, encyclopedias, gazetteers, handbooks, school yearbooks and similar publications.

EXAMPLES: *Congressional Directory, Webster's New World College Dictionary, the AP Stylebook*. But: "*The Careful Writer*" and "*The Elements of Style*."

See the bibliography for the principal reference works used in preparing this book.

referendum, referendums

reformatory See **prison, jail**.

refugee A person who is forced to leave his home or country to escape war, persecution or natural disaster.

refute See **rebut, refute**.

regifting Passing along an unwanted present to someone else.

regime See **government, junta, regime, administration**.

regions See **directions and regions**.

reign, rein The leather strap for controlling a horse is a *rein*, hence figuratively: *seize the reins, give free rein to*.

Reign is the period a ruler is on the throne: *The king began his reign*.

religious references The basic guidelines:

DEITIES: Capitalize the proper names of monotheistic deities: *God, Allah, the Father, the Son, Jesus Christ, the Son of God, the Redeemer, the Holy Spirit*, etc.

Lowercase pronouns referring to the deity: *he, him, his, thee, thou, who, whose, thy*, etc.

Lowercase *gods* in referring to the deities of polytheistic religions.

Capitalize the proper names of pagan and mythological gods and goddesses: *Neptune, Thor, Venus*, etc.

Lowercase such words as *god-awful, goddamn, godlike, godliness, godsend*.

LIFE OF CHRIST: Capitalize the names of major events in the life of Jesus Christ in references that do not use his name: *The doctrines of the Last Supper, the Crucifixion, the Resurrection and the Ascension are central to Christian belief*.

But use lowercase when the words are used with his name: *The ascension of Jesus into heaven took place 40 days after his resurrection from the dead.*

Apply the principle also to events in the life of his mother: *He cited the doctrines of the Immaculate Conception and the Assumption.* But: *She referred to the assumption of Mary into heaven.*

RITES: Capitalize proper names for rites that commemorate the Last Supper or signify a belief in Christ's presence: *the Lord's Supper, Holy Communion, Holy Eucharist.*

Lowercase the names of other sacraments. See **sacraments** in the **Religion** chapter.

Capitalize *Benediction* and *Mass.* But: *a high Mass, a low Mass, a requiem Mass.*

HOLY DAYS: Capitalize the names of holy days. See **holidays and holy days** and separate entries for major Christian, Jewish and Muslim feasts in the **Religion** chapter.

OTHER WORDS: Lowercase *heaven, hell, devil, angel, cherub, an apostle, a priest,* etc.

Capitalize *Hades* and *Satan.*

For additional details, see **Bible**, entries for frequently used religious terms, the entries for major denominations, **religious movements** and **religious titles** and the **Religion** chapter.

religious titles The first reference to a clergyman or clergywoman normally should include a capitalized title before the individual's name.

In many cases, *the Rev.* is the designation that applies before a name on first reference. Use *the Rev. Dr.* only if the individual has an earned doctoral degree (doctor of divinity degrees frequently are honorary) and reference to the degree is relevant.

On second reference to members of the clergy, use only a last name: *the Rev. Billy Graham* on first reference, *Graham* on second. If known only by a religious name, repeat the title: *Pope John XXIII* on first reference, *John, the pope* or *the pontiff* on second; *Pope Emeritus Benedict XVI* or *Benedict XVI, the pope emeritus. Benedict* alone on second reference. *Metropolitan Herman* on first reference, *Metropolitan Herman* or *the metropolitan* on second.

Detailed guidance on specific titles and descriptive words such as *priest* and *minister* is provided in the entries for major denominations in the **Religion** chapter. In general, however:

CARDINALS, ARCHBISHOPS, BISHOPS: The preferred form for first reference is to use *Cardinal, Archbishop* or *Bishop* before the individual's name: *Cardinal Daniel DiNardo, archbishop of Galveston-Houston.* On second reference: *DiNardo* or *the cardinal.*

Substitute *the Most Rev.* if applicable and appropriate in the context: *He spoke to the Most Rev. Jose Gomez, archbishop of Los Angeles.* On second reference: *Gomez* or *the archbishop.*

Entries for individual denominations tell when *the Most Rev., the Very Rev.,* etc., are applicable. See **Religion** chapter.

MINISTERS AND PRIESTS: Use *the Rev.* before a name on first reference.

Substitute *Monsignor* before the name of a Roman Catholic priest who has received this honor.

Do not routinely use *curate, father, pastor* and similar words before an individual's name. If they appear before a name in a quotation, capitalize them.

RABBIS: Use *Rabbi* before a name on first reference. On second reference, use only the last name.

NUNS: Always use *Sister*, or *Mother* if applicable, before a name: *Sister Agnes Rita* in all references if the nun uses only a religious name; *Sister Mary Ann Walsh* on first reference if she uses a surname. *Walsh* on subsequent references.

OFFICEHOLDERS: The preferred first-reference form for those who hold church office but are not ordained clergy in the usual sense is to use a construction that sets the title apart from the name by commas. Capitalize the formal title of an office, however, if it is used directly before an individual's name.

reluctant, reticent

Reluctant means unwilling to act: *He is reluctant to enter the primary.*

Reticent means unwilling to speak: *The candidate's husband is reticent.*

reply

On Twitter, an @ reply is a common technique to speak to other people directly. A tweet that begins with @username can be seen in Twitter feeds by people that follow both parties, though it can also be viewed on an individual's profile page. Example: *@APStylebook I have a style question that I need help with.*

representative, Rep.

See **legislative titles** and **party affiliation**.

republic

Capitalize *republic* when used as part of a nation's full, formal name: *the Republic of Argentina.*

See **datelines**.

Republic Airways Holdings Inc.

Headquarters of this airline is in Indianapolis.

Republican Governors Association

No apostrophe.

Republican National Committee

On second reference: *the national committee, the committee* and *the RNC.*

Similarly: *Republican State Committee, Republican County Committee, Republican City Committee, the state committee, the county committee, the city committee, the committee.*

Republican, Republican Party

GOP may be used on second reference.

See **political parties and philosophies** and **GOP**.

reputation

See **character, reputation**.

rescission

Reserve

Capitalize when referring to U.S. armed forces, as in *Army Reserve.* Lowercase in reference to members of these backup forces: *reserves*, or *reservists*.

Reserve Officers' Training Corps

The *s'* is military practice. *ROTC* is acceptable in all references.

When the service is specified, use *Army ROTC, Navy ROTC* or *Air Force ROTC*, not *AROTC, NROTC* or *AFROTC.*

resident

See **citizen, resident, subject, national, native**.

resistible

restaurateur

restrictive clauses

See **essential clauses, nonessential clauses**.

restrictive phrases

See **essential phrases, nonessential phrases**.

retail sales

The sales of retail stores, including merchandise sold and receipts for repairs and similar services.

A business is considered a *retail store* if it is engaged primarily in selling merchandise for personal, household or farm consumption.

retweet The practice, on Twitter, of sharing a tweet by someone else to your followers. Users can either click on a retweet button to simply relay the tweet exactly as written and labeled as coming from the original tweeter, or use the informal conventions of "RT @ username": at the beginning, or "via @username" at the end, to share the tweet, which allows the user to edit and/or add comment. Spelled out in all references, though common usage on Twitter abbreviates to RT. If you amend the tweet before forwarding, use the abbreviation MT for "modified tweet."

For AP staffers, retweets, like original tweets, should not be written in a way that looks like an expression of personal opinion on the issues of the day. However, AP staffers can judiciously retweet opinionated material by making clear it is being reported, much like a quote in a story. Add this context before the RT in the manual retweet, or write a new tweet that includes the original in quote marks.

Original tweet example:

@jonescampaign: Smith's policies would destroy our schools.

Example amended for AP retweet:

Jones campaign now denouncing Smith on education. RT @jonescampaign: Smith's policies would destroy our schools.

A tweet from @jonescampaign contends, "Smith's policies would destroy our schools."

Reuters See **Thomson Reuters Corp.**

Rev. When this description is used before an individual's name, precede it with the word *"the"* because, unlike the case with *Mr.* and *Mrs.*, the abbreviation *Rev.* does not stand for a noun.

If an individual also has a secular title such as *Rep.*, use whichever is appropriate to the context.

See **religious titles**.

revenue See **profit terminology**.

revenue bond See **loan terminology**.

reverse auction An auction where the winning bidder is the one willing to take the lowest price. In a reverse auction for subprime mortgage loans, for instance, a bank offering to sell a bundle of bad loans for 50 cents on the dollar would beat a bank offering to sell its loans for 60 cents on the dollar.

Reverse 911 Capitalized trademark for an automated phone alert system.

Use the generic form if the brand is uncertain.

revolution Capitalize when part of a name for a specific historical event: *the American Revolution, the Bolshevik Revolution, the French Revolution.*

The Revolution, capitalized, also may be used as a shorthand reference to the *American Revolution.* Also: *the Revolutionary War.*

Lowercase in other uses: *a revolution, the revolution, the American and French revolutions.*

revolutions per minute The abbreviation *rpm* is acceptable on first reference in specialized contexts such as an auto column. Otherwise do not use it until second reference.

revolving credit Describes an account on which the payment is any amount less than the total balance, and the remaining balance carried forward is subject to finance charges.

Rh factor Also: *Rh negative, Rh positive.*

Rhode Island Abbreviate *R.I.* in datelines only; spell out in stories. Postal code: *RI*
See **state names**.

Rhodes scholar Lowercase *scholar* and *scholarship.*

rhythm and blues *R&B* is acceptable on second reference.

RIA Novosti A Russian government news agency, based in Moscow. Successor to the Soviet Information Bureau (1941-1960) and the Novosti Press Agency (1961-1990).

Richter scale No longer widely used. See **earthquakes**.

RICO An acronym for *Racketeer Influenced and Corrupt Organizations Act.* Acceptable on second reference, but *anti-racketeering* or *anti-corruption law* is preferred.

ride-sharing See **Uber**.

rifle See **weapons**.

rifle, riffle *To rifle* is to plunder or steal.
To riffle is to leaf rapidly through a book or pile of papers.

right hand (n.) **right-hander** (n.) **right-handed** (adj.)

rightist, ultra-rightist In general, avoid these terms in favor of more precise descriptions of an individual's political philosophy.
Ultra-rightist suggests an individual who subscribes to rigid interpretations of a conservative doctrine

or to forms of fascism that stress authoritarian, often militaristic, views.
See **radical** and **leftist, ultra-leftist**.

right of way, rights of way

right-to-work (adj.) A *right-to-work* law prohibits a company and a union from signing a contract that would require the affected workers to be union members.
See **closed shop** for definitions of various agreements that require union membership.

right wing (n.) **right-winger** (n.) **right-wing** (adj.) Generally try to avoid in describing political leanings.

Ringling Bros. and Barnum & Bailey Note the *and, &.*
The circus is owned by Feld Entertainment Inc., headquartered in Palmetto, Florida.

Rio de Janeiro The city in Brazil stands alone in datelines.

Rio Grande Not *Rio Grande River. Rio* means river in Spanish.

rip-off (n. and adj.) **rip off** (v.)

river Capitalize as part of a proper name: *the Mississippi River.*
Lowercase in other uses: *the river, the Mississippi and Missouri rivers.*

road Do not abbreviate. See **addresses**.

robbery See **burglary, larceny, robbery, theft**.

Roche Holding AG Headquarters is in Basel, Switzerland.

rock 'n' roll But *Rock and Roll Hall of Fame.*

Rocky Mountains Or simply: *the Rockies*.

roll call (n.) **roll-call** (adj.)

Rollerblade A trademark for a brand of in-line skates.

roller coaster

rollover The selling of new securities to pay off old ones coming due or the refinancing of an existing loan.

Rolls-Royce Note the hyphen in this trademark for a make of automobile.

Rolodex A trademark for a brand of rotary card file.

ROM Acronym for *read-only memory*, computer memory whose contents cannot be modified. *ROM* acceptable in all references.

Roma Capitalize references to the nomadic ethnic group also known as *Gypsies*. Either is acceptable. In the United States, they are widely referred to as *Gypsies*. The word should be explained: *Roma, also known as Gypsies*. See **Gypsy, Gypsies**.

Roman Catholic Church The church teaches that its bishops have been established as the successors of the apostles through generations of ceremonies in which authority was passed down by a laying-on of hands.

Responsibility for teaching the faithful and administering the church rests with the bishops. However, the church holds that the pope has final authority over their actions because he is the bishop of Rome, the office it teaches was held by the Apostle Peter at his death.

The Curia serves as a form of governmental cabinet. Its members, appointed by the pope, handle both administrative and judicial functions.

The pope also chooses members of the College of Cardinals, who serve as his principal counselors. When a new pope must be chosen, they meet in a conclave to select a new pope by majority vote. In practice, cardinals are mostly bishops, but there is no requirement that a cardinal be a bishop.

In the United States, the church's principal organizational units are archdioceses and dioceses. They are headed, respectively, by archbishops and bishops, who have final responsibility for many activities within their jurisdictions and report directly to Rome.

The church counts more than 1 billion members worldwide. In the United States it has more than 66 million members, making it the largest single body of Christians in the nation.

Roman Catholics believe in the Trinity — that there is one God who exists as three divine persons — the Father, the Son and the Holy Spirit. They believe that the Son became man as Jesus Christ.

In addition to the Holy Eucharist, there are six other sacraments — baptism, confirmation, penance (often called the sacrament of reconciliation), matrimony, holy orders, and the sacrament of the sick (formerly extreme unction).

The clergy below pope are, in descending order, cardinal, archbishop, bishop, monsignor, priest and deacon. In religious orders, some men who are not priests have the title *brother*.

Capitalize *pope* when used as a title before a name: *Pope John XXIII, Pope Francis*. Lowercase in all other uses. See **religious titles**.

The first-reference forms for other titles follow. Use only last names on second reference.

Cardinals: *Cardinal Daniel DiNardo*. The usage *Daniel Cardinal DiNardo*, a practice traceable to the nobility's custom of identifications such as *William, Duke of Norfolk*, is still used in formal documents but otherwise is considered archaic.

Archbishops: *Archbishop Gregory Aymond*, or *the Most Rev. Gregory Aymond, archbishop of New Orleans*.

Bishops: *Bishop Thomas Paprocki*, or *the Most Rev. Thomas Paprocki, bishop of Springfield, Illinois*.

Monsignors: *Monsignor Martin Krebs*. Do not use the abbreviation *Msgr.* Do not use *the Rt. Rev.* or *the Very Rev.* — this distinction between types of monsignors no longer is made.

Priests: *the Rev. James Martin*. See **religious titles**.

Romania

Roman numerals The Roman letters (*I*, *X*, etc.) were used as numerals until the 10th century.

Use Roman numerals for wars and to establish personal sequence for people and animals: *World War I, Native Dancer II, King George V.* Also for certain legislative acts (*Title IX*).

Except in formal reference, pro football Super Bowls should be identified by the year, rather than the Roman numerals: *1969 Super Bowl*, not *Super Bowl III*.

Use Arabic numerals in all other cases. See **Arabic numerals** and **numerals**.

In Roman numerals, the capital letter *I* equals 1, *V* equals 5, *X* equals 10, *L* equals 50, *C* equals 100, *D* equals 500 and *M* equals 1,000.

Other numbers are formed from these by adding or subtracting as follows:

—The value of a letter following another of the same or greater value is added: *III* equals 3.

—The value of a letter preceding one of greater value is subtracted: *IV* equals 4.

Rome The city in Italy stands alone in datelines.

room numbers Use figures and capitalize *room* when used with a figure: *Room 2, Room 211.*

rooms Capitalize the names of specially designated rooms: *Blue Room, Lincoln Room, Oval Office, Persian Room.*

Rosh Hashana The Jewish new year. Occurs in September or October.

rostrum See **lectern, podium, pulpit, rostrum**.

ROTC See **Reserve Officers' Training Corps**.

roundtable

roundup (n.) **round up** (v.)

route numbers Do not abbreviate *route*. Use figures and capitalize route when used with a figure: *U.S. Route 70, state Route 1A.*

See **highway designations**.

Royal Dutch Shell PLC A 2005 unification of Royal Dutch Petroleum and Shell Transport & Trading Co., with headquarters in The Hague, Netherlands. The company specializes in petroleum and related products. Holdings include Shell Oil Co., a U.S. corporation, with headquarters in Houston.

royal titles See **nobility**.

RSS An abbreviation for *Really Simple Syndication*. A protocol for subscribing to and distributing feeds that notify people of new entries on news sites, blogs, podcasts or other online information sources. Also *RSS feed*. *RSS* is acceptable in all references.

RSVP The abbreviation for the French *repondez s'il vous plait*, it means *please reply*.

rubber stamp (n.) **rubber-stamp** (v. and adj.)

rubella Also known as *German measles*.

runner-up, runners-up

running mate

rush hour (n.) **rush-hour** (adj.)

Russia See **Commonwealth of Independent States**.

Russian names When a first name in Russian has a close phonetic equivalent in English, use the equivalent in translating the name: *Alexander Solzhenitsyn* rather than *Aleksandr*, the spelling that would result from a transliteration of the Russian letter into the English alphabet.

When a first name has no close phonetic equivalent in English, express it with an English spelling that approximates the sound in Russian: *Dmitry, Nikita, Sergei*, for example. If an individual has a preference for an English spelling that is different from the one that would result by applying these guidelines, follow the individual's preference. Example: *Foreign Minister Sergey Lavrov*.

For last names, use the English spelling that most closely approximates the pronunciation in Russian.

Exception: the *"ev"* ending of names like Gorbachev may be pronounced "yov."

If an individual has a preference for an English spelling that is different from the one that would result by applying these guidelines, follow the individual's preference.

Women's last names often have the feminine ending *"-a."* But use this ending only if the woman is not married or if she is known under that name (the tennis player *Anna Kournikova*). Otherwise, use the masculine form: *Mrs. Medvedev*.

Russian names never end in *off*, except for common mistransliterations such as *Rachmaninoff*. Instead, the transliterations should end in *ov*: *Romanov*. Also, Russian names end in *"sky,"* rather than *"ski"* typical of Polish surnames.

Russian Revolution Also: *the Bolshevik Revolution*.

Rust Belt Areas of the Midwest and Northeast where factories are old and closed.

Ryanair Holdings PLC Headquarters of this airline is in Dublin, Ireland.

saboteur

Sacagawea

Saddam Use *Saddam* in second reference to Iraq's former leader Saddam Hussein.

safety belt Also: *seat belt*.

Safeway Supermarket chain that has stores under names including Safeway, Vons, Pavilion's, Randall's, Tom Thumb and Carrs. In March 2014, the company agreed to be acquired by an investor group led by Cerberus Capital Management, which owns several other supermarket chains. The acquisition closed in January 2015. The combined company has corporate offices in Phoenix, Arizona; Boise, Idaho, and Pleasanton, California.

saint Abbreviate as *St.* in the names of saints, cities and other places: *St. Jude*; *St. Paul, Minnesota*; *St. John's, Newfoundland*; *St. Lawrence Seaway*.
But see the entries for **Saint John** and **Sault Ste. Marie**.

Saint John The spelling for the city in New Brunswick.
To distinguish it from *St. John's, Newfoundland*.

salable

SALT See **Strategic Arms Reduction Treaty (START)**

Salt Lake City The city in Utah stands alone in datelines.

salvo, salvos

SAM, SAMs Acceptable on second reference for *surface-to-air missile(s)*.

Samsung Electronics Headquarters is in Seoul, South Korea.

Sanaa The capital of Yemen. The double-a reflects the Arabic pronunciation of *San'a*.

San Antonio The city in Texas stands alone in datelines.

sandbag (n. and v.) The verbs: *sandbagged, sandbagging*. And: *sandbagger*.

San Diego The city in California stands alone in datelines.

sandstorm See **weather terms**.

San Francisco The city in California stands alone in datelines.

San Marino Use alone in datelines on stories from the Republic of San Marino.

Santa Claus

Sao Paulo The city in Brazil stands alone in datelines.

Sardinia Use instead of Italy in datelines on stories from communities on this island.

SARS Acceptable in all references for *severe acute respiratory syndrome*, but it should be spelled out somewhere in the story.

Saskatchewan A province of Canada north of Montana and North Dakota. Do not abbreviate.
See **datelines**.

SAT Use only the initials in referring to the previously designated Scholastic Aptitude Test or the Scholastic Assessment Test. Example: *The students scored above average on the SAT.*

Satan But lowercase *devil* and *satanic*.

satellite communications The following are some generally used technical terms dealing with satellite communications.
uplink The transmission from the ground to the satellite.
downlink The transmission from the satellite to the ground.
footprint The area on the ground in which a transmission from a particular satellite can be received.
earth station Sending or receiving equipment on the ground for a satellite.
transponder The equipment on a satellite that receives from the ground and sends to the ground. A satellite usually has a number of *transponders*.
geosynchronous A satellite orbit in which the satellite appears to always be in the same place in reference to the Earth. Most communications satellites are in geosynchronous orbits. Also *geostationary*.

satellites See **spacecraft designations**.

Saturday night special See **weapons**.

Saudi Arabia Use *Saudi* as the adjective in referring to the people or culture of Saudi Arabia. It's *Saudi diplomacy*, not *Saudi Arabian diplomacy*. For the Saudi monarchy, follow the style on British and other monarchies. *Foreign Minister Prince Saud Al-Faisal* would be *Prince Saud* on first reference and *Saud* on second reference.

Saudi Arabian Oil Co. *Saudi Aramco* is acceptable on second reference. Formerly the Arabian American Oil Co.

Sault Ste. Marie, Mich., Sault Ste. Marie, Ontario The abbreviation is *Ste.* instead of *St.* because the full name is *Sault Sainte Marie*.

savings and loan associations Also called *thrifts* or *savings and loans*. Differ from banks in that they are required by law to have a large proportion of their lending in mortgages and other consumer loans. They are regulated by the Federal Deposit Insurance Corp. and the Treasury Department's Office of the Comptroller of the Currency.

scene numbers Capitalize scene when used with a figure: *Scene 2; Act 2, Scene 4.*
But: *the second scene, the third scene.*
See **numerals**.

scheme Do not use as a synonym for *a plan* or *a project*.

Schengen Area A group of European countries that have agreed to abolish passport and customs controls among one another. Created by the 1985 Schengen Agreement, it has grown to encompass 26 countries: 22 of the 28 EU member nations plus non-EU nations Norway, Iceland, Switzerland and Liechtenstein. EU members Great Britain and Ireland opted out of the agreement, while four other EU nations — Bulgaria, Croatia, Cyprus and Romania — are candidates to join once all EU member countries give their approval.

school Capitalize when part of a proper name: *Public School 3, Madison Elementary School, Doherty Junior High School, Crocker High School.*

scissors Takes plural verbs and pronouns: *The scissors are on the table. Leave them there.*

Scotch tape A trademark for a brand of transparent tape.

Scotland Use *Scotland* after the names of Scottish communities in datelines.
See **datelines** and **United Kingdom**.

Scot, Scots, Scottish A native of Scotland is a *Scot.* The people are the *Scots*, not the *Scotch.*
Somebody or something is *Scottish.*

scraping, mirroring The method of copying video, photo or audio content from an account and reposting it to a different one.

Screen Actors Guild-American Federation of Television and Radio Artists *SAG-AFTRA* is acceptable on second reference.

National offices in Los Angeles and New York.

screen saver

E.W. Scripps Co. In July 2014 Scripps agreed with Journal Communications to combine broadcasting operations and spin off newspaper holdings into a separate public entity. The deal is expected to be finalized in 2015. Under terms of the deal, E.W. Scripps will remain based in Cincinnati. The company will own and operate TV and radio stations serving various markets. It will continue to sponsor the annual spelling bee.

Scripps Networks Interactive Inc. Owner of HGTV, Food Network, DIY Network and other national television networks. Headquarters is in Knoxville, Tennessee.

Scripture, Scriptures Capitalize when referring to the religious writings in the Bible.
See **Bible**.

scuba Lowercased acronym for *self-contained underwater breathing apparatus.*

Scud missile

sculptor Use for both men and women.

scurrilous

Sea Islands A chain of islands off the coasts of South Carolina, Georgia and Florida.
Islands within the boundaries of South Carolina include Parris Island, Port Royal Island, and St. Helena Island.
Those within Georgia include Cumberland Island (largest in the chain), St. Simons Island and St.

Catherines Island (no apostrophes), and Sea Island.

Amelia Island is within the boundaries of Florida.

Several communities have names taken from the island name — Port Royal is a town on Port Royal Island, Sea Island is a resort on Sea Island, and St. Simons Island is a village on St. Simons Island.

In datelines:
PORT ROYAL, S.C. (AP) —
ST. SIMONS ISLAND, Ga. (AP) —

SEAL(s) A special operations force of the Navy. The acronym is for *sea, air, land*.
See **special forces**.

seaman See **military titles**.

search engine optimization Any of a number of methods, both informal and algorithmic, used to ensure that online content shows up in search engines such as Google and Bing, thus increasing traffic to the content. *SEO* is acceptable on second reference.

Sears Holdings Corp. The company formed when Kmart Holding Corp. bought Sears, Roebuck & Co. in 2005. Headquarters is in Hoffman Estates, Illinois.

seasons Lowercase *spring, summer, fall, winter* and derivatives such as *springtime* unless part of a formal name: *Dartmouth Winter Carnival, Winter Olympics, Summer Olympics*.

seat belt Two words.

Seattle The city in the state of Washington stands alone in datelines.

second guess (n.) The verb form: *second-guess*. Also: *second-guesser*.

second hand (n.) **secondhand** (adj. and adv.)

second-rate (adj.)

second reference When used in this book, the term applies to all subsequent references to an organization or individual within a story.

Acceptable abbreviations and acronyms for organizations frequently in the news are listed under the organization's full name. A few prominent acronyms acceptable on first reference also are listed alphabetically according to the letters of the acronym.

The listing of an acceptable term for second reference does not mean that it always must be used after the first reference. Often a generic word such as *the agency, the commission* or *the company* is more appropriate and less jarring to the reader. At other times, the full name may need to be repeated for clarity.

For additional guidelines that apply to organizations, see **abbreviations and acronyms** and **capitalization**.

For additional guidelines that apply to individuals, see **courtesy titles** and **titles**.

secretary Capitalize before a name only if it is an official corporate or organizational title. Do not abbreviate.
See **titles**.

secretary-general With a hyphen. Capitalize as a formal title before a name: *Secretary-General Ban Ki-moon*.
See **titles**.

secretary of state Capitalize as a formal title before a name.
See **titles**.

secretary-treasurer With a hyphen. Capitalize as a formal title before a name.
See **titles**.

Secret Service A federal agency administered by the Department of Homeland Security.

The *Secret Service Uniformed Division*, which protects the president's residence and offices and the embassies in Washington, formerly was known as the Executive Protective Service.

section Capitalize when used with a figure to identify part of a law or bill: *Section 14B of the Taft-Hartley Act*.

Securities and Exchange Commission *SEC* is acceptable on second reference.

The related legislation is the *Securities Exchange Act* (no *and*).

securitization Bundling together individual assets, such as mortgages, and selling stakes to investors.

Security Council (U.N.) *Security Council* may be used on first reference in stories under a United Nations dateline. Use *U.N. Security Council* in other first references.

Retain capitalization of *Security Council* in all references.

Lowercase *council* whenever it stands alone.

Seeing Eye dog A trademark for a guide dog trained by Seeing Eye Inc. of Morristown, New Jersey. *Guide dog* is preferred in all references.

seesaw

self- Always hyphenate:
self-assured   self-government
self-defense

selfie A self-portrait photo generally taken with a camera-equipped phone or webcam. A photo is most commonly called a *selfie* when shared over a social network.

sellout (n.) **sell out** (v.)

semi- The rules in **prefixes** apply, but in general, no hyphen.
Some examples:
semifinal   semiofficial
semi-invalid   semitropical
But semi-automatic.

semiannual Twice a year, a synonym for *biannual*.
Do not confuse it with *biennial*, which means every two years.

semicolon See entry in **Punctuation** chapter.

semitrailer Or *semitractor-trailer*, but not *semi-tractor trailer*.

Senate Capitalize all specific references to governmental legislative bodies, regardless of whether the name of the state or nation is used: *the U.S. Senate, the Senate, the Virginia Senate, the state Senate, the Senate*.

Lowercase plural uses: *the Virginia and North Carolina senates*.
See **governmental bodies**.

Lowercase references to nongovernmental bodies: *the student senate at Yale*.

senatorial Always lowercase.

senator, Sen. See **legislative titles** and **party affiliation**.

send-off (n.) **send off** (v.)

senior See **junior, senior**.

senior citizen Use the term sparingly. See **elderly**.

sentences Capitalize the first word of every sentence, including quoted statements and direct questions:

Patrick Henry said, "I know not what course others may take, but as for me, give me liberty or give me death."

Capitalize the first word of a quoted statement if it constitutes a sentence, even if it was part of a larger sentence in the original: *Patrick Henry said, "Give me liberty or give me death."*

In direct questions, even without quotation marks: *The story answers the question, Where does true happiness really lie?*

Use a single space between sentences.

See **ellipsis** in **Punctuation** chapter and **poetry**.

Sept. 11 The term for describing the attacks in the United States on Sept. 11, 2001. Use 2001 if needed for clarity. Also acceptable is 9/11. See **9/11**.

Sept. 11 memorial Acceptable in all references to the *National September 11 Memorial & Museum* at *ground zero*. Add location for other memorials with similar names.

sergeant See **military titles**.

sergeant-at-arms

serial numbers Use figures and capital letters in solid form (no hyphens or spaces unless the source indicates they are an integral part of the code): *A1234567*.

server A computer program that responds to requests from remote computers on a network. A Web server, for instance, hosts websites and delivers pages to users upon demand. A file server, in another example, stores and delivers documents to users on a network. A server typically runs on a specialized computer, though most of today's PCs are capable of running such software.

serviceable

service clubs See **fraternal organizations and service clubs**.

Service Employees International Union A Washington, D.C.-based labor organization that represents a wide array of service-industry workers in the United States, Puerto Rico and Canada. *SEIU* is acceptable on second reference.

serviceman, servicewoman But *service member*.

sesquicentennial A 150-year period.

setup (n. and adj.) **set up** (v.)

Seven Seas Arabian Sea, Atlantic Ocean, Bay of Bengal, Mediterranean Sea, Persian Gulf, Red Sea, South China Sea.

Seven Wonders of the World The Egyptian pyramids, the hanging gardens of Babylon, the Mausoleum at Halicarnassus, the temple of Artemis at Ephesus, the Colossus of Rhodes, the statue of Zeus by Phidias at Olympia and the Pharos or lighthouse at Alexandria.

sewage Use this term, not *sewerage*, for both the waste matter and the drainage system.

sexual assault See **privacy**.

sexually transmitted diseases *STDs* is acceptable on second reference.

shah Capitalize when used as a title before a name: *Shah Mohammad Reza Pahlavi of Iran.*

The Shah of Iran commonly is known only by this title, which is, in effect, an alternate name. Capitalize *Shah of Iran* in references to the holder of the title; lowercase subsequent references as *the shah.*

The practice is based on the guidelines in the **nobility** entry.

shake-up (n. and adj.) **shake up** (v.)

shall, will Use *shall* to express determination: *We shall overcome. You and he shall stay.*

Either *shall* or *will* may be used in first-person constructions that do not emphasize determination: *We shall hold a meeting. We will hold a meeting.*

For second- and third-person constructions, use *will* unless determination is stressed: *You will like it. She will not be pleased.*

See **should, would** and **subjunctive mood**.

Shanghai The city in China stands alone in datelines.

shape-up (n. and adj.) **shape up** (v.)

she Do not use this pronoun in references to ships or nations. Use *it* instead.

Sheetrock A trademark for a brand of gypsum wallboard or plasterboard.

sheikh A title for a religious or tribal leader. Also used as a term of respect. *Sheikh* is also used in certain Arab names, such as the Egyptian city of *Sharm el-Sheikh.*

shell See **weapons**.

sheriff Capitalize when used as a formal title before a name. See **titles**.

ships See **boats, ships**.

shoeshine, shoestring

short An investment term used to describe the position held by individuals who sell stock that they do not yet own by borrowing from their broker in order to deliver to the purchaser.

A person selling short is betting that the price of the stock will fall.

shortchange

short covering The purchase of a security to repay shares of a security borrowed from a broker.

short-lived (adj.) *A short-lived plan. The plan was short-lived.*

short sale In financial markets, a sale of securities that are not owned by the sellers at the time of sale but which they intend to purchase or borrow in time to make delivery. *Short selling* is a bet that a stock's price will fall. In real estate, a *short sale* is when a bank lets homeowners sell their homes for less than they owe on the mortgage.

short ton Equal to 2,000 pounds. See **ton**.

shot See **weapons**.

shotgun See **weapons**.

should, would Use *should* to express an obligation: *We should help the needy.*

Use *would* to express a customary action: *In the summer we would spend hours by the seashore.*

Use *would* also in constructing a conditional past tense, but be careful:

Wrong: *If Soderholm would not have had an injured foot, Thompson would not have been in the lineup.*

Right: *If Soderholm had not had an injured foot, Thompson would not have been in the lineup.*

See **subjunctive mood**.

shoutout (n.) **shout out** (v.)

showcase, showroom, showtime

showoff (n.) **show off** (v.)

shrubs See **plants**.

shutdown (n.) **shut down** (v.)

shut-in

shut-off (n.) **shut off** (v.)

shutout (n.) **shut out** (v.)

(sic) Use the Latin word meaning *thus* or *so* to show that quoted material or person's words include a misspelling, incorrect grammar or peculiar usage. Place (*sic*) in the text directly after the problem to show that the passage is precisely reproduced. Do not insert (*sic*) for quoted material that may be open to challenge, such as a political assertion. Specify that outside the quote in a separate sentence.

To call attention to (*sic*) in wire versions of the story, use an editor's note atop the story. The Eds. note will not appear in the online version.

— — —

Eds. note: [Eds: (sic) in a quote indicates a grammatical error in the original document]

or

Eds. note: [Eds: (sic) indicates the spelling Jorga is correct]

Sicily Use instead of Italy in datelines on stories from communities on this island.

side by side, side-by-side *They walked side by side. The stories received side-by-side display.*

Siemens AG Headquarters is in Munich.

Sierra Nevada, the Not *Sierra Nevada mountains* or *Sierra Nevada mountain range.* (*Sierra* means mountain range.)

sightseeing, sightseer

sign-up (n. and adj.) **sign up** (v.)

Silicon Valley High-tech region encompassing the northern Santa Clara Valley and adjacent areas of Northern California.

Sinai Not *the Sinai.* But: *the Sinai Desert, the Sinai Peninsula.*

Singapore Stands alone in datelines.

Singapore Airlines Headquarters of this airline is in Singapore.

single-handed, single-handedly

sir See **nobility**.

sister-in-law, sisters-in-law

sit-down (n. and adj.) **sit down** (v.)

sit-in (n. and adj.) **sit in** (v.)

situp (n.) **sit up** (v.)

sizable

sizes Use figures: *a size 8 dress, size 40 long, 10 1/2B shoes, a 34 1/2 sleeve.*

skeptic See **cynic, skeptic**.

Skid Road, Skid Row The term originated as *Skid Road* in the Seattle area, where dirt roads were used to skid logs to the mill. Over the years, *Skid Road* became a synonym for the area where loggers gathered, usually down among the rooming houses and saloons.

In time, the term spread to other cities as a description for sections, such as the Bowery in New York, that were havens for derelicts. In the process, *row* replaced *road* in many references.

Use *Skid Road* for this section in Seattle; either *Skid Road* or *Skid Row* for other areas.

skillful

ski, skis, skier, skied, skiing Also: *ski jump, ski jumping.*

Skype A service that allows users to communicate by voice, video and instant message over the Internet. *Skype* is used informally as a verb for using the service, particularly when communicating on video.

SkyWest Inc. Headquarters of this airline is in St. George, Utah.

slang In general, avoid slang, the highly informal language that is outside of conventional or standard usage.
See **colloquialisms** and **dialect**.

slash Acceptable in descriptive phrases such as 24/7 or 9/11, but otherwise confine its use to special situations, as with fractions or denoting the ends of a line in quoted poetry.

slaying See **homicide, murder, manslaughter**.

sledgehammer

sleet See **weather terms**.

sleight of hand

slideshow

slowdown (n.) **slow down** (v.)

slumlord

slush fund

small-arms fire

small-business man/woman

smartphone An advanced mobile device, such as an iPhone, that can be used to check email, browse the Web and download applications.

smashup (n. and adj.) **smash up** (v.)

Smithsonian Institution Not *Smithsonian Institute.*

smoke bomb, smoke screen

smokejumper One word, lowercase, for the firefighter who gets to fires by aircraft and parachute.

Smokey Or *Smokey Bear.* Not *Smokey the Bear.*
But: *A smoky room.*

smolder Not *smoulder.*

SMS An abbreviation for *Short Message Service. Text messaging* is preferred.

Snapchat A mobile messaging app in which users can capture photos or brief video clips, add text or drawings and share them with friends, who will then be able to see them for a brief period of time defined by the sender. Snapchat "stories" give users the option of publishing content and making it viewable for a full 24 hours.

sneaked Preferred as past tense of *sneak*. Do not use the colloquial *snuck*.

snowdrift, snowfall, snowflake, snowman, snowplow, snowshoe, snowstorm, snowsuit

so called (adv.) **so-called** (adj.) Use sparingly. Do not follow with quotation marks. Example: *He is accused of trading so-called blood diamonds to finance the war.*

socialist, socialism See **political parties and philosophies**.

social media Online tools and services that people use to connect with one another, including social networks. See section on **Social Media Guidelines**.

social media optimization Any of a number of methods used to ensure that online content is shared on social networks, thus increasing click-thru traffic to the originating website. *SMO* is acceptable on second reference.

social networking A practice by which people meet, interact and share information online through the use of such sites as *Facebook* or *Twitter*.

social networks Online networks such as Facebook or Twitter where people share personal and professional information and content, and connect with friends and colleagues.

Social Security Capitalize all references to the U.S. system.

The number groups are hyphenated: *123-45-6789*

Lowercase generic uses such as: *Is there a social security program in Sweden?*

Society for the Prevention of Cruelty to Animals *SPCA* is acceptable on second reference.

The *American Society for the Prevention of Cruelty to Animals* is limited to the five boroughs of New York City.

The autonomous chapters in other cities ordinarily precede the organization by the name of the city: On first reference, *the San Francisco Society for the Prevention of Cruelty to Animals*; on second, *the San Francisco SPCA* or *the SPCA* as appropriate in the context.

Society of Professional Journalists (no longer the Society of Professional Journalists, Sigma Delta Chi). On second reference: *SPJ.*

soft-spoken

software titles Capitalize but do not use quotation marks around such titles as WordPerfect or Windows, but use quotation marks for computer games: *"Where in the World Is Carmen Sandiego?"*

solicitor See **lawyer**.

soliloquy, soliloquies

solvency The ability to pay expenses and debt on time and continue operating. An insolvent company typically has to seek bankruptcy protection from creditors.

Somali A person from Somalia, or an adjective for something linked to Somalia. Do not use *Somalian*.

song titles See **composition titles**.

son-in-law, sons-in-law

SOS The distress signal.
S.O.S (no final period) is a trademark for a brand of soap pad.

sound barrier The speed of sound is no longer a true barrier because aircraft have exceeded it. See **Mach number**.

soundstage

source Avoid the term if possible. Be as specific as possible about the source of information. If space is limited, use *source* as a last resort. *Official* or a similar word will often suffice, including in headlines. See **anonymous sources**.

source code The basic blueprint of a computer program.

South As defined by the U.S. Census Bureau, the 16-state region is broken into three divisions.
The four *East South Central* states are Alabama, Kentucky, Mississippi and Tennessee.
The eight *South Atlantic* states are Delaware, Florida, Georgia, Maryland, North Carolina, South Carolina, Virginia and West Virginia.
The four *West South Central* states are Arkansas, Louisiana, Oklahoma and Texas.
There is no official U.S. Census Bureau definition of Southeast.
See **Midwest region; Northeast region**; and **West** for the bureau's other regional breakdowns.

South America See **Western Hemisphere**.

South Carolina Abbreviate *S.C.* in datelines only; spell out in stories. Postal code: *SC*
See **state names**.

South Dakota Abbreviate *S.D.* in datelines only; spell out in stories. Postal code: *SD*
See **state names**.

Southeast Asia The nations of the Indochina Peninsula and the islands southeast of it: Cambodia, Indonesia, Laos, Malaysia, Myanmar, Papua New Guinea, the Philippines, Singapore, Thailand and Vietnam.
See **Asian subcontinent** and **Far East**.

south, southern, southeast, southwest See **directions and regions**.

Southwest Airlines Co. Headquarters of this airline is in Dallas.

Soviet Union See **Commonwealth of Independent States**.

Space Age It began with the launching of Sputnik 1 on Oct. 4, 1957.

space agency See **National Aeronautics and Space Administration**.

space centers See **John F. Kennedy Space Center** and **Lyndon B. Johnson Space Center**.

spacecraft designations Use Arabic figures and capitalize the name: *Gemini 7, Apollo 11, Pioneer 10*. See **numerals**.

spaceship

space shuttle Lowercase *space shuttle*, but capitalize a proper name.

The space shuttle was a reusable winged spaceship capable of carrying people and cargo into Earth orbit. NASA'S shuttles flew from 1981 until 2011, logging 135 missions. Two of the five shuttles were destroyed in flight, Challenger in 1986 and Columbia in 2003.

spacewalk

spam, Spam Use *spam* in all references to unsolicited commercial or bulk email, often advertisements. Use *Spam*, a trademark, to refer to a canned meat product.

Spanish-American War

Spanish names The family names of both the father and mother usually are considered part of a person's full name. In everyday use, customs sometimes vary with individuals and countries.

The normal sequence is given name, father's family name, mother's family name: *Gabriel Garcia Marquez*.

On second reference, use only the father's family name (*Garcia*), unless the individual prefers or is widely known by a multiple last name (*Garcia Marquez*).

Some individuals use a *y* (for *and*) between the two surnames to ensure that both names are used together (including second references): *Gabriel Garcia y Marquez*.

A married woman sometimes uses her father's name, followed by the particle *de* (for *of*) and her husband's name. A woman named *Irma Perez* who married a man named *Anibal Gutierrez* would be known as *Irma Perez de Gutierrez*.

speaker Capitalize as a formal title before a name. Generally, it is a formal title only for the speaker of a legislative body: *Speaker John Boehner*.

See **titles**.

special contexts When this term is used in this book, it means that the material described may be used in a regular column devoted to a specialized subject or when a particular literary effect is suitable.

Special literary effects generally are suitable only in feature copy, but even there they should be used with care. Most feature material should follow the same style norms that apply to regular news copy.

special forces Do not use interchangeably with *special operations forces*. Capitalize when referring specifically to the *U.S. Army Special Forces*, also known as Green Berets. Others, such as Navy SEALs or Army Rangers, should be called *special operations forces*.

species Same in singular and plural. Use singular or plural verbs and pronouns depending on the sense: *The species has been unable to maintain itself. Both species are extinct.*

See **genus, species**.

speeches Capitalize and use quotation marks for their formal titles, as described in **composition titles**.

speechmaker, speechmaking

speed of sound See **Mach number**.

speeds Use figures. *The car slowed to 7 mph, winds of 5 to 10 mph, winds of 7 to 9 knots, 10-knot wind.*

Avoid extensively hyphenated constructions such as *5-mile-per-hour winds*.

See **numerals**.

speedup (n. and adj.) **speed up** (v.)

spelling The basic rule when in doubt is to consult this book followed by, if necessary, a dictionary under conditions described in the **dictionaries** entry.

Memory aid: Noah Webster developed the following rule of thumb for the frequently vexing question of whether to double a final consonant in forming the present participle and past tense of a verb:

—If the stress in pronunciation is on the first syllable, do not double the consonant: *combat, combating, combated; cancel, canceling, canceled.*

—If the stress in pronunciation is on the second syllable, double the consonant unless confusion would result: *incur, incurred, incurring.* An exception, to avoid confusion with *buss*, is *bus, bused, busing.*

Avoid spelling simplifications such as *lite.* Exception: *thru* allowed in some compounds: *drive-thru, writethru.*

British spellings, when they differ from American, are acceptable only in particular cases such as formal or composition titles: *Jane's Defence Weekly, Labour Party, Excel Centre, London Palladium Theatre, Wimbledon's Centre Court.*

spill, spilled, spilling Not *spilt* in the past tense.

spinoff (n.) A distribution that occurs when the company forms a separate company out of a division, a subsidiary or other holdings. The shares of the new company are distributed proportionately to the parent company holders.

Spirit Airlines Headquarters is in Miramar, Florida.

split infinitive See **verbs**.

spokesman, spokeswoman But not *spokesperson.* Use *representative* if you do not know the sex of the individual.

sports writer This is an exception to Webster's New World College Dictionary.

sport utility vehicle No plural *s* in *sport*; no hyphen.

SUV is acceptable on first reference.

spot market A market for buying or selling commodities or foreign exchange for immediate delivery and for cash payment.

spot price The price of a commodity available for immediate sale and delivery. The term is also used to refer to foreign exchange transactions.

spouse Use when some of the people involved may be either gender. For example: *physicians and their spouses,* not *physicians and their wives.*

spring See **seasons**.

springtime

sputnik Usually lowercase, but capitalize when followed by a figure as part of a proper name: *Sputnik 1.*

It is Russian for *satellite.*

squall See **weather terms**.

square Do not abbreviate. Capitalize when part of a proper name: *Washington Square.*

Sri Lanka Formerly Ceylon. Use *Sri Lanka* in datelines and other references to the nation.

The people may be called either *Sri Lankans* or *Ceylonese.*

Before the nation was called Ceylon, it was Serendip, whence comes the word *serendipity*.

SRO Acceptable on second reference for *standing room only*.

SST Acceptable in all references for a *supersonic transport*.

stadium, stadiums Capitalize only when part of a proper name: *Dodger Stadium*.

Stalin, Josef Not *Joseph*.

stall Use care when using *stall* in this sense: when an automobile *stalls*, the engine stops. This may not be true when an airplane *stalls*; it pitches forward or sideways because of a lack of air speed.

stamp, stomp Both are acceptable, but *stamp* is preferred.

stanch, staunch *Stanch* is a verb: *He stanched the flow of blood.*
Staunch is an adjective: *She is a staunch supporter of equality.*

stand-alone (adj.)

Standard & Poor's 500 index The market indicator most professional investors use to determine how stocks are performing. It encompasses 500 top companies in leading U.S. industries. Many mutual funds use it as the benchmark they measure their own performance against. Always use the full name on first reference. On subsequent references, use *S&P 500*.

standard-bearer

standard time Capitalize *Eastern Standard Time*, *Pacific Standard Time*, etc., but lowercase *standard time* when standing alone.
See **time zones**.

stand-in (n. and adj.) **stand in** (v.)

standoff (n. and adj.) **stand off** (v.)

standout (n. and adj.) **stand out** (v.)

starboard Nautical for *right*, when facing the bow, or forward. See **port, starboard**.

"The Star-Spangled Banner" But lowercase *the national anthem*.

startup One word (n. and adj.) to describe a new business venture. An exception to Webster's New World College Dictionary preference.

state Lowercase in all *state of* constructions: *the state of Maine, the states of Maine and Vermont*.
Four states — Kentucky, Massachusetts, Pennsylvania and Virginia — are legally commonwealths rather than states. The distinction is necessary only in formal uses: *The commonwealth of Kentucky filed a suit.* For simple geographic reference: *Tobacco is grown in the state of Kentucky.*
Do not capitalize *state* when used simply as an adjective to specify a level of jurisdiction: *state Rep. William Smith, the state Transportation Department, state funds*.
Apply the same principle to phrases such as *the city of Chicago, the town of Auburn*, etc.
See also **state names**.

statehouse Capitalize all references to a specific statehouse, with or without the name of the state: *The Vermont Statehouse is in Montpelier. The governor will visit the Statehouse today.*
Lowercase plural uses: *the Massachusetts and Rhode Island statehouses.*

state names Follow these guidelines:

SPELL OUT: The names of the 50 U.S. states should be spelled out when used in the body of a story, whether standing alone or in conjunction with a city, town, village or military base. No state name is necessary if it is the same as the dateline. This also applies to newspapers cited in a story. For example, a story datelined Providence, R.I., would reference the *Providence Journal*, not the *Providence (Rhode Island) Journal*. See **datelines**.

EIGHT NOT ABBREVIATED: The names of eight states are never abbreviated in datelines or text: *Alaska, Hawaii, Idaho, Iowa, Maine, Ohio, Texas* and *Utah*.

Memory aid: Spell out the names of the two states that are not part of the contiguous United States and of the continental states that are five letters or fewer.

IN THE BODY OF STORIES: Except for cities that stand alone in datelines, use the state name in textual material when the city or town is not in the same state as the dateline, or where necessary to avoid confusion: *Springfield, Massachusetts*, or *Springfield, Illinois*. Provide a state identification for the city if the story has no dateline, or if the city is not in the same state as the dateline. However, cities that stand alone in datelines may be used alone in stories that have no dateline if no confusion would result.

ABBREVIATIONS REQUIRED: Use the state abbreviations listed at the end of this section:

—In conjunction with the name of a city, town, village or military base in most datelines. See **datelines** for examples and exceptions for large cities.

—In lists, agate, tabular material, nonpublishable editor's notes and credit lines.

—In short-form listings of party affiliation: *D-Ala., R-Mont.* See **party affiliation** entry for details.

Following are the state abbreviations, which also appear in the entries for each state (postal code abbreviations in parentheses):

Ala. (AL)	Md. (MD)	N.D. (ND)
Ariz. (AZ)	Mass. (MA)	Okla. (OK)
Ark. (AR)	Mich. (MI)	Ore. (OR)
Calif. (CA)	Minn. (MN)	Pa. (PA)
Colo. (CO)	Miss. (MS)	R.I. (RI)
Conn. (CT)	Mo. (MO)	S.C. (SC)
Del. (DE)	Mont. (MT)	S.D. (SD)
Fla. (FL)	Neb. (NE)	Tenn. (TN)
Ga. (GA)	Nev. (NV)	Vt. (VT)
Ill. (IL)	N.H. (NH)	Va. (VA)
Ind. (IN)	N.J. (NJ)	Wash. (WA)
Kan. (KS)	N.M. (NM)	W.Va. (WV)
Ky. (KY)	N.Y. (NY)	Wis. (WI)
La. (LA)	N.C. (NC)	Wyo. (WY)

These are the postal code abbreviations for the eight states that are not abbreviated in datelines or text: AK (Alaska), HI (Hawaii), ID (Idaho), IA (Iowa), ME (Maine), OH (Ohio), TX (Texas), UT (Utah). Also: District of Columbia (DC).

Use the two-letter Postal Service abbreviations only with full addresses, including ZIP code.

PUNCTUATION: Place one comma between the city and the state name, and another comma after the state name, unless ending a sentence or indicating a dateline: *He was traveling from Nashville, Tennessee, to Austin, Texas, en route to his home in Albuquerque, New Mexico. She said Cook County, Illinois, was Mayor Daley's stronghold.*

HEADLINES: Avoid using state abbreviations in headlines whenever possible.

MISCELLANEOUS: Use *New York state* when necessary to distinguish the state from New York City.

Use *state of Washington* or *Washington state* when necessary to distinguish the state from the District of Columbia. (*Washington State* is the name of a university in the state of Washington.)

State of the Union Capitalize all references to the president's annual address.

Lowercase other uses: *"The state of the union is confused,"* the editor said.

state police Capitalize with a state name if part of the formal description for a police agency: *the New York State Police, the Virginia State Police.*

In most cases, state police standing alone is a shorthand reference for *state policemen* rather than a reference to the agency. For consistency and to avoid hairline distinctions about whether the reference is to the agency or the officers, lowercase the words *state police* whenever they are not preceded by a state name.

See **highway patrol.**

states' rights

statewide

stationary, stationery To stand still is to be *stationary.*

Writing paper is *stationery.*

station wagon

status A text update posted on a social network to alert followers to a user's recent activities or point them to something of interest.

statute mile It equals 5,280 feet, or approximately 1.6 kilometers.

To convert to approximate nautical miles, multiply the number of statute miles by .869.

See **kilometer; knot; mile;** and **nautical mile.**

staunch See **stanch, staunch.**

stealth When used in connection with military aircraft, ships and vehicles it means the equipment is masked from various types of electronic detection. Stealth equipment can range from radar wave absorbing paint to electronic jamming devices. Like the *cruise missile,* always lowercase, no quotation marks.

stem cell

stepbrother, stepfather Also: *stepsister, stepmother.*

steppingstone

stifling

St. John's The city in the Canadian province of Newfoundland and Labrador.

Not to be confused with *Saint John, New Brunswick.*

St. Louis The city in Missouri stands alone in datelines.

stockbroker

Stockholm The city in Sweden stands alone in datelines.

stock index futures Futures contracts valued on the basis of indexes that track the prices of a specific group of stocks. The most widely traded is the future based on the Standard & Poor's 500 stock index. Speculators also trade options on index futures.

stock prices Prices are quoted in dollars and cents. Use active verbs: *Microsoft stock fell 10 cents to $38.01 in afternoon trading.* Avoid rounding individual stock prices in stories. If individual stock prices are rounded, the story should include context. *The stock rose above $100 for the first time.* In headlines, rounding down is acceptable.

When writing about indices, carry out decimals two places. *The Dow Jones industrial average rose*

78.73 points, or 0.5 percent, to close at 16,438.91. However, it is acceptable to round down in shorter stories. *The Dow rose to 16,438.*

stopgap

storm See **weather terms**.

stormwater

storyline

storyteller

straight-laced, strait-laced
Use *straight-laced* for someone strict or severe in behavior or moral views.

Reserve *strait-laced* for the notion of confinement, as in a corset.

strait Capitalize as part of a proper name: *Bering Strait, Strait of Gibraltar.*

But: *the Bosporus* and *the Dardanelles.* Neither is followed by *Strait.*

straitjacket

Strategic Arms Reduction Treaty *START* is acceptable on first reference to the treaty as long as it is made immediately clear which is being referred to.

Use the *strategic arms treaty* or the *treaties* in some references to avoid alphabet soup.

There are three START treaties:
—START I, signed in 1991.
—START II, signed in 1992. Ratified by U.S. Senate, but never took effect because Senate did not adopt the 1997 protocol and several amendments to Anti-Ballistic Missile treaty demanded by Russian Duma. Shelved by Russia in 2002 after U.S withdrew from ABM treaty.
—New START, signed in 2010.

Do not confuse with the *Strategic Arms Limitation Treaty* of 1979, known as *SALT.*

streaming The delivery of audio or video in real time over the Internet. Videos on YouTube are an example of streaming content, as are many on-demand services like Netflix and Hulu.

street Abbreviate only with a numbered address. See **addresses**.

strikebreaker

strong-arm (v. and adj.)

strong-willed

stylebook One word when referring to the *AP Stylebook* and to *stylebooks* generically.

Styrofoam A trademark for a brand of plastic foam. Use the term *plastic foam* unless referring specifically to the trademarked product. (Note: Cups and other serving items are not made of *Styrofoam* brand plastic foam.)

sub- The rules in **prefixes** apply, but in general, no hyphen. Some examples:

subbasement	submachine gun
subcommittee	suborbital
subculture	subtotal
subdivision	subzero

subcommittee Lowercase when used with the name of a legislative body's full committee: *a Ways and Means subcommittee.*

Capitalize when a subcommittee has a proper name of its own: *the Senate Permanent Subcommittee on Investigations.*

subject See **citizen, resident, subject, national, native**.

subjunctive mood Use the subjunctive mood of a verb for contrary-to-fact conditions, and expressions of doubts, wishes or regrets:

If I were a rich man, I wouldn't have to work hard.

I doubt that more money would be the answer.

I wish it were possible to take back my words.

Sentences that express a contingency or hypothesis may use either the subjunctive or the indicative mood depending on the context. In general, use the subjunctive if there is little likelihood that a contingency might come true:

If I were to marry a millionaire, I wouldn't have to worry about money.

If the bill passes as expected, it will provide an immediate tax cut.

See **should, would**.

submachine gun See **weapons**.

subpoena, subpoenaed, subpoenaing

subprime A class of borrowers characterized by tarnished credit histories. These borrowers usually entail greater risk for lenders so they are charged a higher interest rate for a loan.

successor

Sudan Use *Sudan* for the East African country whose capital is *Khartoum*. *South Sudan* is the country in the southern region that declared independence July 9, 2011. Its capital is *Juba*.

suffixes See separate listings for commonly used suffixes.

Follow Webster's New World College Dictionary for words not in this book.

If a word combination is not listed in Webster's New World College Dictionary, use two words for the verb form; hyphenate any noun or adjective forms.

suicide Generally, AP does not cover suicides or suicide attempts, unless the person involved is a well-known figure or the circumstances are particularly unusual or publicly disruptive. Suicide stories, when written, should not go into detail on methods used.

Avoid using *committed suicide* except in direct quotations from authorities. Alternate phrases include *killed himself, took her own life* or *died by suicide*. The verb *commit* with *suicide* can imply a criminal act. Laws against suicide have been repealed in the United States and many other places.

Do not refer to an *unsuccessful suicide attempt*. Refer instead to an *attempted suicide*.

Medically assisted suicide is permitted in some states and countries. Advocacy groups call it *death with dignity*, but AP doesn't use that phrase on its own. When referring to legislation whose name includes *death with dignity* or similar terms, just say *the law allows the terminally ill to end their own lives* unless the name itself of the legislation is at issue.

suit, suite You may have a *suit* of clothes, a *suit* of cards, or be faced with a *lawsuit*.

There are *suites* of music, rooms and furniture.

summer See **seasons**.

summertime

sun Lowercase. See **heavenly bodies**.

sunbathe The verb forms: *sunbathed, sunbathing*. Also: *sunbather*.

Sun Belt Generally those states in the South and West, ranging from

Florida and Georgia through the Gulf states into California.

super Avoid the slang tendency to use it in place of *excellent, wonderful*, etc.

super- The rules in **prefixes** apply, but in general, no hyphen. Some frequently used words:

superagency	superhighway
supercarrier	superpower
supercharge	supertanker

As with all prefixes, however, use a hyphen if the word that follows is capitalized: *super-Republican*.

Super Bowl

superconducting super collider

superintendent Do not abbreviate. Capitalize when used as a formal title before a name.
See **titles**.

superior court See **court names**.

supersede

supersonic See **Mach number**.

supersonic transport *SST* is acceptable in all references.

Supreme Court of the United States
Capitalize *U.S. Supreme Court* and also *the Supreme Court* when the context makes the *U.S.* designation unnecessary.

The chief justice is properly the *chief justice of the United States*, not *of the Supreme Court*: *Chief Justice John Roberts*.

The proper title for the eight other members of the court is *associate justice*. When used as a formal title before a name, it should be shortened to justice unless there are special circumstances: *Justice Ruth Bader Ginsburg, Associate Justice Ruth Bader Ginsburg*.
See **judge**.

supreme courts of the states
Capitalize with the state name (*the New Jersey Supreme Court*) and without the state name when the context makes it unnecessary: *the state Supreme Court, the Supreme Court*.

If a court with this name is not a state's highest tribunal, the fact should be noted. In New York, for example, the Supreme Court is a trial court. Appeals are directed to the Appellate Division of the Supreme Court. The state's highest court is the Court of Appeals.

surface-to-air missile(s)
SAM(s) may be used on second reference. Avoid the redundant *SAM missiles*.

SUV See **sport utility vehicle**.

swag Sometimes used to describe the free stuff at gift suites and in gift bags given to presenters and other award-show participants.

Swarm A location-based social network. Users check in at certain places or businesses, collect rewards for visits and track friends who use the service.

swastika

SWAT Acronym for *Special Weapons and Tactics*.

sweatpants, sweatshirt, sweatsuit

swing states States where voters have vacillated between Republican and Democratic candidates in the last three or four presidential elections.

Swiss International Air Lines
Switzerland's national carrier. Headquarters in Basel, Switzerland.

Sydney The city in Australia
stands alone in datelines.

syllabus, syllabuses

sync Short for synchronization;
not *synch*. Also, *syncing*.

T

tablecloth

tablespoon, tablespoonfuls
Equal to three teaspoons or one-half a fluid ounce.
 The metric equivalent is approximately 15 milliliters.
 See **liter** and **recipes**.

table tennis See **pingpong**.

tablet A touch-screen device, such as an Apple iPad, Amazon Kindle Fire or Microsoft Surface, that can be connected to the Internet.

tabular matter Exceptions may be made to the normal rules for abbreviations as necessary to make material fit. But make any abbreviations as clear as possible.

tag To identify someone or something in a post or piece of content. Photos are often tagged to identify people and objects in them.

tailspin

tail wind

Taiwan Use *Taiwan*, not *Formosa*, in references to the government in Taiwan and to the island itself.
 See **China**.

take-home pay

takeoff (n. and adj.) **take off** (v.)

takeout (n. and adj.) **take out** (v.)

takeover (n. and adj.) **take over** (v.)

takeup (n. and adj.) **take up** (v.)

Taliban Extremist Islamic movement that ruled Afghanistan until ousted by U.S.-led coalition after the Sept. 11, 2001, attacks. The *Taliban* continue to operate as an insurgent force with adherents in Afghanistan and Pakistan. The name derives from the Arabic word for religious students. The word *Taliban* normally takes a plural verb.

Talmud The collection of writings that constitute the Jewish civil and religious law.

tanks Use Arabic figures, separated from letters by a hyphen: *M-60*. Plural: *M-60s*.

tape recording (n.) **tape-record** (v.)

taps Lowercase (without quotation marks) the bugle call for "lights out," also sounded at military funerals.

Target Corp. Headquarters is in Minneapolis.

Taser Trademark for stun gun. (Acronym for *Thomas A. Swift's*

Electric Rifle.) Use the generic form if the brand is uncertain. Don't use verbs like *tasered*. Exception: When verb forms appear in direct quotations, use lowercase.

Tass Acceptable on first reference for the Russian government's news agency that is officially *ITAR-Tass*. ITAR is an acronym for *Information Telegraph Agency of Russia*.

tattletale

tax-free (adj.)

tea party Populist movement in the United States that opposes the Washington political establishment and espouses conservative and libertarian philosophy, including reduced government spending, lower taxes and reduction of the national debt and the federal budget deficit. Adherents are *tea partyers*. Formally named groups in the movement are capitalized: *Tea Party Express*.

teachers college No apostrophe.

team Use singular verb and pronoun "it" when referring to the team as a collective unit. However, the team name takes a plural verb: *The Orlando Magic are close to setting a franchise record.*
See **collective nouns**.

teammate

teamster Capitalize *teamster* only if the intended meaning is that the individual is a member of the International Brotherhood of Teamsters, Chauffeurs, Warehousemen and Helpers of America.

Teamsters union Acceptable in all references to the *International Brotherhood of Teamsters*.
See the entry under that name.

tear gas Two words. See also **Chemical Mace**.

teaspoon Equal to one-sixth of a fluid ounce, or one-third of a tablespoon.
The metric equivalent is approximately 5 milliliters.
See **liter**.

teaspoonful, teaspoonfuls Not *teaspoonsful*. See **recipes**.

teen, teenager (n.) **teenage** (adj.) Do not use *teen-aged*.

Teflon A trademark for a type of nonstick coating.

telecast (n.) **televise** (v.)

telephone numbers Use figures. The form: *212-621-1500*. For international numbers use *011* (from the United States), the country code, the city code and the telephone number: *011-44-20-7535-1515*. Use hyphens, not periods.
The form for toll-free numbers: *800-111-1000*.
If extension numbers are needed, use a comma to separate the main number from the extension: *212-621-1500, ext. 2*.

teleprompter A generic term for an electronic device that rolls a prepared speech or script in front of politicians, award show hosts, presenters and other speakers.

television program titles Follow the guidelines in **composition titles**.
Put quotation marks around *show* only if it is part of the formal name. The word *show* may be dropped when it would be cumbersome, such as in a set of listings.

(Italics are used here only to illustrate examples; do not use italics on the wires.)

In text or listing, treat programs named after the star in any of the following ways: *"The Mary Tyler Moore Show," "Mary Tyler Moore"* or *the Mary Tyler Moore show*. But be consistent in a story or set of listings.

Use quotation marks also for the title of an episode: *"The Clean Room Infiltration," an episode of "The Big Bang Theory."* Also: *"NBC Nightly News," the "Today" show, "The Tonight Show."*

television station The call letters alone are frequently adequate, but when this phrase is needed, use lowercase: *television station WTEV*.

telltale

temblor See **earthquakes**.

temperatures Use figures for all except *zero*. Use a word, not a minus sign, to indicate temperatures below zero.

Right: *The day's low was minus 10.*

Right: *The day's low was 10 below zero.*

Wrong: *The day's low was -10.*

Right: *The temperature rose to zero by noon.*

Right: *The day's high was expected to be 9 or 10.*

Also: *5-degree temperatures, temperatures fell 5 degrees, temperatures in the 30s* (no apostrophe).

Temperatures get *higher* or *lower*, but they don't get *warmer* or *cooler*.

Wrong: *Temperatures are expected to warm up in the area Friday.*

Right: *Temperatures are expected to rise in the area Friday.*

See **Fahrenheit**; **Celsius**; **numerals** and **weather terms**.

Temple Mount The walled, elevated area in Jerusalem's Old City that was the site of the ancient Jewish temples. It now houses the centuries-old Dome of the Rock shrine and Al-Aqsa mosque and is known to Muslims as the *Haram al-Sharif*, or *Noble Sanctuary*. Muslims believe the Prophet Muhammad made his night journey to heaven from the site.

tenderhearted

tenfold

Ten Most Wanted Fugitives The FBI's official list.

Tennessee Abbreviate *Tenn.* in datelines only; spell out in stories. Postal code: *TN*

See **state names**.

Tennessee Valley Authority TVA is acceptable on second reference.

Headquarters is in Knoxville, Tennessee.

tera- A prefix denoting 1 trillion units of a measure. Move the decimal point 12 places to the right, adding zeros if necessary, to convert to the basic unit: 5.5 teratons = 5,500,000,000,000 tons.

terabtye See **byte**.

terrace Do not abbreviate. See **addresses**.

Texas Do not abbreviate in datelines or stories. Postal code: *TX*

Second in total land area. See **state names**.

Texas Hold 'em The poker game.

text messaging, instant messaging Increasingly, terms and symbols used in text and instant messaging are showing up in quotations and regular written exchanges. The following are a selection of the most popular symbols, terms and abbreviations used in texting and IMing. Many are also used in social media updates.

2 Shorthand for *to* or *too*, as in *I have something 4 U 2.*

4 Shorthand for *for*.

BFF *Best friend forever*. Often used sarcastically.

BRB *Be right back.*

C Shorthand for *see*, as in *C U later*. Also used in lowercase.

capitalization Normal conventions of capitalization are often ignored in IM and text messages because the use of the shift key slows down letter entry.

IDK *I don't know.*

IMO/IMHO *In my opinion, in my humble opinion.*

LOL *Laugh out loud* or *laughing out loud*. Use to indicate that the sender has found something funny. See also **ROFL**.

NSFW *Not safe for work.* Used to alert recipients that upcoming material or attachments may be objectionable in an office environment. Often used to warn recipients of impending coarse or pornographic images being sent.

R Shorthand for *are*, as in, *R U kidding?* Also used in lowercase.

removal of punctuation, characters It is acceptable in instant-message and texting conventions to remove punctuation and characters, most often vowels, to save time typing or thumbing in letters. Thus, a word like *remember* could become *rmbr*.

ROFL *Rolling on the floor laughing.* One step beyond *LOL*.

thx Shorthand for *thanks*. Also *tnx*.

U Shorthand for *you*.

Y Shorthand for *why*.

text, texting, texted Acceptable in all usages as a verb for *to send a text message*.

texts, transcripts Follow normal style guidelines for capitalization, spelling and abbreviations in handling a text or transcript. Do not use a dateline.

Use quotation marks only for words or phrases that were quoted in the text or by the person who spoke.

Identify a change in speakers by starting a paragraph with the new speaker's name and a colon. Use normal second-reference forms if the speaker has been identified earlier; provide a full name and identification if the individual is being mentioned for the first time.

Use Q: for *question* and A: for *answer* at the start of paragraphs when these notations are adequate to identify a change in speakers.

See **ellipsis** in the **Punctuation** chapter for guidelines on condensing texts and transcripts.

Thai A native or the language of Thailand.

Siam and *Siamese* are historical only.

Use *siamese* for the cat.

Thai Airways International PLC Headquarters of this airline is in Bangkok, Thailand.

Thanksgiving, Thanksgiving Day The fourth Thursday in November.

that (conjunction) Use the conjunction *that* to introduce a dependent clause if the sentence sounds or looks awkward without it. There are no hard-and-fast rules, but in general:

—*That* usually may be omitted when a dependent clause immediately follows a form of the verb *to say*: *The president said he had signed the bill.*

—*That* should be used when a time element intervenes between the verb and the dependent clause: *The president said Monday that he had signed the bill.*

—*That* usually is necessary after some verbs. They include: *advocate, assert, contend, declare, estimate, make clear, point out, propose* and *state.*

—*That* is required before subordinate clauses beginning with conjunctions such as *after, although, because, before, in addition to, until* and *while*: *Haldeman said that after he learned of Nixon's intention to resign, he sought pardons for all connected with Watergate.*

When in doubt, include *that.* Omission can hurt. Inclusion never does.

that, which (pronouns) Use *that* and *which* in referring to inanimate objects and to animals without a name. Use *that* for essential clauses, important to the meaning of a sentence, and without commas: *I remember the day that we met.* Use *which* for nonessential clauses, where the pronoun is less necessary, and use commas: *The team, which finished last a year ago, is in first place.*

(Tip: If you can drop the clause and not lose the meaning of the sentence, use *which*; otherwise, use *that.* A *which* clause is surrounded by commas; no commas are used with *that* clauses.)

See the **essential clauses, nonessential clauses** entry for guidelines on using *that* and *which* to introduce phrases and clauses.

theater Use this spelling unless the proper name is *Theatre*: *Shubert Theatre.*

theft See **burglary, larceny, robbery, theft**.

their, there, they're *Their* is a plural possessive pronoun and must agree in number with the antecedent. Wrong: *Everyone raised their hands.* Right: *They raised their hands.* See **every one, everyone** for the pronoun that takes singular verbs and pronouns.

There is an adverb indicating direction: *We went there for dinner.*

There also is used with the force of a pronoun for impersonal constructions in which the real subject follows the verb: *There is no food on the table.*

They're is a contraction for *they are.*

thermos Formerly a trademark, now a generic term for any vacuum bottle, although one manufacturer still uses the word as a brand name.

Lowercase *thermos* when it is used to mean any vacuum bottle; use *Thermos* when referring to the specific brand.

Third World Avoid use of this term. *Developing nations* is more appropriate when referring to the economically developing nations of Africa, Asia and Latin America. Do not confuse with *nonaligned*, which is a political term. See **nonaligned nations**.

Thomson Reuters Corp. A news and data provider based in New York. The company was formed out of Thomson Corp.'s 2008 acquisition of Reuters Group PLC, which includes the news agency named for Baron Paul Julius von Reuter, the founder. Use *Reuters* when referring to the news agency.

3M Trademark and name of the company formerly known as Minnesota Mining & Manufacturing. Many of its products are known under the names *3M* and *Scotch*. Headquarters of 3M Co. is in St. Paul, Minnesota.

three R's They are: *reading, 'riting and 'rithmetic.*

throwaway (n. and adj.)

thumbs-up, thumbs-down

thunderstorm See **weather terms**.

Tiananmen Square Large public square in central Beijing. Site of pro-democracy demonstrations in 1989 that ended in bloodshed.

tidbit

tie-in (n. and adj.) **tie in** (v.)

tie, tied, tying

tie-up (n. and adj.) **tie up** (v.)

tilde Do not use the symbol in standard AP wire transmissions. If necessary for Internet addresses, write out the word and put it in parentheses.

till Or *until*. But not *'til*.

time element Use the days of the week, not *today* or *tonight*, in print copy.

Use *Monday, Tuesday*, etc., for days of the week within seven days before or after the current date.

Use the month and a figure where appropriate. See **months** for forms and punctuation.

Avoid such redundancies as *last Tuesday* or *next Tuesday*. The past, present or future tense used for the verb usually provides adequate indication of which Tuesday is meant:

He said he finished the job Tuesday. She will return Tuesday.

Avoid awkward placements of the time element, particularly those that suggest the day of the week is the object of a transitive verb: *The police jailed Tuesday.* Potential remedies include the use of the word *on* (see the **on** entry), rephrasing the sentence, or placing the time element in a different sentence.

time of day The exact time of day that an event has happened or will happen is not necessary in most stories. Follow these guidelines to determine when it should be included and in what form:

SPECIFY THE TIME:

—Whenever it gives the reader a better picture of the scene: Did the earthquake occur when people were likely to be home asleep or at work? A clock reading for the time in the datelined community is acceptable although *pre-dawn hours* or *rush hour* often is more illustrative.

—Whenever the time is critical to the story: When will the rocket be launched? When will a major political address be broadcast? What is the deadline for meeting a demand?

DECIDING ON CLOCK TIME: When giving a clock reading, use the time in the datelined community.

If the story has no dateline, use the clock time in force where the event happened or will take place.

The only exception is a nationwide story or tabular listing that involves television or radio programs. Always use Eastern time, followed by *EDT* or *EST*, and specify whether the program will be broadcast simultaneously nationwide or whether times will vary because of separate transmissions for different time zones. If practical, specify those times in a separate paragraph.

ZONE ABBREVIATIONS: Use *EST, CDT, PST*, etc., after a clock time only if:

—The story involves travel or other activities, such as the closing hour for polling places or the time of a televised speech, likely to affect people or developments in more than one time zone.

—The item involves television or radio programs. (See above.)

—The item has no dateline.

—The item is an advisory to editors.

CONVERT TO EASTERN TIME? Do not convert clock times from other time zones in the continental United States to Eastern time. If there is high interest in the precise time, add *CDT, PST*, etc., to the local reading to help readers determine their equivalent local time.

If the time is critical in a story from outside the continental United States, provide a conversion to Eastern time using this form:

The kidnappers set a 9 a.m. (3 a.m. EDT) deadline.

See **time zones** for additional guidance on forms.

timeout

times Use figures except for *noon* and *midnight*. Use a colon to separate hours from minutes: *11 a.m., 1 p.m., 3:30 p.m., 9-11 a.m., 9 a.m. to 5 p.m.*

Avoid such redundancies as *10 a.m. this morning, 10 p.m. tonight* or *10 p.m. Monday night*. Use *10 a.m.* or *10 p.m. Monday*, etc., as required by the norms in time element.

The construction *4 o'clock* is acceptable, but time listings with *a.m.* or *p.m.* are preferred.

See **midnight**; **noon**; **numerals** and **time zones**.

time sequences Spell out: *50 hours, 23 minutes, 14 seconds*. When

using the abbreviated form, as in sports statistics or similar agate use, or subsequent references, the form is: 2:30:21.65 (hours, minutes, seconds, tenths, hundredths).

Time Warner Inc. Media company that owns the *Warner Bros.* movie and TV studio; the *Time Inc.* magazine publishing business, including *Time, Sports Illustrated, People* and *Fortune*; and pay TV networks including *HBO, CNN, TBS* and *TNT*. It spun off Time Warner Cable Inc. in 2009. The company was briefly known as AOL Time Warner Inc. after agreeing to be acquired by America Online Inc. in 2000, but changed its name back to *Time Warner Inc.* in 2003. AOL was spun off in 2009. The company spun off its Time Inc. magazine unit into a separate, publicly traded company in 2014. Headquarters is in New York.

time zones Capitalize the full name of the time in force within a particular zone: *Eastern Standard Time, Eastern Daylight Time, Central Standard Time*, etc.

Lowercase all but the region in short forms: *the Eastern time zone, Eastern time, Mountain time*, etc.

See **time of day** for guidelines on when to use clock time in a story.

Spell out *time zone* in references not accompanied by a clock reading: *Chicago is in the Central time zone.*

The abbreviations *EST, CDT*, etc., are acceptable on first reference for zones used within the continental United States, Canada and Mexico only if the abbreviation is linked with a clock reading: *noon EST, 9 a.m. PST*. (Do not set off the abbreviations with commas.)

Spell out all references to time zones not used within the contiguous United States: *When it is noon EDT, it is 1 p.m. Atlantic Standard*

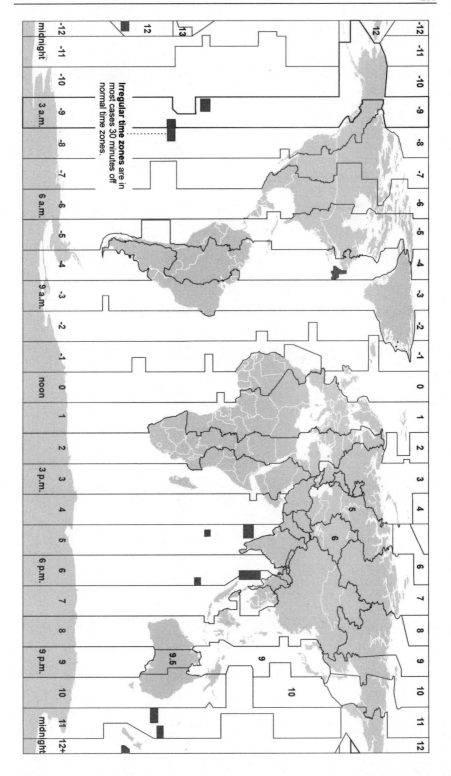

Irregular time zones are in most cases 30 minutes off normal time zones.

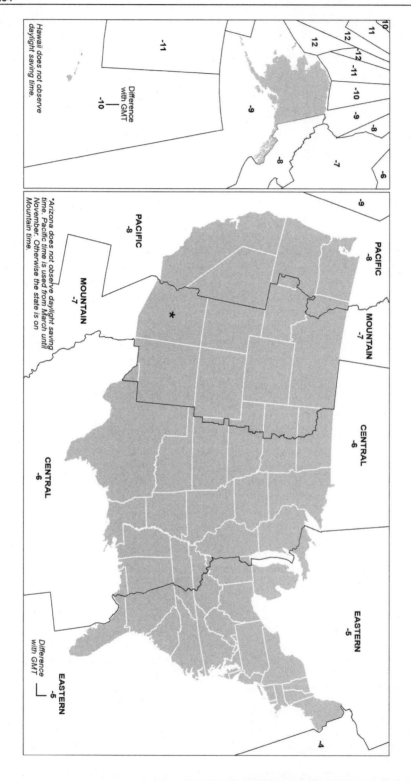

Hawaii does not observe daylight saving time.

Difference with GMT
-10

-11

*Arizona does not observe daylight saving time. Pacific time is used from March until November. Otherwise the state is on Mountain time.

PACIFIC
-8

MOUNTAIN
-7

CENTRAL
-6

EASTERN
-5

PACIFIC
-8

MOUNTAIN
-7

CENTRAL
-6

EASTERN
-5

Difference with GMT

Time and 8 a.m. Alaska Standard Time.

One exception to the spelled-out form: *Greenwich Mean Time* may be abbreviated as *GMT* on second reference if used with a clock reading. See **GMT**.

tipoff (n. and adj.) **tip off** (v.)

tiptop

titleholder

titles In general, confine capitalization to formal titles used directly before an individual's name.

The basic guidelines:

LOWERCASE: Lowercase and spell out titles when they are not used with an individual's name: *The president issued a statement. The pope gave his blessing.*

Lowercase and spell out titles in constructions that set them off from a name by commas: *The vice president, Joe Biden, was re-elected in 2012. Pope Francis, the current pope, was born in Argentina.*

COURTESY TITLES: See **courtesy titles** for guidelines on when to use *Miss, Mr., Mrs., Ms.* or no titles.

The forms *Mr., Mrs., Miss* and *Ms.* apply both in regular text and in quotations.

FORMAL TITLES: Capitalize formal titles when they are used immediately before one or more names: *Pope Francis, President Barack Obama, Vice Presidents John Jones and William Smith.*

A formal title generally is one that denotes a scope of authority, professional activity or academic activity: *Sen. Dianne Feinstein, Dr. Benjamin Spock, retired Gen. Colin Powell.*

Other titles serve primarily as occupational descriptions: *astronaut John Glenn, movie star John Wayne, peanut farmer Jimmy Carter.*

A final determination on whether a title is formal or occupational depends on the practice of the governmental or private organization that confers it. If there is doubt about the status of a title and the practice of the organization cannot be determined, use a construction that sets the name or the title off with commas.

ABBREVIATED TITLES: The following formal titles are capitalized and abbreviated as shown when used before a name both inside and outside quotations: *Dr., Gov., Lt. Gov., Rep., Sen.* and certain military ranks listed in **military titles**.

All other formal titles are spelled out in all uses.

GOVERNMENT OFFICIALS: In stories with U.S. datelines, do not include *U.S.* before the titles of Secretary of State or other government officials, except where necessary for clarity. Examples: *Secretary of State John Kerry, Attorney General Eric Holder.*

In stories with international datelines, include *U.S.* before the titles: *U.S. Secretary of State John Kerry, U.S. Attorney General Eric Holder.* Exceptions: *President Barack Obama, Vice President Joe Biden.*

ROYAL TITLES: Capitalize *king, queen,* etc., when used directly before a name. See individual entries and **nobility**.

TITLES OF NOBILITY: Capitalize a full title when it serves as the alternate name for an individual. See **nobility**.

PAST AND FUTURE TITLES: A formal title that an individual formerly held, is about to hold or holds temporarily is capitalized if used before the person's name. But do not capitalize the qualifying word: *former President George W. Bush, deposed King Constantine, Attorney General-designate Griffin B. Bell, acting Mayor Peter Barry.*

LONG TITLES: Separate a long title from a name by a construction that requires a comma: *Charles Robinson, the undersecretary for economic affairs, spoke.* Or: *The undersecretary for economic affairs, Charles Robinson, spoke.*

UNIQUE TITLES: If a title applies only to one person in an organization, insert the word *the* in a construction that uses commas: *John Jones, the deputy vice president, spoke.*

ADDITIONAL GUIDANCE: Many commonly used titles and occupational descriptions are listed separately in this book, together with guidelines on whether and/or when they are capitalized. In these entries, the phrases *before a name* or *immediately before a name* are used to specify that capitalization applies only when a title is not set off from a name by commas.

See **academic titles**; **composition titles**; **legislative titles**; **military titles**; and **religious titles**.

tobacco, tobaccos

Tobago See **Trinidad and Tobago**.

today, tonight Use only in direct quotations and in phrases that do not refer to a specific day: *Customs today are different from those of a century ago.*

Use the day of the week in copy, not *today* or *tonight*.

Tokyo The city in Japan stands alone in datelines.

tomorrow Use only in direct quotations and in phrases that do not refer to a specific day: *The world of tomorrow will need additional energy resources.*

Use the day of the week in other cases.

ton There are three types:

A *short ton* is equal to 2,000 pounds.

A *long ton*, also known as a *British ton*, is equal to 2,240 pounds.

A *metric ton* is equal to 1,000 kilograms, or approximately 2,204.62 pounds.

CONVERSION EQUATIONS:

Short to long: Multiply by 0.89 (5 short tons x 0.89 = 4.45 long tons).

Short to metric: Multiply by 0.9 (5 short tons x 0.9 = 4.5 metric tons).

Long to short: Multiply by 1.12 (5 long tons x 1.12 = 5.6 short tons).

Long to metric: Multiply by 1.02 (5 long tons x 1.02 = 5.1 metric tons).

Metric to short: Multiply by 1.1 (5 metric tons x 1.1 = 5.5 short tons).

Metric to long: Multiply by 0.98 (5 metric tons x 0.98 = 4.9 long tons).

See **metric system**.

See **kiloton** for units used to measure the power of nuclear explosions.

See **oil** for formulas to convert the tonnage of oil shipments to gallons.

tonight See **today, tonight** entry.

tornado(es) See **weather terms**.

Toronto The city in Canada stands alone in datelines.

Tory, Tories An exception to the normal practice when forming the plural of a proper name ending in *y*.

The words are acceptable on second reference to the Conservative Party in Britain and its members.

Total SA Headquarters of French oil company is in Paris.

total, totaled, totaling The phrase *a total of* often is redundant.

It may be used, however, to avoid a figure at the start of a sentence: *A total of 650 people were killed in holiday traffic accidents.*

touch screen (n.) **touch-screen** (adj.)

toward Not *towards*.

town Apply the capitalization principles in **city**.

town council Apply the capitalization principles in **city council**.

Toyota Motor Corp. Headquarters is in Toyota City, Japan.

Toys R Us

trade-in (n. and adj.) **trade in** (v.)

trademark A trademark is a brand, symbol, word, etc., used by a manufacturer or dealer and protected by law to prevent a competitor from using it: *AstroTurf*, for a type of artificial grass, for example.

In general, use a generic equivalent unless the trademark name is essential to the story.

When a trademark is used, capitalize it.

Many trademarks are listed separately in this book, together with generic equivalents.

The International Trademark Association, located in New York, is a helpful source of information about trademarks. See **brand names**.

trade-off (n. and adj.) **trade off** (v.)

trade show

traffic, trafficked, trafficking

trampoline Formerly a trademark, now a generic term.

trans- The rules in **prefixes** apply, but in general, no hyphen. Some examples:

transcontinental   transsexual
transmigrate   transship
transoceanic   trans-Siberian

Also: *trans-Atlantic* and *trans-Pacific*. These are exceptions to Webster's New World College Dictionary in keeping with the general rule that a hyphen is needed when a prefix precedes a capitalized word.

transcripts See **texts, transcripts**.

Trans-Dniester A separatist sliver of land in Moldova on the eastern bank of the River Dniester. Trans-Dniester, then a part of the Soviet Union, was joined with Moldova in 1940 when the Soviet Union annexed Moldova from Romania. It fought a separatist war with Moldova in 1992 and has considered itself independent ever since, though no other country recognizes it as such. Most of the population speaks Russian. In stories, the dateline should be Trans-Dniester, without reference to Moldova: *TIRASPOL, Trans-Dniester*.

transfer, transferred, transferring

transgender Use the pronoun preferred by the individuals who have acquired the physical characteristics of the opposite sex or present themselves in a way that does not correspond with their sex at birth.

If that preference is not expressed, use the pronoun consistent with the way the individuals live publicly. See **LGBT** and **transsexual**.

Transportation Communications International Union Formerly the Brotherhood of Railway, Airline and Steamship Clerks, Freight Handlers, Express and Station Employees. *TCU* is acceptable on second reference.

Headquarters is in Rockville, Maryland.

transsexual Use *transgender* to describe individuals who have acquired the physical characteristics of the opposite sex or present themselves in a way that does not correspond with their sex at birth. See **LGBT** and **transgender**.

travelogue Not *travelog*.

travel, traveled, traveling, traveler

treasurer Capitalize when used as a formal title immediately before a name. See **titles**.

Caution: The secretary of the U.S. Department of the Treasury is not the same person as the U.S. treasurer.

Treasurys Securities sold by the federal government to investors to fund its operations, cover the interest on U.S. government debt and pay off maturing securities. Because they carry the full backing of the government, Treasurys are viewed as the safest investment.

Treasury bills, Treasury bonds, Treasury notes See **loan terminology**.

trees See **plants**.

trending Used to indicate that a particular topic, word, phrase or piece of content is getting a lot of attention on a social network, search engine or website. Often used as a verb. Do not use without context and explanation, including describing the location of users where the topic is trending. *The topic of the Oscars is trending worldwide on Twitter today.*

tribe, tribal Refers to a social group of linked families or communities sharing a common ancestry or culture and who may be part of a larger ethnic group, such as the *Cherokee tribe* of American Indians and the *Ngunnawal tribe* of Aborigines. *Ethnic group* is preferred when referring to ethnicity or ethnic violence. See **nationalities and races**.

Tribune Publishing Co. Newspaper publishing company based in Chicago that publishes Los Angeles Times, Chicago Tribune and other newspapers and digital news sites in various markets. It also operates Spanish language properties Hoy and El Sentinel.

trigger-happy

Trinidad and Tobago In datelines on stories from this nation, use a community name followed by either *Trinidad* or *Tobago* — but not both — depending on which island the community is located.

Trojan horse, Trojan War

troop, troops, troupe A *troop*, in its singular form, is a group of people, often military, or animals. *Troops*, in the plural, means several such groups. But when the plural appears with a large number, it is understood to mean individuals: *There were an estimated 150,000 troops in Iraq.* (But not: *Three troops were injured.*)

Use *troupe* only for ensembles of actors, dancers, singers, etc.

tropical depression See **weather terms**.

Truman, Harry S. With a period after the initial. Truman once said there was no need for the period because the S did not stand for a name.

Asked in the early 1960s about his preference, he replied, "It makes no difference to me."

AP style has called for the period since that time.

trustee A person to whom another's property or the management of another's property is entrusted.

Do not capitalize if used before a name.

trusty A prison inmate granted special privileges as a trustworthy person.

tryout (n.) **try out** (v.)

tsar Use *czar*.

T-shirt

tsunami See **weather terms**.

tuberculosis *TB* is acceptable on second reference.

Tumblr A digital platform where users post written blog entries, photos, videos and music. Users can choose other users to follow, and can interact with posts by "liking" them, replying to them or "reblogging" them to their own followers. Yahoo bought Tumblr in May 2013.

tuneup (n. and adj.) **tune up** (v.)

turboprop See **aircraft terms**.

Turkmen, Turkmens Used to describe the people of Turkmenistan and neighboring regions. *He is Turkmen. They are Turkmens.*

turnpike Capitalize as part of a proper name: *the Pennsylvania Turnpike*. Lowercase *turnpike* when it stands alone.

See **highway designations**.

TV Acceptable as an abbreviated form of *television*, as a noun or adjective.

tweet A public message of up to 140 characters on Twitter. Also usable as a verb: to tweet.

Twenty-First Century Fox Inc.
Entertainment conglomerate controlled by Rupert Murdoch. The company includes the former entertainment businesses of News Corp., such as its movie studio and television networks, which were split off into a separate publicly traded company in June 2013. The company's preference is to use the spelling *21st Century Fox*, but for corporate stories AP uses the legal name reflected in Securities and Exchange Commission filings: Twenty-First Century Fox Inc.

Twentieth Century Fox Film Corp., also known as 20th Century Fox, is the film studio unit of Twenty-First Century Fox. Twentieth Century Fox Film Co. Ltd. operates as a British-based subsidiary of Twenty-First Century Fox Inc.

20-something

24/7

twin towers The two tallest buildings in the World Trade Center complex destroyed in the 9/11 attack. Also lowercase *north tower* and *south tower*.

Twitter A microblogging platform that allows users to post updates of up to 140 characters to their followers. They can also share photos or video, as well as links to outside content. The verb is *to tweet, tweeted*. A Twitter message is known as a *tweet*.

two-by-four Spell out the noun, which refers to any length of un-trimmed lumber approximately 2 inches thick by 4 inches wide.

typhoons Capitalize typhoon when it is part of the name that weather forecasters assign to a storm: *Typhoon Tilda.*
But use *it* and *its* — not *she, her* or *hers* — in pronoun references.
See **weather terms**.

Uber Ride-hailing services such as Uber and Lyft let people use smartphone apps to book and pay for a private car service or, in some cases, a taxi. They may also be called *ride-booking services*. Do not use *ride-sharing*.

U-boat A German submarine. Anything referring to a submarine should be *submarine* unless directly referring to a German vessel of World War I or II vintage.

UFO, UFOs Acceptable in all references for *unidentified flying object(s)*.

ukulele

Ulaanbaatar The preferred spelling for the capital of Mongolia, previously known as *Ulan Bator*.

Ulster Historically, one of the four Irish provinces, covering nine counties. Six of the counties became Northern Ireland, three became part of the Republic of Ireland. Avoid use as a synonym for *Northern Ireland*. See **United Kingdom**.

ultra- The rules in **prefixes** apply, but in general, no hyphen. Some examples:

ultramodern	ultrasonic
ultranationalism	ultraviolet

umlaut This diacritical mark (two dots placed over the vowel to change its sound) should not be used in standard AP transmissions. Instead, use two regular letters when needed.

U.N. Use periods in *U.N.*, for consistency with U.S. within texts. In headlines, it's *UN* (no periods). See **United Nations**.

un- The rules in **prefixes** apply, but in general, no hyphen. Some examples:

un-American	unnecessary
unarmed	unshaven

Uncle Sam

Uncle Tom A term of contempt applied to a black person, taken from the main character in Harriet Beecher Stowe's novel "Uncle Tom's Cabin." It describes the practice of kowtowing to whites to curry favor.

Do not apply it to an individual. It carries potentially libelous connotations of having sold one's convictions for money, prestige or political influence.

under- The rules in **prefixes** apply, but in general, no hyphen. Some examples:

underdog	undersheriff
underground	undersold

underscore Do not use the symbol in Internet addresses; write out the word and put it in parentheses.

undersecretary One word. See **titles**.

underwater In the housing industry, the term for homeowners who owe more on their mortgages than their homes are worth.

underway One word in all uses.

unemployment rate In the United States, this estimate of the number of unemployed residents seeking work is compiled monthly by the Bureau of Labor Statistics, an agency of the Labor Department.

Each month the bureau selects a nationwide cross section of the population and conducts interviews to determine the size of the U.S. workforce. The workforce is defined as the number of people with jobs and the number looking for jobs.

The unemployment rate is expressed as a percentage figure. The essential calculation involves dividing the total workforce into the number of people looking for jobs, followed by adjustments to reflect variable factors such as seasonal trends.

UNESCO Acceptable in all reference for the *United Nations Educational, Scientific and Cultural Organization*.

unfollow To remove an account from the list of accounts that populate one's feed on a social network. Note that *unfollowing* is generally a one-way action: I may unfollow you, but you may continue to follow me.

unfriend To remove someone from a list of friends that one is connected to, usually on Facebook.

UNICEF Acceptable in all references for the *United Nations Children's Fund*. The words *International*

and *Emergency*, originally part of the name, have been dropped.

unidentified flying object(s) *UFO* and *UFOs* are acceptable in all references.

Uniform Code of Military Justice The laws covering members of the U.S. armed forces.

uninterested See **disinterested, uninterested**.

union Capitalize when used as a proper name of the Northern states during the Civil War: *The Union defeated the Confederacy*.

union names The formal names of unions may be condensed to conventionally accepted short forms that capitalize characteristic words from the full name followed by union in lowercase.

Follow union practice in the use of the word worker in shortened forms: United Auto Workers, United Mine Workers.

When worker is used generically, make autoworkers and steelworkers one word in keeping with widespread practice; use two words for other job descriptions: bakery workers, mine workers.

Some unions frequently in the news:

Amalgamated Transit Union
American Federation of Government Employees
American Federation of Labor and Congress of Industrial Organizations
American Federation of Musicians
American Federation of State, County and Municipal Employees
American Federation of Teachers
American Postal Workers Union
Communications Workers of America
International Association of Machinists and Aerospace Workers

International Brotherhood of Electrical Workers
International Brotherhood of Teamsters
International Longshore and Warehouse Union
International Longshoremen's Association
International Union of Bricklayers and Allied Craftworkers
International Union of Painters and Allied Trades
Laborers' International Union of North America
National Association of Letter Carriers
National Education Association
Newspaper Guild, The
Screen Actors Guild-American Federation of Television and Radio Artists
Service Employees International Union
Sheet Metal Workers International Association
UNITE HERE (no hyphen), a merger of the Union of Needletrades, Industrial and Textile Employees with the Hotel Employees and Restaurant Employees.
United Auto Workers
United Brotherhood of Carpenters
United Electrical, Radio and Machine Workers of America
United Farm Workers
United Food and Commercial Workers International Union
United Mine Workers of America
United Steelworkers

Union Pacific Corp. Freight railroad, with headquarters in Omaha, Nebraska.

union shop See **closed shop**.

unique It means one of a kind. Do not describe something as *rather unique, most unique* or *very unique*.

United Airlines Headquarters is in Chicago. The parent company is United Continental Holdings Inc.

United Arab Emirates Spell out on first reference in stories and in datelines. *UAE* (no periods) is acceptable on second reference.

United Auto Workers The shortened form of the United Automobile, Aerospace and Agricultural Implement Workers of America is acceptable in all references. Headquarters is in Detroit.

United Farm Workers Headquarters is in Keene, California.

United Kingdom It consists of Great Britain and Northern Ireland.
Great Britain (or Britain) consists of England, Scotland and Wales.
Ireland is independent of the United Kingdom.
The abbreviation *U.K.* is acceptable as a noun or adjective. Use *UK* (no periods) in headlines.
See **datelines** and **Ireland**.

United Mine Workers of America The shortened forms *United Mine Workers* and *United Mine Workers union* are acceptable in all references.
UMW and *Mine Workers* are acceptable on second reference.
Use *mine workers* or *miners*, lowercase, in generic references to workers in the industry.
Headquarters is in Washington.

United Nations Abbrev: *U.N.* (no space). Use periods in *U.N.*, for consistency with U.S. within texts. In headlines, it's *UN* (no periods).
In datelines: *UNITED NATIONS (AP) —*
Use *U.N. General Assembly, U.N. Secretariat* and *U.N. Security Council*

in first references not under a United Nations dateline.

General Assembly, the Secretariat and *Security Council* are acceptable in all references under a United Nations dateline and on second reference under other datelines.

Lowercase *the assembly* and *the council* when they stand alone.

See **UNESCO** and **UNICEF**.

United Press International

A privately owned news agency formed in 1958 as a merger of United Press and International News Service.

Use the full name on first reference. *UPI* is acceptable on second reference.

Headquarters is in Washington.

United Service Organizations

USO is acceptable in all references.

United States
Use periods in the abbreviation, *U.S.* within texts. In headlines, it's *US* (no periods).

United States Conference of Catholic Bishops
Formerly the National Conference of Catholic Bishops, it is the national organization of Roman Catholic bishops.

United Steelworkers
The shortened form of the United Steel, Paper and Forestry, Rubber, Manufacturing, Energy, Allied Industrial and Service Workers International Union is acceptable in all references. Headquarters is in Pittsburgh, Pennsylvania.

unprecedented It means having no precedent, unheard of. Often misused.

-up Follow Webster's New World College Dictionary. Hyphenate if not listed there.

Some frequently used words (all are nouns, some also are used as adjectives):

breakup	makeup
call-up	mix-up
change-up	mock-up
checkup	pileup
cleanup	pushup
close-up	roundup
cover-up	runners-up
crackup	setup
follow-up	shake-up
frame-up	shape-up
grown-up	smashup
hang-up	speedup
holdup	tie-up
letup	walk-up
lineup	windup

Use two words when any of these occurs as a verb.

See **suffixes**.

up- The rules in **prefixes** apply, but in general, no hyphen. Some examples:

upend	upstate
upgrade	uptown

UPI See **United Press International**.

uppercase One word (n., v., adj.) when referring to the use of capital letters, in keeping with printers' practice.

UPS Inc. Acceptable in all references to *United Parcel Service Inc.* Headquarters is in Atlanta.

upside down (adv.) **upside-down** (adj.) *The car turned upside down. The book is upside-down.*

upstage

upstate Always lowercase: *upstate New York.*

upward Not *upwards.*

URL *Uniform Resource Locator*, an Internet address. An example: *http://politics.ap.org/states/mi.html*

http: is the protocol, or method of transfer.

// indicates a computer name follows.

politics is the server.

ap.org is the domain.

/states is the folder.

/mi.html indicates a file (*.html* is the file type).

When the *URL* does not fit entirely on one line, break it into two or more lines without adding a hyphen or other punctuation mark.

See **Sending Text Stories** chapter.

U.S. The abbreviation is acceptable as a noun or adjective for *United States*. In headlines, it's *US* (no periods).

USA No periods in the abbreviated form for *United States of America*.

U.S. Agency for International Development *USAID* is acceptable on second reference.

U.S. Air Force See **air force**; **military academies**; and **military titles**.

US Airways Group Merged in 2013 with American Airlines to form American Airlines Group Inc., based in Fort Worth, Texas. The company plans to phase out the US Airways name.

U.S. Army See **army**; **military academies**; and **military titles**.

U.S. Chamber of Commerce
On second reference, *the Chamber* is acceptable. Lowercase when referring to a local chamber of commerce: *the Seattle Metropolitan Chamber of Commerce*, but *the chamber* on second reference.

U.S. Coast Guard See **coast guard**; **military academies**; and **military titles**.

U.S. Conference of Mayors
The members are the mayors of cities with 30,000 or more residents.

Use *the conference* or *the mayors' conference* on second reference.

There is no organization with the name *National Mayors' Conference*.

See **National League of Cities**.

U.S. Court of Appeals The court is divided into 13 circuits as follows:

District of Columbia Circuit.

Federal Circuit.

1st Circuit: Maine, Massachusetts, New Hampshire, Rhode Island, Puerto Rico. Based in Boston.

2nd Circuit: Connecticut, New York, Vermont. Based in New York.

3rd Circuit: Delaware, New Jersey, Pennsylvania, Virgin Islands. Based in Philadelphia.

4th Circuit: Maryland, North Carolina, South Carolina, Virginia, West Virginia. Based in Richmond, Va.

5th Circuit: Louisiana, Mississippi, Texas. Based in New Orleans.

6th Circuit: Kentucky, Michigan, Ohio, Tennessee. Based in Cincinnati.

7th Circuit: Illinois, Indiana, Wisconsin. Based in Chicago.

8th Circuit: Arkansas, Iowa, Minnesota, Missouri, Nebraska, North Dakota, South Dakota. Based in St. Louis.

9th Circuit: Alaska, Arizona, California, Hawaii, Idaho, Montana, Nevada, Oregon, Washington, Guam. Based in San Francisco.

10th Circuit: Colorado, Kansas, New Mexico, Oklahoma, Utah, Wyoming. Based in Denver.

11th Circuit: Alabama, Florida and Georgia. Based in Atlanta.

The courts do not always sit in the cities where they are based. Sessions may be held in other major cities within each region.

REFERENCE FORMS: A phrase such as a *federal appeals court* is acceptable on first reference.

On first reference to the full name, use *U.S. Court of Appeals* or a full name: *8th U.S. Circuit Court of Appeals* or *the U.S. Court of Appeals for the 8th Circuit.*

U.S. Circuit Court of Appeals without a circuit number is a misnomer and should not be used.

In shortened and subsequent references: *the Court of Appeals, the 2nd Circuit, the appeals court, the appellate court(s), the circuit court(s), the court.*

Do not create nonexistent entities such as *the San Francisco Court of Appeals.* Make it *the U.S. Court of Appeals in San Francisco.*

JURISTS: The formal title for the jurists on the court is *judge: U.S. Circuit Judge Homer Thornberry* is preferred to *U.S. Appeals Judge Homer Thornberry,* but either is acceptable. See **judge**.

U.S. Court of Appeals for the Armed Forces
This court, not part of the judicial branch as such, is a civilian body established by Congress to hear appeals from actions of the Defense Department. It is based in Washington. (Formerly the U.S. Court of Military Appeals.)

U.S. Court of Appeals for the Federal Circuit
Commonly known as the CAFC, it replaced U.S. Court of Claims and U.S. Court of Customs and Patent Appeals. It handles lawsuits against the federal government and appeals involving customs, patents and copyright. It is based in Washington.

U.S. Customs and Border Protection
An agency of the Department of Homeland Security, it includes the Border Patrol.

U.S. Court of Military Appeals
See **U.S. Court of Appeals for the Armed Forces**.

U.S. Customs Court
This court, based in New York City, handles disputes over customs duties that arise at any U.S. port of entry.

U.S. District Courts
There are 94. In shortened and subsequent references: *the District Court, the District Courts, the court.*

Judge is the formal title for District Court jurists: *U.S. District Judge Frank Johnson.* See **judge**.

usher Use for both men and women.

U.S. Immigration and Customs Enforcement
ICE is the acronym for this investigative arm of the Department of Homeland Security. It incorporates the functions of the former Immigration and Naturalization Service and the former Customs service.

U.S. Marshals Service
No apostrophe.

U.S. Military Academy
See **military academies**.

U.S. Navy
See **navy**; **military academies**; and **military titles**.

U.S. Postal Service
Use *U.S. Postal Service* or *the Postal Service* on first reference. Retain capitalization of *Postal Service* in subsequent references to the agency.

Lowercase *the service* when it stands alone. Lowercase *post office* in generic references to the agency and to an individual office: *I went to the post office.*

USS For *United States Ship, Steamer* or *Steamship*, preceding the name of a vessel: *the USS Iowa.*
In datelines:
ABOARD USS IOWA (AP) —

U.S. Supreme Court See **Supreme Court of the United States**.

U.S. Tax Court This court handles appeals in tax cases.

user interface The features of a device, program or website that enable control by a human. *UI* is acceptable on second reference. Also called user experience or *UX*.

Utah Do not abbreviate in datelines or stories. Postal code: *UT*
See **state names**.

U-turn (n. and adj.)

vacuum

Valium A trademark for a brand of tranquilizer and muscle relaxant. It also may be called *diazepam*.

valley Capitalize as part of a full name: *the Mississippi Valley*.

Lowercase in plural uses: *the Missouri and Mississippi valleys*.

Vaseline A trademark for a brand of petroleum jelly.

Vatican City Stands alone in datelines.

VCR Acceptable in all references to *videocassette recorder*.

V-E Day May 8, 1945, the day the surrender of Germany was announced, officially ending the European phase of World War II.

vegetables See **food**.

vegetative state A condition in which the eyes are open and can move, and the patient has periods of sleep and periods of wakefulness, but remains unconscious, unaware of self or others. The patient can't think, reason, respond, do anything on purpose, chew or swallow. Reaction to a sound or a sight is reflex. A vegetative state is labeled "persistent" if it lasts more than a month. It's generally considered permanent if it lasts longer than three months

and was caused by lack of oxygen to the brain, or longer than 12 months when caused by traumatic injury.

See **coma** and **minimally conscious state**.

V-8 The engine.

Velcro Trademark for a nylon material that can be pressed together or pulled apart for easy fastening and unfastening. Use a generic term such as *fabric fastener*.

vendor

verbal See **oral, verbal, written**.

verbs The abbreviation *v.* is used in this book to identify the spelling of the verb forms of words frequently misspelled.

SPLIT FORMS: In general, avoid awkward constructions that split infinitive forms of a verb (*to leave, to help*, etc.) or compound forms (*had left, are found out*, etc.)

Awkward: *She was ordered to immediately leave on an assignment.*

Preferred: *She was ordered to leave immediately on an assignment.*

Awkward: *There stood the wagon that we had early last autumn left by the barn.*

Preferred: *There stood the wagon that we had left by the barn early last autumn.*

Occasionally, however, a split is not awkward and is necessary to convey the meaning:

He wanted to really help his mother.
Those who lie are often found out.
How has your health been?
The budget was tentatively approved.

Verizon Communications Inc.
Headquarters is in New York.

Vermont Abbreviate *Vt.* in datelines only; spell out in stories. Postal code: *VT*
See **state names**.

verses See **poetry** for guidelines on how to handle verses of poetry typographically.

versus Spell it out in ordinary speech and writing: *The proposal to revamp Medicare versus proposals to reform Medicare and Medicaid at the same time* ... In short expressions, however, the abbreviation *vs.* is permitted: *The issue of guns vs. butter has long been with us.*
For court cases, use *v.*: *Marbury v. Madison.*

Veterans Affairs Formerly
Veterans Administration, it became Cabinet level in March 1989 with the full title Department of Veterans Affairs. *VA* (no periods) is still used on second reference.

Veterans Day Formerly Armistice Day, Nov. 11, the anniversary of the armistice that ended World War I in 1918.
The federal legal holiday, observed on the fourth Monday in October during the mid-1970s, reverted to Nov. 11 in 1978.

Veterans of Foreign Wars
VFW is acceptable on second reference.
Headquarters is in Kansas City, Missouri.

veto, vetoes (n.) The verb forms: *vetoed, vetoing.*

Viacom Inc. Media conglomerate based in New York. Owns *Paramount Pictures* movie studio and pay TV channels such as *MTV, Nickelodeon, Comedy Central* and *BET*.

vice Use two words: *vice admiral, vice chairman, vice chancellor, vice consul, vice president, vice principal, vice regent, vice secretary.*
Several are exceptions to Webster's New World College Dictionary. The two-word rule has been adopted for consistency in handling the similar terms.

vice president Capitalize or lowercase following the same rules that apply to *president*. See **president** and **titles**.

vice versa

videocassette recorder *VCR* is acceptable in all references.

video game Two words in all uses.

video recording Term for digital audio and visual recording. Digital has largely replaced videotaping.

videotape (n. and v.)

Vienna The city in Austria stands alone in datelines.

Vietnam

Vietnam War

vie, vied, vying

village Apply the capitalization principles in **city**.

Vine A Twitter service that allows users to capture and share videos of up to six seconds that play on a loop.

VIP, VIPs Acceptable in all references for *very important person(s)*.

Virgin America Headquarters of this airline is in Burlingame, California.

Virgin Atlantic Airways Ltd. Headquarters is in Crawley, England.

Virginia Abbreviate *Va.* in datelines only; spell out in stories. Postal code: *VA*
See **state names**.

Virgin Islands Use with a community name in datelines on stories from the U.S. Virgin Islands. Do not abbreviate.
Identify an individual island in the text if relevant.
See **datelines** and **British Virgin Islands**.

virus, worm A computer *virus* is any malicious, invasive program designed to infect and disrupt computers. A *worm* is a type of virus that spreads on networks such as the Internet, copying itself from one computer to another without human intervention.

viscount, viscountess See **nobility**.

V-J Day Sept. 2, 1945, the day of formal surrender by Japan to Allied forces in World War II. Some commemorations recognized the date as Aug. 14, 1945, the day fighting with Japan ended and the armistice was declared, but the formal proclamation was not until Sept. 2.

voice mail Two words.

Voice of America *VOA* is acceptable on second reference.

VoIP *Voice over Internet Protocol.* A method of transmitting sound as data over the Internet, allowing for inexpensive phone conversations. *VoIP* is acceptable on second reference.

Volkswagen AG Headquarters is in Wolfsburg, Germany.

Volkswagen of America Inc. The name of the U.S. subsidiary of the German company *Volkswagen AG*.
U.S. headquarters is in Herndon, Virginia.

volley, volleys

vote-getter

vote tabulations Always use figures for the totals.
Spell out below 10 in other phrases related to voting: *by a five-vote majority, with three abstentions, four votes short of the necessary two-thirds majority.*
For results that involve fewer than 1,000 votes on each side, use these forms: *The House voted 230-205, a 230-205 vote.*
To make totals that involve more than 1,000 votes on a side easier to read, separate the figures with the word *to* to avoid hyphenated adjectival constructions. See **election returns** for examples.

vulgarities See **obscenities, profanities, vulgarities**.

wacky

waitlist (n.) **wait-list** (v.)

wake-up call

Wales Use *Wales* after the names of Welsh communities in datelines.
See **datelines** and **United Kingdom**.

walk-up (n. and adj.) **walk up** (v.)

Wall Street When the reference is to the entire complex of financial institutions in the area rather than the actual street itself, *the Street* is an acceptable short form.

Wal-Mart Stores Inc. Headquarters is in Bentonville, Arkansas. The company's name is spelled *Wal-Mart* in all uses, whether referring to the corporation or an individual store.

Walt Disney Co., The Family entertainment company that owns TV networks *ESPN* and *ABC*, theme parks and brands such as *Marvel* and *Pixar*. Headquarters is in Burbank, California.

war Capitalize as part of the name of a specific conflict: *the Afghanistan War, the Iraq War, the Civil War, the Cold War, the Korean War, the Vietnam War, the War of 1812,* *World War I, World War II, the Gulf War.*

warden Capitalize as a formal title before a name. See **titles**.

wards Use figures. See **political divisions**.

warhead

war horse, warhorse Two words for a horse used in battle.
One word for a veteran of many battles: *He is a political warhorse.*

warlike

warlord

warrant officer See **military titles**.

wartime

washed-up (adj.)

Washington Abbreviate *Wash.* in datelines only; spell out in stories. Postal code: *WA*
See **state names**.

The Washington Post Co. The newspaper was sold to Amazon.com Inc. founder Jeff Bezos in October 2013. It's now part of privately held WP Express Publications LLC, a division of Nash Holdings LLC. The newspaper's former owner, The Washington Post Co., changed its name to Graham Holdings Co. to reflect the sale.

Washington's Birthday Capitalize *birthday* in references to the holiday.

The date President George Washington was born is computed as Feb. 22. The federal legal holiday is the third Monday in February.

Some states and some organizations refer to it as *Presidents Day,* but the formal name has not changed.

wastebasket

waterspout See **weather terms**.

watt A unit of power, mostly associated with electricity. Electrical energy is measured in watt-hours (or kilowatt-hours or megawatt-hours). Do not use *megawatts per hour*. Abbreviate *W, kW, MW*.

weapons *Gun* is an acceptable term for any firearm. Note the following definitions and forms in dealing with weapons and ammunition:

anti-aircraft A cannon or other weapon designed for defense against air attack. The form: *a 105 mm anti-aircraft gun.*

artillery A carriage-mounted cannon.

assault rifle, assault weapon Terms for military or police-style weapons that are shorter than a conventional rifle and technically known as carbines. The precise definitions may vary from one law or jurisdiction to another. Although the terms are often used interchangeably, some make the distinction that *assault rifle* is a military weapon with a selector switch for firing in either fully automatic or semi-automatic mode from a detachable, 10- to 30-round magazine. Comparatively lightweight and easy to aim, this carbine was designed for tactical operations and is used by some law enforcement agencies. The form: *an M16 assault rifle, an AK-47 assault rifle, a Kalashnikov assault rifle.* An *assault weapon* is the civilian version of the military carbine with a similar appearance. This gun is semi-automatic, meaning one shot per trigger pull. Ammunition magazines ranging from 10 to 30 rounds or more allow rapid-fire capability. Other common characteristics include folding stock, muzzle flash suppressor, bayonet mount and pistol grip. Assault weapon sales were largely banned under federal law from 1994 to 2004 to curb gun crimes. The form: *AR-15 carbine with military-style appearance.*

Examples:

Each soldier carried an M16 assault rifle into combat, facing enemy troops armed with AK-47 assault rifles.

Politicians debated sales restrictions on assault weapons, including military-style AR-15 carbines for gun hobbyists.

automatic A firearm that reloads automatically after each shot. The term should not be used to describe the rate of fire. To avoid confusion, specify *fully automatic* or *semi-automatic* rather than simply automatic. Give the type of weapon or model for clarity.

bolt-action rifle A manually operated handle on the barrel opens and closes the breech, ejecting a spent round, loading another and cocking the weapon for triggering. Popular for hunting and target-shooting. Example: *Remington 700.* Some shotguns are bolt-action.

buckshot See **shot**.

bullet The projectile fired by a rifle, pistol or machine gun. Together with metal casing, primer and propellant, it forms a *cartridge.*

caliber A measurement of the diameter of the inside of a gun barrel except for most shotguns. Measurement is in either millimeters or decimal fractions of an inch. The word *caliber* is not used when giving the metric measurement. The forms: *a 9 mm pistol, a .22-caliber rifle.*

cannon A weapon, usually supported on some type of carriage, that fires explosive projectiles. The form: *a 105 mm cannon.* Plural is *cannons.*

carbine A short, lightweight rifle, usually having a barrel length of less than 20 inches. The form: *an M3 carbine.*

cartridge See **bullet**.

clip A device to store multiple rounds of ammunition together as a unit, ready for insertion into the gun. Clips are generally used to load obsolete military rifles. *Clip* is not the correct term for a detachable *magazine* commonly used in modern military rifles, assault rifles, assault weapons, submachine guns and semi-automatic pistols. See **magazine**.

Colt Named for Samuel Colt, it designates a make of weapon or ammunition developed for Colt handguns. The forms: *a Colt .45-caliber revolver, .45 Colt ammunition.*

fully automatic A firearm that fires continuously as long as the trigger is depressed. Examples include *machine guns* and *submachine guns.*

gauge The measure of the size of a shotgun. Gauge is expressed in terms of the number per pound of round lead balls with a diameter equal to the size of the barrel. The bigger the number, the smaller the shotgun.

The forms: *a 12-gauge shotgun, a .410-gauge shotgun.* The .410 actually is a caliber, but commonly is called a gauge. The ball leaving the barrel is 0.41" in diameter.

handgun A *pistol* or a *revolver.*

howitzer A cannon shorter than a gun of the same caliber employed to fire projectiles at relatively high angles at a target, such as opposing forces behind a ridge. The form: *a 105 mm howitzer.*

lever-action rifle A handle on the stock ejects and loads cartridges and cocks the rifle for triggering. A firearm often associated with the Old West. Example: *Winchester 94.*

M1, M16 These and similar combinations of a letter and figure(s) designate rifles used by the military. The forms: *an M1 rifle, an M16 rifle.*

machine gun A fully automatic gun that fires as long as the trigger is depressed and bullets are chambered. Such a weapon is generally so large and heavy that it rests on the ground or a mount. A submachine gun is hand-held. The form: *a .50-caliber Browning machine gun.*

magazine The ammunition storage and feeding device within or attached to a firearm. It may be fixed to the firearm or detachable. It is not a *clip.*

Magnum A trademark for a type of high-powered cartridge with a larger case and a larger powder charge than other cartridges of approximately the same caliber. The form: *a .357 Magnum, a .44 Magnum.*

mortar Device used to launch a mortar shell; it is the shell, not the mortar, that is fired.

musket A heavy, large-caliber shoulder firearm fired by means of a matchlock, a wheel lock, a flintlock or a percussion lock. Its ammunition is a musket ball.

pistol A handgun that can be a single shot or a semi-automatic. Differs from a revolver in that the chamber and barrel are one integral part. Its size is measured in calibers. The form: *a .45-caliber pistol.*

revolver A handgun. Differs from a pistol in that cartridges are held in chambers in a cylinder that revolves through the barrel. The form: *a .45-caliber revolver.*

rifle A firearm designed or made to be fired from the shoulder and having a rifled bore. It uses bullets or cartridges for ammunition. Its size is measured in calibers. The form: *a .22-caliber rifle.*

Saturday night special A compact, relatively inexpensive handgun.

semi-automatic A firearm that fires only once for each pull of the trigger. It reloads after each shot. The form: *a semi-automatic rifle, a semi-automatic weapon, a semi-automatic pistol.* The hyphen is an exception to general guidance against hyphenating words formed with *semi-*.

shell The word applies to military or naval ammunition and to shotgun ammunition. For small arms, bullet or round is the common term for ammunition.

shot Small lead or steel pellets fired by shotguns. A shotgun shell usually contains 1 to 2 ounces of shot. Do not use *shot* interchangeably with *buckshot*, which refers only to the largest shot sizes.

shotgun A firearm typically used to fire small spherical pellets called shot. *Shotguns* usually have a smooth bore barrel, but some contain a rifled barrel, which is used to fire a single projectile. Size is measured according to gauge, except for the .410, which is measured according to caliber, meaning the ball leaving the barrel is 0.41" in diameter. The form: *a 12-gauge shotgun, a .410 shotgun.*

submachine gun A lightweight fully automatic gun firing handgun ammunition.

weather-beaten

weather bureau See **National Weather Service**.
Online:
www.noaa.gov

weatherman The preferred term is *weather forecaster.*

weather terms The following are based on definitions used by the National Weather Service. All temperatures are Fahrenheit. The federal weather glossary is at http://forecast.weather.gov/glossary.php

blizzard Wind speeds of 35 mph or more and considerable falling and/or blowing of snow with visibility of less than one-quarter mile for three or more hours.

coastal waters The waters within 100 miles of the coast, including bays, harbors and sounds.

cyclone A storm with strong winds rotating about a moving center of low atmospheric pressure.

The word sometimes is used in the United States to mean *tornado* and in the Indian Ocean area to mean *hurricane.*

degree-day A measure of the amount of heating or cooling needed for a building. It is based on the difference between the average daily temperature and 65 degrees. Positive values are cooling degree days and negative values are heating degree days.

derecho A widespread and usually fast-moving straight-line windstorm. It is usually more than hundreds of miles long and more than 100 miles across. Plural: *derechos.*

dew point The temperature to which air must be cooled for dew to form. The higher the *dew point*, the more moisture in the air.

dust devil A small, rapidly rotating wind that is made visible by the dust, dirt or debris it picks up. Also called a *whirlwind*, it develops best on clear, dry, hot afternoons.

dust storm Visibility of one-half mile or less due to dust, wind speeds of 30 mph or more.

flash flood A sudden, violent flood. It typically occurs after a heavy rain or the melting of a heavy snow.

flash flood warning Warns that flash flooding is imminent or in progress or is highly likely. Those in the affected area should take necessary precautions immediately.

flash flood watch Alerts the public that conditions are favorable for flash flooding. Those in the affected area are urged to be ready to take additional precautions if a flash flood warning is issued or if flooding is observed.

flood Stories about floods usually tell how high the water is and where it is expected to crest. Such a story should also, for comparison, list flood stage and how high the water is above, or below, flood stage.

Wrong: *The river is expected to crest at 39 feet.*

Right: *The river is expected to crest at 39 feet, 12 feet above flood stage.*

freeze Describes conditions when the temperature at or near the surface is expected to be below 32 degrees during the growing season. Adjectives such as *severe* or *hard* are used if a cold spell exceeding two days is expected. A *hard freeze* is when the temperature drops to 28 degrees in areas that don't normally freeze.

A freeze may or may not be accompanied by the formation of frost. However, use of the term *freeze* usually is restricted for occasions when wind or other conditions prevent frost.

freezing drizzle, freezing rain A drizzle or rain that falls as a liquid but freezes into glaze upon contact with the cold ground or surface structures.

frost Describes the formation of very small ice crystals, which might develop under conditions similar to dew except for the minimum temperatures involved. Phrases such as

frost in low places or *scattered light frost* are used when appropriate.

funnel cloud A violent, rotating column of air that does not touch the ground, usually a pendant from a cumulonimbus cloud.

gale Sustained winds within the range of 39 to 54 mph (34 to 47 knots).

hail Showery precipitation in the form of irregular pellets or balls of ice more than 5 mm in diameter, falling from a cumulonimbus cloud.

heavy snow It generally means:
a. A fall accumulating to 4 inches or more in depth in 12 hours, or
b. A fall accumulating to 6 inches or more in depth in 24 hours.

high wind Normally indicates that sustained winds of 40 mph or greater are expected to last one hour or longer; or winds of 58 mph regardless of how long they last.

hurricane categories Hurricanes are ranked 1 to 5 according to what is known as the Saffir-Simpson Hurricane Wind Scale.

Category 1 — Hurricane has winds of 74 to 95 mph. Some damage will occur.

Category 2 — Winds from 96 to 110 mph. Extensive damage will occur.

Category 3 — Winds from 111 to 129 mph. Devastating damage will occur.

Category 4 — Winds from 130 to 156 mph. Catastrophic damage will occur.

Category 5 — Winds of 157 mph or higher. Catastrophic damage will occur.

Only three *Category 5* storms have hit the United States since record-keeping began: the 1935 Labor Day hurricane that hit the Florida Keys and killed 600 people; Hurricane Camille, which devastated the Mississippi coast in 1969, killing 256 and leaving $1.4 billion damage, and Hurricane Andrew, which hit South Florida in 1992, killing 43 and causing $30.5 billion in damage. Hurricane Katrina in 2005, which killed 1,200 people and caused $108 billion in damage, reached Category 5 in open water but hit the coast as a Category 3.

Categories 3, 4 and 5 hurricanes are considered major hurricanes.

hurricane eye The relatively calm area in the center of the storm. In this area winds are light and the sky often is covered only partly by clouds.

hurricane or typhoon A warm-core tropical cyclone in which the minimum sustained surface wind is 74 mph or more.

Hurricanes are spawned east of the international date line. Typhoons develop west of the line. They are known as cyclones in the Indian Ocean and Australia.

When a hurricane or typhoon loses strength (wind speed), usually after landfall, it is reduced to *tropical storm* status.

hurricane season The portion of the year that has a relatively high incidence of hurricanes. In the Atlantic, Caribbean and Gulf of Mexico, this is from June through November. In the eastern Pacific, it is May 15 through Nov. 30. In the central Pacific, it is June 1 through Nov. 30.

hurricane warning An announcement that sustained winds of 74 mph (119 km/hr) or higher are expected somewhere within the specified area in association with a tropical, subtropical or post-tropical cyclone. The warning is issued 36 hours before tropical-storm-force winds are expected to arrive.

hurricane watch An announcement that sustained winds of 74 mph (119 km/hr) or higher are possible within the specified area in association with a tropical, subtropical or post-tropical cyclone. A hurricane watch is issued 48 hours in advance

of the expected onset of tropical-storm-force winds.

ice storm warning Reserved for occasions when significant, and possibly damaging, accumulations of ice are expected.

ice storm, freezing drizzle, freezing rain Describes the dangerous freezing of drizzle or rain on objects as it strikes them. *Freezing drizzle* and *freezing rain* are synonyms for *ice storm*. Significant accumulations, which can take down power lines, are usually one-quarter of an inch or greater.

microburst Occurs when a mass of cooled air rushes downward out of a thunderstorm, hits the ground and rushes outward in all directions. Peak winds last less than five minutes and are less 2.5 miles wide. A plane flying through a *microburst* at low altitude, as on final approach or takeoff, would at first experience a strong headwind and increased lift, followed by a strong tail wind and sharply decreased lift.

monsoon Usually refers to a regular season of heavy rain and wind for a particular region, such as in India or Arizona and New Mexico. It is a seasonal warm wind created by temperature difference on land and nearby ocean. It reverses directions with the seasons, so there are dry phases of monsoons, but people don't usually think of the seasonal dry period as a monsoon.

National Hurricane Center The National Weather Service's National Hurricane Center in Miami has overall responsibility for tracking and providing information about tropical depressions, tropical storms and hurricanes in the Atlantic Ocean, Gulf of Mexico, Caribbean Sea and eastern Pacific Ocean.

The service's Central Pacific Hurricane Center in Honolulu is responsible for hurricane information in the Pacific Ocean area north of the equator from 140 degrees west longitude to 180 degrees.

Online:
www.nhc.noaa.gov

nearshore waters The waters extended to five miles from shore.

nor'easter The term used by the National Weather Service for storms that either exit or move north along the East Coast, producing winds blowing from the northeast.

offshore waters The waters extending to about 250 miles from shore.

polar vortex Usually refers to the gigantic circular upper air weather pattern in the Arctic region, enveloping the North Pole (but it can apply to the South Pole, too). It is a normal pattern that is stronger in the winter and keeps some of the coldest weather bottled up near the North Pole. The jet stream usually pens the polar vortex in and keeps it north. But at times some of the vortex can break off or move south, bringing unusually cold weather south and permitting warmer weather to creep up north.

sandstorm Visibility of one-half mile or less due to sand blown by winds of 30 mph or more.

Santa Ana wind In Southern California, a weather condition in which strong, hot, dry, dust-bearing winds descend to the Pacific Coast from inland desert regions.

severe thunderstorm Describes either of the following:

a. Winds — Thunderstorm-related surface winds sustained or gusts 58 mph or greater.

b. Hail — Surface hail 1 inch in diameter or larger. The word *hail* in a watch implies hail at the surface and aloft unless qualifying phrases such as *hail aloft* are used.

sleet (one form of ice pellet) Describes generally solid grains of ice formed by the freezing of raindrops or the refreezing of largely melted snowflakes before reaching the ground. Sleet, like small hail, usually bounces when hitting a hard surface.

sleet (heavy) Heavy sleet is a fairly rare event in which the ground is covered to a depth of one-half inch or more or a depth of significance to motorists and others.

squall A sudden increase of wind speed by at least 18 mph (16 knots) and rising to 25 mph (22 knots) and lasting for at least one minute.

storm surge An abnormal rise of water above the normal tide, generated by a storm.

storm tide Water level rise due to the combination of storm surge and the astronomical tide.

tidal wave Often used incorrectly as a synonym for *tsunami*. A large wave created by rising tide in a funnel-shaped inlet is called a *tidal bore*. Unusually large waves at sea are sometimes called *rogue waves*.

tornado A violent rotating column of air forming a pendant, usually from a cumulonimbus cloud, and touching the ground. It is often, but not always, visible as a funnel cloud, and usually is accompanied by a loud roaring noise. On a local scale, it is the most destructive of all atmospheric phenomena. Tornadoes can appear from any direction, but in the U.S. most move from southwest to northeast.

Tornado strength is measured by an enhanced F-scale rating from EF0 to EF5, which considers 28 different types of damage to structures and trees. It updates the original scale, which estimated wind strength. An EF2 or higher is considered a significant tornado.

Plural is *tornadoes*.

tornado warning A *tornado warning* is issued by a local National Weather Service office to warn the public of an existing tornado.

tornado watch A *tornado watch* alerts the public to the possibility of a tornado in the next several hours.

traveler's advisory Alerts the public that difficult traveling or hazardous road conditions are expected to be widespread.

tropical depression A tropical cyclone in which the maximum sustained surface wind is 38 mph (33 knots) or less.

tropical storm A warm-core tropical cyclone in which the maximum sustained surface winds range from 39 to 73 mph (34 to 63 knots) inclusive.

tsunami (s.), **tsunamis** (pl.) A great sea wave or seismic sea wave caused by an underwater disturbance such as an earthquake, landslide or volcano. It can cause massive death and destruction as was seen in the Indian Ocean *tsunami* in December 2004. It is different from a tidal wave.

typhoon See **hurricane or typhoon** in this listing.

waterspout A tornado over water.

wind chill factor No hyphen. The *wind chill* is a calculation that describes the combined effect of the wind and cold temperatures on exposed skin. The *wind chill fac-*

Heat index table

RELATIVE HUMIDITY

TEMP. F	40%	45%	50%	55%	60%	65%	70%	75%	80%	85%	90%	95%	100%
110	136												
108	130	137											
106	124	130	137										
104	119	124	131	137			APPARENT TEMPERATURE						
102	114	119	124	130	137								
100	109	114	118	124	129	136							
98	105	109	113	117	123	128	134						
96	101	104	108	112	116	121	126	132					
94	97	100	102	106	110	114	119	124	129	135			
92	94	96	99	101	105	108	112	116	121	126	131		
90	91	93	95	97	100	103	106	109	113	117	122	127	132
88	88	89	91	93	95	98	100	103	106	110	113	117	121
86	85	87	88	89	91	93	95	97	100	102	105	108	112
84	83	84	85	86	88	89	90	92	94	96	98	100	103
82	81	82	83	84	84	85	86	88	89	90	91	93	95
80	80	80	81	81	82	82	83	84	84	85	86	86	87

Wind chill factor table

AIR TEMPERATURE

WIND MPH	40	35	30	25	20	15	10	5	0	-5	-10	-15	-20	-25	-30	-35	-40	-45
	APPARENT TEMPERATURE																	
5	36	31	25	19	13	7	1	-5	-11	-16	-22	-28	-34	-40	-46	-52	-57	-63
10	34	27	21	15	9	3	-4	-10	-16	-22	-28	-35	-41	-47	-53	-59	-66	-72
15	32	25	19	13	6	0	-7	-13	-19	-26	-32	-39	-45	-51	-58	-64	-71	-77
20	30	24	17	11	4	-2	-9	-15	-22	-29	-35	-42	-48	-55	-61	-68	-74	-81
25	29	23	16	9	3	-4	-11	-17	-24	-31	-37	-44	-51	-58	-64	-71	-78	-84
30	28	22	15	8	1	-5	-12	-19	-26	-33	-39	-46	-53	-60	-67	-73	-80	-87
35	28	21	14	7	0	-7	-14	-21	-27	-34	-41	-48	-55	-62	-69	-76	-82	-89
40	27	20	13	6	-1	-8	-15	-22	-29	-36	-43	-50	-57	-64	-71	-78	-84	-91
45	26	19	12	5	-2	-9	-16	-23	-30	-37	-44	-51	-58	-65	-72	-79	-86	-93
50	26	19	12	4	-3	-10	-17	-24	-31	-38	-45	-52	-60	-67	-74	-81	-88	-95
55	25	18	11	4	-3	-11	-18	-25	-32	-39	-46	-54	-61	-68	-75	-82	-89	-97
60	25	17	10	3	-4	-11	-19	-26	-33	-40	-48	-55	-62	-69	-76	-84	-91	-98

FROSTBITE TIME   30 min.   10 min.   5 min.

tor would be minus 4, for example, if the temperature was 15 degrees and the wind was blowing at 25 mph — in other words, a temperature of 4 below zero with no wind.

The higher the wind at a given temperature, the lower the wind chill reading, although wind speeds above 40 mph have little additional cooling effect.

wind shear A sudden shift in wind direction and/or speed.

winter storm warning Notifies the public that a winter storm is producing, or is forecast to produce, heavy snow or significant ice accumulations.

winter storm watch Alerts the public that there is a potential for heavy snow or significant ice accumulations. The watch is usually issued at least 24 to 36 hours in advance.

weather vane

Web Short form of *World Wide Web*, it is a service, or set of standards, that enables the publishing of multimedia documents on the Internet. The Web is not the same as the Internet, but is a subset; other applications, such as email, exist on the Internet.

Also, *website, webcam, webcast* and *webmaster*. But as a short form and in terms with separate words, *the Web, Web page* and *Web browser*.

See **Internet**.

Web browser Software for viewing and interacting with websites. Leading browsers include Microsoft Corp.'s Internet Explorer, Mozilla's Firefox, Google Inc.'s Chrome and Apple Inc.'s Safari. Some browsers have been adapted for smartphones and tablet computers, although applications designed for specific services such as Facebook have become more popular

for accessing content on mobile devices.

website A location on the World Wide Web that maintains one or more pages at a specific address. Also, *webcam, webcast* and *webmaster*. But as a short form and in terms with separate words, *the Web, Web page* and *Web feed*. See **Web**.

Webster's New World College Dictionary See **dictionaries**.

weekend

weeklong, weekslong One word as an adjective.

weights Use figures: *The baby weighed 9 pounds, 7 ounces. She had a 9-pound, 7-ounce boy.*

weird

well Hyphenate as part of a compound modifier: *She is a well-dressed woman. He is well-fed.*

See **hyphen** in the **Punctuation** chapter for guidelines on compound modifiers.

well-being

well-informed

Wells Fargo & Co. Acquired Wachovia Corp. in 2009. Headquarters is in San Francisco.

well-to-do

well-wishers

West, Western, west, western Use *West* to cover the 13-state region as defined by the U.S. Census Bureau and broken into two divisions.

The eight Mountain division states are Arizona, Colorado, Idaho,

Montana, Nevada, New Mexico, Utah and Wyoming.

The five Pacific division states are Alaska, California, Hawaii, Oregon and Washington.

Capitalize *Western* for the film or book genre, but lowercase the style of music better known as country.

For directions, *west* and *western*. See **directions and regions**.

Western Hemisphere

Western Hemisphere The continents of North and South America, and the islands near them.

It frequently is subdivided as follows:

Caribbean The islands from the tip of Florida to the continent of South America, plus French Guiana, Guyana and Suriname on the northeastern coast of South America.

Major island elements are Cuba, Hispaniola (the island shared by the Dominican Republic and Haiti), Jamaica, Puerto Rico, and the West Indies islands.

Central America The narrow strip of land between Mexico and Colombia. Located there are Belize, Costa Rica, El Salvador, Guatemala, Honduras, Nicaragua and Panama.

Latin America The area of the Americas south of the United States where Romance languages (those derived from Latin) are dominant. It applies to most of the region south of the United States except areas with a British heritage: the Bahamas, Barbados, Belize, Grenada, Guyana, Jamaica, Trinidad and Tobago, and various islands in the West Indies. Suriname, the former Dutch Guiana, is an additional exception.

North America Canada, Mexico, the United States and the Danish territory of Greenland. When the term is used in more than its continental sense, it also may include the islands of the Caribbean.

South America Argentina, Bolivia, Brazil, Chile, Colombia, Ecuador, Paraguay, Peru, Uruguay, Venezuela, and in a purely continental sense, French Guiana, Guyana and Suriname. Politically and psychologically, however, the latter three regard themselves as part of the Caribbean.

West Indies An island chain extending in an eastward arc between the southeastern United States and the northern shore of South America, separating the Caribbean Sea from the Atlantic Ocean and including the Bahamas, the Greater Antilles, and the Lesser Antilles.

Major island elements are the nations of Barbados, Grenada, and Trinidad and Tobago, plus smaller islands dependent in various degrees on:

—Britain: British Virgin Islands, Anguilla, and the West Indies Associated States, including Antigua, Dominica, St. Lucia, St. Vincent and St. Christopher-Nevis.

—France: Guadeloupe (composed of islands known as Basse-Terre and Grande-Terre, plus five other islands) and Martinique.

—Netherlands: Netherlands Antilles, composed of Aruba, Bonaire, Curacao, Saba, St. Eustatius and the southern portion of St. Martin Island (the northern half is held by France and is part of Guadeloupe).

—United States: U.S. Virgin Islands, principally St. Croix, St. John and St. Thomas.

West Indies See **Western Hemisphere**.

West Point Acceptable on second reference to the *U.S. Military Academy*.
See **military academies**.
In datelines:
WEST POINT, N.Y. (AP) —

West Virginia Abbreviate *W.Va.* in datelines only; spell out in stories. Postal code: *WV*

See **state names**.

Weyerhaeuser Co. Headquarters is in Federal Way, Washington.

wheat It is measured in bushels domestically, in metric tons for international trade.

There are 36.7 bushels of wheat in a metric ton.

wheelchair See **disabled, handicapped**.

whereabouts Takes a singular verb:

His whereabouts is a mystery.

wherever

which See **essential clauses, nonessential clauses**; **that, which**; and **who, whom**.

whip Capitalize when used as a formal title before a name. See **legislative titles** and **titles**.

whistleblower

white-collar (adj.)

white paper Two words, lowercase, when used to refer to a special report.

whitewash (n., v. and adj.)

WHO The World Health Organization is the specialized health agency of the United Nations and is based in Geneva. It sets internationally accepted guidelines for treating diseases and coordinates responses to disease outbreaks globally. *WHO* is acceptable on second reference and takes a singular verb. Online: www.who.int

wholehearted

wholesale price index A measurement of the changes in the average prices that businesses pay for a selected group of industrial commodities, farm products, processed foods and feed for animals.

Do not capitalize when referring to the U.S. producer price index, issued monthly by the Bureau of Labor Statistics, an agency of the Labor Department.

who's, whose *Who's* is a contraction for *who is*, not a possessive: *Who's there?*

Whose is the possessive: *I do not know whose coat it is.*

who, whom *Who* is the pronoun used for references to human beings and to animals with a name. It is grammatically the subject (never the object) of a sentence, clause or phrase: *The woman who rented the room left the window open. Who is there?*

Whom is used when someone is the object of a verb or preposition: *The woman to whom the room was rented left the window open. Whom do you wish to see?*

See **essential clauses, nonessential clauses** for guidelines on how to punctuate clauses introduced by *who, whom, that* and *which*.

-wide No hyphen. Some examples:

citywide	nationwide
continentwide	statewide
countrywide	worldwide
industrywide	

wide- Usually hyphenated. Some examples:

wide-angle	wide-eyed
wide-awake	wide-open
wide-brimmed	

Exception: *widespread*.

widget A small module with a specific purpose that appears on a website, desktop or other interface and allows access to content or functions.

widow, widower In obituaries: A man is *survived by his wife*, or *leaves his wife*. A woman is *survived by her husband*, or *leaves her husband*.

In same-sex marriages, a man is *survived by his husband*, or *leaves his husband*. A woman is *survived by her wife*, or *leaves her wife*.

Guard against the redundant *widow (widower) of the late*.

widths See **dimensions**.

Wi-Fi For the wireless networking standards.

wiki Software that allows a group of users to add, delete, edit and share information on an intranet or Internet website.

WikiLeaks

Wikipedia An online encyclopedia whose entries are created and edited by its users, regardless of a person's expertise. May contain useful links but should not be used as a primary source of information.

wildfires Use square miles to describe the size of fires. *The fire has burned nearly 4 1/2 square miles of hilly brush land.* Use acres only when the fire is less than a square mile. When possible, be descriptive: *The fire is the size of Denver.*

wildlife

will See **shall, will** and **subjunctive mood**.

windbreaker

wind chill factor See **weather terms**.

wind-swept

windup (n. and adj.) **wind up** (v.)

wingspan

winter See **seasons**.

wintertime

wiretap, wiretapper (n.) The verb forms: *wiretap, wiretapped, wiretapping*.

Wisconsin Abbreviate *Wis.* in datelines only; spell out in stories. Postal code: *WI*
See **state names**.

-wise No hyphen when it means *in the direction of* or *with regard to*. Some examples:

clockwise	otherwise
lengthwise	slantwise

Avoid contrived combinations such as *moneywise, religionwise*.

The word *penny-wise* is spelled with a hyphen because it is a compound adjective in which *wise* means *smart*, not an application of the suffix *-wise*. The same for *street-wise* in *the street-wise youth* (an exception to Webster's New World College Dictionary).

WMD Acceptable on second reference for *weapons of mass destruction*.

woman, women Use *female* as an adjective, not *woman*. *She is the first female governor of North Carolina.*

Women should receive the same treatment as men in all areas of coverage. Physical descriptions, sexist references, demeaning stereotypes and condescending phrases should not be used.

To cite some examples, this means that:

—Copy should not assume maleness when both sexes are involved, as in *Jackson told newsmen* or in *the taxpayer ... he* when it easily can be said *Jackson told reporters* or *taxpayers ... they.*

—Copy should not express surprise that an attractive woman can be professionally accomplished, as in: *Mary Smith doesn't look the part, but she's an authority on ...*

—Copy should not gratuitously mention family relationships when there is no relevance to the subject, as in: *Golda Meir, a doughty grandmother, told the Egyptians today ...*

—Use the same standards for men and women in deciding whether to include specific mention of personal appearance or marital and family situation.

In other words, treatment of the sexes should be evenhanded and free of assumptions and stereotypes. This does not mean that valid and acceptable words such as *mankind* or *humanity* cannot be used. They are proper.

See **courtesy titles; divorce; man, mankind;** and **-persons**.

word-of-mouth (n. and adj.)

word processing (adj.)

workbook, workday, workforce, workhorse, workout, workplace, workstation, workweek

workers' compensation

working class (n.)
working-class (adj.)

World Bank Acceptable in all references for *International Bank for Reconstruction and Development.*

World Health Organization *WHO* is acceptable on second reference.

Headquarters is in Geneva.

World Series Or *the Series* on second reference. A rare exception to the general principles under **capitalization**.

World War I, World War II

worldwide

worn-out (adj.)

worthwhile

would See **should, would**.

wrack See **rack, wrack**.

wracked The preferred spelling when used to say a person is *wracked with pain*. Also, *nerve-wracking*.

write-down (n. and adj.) **write down** (v.) An accounting step a company makes when an asset or class of assets it holds falls in value. The decline in value is reflected in a reduction on the asset side of a company's balance sheet.

write-in (n. and adj.) **write in** (v.)

wrongdoing

Wyoming Abbreviate *Wyo.* in datelines only; spell out in stories. Postal code: *WY*

See **state names**.

XYZ

Xerox A trademark for a brand of photocopy machine. Never a verb. Use a generic term, such as *photocopy*.

Headquarters of *Xerox Corp.* is in Norwalk, Connecticut.

Xinhua News Agency The official news agency of the Chinese government is based in Beijing. It was founded in 1931 as the Red China News Agency and adopted its current name in 1937. *Xinhua* is acceptable on second reference.

Xmas Don't use this abbreviation for *Christmas*.

XML For *Extensible Markup Language*, used to sort, search and format information.

X-ray (n., v. and adj.) Use for both the photographic process and the radiation particles themselves.

Yahoo A trademark for an online computer service. Headquarters of Yahoo Inc. is in Sunnyvale, California. Do not use the exclamation point in the formal corporate name.

yard Equal to 3 feet.

The metric equivalent is approximately 0.91 meter.

To convert to meters, multiply by 0.91 (5 yards x 0.91 = 4.55 meters).

See **foot**; **meter**; and **distances**.

year-end (n. and adj.)

yearlong, yearslong

year-round (adj. and adv.)

years Use figures, without commas: *1975*. When a phrase refers to a month, day and year, set off the year with a comma: *Feb. 14, 1987, is the target date*. Use an *s* without an apostrophe to indicate spans of decades or centuries: *the 1890s, the 1800s*.

Years are the lone exception to the general rule in numerals that a figure is not used to start a sentence: *1976 was a very good year.*

See **A.D.**; **B.C.**; **century**; **historical periods and events**; **months** and **numerals**.

Yellow Pages Capitalize in describing the business telephone directory.

yesterday Use only in direct quotations and in phrases that do not refer to a specific day: *Yesterday we were young.*

Use the day of the week in other cases.

yesteryear

Yom Kippur The Jewish Day of Atonement. Occurs in September or October.

Young Men's Christian Association The term *the Y* is acceptable in all references to the main organization, which has its headquarters in

Chicago. Use *YMCA* when referring to a specific location: *the YMCA of Greater Louisville.*

Young Women's Christian Association *YWCA* is acceptable in all references.

Headquarters is in New York.

youth Applicable to boys and girls from age 13 until 18th birthday. Use *man* or *woman* for individuals 18 and older.

YouTube A video-serving network owned by Google that allows users to upload their own videos for access by anyone with a network connection.

yo-yo Formerly a trademark, now a generic term.

Yukon A territorial section of Canada. Do not abbreviate. Use in datelines after the names of communities in the territory.

See **Canada**.

Yule, Yuletide Old English name for Christmas season. Uppercase is an exception to Webster's New World College Dictionary.

Yum Brands Inc. Owner of the Pizza Hut, KFC and Taco Bell restaurant chains. Do not use the formal exclamation point in the corporate name. Headquarters of Yum Brands is in Louisville, Kentucky.

zero, zeros

zigzag

ZIP code Use all-caps *ZIP* for *Zoning Improvement Plan*, but always lowercase the word *code.*

Run the five digits together without a comma, and do not put a comma between the state name and the ZIP code: *New York, NY 10020.*

zip line

Zurich The city in Switzerland stands alone in datelines.

A GUIDE TO PUNCTUATION

There is no alternative to correct punctuation. Incorrect punctuation can change the meaning of a sentence, the results of which could be far-reaching.

Even if the meaning is not changed, bad punctuation, however inconsequential, can cause the reader to lose track of what is being said and give up reading a sentence.

The basic guideline is to use common sense.

—Punctuation is to make clear the thought being expressed.

—If punctuation does not help make clear what is being said, it should not be there.

"The Elements of Style" by William Strunk Jr. and E.B. White is a bible of writers. It states:

"Clarity, clarity, clarity. When you become hopelessly mired in a sentence, it is best to start fresh; do not try to fight your way through against terrible odds of syntax. Usually what is wrong is that the construction has become too involved at some point; the sentence needs to be broken apart and replaced by two or more shorter sentences."

This applies to punctuation. If a sentence becomes cluttered with commas, semicolons and dashes, start over.

These two paragraphs are full of commas and clauses; all of it equals too much for the reader to grasp:

The Commonwealth Games Federation, in an apparent effort to persuade other nations to ignore the spiraling boycott, ruled Sunday that Budd, a runner who has had a storied past on and off the track, and Cowley, a swimmer who competes for the University of Texas, were ineligible under the Commonwealth Constitution to compete for England in the 10-day event to be held in Edinburgh, Scotland, beginning July 24.

The decision on Budd, who has been the object of a number of demonstrations in the past, and Cowley followed an earlier announcement Sunday by Tanzania that it was joining Nigeria, Kenya, Ghana and Uganda in boycotting the games because of Britain's refusal to support economic sanctions against South Africa's government.

PUNCTUATION MARKS AND HOW TO USE THEM

apostrophe (') Follow these guidelines:

POSSESSIVES: See the **possessives** entry in main section.

PLURAL NOUNS NOT ENDING IN S: Add *'s*: *the alumni's contributions, women's rights.*

PLURAL NOUNS ENDING IN S: Add only an apostrophe: *the churches' needs, the girls' toys, the horses' food, the ships' wake, states' rights, the VIPs' entrance.*

NOUNS PLURAL IN FORM, SINGULAR IN MEANING: Add only an apostrophe: *mathematics' rules, measles' effects.* (But see INANIMATE OBJECTS below.)

Apply the same principle when a plural word occurs in the formal name of a singular entity: *General Motors' profits, the United States' wealth.*

NOUNS THE SAME IN SINGULAR AND PLURAL: Treat them the same as plurals, even if the meaning is singular: *one corps' location, the two deer's tracks, the lone moose's antlers.*

SINGULAR NOUNS NOT ENDING IN S: Add *'s*: *the church's needs, the girl's toys, the horse's food, the ship's route, the VIP's seat.*

Some style guides say that singular nouns ending in *s* sounds such as *ce*, *x*, and *z* may take either the apostrophe alone or *'s*. See SPECIAL EXPRESSIONS, but otherwise, for consistency and ease in remembering a rule, always use *'s* if the word does not end in the letter *s*: *Butz's policies, the fox's den, the justice's verdict, Marx's theories, the prince's life, Xerox's profits.*

SINGULAR COMMON NOUNS ENDING IN S: Add *'s* unless the next word begins with *s*: *the hostess's*

invitation, the hostess' seat; the witness's answer, the witness' story.

SINGULAR PROPER NAMES ENDING IN S: Use only an apostrophe: *Achilles' heel, Agnes' book, Ceres' rites, Descartes' theories, Dickens' novels, Euripides' dramas, Hercules' labors, Jesus' life, Jules' seat, Kansas' schools, Moses' law, Socrates' life, Tennessee Williams' plays, Xerxes' armies.* (An exception is *St. James's Palace.*)

SPECIAL EXPRESSIONS: The following exceptions to the general rule for words not ending in *s* apply to words that end in an *s* sound and are followed by a word that begins with *s*: *for appearance' sake, for conscience' sake, for goodness' sake.* Use *'s* otherwise: *the appearance's cost, my conscience's voice.*

PRONOUNS: Personal interrogative and relative pronouns have separate forms for the possessive. None involves an apostrophe: *mine, ours, your, yours, his, hers, its, theirs, whose.*

Caution: If you are using an apostrophe with a pronoun, always double-check to be sure that the meaning calls for a contraction: *you're, it's, there's, who's.*

Follow the rules listed above in forming the possessives of other pronouns: *another's idea, others' plans, someone's guess.*

COMPOUND WORDS: Applying the rules above, add an apostrophe or *'s* to the word closest to the object possessed: *the major general's decision, the major generals' decisions, the attorney general's request, the attorneys general's request.* See the **plurals** entry for guidelines on forming the plurals of these words.

Also: *anyone else's attitude, John Adams Jr.'s father, Benjamin Franklin of Pennsylvania's motion.* Whenever practical, however, recast the phrase to avoid ambiguity: *the motion by Benjamin Franklin of Pennsylvania.*

JOINT POSSESSION, INDIVIDUAL POSSESSION: Use a possessive form after only the last word if ownership is joint: *Fred and Sylvia's apartment, Fred and Sylvia's stocks.*

Use a possessive form after both words if the objects are individually owned: *Fred's and Sylvia's books.*

DESCRIPTIVE PHRASES: Do not add an apostrophe to a word ending in *s* when it is used primarily in a descriptive sense: *citizens band radio, a Cincinnati Reds infielder, a teachers college, a Teamsters request, a writers guide.*

Memory aid: The apostrophe usually is not used if *for* or *by* rather than *of* would be appropriate in the longer form: *a radio band for citizens, a college for teachers, a guide for writers, a request by the Teamsters.*

An *'s* is required however, when a term involves a plural word that does not end in *s*: *a children's hospital, a people's republic, the Young Men's Christian Association.*

DESCRIPTIVE NAMES: Some governmental, corporate and institutional organizations with a descriptive word in their names use an apostrophe; some do not. Follow the user's practice: *Actors' Equity, Diners Club, the Ladies' Home Journal, the National Governors Association.*

QUASI POSSESSIVES: Follow the rules above in composing the possessive form of words that occur in such phrases as *a day's pay, two weeks' vacation, three days' work, your money's worth.*

Frequently, however, a hyphenated form is clearer: *a two-week vacation, a three-day job.*

DOUBLE POSSESSIVE: Two conditions must apply for a double possessive — a phrase such as *a friend of John's* — to occur: 1. The word after *of* must refer to an animate object, and 2. The word before *of* must involve only a portion of the animate object's possessions.

Otherwise, do not use the possessive form of the word after *of*: *The friends of John Adams mourned his death.* (All the friends were involved.) *He is a friend of the college.* (Not *college's*, because *college* is inanimate).

Memory aid: This construction occurs most often, and quite naturally, with the possessive forms of personal pronouns: *He is a friend of mine.*

INANIMATE OBJECTS: There is no blanket rule against creating a possessive form for an inanimate object, particularly if the object is treated in a personified sense. See some of the earlier examples, and note these: *death's call, the wind's murmur.*

In general, however, avoid excessive personalization of inanimate objects, and give preference to an *of* construction when it fits the make-up of the sentence. For example, the earlier references to *mathematics' rules* and *measles' effects* would better be phrased: *the rules of mathematics, the effects of measles.*

OMITTED LETTERS: *I've, it's, don't, rock 'n' roll, 'tis the season to be jolly. He is a ne'er-do-well.* See **contractions** in main section.

OMITTED FIGURES: *The class of '62. The Spirit of '76. The '20s.*

PLURALS OF A SINGLE LETTER: *Mind your p's and q's. He learned the three R's and brought home a report card with four A's and two B's. The Oakland A's won the pennant.*

DO NOT USE: For plurals of numerals or multiple-letter combinations. See **plurals**.

brackets [] They cannot be transmitted over news wires. Use parentheses or recast the material.

See **parentheses**.

colon (:) The most frequent use of a colon is at the end of a sentence to introduce lists, tabulations, texts, etc.

Capitalize the first word after a colon only if it is a proper noun or the start of a complete sentence: *He promised this: The company will make good all the losses.* But: *There were three considerations: expense, time and feasibility.*

EMPHASIS: The colon often can be effective in giving emphasis: *He had only one hobby: eating.*

LISTINGS: Use the colon in such listings as time elapsed (*1:31:07.2*), time of day (*8:31 p.m.*), biblical and legal citations (*2 Kings 2:14; Missouri Code 3:245-260*).

DIALOGUE: Use a colon for dialogue. In coverage of a trial, for example:

Bailey: What were you doing the night of the 19th?

Mason: I refuse to answer that.

Q AND A: The colon is used for question-and-answer interviews:

Q: Did you strike him?

A: Indeed I did.

INTRODUCING QUOTATIONS: Use a comma to introduce a direct quotation of one sentence that remains within a paragraph. Use a colon to introduce long quotations within a paragraph and to end all paragraphs that introduce a paragraph of quoted material.

PLACEMENT WITH QUOTATION MARKS: Colons go outside quotation marks unless they are part of the quotation itself.

MISCELLANEOUS: Do not combine a dash and a colon.

comma (,) The following guidelines treat some of the most frequent questions about the use of commas. Additional guidelines on specialized uses are provided in separate entries such as **dates** and **scores**.

For detailed guidance, consult the punctuation section in the back of Webster's New World College Dictionary.

IN A SERIES: Use commas to separate elements in a series, but do not put a comma before the conjunction in a simple series: *The flag is red, white and blue. He would nominate Tom, Dick or Harry.*

Put a comma before the concluding conjunction in a series, however, if an integral element of the series requires a conjunction: *I had orange juice, toast, and ham and eggs for breakfast.*

Use a comma also before the concluding conjunction in a complex series of phrases: *The main points to consider are whether the athletes are skillful enough to compete, whether they have the stamina to endure the training, and whether they have the proper mental attitude.*

See **dash** and **semicolon** for cases when elements of a series contain internal commas.

WITH EQUAL ADJECTIVES: Use commas to separate a series of adjectives equal in rank. If the commas could be replaced by the word *and* without changing the sense, the adjectives are equal: *a thoughtful, precise manner; a dark, dangerous street.*

Use no comma when the last adjective before a noun outranks its predecessors because it is an integral element of a noun phrase, which is the equivalent of a single noun: *a cheap fur coat* (the noun phrase is *fur coat*); *the old oaken bucket; a new, blue spring bonnet.*

WITH NONESSENTIAL CLAUSES: A nonessential clause must be set off by commas. An essential clause must not be set off from the rest of a sentence by commas.

See **essential clauses, nonessential clauses** in the main section.

WITH NONESSENTIAL PHRASES: A nonessential phrase must be set off by commas. An essential phrase must not be set off from the rest of a sentence by commas.

See **essential phrases, nonessential phrases** in the main section.

WITH INTRODUCTORY CLAUSES AND PHRASES: A comma is used to separate an introductory clause or phrase from the main clause: *When he had tired of the mad pace of New York, he moved to Dubuque.*

The comma may be omitted after short introductory phrases if no ambiguity would result: *During the night he heard many noises.*

But use the comma if its omission would slow comprehension: *On the street below, the curious gathered.*

WITH CONJUNCTIONS: When a conjunction such as *and, but* or *for* links two clauses that could stand alone as separate sentences, use a comma before the conjunction in most cases: *She was glad she had looked, for a man was approaching the house.*

As a rule of thumb, use a comma if the subject of each clause is expressly stated: *We are visiting Washington, and we also plan a side trip to Williamsburg. We visited Washington, and our senator greeted us personally.* But no comma when the subject of the two clauses is the same and is not repeated in the second: *We are visiting Washington and plan to see the White House.*

The comma may be dropped if two clauses with expressly stated subjects are short. In general, however, favor use of a comma unless a particular literary effect is desired or if it would distort the sense of a sentence.

INTRODUCING DIRECT QUOTES: Use a comma to introduce a complete one-sentence quotation within a paragraph: *Wallace said, "She spent six months in Argentina and came back speaking English with a Spanish accent."* But use a colon to introduce quotations of more than one sentence. See **colon**.

Do not use a comma at the start of an indirect or partial quotation: *He said the victory put him "firmly on the road to a first-ballot nomination."*

BEFORE ATTRIBUTION: Use a comma instead of a period at the end of a quote that is followed by attribution: *"Rub my shoulders," Miss Cawley suggested.*

Do not use a comma, however, if the quoted statement ends with a question mark or exclamation point: *"Why should I?" he asked.*

WITH HOMETOWNS AND AGES: Use a comma to set off an individual's hometown when it is placed in apposition to a name (whether *of* is used or not): *Mary Richards, Minneapolis, and Maude Findlay, Tuckahoe, New York, were there.*

If an individual's age is used, set it off by commas: *Maude Findlay, 48, Tuckahoe, New York, was present.*

WITH PARTY AFFILIATION, ACADEMIC DEGREES, RELIGIOUS AFFILIATIONS: See separate entries under each of these terms.

NAMES OF STATES AND NATIONS USED WITH CITY NAMES: *His journey will take him from Dublin, Ireland, to Fargo, North Dakota, and back. The Selma, Alabama, group saw the governor.*

Use parentheses, however, if a state name is inserted within a proper name: *The Huntsville (Alabama) Times.*

WITH YES AND NO: *Yes, I will be there.*

IN DIRECT ADDRESS: *Mother, I will be home late. No, sir, I did not take it.*

SEPARATING SIMILAR WORDS: Use a comma to separate duplicated words that otherwise would be confusing: *What the problem is, is not clear.*

IN LARGE FIGURES: Use a comma for most figures greater than 999. The major exceptions are street addresses (*1234 Main St.*), broadcast frequencies (*1460 kilohertz*), room numbers, serial numbers, telephone numbers, and years (*1876*). See separate entries under these headings.

PLACEMENT WITH QUOTES: Commas always go inside quotation marks.

WITH FULL DATES: When a phrase refers to a month, day and year, set off the year with a comma: *Feb. 14, 1987, is the target date.*

See **semicolon**.

compound adjectives See the **hyphen** entry.

dash (—) Follow these guidelines:

ABRUPT CHANGE: Use dashes to denote an abrupt change in thought in a sentence or an emphatic pause: *Through her long reign, the queen and her family have adapted — usually skillfully — to the changing taste of the time.* But avoid overuse of dashes to set off phrases when commas would suffice.

SERIES WITHIN A PHRASE: When a phrase that otherwise would be set off by commas contains a series of words that must be separated by commas, use dashes to set off the full phrase: *He listed the qualities — intelligence, humor, conservatism, independence — that he liked in an executive.*

ATTRIBUTION: Use a dash before an author's or composer's name at the end of a quotation: *"Who steals my purse steals trash." — Shakespeare.*

IN DATELINES:
NEW YORK (AP) — The city is broke.

IN LISTS: AP uses dashes instead of bullets to introduce individual sections of a list. Capitalize the first word following the dash. Use periods, not semicolons, at the end of each section, whether it is a full sentence or a phrase. Example:
Jones gave the following reasons:
—He never ordered the package.
—If he did, it didn't come.
—If it did, he sent it back.

WITH SPACES: Put a space on both sides of a dash in all uses except the start of a paragraph and sports agate summaries.

ellipsis (…) In general, treat an ellipsis as a three-letter word, constructed with three periods and two spaces, as shown here.

Use an ellipsis to indicate the deletion of one or more words in condensing quotes, texts and documents. Be especially careful to avoid deletions that would distort the meaning.

An ellipsis also may be used to indicate a thought that the speaker or writer does not complete. Substitute a dash for this purpose, however, if the context uses ellipses to indicate that words actually spoken or written have been deleted.

Brief examples of how to use ellipses are provided after guidelines are given. More extensive examples, drawn from the speech in which President Richard Nixon announced his resignation, are in the sections below marked CONDENSATION EXAMPLE and QUOTATIONS.

PUNCTUATION GUIDELINES: If the words that precede an ellipsis constitute a grammatically complete sentence, either in the original or in the condensation, place a period at the end of the last word before the ellipsis. Follow it with a regular space and an ellipsis: *I no longer have a strong enough political base. …*

When the grammatical sense calls for a question mark, exclamation point, comma or colon, the sequence is word, punctuation mark, regular space, ellipsis: *Will you come? ...*

When material is deleted at the end of one paragraph and at the beginning of the one that follows, place an ellipsis in both locations.

CONDENSATION EXAMPLE: Here is an example of how the spacing and punctuation guidelines would be applied in condensing President Richard Nixon's resignation announcement:

Good evening. ...

In all the decisions I have made in my public life, I have always tried to do what was best for the nation. ...

... However, it has become evident to me that I no longer have a strong enough political base in ... Congress.

... As long as there was ... a base, I felt strongly that it was necessary to see the constitutional process through to its conclusion, that to do otherwise would be ... a dangerously destabilizing precedent for the future.

QUOTATIONS: In writing a story, do not use ellipses at the beginning and end of direct quotes:

"It has become evident to me that I no longer have a strong enough political base," Nixon said.

Not *"... it has become evident to me that I no longer have a strong enough political base ... ," Nixon said.*

SPECIAL EFFECTS: Ellipses also may be used to separate individual items within a paragraph of show business gossip or similar material. Use periods after items that are complete sentences.

exclamation point (!) Follow these guidelines:

EMPHATIC EXPRESSIONS: Use the mark to express a high degree of surprise, incredulity or other strong emotion.

AVOID OVERUSE: Use a comma after mild interjections. End mildly exclamatory sentences with a period.

PLACEMENT WITH QUOTES: Place the mark inside quotation marks when it is part of the quoted material: *"How wonderful!" he exclaimed. "Never!" she shouted.*

Place the mark outside quotation marks when it is not part of the quoted material: *I hated reading Spenser's "Faerie Queene"!*

MISCELLANEOUS: Do not use a comma or a period after the exclamation mark:

Wrong: *"Halt!", the corporal cried.*
Right: *"Halt!" the corporal cried.*

hyphen (-) Hyphens are joiners. Use them to avoid ambiguity or to form a single idea from two or more words.

Use of the hyphen is far from standardized. It is optional in most cases, a matter of taste, judgment and style sense. But the fewer hyphens the better; use them only when not using them causes confusion. (*Small-business owner*, but *health care center*.) See individual entries in this book. If not listed here, use the first listed entry in Webster's New World College Dictionary. (amended example from small-businessman, in line with entry below.)

Some guidelines:

AVOID AMBIGUITY: Use a hyphen whenever ambiguity would result if it were omitted: *The president will speak to small-business men.* (*Businessmen* normally is one word. But *the president will speak to small businessmen* is unclear.)

Others: *He recovered his health. He re-covered the leaky roof.*

COMPOUND MODIFIERS: When a compound modifier — two or more words that express a single concept — precedes a noun, use hyphens to link all the words in the compound except the adverb *very* and all adverbs that end in *-ly*: *a* *first-quarter touchdown, a bluish-green dress, a full-time job, a well-known man, a better-qualified woman, a know-it-all attitude, a very good time, an easily remembered rule.*

Many combinations that are hyphenated before a noun are not hyphenated when they occur after a noun: *The team scored in the first quarter. The dress, a bluish green, was attractive on her. She works full time. His attitude suggested that he knew it all.*

But when a modifier that would be hyphenated before a noun occurs instead after a form of the verb *to be*, the hyphen usually must be retained to avoid confusion: *The man is well-known. The woman is quick-witted. The children are soft-spoken. The play is second-rate.*

The principle of using a hyphen to avoid confusion explains why no hyphen is required with *very* and *-ly* words. Readers can expect them to modify the word that follows. But if a combination such as *little-known man* were not hyphenated, the reader could logically be expecting *little* to be followed by a noun, as in *little man.* Instead, the reader encountering *little known* would have to back up mentally and make the compound connection on his own.

TWO-THOUGHT COMPOUNDS: *serio-comic, socio-economic.*

COMPOUND PROPER NOUNS AND ADJECTIVES: Use a hyphen to designate dual heritage: *Italian-American, Mexican-American.*

No hyphen, however, for *French Canadian* or *Latin American.*

PREFIXES AND SUFFIXES: See the **prefixes** and **suffixes** entries, and separate entries for the most frequently used prefixes and suffixes.

AVOID DUPLICATED VOWELS, TRIPLED CONSONANTS: Examples: *anti-intellectual, pre-empt, shell-like.*

WITH NUMERALS: Use a hyphen to separate figures in **odds**, **ratios**, **scores**, some **fractions** and some **vote tabulations**. See examples in entries under these headings.

When large numbers must be spelled out, use a hyphen to connect a word ending in *-y* to another word: *twenty-one, fifty-five*, etc.

SUSPENSIVE HYPHENATION: The form: *He received a 10- to 20-year sentence in prison.*

parentheses ( ) In general, use parentheses around logos, as shown in **datelines**, but otherwise be sparing with them.

Parentheses are jarring to the reader. Because they do not appear on some news service printers, there is also the danger that material inside them may be misinterpreted.

The temptation to use parentheses is a clue that a sentence is becoming contorted. Try to write it another way. If a sentence must contain incidental material, then commas or two dashes are frequently more effective. Use these alternatives whenever possible.

There are occasions, however, when parentheses are the only effective means of inserting necessary background or reference information. When they are necessary, follow these guidelines:

WITHIN QUOTATIONS: If parenthetical information inserted in a direct quotation is at all sensitive, place an editor's note under a dash at the bottom of a story alerting copy desks to what was inserted.

PUNCTUATION: Place a period outside a closing parenthesis if the material inside is not a sentence (*such as this fragment*).

(*An independent parenthetical sentence such as this one takes a period before the closing parenthesis.*)

When a phrase placed in parentheses (*this one is an example*) might normally qualify as a complete sentence but is dependent on the surrounding material, do not capitalize the first word or end with a period.

INSERTIONS IN A PROPER NAME: Use parentheses if a state name or similar information is inserted within a proper name: *The Huntsville (Alabama) Times.* But use commas if no proper name is involved: *The Selma, Alabama, group saw the governor.*

NEVER USED: Do not use parentheses to denote a political figure's party affiliation and jurisdiction. Instead, set them off with commas, as shown under **party affiliation**.

Do not use *(cq)* or similar notation to indicate that an unusual spelling or term is correct. Include the confirmation in an editor's note at the top of a story.

periods (.) Follow these guidelines:

END OF DECLARATIVE SENTENCE: *The stylebook is finished.*

END OF A MILDLY IMPERATIVE SENTENCE: *Shut the door.*

Use an exclamation point if greater emphasis is desired: *Be careful!*

END OF SOME RHETORICAL QUESTIONS: A period is preferable if a statement is more a suggestion than a question: *Why don't we go.*

END OF AN INDIRECT QUESTION: *He asked what the score was.*

MANY ABBREVIATIONS: For guidelines, see **abbreviations and acronyms**. For the form of frequently used abbreviations, see the entry under the full name, abbreviation, acronym or term.

INITIALS: *John F. Kennedy, T.S. Eliot* (No space between *T.* and *S.*, to prevent them from being placed on two lines in typesetting.)

Abbreviations using only the initials of a name do not take periods: *JFK, LBJ.*

ELLIPSIS: See **ellipsis**.

ENUMERATIONS: After numbers or letters in enumerating elements of a summary: *1. Wash the car. 2. Clean the basement.* Or: *A. Punctuate properly. B. Write simply.*

PLACEMENT WITH QUOTATION MARKS: Periods always go inside quotation marks. See **quotation marks**.

SPACING: Use a single space after a period at the end of a sentence.

question mark (?) Follow these guidelines:

END OF A DIRECT QUESTION: *Who started the riot?*

Did he ask who started the riot? (The sentence as a whole is a direct question despite the indirect question at the end.)

You started the riot? (A question in the form of a declarative statement.)

INTERPOLATED QUESTION: *You told me — Did I hear you correctly? — that you started the riot.*

MULTIPLE QUESTIONS: Use a single question mark at the end of the full sentence:

Did you hear him say, "What right have you to ask about the riot?"

Did he plan the riot, employ assistants, and give the signal to begin?

Or, to cause full stops and throw emphasis on each element, break into separate sentences: *Did he plan the riot? Employ assistants? Give the signal to begin?*

CAUTION: Do not use question marks to indicate the end of indirect questions:

He asked who started the riot. To ask why the riot started is unnecessary. I want to know what the cause of the riot was. How foolish it is to ask what caused the riot.

QUESTION-AND-ANSWER FORMAT: Do not use quotation

marks. Paragraph each speaker's words:

Q: *Where did you keep it?*
A: *In a little tin box.*

PLACEMENT WITH QUOTATION MARKS: Inside or outside, depending on the meaning:

Who wrote "Gone With the Wind"?
He asked, "How long will it take?"

MISCELLANEOUS: The question mark supersedes the comma that normally is used when supplying attribution for a quotation: *"Who is there?" she asked.*

quotation marks (" ") The basic guidelines for open-quote marks (") and close-quote marks ("):

FOR DIRECT QUOTATIONS: To surround the exact words of a speaker or writer when reported in a story:

"I have no intention of staying," he replied.

"I do not object," he said, "to the tenor of the report."

Franklin said, "A penny saved is a penny earned."

A speculator said the practice is "too conservative for inflationary times."

RUNNING QUOTATIONS: If a full paragraph of quoted material is followed by a paragraph that continues the quotation, do not put close-quote marks at the end of the first paragraph. Do, however, put open-quote marks at the start of the second paragraph. Continue in this fashion for any succeeding paragraphs, using close-quote marks only at the end of the quoted material.

If a paragraph does not start with quotation marks but ends with a quotation that is continued in the next paragraph, do not use close-quote marks at the end of the introductory paragraph if the quoted material constitutes a full sentence.

Use close-quote marks, however, if the quoted material does not constitute a full sentence. For example:

He said, "I am shocked and horrified by the incident.

"I am so horrified, in fact, that I will ask for the death penalty."

But: *He said he was "shocked and horrified by the incident."*

"I am so horrified, in fact, that I will ask for the death penalty," he said.

DIALOGUE OR CONVERSATION: Each person's words, no matter how brief, are placed in a separate paragraph, with quotation marks at the beginning and the end of each person's speech:

"Will you go?"
"Yes."
"When?"
"Thursday."

NOT IN Q-and-A: Quotation marks are not required in formats that identify questions and answers by Q: and A:. See **question mark** for example.

NOT IN TEXTS: Quotation marks are not required in full texts, condensed texts or textual excerpts. See **ellipsis**.

COMPOSITION TITLES: See **composition titles** for guidelines on the use of quotation marks in book titles, movie titles, etc.

NICKNAMES: See **nicknames**.

IRONY: Put quotation marks around a word or words used in an ironical sense: *The "debate" turned into a free-for-all.*

UNFAMILIAR TERMS: A word or words being introduced to readers may be placed in quotation marks on first reference:

Broadcast frequencies are measured in "kilohertz."

Do not put subsequent references to *kilohertz* in quotation marks. See **foreign words**.

AVOID UNNECESSARY FRAGMENTS: Do not use quotation marks to report a few ordinary

words that a speaker or writer has used:

Wrong: *The senator said he would "go home to Michigan" if he lost the election.*

Right: *The senator said he would go home to Michigan if he lost the election.*

PARTIAL QUOTES: When a partial quote is used, do not put quotation marks around words that the speaker could not have used.

Suppose the individual said, *"I am horrified at your slovenly manners."*

Wrong: *She said she "was horrified at their slovenly manners."*

Right: *She said she was horrified at their "slovenly manners."*

Better when practical: Use the full quote.

QUOTES WITHIN QUOTES: Alternate between double quotation marks ("or") and single marks ('or'):

She said, "I quote from his letter, 'I agree with Kipling that "the female of the species is more deadly than the male," but the phenomenon is not an unchangeable law of nature,' a remark he did not explain."

Use three marks together if two quoted elements end at the same time: *She said, "He told me, 'I love you.'"*

PLACEMENT WITH OTHER PUNCTUATION: Follow these long-established printers' rules:

—The period and the comma always go within the quotation marks.

—The dash, the semicolon, the question mark and the exclamation point go within the quotation marks when they apply to the quoted matter only. They go outside when they apply to the whole sentence.

See **comma**.

semicolon (;) In general, use the semicolon to indicate a greater separation of thought and information than a comma can convey but less than the separation that a period implies.

The basic guidelines:

TO CLARIFY A SERIES: Use semicolons to separate elements of a series when the items in the series are long or when individual segments contain material that also must be set off by commas:

He is survived by a son, John Smith, of Chicago; three daughters, Jane Smith, of Wichita, Kansas, Mary Smith, of Denver, and Susan, of Boston; and a sister, Martha, of Omaha, Nebraska.

Note that the semicolon is used before the final *and* in such a series.

Another application of this principle may be seen in the cross-references at the end of entries in this book. Because some entries themselves have a comma, a semicolon is used to separate references to multiple entries, as in: See the **felony, misdemeanor** *entry*; **pardon, parole, probation**; *and* **prison, jail**.

See **dash** for a different type of connection that uses dashes to avoid multiple commas.

TO LINK INDEPENDENT CLAUSES: Use semicolon when a coordinating conjunction such as *and, but* or *for* is not present: *The package was due last week; it arrived today.*

If a coordinating conjunction is present, use a semicolon before it only if extensive punctuation also is required in one or more of the individual clauses: *They pulled their boats from the water, sandbagged the retaining walls, and boarded up the windows; but even with these precautions, the island was hard-hit by the hurricane.*

Unless a particular literary effect is desired, however, the better approach in these circumstances is to break the independent clauses into separate sentences.

PLACEMENT WITH QUOTES: Place semicolons outside quotation marks.

THE ASSOCIATED PRESS STATEMENT OF NEWS VALUES AND PRINCIPLES

For more than a century and a half, men and women of The Associated Press have had the privilege of bringing truth to the world. They have gone to great lengths, overcome great obstacles — and, too often, made great and horrific sacrifices — to ensure that the news was reported quickly, accurately and honestly. Our efforts have been rewarded with trust: More people in more places get their news from the AP than from any other source.

In the 21st century, that news is transmitted in more ways than ever before — in print, on the air and on the Web, with words, images, graphics, sounds and video. But always and in all media, we insist on the highest standards of integrity and ethical behavior when we gather and deliver the news.

That means we abhor inaccuracies, carelessness, bias or distortions.

It means we will not knowingly introduce false information into material intended for publication or broadcast; nor will we alter photo or image content. Quotations must be accurate, and precise.

It means we always strive to identify all the sources of our information, shielding them with anonymity only when they insist upon it and when they provide vital information — not opinion or speculation; when there is no other way to obtain that information; and when we know the source is knowledgeable and reliable.

It means we don't plagiarize.

It means we avoid behavior or activities that create a conflict of interest and compromise our ability to report the news fairly and accurately, uninfluenced by any person or action.

It means we don't misidentify or misrepresent ourselves to get a story. When we seek an interview, we identify ourselves as AP journalists.

It means we don't pay newsmakers for interviews, to take their photographs or to film or record them. It means we must be fair. Whenever we portray someone in a negative light, we must make a real effort to obtain a response from that person. When mistakes are made, they must be corrected — fully, quickly and ungrudgingly.

And ultimately, it means it is the responsibility of every one of us to ensure that these standards are upheld. Any time a question is raised about any aspect of our work, it should be taken seriously.

"I have no thought of saying The Associated Press is perfect. The frailties of human nature attach to it," wrote Melville Stone, the great general manager of the AP. But he went on to say that "the thing it is striving for is a truthful, unbiased report of the world's happenings ... ethical in the highest degree."

He wrote those words in 1914. They are true today.

* * *

The policies set forth in these pages are central to the AP's mission; any failure to abide by them is subject to review, and could result in disciplinary action, ranging from admonishment to dismissal, depending on the gravity of the infraction.

STANDARDS AND PRACTICES

ANONYMOUS SOURCES

Transparency is critical to our credibility with the public and our subscribers. Whenever possible, we pursue information on the record. When a newsmaker insists on background or off-the-record ground rules, we must adhere to a strict set of guidelines, enforced by AP news managers.

Under AP's rules, material from anonymous sources may be used only if:
1. The material is information and not opinion or speculation, and is vital to the news report.

2. The information is not available except under the conditions of anonymity imposed by the source.

3. The source is reliable, and in a position to have accurate information.

Reporters who intend to use material from anonymous sources must get approval from their news manager before sending the story to the desk. The manager is responsible for vetting the material and making sure it meets AP guidelines. The manager must know the identity of the source, and is obligated, like the reporter, to keep the source's identity confidential. Only after they are assured that the source material has been vetted should editors allow it to be transmitted.

Reporters should proceed with interviews on the assumption they are on the record. If the source wants to set conditions, these should be negotiated at the start of the interview. At the end of the interview, the reporter should try once again to move some or all of the information back on the record.

Before agreeing to use anonymous source material, the reporter should ask how the source knows the information is accurate, ensuring that the source has direct knowledge. Reporters may not agree to a source's request that AP not pursue additional comment or information.

The AP routinely seeks and requires more than one source. Stories should be held while attempts are made to reach additional sources for confirmation or elaboration. In rare cases, one source will be sufficient — when material comes from an authoritative figure who provides information so detailed that there is no question of its accuracy.

We must explain in the story why the source requested anonymity. And, when it's relevant, we must describe the source's motive for disclosing the information. If the story hinges on documents, as opposed to interviews, the reporter must describe how the documents were obtained, at least to the extent possible.

The story also must provide attribution that establishes the source's credibility; simply quoting "a source" is not allowed. We should be as descriptive as possible: "according to top White House aides" or "a senior official in the British Foreign Office." The description of a source must never be altered without consulting the reporter.

We must not say that a person declined comment when he or she is already quoted anonymously. And we should not attribute information to anonymous sources when it is obvious or well known. We should just state the information as fact.

Stories that use anonymous sources must carry a reporter's byline. If a reporter other than the bylined staffer contributes anonymous material to a story, that reporter should be given credit as a contributor to the story.

And all complaints and questions about the authenticity or veracity of anonymous material — from inside or outside the AP — must be promptly brought to the news manager's attention.

Not everyone understands "off the record" or "on background" to mean the same things. Before any interview in which any degree of anonymity is expected, there should be a discussion in which the ground rules are set explicitly.

These are the AP's definitions:

On the record. The information can be used with no caveats, quoting the source by name.

Off the record. The information cannot be used for publication.

Background. The information can be published but only under conditions negotiated with the source. Generally, the sources do not want their names published but will agree to a description of their position. AP reporters should object vigorously when a source wants to brief a group of reporters on background and try to persuade the source to put the briefing on the record. These background briefings have become routine in many venues, especially with government officials.

Deep background. The information can be used but without attribution. The source does not want to be identified in any way, even on condition of anonymity.

In general, information obtained under any of these circumstances can be pursued with other sources to be placed on the record.

ANONYMOUS SOURCES IN MATERIAL FROM OTHER NEWS SOURCES

Reports from other news organizations based on anonymous sources require the most careful scrutiny when we consider them for our report.

AP's basic rules for anonymous-source material apply to pickups as they do in our own reporting: The material must be factual and obtainable no other way. The story must be truly significant and newsworthy. Use of sourced material must be authorized by a manager. The story must be balanced, and comment must be sought.

Further, before picking up such a story we must make a bona fide effort to get it on the record, or, at a minimum, confirm it through our own sources. We shouldn't hesitate to hold the story if we have any doubts. If the source material is ultimately used, it must be attributed to the originating member and note their description of their sources.

AUDIO

AP's audio actualities must always tell the truth. We do not alter or manipulate the content of a newsmaker actuality in any way. Voice reports by AP correspondents may be edited to remove pauses or stumbles.

With the permission of a manager, overly long pauses by news subjects may be shortened.

The AP does permit the use of the subtle, standard audio processing methods of normalization of levels, general volume adjustments, equalization to make the sound clearer, noise reduction to reduce extraneous sounds such as telephone line noise, and fading in and out of the start and end of sound bites — provided the use of these methods does not conceal, obscure, remove or otherwise alter the content, or any portion of the content, of the audio. When an employee has questions about the use of such methods or the AP's requirements and limitations on audio editing, he or she should contact the desk supervisor prior to the transmission of any audio.

BYLINES

Bylines may be used only if the journalist was in the datelined location to gather the information reported. If a reporter in the field provides information to a staffer who writes the story, the reporter in the field gets the byline, unless the editor in charge determines that the byline should more properly go to the writer.

We give bylines to photographers, broadcast reporters and TV crew members who provide information without which there would be no story.

If multiple staffers report the story, the byline is the editor's judgment call. In general, the byline should go to the staffer who reported the key facts. Or, one staffer can take the byline for one cycle, and another for the following cycle.

A double byline or editor's note also can be used when more than one staffer makes a substantial contribution to the reporting or writing of a story. Credit lines recognize reporting contributions that are notable but don't call for a double byline.

If either of the staffers with a double byline was not in the datelined location, we should say who was where in a note at the story's end.

For roundups, the byline goes to the writer, with credit in an editor's note to the reporters who contributed substantial information.

Regarding credits for staffers who do voice or on-camera work: We do not use pseudonyms or "air names." Any exceptions — for instance, if a staffer has been known professionally by an air name for some time — must be approved by a manager.

CORRECTIONS/CORRECTIVES

Staffers must notify supervisory editors as soon as possible of errors or potential errors, whether in their work or that of a colleague. Every effort should be made to contact the staffer and his or her supervisor before a correction is moved.

When we're wrong, we must say so as soon as possible. When we make a correction in the current cycle, we point out the error and its fix in the editor's note. A correction must always be labeled a correction in the editor's note. We do not use euphemisms such as "recasts," "fixes," "clarifies" or "changes" when correcting a factual error.

A corrective corrects a mistake from a previous cycle. The AP asks papers or broadcasters that used the erroneous information to use the corrective, too.

For corrections on live, online stories, we overwrite the previous version. We send separate corrective stories online as warranted.

For graphics, we clearly label a correction with a FIX logo or bug, and clearly identify the material that has been corrected.

For photos, we move a caption correction and retransmit the photo with a corrected caption, clearly labeled as a retransmission to correct an error.

For video, corrections in scripts and/or shotlists are sent to clients as an advisory and are labeled as such.

For live broadcasts, we correct errors in the same newscast if at all possible. If not, we make sure the corrected information is used in the next appropriate live segment. Audio correspondent reports that contain factual errors are eliminated and, when possible, replaced with corrected reports.

DATELINES

A dateline tells the reader where we obtained the basic information for a story. In contrast, a byline tells the reader that a reporter was at the site of the dateline.

When a datelined story contains supplementary information obtained in another location — say, when an official in Washington comments on a disaster elsewhere — we should note it in the story.

The dateline for video or audio must be the location where the events depicted actually occurred. For voice work, the dateline must be the location from which the reporter is speaking; if that is not possible, the reporter should not use a dateline. If a reporter covers a story in one location but does a live report from a filing point in another location, the dateline is the filing point.

FABRICATIONS

Nothing in our news report — words, photos, graphics, sound or video — may be fabricated. We don't use pseudonyms, composite characters or fictional names, ages, places or dates. We don't stage or re-enact events for the camera or microphone, and we don't use sound effects or substitute video or audio from one event to another. We do not "cheat" sound by adding audio to embellish or fabricate an event. A senior editor must be consulted prior to the introduction of any neutral sound (ambient sound that does not affect the editorial meaning but corrects a technical fault).

We do not ask people to pose for photos unless we are making a portrait and then we clearly state that in the caption. We explain in the caption the circumstances under which photographs are made. If someone is asked to pose for photographs by third parties and that is reflected in AP-produced images, we say so in the caption. Such wording would be: "XXX poses for photos."

GRAPHICS

We use only authoritative sources. We do not project, surmise or estimate in a graphic. We create work only from what we know.

We post or move a locator map only when we can confirm the location ourselves.

We create charts at visually proper perspectives to give an accurate representation of data. The information must be clear and concise. We do not skew or alter data to fit a visual need.

We credit our sources on every graphic, including graphics for which AP journalists have created the data set or database.

IMAGES

AP pictures must always tell the truth. We do not alter or digitally manipulate the content of a photograph in any way.

The content of a photograph must not be altered in Photoshop or by any other means. No element should be digitally added to or subtracted from any photograph. The faces or identities of individuals must not be obscured by Photoshop or any other editing tool. Only retouching or the use of the cloning tool to eliminate dust on camera sensors and scratches on scanned negatives or scanned prints are acceptable.

Minor adjustments in Photoshop are acceptable. These include cropping, dodging and burning, conversion into grayscale, and normal toning and color adjustments that should be limited to those minimally necessary for clear and accurate reproduction (analogous to the burning and dodging previously used in darkroom processing of images) and that restore the authentic nature of the photograph. Changes in density, contrast, color and saturation levels that substantially alter the original scene are not acceptable. Backgrounds should not be digitally blurred or eliminated by burning down or by aggressive toning. The removal of "red eye" from photographs is not permissible.

When an employee has questions about the use of such methods or the AP's requirements and limitations on photo editing, he or she should contact a senior photo editor prior to the transmission of any image.

On those occasions when we transmit images that have been provided and altered by a source — the faces obscured, for example — the caption must clearly explain it. Transmitting such images must be approved by a senior photo editor.

Except as described herein, we do not stage, pose or re-enact events. When we shoot video, environmental portraits, or photograph subjects in a studio care should be taken to avoid, misleading viewers to believe that the moment was spontaneously captured in the course of gathering the news. In the cases of portraits, fashion or home design illustrations, any intervention should be revealed in the caption and special instructions box so it can't be mistaken as an attempt to deceive.

For video, the AP permits the use of subtle, standard methods of improving technical quality, such as adjusting video and audio levels, color correcting due to white balance, eliminating buzzing, hums, clicks, pops, or overly long pauses or other technical faults, and equalization of audio to make the sound clearer — provided the use of these methods does not conceal, obscure, remove or otherwise alter the content, or any portion of the content, of the image. The AP also allows digitally obscuring faces to protect a subject's identity under certain circumstances. Such video must not be distributed without approval of the Editor of the Day or senior manager. In addition, video for online use and for domestic broadcast stations can be fonted with titles and logos.

Graphics, including those for television, often involve combining various photographic elements, which necessarily means altering portions of each photograph. The background of a photograph, for example, may be removed to leave the headshot of the newsmaker. This may then be combined with a logo representing the person's company or industry, and the two elements may be layered over a neutral background.

Such compositions must not misrepresent the facts and must not result in an image that looks like a photograph — it must clearly be a graphic.

Similarly, when we alter photos to use as graphics online, we retain the integrity of the image, limiting the changes to cropping, masking and adding elements like logos. Videos for use online can be altered to add graphical information such as titles and logos, to tone the image and to improve audio quality. It is permissible to display photos online using techniques such as 360-degree panoramas or dissolves as long as they do not alter the original images.

OBSCENITIES, PROFANITIES, VULGARITIES

We do not use obscenities, racial epithets or other offensive slurs in stories unless they are part of direct quotations and there is a compelling reason for them.

If a story cannot be told without reference to them, we must first try to find a way to give the reader a sense of what was said without using the specific word or phrase. If a profanity, obscenity or vulgarity is used, the story must be flagged at the top, advising editors to note the contents.

A photo containing something that could be deemed offensive must carry an editor's note flagging it.

When a piece of video or audio contains something that might be deemed offensive, we flag it in the written description (rundown, billboard and/or script) so clients know what they are getting. Recognizing that standards differ around the world, we tailor our advisories and selection of video and audio according to customer needs.

We take great care not to refer readers to Web sites that are obscene, racist or otherwise offensive, and we must not directly link our stories to such sites.

In our online service, we link the least offensive image necessary to tell the story. For photo galleries and interactive presentations we alert readers to the nature of the material in the link and on the opening page of the gallery or interactive. If an obscene image is necessary to tell the story, we blur the portion of the image considered offensive after approval of the department manager, and flag the video.

PRIVACY

We do not generally identify those who say they have been sexually assaulted or pre-teenage children who are accused of crimes or who are witnesses to them, except in unusual circumstances. Nor do we transmit photos or video that identify such persons. An exception would occur when an adult victim publicly identifies him/herself.

Senior editors/managers must be consulted about exceptions.

PROVIDING ATTRIBUTION

We should give the full name of a source and as much information as needed to identify the source and explain why he or she is credible. Where appropriate, include a source's age; title; name of company, organization or government department; and hometown.

If we quote someone from a written document — a report, email or news release — we should say so. Information taken from the Internet must be vetted according to our standards of accuracy and attributed to the original source. File, library or archive photos, audio or videos must be identified as such.

For lengthy stories, attribution can be contained in an extended editor's note, usually at the end, detailing interviews, research and methodology. The goal is to provide a reader with enough information to have full confidence in the story's veracity.

QUOTATIONS

The same care that is used to ensure that quotes are accurate should also be used to ensure that quotes are not taken out of context.

We do not alter quotations, even to correct grammatical errors or word usage. If a quotation is flawed because of grammar or lack of clarity, the writer must be able to paraphrase in a way that is completely true to the original quote. If a quote's meaning is too murky to be paraphrased accurately, it should not be used.

Ellipses should be used rarely.

When relevant, stories should provide information about the setting in which a quotation was obtained — for example, a press conference, phone interview or hallway conversation with the reporter. The source's affect and body language — perhaps a smile or deprecatory gesture — is sometimes as important as the quotation itself.

Use of regional dialects with nonstandard spellings should generally be limited to a writer's effort to convey a special tone or sense of place. In this case, as in any interview with a person not speaking his or her native language, it is especially important that their ideas be accurately conveyed. Always, we must be careful not to mock the people we quote.

Quotes from one language to another must be translated faithfully. If appropriate, we should note the language spoken.

The video or audio editing of quotations or soundbites must not alter the speaker's meaning. Internal editing of audio soundbites of newsmakers is not permitted. Shortened soundbites by cutaway or other video transition are permitted as long as the speaker's meaning is not altered or misconstrued. Sound edits on videotape are permitted under certain circumstances, such as a technical failure. They must be done only after approval by a senior editorial manager.

RESPONSES

We must make significant efforts to reach anyone who may be portrayed in a negative way in our stories, and we must give them a reasonable amount of time to get back to us before we move the story. What is "reasonable" may depend on the urgency and competitiveness of the story. If we don't reach the parties involved, we must explain in the story what efforts were made to do so.

USE OF OTHERS' MATERIAL

An AP staffer who reports and writes a story must use original content, language and phrasing. We do not plagiarize, meaning that we do not take the work of others and pass it off as our own.

But in some respects, AP staffers must deal with gray areas.

It is common for an AP staffer to include in his or her work passages from a previous AP story by another writer — generally background, or boilerplate. This is acceptable if the passages are short. Regardless, the reporter writing the story is responsible for the factual and contextual accuracy of the material.

Also, the AP often has the right to use material from its members and subscribers; we sometimes take the work of newspapers, broadcasters and other outlets, rewrite it and transmit it without credit.

There are rules, however. When the material is exclusive, controversial or sensitive, we always credit it. And we do not transmit the stories in their original form; we rewrite them, so that the approach, content, structure and length meet our requirements and reflect the broader audience we serve.

Similar rules apply when we use material from news releases. Under no circumstances can releases reach the wire in their original form; we can use information and quotes from releases, but we must check the material, augment it with information from other sources, and then write our own stories.

We apply the same judgment in picking up material from members or from news releases that we use when considering information we receive from other sources. We must satisfy ourselves, by our own reporting, that the material is credible. If it does not meet AP standards, we don't use it.

For video, if another broadcaster's material is required and distributed, the name of that broadcaster shall be advised on the accompanying shotlist.

Pickups of audio and of television graphics are credited in billboards/captions when the member requests it.

CONFLICTS OF INTEREST

The AP respects and encourages the rights of its employees to participate actively in civic, charitable, religious, public, social or residential organizations.

However, AP employees must avoid behavior or activities — political, social or financial — that create a conflict of interest or compromise our ability to report the news fairly and accurately, uninfluenced by any person or action. Nothing in this policy is intended to abridge any rights provided by the National Labor Relations Act.

Here is a sampler of AP practices on questions involving possible conflict of interest. It is not all-inclusive; if you are unsure whether an activity may constitute a conflict or the appearance of a conflict, consult your manager at the onset.

EXPRESSIONS OF OPINION

Anyone who works for the AP must be mindful that opinions they express may damage the AP's reputation as an unbiased source of news. They must refrain from declaring their views on contentious public issues in any public forum, whether in Web logs, chat rooms, letters to the editor, petitions, bumper stickers or lapel buttons, and must not take part in demonstrations in support of causes or movements.

FAVORS

Employees should not ask news sources or others they meet in a professional capacity to extend jobs or other benefits to anyone. They also should not offer jobs, internships or any benefits of being an AP employee to news sources.

FINANCIAL INTERESTS

Associated Press employees who regularly write or edit business or financial news must always avoid any conflict of interest or the appearance of any conflict of interest in connection with the performance of these duties. For these reasons, these employees must abide by the following rules and guidelines when making personal investment and financial decisions.

These employees must not own stock, equities or have any personal financial investment or involvement with any company, enterprise or industry that they regularly cover for the AP. A technology writer, for example, must not own any technology equities; a retail industry writer must not own the stock of any department store or corporate enterprise that includes department stores. Staff members who are temporarily assigned to such coverage or editorial duties must immediately notify a manager of possible conflicts to determine whether the assignment is appropriate. If necessary, employees might be asked either to divest or to suspend any activity involving their holdings.

Editors and writers who regularly cover the financial markets may not own stock in any company. They may invest in equity index-related products and publicly available diversified mutual funds or commodity pools.

Financial news employees must also avoid investment activities that are speculative or driven by day-trading or short-term profit goals because such activities may create the impression that the employee is seeking to drive market factors or is acting upon information that is not available to the public.

Instead, the personal financial activities and investments of these employees must be based upon the longer term and retirement savings. For these reasons, an employee covered by this policy should not buy and sell the same financial product within 60 days, unless he/she gains the permission of the department manager and is able to demonstrate financial need that is unrelated to information discussed or gained in the course of his/her employment. This trading limitation does not apply to equity-index funds, broadly diversified and publicly available mutual funds and commodity pools.

All employees must comply with federal and local laws concerning securities and financial transactions, including statutes, regulations and guidelines prohibiting actions based upon "inside information." All employees are reminded that they may not act upon, or inform any other person of, information gained in the course of AP employment, unless and until that information becomes known to the general public.

Employees should avoid any conflict of interest or the appearance of a conflict of interest in the investments and business interests of their spouses or other members of their household with whom they share finances. They are expected to make every effort to assure that no spouse or other member of their household has investment or business interests that could pose such a conflict.

Employees should be aware that the investment activities and/or financial interests of their spouses or other individuals with whom they share financial interests may make it inappropriate for them to accept certain assignments. Employees must consult with their managers before accepting any such assignment.

Employees who are asked to divest holdings will be given one year from the date of the request to do so, in order to give them the opportunity to avoid market fluctuations.

When this document requires the sale of stock holdings, an employee can satisfy this requirement by putting the shares into a blind trust (or into an equivalent financial arrangement) that meets the same goal: preventing an individual from knowing, at any given time, the specific holdings in the account and blocking an individual from controlling the timing of transactions in such holdings. If AP assigns a staff member to a new job where mandatory divestiture would impose a financial hardship even after the one-year grace period, AP will reimburse the staff member up to a maximum of $500 for the reasonable costs of setting up a blind trust.)

FREELANCE WORK

Individuals who seek to engage in non-AP work are subject to the following restrictions:

• Freelance work must not represent a conflict of interest for either the employee or the AP.

• Such activities may not interfere with the employees' job responsibilities, including availability for newsgathering.

• Such activities may not exploit the name of The Associated Press or the employee's position with the AP without permission of the AP.

• Inevitably, some employees will use material they accumulated in their AP work — notes, stories (either written or broadcast), images, videotape, graphics — for other-than-AP uses. The resulting product must be presented to the AP for its approval prior to submission to any outside publisher, purchaser or broadcaster. And under no circumstances should the AP incur expenses for research material that is not used for AP purposes.

FREE TICKETS

We do not accept free tickets to sports, entertainment or other events for anything other than coverage purposes. If we obtain tickets for a member or subscriber as a courtesy, they must be paid for, and the member should reimburse the AP.

GIFTS

Associated Press offices and staffers are often sent or offered gifts or other items — some of them substantial, some of them modest, some of them perishable — by sources, public relations agencies, corporations and others. Sometimes these are designed to encourage or influence AP news coverage or business, sometimes they are just "perks" for journalists covering a particular event. Whatever the intent, we cannot accept such items; an exception is made for trinkets like caps or mugs that have nominal value, approximately $25 or less. Otherwise, gifts should be politely refused and returned, or if that is impracticable, they should be given to charity.

Books, CDs, DVDs, and other items received for review may be kept for staffers' professional reference or donated to charities, but may not be sold for personal gain. In cases where restrictions forbid transfer to third parties, these items, usually CDs and DVDs should be recycled. Items of more than nominal value that are provided for testing, such as computer gear, must be returned.

AP and its employees may accept discounts from companies only if those discounts are standard and offered to other customers.

We do not accept unsolicited contest awards from any organization that has a partisan or financial interest in our coverage; nor do we enter such contests.

The aim in all dealings should be to underscore the AP's reputation for objectivity.

OFFICIAL SCORERS
Employees may not serve as official scorers at sports events.

OUTSIDE APPEARANCES
Employees frequently appear on radio and TV news programs as panelists asking questions of newsmakers; such appearances are encouraged.

However, there is potential for conflict if staffers are asked to give their opinions on issues or personalities of the day. Advance discussion and clearance from a staffer's supervisor are required.

Employees must inform a news manager before accepting honoraria and/or reimbursement of expenses for giving speeches or participating in seminars at colleges and universities or at other educational events if such appearance makes use of AP's name or the employee represents himself or herself as an AP employee. No fees should be accepted from governmental bodies; trade, lobbying or special interest groups; businesses, or labor groups; or any group that would pose a conflict of interest. All appearances must receive prior approval from a staffer's supervisor.

POLITICAL ACTIVITIES
Editorial employees are expected to be scrupulous in avoiding any political activity, whether they cover politics regularly or not. They may not run for political office or accept political appointment; nor may they perform public relations work for politicians or their groups. Under no circumstances should they donate money to political organizations or political campaigns. They should use great discretion in joining or making contributions to other organizations that may take political stands.

Non-editorial employees must refrain from political activity unless they obtain approval from a manager.

When in doubt, staffers are encouraged to discuss any such concerns with their supervisors.

And a supervisor must be informed when a spouse — or other members of an employee's household — has any ongoing involvement in political causes, either professionally or personally.

TRIPS
If a trip is organized, and we think the trip is newsworthy, we go and pay our way. If we have a chance to interview a newsmaker on a charter or private jet, we reimburse the news source for the reasonable rate of the costs incurred — for example, standard airfare. There may be exceptional circumstances, such as a military trip, where it is difficult to make other travel arrangements or calculate the costs. Consult a manager for exceptions.

* * *

BRIEFING ON MEDIA LAW

INTRODUCTION

The courts significantly changed the legal standards governing the work of reporters and editors during the era of the civil rights movement and the Vietnam War, applying the First Amendment's protection of speech and press with new force and meaning.

In *New York Times v. Sullivan* (1964), the Supreme Court held for the first time that the First Amendment limits the ability of states to impose damages for the publication of a statement even when it is false, in some circumstances. Sixteen years later, in *Richmond Newspapers v. Virginia* (1980), the court reached the equally unprecedented conclusion that the First Amendment establishes an affirmative right for the press and public to compel access to information concerning the exercise of government power. The fallout from these two watershed cases has reshaped a great deal of the law that governs the publication of the news and the way it is gathered.

This chapter addresses some of the key legal issues facing journalists. With respect to newsgathering *activity*, it explores three topics of direct significance:

Access to government information, including the rules governing reporter access to the courts and to government information generally;

Confidential sources, including the law relating to promises of confidentiality and the reporter's privilege; and

Newsgathering conduct, including common law and statutory rules that may create liability for actions taken while a reporter is seeking out the news.

With respect to news *content*, this chapter addresses the legal principles in three branches of the law that govern liability for the publication of information:

Defamation, including the elements of a claim arising from the publication of a *false* statement, and the common law and constitutional defenses to liability;

Privacy, including claims for the disclosure of private facts, misappropriation and "false light," which can arise when the facts reported are *true*; and

Copyright infringement, including the elements of a copyright claim and the "fair use" defense.

While the law can vary in significant ways from one state to another, particularly in its details, the broad principles affecting newsgathering and reporting in the United States are largely consistent, due in part to the federal constitutional principles protecting speech and the press that overlay state law. Reporters and editors naturally will become familiar over time with the particulars of media law in the places where they work, and this chapter is intended only as a general primer on some basic principles that are likely to apply across a range of situations. It should not be construed as legal advice and should not substitute for obtaining legal guidance when you are in doubt.

LEGAL PRINCIPLES OF NEWSGATHERING

Several legal rules have special importance to the way the news is gathered. This chapter takes up three of them: the affirmative rights that can be invoked to compel access to government *proceedings* and the release of government documents; the legal protections that often allow reporters to obtain information through a promise of confidentiality; and, the "laws of general applicability," such as intrusion, trespass, and misrepresentation, that reporters must usually follow, even when they inhibit the ability to seek out the news.

Access to government information

Public access to information about the actions of government is essential in a democracy. James Madison made just this point in 1832:

"A Popular Government, without popular information, or the means of acquiring it, is but a Prologue to a Farce or a Tragedy; or perhaps both. Knowledge will forever govern ignorance: And a people who mean to be their own Governors, must arm themselves with the power which knowledge gives."

The press and public have affirmative rights, both constitutional and statutory, to compel access to the type of government information that is essential to the functioning of our democracy. A right of access extends to official *proceedings*, including court trials, hearings, and the meetings of some legislative bodies and administrative agencies. Access rights also extend to the inspection of *documents* held by the government, with only specific exceptions. Given the independence of the three branches of government, the scope of access to judicial proceedings and court records is largely governed by constitutional and common law principles articulated by judges, while access to information in the executive and legislative branches is largely governed by statutes and administrative regulations.

These access rights are not absolute; they can be abridged in a number of situations. Nonetheless, clear legal standards define the scope of these rights and the procedures available to reporters to enforce them.

• Recognition of a First Amendment right of access

The articulation by the Supreme Court in 1980 of a constitutional *right* to certain information about the exercise of government power, and the delineation of the proper scope and application of that right over the ensuing years, would provide a fascinating case study of the meaning of a "living constitution." In *Richmond Newspapers v. Virginia*, the Supreme Court ruled for the first time that the First Amendment encompasses an affirmative, enforceable right of public access to criminal trials. As the court later explained the rationale for this new constitutional right, "a major purpose" of the First Amendment's protection of free speech, a free press and the right to petition the government is the public's need to know what the government is up to, if democracy is to function. Just as other provisions of the Bill of Rights have been read to imply the right to travel, a right to privacy, and the right to be presumed innocent, the court concluded that the First Amendment implies a right of the public to certain information concerning the direct exercise of government power.

In a series of rulings following *Richmond Newspapers*, the Supreme Court reaffirmed the existence of this constitutional right of access and defined its scope. In 1982, the court said that the right to attend a criminal trial applies even during the testimony of a minor victim of a sex crime. In *Globe Newspaper Co. v. Superior Court* (1982), the court said that the right to attend a criminal trial applies even during the testimony of a minor victim of a sex crime. The court in that case struck down as unconstitutional a Massachusetts statute mandating closed proceedings during all such testimony, saying that the First Amendment right of access requires a judge to determine on a case-by-case basis whether the privacy concerns of a particular victim outweigh the public's right to attend and observe the proceedings. In 1984, the Supreme Court held that the right of public access extends to the proceedings to select a jury in a criminal case, *Press-Enterprise Co. v. Superior Ct. I*, and two years later said the right extends to preliminary hearings in a criminal prosecution. *Press-Enterprise Co. v Superior Ct. II*. The First Amendment protects the public's right to attend such judicial proceedings unless specific findings are made, on the record, demonstrating that a closed proceeding is essential in order to "preserve higher values," and any limitation imposed on public access must be narrowly tailored to serve that interest. In 2010, in *Presley v. Georgia*, the court held a trial judge must ensure that these standards are satisfied before a courtroom is closed to the public, even if no one objects to the closure.

While the Supreme Court has not substantively revisited the right of access in detail since 1986, lower federal and state courts have widely considered and applied the right to a large variety of judicial and administrative proceedings over the intervening years. Courts have recognized a constitutional right to attend a given type of proceeding if public access will generally play a positive role in the performance of the proceeding (encouraging diligent attention by officials, ensuring that proper procedures are followed, preventing perjury or other misconduct, facilitating public understanding of decisions made), and if it is the type of proceeding that historically has been open to the public. This right has been held also to apply to administrative proceedings conducted like trials, such as deportation hearings and agency adjudications.

The constitutional right is generally recognized to apply to all aspects of a criminal prosecution, except to matters involving a grand jury. Grand jury investigations historically have been completely secret, and this secrecy itself advances the important public policy of protecting innocent people in those cases where an investigation does not result in any criminal charge being filed. The right of access has been held to extend to civil trials and proceedings, although in some states there are important exceptions. Family Court proceedings, for example, raise significant privacy concerns, as do juvenile delinquency matters, and these are often closed to the public.

• Limits on constitutional access

As noted, the constitutional right to attend government proceedings is not absolute. That a First Amendment right protects public access to a type of proceeding does not mean that such a proceeding can never be closed to the press and public. The Supreme Court has identified four factors that must each be satisfied before the right of access may be restricted:

1. Those who want to close a proceeding must prove that holding a public proceeding would directly threaten some compelling interest, such as a defendant's right to a fair trial or the right of privacy, that outweighs the public interest in openness.

2. There must be no alternative short of closing the proceeding that could protect the threatened interest.

3. Any limitation on access must be as narrow as possible.

4. The limitation imposed must be effective in protecting the threatened interest or else closure may not be ordered.

Applying these factors, courts have required journalists and the public to be excluded from proceedings in a number of situations, such as during the testimony of a sexual assault victim whose identity has not previously been disclosed to the public, or during testimony by an undercover police officer whose effectiveness or safety would be jeopardized by public identification.

Sidebar conferences between the attorneys and the judge generally involve discussions intended to be kept confidential from the jury, but these discussions should usually be available to the press. A transcript is generally kept of such sidebar discussions and should be available for inspection as part of the record of the proceeding. To withhold the transcript of such a sidebar conference held during an open proceeding, the same four-part test would need to be met.

One recurring but unsettled issue concerns reporters' access to information identifying jurors, and their right to speak to jurors after a verdict. The Supreme Court has said specifically that the First Amendment right of access extends to jury selection proceedings, where names and other identifying information are normally disclosed. Some lower courts have concluded that this principle also requires disclosures of written juror questionnaires when they are used. Nonetheless, in some high profile cases such as the prosecutions of Martha Stewart, Michael Jackson, Illinois Gov. Rod Blagojevich, and baseball slugger Barry Bonds, courts have sought to keep the identities of jurors private during the trial or to minimize press contact with jurors following a verdict. Sometimes a judge will conduct jury selection by reference only to juror numbers, to prevent public disclosure of juror names or addresses before a trial is over. The U.S. Court of Appeals in Philadelphia concluded in *United States v. Wecht* (2008) that the public access right requires juror names to be disclosed before the start of a trial, but this position is not universally embraced. In other cases, courts have barred reporters from speaking with jurors long after a verdict is returned. Limitations on disclosure of juror identities before a verdict is returned are sometimes permitted, but restrictions after a verdict is returned can rarely be squared with the First Amendment right of access.

Reporters confronted with such court orders should seek legal advice on the validity of the restriction imposed.

• What to say if a hearing is about to be closed without prior notice

Because a constitutional right is at stake, the press has a right to be heard before a proceeding is closed to the public. The following statement should be read in court when confronted with an attempt to close a hearing without advance notice. It allows a reporter, when permitted to address the court, to state the basic concerns and to seek time for counsel to appear to make the legal argument. Any parts of the statement that are not applicable to a specific case can be changed or omitted:

May it please the Court, I am (name) of The Associated Press (or other news organization). I respectfully request the opportunity to register on the record an objection to closing this proceeding to the public. The Associated Press (or other organization) requests a hearing at which its counsel may present to the Court legal authority and arguments showing why any closure in this proceeding would be improper.

The press and the public have a constitutional right to attend judicial proceedings, and may not be excluded unless the Court makes findings, on the record, that: (1) closure is required to preserve a compelling constitutional interest, (2) no adequate alternatives to closure exist, and (3) the closure ordered is narrowly tailored to protect the threatened interest effectively.

The Associated Press (or other news organization) submits that these findings cannot be made here, especially given the public interest in this proceeding. The public has a right to be informed of what transpires in this case, the positions being argued by the parties, and the factual basis for rulings made by the Court. The Court should avoid any impression that justice is being carried on in secret. The Associated Press (or other news organization) objects to any closure order and respectfully requests a hearing at which it can present full legal arguments and authority in support of this position. Thank you.

If the court will not allow a reporter to be heard, a brief written statement — handwritten is fine — should be delivered to the courtroom clerk, making these same points.

• A word about gag orders

The tension between the right of a free press and the right of a fair trial is nothing new. Finding an impartial jury for the treason trial of Aaron Burr in 1807 was difficult, the Supreme Court has noted, because few people in Virginia "had not formed some opinions concerning Mr. Burr or his case, from newspaper accounts." Nonetheless, an apparently increasing number of cases involving celebrity defendants or notorious crimes generating intense publicity have led to an increased number of orders preventing lawyers, parties to a case, and sometimes even witnesses, from discussing the case outside of the courtroom.

The Supreme Court has said that speech by attorneys, as officers of the court, may be regulated to protect the integrity of the judicial system. Orders more broadly barring the speech of other trial participants, including the parties and witnesses, are permitted only when absolutely necessary to ensure an accused's right to a fair trial. Such orders have been entered in cases involving extraordinary press coverage that threatens the ability to select an impartial jury, when other measures are not likely to mitigate the effects of unrestrained pretrial publicity.

A typical gag order does not prevent a reporter from asking questions, but it does bar trial participants and court officers from answering them. Because a gag order restricts access to news, a reporter has legal standing to challenge an order, and may be successful if a gag order was entered without adequate factual findings to justify the need for the specific restraint on speech imposed by the court, or if the order is overbroad in the categories of individuals restrained or the range of topics they are prohibited from discussing.

• Media protocols in high-profile cases

Over the years "decorum orders" have been entered by some courts to regulate the conduct of reporters covering high profile trials. Sometimes requested by the parties and sometimes imposed unilaterally by the court, these orders may restrict the use of cameras and recording devices at specific locations in and around the courthouse, direct that witnesses or jurors not be photographed as they come and go from court, restrict the use of cellphones, or impose other restrictions to protect the decorum of a trial and operations at the courthouse. In the aborted Kobe Bryant prosecution, for example, a Colorado state judge imposed a decorum order specifying such details as where cameras could be positioned outside the courthouse, limiting the times when reporters could enter or leave the courtroom, and specifying where reporters could sit, where they could park their cars and how they could enter the courthouse.

Restrictions on the actions of journalists that directly affect their ability to gather news must be narrowly tailored to protect a compelling governmental interest. Decorum orders that become necessary in high-profile cases to ensure safety, protect physical access to the courts by the public, or prevent interference with the integrity of the proceedings in the courtroom, are likely to be allowed as long as their terms are reasonable, content-neutral and limited to clearly defined restrictions on conduct within the courthouse and its immediate environs. A decorum order likely goes too far, however, if it also controls the content of a news report rather than just the conduct of a reporter. For example, for privacy reasons a court might restrict the taking of photographs of jurors as they enter or leave the courthouse, but could not properly bar the press from ever publishing the image of a juror, even if it were obtained through other sources. One restriction is limited to conduct at the courthouse; the other is aimed at the content of a news report.

• The right to attend other types of proceedings

In some instances, the constitutional right of access has been held to extend to proceedings beyond court hearings. For example, the U.S. Court of Appeals in Cincinnati has held that the public had a constitutional right to attend deportation proceedings conducted by the Immigration and Naturalization Service. (*Detroit Free Press v. Ashcroft*, 2002.) The U.S. Court of Appeals in New York has held that the right of access applies in transit agency tribunals to assess fines. (*New York Civ. Lib. Union v. N.Y.C. Transit Authority*, (2011)). The First Amendment right of access similarly has been found to extend to military courts-martial, proceedings of judicial review boards and hearings of the Federal Mine Safety and Health Administration.

Most states and the federal government also have statutes known as "open meetings laws" or "government in the sunshine" acts that protect the right of the public and the press to attend meetings of public authorities. These laws essentially provide that every meeting where a public board or public authority convenes to conduct business must be open to the public, with only limited exception. The federal law, for example, allows a meeting to be closed only if one of 10 identified categories of information is to be discussed, such as personnel and salary decisions. Even when a portion of a meeting is closed, a transcript or minutes must be prepared, and must be disclosed to the extent that disclosure would not reveal the exempt information.

These access laws typically apply to executive agencies, but not to the legislative bodies, in most cases. Most state constitutions separately require open legislative sessions, although each house is usually free to make its own rules about access to committee meetings.

• The right of access applies to court records

The right of access generally includes the right to inspect transcripts of open proceedings, evidence introduced at a trial and most motion papers, orders and other records of open court proceedings. Some courts have concluded that this right to inspect judicial records is implicit in the First Amendment right of access, holding that the right covers any documents relating to a proceeding that is itself subject to the First Amendment right of access.

Other courts analyze the right of access to documents filed with the court as a common law right that may be more easily restricted, sometimes with unfortunate results. For example, in the famous case of *McConnell v. Federal Election Commission* (2003), a challenge to the constitutionality of the McCain-Feingold campaign finance reform act was decided by the courts entirely on the basis of written submissions, without any public evidentiary hearing. A massive record of some 100,000 pages was presented to the court, apparently detailing the types of campaign abuses that Congress found to justify restrictions on election speech. Despite the public interest in knowing the factual basis for the competing arguments being made, the District of Columbia court concluded that the public had only a common law right to inspect the documents presented to the court, and that this right extended only to information "relied upon" by the court in reaching its decision. The court therefore rejected an application by several news organizations to inspect the evidence filed with the court, saying the public was only entitled to inspect specific pages of the record actually cited in the court's opinions. Other courts have rejected this limitation and have found a constitutional right of access to records submitted to courts in support of requests for judicial action, regardless of whether the court ultimately relies on the record, an approach embraced by the U.S. Court of Appeals in New York (*Lugosh v. Pyramid Corp.*).

Whether the right to inspect court records is a constitutional right or a common law right is not fully settled in some areas of the country. Whatever the scope of the right to inspect court records, however, it does not generally extend to pretrial discovery documents and other litigation records that are not filed with the courts. While compelled public access to discovery has been afforded on rare occasions, involving highly newsworthy disputes, reporters generally have no right to require parties to a lawsuit to allow inspection of litigation material that is never filed with the court.

• Access to other government records

The federal Freedom of Information Act (FOIA), originally passed by Congress in 1966, creates a presumptive right of access to all documents held in the executive branch, other than documents in the possession of the president and his immediate staff. It does not cover Congress or the courts. All Cabinet agencies, independent agencies, regulatory commissions and government-owned corporations are covered.

Records made available for inspection under the act include virtually anything recorded in a physical medium that can be reproduced. This includes all documents, papers, reports, and letters in the government's possession, as well as films, photographs, sound recordings, databases, computer disks and tapes. A 1996 law expanded FOIA to require federal agencies, whenever possible, to share data in a specific format, such as on computer diskette or CD-ROM. The 1996 amendments also broadened citizen access to government by placing more information directly online.

The act contains nine exemptions that permit — but do not require — agencies to withhold information. Those exemptions are: (1) national security; (2) internal agency personnel rules; (3) information specifically exempt from disclosure by another law; (4) trade secrets; (5) internal agency memorandums and policy deliberations; (6) personal privacy; (7); law enforcement investigations; (8) federally regulated bank information; and (9) oil and gas well data.

Different agencies apply these exemptions in different ways even when issues ostensibly have already been settled in court. If you want something, ask for it. Let the government decide whether it has any grounds or willingness to deny your request. The statutory exemptions allow information to be withheld, but do not require it. Even an exempt document can be released at the government's discretion.

Because of the various exemptions, documents are often produced with large sections blacked out as "exempt." And, because of a lack of manpower assigned to implement the act, there are often long delays in getting documents at all. Under the law, information is supposed to be produced within 20 days, but there is no effective enforcement mechanism when an agency misses this deadline, short of going to court.

• Making a request under FOIA

There is no set format for making a FOIA request for documents. Although most agencies have adopted regulations describing specific steps to follow, any reasonably precise identification of the information sought, submitted to the proper person, will trigger an obligation for an agency to respond. Here are a few elementary steps to consider in making a FOIA request that may help avoid problems:

—Call the public information office of the agency you believe has the records before filing your request, to make sure you have the right agency and the right address for filing it. Ask if the information you are seeking could be released without a written FOIA request.

—Be as specific as possible about what you want. Give dates, titles, and authors for documents if you know them. In your letter, provide your telephone number, email address, and offer to supply any other information that might help narrow the search.

—Even if you are using the letterhead stationery of a news organization, state specifically that you are a reporter for that organization and plan to use the material in news stories. The act does not require you to state your purpose, but disclosures in the public interest are eligible for fee waivers, exemption waivers and in some cases expedited handling.

—Request a waiver of search and copying fees. To avoid delays if the waiver is denied, also state a limit you are prepared to pay, such as $100, without the agency's need to obtain your prior, specific consent.

—If you want field office files checked as well as those at headquarters, be sure to request that specifically. Some agencies, such as the FBI, will not check beyond the office where the request is submitted, unless asked. It is good practice to send a separate request directly to the FOI officer at the field office of an agency in any event, if you think relevant documents exist there.

—Ask the agency to cite specific exemptions for each item it withholds in the event that any part of the request is denied.

—Request that redacted copies of documents be provided if only a specific portion of a document is subject to an exemption.

—If your initial request is denied, file an administrative appeal. Some agencies take a very different view on appeal. The denial letter will specify to whom the appeal must be sent and the deadline for making an appeal. If you do not first pursue an administrative appeal, you cannot go to court to compel release of the information.

—An appeal can be made through a simple letter that explains why the public will benefit from disclosure and asks for a review of the grounds on which the request was denied. Several exemptions require a balancing of private and public interests, and reviewers on an administrative appeal may be more likely to exercise their right to waive an exemption if a good case for disclosure is made.

You may want to consult FOIA experts or manuals before proceeding with a request. A FOI Service Center is maintained by the Reporters Committee for Freedom of the Press. The committee publishes a pamphlet with sample FOIA letters and appeal forms as well as analyses of the act. (Available on the Web at: http://www.rcfp.org/foiact/index.html.) The committee maintains a toll-free hot line (800-336-4243), 24 hours a day, seven days a week, with attorneys available to provide FOIA advice to journalists.

On the Web, the U.S. Department of Justice publishes a "Guide to the Freedom of Information Act," which gives the current government understanding of what is covered and not covered by each exemption, http://www.justice.gov/oip/foia-guide.html. Also on the Web, the U.S. Department of Justice publishes a collection of "FOIA Resources," which includes up-to-date copies of relevant statutes and recent court decisions, http://www.justice.gov/oip/foia-resources.html.

It is advisable to check on specific state freedom of information laws. Each individual state has its own freedom of information laws that apply to state and local government agencies.

Issues concerning sources

For better or worse, some sources who possess important information of great public significance will speak to a journalist only if they are promised confidentiality. This has been true from the earliest history of an independent press in America. John Peter Zenger, whose New York trial in 1735 is best remembered for establishing the principle that truth is a defense to a claim for libel, was also the first American newspaperman to establish the tradition that journalists will protect their sources to the point of imprisonment. Zenger refused to divulge to British authorities the identities of those who made the statements that authorities considered libelous.

The use of confidential sources remains an important means for reporters to uncover the news. Such sources make available to the public more than the sanitized "spin" of government and corporate press releases. Yale professor Alexander Bickel noted:

"Indispensable information comes in confidence from officeholders fearful of superiors, from businessmen fearful of competitors, from informers operating at the edge of the law who are in danger of reprisal from criminal associates, from people afraid of the law and government — sometimes rightly afraid, but as often from an excess of caution — and from men in all fields anxious not to incur censure for unorthodox or unpopular views." ("The Morality of Consent," 1975.)

In one study of some 10,000 news reports conducted in 2005, 13 percent of the front-page newspaper articles reviewed were based, at least in part, on anonymous sources.

Promising confidentiality to a source always raises a number of issues, legal and journalistic. If a reporter refuses to identify a source, there is always the potential that a publisher may be hauled into court or a reporter thrown into jail. If a publisher is sued for libel, having a story based on sources that were promised confidentiality creates an entirely separate set of concerns: it is hard to prove the "truth" of a statement if the source of the information cannot be revealed. In one case, a Massachusetts court entered a default judgment against the Boston Globe for refusing to reveal its confidential source for a story that became the subject of a libel claim. A jury subsequently awarded the plaintiff $2.1 million — a hefty price to pay to uphold a promise to a source.

• A promise to a source creates an enforceable agreement

A reporter who reveals the name or identity of someone who was promised confidentiality can be held liable for breach of the agreement.

The Supreme Court decided just this issue in *Cohen v. Cowles* (1991), a case involving "dirt" on one political candidate that was provided to a newspaper reporter on the eve of the election by a political consultant for the candidate's opponent. The reporter promised the consultant confidentiality. His editors, however, considered the identification of the source necessary for the public to weigh the significance of the new disclosures, and overruled the reporter. As a result, the no-longer confidential source lost his job, and sued. A jury verdict of $200,000 in favor of the spurned source was upheld by the Supreme Court, which found the First Amendment no defense to a claim for the damages caused by breaking a promise freely made.

The same result was reached by a New York court in a case involving a promise to mask someone's identity in a photograph. A journalist promised a man receiving treatment in an AIDS clinic that he would not be "identifiable" if he allowed his photograph to be taken. The journalist used a rear-angle setup and retouching techniques to obscure his identity, but the man's friends still recognized him when the photograph was published. The New York court held that the burden of carrying out the promise to disguise rested with the journalist who made the promise, and upheld the jury's award of damages to the patient.

Reporters can unwittingly create problems for themselves in making agreements with sources to protect confidentiality, or in failing to clarify with the source the meaning of an agreement. A few common-sense steps can minimize the risk that problems with sources will develop:

-Before making any promise, consider whether it is worth doing: How important is the information that the source is going to provide? Can the information be obtained or confirmed from any "on-the-record" source?

-If a promise of some protection is to be made, express it in terms of the steps that will be taken to protect the source rather than the result to be achieved. For example, promise a source to not use the name, or agree on how the source will be identified in the story (a "high-ranking military officer," or a "knowledgeable Defense Department official"), rather than promising "no one will know you gave me this information." If a photograph or videotape is involved, the key is still to promise a specific action ("I will photograph you only from behind") rather than promising a result ("no one will recognize you").

-Make sure the source has the same understanding of the scope of the promise made, as you do. Avoid using ambiguous terms as a shorthand for an agreement, such as "this will be off the record," or this is "confidential." Instead, be specific about the terms of the agreement and how far the promise extends.

Must confidentiality be maintained if litigation results? If a court order requires disclosure? Or, will the source allow disclosure in certain situations?

-Follow through with any agreement, making sure to inform editors and others who need to know to carry out the promise. The broader the promise, the more the effort needed to make sure that it is upheld.

The bottom line is this: promises of confidentiality or anonymity should be made cautiously, and only after a determination that the risk of such promises is outweighed by the need for the information. When a promise is made, make sure it is as precise as possible, and then make sure it is carried out.

• Reporter's privilege

Given the importance of confidential sources, reporters have long asserted a right to protect the identity of those to whom confidentiality was promised. All states except Wyoming have provided some level of protection for reporters who are called to testify about their sources. Thirty-nine states and the District of Columbia have enacted "shield laws" that provide legal protection against the disclosure of sources; Hawaii's statute recently expired under a sunset provision and it has not as of this writing been re-enacted; nine additional states have recognized some form of a "reporter's privilege" through judicial decisions. About half of the state shield laws provide reporters with an absolute privilege not to disclose confidential sources, while the remainder establish a high standard that must be met before a reporter's promise of confidentiality can be pierced.

The existence and scope of the reporter's privilege is more confused in federal courts. Although significant efforts have been made in recent years, there is no federal shield law, and the Supreme Court has addressed the "reporter's privilege" only once — in a ruling that is far from clear.

In *Branzburg v. Hayes* (1972), the Supreme Court considered claims of privilege asserted by three journalists who had been subpoenaed to reveal confidential information and sources before grand juries investigating possible criminal activity. The reporters had written stories describing the synthesizing of hashish, conversations with admitted drug users, and eyewitness accounts of events at Black Panther headquarters at a time of civil unrest in the surrounding neighborhood. In each instance, the journalist claimed a privilege under the First Amendment not to answer questions concerning confidential information and sources.

A closely divided Supreme Court held in a 5-4 ruling that it did not violate the First Amendment to require these journalists to testify in the grand jury investigations, conducted in good faith, concerning the identities of persons allegedly engaged in criminal conduct. The court, however, did not reject altogether the notion of a First Amendment privilege. To the contrary, the majority opinion expressed the view that its narrow focus should not apply to "the vast bulk of confidential relationships between reporters and their sources," and emphasized that even grand juries "must operate within the limits of the First Amendment as well as the Fifth."

Justice Lewis Powell cast the decisive fifth vote and wrote separately to underscore further the "limited nature" of the court's holding. He explained that reporters would still have access to the courts, and could move to quash a subpoena if confidential source information were being sought "without a legitimate need of law enforcement."

Court decisions over the ensuing decades have embraced a qualified reporter's privilege that accommodates the interests of the press and those who seek to obtain information through judicial process. The United States Courts of Appeals in 10 of the 12 federal circuits have specifically applied the First Amendment reporter's privilege in civil lawsuits.

Courts, however, have read *Branzburg* more restrictively in the criminal context, sometimes declining to recognize a privilege at all, or allowing only a very limited balancing of interests. Three different federal appellate courts affirmed contempt citations requiring reporters to be jailed for refusing to reveal confidential sources sought in criminal investigations. In 2001, freelance writer Vanessa Leggett served nearly six months in a Texas prison for declining to reveal sources of information related to a notorious murder, almost four times longer than any prison term previously imposed on any reporter by any federal court. In 2004, James Taricani, a reporter for WJAR-TV in Rhode Island, completed a four-month sentence of home confinement for declining to reveal who leaked a videotape capturing alleged corruption by public officials in Providence. And, in 2005 The New York Times reporter Judith Miller was jailed in Virginia for several months for refusing to disclose her confidential source for a story she never wrote about CIA operative Valerie Plame.

Most recently, the U.S. Court of Appeals for the Fourth Circuit rejected any First Amendment-based or common law reporter's privilege in a criminal proceeding in which the subpoenaed journalist, James Risen, was an "eyewitness" to a crime. In this case, a confidential source allegedly leaked classified information to Risen and Risen was then subpoenaed to testify whether the criminal defendant was, in fact, his source. (*U.S. v. Sterling*). The U.S. Court of Appeals in Richmond held that Risen had no privilege whatsoever to refuse to testify in this context, and the Supreme Court refused to review the holding. When the case against the source went to trial, however, Attorney General Eric Holder decided that Risen's testimony was not needed, and Risen was not forced to testify. The CIA officer accused of being the source was convicted without compelling the reporter to testify or go to jail.

The aggressive court actions in criminal investigations have encouraged private litigants and federal courts adjudicating their civil cases also to demand confidential information from reporters. In one civil suit, five reporters (including two Pulitzer Prize winners) were held in contempt and subjected to fines of $500 per day each for declining to reveal their confidential sources of information about Dr. Wen Ho Lee, who claimed information about him was provided to reporters by government agents in violation of the Privacy Act.

Because the scope of a reporter's privilege in the federal courts is unsettled, reporters have been aided in federal criminal investigations by Department of Justice guidelines that severely limit the circumstances under which U.S. attorneys may attempt to subpoena reporters. As adopted by Attorney General Elliot Richardson in the wake of the Watergate scandal, these guidelines remain in effect and are published in the Code of Federal Regulations at 28 C.F.R. 50.10. In general, the guidelines imposed a number of criteria governing the issuance of subpoenas directed to journalists, including that:

-All reasonable attempts must be made to obtain the information sought from other sources before a subpoena to a reporter is considered,

-Negotiations for the information should be pursued with the reporter before a subpoena is sought.

-No subpoena may be issued to a reporter without the personal approval of the attorney general.

-The attorney general's approval may not be sought unless the information held by the reporter is essential to the investigation and not reasonably available from other sources.

-Except in exigent circumstances, subpoenas should be used only to verify published information and to confirm the accuracy of the circumstances surrounding published information.

Notwithstanding these guidelines, in 2013, it was disclosed that the Department had secretly subpoenaed the telephone records of the AP in connection with a national security leak investigation and had obtained a search warrant for the email of a Fox News reporter in another leak investigation. The public uproar following these disclosures caused President Barack Obama to direct Attorney General Eric Holder to review and strengthen the guidelines protecting journalists' confidential sources. New guidelines were issued in early 2014 and further revised in early 2015. The regulations are codified at 28 C.F.R. §50.10 and impose additional obligations on federal attorneys who seek to obtain a journalist' s testimony or work product, or to uncover a journalist's confidential source. The guidelines were expanded to cover subpoenas seeking hotel, credit card and other records of businesses used by journalists in the course of their newsgathering, and to require advance notice to the press in most cases before these records are obtained from third parties. The approval requirements of the guidelines were also extended for the first time to cover applications for search warrants as well as subpoenas.

These regulations provide the same types of protection contained in some state shield laws, and the Department of Justice has demonstrated a serious desire to enforce these regulations strictly. Any time a subpoena is received by a reporter from a U.S. attorney, the first question to ask the attorney is: Did you comply with the media guidelines at 28 C.F.R. 50.10 before issuing this subpoena? Not infrequently, just asking the question results in the subpoena being withdrawn.

• Policies and practices for handling subpoenas

AP declines to provide any of its news stories and photos to non-subscribers without a valid subpoena. Although AP does not invite subpoenas, it advises litigants and government officials that it will accept service of a validly issued subpoena narrowly requiring production of news stories and photos as they were transmitted, and will otherwise enforce its rights to resist disclosure to the full extent of the law.

Procedures for responding to a narrow subpoena for published material should be consistently applied, without taking sides, in order to preserve neutrality and objectivity, both in fact and in appearance. In appropriate cases, AP may provide a letter or affidavit authenticating a published story or photo, confirming that a fair and true copy has been provided of an item transmitted by AP on a particular date and time. Whenever possible, AP seeks reimbursement of its copying costs and other costs of compliance.

Subpoenas that go beyond published reports should be resisted routinely by AP reporters in order to avoid becoming perceived as an investigative arm of the government or private litigants. AP does not produce reporters' notes or photos or negatives which have not been moved, nor does it produce drafts or any editorial material, including internal memorandums concerning the newsgathering process. AP never reveals the identity of sources to whom it has promised confidentiality.

AP does not invite sanctions by ignoring subpoenas. It will affirmatively oppose subpoenas that seek privileged work-product and unpublished information of every kind.

A couple of practical pointers that can avoid subpoena problems:

-Always avoid giving out information about stories to lawyers over the phone. Providing information may only whet a lawyer's appetite to serve a subpoena, and it can create an argument that grounds for objecting to a subpoena have somehow been waived. It is always better to refer any questions from lawyers to AP's lawyers in New York.

-Subpoenas from criminal defense attorneys seeking published, local news copy to demonstrate the extent of pretrial publicity can often be deflected by reminding the litigants that AP has no means of determining whether or which AP members used AP copy. The reliable sources for information about what was disseminated to the public are articles stored in news databases and video clips available from television stations and electronic "clipping" services.

• Liability for newsgathering conduct

A reporter for Mother Jones won a national award in 1984 for posing as a job applicant at a chemical factory and covertly taking photographs documenting illegal pesticides being manufactured for the export market. That conduct today would more likely win a lawsuit.

In holding that a reporter's promise of confidentiality is legally binding, the Supreme Court in *Cohen v. Cowles* (1991) announced that "generally applicable" laws having only "incidental effects" on the ability of the press to gather the news do not offend the First Amendment. Ever since, a flow of lawsuits have been filed against reporters asserting claims for such "generally applicable" torts as intrusion, trespass, and fraud, and more recently, asserting claims for accessing password protected computers or voicemail. From the muzzling effect of the tobacco industry's threat of "tortious interference" liability against CBS for an expose based on a confidential source who was party to a standard confidentiality agreement as an employee of a tobacco company, through *Food Lion's* claim of trespass, fraud and breach of duty leveled against ABC and a spate of other hidden camera lawsuits, reporters since *Cohen v. Cowles*, have faced an increased number of claims alleging misconduct in the gathering of the news.

This section highlights briefly some of the legal theories that can create problems for the unwary reporter.

• Intrusion upon seclusion

A claim for intrusion exists in most states if someone intentionally commits a "highly offensive" intrusion upon another's solitude or seclusion, invading either a physical space or the private affairs of the plaintiff, such as reviewing private financial statements or personal email without permission. Intrusion claims against the press most commonly arise in three contexts: (1) surreptitious surveillance; (2) trespass of private property, and (3) instances where consent to enter a private setting for one purpose has been exceeded (as where a reporter gains access to information under false pretenses).

Intrusion is a branch of the law of privacy. Where the potentially offending conduct occurs is therefore important. For example, in the United States a person generally has no legitimate basis to complain if a picture is taken in a public place, but if the picture is taken in or around the person's home, a claim for intrusion may exist if the person had a "reasonable expectation" of privacy where the photograph was taken.

In one noted lawsuit a few years back, the family of an officer of a large health care corporation successfully obtained an injunction against the elaborate efforts of a news organization that was seeking information about the family. The organization's camera crew followed the children to school, and sat in a boat outside the family's Florida home with a camera equipped with a high-powered telescopic lens. In issuing an injunction, the court concluded that "a persistent course of hounding, harassment and unreasonable surveillance, even if conducted in a public or semi-public place," could support a claim for intrusion upon seclusion.

A claim for intrusion generally requires (1) an intentional intrusion, (2) that impinges upon the solitude or seclusion of another, or his private affairs, and (3) that would be highly offensive to a reasonable person. The term "highly offensive" is ill-defined, but can include harassing behavior, surreptitious surveillance, or the use of high-power lenses and listening devices to invade typically private places.

The tort of intrusion is based on wrongful conduct rather than on the publication of any information, so a claim may exist even when the news story being pursued is never published. For this reason, in many states it is no defense to an intrusion claim to assert the newsworthiness of the information that was being sought. The issue is whether a reasonable person would view the conduct as highly offensive under all the circumstances.

Some examples where courts have upheld claims for intrusion illustrate the nature of the tort:

—Two journalists in California, without discussing who they were, gained access to the home of a disabled veteran who purported to provide healing aids in the form of clay, minerals and herbs. While there, they surreptitiously photographed and tape-recorded the veteran, for use in a magazine report. The court allowed a claim for intrusion even though the reporters were invited into the home by the veteran. While a person takes the risk that someone allowed into their home is not what he seems, and even though a visitor is free to repeat anything he sees or hears, the court held that the homeowner's risk does not extend to the risk that secret photographs and recordings will be transmitted to the world at large.

—The unauthorized recording of an unplanned interview conducted when the plaintiff answered his own front door has similarly been held to constitute an actionable "intrusion," while secretly recording an interview of a person who stepped from their home onto a public sidewalk was held not to be an intrusion.

—Televising an image of a person's home is not an intrusion if the broadcast shows no more than what can be seen from the street, and secretly recording a conversation in a place of business was held not to be an intrusion if the reporter was invited into the office and the state wiretap law permitted the secret recording.

• Trespass

A person commits a trespass by entering property that is in the possession of another, without authorization or consent. To avoid a claim, permission must be obtained by an owner, a tenant or someone acting on their behalf. Like intrusion, a trespass claim arises from conduct in gathering news, not from the content of any report that may subsequently be published.

Permission to be on private property can be implied by custom or by the nature of the premises. For example, someone has implied permission to enter a store or restaurant during business hours, even though it may be located on private property. There is similarly an implied right to approach someone's house on a driveway or sidewalk to see if they are home. Permission, whether express or implied, can also be revoked. If a posted sign says "Do Not Enter," or if the owner came to the door and said to leave, remaining on the property would be a trespass.

Trespass is also a strict liability tort. Entering on someone's property without permission, even by accident or mistake, will constitute a trespass. On the other hand, trespass protects only against a physical invasion of property; it does not limit the collection or use of information gathered while on the property. The law of trespass does not restrict a reporter on a public sidewalk from using what can be seen or heard on the adjacent private property.

The impact of trespass on newsgathering is also tempered by the nature of the damages that may be recovered through a claim for trespass. The trespass tort is intended to protect property, not privacy or reputation. A trespasser therefore can be held responsible only for physical harm done while on the land and other injury that is a "natural consequence" of the trespass. Courts generally will not recognize injury to reputation or emotional distress caused by the later publication of a photograph obtained during a trespass to be a "natural consequence" of the trespass itself.

A vivid example of a trespass claim involved a television camera crew that was preparing a report on credit card fraud. The United States Secret Service obtained a warrant to search an apartment for evidence of credit card fraud, and a news magazine camera crew followed the Secret Service into the apartment. Part of the search was taped, including a sequence of a mother and child cowering on the couch asking not be photographed. In refusing to dismiss a lawsuit asserting claims for trespass and a constitutional tort (for improperly accompanying federal agents in executing a search warrant), an outraged court said the reporters "had no greater right than that of a common thief to be in the apartment." Like intrusion, the trespass was complete once the invasion of private property occurred. The trespass claim could be asserted even though the news report being pursued was never broadcast.

In situations rife with the potential for trespass, common sense can once again minimize the risk of litigation:

—Whenever possible, ask the property owner or those who appear to be in charge for permission to enter, or seek their approval to remain. In situations where police or fire officials have taken control of a crime or disaster scene, they may stand in for the owner and grant or deny access. Their presence does not defeat the owner's rights, however, and the owner can still require a reporter to leave private property.

—Always identify yourself — verbally, by displaying a press credential, and through insignias on clothing and cameras — so that those present know you are a reporter and will not assume you are part of any police or emergency response team. If not asked to leave, the fact that your status as a reporter was disclosed may be sufficient to establish an implied consent to remain.

—If asked to leave, retire to the sidewalk, street, or other position on public property.

—Consent obtained through fraud or misrepresentation will not be considered valid consent and will not defeat a claim for trespass.

—Consent obtained from minors or others who are not legally capable of giving consent (mentally incapacitated people, for example) will not defeat a claim for trespass.

• Electronic eavesdropping

Both state and federal law regulate the electronic recording of conversations, including telephone conversations.

Under the federal law, a conversation may not be recorded without the consent of at least one of the participants. That means reporters are not prohibited by federal law from recording any conversation that they participate in, whether or not they disclose that the conversation is being recorded. But, leaving a hidden tape recorder in a room to record a conversation between others, secretly listening in on an extension phone and recording the conversation, or recording a telephone call picked up on a scanner or listening device, is a violation of federal law if done without permission of one of the parties.

The law in most states is similar to the federal law, allowing a conversation to be recorded so long as one party to the conversation consents. The laws in a minority of states are more strict, and prohibit recording any conversation unless permission is given by all the parties to the conversation. States where the consent of all parties is required in order to record a conversation are: California, Connecticut, Florida, Illinois, Maryland, Massachusetts, Michigan, Montana, Nevada, New Hampshire, Pennsylvania, and Washington. (Michigan's statute, which until recently had been thought to require consent of all parties, has been construed by the courts to require consent of only one participant in the conversation.) This requirement of consent extends only to conversations where there is some expectation of privacy, and does not prohibit tape-recording at speeches, press conferences and similar public events.

• Misrepresentation and similar forms of wrongdoing

Laws of general applicability govern the actions of reporters, yet conduct that might sometimes be deemed "deceit," "misrepresentation" or "fraud" can be useful in ferreting out the news. Reporters are often less than candid in dealing with those from whom they want information. Recognizing this reality, some courts have held that claims such as fraud and misrepresentation cannot be pursued against journalists unless the wrong is "particularly egregious," or part of a broader pattern of wrongdoing. For example, courts have rejected claims for fraud based on a false message left on a telephone answering machine to induce the disclosure of information, and for fraudulently promising that no "ambush" techniques would be used if an interview were granted.

Other courts have been less willing to weigh the public interest in a news report against the allegedly wrongful conduct. In one instance, a judge allowed claims for fraud and breach of contract to proceed against Business Week after a reporter gained access to records of a credit reporting agency by misrepresenting that a subscription to the credit service was being sought in order to conduct background checks on potential Business Week employees. In reality, information was sought for an exposé on the credit-reporting industry, and the reporter promptly obtained the credit history of then-Vice President Dan Quayle without his consent. The court held that such "wanton misconduct" can result in liability, and allowed a recovery of the costs incurred by the credit agency as a result of the misrepresentation.

Remember, the basic rule is that reporters must obey rules and regulations when they are gathering the news. While there are some exceptions, the First Amendment will not generally provide a defense to a reporter who violates the law while gathering the news.

• Special Considerations When Dealing with National Security Issues

The Espionage Act (of 1917) makes it a federal crime to publish classified information that either (a) reveals the communications intelligence activities of the United States or any foreign country, or (b) discloses classified information obtained from a foreign government or military force through the "processes of communications intelligence." The Espionage Act also broadly makes it a crime for any unauthorized person either to communicate to another, or to retain possession of "information relating to national defense" if there is "reason to believe" the information could harm the U.S. or help a foreign nation or military force.

In the decades since the statute was enacted, there has never been a prosecution of a news organization for violating the Espionage Act, but there has been sabre-rattling from time to time. In December 2010, for example, Sen. Joseph Lieberman publicly called upon the Justice Department to investigate whether The New York Times had violated the Espionage Act by publishing confidential U.S. diplomatic cables it had obtained from WikiLeaks. And, in June 2013, Rep. Peter King, chairman of the House Subcommittee on Counterterrorism, repeatedly called for the prosecution of journalists who "severely compromise national security," singling out Glenn Greenwald, then a journalist for The Guardian, for publishing news reports based on the documents leaked by Edward Snowden. The application of the Espionage Act to a news organization would raise significant First Amendment issues and might well run afoul of the doctrine barring application of criminal sanctions against the press for publishing truthful information on matters of public concern. It would also raise a number of significant issues, including the propriety of the classification of the information at issue; the vagueness and breadth of the statute when applied to the press; and the lack of the meaning of "harm" to our national security and the burden proving it.

Given the continuing uncertainty surrounding the Espionage Act, special care should be taken before accepting or communicating information known to be classified, and legal guidance sought where appropriate. Because the act is not literally limited to "classified" information, special care should be taken with any nonpublic information concerning official intelligence activities or communications with foreign governments.

In order to avoid exposure for possible conspiracy and "aiding and abetting" liability or both, it is also important to maintain a traditional source-news organization relationship with those individuals who may provide you with national security information, although this is no guarantee of immunity from prosecution.

In 2011, as part of a national security leak investigation, the Justice Department obtained a search warrant for the email of a Fox News reporter who allegedly obtained classified information from a State Department source. In applying for the warrant, the Department told the court that the reporter had asked the source to disclose newsworthy information he knew to be classified, and asserted that in doing so the reporter was aiding and abetting a violation of Espionage Act. When the search warrant application was made public months later, a firestorm erupted over the assertion that a reporter had committed a crime simply by asking for information. Attorney General Holder subsequently acknowledged that the Department had never intended to prosecute the reporter and had over-stepped its bounds in making the allegation of criminality. Holder vowed that no reporter would go to jail for "engaging in journalism" so long as he was Attorney General. Holder then revised the Departmental guidelines to prevent a search warrant from being sought for a reporter's records unless the reporter is indeed the target of an active criminal investigation.

LEGAL PRINCIPLES OF PUBLICATION

When a news report is published, the nature of its content poses three principal legal risks to a journalist: that the report contains incorrect information that harms someone's reputation, contains correct information that invades someone's privacy, or contains material that is subject to someone else's copyright. This section provides an overview of the law of libel, privacy and copyright infringement, by examining what a plaintiff is required to prove against news organizations to succeed on such claims and the defenses that are available.

Defamation

In 1967, shortly after *New York Times v. Sullivan* was handed down, Associate Justice John Harlan remarked that "the law of libel has changed substantially since the early days of the Republic." Unfortunately, the news stories that still generate the most claims of injury to reputation — the basis of libel — are still the run-of-the-mill.

Perhaps 95 of 100 libel suits result from the routine publication of charges of crime, immorality, incompetence or inefficiency. A Harvard Nieman report makes the point: "The gee whiz, slam-bang stories usually aren't the ones that generate libel, but the innocent-appearing, potentially treacherous minor yarns from police courts and traffic cases, from routine meetings and from business reports."

Most lawsuits based on relatively minor stories result from factual error or inexact language — for example, getting the plea wrong or inaccurately making it appear that all defendants in a case face identical charges. Libel even lurks in such innocent-appearing stories as birth notices and wedding announcements. Turner Catledge, former managing editor of The New York Times, noted in his autobiography, "My Life and the Times," that people sometimes would "call in the engagement of two people who hate each other, as a practical joke." The fact that some New York newspapers have had to defend suits for such announcements illustrates the care and concern required in every editorial department.

In publishing, no matter what level of constitutional protection, there is just no substitute for accuracy.

• *What is libel?*

Libel is one side of the coin called "defamation," slander being the flip side. At its most basic, defamation means injury to reputation. Libel is generally distinguished from slander, in that a libel is written, or otherwise printed, whereas a slander is spoken. While defamation published in a newspaper universally is regarded as libel, it is perhaps not so self-evident that, in many states, defamation broadcast by television or radio also is considered libel, rather than slander: Because broadcast defamation is often recorded on tape and carried to a wide audience, it is viewed as more dangerous to reputation than a fleeting, unrecorded conversation, and so is classed with printed defamation. In any case, the term defamation generally includes both libel and slander. Words, pictures, cartoons, photo captions and headlines can all give rise to a claim for defamation.

The various states define libel somewhat differently, but largely to the same effect. In Illinois, for example, libel is defined by the courts as "the publication of anything injurious to the good name or reputation of another, or which tends to bring him into disrepute." In New York, a libelous statement is one that tends to expose a person to hatred, contempt or aversion or to induce an evil or unsavory opinion of the person in the minds of a substantial number of people in the community.

In Texas, libel is defined by statute as anything that "tends to injure a living person's reputation and thereby expose the person to public hatred, contempt or ridicule, or financial injury or to impeach any person's honesty, integrity, virtue, or reputation or to publish the natural defects of anyone and thereby expose the person to public hatred, ridicule, or financial injury."

• Liability for republication: the 'conduit' fallacy

A common misconception is that one who directly quotes a statement containing libelous allegations is immune from suit so long as the quoted statement was actually made, accurately transcribed and clearly attributed to the original speaker. This is not so. In fact, the common law principle is just the opposite — a republisher of a libel is generally considered just as responsible for the libel as the original speaker. That you were simply an accurate conduit for the statement of another is no defense to a libel claim.

In many circumstances, therefore, a newspaper can be called to task for republishing a libelous statement made by someone quoted in a story. This rule can lead to harsh results and therefore exceptions exist. For example, reporting the fact that a plaintiff has filed a libel suit against a defendant could, in certain circumstances, lead to a claim against a newspaper for repeating the libel alleged in the complaint. In most states, a "fair report privilege" shields the publisher of an accurate and impartial report of the contents of legal papers filed in court to avoid this result.

Many states also recognize that newspapers under the pressure of daily deadlines often rely on the research of other reputable news organizations in republishing news items originally appearing elsewhere. In such cases, reliance on a reputable newspaper or news agency often is recognized as a defense to a libel claim. Of course, this so-called "wire service defense" may not be available if the republisher had or should have had substantial reason to question the accuracy or good faith of the original story.

The fair report privilege and the wire service defense are exceptions to the basic rule. When the press reports that X has leveled accusations against Y, the press may be held to account not only for the truth of the fact that the accusations were made, but also for the steps taken to verify the truth of the accusations. Therefore, when accusations are made against a person, it generally is prudent to investigate their truth as well as to obtain balancing comment with some relation to the original charges. Irrelevant counthercharges can lead to problems with the person who made the first accusation.

In short, always bear in mind that a newspaper can be held responsible in defamation for republishing the libelous statement made by another, even when the quote is correct.

• *The five things a successful libel plaintiff must prove*

Although the terminology may differ from state to state, a libel plaintiff suing a reporter or a news organization will have to prove five things in order to prevail on a claim for defamation:

1. A defamatory statement was made.
2. The defamatory statement is a matter of fact, not opinion.
3. The defamatory statement is false.
4. The defamatory statement is about ("of and concerning") the plaintiff.
5. The defamatory statement was published with the requisite degree of "fault."

By developing an understanding of the legal elements of a claim for libel, reporters and editors can fashion guideposts that will assist them in practicing their craft in a way that avoids wrongfully injuring the reputation of the subjects of their stories — and thereby reducing the legal risk to the publications for which they write.

1. A defamatory statement was made

It may seem self-evident that a libel claim cannot exist unless a defamatory statement was made, but subjects of news stories (and their lawyers) often bring claims for libel without being able to demonstrate that what was written about them is capable of conveying a defamatory meaning. Put differently, not every negative news report is defamatory.

Generally, statements accusing someone of being a criminal, an adulterer, insane or infected with a loathsome disease are considered automatically "capable of defamatory meaning," as are statements that injure someone's professional reputation (such as that they are corrupt or incompetent). However, to determine whether any particular statement is susceptible of defamatory meaning, reference must be made, first, to the definition of libel adopted in the relevant state, and second, to the full context in which the challenged statement appeared when it was published.

For example, a New York court found that a statement identifying an attorney as a "flashy entertainment lawyer" was not, without more, defamatory, although a statement that a lawyer was an "ambulance chaser" with an interest only in "slam dunk" cases would be. The reasoning is that the first statement would not necessarily damage a lawyer's reputation, while the latter would. Likewise, in New York, allegations of drunkenness, use of "political clout" to gain governmental benefit, membership in the "Mafia," communist affiliation or that someone has cancer may or may not be defamatory, depending on the circumstances of the case.

In Illinois, courts make determinations about defamatory meaning on a case-by-case basis, though in Illinois, most statements will not be considered defamatory unless they charge a person with commission of a crime, adultery/ fornication, or incompetence or lack of integrity in their business or profession. Under this approach, the statement that plaintiff left his children home at night and lost his job because of drinking was held to be defamatory as an accusation of child neglect and inability to discharge the duties of his job due to alcoholism. Similarly, reporting that an alderman had disclosed confidential information was held to be defamatory as indicating that the official lacked the integrity to properly discharge the duties of his office.

In Texas, a statement may be false, abusive and unpleasant without being defamatory. For example, a Texas court held that describing someone as resembling a "hard boiled egg," referring to baldness and pudginess, was not defamatory. Likewise, describing a political candidate as a "radical," "backed and financed by big-shot labor bosses" was not considered defamatory in Texas. On the other hand, an insinuation that a person is connected with gambling and prostitution was found to be defamatory. The assertion that a person who had made an allegation against another of child molestation had fabricated and since recanted the allegation was defamatory when no recantation had, in fact, been made.

While each potentially defamatory statement must be assessed in its own context, particular caution is in order where the statement involves allegations of crime or similar wrongdoing, incompetence or unprofessionalism, or infidelity.

2. The defamatory statement is a matter of fact, not opinion

To be actionable as libel, a defamatory statement must be provably false (or carry a provably false implication). Stated differently, only factual statements that are capable of being proven true or false can form the basis of a libel claim. "Opinions" that do not include or imply provably false facts cannot be the basis of a libel claim. Similarly, epithets, satire, parody and hyperbole that are incapable of being proven true or false are protected forms of expression.

The Supreme Court, in *Gertz v. Robert Welch Inc.* (1974), recognized a constitutional dimension to the prohibition of libel claims based on opinion, stating that "there is no such thing as a false idea." In a later case, *Milkovich v. Lorain Journal Co.* (1990), the Supreme Court denied that there is a distinct constitutional "opinion privilege," but held that any claim for libel must be based on a statement of fact that is provably false, thus shielding purely subjective opinions from liability. Under this approach, a statement is not protected "opinion" merely because it contains qualifying language such as "I think" or "I believe," if what follows contains an assertion of fact that can be proven true or false (e.g., "I believe he murdered his wife.").

Some examples of actual cases can provide a better sense of the distinction between an actionable false fact and a protected opinion:

In Virginia, "pure expressions of opinion" cannot be the basis of a claim for defamation. Under this standard, the statement "I wouldn't trust him as far as I could throw him" and the caption "Director of Butt-Licking" were held to be nonactionable opinion. The Virginia Supreme Court has found words charging that an architect lacked experience and charged excessive fees, or accusing a charitable foundation with failing to spend a "reasonable portion" of its income on program services, also to be protected opinions rather than to be verifiable facts.

In New York, the test for distinguishing a fact from an opinion asks whether: (1) the statement has a precise core of meaning on which a consensus of understanding exists; (2) the statement is verifiable; (3) the textual context of the statement would cause an average reader to infer a factual meaning; and (4) the broader social context signals usage as either fact or opinion. The first two factors focus on the meaning of the words used, the latter two factors consider whether the content, tone and apparent purpose of the statement should signal to the reader that the statement reflects the author's opinion.

Under these principles, calling a doctor a "rotten apple," for example, is incapable of being proved true or false and is therefore protected as an expression of opinion. Similarly, a statement that someone lacked "talent, ambition, initiative" is a nonactionable expression of opinion, since there is no provable, common understanding of what quantum of talent or ambition constitutes a "lack." In one New York case, a letter to the editor published in a scientific journal submitted by the International Primate Protection League and which warned that a multinational corporation's plans for establishing facilities to conduct hepatitis research using chimpanzees could spread hepatitis to the rest of the chimpanzee population was, given its overall context, protected as opinion.

Even when a fact is implicit in an opinion, the common law often protects the statement from liability. In many states, a statement of opinion based on true facts that are themselves accurately set forth is not actionable. Where the facts underlying the opinion are reported inaccurately, however, and would adversely affect the conclusion drawn by the average reader concerning the opinion expressed, the publication may give rise to a claim for libel. For example, the statement, "I believe he murdered his wife because he was found with a bottle of the same kind of poison that killed her," likely would not be actionable even if the plaintiff could prove he did not murder his wife *if* it is true that he was found with a bottle of the same kind of poison that killed her. The true facts on which the (erroneous) opinion was based were disclosed to the readers. If there was no bottle of poison, however, the suggestion that he was a murderer would certainly be actionable. If an opinion suggests or appears to rely on an undisclosed fact, however, a libel claim may still be brought upon the unstated, implied facts if they are both false and defamatory.

The statement that a sports commentator was a "liar" without reference to specific facts, under this approach, was considered to be protected opinion. Taken in the total context of an article, the statement that the plaintiff was a "neo-Nazi" was protected as opinion. Likewise, a statement calling a plaintiff a "commie," suggesting that he does not understand the subject he teaches and that he is "not traveling with a full set of luggage," was also protected as opinion. Statements accusing doctors of being "cancer con-artists," of practicing "medical quackery," and of promoting "snake oil remedies," were also protected. A newspaper column and editorial characterizing a nudist pageant as "pornography" and as "immoral" were also protected.

One federal appeals court has held that three questions should be considered to distinguish opinion from fact: (1) does the statement use figurative or hyperbolic language that would negate the impression that the statement is serious? (2) does the general tenor of the statement negate the impression that the statement is serious? (3) can the statement be proved true or false?

Under this test, a commentator's statement that a product "didn't work" was not an opinion because, despite the humorous tenor of the comment, it did not use figurative or hyperbolic language, it could reasonably be understood as asserting an objective fact and the fact could be proven true or false. Likewise, a statement made in a newspaper interview that plaintiff was an "extortionist" was not protected as opinion.

The common thread to these variations is that opinions offered in a context presenting the facts on which they are based will generally not be actionable. On the other hand, opinions that imply the existence of undisclosed, defamatory facts (i.e., if you knew what I know) are more likely to be actionable. In addition, a statement that is capable of being proven true or false, regardless of whether it is expressed as an opinion, an exaggeration or hyperbole, may be actionable.

3. The defamatory statement is false

In almost all libel cases involving news organizations, the plaintiff has the burden of proving that the defamatory statement is false. (The states are divided on whether a purely private individual has to prove falsity when the defamatory statement does not involve a matter of public concern.) Nonetheless, as a practical matter, a libel defendant's best defense is often to prove that the statement is true. While this may sound like six-of-one-half-dozen-of-the-other, there is considerable significance to placing on the plaintiff the legal burden of proving falsity: Where a jury feels it cannot decide whether a statement is true or false because the evidence is mixed, it is required to rule against the plaintiff — ties go to the defendant.

In almost all states, the question is not whether the challenged statement is literally and absolutely true, in every jot and tittle, but whether the statement as published is "substantially true." That is, a court will consider whether the gist or sting of the defamatory statement is accurate, or whether the published statement would produce a different effect in the mind of a reader than would the absolutely true version.

For example, most courts will dismiss a libel claim brought by a person charged with second degree burglary, if a newspaper mistakenly reported that he had been charged with first-degree burglary: The gist of the story (that the man is an accused burglar) is true, and most readers would not form a better opinion of the man had they been correctly informed that it was only second degree burglary with which he had been charged. But, where a newspaper mistakenly reports that the accused burglar has been charged with murder (or that a person thus far only accused of murder has been convicted of it), a court might well conclude that the "sting" of the statement is not substantially accurate, and that readers would think less of the person based on the false statement than they would have had the published report been accurate.

4. The defamatory statement is about the plaintiff

Since the law of libel protects the reputation of an individual or a business entity, only the individual or entity whose reputation has been injured is entitled to complain. Thus, a libel plaintiff must prove that the defamatory statement was "of and concerning" the plaintiff. It often is obvious whether a statement is about a particular person (for example, because it gives his or her full name, place of residence and age). But even where no name is used, a libel claim may be brought if some readers would reasonably understand the statement to be about the plaintiff. For example, the statement referring to "the woman who cooks lunch at the diner," when there is only one woman who cooks at that diner, will be considered "of and concerning" the female cook.

In a recent Illinois case, a news report on the commencement of a murder trial referred to the defendant as "suburban car dealer John Doe." While "John Doe" was indeed on trial for murder, he was not a suburban car dealer. His brother, "Joe Doe," was a suburban car dealer, but was not on trial for murder. The court concluded that reasonable readers could have understood the report to be about Joe (despite the fact that Joe's name was never mentioned, while John's was correctly used), and that Joe therefore would have the opportunity to show the statement was understood to be "of and concerning" him.

A few words about "group libel." Where a statement impugns a group of persons, but no individual is specifically identified, no member of the group may sue for libel if the group is large. For example, the statement, in a large city, that "all cab drivers cheat their customers out of money," does not allow any cab driver to sue for libel as a result, no matter how many fares the plaintiff cab driver may have lost because of the published statement. But, beware of publishing the same statement in a newspaper in a town with only a handful of cab drivers, where a court might well conclude the readers would reasonably think the statement was specifically referring to each of the town's four cab drivers, despite the absence of their names in the statement. Some courts have questioned whether the First Amendment permits claims for group libel under any circumstances, because the Supreme Court has said that the requirement that the statement be "of and concerning" the plaintiff is constitutionally required.

In this regard, it is worth noting, most courts have held that a statement about a company is not, without more, "of and concerning" its officers, directors or employees (provided it is not a sole proprietorship). By the same token, a statement about a CEO or other corporate official is not, without more, "of and concerning" the company itself.

Finally, a word about the dead: It is mostly correct that you cannot defame the dead. Again, because libel protects personal reputation, and one has no practical need for a good personal reputation in this world after one has departed it, most states do not permit a person's survivors to bring a claim for statements made after the person's death.

5. The defamatory statement was published with the requisite degree of fault

For almost 200 years, libel in this country was a tort of strict liability. It did not matter whether the defendant was at fault or had acted in some improper way. The mere fact that a libel was printed was sufficient to establish liability

New York Times v. Sullivan changed everything. In that case the Supreme Court first recognized the constitutional requirement that a public official must demonstrate not only that an error was made, but also a high degree of fault by the publisher in order to prevail on a libel claim. Somewhat confusingly referred to as "actual malice," what such a plaintiff is required to prove is that the defendant published a "calculated falsehood" — that is, that the defendant knew the statement was false when published, or published the statement despite having a high degree of awareness that it probably was false (the latter is sometimes called "reckless disregard" for the truth). This additional burden was required under the First Amendment, the court said, in order to provide the "breathing room" for the exercise of free speech that is essential to public discussion by citizens on matters concerning their self-government.

The court considered the *Sullivan* case "against the background of a profound national commitment to the principle that debate on public issues should be uninhibited, robust and wide-open, and that it may well include vehement, caustic and sometimes unpleasantly sharp attacks on government and public officials."

The ruling in *Sullivan* with respect to libel claims by public officials was extended three years later to libel claims by public figures, in *The Associated Press v. Walker*. The court reversed a $500,000 libel judgment won by former Maj. Gen. Edwin A. Walker in a Texas state court against the AP, after it had reported that Walker "assumed command" of rioters at the University of Mississippi and "led a charge of students against federal marshals" when James H. Meredith was admitted to the university in September 1962. Walker alleged those statements to be false.

In ruling for the AP, the Supreme Court found: "Under any reasoning, Gen. Walker was a public man in whose public conduct society and the press had a legitimate and substantial interest." It therefore held that Walker, too, was required to prove higher fault by the publisher even though he was not a public official.

The rulings in *Sullivan* and *Walker* cases were landmark decisions for freedom of the press and speech. They established safeguards not previously defined, but they did not provide news organizations with absolute immunity against libel suits by officials who are criticized. Rather, they stand for the principle that, to encourage public debate on matters of public concern, when a newspaper publishes information about a public official or public figure and publishes it without "actual malice," it should be spared a damage suit even if some of the information turns out to be wrong.

The *Walker* decision made an additional important distinction concerning the context in which an article is prepared. In a companion case consolidated before the Supreme Court, Wallace Butts, former athletic director of the University of Georgia, had obtained a libel verdict against Curtis Publishing Co. His suit was based on an article in the Saturday Evening Post accusing Butts of giving his football team's strategy secrets to an opposing coach prior to a game between the two schools.

The Supreme Court found that Butts was a public figure, but said there was a substantial difference between the two cases. Unlike the AP report on the actions of Walker, "the Butts story was in no sense 'hot news' and the editors of the magazine recognized the need for a thorough investigation of the serious charges. Elementary precautions were, nevertheless, ignored."

Chief Justice Earl Warren, in a concurring opinion, referred to "slipshod and sketchy investigatory techniques employed to check the veracity of the source" in the Butts case. He said the evidence disclosed "reckless disregard for the truth."

The differing outcomes against The Associated Press and the Saturday Evening Post should be noted carefully. Although both involved public figures who were required to establish "actual malice," the evidence sufficient to make this showing differed in the context of a "hot news" report from investigative reporting.

By 1974, in *Gertz v. Robert Welch, Inc.*, the Supreme Court had extended the requirement that a libel plaintiff show some fault on the part of the defendant to include all defamation claims against news organizations, although not all types of plaintiffs must show the highest degree of fault. The level of "fault" that a plaintiff must prove will vary depending on who the plaintiff is.

• *Fault required for public officials and public figures*

If the plaintiff is a public official or public figure, the plaintiff must establish by clear and convincing evidence that the publication was made with "actual malice," which, as noted, is an unfortunate choice of phrase by the Supreme Court for a concept that might better have been called "constitutional fault," since the standard has little to do with whether a reporter harbored spite or ill will against the plaintiff.

The first type of actual malice, "knowing falsity," is easy to understand. "Reckless disregard" has required further elaboration by the courts, the best description of which perhaps is publication of a statement "with a high degree of awareness of its probable falsity." Put differently, a reporter may act with reckless disregard for truth if he or she publishes despite holding serious doubts about the truth of the published statement.

The test for actual malice thus looks to the subjective state of mind of the reporter/publisher at the time of publication. It inquires into whether the reporter or publisher believed the statement was false or whether he/she proceeded to publish despite recognizing that there was a good chance that the statement was false. Because most reporters and publishers are not in the business of publishing news reports unless they have good grounds to believe them to be true, generally speaking, it is difficult for a plaintiff to show that a newspaper published a story with actual malice.

As one Illinois court phrased it, actual malice is shown only when a reporter's investigation "has revealed either insufficient information to support the allegations in good faith or information which creates substantial doubt as to the truth of published allegations."

Thus, as interpreted by most states, "actual malice" cannot be proven simply by showing that a reporter made mistakes (either by getting facts wrong or by failing to talk to one or more key sources), or that the reporter disliked the plaintiff, or that the newspaper frequently published items critical of the plaintiff. Rather, the test focuses on whether the reporter in fact disbelieved, or strongly doubted the truth of, the published statement. In some cases, plaintiffs may establish actual malice if they can show that a reporter willfully turned a blind eye to the truth and, if acting in good faith, would have known that the statement was false.

• Fault required for private individuals

Under the First Amendment, even private individuals must show some degree of fault before they can recover for a libel by a news organization in a report on a matter of public concern. States are free to set the standard of care that must be met in reporting on private individuals, so long as they require at least a showing of negligence.

A number of states have decided to adopt the minimum standard and require a private libel plaintiff to show only that a reporter was negligent. That means the plaintiff must show that the reporter's conduct was less careful than one would expect of a reasonable journalist in similar circumstances. In Texas and California, for example, the question in a private figure libel case is whether the defendant should have known, through the exercise of reasonable care, that a statement was false.

The courts have looked at a number of factors to evaluate whether "negligence" exists. The considerations include:

—Did the reporter follow the standards of investigation and reporting ordinarily adhered to by responsible publishers? In many libel cases plaintiffs will use "expert" witnesses to testify about what are the "acceptable journalistic practices."

—Did the reporter follow his or her own normal procedures? Any time that you do something differently from what you usually do in reporting a story — particularly if the change involves exercising less care, rather than more care — you had better have a good explanation for why that was done.

—Did the reporter have any reason to doubt the accuracy of a source, or any advance warning that the story might not be right? Was it possible to find out the truth? This — like many of the factors the courts consider — is a matter of common sense. If you have received information that just does not ring true to you, and it is something that is easily checked, check it out before you run with the story!

—How *much* did the reporter do to check out the facts? Did the reporter take steps to confirm the information received, or simply run with the story without verifying the facts?

—Who are your sources of information? Are they reliable, and objective — or known "flakes" or people with a clear ax to grind? Are they anonymous sources? How many independent sources do you have (and how do they know the information they are giving you)?

Some courts set different fault levels for private figures depending on whether the publication at issue involved a matter of "public concern" or of "private concern." New York, for example, has held that if the plaintiff is a private individual involved in a matter of legitimate public concern, the plaintiff must establish by a preponderance of the evidence that the publication was made in a "grossly irresponsible" manner without due regard for the standards of information gathering and dissemination ordinarily followed by responsible parties involving similar matters. In cases involving matters of private concern, New York, too, applies a negligence standard, although New York courts typically defer to the press in determining what constitutes a matter of "public concern" (and thus the vast majority of New York private figure cases apply the "gross irresponsibility" standard).

• Who is who?

Needless to say, being able to determine whether the subject of a news story is a public official or figure or a private figure bears directly on the amount of legal risk posed by the story.

While it is clear that not every government employee will be considered a public official for purposes of what they must prove in a libel case, the Supreme Court has yet to lay down definitive standards. Thus, the definition varies somewhat from state to state.

In New York, public officials are those who are elected or appointed to office and who appear to have substantial responsibility for control over public and governmental affairs. Judges, police officers, state troopers and corrections officers have all been held to be public officials under this standard. Similarly, a public official is defined to be one who has, or appears to the public to have, substantial responsibility for or control over the conduct of governmental affairs. In California, people found to be public officers have included a police officer, an assistant public defender and an assistant district attorney.

Texas, in contrast, looks to the following criteria as relevant to determine whether a libel plaintiff is a public official: (1) the public interest in the public position held by the plaintiff; (2) the authority possessed by the plaintiff to act on behalf of a government entity; (3) the amount of governmental funds controlled by the plaintiff; (4) the number of employees the official supervises; (5) the amount of contact between the plaintiff and the public, and (6) the extent to which the plaintiff acts in a representative capacity for the governmental entity or has any direct dealings with the government.

Under this standard, (1) a county sheriff; (2) a Child Protective Services specialist with authority to investigate charges of child abuse, remove children from their homes and place them in foster care; (3) an undercover narcotics agent employed by the state's law enforcement agency; (4) a ranking officer in charge of a narcotics squad of four men; (5) an individual who was a high school athletic director, head football coach and teacher; (6) an assistant regional administrator of a branch office of the Securities and Exchange Commission, and (7) a part-time city attorney have all been found to be public officials.

But under the same Texas test, the following people were found not to be public officials: (1) a high school teacher; (2) a prominent member of two private organizations affiliated with a state university; (3) a former special counsel for a court of inquiry into county fund management; (4) a court reporter, and (5) an appointed justice of the peace (where the article appeared in a city where plaintiff was not justice of the peace and did not refer to plaintiff's official capacity).

While, at least at higher ranks, it is relatively easy to identify public officials, both reporters and the courts have confronted substantial difficulty in the area of public figures, particularly in separating those who are merely socially or professionally prominent from those who, because of their influence over public matters, are properly considered public figures for libel purposes.

For example, the 1976 case of *Time v. Firestone* stemmed from Time magazine's account of the divorce of Russell and Mary Alice Firestone. The magazine said she had been divorced on grounds of "extreme cruelty and adultery." The court made no finding of adultery. She sued. The former Mrs. Firestone was a prominent social figure in Palm Beach, Florida, and held press conferences in the course of the divorce proceedings. Yet, the Supreme Court said she was not a public figure because "she did not assume any role of special prominence in the affairs of society, other than perhaps Palm Beach society, and she did not thrust herself to the forefront of any particular public controversy in order to influence resolution of the issues involved in it."

Similarly, Sen. William Proxmire of Wisconsin was sued for $8 million by Ronald Hutchinson, a research scientist who had received several public grants, including one for $50,000. Proxmire gave Hutchinson a "Golden Fleece" award, saying Hutchinson "has made a fortune from his monkeys and in the process made a monkey of the American taxpayer." The Supreme Court held in 1979 that, despite the receipt of substantial public funds, Hutchinson was not a public figure because he held no particular sway over the resolution of matters of public concern.

Note also the case of Ilya Wolston, who pleaded guilty in 1957 to criminal contempt for failing to appear before a grand jury investigating espionage. A book published in 1974 referred to these events. Wolston alleged that he had been libeled. In ruling on *Wolston v. Reader's Digest*, the Supreme Court said that he was not a public figure. The court said people convicted of crimes do not automatically become public figures. Wolston, the court said, was thrust into the public spotlight unwillingly, long after the events of public concern had ended.

At bottom, although the Supreme Court has yet to definitively resolve the issue, the point appears to be that public figures are those who seek the limelight, who inject themselves into public debate, and who seek to influence public opinion. A person who has widespread influence over public opinion on many matters may be deemed a "general purpose public figure" and required to prove actual malice no matter the subject of a particular allegedly defamatory statement. Oprah Winfrey is an example of someone who likely would be deemed a general purpose public figure.

A person who seeks to influence public opinion in only one area (such as, for example, by leading a campaign to enact animal rights legislation), however, may be deemed a "limited purpose public figure" and required to prove actual malice only with respect to allegedly defamatory statements about his or her animal rights activities. Limited purpose public figures have included: a prominent attorney; religious groups; a belly dancer; and a "stripper for God," among others.

Texas courts generally ask three questions in order to determine whether someone is a limited purpose public figure: (1) is the controversy truly a public controversy? (i.e., (a) are people talking about the controversy and (b) are people other than those immediately involved in the controversy likely to feel the impact of its resolution?); (2) does the plaintiff have more than a trivial or tangential role in the controversy?; (3) is the alleged defamation relevant to the plaintiff's participation in the controversy? Under this standard, an abortion protester on a public street in the vicinity of an abortion clinic was considered a limited purpose public figure, as was a zoologist who appeared on television shows and gave interviews on his controversial work.

On the other hand, a public school teacher whose participation in public controversy did not exceed that which she was required to do by school district regulations (except that she responded to media inquiries), was not a public figure in California. Similarly, a corporation which conducted a closeout sale for a landmark department store was not a public figure simply because it was doing business with a party to a controversy.

A note on corporations: In many states, the same standards that determine whether an individual is a public figure apply to corporations. Some states, however, conclude that corporations are always public figures, while others apply a narrower standard. For example, a British corporation that did not deal in consumer goods and had not received significant past publicity was a private figure for the purposes of a Texas libel claim.

In addition, a few lower courts have embraced the concept of an "involuntary public figure," in which an otherwise private person becomes a public figure by virtue of his or her having become drawn into a significant public controversy.

While this area of the law is freighted with subtleties to which lawyers and judges devote considerable energy, the practical bottom line is that, while public officials and public figures always bear a high burden of proof in making out a libel claim, where a news story concerns a private individual, whether involved in a matter of public concern or not, his or her burden is likely to be lower, perhaps much lower, if the story is wrong. Accordingly, there are more legal risks to publishing reports about private individuals (especially where the matter is not of legitimate public concern).

• Defenses commonly available to news organizations

Where a news story is written in such a way that a plaintiff might be able to prove all five of the elements of a libel, the law nevertheless affords defenses to news organizations in certain circumstances. Among the most prominent are the "fair comment privilege," the "fair and accurate report privilege," and the "neutral report privilege." They are referred to as privileges because, where properly invoked, a news organization is "privileged" to print what otherwise would be an actionable libel.

1. Fair comment

The fair comment (sometimes, "fair criticism") privilege long predates the opinion doctrine and continues, in most states, to exist as an independent matter of state law. The right of fair comment has been summarized as follows: "Everyone has a right to comment on matters of public interest and concern, provided they do so fairly and with an honest purpose. Such comments or criticism are not libelous, however severe in their terms, unless they are written maliciously. Thus it has been held that books, prints, pictures and statuary publicly exhibited, and the architecture of public buildings, and actors and exhibitors are all the legitimate subjects of newspapers' criticism, and such criticism fairly and honestly made is not libelous, however strong the terms of censure may be." (*Hoeppner v. Dunkirk Pr. Co.*, 1930.)

Some states, such as Texas, have recognized the fair comment privilege as a matter of statutory law. The Texas statute protects reasonable and fair comment or criticism of the official acts of public officials and of other matters of public concern when published for general information.

Not all states recognize this privilege, and the specifics of its application vary among the states that do recognize it. But where an otherwise potentially libelous story is important to the public interest, careful consideration of whether this privilege might protect publication of the report may be appropriate.

2. Fair and accurate report

Under this privilege, a fair and accurate report of a public proceeding (such as a city council hearing) or document (such as a pleading filed in court) generally cannot be the basis of a libel suit.

Pursuant to the Texas fair report statute, for example, the privilege applies to "a fair, true and impartial account" of: (a) judicial proceedings; (b) an official proceeding to administer the law; (c) all executive and legislative proceedings; and (d) the proceedings of public meetings dealing with public purposes. New York and several other states likewise have created the privilege by statute along similar lines; in some states, the privilege is a product of judge-made law.

In order to qualify for the privilege in the states that recognize it, the account must be both substantially accurate and fair. This does not mean the newspaper is required to publish a verbatim account of an official proceeding or the full text of a government document, but any abridgement or synopsis must be substantially accurate and fairly portrayed. Where it applies, the privilege relieves a news organization of responsibility for determining the underlying truth of the statements made by the participants in these contexts, precisely because the very fact that the comments were made in an official proceeding is newsworthy regardless of whether the statements are actually true.

Some jurisdictions require that, to be privileged, the report expressly identify the official proceeding or document being reported upon.

It bears emphasis that the privilege is limited to statements made in the contexts defined under state law, and it behooves reporters to learn the particulars of the privilege in the states in which they practice journalism.

Statements made by government officials outside of official proceedings (e.g., statements by police or a prosecutor or an attorney on the courthouse steps), or in documents that have not been officially made part of the government record (e.g., a draft pleading provided by a lawyer that has not yet been filed with the court) may or may not qualify as privileged, depending on what state you are in and on the circumstances in which the statements are made.

Some states only extend the privilege to such out of court statements if made by specified top officials. At least one New York trial court, however, has applied this fair report privilege to a news report based on information provided "off the record" by police sources.

In New York and some other states, court rules provide that the papers filed in matrimonial actions are sealed and thus not open to inspection by the general public. It is not clear whether the fair report privilege will attach to publication of the contents of such papers, which by court rule, or order of the judge, are to be kept confidential.

In one case where this very situation arose, the vice president of a company filed a libel suit in New York alleging that he was fired because a newspaper published his wife's charges of infidelity set forth in divorce proceedings. The newspaper responded that its report was a true and fair account of court proceedings. The New York Court of Appeals rejected that argument on grounds that the law makes details of marital cases secret because spatting spouses frequently make unfounded charges.

The lesson of this case is that information gleaned from "confidential" court documents might not be covered under the fair report privilege. In such a case, the paper will be put to the test of proving that it made a reasonable effort to determine the truth of the allegations before publishing them.

Similarly, not all U.S. states recognize a privilege for reporting the contents of foreign government proceedings or documents, at least in part because, according to some courts, it is not clear that the records of foreign governmental entities are as reliable as the records of American governmental units.

There are other "traps" to be aware of when relying on this privilege. For example, statements made on the floor of convention sessions or from speakers' platforms organized by private organizations may not be privileged under the fair report privilege. Strictly speaking, conventions of private organizations are not "public and official proceedings" even though they may be forums for discussions of public questions.

Similarly, while statements made by a governor in the course of executive proceedings have absolute privilege for the speaker (even if false or defamatory), the press' privilege to report all such statements is not always absolute. For example, after a civil rights march, George Wallace, then governor of Alabama, appeared on a television show and said some of the marchers were members of communist and communist-front organizations. He gave some names, which newspapers carried. Some libel suits resulted.

3. Neutral reportage
Once viewed as a promising development in the law likely to spread across most states, the advancement of the neutral report privilege has not proceeded as once anticipated. Many states have declined to consider whether the privilege should exist, while others have rejected it outright (most recently, in Pennsylvania in 2004). Where recognized, the neutral report privilege protects a fair, true and impartial account of newsworthy statements, regardless of whether the reporter knows or believes those statements to be true, if the statements have been made by prominent and typically responsible persons or organizations. The rationale is that some statements are newsworthy, and should receive public attention just because of who has made them.

Thus, for example, a news report concerning a statement by Michael Jordan concerning corruption in basketball, or by the NAACP regarding discrimination committed by a business, likely would be privileged as a neutral report, even if it should later turn out that Jordan or the NAACP were mistaken, since the mere leveling of charges by such prominent sources typically is of public concern.

Significantly, the privilege, where it exists, does not apply when the author of an article goes beyond reporting the fact the statements were made and espouses or adopts the charges as the author's own.

California is one of the few states to recognize the neutral report privilege. There, the privilege is available when the plaintiff is a public figure, the defamatory statement is made by one who is a party to a public controversy and the publication is accurate and neutral. One California court applying the privilege found that a newspaper's account of an accusation that a police officer had improperly obtained a false confession to a crime from a person later released as innocent was not actionable where the newspaper also printed the officer's denial of the charge.

In some states, courts appear to have applied the principle without naming the privilege as such. In one 1997 case in Texas, for example, the court held that a story that accurately reported that parents of school children had accused a school teacher of physically threatening and verbally abusing their children was substantially true regardless of whether the parents' allegations themselves were accurate. More recently, in 2013, the Texas Supreme Court cast doubt on this line of cases, but it declined to completely "foreclose" the possibility that a news report, the sole purpose of which was to report allegations, could be tested for truth by examining whether it had accurately conveyed the allegations. Similarly, in Illinois, a federal appeals court in 2004 held that several stories that accurately reported that a charitable organization was the target of a federal investigation into terrorism funding were not actionable because the fact that the organization was under investigation was true, regardless of whether it was actually guilty of funding terrorism.

New York state courts do not recognize a privilege for neutral reportage, though a federal court in New York has actually found a neutral reportage privilege grounded in the U.S. Constitution. As the federal court described the neutral report privilege in that case, "when a responsible, prominent organization ... makes serious charges against a public figure, the First Amendment protects the accurate and disinterested reporting of those charges, regardless of the reporter's private views regarding their validity." (*Edwards v. National Audubon Society*, 1977.)

• Summary of practical points

Although every AP story is expected to be accurate and fair, stories that involve negative reports about individuals or companies warrant particular attention. When evaluating such a story, it usually is prudent to ask these questions:

1. Are any statements in the story capable of defamatory meaning? In this regard pay close attention to the use of certain "red flag" words that may sound more negative (and thereby more defamatory) than if a different, but similar, word had been chosen. Words such as "fraud," "crony," "linked," "suspicious" and "contaminated" may suggest or imply bad conduct or have criminal connotations (like: "connected" to the Mafia or organized crime). Careful editing can ensure that the facts get reported without the use of "buzz words" that may trigger a libel claim.

—Remember that the fact that police are questioning someone about a crime does not necessarily justify the label suspect. Witnesses are obviously also questioned about a crime.

2. Are those statements ones of fact (capable of being proven true or false), or protected as opinion, or simply rhetorical hyperbole that no reasonable reader would understand as a statement of fact?

3. Could someone reading the report reasonably understand it to be about a specific person, whether or not the person is actually named? Could readers understand it to be about more than one person – the person we intend, but also someone else?

—Remember to be careful of descriptive phrases that may give rise to cases of mistaken identity. A report that "an elderly janitor for a local school" was arrested could lead to suits from every elderly janitor in the school district.

4. Could you prove that the statements in question are true (and do so without violating promises to any confidential sources)?

5. If it turns out that you have the facts wrong, would a jury think you failed to do something that any reasonable journalist would have done to get it right?

6. Assuming there is some possibility that the first five questions could be answered in the plaintiff's favor, is there a privilege that nevertheless justifies proceeding to publish? For example, is the report a fair and accurate report of an official government proceeding or document?

—If a privilege applies, remember that the privilege does not remove the need for careful reporting and the use of editorial judgment. In many cases, courts have held that it is up to the jury to decide whether a particular publication was a fair and accurate report or whether there was "actual malice."

Headlines, photos and captions must be as accurate and objective as news stories. Remember that each of these elements of a story can also give rise to claims of libel.

• Corrections and retraction demands

A correction acknowledges an error in a story and sets the record straight. (A retraction, in contrast, is the withdrawal of a story or a statement within a story.) Published studies have shown that lawsuits against the press can sometimes be avoided if requests for corrections, clarifications or retractions are dealt with seriously, promptly and fairly. Anyone making a correction or retraction demand should be dealt with courteously, and the request should be communicated promptly to the appropriate editor.

Do not be too hasty in drafting a correction, however. It is important to ensure that the correction is actually warranted, that it corrects all aspects of the story that may need correction, and that the correction itself is accurate. Some states have "retraction statutes" that limit the damages a plaintiff can recover or provide other benefits if an error is corrected when brought to the attention of the publisher. You should be aware of any legal requirement in your state setting a time within which a correction must appear.

Transmitting a corrective does not necessarily safeguard the AP against legal action. In fact, transmission of a corrective may itself have legal consequences because it formally acknowledges an error. Because of potential legal implications, a news manager or supervisor at a regional hub or vertical needs to approve all correctives and clarifications, before they are transmitted. Consult with the Standards Center in New York, or the News Center manager in off hours, if the issue involves libel, defamation or other legal issue, or a complicated member issue.

Any time that a kill or corrective is filed, it is crucial to ensure that it is transmitted on all wires that transmitted that original report. In addition, the bureau chief or news editor must prepare and maintain a file containing:

1. Wire copy of the original story and of the kill or corrective that was sent.

2. Wire copy of the substitute story, corrective or clarification filed.

3. A copy of any source material used by the writer or editor in preparation of the story, including member clip, reporter's notes and the like.

In addition, the bureau chief or the news editor, in consultation with the staff members involved, should prepare a statement on the circumstances. If legal action is a possibility, this explanation should not be prepared without prior consultation with the Standards Center or a senior news manager.

The statement should include relevant details, such as any contact with outsiders on the matter. The letter should be a factual report of what happened. It is not the place for extraneous comments about staff members or bureau procedures. Nor is it the place for apologies, nor any legal or factual speculation or conclusions.

Do not make any response to any letter or other communication in connection with any case where legal action seems possible, especially if a lawyer is involved, without first seeking advice from AP's lawyers in New York.

• Document preservation and discovery

A 1979 Supreme Court ruling, *Herbert v. Lando*, has had a significant impact on what materials a libel plaintiff can compel a news organization to disclose. The case ruled that retired Army Lt. Col. Anthony Herbert, a Vietnam veteran, had the right to inquire into the editing process of a CBS "60 Minutes" segment, produced by Barry Lando, which provoked his suit. Herbert had claimed the right to do this so that he could establish actual malice.

The decision formalized and called attention to something that was at least implicit in *New York Times v. Sullivan*: that a plaintiff had the right to try to prove the press was reckless or even knew that what it was printing was a lie. How else could this be done except through inquiry about a reporter's or editor's state of mind?

Despite an admonition in *Herbert v. Lando* that lower courts should carefully monitor (and, if necessary, rein in) discovery in libel cases, reporters and publications involved in libel suits are often forced to expend significant time and resources on discovery concerning their newsgathering, writing and editing activities.

Different reporters follow different practices about retaining their notes. There are potential litigation advantages and disadvantages from following a policy of either keeping notes for a number of years or disposing of notes as soon as they are no longer needed for reporting. The best practice is the one that best advances a reporter's journalistic goals. Whatever practice you follow, however, should be followed uniformly. A difficult issue is presented in litigation if a reporter generally keeps notes, but just doesn't happen to have the notes for a disputed story. Similarly, a reporter who never keeps notes, but happens to save them for a story that ends in litigation, can send a message that the story posed some unique concerns. Adopt a policy and follow it consistently.

Of course, once a lawsuit arrives, no documents (including electronic files, notes, email messages and the like) should be destroyed or deleted, regardless of your usual practice. At that point any notes and drafts are potential evidence and their destruction, with knowledge of the lawsuit, may be illegal.

• Motions practice

If litigation arises, lawyers for a reporter will often seek to dispose of the claims without the necessity of a trial. A number of issues, such as whether a story is "of and concerning" the plaintiff or conveys the defamatory meaning alleged, can often be decided by a judge as a matter of law before any litigation discovery begins.

Courts also can impose "summary judgment" dismissing a case at any point when the evidence developed by the parties demonstrates that the plaintiff's claims are legally defective. A judge may not enter summary judgment if it rests on any facts in dispute. Only the jury may decide disputed issues of fact.

In a 1986 decision, *Anderson v. Liberty Lobby*, the Supreme Court held that summary judgment should be granted in libel actions against public officials and public figures unless the plaintiff can prove actual malice with "convincing clarity" or by "clear and convincing evidence." This rule further facilitates the dismissal of unmeritorious claims without the expense and burden of proceeding to trial.

Over the past twenty years, some states have gone one step further, enacting so-called anti-SLAPP statutes to bring to an end more expeditiously libel lawsuits involving issues of public concern that lack significant merit. The concept initially was to prevent baseless claims asserted by plaintiffs who did not hope to win the lawsuit, but who used litigation to intimidate and censor others. Prime examples were unscrupulous real estate developers seeking to silence opponents of a zoning variance, and others engaged in "strategic litigation against public participation." Anti-SLAPP statutes typically require a defamation plaintiff at the outset of a case to convince the court that reasonable grounds exist to believe a valid defamation claim exists, and they provide for an award of attorneys' fees to the defendant if the claim is found to be meritless. California has one of the broadest statutes, which applies its rules and procedures to any lawsuit challenging defendants for exercising their right of free speech "in connection with a public issue." The California law can be invoked in certain situations to strike lawsuits challenging news reports on public issues, and in recent years some other jurisdictions have adopted similar broad press protections.

• Trials and damages

The huge jury verdicts that sometimes occur in libel cases have caused much concern among legal commentators and the press. A number of remedies have been proposed, including statutory caps on both compensatory and punitive damages. A 1996 non-press Supreme Court case, holding that some excessive damage verdicts might violate the Constitution, holds out some possible promise of relief.

The Supreme Court addressed libel damages in *Gertz v. Robert Welch, Inc.* (1974), and held that in private figure cases, where "actual malice" has not been proven, any award of damages must be supported by competent evidence, represent compensation only for actual damages, must not be "presumed," and must not be punitive. "Actual damages," however, may include compensation for injury to reputation and standing in the community, personal humiliation, and mental anguish and suffering — all items to which a jury assigns a dollar value. In cases where a plaintiff has proved "actual malice," he or she may also recover "presumed" and "punitive" damages.

While the First Amendment imposes severe restrictions on libel claims, and court rules encourage the dismissal of meritless cases at the earliest point, litigation can be a long, expensive, and disruptive process. The key to avoiding the distraction of litigation is always to remember AP's credo: Get it fast, but get it right.

• Invasion of privacy

The roots of the right of privacy are often traced to an article titled "The Right to Privacy" that appeared in the Harvard Law Review in 1890, and was co-authored by Louis D. Brandeis, who later became a Supreme Court justice. The article asserted that the press of the day was "overstepping in every direction the obvious bounds of propriety and decency," and urged courts to recognize a distinct cause of action that would protect the individual's "right of privacy." As a Supreme Court justice, Brandeis later wrote:

"The makers of our Constitution recognized the significance of man's spiritual nature, of his feelings and of his intellect. They knew that only a part of the pain, pleasure and satisfactions of life are to be found in material things. They sought to protect Americans in their beliefs, their thoughts, their emotions and their sensations. They conferred, as against the government, the right to be let alone — the most comprehensive of rights and the right most valued by civilized men." (*Olmstead v. United States*, Brandeis, J. dissenting.)

Over the following decades, legal commentators have vigorously debated the scope and nature of a cause of action for privacy, and identified four distinct forms of the "right of privacy:" (1) misappropriation of someone's name or likeness for a commercial purpose; (2) public disclosure of private facts; (3) unreasonable intrusion upon seclusion, and (4) false light in the public eye. In recent times, these causes of action have taken on significance to the press as plaintiffs have attempted to avoid the heavy burdens of proof placed on the libel plaintiff by alleging an invasion of a form of the right of privacy, instead.

The four distinct "branches" of the privacy tort each seek to protect a different aspect of an individual's privacy. The "intrusion" tort, which is discussed in more detail above, primarily seeks to protect against physical intrusions into a person's solitude or private affairs. The tort does not require publication of information for recovery, and it therefore is referred to as a "newsgathering tort." The other three branches of privacy all require publication of some information in order for the plaintiff to have a claim.

States vary widely both in terms of their acceptance of any of these right to privacy claims and in terms of the rules governing any such claims. Of the four forms of the "privacy" cause of action, New York only recognizes the claim for misappropriation of name or likeness for commercial purposes. Texas recognizes claims for intrusion upon seclusion, public disclosure of private facts and misappropriation of name or likeness for commercial purposes. The California state constitution expressly incorporates a right of privacy and California courts recognize all four forms of the right of privacy cause of action. Illinois courts also recognize all four privacy torts.

The right of privacy creates liability for the publication of facts that are true, and thus raises particular concerns under the First Amendment. In a number of contexts the Supreme Court has struck down rulings imposing liability for reporting information that was both true and newsworthy, but it has consistently declined to hold that the First Amendment always bars such liability altogether.

It can generally be said that when people become involved in a news event, voluntarily or involuntarily, they forfeit aspects of the right to privacy. A person somehow involved in a matter of legitimate public interest, even if not a bona fide spot news event, normally can be written about with safety. However, the same cannot be said about a story or picture that dredges up the sordid details of a person's past and has no current newsworthiness.

Paul P. Ashley, then president of the Washington State Bar Association, summarized the privacy concern for reporters at a meeting of the Associated Press Managing Editors association:

"The essence of the wrong will be found in crudity, in ruthless exploitation of the woes or other personal affairs of private individuals who have done nothing noteworthy and have not by design or misadventure been involved in an event which tosses them into an arena subject to public gaze."

• Publication of private facts

When most people speak of an "invasion of privacy," they have in mind the public disclosure of highly embarrassing private facts. In those states where such a claim is recognized, the elements of a cause of action generally include: (1) "publicity" given to private information, (2) that a reasonable person would find highly offensive, and (3) which is not of any legitimate public interest.

In some states the lack of "legitimate public interest" or lack of "newsworthiness" is an element of the tort, meaning it is a plaintiff's burden to prove. In others, this element is an affirmative defense and the defendant must show how the information was indeed a matter of legitimate public concern. In all cases, newsworthiness is a complete defense to the tort. The First Amendment bars a claim for the true and accurate disclosure of a private fact so long as the information is newsworthy.

The first element of the tort requires "publicity" given to private information. This requires some element of widespread disclosure to the general public, not simply a communication to a single person or small group of people. Conversely, facts that are already known to the general public cannot be the basis of a public disclosure claim, while facts known only to a small group can be.

For example, a California court allowed a privacy claim to be based upon the publication of a photograph of a Little League team in a national magazine to illustrate a story about the team's coach who had sexually abused some of the athletes. Although the photograph had been given to all the members of the team, the identities of the minors shown in the photograph were not known to a broader national audience. The court said their identities could therefore be considered "private" in the context of the story about sex abuse. Some courts have similarly ruled that a person who is recognizable in a picture of a crowd in a public place is not entitled to the right of privacy, but if the camera singled him out for no news-connected reason, then his privacy might be invaded.

The second element of the tort requires that the disclosure be "highly offensive" to a reasonable person. This factor goes to the embarrassing nature of the information itself. Reporting someone's age, for example, would not be highly offensive to a reasonable person, even if that information were not widely known. Reporting, over their objection, that someone was a victim of sexual abuse or suffered from an incurable disease might be.

Finally, no claim will lie if the information is newsworthy, or of legitimate public concern. Courts generally will defer to reporters and editors to determine what is "newsworthy," but the line is not always clear. Even in the context of a report on a plainly newsworthy topic, the disclosure of a highly embarrassing private fact may give rise to a claim for invasion of privacy if the facts are not logically related to the matter of public concern. For example, disclosure of the intimate sexual practices of a celebrity might support a claim for invasion of privacy if it were unrelated to any newsworthy report and amounted to prying into someone's life for its own sake.

Some examples can help to demonstrate the nature of this branch of the privacy tort:

—In a case against a Chicago newspaper, an Illinois trial court held that a mother had stated a cause of action for invasion of privacy when she alleged that she told the newspaper reporter that she did not want to make any public statement about her son's death and where the reporter nevertheless remained in the private hospital room with the mother, recorded her grief-stricken last words to her son and subsequently published a picture of the son's dead body and the mother's "last words" to her son.

—The unsavory incidents of the past of a former prostitute, who had been tried for murder, acquitted, married and lived a respectable life, were featured in a motion picture. She sued for invasion of privacy by public disclosure of private facts. The court ruled that the use of her name in the picture and the statement in advertisements that the story was taken from true incidents in her life violated her right to pursue and obtain happiness.

—Another example of spot news interest: A child was injured in an auto accident in Alabama. A newspaper took a picture of the scene before the child was removed and ran it. That was spot news. Twenty months later a magazine used the picture to illustrate an article. The magazine was sued for public disclosure of private facts and lost the case, the court ruling that 20 months after the accident the child was no longer "in the news."

—In another case, a newspaper photographer in search of a picture to illustrate a hot weather story took a picture of a woman sitting on her front porch. She wore a house dress, her hair in curlers, her feet in thong sandals. The picture was taken from a car parked across the street from the woman's home. She sued, charging invasion of privacy by intrusion upon seclusion and public disclosure of private facts. A court, denying the newspaper's motion for dismissal of the suit, said the scene photographed "was not a particularly newsworthy incident," and the limits of decency were exceeded by "surreptitious" taking and publishing of pictures "in an embarrassing pose."

• False light invasion of privacy

A claim for false light basically complains about publicity that places the plaintiff in a false light in the public eye. In those states that recognize this tort, the publicity must be of a kind that would be highly offensive to a reasonable person, and the defendant generally must have acted with the same level of fault that would be required if the plaintiff had filed a libel claim.

One form in which a claim for false light occasionally arises occurs when an opinion or utterance is falsely attributed to the plaintiff. In another version of the claim, the plaintiff's picture is used to illustrate an article to which he has no reasonable connection, as where the picture of an honest taxi driver is used to illustrate an article about the cheating propensities of cab drivers.

The Supreme Court of the United States ruled in 1967 that the constitutional guarantees of freedom of the press are applicable to claims for invasion-of-privacy by false light involving reports of newsworthy matters. *Time, Inc. v. Hill* (1967). The ruling arose out of a reversal by the Supreme Court of a decision of a New York court that an article with photos in Life magazine reviewing a play,

"The Desperate Hours," violated the privacy of a couple who had been held hostage in a real-life incident. In illustrating the article, Life posed the actors in the house where the real family had been held captive.

The family alleged violation of privacy by false light in the public eye, saying the article gave readers the false impression that the play was a true account of their experiences. Life said the article was "basically truthful."

The court said:

"We create grave risk of serious impairment of the indispensable service of a free press in a free society if we saddle the press with the impossible burden of verifying to a certainty the facts associated in a news article with a person's name, picture or portrait, particularly as related to non-defamatory matter."

The court added, however, that these constitutional guarantees do not extend to "knowing or reckless falsehood." A newspaper still may be liable for invasion of privacy if the facts of a story are changed deliberately or recklessly, or "fictionalized." As with The New York Times and The Associated Press decisions in the field of libel, "The Desperate Hours" case does not confer a license for defamatory statements or for reckless disregard of the truth.

An Illinois court allowed a "false light" claim to proceed where a news report allegedly broadcast the plaintiff's comments (which were covertly recorded) out of context. In a more famous case, a federal appeals court concluded that Gennifer Flowers could maintain a false light claim against James Carville for publishing facts suggesting she had lied about the nature of her relationship with President Bill Clinton. The court said the false light claim could compensate for emotional injury that would not be covered by a claim for defamation.

• Misappropriation

The final of the three "publication"-related forms of invasion of privacy recognized by the courts is misappropriation of the name or likeness of a living person for purposes of trade or advertising without that person's consent. In recent years, some states have included voice as well as name or likeness. This tort is intended to allow people to control the commercial use and exploitation of their own identities. The First Amendment provides for at least some exceptions to such a right — as where a candidate for public office includes his opponent's name and likeness in campaign advertisements.

The misappropriation tort is not generally a concern to reporters because it applies to the *commercial* exploitation of a person's name and likeness. It does not bar editorial uses and provides no remedy when a person's name or image (questions of copyright aside) is used in a news report. This branch of privacy is of little concern outside of the advertising department of a news organization.

• Publishing on the Internet and Social Media

Content published on the Internet in blogs, chat rooms, discussion groups, social media sites and the like is generally subject to the same rules and standards for libel, privacy and other legal actions as any print publication.

AP has adopted Social Media Guidelines that are intended to be followed by its employees. Those Guidelines require, among other things, that AP employees always "identify themselves as being from the AP if they are using [social networking site] accounts for work in any way." And, "if you or your department covers a subject . . . you have a special obligation to be even-handed in your tweets." The Guidelines also restrict AP employees from "declaring their views on contentious public issues in any public forum and must not take part in demonstrations in support of causes or movements. This includes 'liking' and 'following' pages and groups that are associated with these causes or movements." This means that AP employees should not "friend" or "like" political candidates or causes without a journalistic reason for doing so. (To keep track of tweets by newsmakers, a Twitter list will allow you to receive postings without joining the person's official list of followers. Reporters covering a specific politician may also "friend" the politician if essential to their reporting duties.) AP employees are also cautioned to avoid retweeting in a way that makes it look like they are expressing a personal opinion on the issues of the day. "A retweet with no comment can easily be seen as sign of approval of what you're relaying."

Because of the difficulty in verifying the authenticity of material posted on social media sites, it is important not simply to lift quotes, photos or video from social networking sites and attribute them to the domain or feed where the information was found. Before photos, videos or other online content is used, it is important to both verify its authenticity and ensure that any necessary rights for the reuse are obtained. (See discussion of Copyright, below).

• *Material Posted To Your Site(s) by Others*

Monitor any site you operate and remove material that violates the terms of use or is inconsistent with your journalistic standards. The AP's Social Media Guidelines encourage AP staffers to engage in dialogue with those who benefit from or critique AP content: "Any substantive criticism of our content should be taken seriously, however it may be phrased."

Postings to AP's, or your personal websites, Twitter accounts, Facebook wall, or other online platform by third parties who do so anonymously or using a pseudonym could result in legal actions seeking to identify the source of those comments. Courts have offered protection to some anonymous posters, and have generally required a showing of legitimate need before ordering disclosure of an anonymous poster's identity. If you receive such a subpoena or other legal document seeking information to identify the source of an anonymous or pseudonymous posting, please follow the policies and practices for handling subpoenas discussed above.

Copyright infringement

Copyright is the right of an author to control the reproduction and use of any creative expression that has been fixed in tangible form, such as on paper or computer disk. The right of Congress to pass laws protecting copyright is itself protected in the Constitution, and the First Amendment is therefore no defense to a valid claim for copyright infringement under the Copyright Act.

The types of creative expression eligible for copyright protection include literary, graphic, photographic, audiovisual, electronic and musical works. In this context, "tangible forms" range from film to videotape to material posted on the Internet. Personal letters or diaries may be protected by copyright even though they may not have been published and may not contain a copyright notice. Probably of greatest concern to reporters and editors are the copyrights in photographs used to illustrate a news report.

A copyright comes into existence the moment an original work of expression is captured in a tangible form. No government approval or filing is required for a work to be protected by copyright. Upon creation of the work, ownership of the copyright in that work is vested in the "author" of a work — the person to whom the work owes its origin.

The owner will generally be the author of the work, or the photographer in the case of an image. Under certain circumstances, however, someone other than the person who actually created the work may be deemed to be the work's "author" and thereby own the copyright. Under the work made for hire doctrine, copyright ownership of a particular work vests with the employer of the author when the work is created by an employee who is acting within the scope of his or her employment.

The owner of a copyright is given the exclusive right to reproduce, distribute, display and prepare "derivative works" of the copyright material. These rights exist for the life of the author plus 70 years. In the case of a "work for hire" owned by a corporation, the right exists for 95 years from the first publication or 120 years from creation, whichever is shorter.

• Limitations on copyright

Not all uses of copyright material constitute infringement. The most important limitation on the reach of copyright law for journalists is that ideas and facts are never protected by a copyright. What is protected by the copyright law is the manner of expression. The copyright pertains only to the literary, musical, graphic or artistic form in which an author expresses intellectual concepts.

For example, an author's analysis or interpretation of events, the way the material is structured and the specific facts marshaled, the choice of particular words and the emphasis given to specific developments, may all be protected by copyright. The essence of a claim for copyright infringement lies not in taking a general theme or in covering specific events, but in appropriating particular expression through similarities of treatment, details, scenes, events and characterizations.

This printed page illustrates the distinction between protected expression and nonprotected ideas and facts. Despite the copyright protecting this page, a subsequent author is free to report any of the facts it contains. The subsequent author may not, however, employ the same or essentially the same combination of words, structure, and tone, which constitute the expression of those facts.

A second limitation on the reach of copyright is the doctrine of "fair use." This doctrine permits, in certain circumstances, the use of copyright material without its author's permission. Courts will invoke "fair use" when a rigid application of the copyright law would stifle the very creativity the law is designed to foster.

To determine whether a particular use is "fair" and hence permitted, courts are required to evaluate and balance such factors as: (1) the purpose of the use; (2) the nature of the copyrighted work that is being used; (3) the amount and substantiality of the portion used in relation to the copyrighted work as a whole; and (4) the effect of the use upon the potential value of the copyrighted work. Courts generally consider how "transformative" the use is. Uses that can be said to have transformed portions of the original work into something entirely new by "altering the first [work] with new expression, meaning or message" would factor in to a fair use finding. (See *Campbell v. Acuff-Rose Music Inc.*) Uses that merely supplant the work by presenting it essentially as it was in the original version tend not to be fair.

News reporting, criticism and comment are favored purposes under the fair-use doctrine, but "scooping" a copyright holder's first use of previously unpublished material is not. Note, though, that "purpose" is only one of the fair-use factors. Thus, a use for a proper purpose may nevertheless constitute an infringement if other factors weigh against that use being fair.

Here are some general guidelines to keep in mind when dealing with material written by others:

—Content created by the federal government is not protected by copyright, but content created by state and local governments may be.

—The greater the amount of the copyrighted work used, the less likely that a court will characterize the use as fair. The amount of use alone, however, is not necessarily decisive; courts have found uses not to be fair when the portion used was small but so important that it went to the heart of the copyrighted work.

—Uses that decrease any potential market for the copyrighted work weigh against a finding of fairness. For instance, if a literary critic reproduces all five lines of a five-line poem, the potential market for the poem will be diminished because any reader of the critic's piece can also obtain a copy of the poem for free.

Reporters and editors having questions about whether their use in a news story or column of copyrighted material is a fair use should review these factors. No mathematical formula can yield the answer. Where there is a question as to whether a particular use is fair, consideration may be given to seeking permission (or a license) from the copyright owner.

It bears emphasis that the First Amendment provides no greater right to use copyrighted materials than those provided by the copyright law. If a use is not "fair" within the meaning of copyright law, it will be no defense to claim the use of the copyrighted material was newsworthy and therefore protected by the First Amendment. Moreover, proper attribution alone cannot transform an infringing use into a fair one.

In using copyrighted material in a news story or column, writers should make sure that no more of a copyrighted work than is necessary for a proper purpose is used, and that the work is not used in a way that impairs its value.

In this regard, many people who post material to the Internet (photographs, descriptions of events they have witnessed, or other creative works) intend for people to copy and pass them along. It is important to remember, however, that, absent express permission, copying or distributing those works will constitute infringement of copyright unless the fair use doctrine applies. (It also may constitute breach of contract, since the terms of use of many social media sites contain restrictions on use that may be made of material posted there.) And it is often particularly difficult to determine who is the actual owner of the copyright in material posted on the Internet, precisely because it is so often reproduced (or re-posted) by others. For these reasons, special care is required when considering the use of material posted by others to the Web or on social media platforms.

PROCEDURES FOR HANDLING KILLS, DISREGARDS, CLARIFICATIONS AND CORRECTIVES

This chapter summarizes how to make critical corrections to stories that have already been sent, and how to remove them from the news report if needed. We use KILLS, CORRECTIVES and CLARIFICATIONS in these cases. The rules for the use of these items are more complex than for ordinary in-cycle corrections.

Managers of regional hubs and verticals approve correctives, clarifications and kills for issues that originate in their areas. The Standards Center in New York or global news managers must approve any KILL, CORRECTIVE or CLARIFICATION that involves a legal issue, such as libel or defamation. The New York Photo Desk must be consulted for photo problems.

In many cases, the story involved may have been transmitted over more than one service. Any corrective action must be taken on all services where the story was sent.

1. KILLS and DISREGARDS

KILLS AND DISREGARDS are used to permanently remove from the wire material that is still "live" — usually, copy that has been transmitted in the current 24-hour cycle. For material transmitted in a previous cycle, use a CORRECTIVE or CLARIFICATION.

KILLS replace the erroneous story on websites that automatically post AP copy. They also advise AP members not to use stories at all in their publication or broadcasts. They may be used when the entire basis of the story is found to be wrong, and on stories with particularly damaging errors or that are potentially libelous.

DISREGARDS are communications to subscriber editors and are used in less serious cases — for instance, when an old story is retransmitted inadvertently or material is sent on a service where it is not supposed to appear. However, unlike kills, disregards have no effect on a story that has been automatically posted on a subscriber site. If an item has moved online and must be removed from the view of online readers, a kill is required.

2. FORMATS FOR KILLS and DISREGARDS

Workbench and ELVIS templates and the formats below should be used. For broadcast services, follow broadcast style.

Datelines on kills should be the same as on the original stories. Disregards and kills should carry the same category selections as the original story.

KILLS

A KILL should say succinctly what was wrong with the original story - for example, "Smith was charged with robbery, not murder." Do not make any legal conclusions in the KILL — e.g., "the story is potentially libelous" — when transmitting the KILL.

The form for a KILL:

Slug: BC-US--Smith Charged, KILL
Headline: STORY REMOVED: Smith Charged
Ext. Headline: STORY REMOVED: Smith Charged
Eds. Note: BULLETIN KILL. Do NOT use BC-US--Smith Charged. A kill is mandatory.
Dateline: NEW YORK
The Associated Press has withdrawn its story about charges being filed against Joe Smith. Smith was charged with robbery, not murder.

If a substitute story is sent, mark it as the next lead-writethru to the previous story. Include a nonpublishable editor's note advising that it replaces an earlier story that was KILLED.

The form is:

Slug: BC-US--Smith Charged, 4th Ld-Writethru
Headline: Smith charged with robbery in Philadelphia incident
Ext. Headline: Smith charged with robbery; Philadelphia police may also levy other charges in incident
Eds. Note: CORRECTS previous version, which was KILLED, to show that Smith was charged last year with armed robbery but was not convicted.

Use this format for killing an APNewsAlert:

Slug: BC-US--APNewsAlert, KILL
Headline: STORY REMOVED: BC-US--APNewsAlert
Ext. Headline: STORY REMOVED: BC-US--APNewsAlert
Eds. Note: BULLETIN KILL. Do NOT use BC-US--APNewsAlert. A kill is mandatory.
Dateline: NEW YORK
The Associated Press has withdrawn its APNewsAlert about a bankruptcy filing by XYZ Corp. The company has not filed for bankruptcy.
The AP

DISREGARDS
The form for a DISREGARD is:

Slug: BC-US--Practical Joke, DISREGARD
Editors:
Disregard BC-Practical Joke. The story was sent Tuesday and was inadvertently repeated today.
The AP

3. CORRECTIVES and CLARIFICATIONS

A CORRECTIVE is a publishable story that acknowledges an error in a story and sets the record straight. Regional hubs and verticals approve correctives and clarifications. Advise the Standards Center if the corrective involves a legal issue or other complication.

Do not be hasty in transmitting a CORRECTIVE. It is important to ensure that the correction is actually warranted, that it corrects all aspects of the story that may need correction and that the correction itself is accurate.

Transmission of a CORRECTIVE does not necessarily safeguard the AP against legal action. In fact, transmission of a CORRECTIVE may itself have legal consequences because it formally acknowledges an error.

You should be aware of any legal requirement in your region setting a time within which a correction must appear.

CORRECTIVES and CLARIFICATIONS should identify the previous incorrect story by keyword and date. They should carry the dateline and category code of the original story. Use ELVIS templates and the formats below. For broadcast services, follow broadcast style.

CORRECTIVES and CLARIFICATIONS should carry headlines. The headlines should begin with the word Correction or Clarification, followed by a colon. In most cases, the slug and the word story will follow.

Slug:	**BC-US--Church Expenses, CORRECTIVE**
Headline:	**Correction: Church Expenses story**
Ext. Headline:	**Correction: Church Expenses story**

or

Slug:	**BC-US--Church Expenses, CLARIFICATION**
Headline:	**Clarification: Church Expenses story**
Ext. Headline:	**Clarification: Church Expenses story**

Note the slug of the story, *Church Expenses*, is uppercase, while *story* is down.

Occasionally, you will want to use something other than the slug after the word Correction or Clarification, to help online readers know what the content is. For example, the slug on a Benton Harbor riots story was *Crash Death-Disturbance*. An appropriate corrective headline in that case might be:

Slug:	**BC-US--Michigan Crash Death-Disturbance, CORRECTIVE**
Headline:	**Correction: Michigan Riots story**
Ext. Headline:	**Correction: Michigan Riots story**

The format for a corrective:

Slug:	**BC-US--Fed-Indictments, CORRECTIVE**
Headline:	**Correction: Fed-Indictments story**
Ext. Headline:	**Correction: Fed-Indictments story**
Eds. note:	**Eds: Editors who used BC-Fed-Indictments, sent Oct. 22 and datelined in New York, are asked to use the following story.**
Dateline:	**NEW YORK**

In an Oct. 22 story about federal indictments of city officials, The Associated Press reported erroneously the first name of one of those indicted. The correct name is Joseph Arnold, not John Arnold.

For correctives on stories that don't carry a dateline, use: **By The Associated Press**.

The proper form for a CORRECTIVE story often will be the straightforward statement that a previous AP report contained an error. However, where the AP did not originate the error, the CORRECTIVE should make that clear. For instance, "In a March 22 story about an embezzlement case, The Associated Press, quoting state police, erroneously identified the man charged. His correct name is Robert Smith, not Reginald Smith." When the original story cited a member as a source, consult with the member. We will usually cite the member in the corrective. If the original story used member material as a source but did not attribute it to the member, we sometimes must handle the corrective as if the AP itself made the error. Consult local news managers or the Standards Center if necessary.

CLARIFICATIONS

A clarification is a publishable story used to clarify or expand upon a previous story which, while factually correct, may be unfair or subject to misinterpretation.

A clarification must NOT be used as a substitute for a kill or a corrective. The clarification is used to provide background or detail in the interest of clarity or fairness. It is not used to correct factual errors in copy.

The format:

Slug: **BC-US--Airfares, CLARIFICATION**
Headline: **Clarification: Airfares story**
Ext. Headline: **Clarification: Airfares story**
Eds. note: **Eds: Editors who used BC-Airfares of May 8 may wish to use the following, which explains that not all fares on domestic flights are subject to change.**
Dateline: **WASHINGTON**

In a story May 8, The Associated Press reported that fares on domestic flights will increase beginning in April. The story should have specified that fares will increase for flights in the continental United States, but not for flights to Hawaii and Alaska.

For clarifications on stories without datelines, in the byline field use: **By The Associated Press**

4. Sending KILLS, CORRECTIVES AND CLARIFICATIONS

Every KILL, CORRECTIVE and CLARIFICATION must be sent to the same services as the original story. The news editor in charge of the hub, bureau or vertical where the problem arose should ensure that distribution of kill, corrective or clarification is complete. If it involves a legal or membership issue, coordinate with the Standards Center or a global news manager, confirming transmission to all services to which the original item was sent.

The text news desks and editors overseeing broadcast, digital, photo, interactive and radio services are responsible for ensuring that these items are sent wherever necessary in their services.

5. Report Requirements

Any time that a kill or corrective is filed, the bureau chief or news editor must maintain a file for the period of the statute of limitations for defamation claims in your state or country, plus three months. The file must contain:

1. Wire copy of the original story and the KILL and substitute story that were sent. Include material transmitted on broadcast.

2. Wire copy of the original story and CORRECTIVE filed.

3. A copy of any source material used by the writer or editor in preparation of the story, including member clip, handout and the like.

In the case of a KILL or a CORRECTIVE with potential ramifications, include a factual statement by the bureau chief or the news editor, in consultation with staff members involved, on the circumstances. If legal action is a possibility, the explanation should be prepared in consultation with the Standards Center or the Legal Department.

The statement should cite relevant details, such as any contact with outsiders on the matter. Do not include extraneous comments about staff members or bureau procedures. It is not the place for apologies, or any legal or factual speculation or conclusions. Do not respond to any letter or other communication in connection with any case where legal action seems possible, especially if a lawyer is involved, without prior consultation with the Standards Center.

Immediately after transmitting any CORRECTIVE, CLARIFICATION or KILL, record in the Correctives Database, along with the required explanations. You can access the database via staff-only links in Inside AP.

SENDING TEXT STORIES

AP text news is sent in a 24-hour cycle. The cycle begins around 1 a.m. Eastern time on U.S. national and state wires, and usually at 1 a.m. local time on state wires. On international wires, the cycle starts at 0400 or 0500 GMT.

The first story of the cycle might carry the keyword (also known as the "slug") BC-US--Alabama Fire. As the story develops, the number advances to BC-US--Alabama Fire, 1st Ld-Writethru, to BC-US--Alabama Fire, 2nd Ld-Writethru, etc. Once the new cycle begins, the first new story will once again be simply BC-US--Alabama Fire. (Ld-Writethru is used if the story completely replaces the previous story; "Ld" alone is used if the material replaces just the top of the previous story.)

It's important to retain the same basic keyword (BC-US--Alabama-Fire in this case) throughout the cycle and into subsequent ones so that stories land in the proper place on subscriber websites and mobile apps. If a keyword must change, start a new numbering sequence with the new keyword and make reference to the earlier series:

Slug: **BC-US--Nevada Town Burns**
Eds. Note: **Incorporates BC-NV--Hawthorne Block Burns**

Also send an advisory noting the keyword change.

Keep a geographical element in the slug where possible. This makes the keyword more distinctive from keywords on other stories.

URGENT STORIES

Urgent stories begin with an APNewsAlert. Use the ELVIS template, which sets the keyword to "APNewsAlert." Be sure the urgency level of "Bulletin" has been selected on the Prepare to Publish screen.

In the case of exceptionally important news, AP may send a "Flash." The only difference for editors is to select the "Flash" urgency option instead of "Bulletin." The word "Flash" will be added to the item automatically.

APNewsAlerts should conform to AP practices on attribution, even when sourcing is anonymous. In those cases, if the sourcing does not fit within the length limitations, use "Official:" or a similar term. Avoid "Source:" whenever possible. The NewsAlert also should indicate the geographic location, for the benefit of mobile and headline services that lack datelines.

APNewsAlerts should be written in a present-tense style that broadcasters can use immediately on the air. Place the attribution at the beginning.

The APNewsAlert is followed by an APNewsNow. It's essential to use the APNewsNow template in ELVIS. For truly urgent material, the APNewsNow should be only one or two paragraphs. See the section below on APNewsNows for details.

The initial APNewsNow can be followed by a longer APNewsNow (a 1st Ld-Writethru to the previous APNewsNow) or a longer story.

The APNewsNow template will sometimes pull into the file the earlier version of the story with the text "This is a breaking news update. AP's previous story is below." Do not delete this material unless there is a major error in the previous story.

Full writethrus to breaking stories should be sent as soon as possible. A short APNewsNow on a website, even with AP's earlier story below, is not satisfying to a reader. A reader wants a full story that's up-to-date throughout.

Other guidance on sending text stories:

ADDS
Use adds only to break up copy that is too long for transmission in a single piece (more than 4,000 words). The format for the keyword:

Slug: BC-AS--Smith Text, 1st Add

ADVANCE STORIES
AP transmits some stories in advance of the date they are to be used. This is to allow subscribers to reserve space and do design work in advance.

The release date in such cases is determined solely by AP. For stories whose release date is set by the source, see the guidance below on embargoes and hold-for-release stories.

The ELVIS system contains functionality to mark stories as advance stories. Do not manually type any advance coding.

ADVISORIES AND DIGESTS
Use the ELVIS "Advisory" template for all advisories and digests. Most advisories have the word "ADVISORY" in the version field, separated from the keyword by a comma. Advisories and digests are not intended for publication, although there have been many cases where they have wound up appearing online.

An example of an advisory:

Slug: BC-US--Airfares, ADVISORY

EDITORS:

The embargo on BC-US--Airfares has been broken. The story is available for immediate use.

The AP

An example of a digest:

Slug: BC-AP News Digest
The world at 2 p.m. Times EST.
At the Nerve Center, news producers ...

ANALYSES
Stories written as analyses must include "-Analysis" at the end of the keyword: "BC-ML--Egypt-Iran-Analysis." In addition, the word "Analysis:" must appear at the start of each headline, and "An AP News Analysis" must appear in

the Pub. Eds. Note field. In addition there should be an EDITOR'S NOTE _ at the bottom of the story giving the writer's credentials to analyze the situation.

AP NEWSBREAKS, AP EXCLUSIVES, AP IMPACTS AND AP INTERVIEWS

These terms, followed by a colon, are used in headlines of stories. They are not used in APNewsAlerts. Their capitalization is as follows: *APNewsBreak, AP Exclusive, AP Impact, AP Interview.*

Never shorten these terms to "AP:" to save space in a a headline. This could imply AP itself is the source of the information in the story, rather than the actual sources.

An APNewsBreak is significant, competitive, breaking news that we're confident we're reporting first, and that competitors will have to match. It implies some degree of enterprise or exclusivity in getting a spot news development. The text of the story should explain AP's exclusivity. An AP Exclusive consists of reporting gathered over a period of time that breaks significant new ground and results from exclusive AP access to people, a location or data. AP Impact stories must satisfy the criteria for AP Exclusive stories, but in addition must be top-level work that is likely to be among our best enterprise of the year. An AP Interview is a substantive and lengthy interview that stands out in terms of what the interviewee says or the depth in which we portray him or her.

APNEWSNOWS

An APNewsNow is a short news story — 130 words maximum — designed to get the news out to three formats — print, broadcast and online — as quickly as possible. It is used as one element in sending urgent stories (see "Urgent Stories"), and also for non-urgent routine stories that can be told in only 130 words. APNewsNows can and should carry photo, graphic and video links.

APNewsNows follow many of AP's print style conventions but must be easily readable on the air by broadcasters. Therefore, attribution is at the front of sentences, and use of quotes is limited. APNewsNows are written primarily in the present or future tense. Also, they should include a location where the story is taking place in the lead, since broadcasters do not read datelines on the air. Use the day of the week, not "today."

All APNewsNows should include "APNewsNow" in the Eds. Note field. This word is added automatically by the ELVIS NewsNow template. The Eds. Note should also indicate if the story is going to be updated.

A sample:

Slug: [BC-US--Flu Season]
Headline: [Flu season, and vaccine, looking worse]
Ext. Headline: [CDC says flu season, and the vaccine, looking worse]
Eds. Note: [Eds: APNewsNow. Will be updated with additional comments.]
Byline: [By MIKE STOBBE]
Bytitle: [AP Medical Writer]

ATLANTA (AP) _ The U.S. flu season ...

While APNewsNows were designed for breaking news, they can also be used for short, lower-tier stories that can stand, without updating, as briefs. In these cases, they must be written so the story will stand the next day when published in a newspaper or website. In other words, you would not write "Seattle fire-fighters are battling a downtown fire." You might write instead: "A downtown Seattle office building has been damaged in a fire ..."

Before writing an APNewsNow, always select the NewsNows template. The template will sometimes pull into the file the earlier version of the story with the text "This is a breaking news update. AP's previous story is below." Do not delete this material unless there is a major error in the previous material

BYLINES

Except for particles such as *Mac*, *Mc*, *Le*, or *De* (writer's preference) and *Sr.* or *Jr.*, a writer's name is entirely in capital letters.

The standard underline is *Associated Press*. Abbreviate *Associated Press* to *AP* for specialty underlines such as *AP Sports Writer*.

For stories without datelines when a writer's name is not used:

Byline: By The Associated Press

For dual bylines, put the word *and* on the same line between the names.

Byline: By SAMPLE AUTHOR and EXAMPLE WRITER
Bytitle: Associated Press

When a writer works for another news outlet, use the byline with the name of the outlet:

Byline: By NEWSPAPER WRITER
Bytitle: Hometown Citizen-Times

CREDIT LINES

Use credit lines at the end of a story to credit people who contributed significantly to the story other than the byliner. Place them under an indented three-underscore line.

———

AP photographer John Jones in Omaha, Nebraska, AP Business Writer Bill Smith in Paris, AP video journalist Jose Martin in Topeka, Kansas, and AP writer Jane Brown in Dallas contributed to this story. For stringers: AP contributor John Jones provided reporting for this story, or simply John Jones reported from Tegucigalpa. (Other variations may be approved by news managers depending on specific circumstances.)

DATELINES

Most stories should have a dateline. However, some stories that are based on information from many points, or where the location of the writer is not important, are transmitted without datelines.

When a story is transmitted without a dateline, it must have a byline or, alternatively, "By The Associated Press" in the byline field.

If a lead to a story changes the original dateline, note the change in the editor's note:

Slug: **BC-US--Airfares, 6th Ld-Writethru**
Eds note: **Eds: Changes dateline from WASHINGTON**

The lead sequence — *2nd, 3rd, 4th Ld*, etc. — continues uninterrupted even if the dateline changes on a story.

DISREGARDS

Disregards may be used to point out material that has moved inadvertently on the wire and that may be confusing to newspaper editors. However, disregards are not seen by online readers. If an item has moved online and needs to be removed, a kill is required. Use the functionality in ELVIS to set up disregards. Note in particular that the story slug needs to be in the keyword field; otherwise, subscriber editors looking at our stories in directories won't know what story the disregard concerns.

The form:

Slug: **BC-EU--Turkey-Quake Survivors, DISREGARD**

EDITORS:

Disregard BC-EU--Turkey-Quake, Advisory. The advisory is from last week and moved in error.

The AP

HEADLINES

Because of the needs of different products, all stories need two headlines — a short one with no more than 60 characters and a longer, or extended, one with a maximum of 94 characters. Try to make each headline as close to the maximum length as possible.

Only the first word and proper nouns are capitalized. Exception: First word after colon is always uppercase in headlines.

Follow story style in spelling but use numerals for all numbers and single quotes for quotation marks and also for APNewsAlerts. Exception: Use *US, UK* and *UN* (no periods) in all headlines.

Label opinion pieces. Short and long headlines for news analyses must begin with "*Analysis:*" followed by a colon. Likewise, reviews must begin with "*Review:*"

Attribute carefully. Attribution is as important in headlines as in stories.

Use locators when necessary. They should be spelled out if there is room or abbreviated according to AP style. For U.S. states in headlines, no periods for those abbreviated with two capital letters: NY, NJ, NH, NM, NC, SC, ND, SD and RI. Also DC. Other states retain periods: Ga., Ky., Mont., Conn. Do not use postal abbreviations.

Other headline tips:

- Acronyms. Acceptable in headlines only for universally known entities such as *EU*, *IRS*, *FBI*.
- Co. Try not to use this or *cos.* to abbreviate for company or companies.
- Federal Reserve. *Fed* is acceptable in headlines.
- Government. Can be abbreviated to *govt* in headlines as a last resort, but it is preferable to list the specific agency, such as *SEC* or *IRS*.
- Millions, billions. These figures can be abbreviated in headlines. For example, $45 million would be *$45M*, and $5 billion would be *$5B*.
- Numerals. Use numerals; do not spell out numbers except in casual uses: "hundreds" instead of "100s"
- Percent. Try not to abbreviate. If necessary, use *pct.*, not %.
- Quarters. Use 4Q, not Q4.
- Quotes. Always use single quotation marks

HOLD-FOR-RELEASE STORIES
All embargoed copy contains *HFR* (Hold for Release) in the keyword line. Use the functionality in ELVIS to set up the release time on the story. Do not manually type any hold-for-release coding.

INTERNET URLS
Place them at the ends of stories, on a separate line or lines under an indented three-underscore line. Give the title or a brief description of the website if the URL is ambiguous to tell readers what to expect. Always start URLs with http://. Example:

———

Online:

Full UK government report: http://bit.ly/rrtrp

If the Web address is longer than half a line, use bit.ly to shorten.
If there is other material to put at the end of a story, such as the names of other staffers contributing, put the Internet citation last.
All symbols in an Internet URL, including underscores, tildes, etc., may be typed in ELVIS. They will be automatically converted into plain language ("tilde") on services where this is necessary (see non-transmitting symbols).

NONTRANSMITTING AND SPECIAL SYMBOLS
accent marks Do not use them except in Spanish-language services; they can cause garbled copy for some subscribers. If an accent is essential to a story, make note of it in an Eds. Note.
The German umlaut (two dots placed over the vowel to change its sound) is represented by using two regular letters when needed: In "Goetterdaemmerung" the "oe" replaces the "o" with an umlaut and "ae" replaces "a" with an umlaut.

asterisk * Rarely translates and in many cases cannot be sent by AP computers or received by newspaper computers. Converted by ELVIS to (asterisk).

at sign @ Can be typed in ELVIS; for some subscribers, it will be converted to (at).

brackets [ ] Rarely translates and in many cases cannot be sent by AP computers or received by subscriber computers. Use parentheses.

bullets Do not use because they cannot be transmitted without causing problems with some newspaper computers. Use underscore instead.

cent sign (¢) Does not exist. Spell out.

equals = Can be typed in ELVIS; for some subscribers, it will be converted to (equals).

percent % Rarely translates and in many cases cannot be sent by AP computers or received by subscriber computers. Type "percent."

Pound/hash sign or # Can be typed in ELVIS; for some subscribers, it will be converted to (hash).

tilde ~ Can be typed in ELVIS; for some subscribers, it will be converted to (tilde).

underscore _ Can be used in Internet addresses, in place of bullets, and in dash lines.

Typefaces such as **bold** and *italic* cannot be sent on AP news wires.

OPTIONAL LEADS

An optional lead is a separate, complete version of a story, used to offer a different approach for those desiring it. An Eds: note should be used to explain this. Like the main story, it needs to be updated with new developments. Optional leads are not sent online.

Slug:	**BC-US--Presidential Helicopters-Optional**
Headline:	**[Lockheed Martin wins $500 million contract]**
Ext. Headline:	**[Lockheed Martin wins presidential helicopter contract]**
Eds. Note:	**[Eds: For those desiring an alternative approach]**

PACKAGE ADVISORIES

If a story is strongly developing with many elements, use a Package Advisory to keep subscribers up to date. Package Advisories also provide a place to tell members about how AP is covering a story; to advise on coverage plans; and to draw attention to exceptional AP work. If the items in a package advisory come from different regions, do not use a regional code in the keyword.

Example:

Slug: [BC-Sandy, Package Advisory]
EDITORS:
Our package on Hurricane Sandy:

MAIN STORY: ...

PHOTO GALLERIES

For a text story accompanying a large photo package, the keyword should end with the words "-Photo Gallery" and both headlines should begin with "AP PHOTOS:"

PUBLISHABLE EDITOR'S NOTES

Publishable editor's notes should appear in two locations on a story: in the Pub. Eds. Note field and in the story text after the second, third or fourth paragraph, set off with three indented underscores above and below. The editor's note must be inserted into the text by manual typing. ELVIS does not do this automatically. This is intentional so that the publishable editor's note can be placed wherever it's better for the story flow. The text of the editor's notes should be the same in both locations. The text should begin with EDITOR'S NOTE in all caps, followed by a space, an underscore and a space, followed by the text of the note.

REGIONAL CODES

Regional codes in keywords identify the country or region the story is from. They are CN-- for Canada, UN-- for the United Nations, EU-- for Europe, AF-- for Africa, ML-- for the Middle East, AS-- for Asia, LT-- for Latin America, CB-- for the Caribbean and AA-- for Antarctica. U.S. stories on national wires carry US-- in keywords. Stories sent only to U.S. state wires carry a state postal code in the slug: BC-AK--Alaska Fire.

Sports stories do not carry regional codes.

If a story is expected to change its dateline from one region to another in the course of the day, it should not carry a regional code. If a story with a regional code unexpectedly changes its dateline to another region, keep the original regional code in the keyword.

STORY CHAINS

Editors should make every effort to preserve "story chains," the linkages among the various leads to a story on a specific news service. These are important to keeping the story properly updated on websites and in other situations.

NEW STORY FORMS

What makes a story, in any format, "friendly" to the experience of consuming news on a mobile app?

To capture a reader's attention and cut through an endless array of distractions, a story needs to be presented in a compact yet compelling way. This can take myriad forms.

A successful mobile story could distill the news in various ways, from a distinct entry-point down to accessible bites that can be easily digested while walking. Think of them as "to-go" versions, packaged specifically for and delivered directly to the news consumer on the move.

Glances, such as quote boxes, bullet points, Q&As and timelines work well on mobile as long as they are infused with the best of AP expertise and reporting. In other words, shorter doesn't mean a light lift when it comes to reporting and crafting.

Some other examples:

News Guide: One-stop shopping for background and context on an ongoing news story that gives readers orientation and an understanding of where the story stands. It can start small and build up, growing as the story does and being retooled as events evolve. It should have a standard intro but, after that, can go in any direction the facts take us.

NEWS GUIDE: The Ebola crisis

President Barack Obama turned to a trusted adviser to lead the nation's Ebola response as public-health officials ...

Here's a look at the top Ebola developments worldwide Friday:

THE LATEST

Facing renewed criticism of his handling of the crisis, Obama ...

———

CARIBBEAN CRUISE SHIP

Government officials sought to remove from a Caribbean cruise ship ...

———

TRAINING SURVIVORS

The United Nations has begun training Ebola survivors ...

Why it matters: A chunky-text distillation of an important news story that focuses explicitly on how the story impacts all readers. This approach has broad appeal and engages readers by showing them how a faraway news event has relevance in their lives.

WHY IT MATTERS: The Syrian conflict

Syria's conflict is the most violent to emerge from last year's Arab Spring ...

———

THE ISSUE

The fighting has escalated into a civil war that has killed more than ...

———

WHERE THEY STAND

President Barack Obama called for Assad to step down ...

By the numbers: A glance that highlights numerical figures relating to a news story, anything from financial numbers to death tolls and troop sizes.

BY THE NUMBERS: Obama's summer vacation

After two weeks away from the White House, President Barack Obama's vacation ... Here's a look, by the numbers, at how Obama spent the time while juggling ....

———

15: Days, all or part, spent on the island

———

9: Rounds of golf played

———

2: Golf courses played

—

1: Beach outing, with Michelle Obama and daughter Malia

Writing to a photo: A short written piece that uses a particular photograph, or a small series of photographs, as the impetus for the narrative. This serves as a jumping-off point to delve deeper into a particular topic or to just describe a particularly powerful photo.

Explainer: Distills the basic knowledge about something into a small (500 words or less) package.
AP EXPLAINS: Stephen Colbert vs. "Stephen Colbert"
Stephen Colbert leaves Comedy Central's satirical political talk show "The Colbert Report" after nine years ... Here's a brief explanation of Stephen Colbert and the alter ego he is retiring:

—

A SATIRICAL SPIN-OFF
The actor and comedian first created his Colbert character in 1997 ...

—

COLBERT FOR PRESIDENT?!
In the first episode, Colbert coined the term "truthiness," defining ...

Q&A: A LOOK AT JAPAN AND 2 BEING HELD BY ISLAMIC STATE GROUP
Two Japanese men have been threatened with death by the Islamic State group if their government doesn't pay a huge ransom. Here's a look at hostages and Japan, and its interests in the Middle East:

—

WHO ARE THE HOSTAGES?
One seems obsessed with weapons and military goods. The other is a freelance journalist who ...

—

WHAT HAS HAPPENED TO JAPANESE HOSTAGES IN THE PAST?
One has been killed; most have been released ...

—

WHAT IS JAPAN DOING ABOUT THE THREAT?
The hostage crisis ambushed Japanese Prime Minister Shinzo Abe as he ...

SOCIAL MEDIA GUIDELINES

Why this section?

Journalists everywhere have looked to The Associated Press Stylebook for advice about how to gather and disseminate news since the guide was first published in 1953. During that time, methods of newsgathering and delivery have changed drastically — quickening the process and allowing people to learn more about the world around them than ever before.

Social networks have changed that even more quickly, establishing an enormous, real-time database of people and thoughts. As daily life plays out all over the world, social networks give us access to the content that hundreds of millions of people choose to share. Users' accounts can include everything from detailed biographical information to pinpoint snapshots of major life events, and users exchange thoughts, observations and content with one another.

Study after study finds that the vast majority of the world's Internet users are active on social networks.

Social media present unprecedented opportunities and challenges to journalists. This section will show ways social media can enhance beat reporting, simplify finding sources for stories and give journalists a direct connection with people who care about the news they cover. But fluency in social media takes time and effort, and challenges journalists to use the networks in a way that doesn't undermine their credibility.

Social networks don't replace other tools of reporting, but their strong footing in daily life proves that they demand our mastery — like typing, driving or using a smartphone. If we as journalists can't comfortably navigate the most popular areas of the Internet, why should our audience trust us with news at all?

While the speed of technological change may be intimidating and the popularity of individual networks may ebb and flow, this guide hopes to present a foundation that is relevant today but can similarly apply to tomorrow's digital landscape.

AP journalists have been governed by the AP Stylebook for decades. The fundamentals of our news cooperative — accuracy, speed and honesty — are set down in the **News Values and Principles**. These goals have remained paramount for nearly 170 years as the AP has become the essential global news network.

This section extends from those same principles, urging journalists to apply the same standards to their use of social networks, while addressing the challenges and opportunities that are specific to these platforms.

What does the term social media mean?

The term refers to tools that allow the sharing of information and content and the formation of communities through online and mobile networks of people.

What are some examples of social media?

There are many different manifestations of social media — and new ones are being developed all the time. Some of the most common types:

* Social networks like Facebook, Google Plus and LinkedIn form communities around common interests and share content, like news stories, videos, photos and general updates on what's going on in users' lives.

* Blogs, which are generally written by a single person or specified group of people, but where comment fields and the ability to follow bloggers and see their updates often allow for a broader discussion among readers.

* Microblogging sites, like Twitter and China's Sina Weibo, where a user can send short bits of information, visuals and links to longer content, which are then seen by those who choose to follow that user and can be found by the service's broader community.

* Wikis, where content is collectively created by those who choose to participate in the process.

* Content-sharing services, like Flickr, Instagram and YouTube, where anyone can upload content for easy sharing and discussion with others on the Web.

* Messaging apps like Snapchat, WhatsApp Messenger and WeChat, where users share short messages privately with individuals or with specified groups of fellow users.

* Online forums, where participants can share ideas, debate topics and get help with everything from how to roast a turkey to how to take apart a laptop.

* Check-in services, like Swarm, where users form communities and find out when fellow users have checked themselves into certain locations, events or activities. (Many general-purpose social networks offer check-in functions as well.)

* All sorts of other sites, from dating services to electronic pinboards to collaborative essay-writing projects.

How do journalists use social media in their work?

It varies from journalist to journalist, but these are some common uses:

* To track down sources — in particular, people who witnessed a news event or were directly affected by it.

* To gather user-generated content, like photos or videos, that a news provider may want to acquire and distribute/publish as part of its news report.

* To look for news tips or discussion trends that might lead to or form a story.

* To produce short-format original content, such as blog items.

* To find new sources and keep up with existing ones.

* To interact with news consumers directly to inform their reporting and to promote their work.

* To share links and content that provide an additional entry point to existing journalism.

* To get a preliminary sense of how members of the public — or at least social media users — are reacting to an event.

How, as a journalist, should I balance my public, professional presence with my personal privacy?

There are no one-size-fits-all answers to how journalists should manage their social media accounts with respect to their personal privacy. But journalists should consider various factors, including their newsroom's conduct and ethics policy, and approach social networks with clarity regarding their personal feelings and professional needs. At the AP, our social policies are built atop the foundation of our **News Values and Principles**. Some things to consider:

* Not all social networks allow users to create more than one profile.

* Posts or messages that are intended to be personal can easily be shared, just like emails can be forwarded and conversations recorded. Journalists should never violate their newsroom's conduct or ethics policy under the assumption that their posts are personal, not professional. Social networks bring into clear focus that journalists are considered journalists by the public 24/7.

* Those reluctant to share at all on social media should think about whether they share parts of themselves outside of social media — and when and how. Are you comfortable enough with a source to share small talk about last night's baseball game or some new music? Perhaps sharing some of that during social media interactions with others won't stray too far from what you're comfortable with. There may be subjects that are off-limits for you — that's OK, too.

* Social credibility: When approaching sources on the street, a journalist often gains credibility by presenting a business card or identifying him or herself. On social networks, credibility is gained through consistency and by building connections through interaction and sharing.

How, in all formats, do you vet sources found through social media?

The general rule of thumb is that you should apply the same principles used in vetting a source found any other way. But there can be additional challenges, since it can be difficult to verify the identity of sources found online.

Most importantly, you should never simply lift quotes, photos or video from social networking sites and attribute them to the name on the profile or feed you found them under. Most social media sites offer a way to send a message to a user — use this to establish direct contact, over email or phone, so you can explain what you're working on and get more detailed information about the source.

If a source claims to be an official from a company, organization or government agency, call the place of business to confirm identity, just as you would if a source called on the phone. And if the source provides factual information that's central to a story, always pursue at least one additional source for confirmation.

If you come across photos, videos or other multimedia content that you would like to use in your news report, you'll need to verify the authenticity of the piece of content. You'll then need to determine who controls the copyright of the material and get permission from that person/organization to use it.

Use particular caution if you find a social networking page or feed that appears to belong to a person who is central to a story, especially if you can't get confirmation from that person. Phony accounts are rampant in the social media world, so examine the details to determine whether the page could have just as easily been created by somebody else.

How should social media not be used?

Social networks should never be used as a reporting shortcut when another method, like picking up a phone or knocking on a door, would yield more reliable or comprehensive information. For example, if a key question in a story is only partly or indirectly answered by a tweet sent by a government official, don't settle for that — reach out to the official to find out more. (Though the tweet might also be reported.)

THE BASICS

Each social network has unique characteristics, but a few basic rules generally apply:

HANDLE/USERNAME: When deciding on a username, choose something clear-cut and easy to remember. First name, last name is always a good option. AP may be used for its staffers, though it is not required.

PHOTO: Upload a professional-looking photo of yourself and use it on all networks. People won't take you seriously without one.

BIO: Write a bio that accurately describes who you are. Feel free to include a personal tidbit or two, but remember that you are always representing the AP. You may want to include your email address so people can easily get in touch with you privately.

GOALS: Define some goals about how often you post or tweet and strike a balance among personal and professional posts, responses, links to stories, retweets or reposts.

BUILD CREDIBILITY: It comes through posting regularly. Show you're active, engaged and committed to the tool. You can't parachute in and expect to instantly have people's trust.

CONNECT AND INTERACT: Seek out people who have the same interests as you and pay attention when they post.

BE YOURSELF: No one wants to interact with a robot. You can control how much of you to share, but you need to make it clear that you're human. Use colorful, persuasive language, insert some personality and use humor. Entice users to click your links.

SHARE WHAT YOU SEE: Journalists have a front row seat to history. Use that vantage point to engage with people. If you witness a major news development, report it to the relevant AP desk first; otherwise, you're welcome to share general observations of what's going on around you.

USING LISTS TO STAY ORGANIZED AND PROTECT YOUR PRIVACY

Twitter

Twitter lists are a powerful, convenient way to organize and find new people. When you view a list you've created, you'll only see updates from the users you chose for that list. If you're using a third-party program like TweetDeck or HootSuite, you can organize lists into different columns, so you don't have to search through one long feed to find certain types of tweets. This can make things much easier if you're organizing information from lots of users. Lists can be public or private, allowing you to track users discreetly without directly following them or even share feeds of entire groups of people with the Twitterverse.

For reporters, private lists are an easy way to see tweets by newsmakers, regardless of whether you actually follow them. You may want to start organizing a private list by adding sources you already know. For a legislative reporter, that could include lawmakers and their staffs, party officials, legislative research staffers, the top elected officials and their key staffers, lobbyists, other reporters and bloggers. For a crime reporter, prosecuting and defense attorneys, court staff (clerks, bailiffs, court administrators), other reporters or incarcerated criminals. If you are sharing a list with colleagues you should come back to it regularly to ensure it is always up-to-date. Browsing through lists others have created is a smart way to find other people who might be relevant to you.

Twitter's help section is a great resource for managing your account, finding and following people and creating lists.

Facebook

With Facebook, it's easy to keep friends separate from work contacts by putting people in lists. For example, you can allow people listed as family and friends to post to your timeline, comment about photos posted by you or tagged by other people and even see your friends. But you can restrict access to your work list, so they see very little about you. Facebook's help section offers detailed instructions on managing your privacy settings.

See **Social Media Guidelines for AP Employees**.

SEARCH FOR PEOPLE – AND THEIR PHOTOS AND VIDEOS

Regardless of where and when news develops, it will likely be shared using social networks. Journalists should be able to quickly use social media tools to find people, photos and video related to news. Even routine stories can benefit from sources found through social media.

Quick, smart reaction to breaking news can be key to finding people or securing exclusive photos and video. It can also help save time and resources. And often, it's the only way to reach people.

To get strong results from a social network search, be thoughtful about your search terms and refine them as you gauge your results. People who aren't journalists don't always think like journalists, so simplify your language and try to think of what they might say.

For example, if you're seeking user-generated content from passengers trapped on a cruise ship, try to think of what tourists, their friends and families might say. You might try different combinations of words: "Carnival," "Splendor" "cruise," "stuck," "vacation," "port," "aboard," "sick" or "miserable." Also consider the expletives that someone might be inclined to utter when trapped in an uncomfortable situation.

The **Facebook** search page field near the top of the page makes it easy to type in what you're looking for and then refine the search by type of result (people, pages, posts, etc.). When you find someone, message them privately or comment on the post that you're contacting them about (while logged in), identify yourself and give the person a way to reach you through phone or email.

Note that Facebook messages sent to strangers will usually go to their "other" folder, which most users don't even realize they have. Facebook sometimes gives you the option of sending the message to their regular inbox for a small fee. You can also try to find other ways to contact the user – maybe they have a link to a blog or an email address, or perhaps you can find the same person on Twitter or LinkedIn. Or a public records search might turn up a phone number.

You can do people and keyword searches on **Twitter** and save them. When you find someone, hit "Reply" (while logged into Twitter) and write something like:

You may also follow people and ask them to follow you, so they can direct message you and make contact privately. Stakes in each situation will vary, but feel free to err on the side of private direct messages if the topic or your discovery seems competitive. Don't forget: Other media outlets can follow your tweets for tips and clues to what you're pursuing and can find what you write when you reply to someone.

Most days, it's pretty easy to find a reporter on a social network post something like: *"Are you or do you know anyone who's affected by Event X? If so, please msg me, I may want to talk with you for my story."*

That method can sometimes yield results, especially if a reporter has a specialized, tuned-in audience of people willing to either share the request or offer themselves up as sources without hesitation. But it's somewhat limiting.

Think about it: If you were on assignment doing a story about voters on Election Day (and were prohibited from using social media), would you simply walk outside your office and shout: "Hey, has anyone voted today?" Probably not. More likely, you'd head to a local polling place, watch voters walk in and out and try to speak with them there.

Finding people through social media requires the same detective-like mentality reporters use when they're wielding nothing more than a notepad and pencil.

Advanced searches allow you to narrow results by location, weed out posts by people simply passing along news links of a story you're working on, and quickly pinpoint relevant, real-world people with the ability to give firsthand contributions to your story.

The **Twitter Advanced Search** (https://twitter.com/search-advanced), in particular, is simple but powerful. Try different combinations of keywords to find what you're looking for.

General tips:

—Put keywords and hashtags (the number # symbol followed by a keyword, which is used to convey the subject a user is addressing) in the top boxes. You can use "and" and "or" in the searches and also choose among several languages.

—Under "None of these words" put "http" to eliminate people who are passing along story links — but note that this will also eliminate many tweets that contain photos and video, since sharing such content often involves a link. You can also focus your search here. Considering the cruise ship example, if you're searching for a Carnival ship you might put "church" in this box to eliminate tweets about church carnivals.

—The "People" search area lets you look for tweets from or to specific user accounts.

—Under "Places," put the city, ZIP code or landmark. The default area is 15 miles, but you can change that after the results are returned by changing the 15 to another number in the gray search box. Start nearby and expand, depending on how many results you get.

—There's also a save option on top of the search results page.

Video Searches

Besides Twitter, Facebook and other networks, there are some good sites to specifically search for mobile video.

On **YouTube**, conduct a search using the search box and click "Filter" when the results are returned. You can then narrow the results by time frame or change how they are displayed.

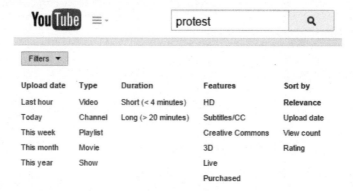

Display your results by upload date and refresh the page frequently to see new postings. Make sure you find the earliest example of a video to make sure you are chasing original content. Consider the words someone uploading video may use, as well as the city and specific streets or landmarks they may refer to.

To contact the person who posted the video, click on his or her username and go to their "About" page. Then you'll find a button for sending a message.

On **Vimeo** (http://vimeo.com), put in your search terms and click enter. On the page that comes up, click "Advanced Filters" on the right to limit the results to the last 24 hours, last week or beyond.

Photo Searches

Several sites are available to search for photos posted to social networks. Photos shared through Facebook or Twitter can be search using those networks' own search functions, which allow you to narrow results to zero in on images. Some other sites worth searching for photos:

—**Flickr** (http://www.flickr.com) has a wealth of visual content. You can search it without logging in, but you'll need a Yahoo account to reach out to users to ask about using their content.

—**Google Plus** (https://plus.google.com) also draws a lot of user-generated content.

—**Ink361** (https://ink361.com) makes it fairly easy to search for Instagram photos and videos by hashtag. (General keyword searching is not possible on Instagram.)

—**Gramfeed** (http://www.gramfeed.com) allows you to search Instagram content by geographic location.

Old Tweets

Trying to find old tweets, so you can capture an image of them, delete them or simply have a look? This used to be challenging and require third-party tools. But now, the Twitter Advanced Search page (see above) will return results going back to the very first tweets. Be sure to specify a range of dates at the bottom of the search page.

USER-GENERATED CONTENT

User-generated content, or UGC, is the term commonly used in the news industry for content that has been produced by anyone who isn't working as a professional journalist. Sometimes this is also referred to as citizen journalism, when members of the public capture news events on their own devices either by chance or by pursuing a story. User-generated content may be found via social networks but could equally be given to a reporter on the scene of a news event. It is essential to hold UGC to the same standards as all other information taken in and reported by the AP.

There are a number of challenges that face journalists handling UGC, most notably the issue of verification. Most broadly, do we know exactly what we are seeing, and how we have determined this? We should seek to tell the story surrounding each piece of video and audio and every photo we acquire with the level of accuracy people expect from the AP. This means tapping into our considerable knowledge base, drawing on the expertise of AP staff around the world.

Securing access to content can often be a challenge, especially in a breaking news situation when video or photos have been posted to social networks. You must always strive to seek the original source of the media you are seeking to acquire. Once that content owner has been identified, ask for permission to use the material, following all the established protocols the AP has in place. Also ask tough questions about when they captured material, why there were there, and anything else that can help you determine the authenticity of the content.

When publishing UGC, you should make every effort to give due credit to the person who has created that content. Use the person's name if he or she is happy for you to do so, or a username (from a social network or platform) if it is applicable or the preference of the individual.

It can sometimes be useful for AP or individual journalists to put out tweets or posts asking the public to come forward with UGC related to a particular story. When doing so, emphasize that members of the public should not put themselves in danger gathering content for AP. The same caution should be taken when directly communicating with these content owners privately.

REFERENCING USER-GENERATED CONTENT

When using or referencing UGC in the AP report, we must be consistent about how we refer to the content. Here is some recommended language for use in various formats. The material in parentheses will need to be adjusted based on individual circumstances.

VIDEO OR PHOTOS REFERENCED IN TEXT
The video (or photo) was supplied to The Associated Press by (local activists, a local videographer, etc.). It has been authenticated, based on (the AP's examination of the evidence) and was consistent with (AP's own reporting on the incident, human rights officials' accounts of the event, etc.).

PHOTO CAPTIONS
This photo, which AP obtained from (an activist group / the activist group xxxxx / a local photographer on the scene / etc.), has been authenticated based on its contents and other AP reporting.

This photo, which AP obtained from (an activist group / the activist group xxxxx / a local photographer on the scene / etc.), has been authenticated based on details in it. (For situations where we don't have other AP reporting)

VIDEO SCRIPTS AND SHOTLISTS
Use whichever of the following apply in the form of caveats or worked into a storyline:

Video and audio translated and content checked by regional experts against known locations and events.

Video is consistent with independent AP reporting.

Video cleared for use by all AP clients by content creator (or via third-party permission — insert as appropriate).

TO BE READ IN VOICED VIDEO REPORTS
An amateur videographer/activists (as appropriate — and name the group when possible) says/say this video shows (whatever it may be). It has been authenticated based on its contents and other AP reporting.

DIGITAL SECURITY FOR JOURNALISTS

It's impossible to be a productive journalist without extensive use of digital communication and production tools. But journalists are not always aware of how to keep their online accounts and private material secure.

Strong security is a combination of good technology and meticulous habits. It might sound attractive to employ the best possible security on all files and every communication channel, but this isn't practical because security always has a cost in terms of time, money or inconvenience. But you can secure your data against some types of unauthorized access.

Here are some basic techniques that will make your data more secure and help you to understand what is not protected. Probably, many of them will already be familiar to you. They may seem simplistic, but most security compromises are the result of lapses in good habits, not high-tech hacking.

1) Use secure passwords. If your passwords are easy to break, nothing else matters.

It is possible to log into an astonishing number of systems with the passwords "123456," "password" and "qwerty." Needless to say, these are terrible choices. But words in the dictionary are also no good because automated password crackers can make thousands of guesses per second. Passwords with letters replaced by numbers (such as zero for "o," three for "e" and one for "l") are also easily guessed by computer. The best passwords are actually passphrases, short sentences that are personally relevant and therefore memorable. If that's too long to type, you can make an acronym from the first letter of each word in your passphrase. Ideally, every password should contain at least one capital letter, lowercase letter, number and symbol.

Particularly protect your email password. Most online services will email you a new password in case you forget yours, so if someone has control of your email, they pretty much have control of all of your accounts. Make sure your email password is well chosen and different from all other passwords. Change it immediately if you suspect someone has compromised your account. In fact you should change your important passwords several times a year to put a time limit on the damage that a stolen password can do.

Social networking and instant messenger passwords are also frequently compromised. Be sure to use a different password for each account. Otherwise, an attacker could gain control of all of your accounts simultaneously – and then change all the passwords, leaving you with few public channels to contest the identity theft!

Ideally, each place you log in should use a different password. No one can remember dozens of different passwords, but you can use a program like 1Password to securely store a completely random and un-guessable password for each service. The downside is that you must have your personal password database with you at all times, your master password exposes everything at once if it is compromised, and if you lose your master password you lose all of your access simultaneously.

Never share your password with anyone over email. If you need to share your password with someone you trust — such as a tech support staffer or a colleague with whom you co-manage a social account — do so verbally.

2) Some computers and networks are more secure than others.

Sending an email at the office to a colleague is very secure if your organization runs its own mail servers (rather than using cloud-based email), because the message only travels across the internal network, not the Internet. But an email sent over WiFi at a coffee shop can be intercepted by anyone nearby, if they have the right software on their laptop.

In general, different networks have different levels of security. A computer attached directly to the public Internet is quite vulnerable, whereas a computer on an internal network, talking only to other internal servers, is quite insulated from the outside world.

VPN software creates a "virtual private network" that connects a remote computer to an internal network over an encrypted channel. It is quite secure — as long as you trust the computer you are running it on and don't forget to log out.

Other people's computers might have viruses, key-logging software or other malware installed. Avoid doing sensitive work on machines you can't vouch for. Especially try to avoid typing your passwords on a public computer or other system that might have key-logging software installed. If you must log in from an untrusted machine, change your password later from a secure computer.

3) Be suspicious of people sending you links with generic descriptions, and always read the URL before you log in.

"Phishing" is the practice of tricking someone into revealing their password, and it's the most common method of gaining unauthorized access. There are many different ways to phish, but all of them are based on sending you a message with a link in it.

The original phishing scams involved an email or other message asking you to re-enter your password for "security purposes" that contained a link to a fake login screen that looks like a legitimate bank or social networking site. It's very easy to create a copy of a website at a fake address, and most people won't notice that the URL is wrong before happily typing in their passwords. For example, if the login screen looks like Twitter, the URL displayed in your browser must start with "twitter.com." Other addresses such as "itwitter.com" are scams. Be very wary of messages with links that take you to a login screen of any sort, and get into the habit of reading the URL before typing in your password.

Other phishing schemes are even more insidious because they exploit security flaws to steal passwords stored in your browser without ever asking you to log in. These attacks still come in the form of links, usually accompanied by very generic messages such as "check out this picture of you" or "did you see this site?" Be very suspicious of such generic links even if they come from a trusted source — your friends' accounts may have been compromised, and if you click the bad link, your account may be compromised too. Also, keep your Web browser up to date, including automatically downloaded updates to minimize your vulnerability to these types of attacks.

There have been hundreds of phishing scams, and there are sure to be more variants in the future. The only protection is to understand how these scams operate, read URLs before logging in and be wary of generic links delivered by email, Twitter, Facebook or any other messaging system.

4) Different communications tools have different levels of security.

Email has the weakest security of any communication method. It's transmitted unencrypted, so it's no more secure than sending a post card. Emails can be intercepted by any network operator between the source and destination, viewed by the administrators of the mail servers at either end or snooped by someone on the same public wireless network. Instant messages are often vulnerable in the same way.

All Web traffic is similarly transmitted without encryption, except for sites that can be accessed using "https" instead of "http," which is normally indicated by a little "lock" icon in the browser. When a website offers both, a URL starting with https is greatly preferable because https connections are encrypted, which makes it harder for eavesdroppers to record your password or other sensitive information. Standard mobile phones are difficult to intercept over the air, but of course the telecommunications company has full access to the connection, as well as your location (even when no calls are made). This may or may not be a problem depending on who wants to listen.

Skype connections are encrypted so that they cannot be intercepted en route by telecommunications companies or anyone else. Skype can be more secure than regular telephone calls in many situations, but it depends on who wants to eavesdrop and that person's relationship to Skype. Skype could still decrypt recorded conversations if it wants to — or if it is compromised or compelled by a third party. Other digital-telephony services have similar security profiles.

Email encrypted using the popular encryption program PGP can be very secure, but PGP is quite difficult to set up and use correctly — and can be compromised after the fact if a private key leaks.

The best solution for truly private communication is the OTR ("off the record") instant messaging system. OTR is built into many IM programs, including the popular Adium application. It is quite secure, even against state-level attackers and about as simple as secure communication gets. But it still demands good habits.

OTR will not hide whom you are communicating with, only what you are saying. Similarly, it's easy to pretend to be someone else over IM. The first time you connect, use another channel simultaneously (such as the phone) to ensure that the person on the other end is really who you think it is. Finally, no amount of communication security will help if someone later reads the chat logs stored on your computer. With Microsoft Office Communicator, chat logs are in the "Conversation History" folder in Outlook. You need to find where such logs are for OTR or other instant messaging programs.

5) Think about what data is stored and where. Caution on cloud computing.

How many copies of that sensitive chat log, photograph or private message are floating around on your laptop? Are there any on other computers? Did you give a copy to someone who might store it insecurely? Are there any copies in the cloud?

Many communications programs make automatic copies. There could be a sensitive email in a saved folder, or an online service might be saving your chat logs (as gchat does by default). Your organization may already have data retention policies or guidance on best practices. If your organization doesn't, consult with your own attorney about types of data to keep while reporting.

It's also important to know where your data are stored. Cloud computing can solve many problems, but whenever you store sensitive information on someone else's computer you are depending on them to keep it safe. In essence, you are betting on their competence and will to resist your attackers. Even if a cloud computing provider is honest and smart, do you know what they will do when served with a subpoena? It's best to consult with an attorney before placing sensitive material in the cloud.

This applies especially to email and social networking service providers, most of whom routinely turn their user's data over to law enforcement agencies if asked. In many circumstances, this happens without any sort of warrant or other judicial oversight, or even notification to the user that their privacy has been compromised. This includes major vendors, such as Facebook, Google and Yahoo, and applies in many countries including the United States.

Further, many governments operate massive Internet surveillance operations, so anything transmitted unencrypted must be assumed to be in the hands of one state agency or another.

6) Consider what might happen if your equipment falls into the wrong hands.

Communication security is important, but many people neglect physical security. A laptop can be lost or stolen, or someone might wander into the office while you are at lunch or even sneak into your hotel room. Computers and other electronics are also routinely seized by authorities of all stripes, including law enforcement and international customs. Encrypt your hard drive if you have sensitive material on your computer, and be careful to track all copies of critical files, including those on thumb drives or other media. The same precautions apply to camera memory cards, phones containing images or video, etc.

7) If a security breach might cause serious harm, you need expert advice.

Tools such as OTR instant messaging and the Tor anonymity network can be enormously powerful and offer the possibility of truly secure communication, but they require considerable thought and care to use them correctly. Encryption systems come in many flavors, but even the most sophisticated software is useless if you forget to log out at the right time. And digital security is just one part of operational security — it takes more than technology to keep secrets.

This little guide is no substitute for specialized training, technology and procedures. If the stakes are high, you need to consult an expert.

SOCIAL MEDIA GUIDELINES FOR AP EMPLOYEES

REVISED MAY 2013

AP's Social Media Guidelines are based on our Statement of News Values and Principles. The guidelines below apply these long-tested principles to the social media space. The Social Media Guidelines are designed to advance the AP's brand and staffers' personal brands on social networks. They encourage staffers to be active participants in social networks while upholding our fundamental value that staffers should not express personal opinions on controversial issues of the day.

Any exceptions to the guidelines below must be approved by a senior AP manager. Nothing in this policy is intended to abridge any rights provided by the National Labor Relations Act.

ACCOUNTS

All AP journalists are encouraged to have accounts on social networks. They have become an essential tool for AP reporters to gather news and share links to our published work. We recommend having one account per network that you use both personally and professionally.

Many AP journalists have had great success with this strategy.

Employees must identify themselves as being from AP if they are using their accounts for work in any way. You don't have to include AP in your Twitter or other usernames, and you should use a personal image (not an AP logo) for the profile photo. But you should identify yourself in your profile as an AP staffer.

Posting AP proprietary or confidential material is prohibited.

Employees may not include political affiliations in their profiles and should not make any postings that express political views.

OPINION

AP staffers must be aware that opinions they express may damage the AP's reputation as an unbiased source of news. AP employees must refrain from declaring their views on contentious public issues in any public forum and must not take part in organized action in support of causes or movements.

Sometimes AP staffers ask if they're free to comment in social media on matters like sports and entertainment. The answer is yes, but there are some important things to keep in mind:

First, trash-talking about anyone (including a team, company or celebrity) reflects badly on staffers and the AP. Assume your tweet will be seen by the target of your comment. The person or organization you're deriding may be one that an AP colleague is trying to develop as a source.

Second, if you or your department covers a subject — or you supervise people who do — you have a special obligation to be even-handed in your tweets. Whenever possible, link to AP copy, where we have the space to represent all points of view.

Posts and tweets aimed at gathering opinions for a story must make clear that we are looking for voices on all sides of an issue.

PRIVACY

Employees should be mindful that any opinions or personal information they disclose about themselves or colleagues may be linked to the AP's name. That's true even if staffers restrict their pages to viewing only by friends.

We recommend customizing your privacy settings on Facebook to determine what you share and with whom.

However, as multitudes of people have learned all too well, virtually nothing is truly private on the Internet. It's all too easy for someone to copy material out of restricted pages and redirect it elsewhere for wider viewing.

FRIENDING/FOLLOWING

It is acceptable to extend and accept Facebook friend requests from sources, politicians and newsmakers if necessary for reporting purposes, and to follow them on Twitter.

However, friending and "liking" political candidates or causes may create a perception among people unfamiliar with the protocol of social networks that AP staffers are advocates. Therefore, staffers should try to make this kind of contact with figures on both sides of controversial issues.

We should avoid interacting with newsmakers on their public pages – for instance, commenting on their posts.

AP managers should not issue friend requests to subordinates. It's fine if employees want to initiate the friend process with their bosses or other managers.

PUBLISHING

AP staff are encouraged to link to AP content in all formats. They can also link to content from other media organizations, except if the material spreads rumors or is otherwise inappropriate. Staffers should always refrain from spreading unconfirmed rumors online, regardless of whether other journalists or news outlets have shared the reports; because of staffers' affiliation with AP, doing so could lend credence to reports that may well be incorrect.

Be mindful of competitive and corporate issues as you post links. And while we compete vigorously with other news organizations, you should think twice before you tweet or post anything that disparages them. This may affect perceptions of your objectivity.

Staffers should link to content that has been published online, rather than directly uploading or copying and pasting the material.

AP journalists have live-tweeted news events on several occasions with great success. Here are some guidelines on live-tweeting:

— News events (press conferences, sports events, etc.) that are being broadcast live: AP staffers are welcome to live-tweet these events. However, when major news breaks, a staffer's first obligation is to provide full details to the appropriate news desk for use in AP services if the desk isn't tuned in already. After providing this information and handling any other immediate AP work, the staffer is then free to tweet or post information about the news development.

— Exclusive material: AP news services must have the opportunity to publish exclusive text, photo and video material before it appears on social networks. Once that material has been published, staffers are welcome to tweet and post a link to it on AP or subscriber platforms.

— Incremental reporting threads: AP staffers should never share on social networks incremental information that, if closely held, could lead to important, exclusive content.

— Other content: Other material you have gathered may be shared on social networks. This includes material we commonly refer to as "cutting room floor" content — material that is not needed for a specific AP product.

A note about the safety of AP staff: Staffers must not post on social networks any information that could jeopardize the safety of AP staff — for example, the exact location of staffers reporting from a place where journalists may be kidnapped or attacked. This also applies to reports of the arrest or disappearance of staffers. In some cases, publicity may in fact help a staffer, but this determination must be made by AP managers handling the situation.

RETWEETING

Retweets, like tweets, should not be written in a way that looks like you're expressing a personal opinion on the issues of the day. A retweet with no comment of your own can easily be seen as a sign of approval of what you're relaying.

Examples of retweets that can cause problems:

1. RT *@jonescampaign*: Smith's policies would destroy our schools
2. RT *@dailyeuropean*: At last, a euro plan that works

These kinds of unadorned retweets must be avoided.

However, we can judiciously retweet opinionated material if we make clear we're simply reporting it, much as we would quote it in a story. Introductory words help make the distinction.

Examples:

1. Jones campaign now denouncing Smith on education. RT *@jonescampaign*: Smith's policies would destroy our schools
2. Big European paper praises euro plan. RT *@dailyeuropean*: At last, a euro plan that works

These cautions apply even if you say on your Twitter profile that retweets do not constitute endorsements. Many people who see your tweets and retweets will never look at your Twitter bio.

Staffers should steer clear of retweeting rumors and hearsay. They can, however, feel free to reply to such tweets in order to seek further information, as long as they're careful to avoid repeating the questionable reports.

When a newsmaker breaks significant news on a social network, a staffer who sees this should report it to the appropriate AP news desk and do any related reporting work asked of him or her. The staffer can then feel free to retweet or share the original tweet or post, if the newsmaker account is judged to be authentic. Policies and best practices on verifying accounts are outlined in more detail below.

SHOWCASING AP WORK ON PERSONAL SITES, BLOGS AND SOCIAL NETWORKS

AP staffers may wish to share their work on their personal websites and blogs. Staffers may post a sampling of their text stories, photos, videos or interactives once they have been published by AP. The material must be clearly identified as AP content.

When highlighting their work on social networks or other sites and services that are focused on the sharing of content among users, staffers must link to the content rather than uploading it directly.

Non-AP content created by AP staffers, such as personal photos, videos and writings, can be shared on personal websites, blogs and social networks. All postings must be consistent with the rules in the AP News Values and Principles and Social Media Guidelines, including those on expressing opinions on contentious public issues. Staffers working in a hostile or otherwise sensitive environment should be mindful of security issues, as well as the impact on AP's ability to gather the news, when deciding what personal content to share online.

SOURCING

It can be difficult to verify the identity of sources found on social networks. Sources discovered there should be vetted in the same way as those found by any other means. If a source you encounter on a social network claims to be an official from a company, organization or government agency, call the place of business to confirm the identity, just as you would if a source called on the phone.

You must never simply lift quotes, photos or video from social networking sites and attribute them to the name on the profile or feed where you found the material. Most social media sites offer a way to send a message to a user; use this to establish direct contact, over email or by phone, so you can get more detailed information about the source.

Use particular caution if you find a social networking account that appears to belong to a person who is central to a story, especially if you can't get confirmation from that person. Fake accounts are rampant in the social media world and can appear online within minutes of a new name appearing in the news. Examine the details to determine whether the page could have just as easily been created by somebody else.

Many athletes, celebrities and politicians have verified Twitter accounts, identified by a white-on-blue check mark on the profile page, which means Twitter has determined that the account really does belong to that person. However, Twitter's verification process has been fooled, meaning we should still do our own checking with the newsmaker. The same goes for verified Google Plus pages, which have a check mark — we need to verify the page through our own reporting.

Also, before you quote from newsmaker's tweets or posts, confirm who is managing the account. Is it the famous person? His or her handlers? A combination? Knowing the source of the information will help you determine just how newsworthy the tweet or post is and how to characterize it.

To include photos, videos or other multimedia content from social networks in our news report, we must determine who controls the copyright to the material and get permission from that person or organization to use it. Any exceptions must be discussed with the Nerve Center and Legal. The authenticity of the content also needs to be verified to AP's standards.

Staffers should take a sensitive and thoughtful approach when using social networks to pursue information or user-generated content from people in dangerous situations or from those who have suffered a significant personal loss. They should never ask members of the public to put themselves in danger, and in fact should remind them to stay safe when conditions are hazardous. Staffers should use their journalistic instincts to determine whether inquiring through social media is appropriate at all given the source's difficult circumstances, and should consult with a manager in making this decision. For more details on how to handle this situation, see the broader memo that was distributed to AP staff.

INTERACTING WITH USERS

AP is strongly in favor of engaging with those who consume our content. Staffers should feel free to ask their followers on social networks for their opinions on news stories, or to put out a call for witnesses and other sources, including people who have captured photos or video that AP might want to authenticate and use. They're also encouraged to answer questions about their areas of coverage that are directed their way on social media, as long as they answer in a way that's consistent with AP's News Values and Principles and Social Media Guidelines.

Most feedback we receive is constructive, and any substantive criticism of our content should be taken seriously, however it may be phrased.

AP's News Values and Principles say, "Staffers must notify supervisory editors as soon as possible of errors or potential errors, whether in their work or that of a colleague." Beyond that, responses to our audience can largely be guided by the nature of the comments that come in.

A thoughtful note from a reader or viewer that leads to a correction by us deserves an email or tweet of thanks (try to avoid repeating the original error). If someone offers a businesslike criticism of a story or image but has their facts wrong, it's good to reply, time permitting, to clarify the facts.

However, it's best to avoid protracted back-and-forth exchanges with angry people that become less constructive with each new round. Abusive, bigoted, obscene and/or racist comments should be flagged to the Nerve Center immediately and, if appropriate, to AP Global Security (contact dspriggs@ap.org).

OTHER THINGS TO KEEP IN MIND:

1. Any response we make to a reader or viewer could go public. Email, Facebook messages and Twitter direct messages may feel like private communications, but may easily find their way to blogs and political pressure groups, attorneys and others. In the case of a story or image that stirs significant controversy, the editor is likely the best person to reply, rather than the person who created the content. The Standards Center can also reply.

2. Any incoming message that raises the possibility of legal action should be reviewed by an AP attorney before a response is made

INTERACTING WITH AP ACCOUNTS

Staff are welcome to retweet and share material posted by official AP-branded accounts on social networking sites (e.g. @AP or an AP Facebook or Google Plus page). We ask that AP staff refrain from liking or commenting on official AP-branded Facebook or Google Plus posts and chats. These accounts are official, public-facing channels of communication, and we want to reserve the comments and interactions for the public, not for journalists talking among themselves in a public-facing spot. It can be off-putting for an average Facebook user to click on a post and see conversations between colleagues or virtual insider pats on the back.

DELETING TWEETS

Twitter.com allows us to delete tweets we've sent. Deletion, however, removes the tweet only from Twitter.com and perhaps some other Twitter clients. Tweets of ours that have been retweeted or reposted elsewhere will still remain publicly visible. If you believe a tweet should be deleted, contact a Nerve Center manager to discuss the situation.

CORRECTIONS

Erroneous tweets or other social media posts need to be corrected as quickly and transparently as errors in any other AP service. This applies to AP-related tweets or posts on personal accounts as well.

The thing to do is to tweet or post that we made a mistake and explain exactly what was wrong.

Example:

Correction: U.S. Embassy in Nigeria says bombings could happen this week at luxury hotels in Abuja (previously we incorrectly said Lagos): apne.ws/uxr9ph

Serious errors need to be brought to the attention of a Nerve Center manager and the appropriate regional or vertical desk.

SPORT IDENTIFICATION CODES

ARC — Archery
ATH — Athletics (Track & Field)
BAD — Badminton
BBA — Baseball-American League
BBC — Baseball-College
BBM — Baseball-Minor Leagues
BBN — Baseball-National League
BBO — Baseball-Other
BBH — Baseball-High School
BBI — Baseball-International
BBW — Baseball-Women's
BBY — Baseball-Youth
BIA — Biathlon
BKC — Basketball-College
BKH — Basketball-High School
BKL — Basketball-Women's Pro
(WNBA)
BKN — Basketball-NBA
BKO — Basketball-Other
BKW — Basketball-Women's College
BOB — Bobsled
BOX — Boxing
BVL — Beach Volleyball
CAN — Canoeing
CAR — Auto Racing
CRI — Cricket
CUR — Curling
CYC — Cycling
DIV — Diving
EQU — Equestrian
FEN — Fencing
FIG — Figure Skating
FHK — Field Hockey
FBC — (American) Football-College
FBH — (American) Football-High
School
FBN — (American) Football-NFL
FBO — (American) Football-Other
GLF — Golf
GYM — Gymnastics
HNB — Handball
HKC — (Ice) Hockey-College
HKN — (Ice) Hockey-NHL
HKO — (Ice) Hockey-Other
JUD — Judo
LUG — Luge

MMA — Mixed Martial Arts
PEN — Modern Pentathlon
MOT — Motorcycling
OLY — Olympics (with a specific
sport code added where ap-
plicable)
RAC — (Horse) Racing
ROW — Rowing
RGL — Rugby League
RGU — Rugby Union
SAI — Sailing
SHO — Shooting
SKE — Skeleton
SKI — Skiing
SPD — Speed Skating
SBD — Snowboarding
SOC — Soccer
SOF — Softball
SQA — Squash
SUM — Sumo Wrestling
SWM — Swimming
TAE — Taekwondo
TEN — Tennis
TRI — Triathlon
TTN — Table Tennis
VOL — Volleyball
WPO — Water Polo
WEI — Weightlifting
WRE — Wrestling

SPORTS GUIDELINES AND STYLE

A

abbreviations It is not necessary to spell out the most common abbreviations on first reference: *NFL, AFC, NFC, NBA, NHL, NCAA, PGA, LPGA, USGA, NASCAR, MLB, AL, NL, FIFA.*

Achilles tendon No apostrophe for the tendon connecting the back of the heel to the calf muscles. But it's *Achilles' heel*, with an apostrophe, for a vulnerable spot.

ACL When describing injuries, acceptable in all references to the *anterior cruciate ligament.*

-added Follow this form in sports stories: *The $500,000-added sweepstakes.*

agate See **basic summary** and **match summary**.

air ball

All-America, All-American The Associated Press recognizes only one All-America football and basketball team each year. In football, only Walter Camp's selections through 1924, and the AP selections after that, are recognized. Do not call anyone not listed on either the Camp or AP roster an *All-America* selection.

Similarly do not call anyone who was not an AP selection an *All-America basketball player*. The first All-America basketball team was chosen in 1948.

Use *All-American* when referring specifically to an individual: *All-American Michael Jordan*, or *He is an All-American.*

Use *All-America* when referring to the team: *All-America team*, or *All-America selection.*

all-star, All-Star, All-Star Game Use uppercase All-Star only when referring to players who have been officially named All-Stars in a sport that refers to its best players each season as All-Stars. The term does not apply in pro football, where players selected to The Associated Press NFL All-Pro team should be referred to as *All-Pro*, while those selected to the Pro Bowl should be referred to as *Pro Bowl players* or *Pro Bowlers*. Use lowercase all-star sparingly to refer informally to performances or players in casual constructions. Use All-Star Game in references where it is the official title of the game.

Alpine skiing In Olympics, slalom, giant slalom, super-G, downhill, Alpine combined

apostrophe See the **possessives** entry in main section and the **apostrophe** entry in the Punctuation Guide, including its descriptive phrases section. Use only in constructions where warranted: *Patriots quarterback Tom Brady* doesn't get an apostrophe as a descriptive but *Tom Brady, the Patriots' quarterback*, gets an apostrophe as a possessive.

archery At the Summer Olympics, individual and team events for men and women. Use a **basic summary**.

AstroTurf A trademark for a type of artificial grass.

athlete's foot, athlete's heart

athletic club Abbreviate as *AC* with the name of a club, but only in sports summaries: *Illinois AC.* See **volleyball** for an example of such a summary.

athletic director Use the singular *athletic* unless otherwise in a formal title.

athletic teams Capitalize teams, associations and recognized nicknames: *Red Sox, the Big Ten, the A's, the Colts.*

athletic trainers Health care professionals who are licensed or otherwise regulated to work with athletes and physically active people to prevent, diagnose and treat injuries and other emergency, acute and chronic medical conditions including cardiac abnormalities and heat stroke. Specify where necessary to distinguish from personal trainers, who focus primarily on fitness.

auto racing Common terms include *victory lane, pit road.*
Follow the forms below for all major auto races:

NASCAR
LINEUP
NASCAR-Sprint Cup-Daytona 500 Lineup
By The Associated Press
After Thursday qualifying; race Sunday
At Daytona International Speedway
Daytona Beach, Fla.
Lap length: 2.5 miles
(Car number in parentheses)
1. (99) Carl Edwards, Ford, 194.738.
2. (16) Greg Biffle, Ford, 194.087.
3. (14) Tony Stewart, Chevrolet, 193.607.

RESULTS
NASCAR Sprint Cup-Daytona 500 Results
By The Associated Press

Monday
At Daytona International Speedway
Daytona Beach, Fla.
Lap length: 2.5 miles
(Start position in parentheses)
 1. (4) Matt Kenseth, Ford, 202 laps, 100.9 rating, 47 points, $1,589,387.
 2. (5) Dale Earnhardt Jr., Chevrolet, 202, 99.5, 42, $1,102,175.
 3. (2) Greg Biffle, Ford, 202, 126.2, 42, $804,163.

For cars not finishing the race, include reason:
 41. (17) Robby Gordon, Dodge, engine, 25, 30.5, 3, $268,150.
 42. (8) Jimmie Johnson, Chevrolet, accident, 1, 28.3, 2, $327,149.
 43. (25) David Ragan, Ford, accident, 1, 25.9, 1, $267,637.

After the final driver, add:
Race Statistics
Average Speed of Race Winner: 140.256 mph.
Time of Race: 3 hours, 36 minutes, 2 seconds.
Margin of Victory: 0.210 seconds.
Caution Flags: 10 for 42 laps.
Lead Changes: 25 among 13 drivers.
Lap Leaders: G.Biffle 1-9; R.Smith 10-11; G.Biffle 12-14; P.Menard 15-16; D.Hamlin 17-40; J.Burton 41-57; J.Gordon 58; T.Stewart 59-60; J.Burton 61-67; G.Biffle 68-76; M.Truex Jr. 77-81; G.Biffle 82; T.Labonte 83-85; G.Biffle 86-99; M.Truex Jr. 100-101; D.Hamlin 102-129; G.Biffle 130; M.Martin 131-132; G.Biffle 133-138; D.Hamlin 139-143; J.Logano 144-145; M.Kenseth 146-157; G.Biffle 158; D.Blaney 159-164; M.Kenseth 165-202.
Leaders Summary (Driver, Times Led, Laps Led): D.Hamlin, 3 times for 57 laps; M.Kenseth, 2 times for 50 laps; G.Biffle, 8 times for 44 laps; J.Burton, 2 times for 24 laps; M.Truex Jr., 2 times for 7 laps; D.Blaney, 1 time for 6 laps; T.Labonte, 1 time for 3 laps; P.Menard, 1 time for 2 laps; J.Logano, 1 time for 2 laps; M.Martin, 1 time for 2 laps; T.Stewart, 1 time for 2 laps; R.Smith, 1 time for 2 laps; J.Gordon, 1 time for 1 lap.
Top 12 in Points: 1. M.Kenseth, 47; 2. D.Earnhardt Jr., 42; 3. G.Biffle, 42; 4. D.Hamlin, 42; 5. J.Burton, 40; 6. P.Menard, 39; 7. K.Harvick, 37; 8. C.Edwards, 36; 9. J.Logano, 36; 10. M.Martin, 35; 11. C.Bowyer, 33; 12. M.Truex Jr., 33.

Formula One-Abu Dhabi Grand Prix Results
By The Associated Press
Sunday
At Yas Marina circuit
Abu Dhabi, United Arab Emirates
Lap length: 3.45 miles
 1. Kimi Raikkonen, Finland, Lotus, 55 laps, 1:45:58.667, 107.421 mph.
 2. Fernando Alonso, Spain, Ferrari, 55, 1:45:59.519.

Constructors Standings
1. Red Bull, 460 points.
2. Ferrari, 400.

IndyCar-MAVTV 500 Results

By The Associated Press

Saturday

At Auto Club Speedway

Fontana, Calif.

Lap length: 2 miles

(Starting position in parentheses)

1. (5) Ed Carpenter, Dallara-Chevrolet, 250, Running.

2. (9) Dario Franchitti, Dallara-Honda, 250, Running.

24. (13) Will Power, Dallara-Chevrolet, 66, Contact.

25. (11) E.J. Viso, Dallara-Chevrolet, 65, Mechanical.

—

Race Statistics

Winners average speed: 168.939.

Time of Race: 2:57:34.7433.

Margin of Victory: Under Caution.

Cautions: 7 for 43 laps.

Lead Changes: 29 among 12 drivers.

Lap Leaders: Kanaan 1, Andretti 2-4, Hildebrand 5-35, Briscoe 36-37, Sato 38-39, Newgarden 40, Hildebrand 41-65, Carpenter 66-75, Jakes 76-85, Carpenter 86-109, Dixon 110, Carpenter 111-122, Dixon 123-133, Kanaan 134-147, Castroneves 148-149, Sato 150-152, Kanaan 153-184, Dixon 185-195, Carpenter 196, Dixon 197-198, Carpenter 199-203, Tagliani 204-217, Carpenter 218, Tagliani 219-223, Franchitti 224-225, Tagliani 226-227, Sato 228, Carpenter 229-236, Franchitti 237-249, Carpenter 250.

Points: Hunter-Reay 468, Power 465, Dixon 435, Castroneves 431, Pagenaud 387, Briscoe 370, Franchitti 363, Hinchcliffe 358, Kanaan 351, Rahal 333.

NHRA Results

By The Associated Press

Sunday

At Firebird International Raceway

Chandler, Ariz.

Final Results

Top Fuel_Tony Schumacher, 4.606 seconds, 213.20 mph def. Morgan Lucas, 4.652 seconds, 258.67 mph.

Funny Car_Ron Capps, Dodge Charger, 4.064, 314.90 def. Matt Hagan, Charger, 4.158, 300.33.

Pro Stock_Erica Enders-Stevens, Chevy Cobalt, 6.538, 211.99 def. Mike Edwards, Chevy Camaro, 6.520, 213.74.

B

backboard, backcourt, backfield, backhand, backspin, backstop, backstretch, backstroke Some are exceptions to Webster's New World, made for consistency in handling sports stories.

badminton Games are won by the first player to score 21 points, unless it is necessary to continue until one player has a two-point spread. Most matches go to the first winner of two games.

Use a **match summary**.

ball carrier

ballclub, ballgame, ballpark, ballplayer

baseball The spellings for some frequently used words and phrases, some of which are exceptions to Webster's New World College Dictionary:

backstop	passed ball
baseline	pinch hit
bullpen	pinch hitter (n.)
center field (n., adj.)	pitchout
center fielder	put out (v.) putout (n.)
designated hitter	RBI (s.), RBIs (pl.)
doubleheader	right field (n., adj.)
double play	rundown (n.)
fair ball	sacrifice
fastball	sacrifice fly
first baseman	sacrifice hit
foul ball line	shortstop
foul tip	shut out (v.)
ground-rule double	shutout (n., adj.)
home plate	slugger
home run	squeeze play
left field (n., adj)	strike
line drive	strike zone
line up (v.)	Texas leaguer
lineup (n.)	third base coach
major league(s) (n.)	triple play
major league (adj.)	twinight doubleheader
major leaguer (n.)	walk-off
outfielder	wild pitch

NUMBERS: Some sample uses of numbers: *first inning, seventh-inning stretch, 10th inning, first base, second base, third base, first home run, 10th home run, first place, one RBI, 10 RBIs. The pitcher's record is now 6-5. The final score was 1-0.*

LEAGUES: Use *American League, National League, American League West, National League East,* or *AL West* and *AL East,* etc. On second reference: *the league, the pennant in the West, the league's West Division,* etc.

Note: No hyphen in *major league, minor league, big league* (n. or adj.)

PLAYOFFS: Use *American League Championship Series,* or *ALCS* on second reference; *National League Championship Series,* or *NLCS; AL Division Series,* or *ALDS*; and *NL Division Series,* or *NLDS*. In the early rounds, use *series* lowercase. Use uppercase *Series* only to refer to the World Series.

ERA Acceptable in all references for earned run average.

Green Monster Acceptable in all references to the left field wall at Fenway Park, home of the Boston Red Sox.

BOX SCORES: A sample follows. The visiting team always is listed on the left, the home team on the right.

Only one position, the first he played in the game, is listed for any player.

BC-BBN--BOX-Atl-SD

BRAVES 8, PADRES 3

ATLANTA	ab	r	h	bi	SAN DIEGO	ab	r	h	bi
Ogllen ss	5	1	1	1	QVeras 2b	4	1	0	0
Lckhrt 2b	5	2	2	0	SFinley cf	4	0	1	0
ChJnes 3b	4	2	2	1	Gwynn rf	4	1	1	0
Glrrga 1b	2	1	1	4	Cminiti 3b	3	0	1	0
Klesko lf	4	0	1	1	Leyritz 1b	3	1	2	2
Rocker p	0	0	0	0	Joyner 1b	1	0	1	0
Perez p	0	0	0	0	CHrndz c	4	0	1	0
Seanez p	0	0	0	0	RRivra lf	3	0	1	0
Lgtnbr p	0	0	0	0	MaSwy ph	1	0	0	0
JLopez c	4	1	1	1	Gomez ss	3	0	0	0
AJones cf	4	1	2	0	Miceli p	0	0	0	0
Tucker rf	2	0	1	0	Bhrngr p	0	0	0	0
GerWm rf	2	0	1	0	Lngstn p	0	0	0	0
Neagle p	2	0	0	0	GMyrs ph	0	0	0	0
DeMrtz p	0	0	0	0	JHmtn p	2	0	0	0
Clbrnn ph	1	0	0	0	RayMys p	0	0	0	0
DBtsta lf	1	0	0	0	Sheets ss	1	0	0	0
VnWal ph	1	0	0	0					
Totals	36	8	12	8		34	3	8	3

Atlanta	000 101 600 - 8
San Diego	000 200 000 - 2

DP_Atlanta 1, San Diego 2. LOB_Atlanta 4, San Diego 7. 2B_ChJones (1), Gwynn (1), RRivera (2). 3B_Lockhart (1). HR_Galarraga (1), JLopez (1), Leyritz (1).

	IP	H	R	ER	BB	SO
Atlanta						
Neagle	5 2-3	7	3	3	1	7
DeMrtz W, 1-0	1-3	0	0	0	0	0
Rocker	1 1-3	0	0	0	0	3
Perez	0	1	0	0	1	0
Seanez	2-3	0	0	0	0	0
Ligtenberg	1	0	0	0	1	2
San Diego						
JHamilton L, 0-1	6	7	4	4	2	5
RaMyers	2-3	2	3	3	1	0
Miceli	1-3	1	1	1	0	1
Boehringer	1	2	0	0	0	0
Langston	1	0	0	0	0	0

Perez pitched to 2 batters in the 8th, JHamilton pitched to 2 batters in the 7th.

Umpires_Home, Bonin; First, Davis; Second, Rippley; Third, Tata; Left, Poncino; Right, Hallion.

T_2:58. A_65,042 (59,772).

Example of an expanded box score:

BC-BBA--EXP-BOX-Ana-Tex

Rangers 3, Angels 2

Anaheim	AB	R	H	BI	BB	SO	Avg.
Erstad cf	4	0	3	2	0	0	.750
Gil ss	3	0	0	0	0	0	.000
a-OPalmeiro ph	1	0	0	0	0	0	.000
Nieves ss	0	0	0	0	0	0	.000
Salmon rf	4	0	1	0	0	1	.250
Glaus 3b	4	0	1	0	0	1	.250
GAnderson lf	3	0	1	0	1	0	.333
GHill dh	4	0	0	0	0	1	.000
BMolina c	4	1	1	0	0	1	.250
Spiezin 1b	3	1	1	0	0	1	.333
Eckstein 2b	3	0	1	0	0	0	.333
Totals	33	2	9	2	1	5	

Texas	AB	R	H	BI	BB	SO	Avg.
Greer lf	3	0	0	1	0	1	.143
Velarde 2b	4	0	1	0	0	1	.250
ARodriguez ss	4	0	1	0	0	3	.375
RPalmeiro 1b	2	0	0	0	2	0	.167
IRodriguez c	4	1	2	0	0	0	.250
Galarraga dh	3	1	1	1	0	0	.167
Caminiti 3b	2	0	1	0	1	0	.500
Curtis cf	2	1	1	0	0	0	.500
Mateo rf	3	0	1	0	0	1	.429
^Totals	27	3	8	2	3	6	

Anaheim	001 000 010_2 9 2
Texas	020 000 10X_3 8 0

a-grounded into double play for Gil in the 8th.

LOB_Anaheim 5, Texas 5. 2B_Erstad 2 (2), Glaus (1), BMolina (1), Spiezio (1), Velarde (1), IRodriguez (1), Galarraga (1). RBIs_Erstad 2 (2), Greer (1), Galarraga (1). SB_ARodriguez (1).

SF_Greer. GIDP_OPalmeiro, GHill 2, IRodriguez, Curtis, Mateo.

Runners left in scoring position_Anaheim 4 (Salmon, Glaus, BMolina 2); Texas 3 (Greer, RPalmeiro, Caminiti). RISP_L.A. Angels 2 for 12; Texas 2 for 9.

Runners moved up_Gil 2, Eckstein.

DP_Anaheim 3 (Gil, Eckstein and Spiezio), (Gil, Eckstein and Spiezio), (Eckstein, Gil and Spiezio); Texas 3 (ARodriguez, Velarde and RPalmeiro), (Velarde, ARodriguez and RPalmeiro), (Caminiti, IRodriguez and RPalmeiro).

	IP	H	R	ER	BB	SO	NP	ERA
Anaheim								
Schoeneweis L, 0-1	7	8	3	3	3	5	108	3.86
Weber	1	0	0	0	0	1	13	0.00
Texas								
Rogers W, 1-0	7 1-3	7	2	2	0	5	96	2.45
JRZimmermn H, 4	2-3	0	0	0	0	2		0.00
Crabtree S, 1	1	2	0	0	1	0	12	0.00

Inherited runners-scored_JRZimmermn 2-0.

IBB_off Crabtree (GAnderson) 1. HBP_by Schoeneweis (Curtis).

Umpires_Home, Rippley; First, Winters; Second, Barrett, Ted; Third, Marquez.

T_2:31. A_49,512 (49,115).

LINESCORE: When a bare linescore summary is required, use this form:

Philadelphia	010 200 000 - 3 4 1
San Diego	000 200 000 - 2 9 1

K. Gross, Tekulve (8) and Virgil; Dravecky, Lefferts (3) and Kennedy. W - KGross, 4-6. LDravecky, 4-3. Sv - Tekulve (3). HRs - Philadelphia, Virgil 2 (8).

LEAGUE STANDINGS: The form:

All Times EDT
NATIONAL LEAGUE

EAST	W	L	Pct.	GB
Pittsburgh	92	69	.571	-
Philadelphia	85	75	.531	61/2

WEST	W	L	Pct.	GB
Cincinnati	108	54	.667	-
Los Angeles	88	74	.543	20

Monday's Results

Chicago 7, St. Louis 5

Atlanta at New York, ppd., rain

Tuesday's Games

Cincinnati (Gullett 14-2 and Nolan 4-4) at New York (Seaver 12-3 and Matlack 6-1) 2, 6 p.m.

Wednesday's Games

Cincinnati at New York, 7:05 p.m.

Chicago at St.Louis, 8:05 p.m.

Only games scheduled.

In subheads for results and future games, spell out day of the week as: *Tuesday's Games*, instead of *Today's Games*.

basic summary This format for summarizing sports events lists winners in the order of their finish. The figure showing the place finish is followed by an athlete's full name, his affiliation or hometown, and his time, distance, points or whatever performance factor is applicable to the sport.

If a contest involves several types of events, the paragraph begins with the name of the event.

A typical example:

60-yard dash – 1, Steve Williams, Florida TC, 6.0. 2, Hasley Crawford, Philadelphia Pioneer, 6.1. 3, Mike McFarland, Chicago TC, 6.2. 4

100 – 1, Steve Williams, Florida TC, 10.1. 2, ...

Most basic summaries are a single paragraph per event, as shown. In some competitions with large fields, however, the basic summary is supplied under a dateline with each winner listed in a single paragraph. See the **auto racing** and **bowling** entries for examples.

Other examples:

Archery
(After 3 of 4 Distances)

1. Darrell Pace, Cincinnati, 914 points.

2. Richard McKinney, Muncie, Ind. 880.

—

Bobsled, Women

1. Kaillie Humphries and Jennifer Ciochetti, Canada, 3 minutes, 48.57 seconds (57.10- 57.07-57.22-57.18).

2. Sandra Kiriasis and Petra Lammert, Germany, 3:48.90 (57.30-57.28-57.21-57.11).

3. Elana Meyers and Katie Eberling, United States, 3:49.57 (57.22-57.45-57.41-57.49).

—

Canoeing, Men

Kayak Singles, 500 meters

Heat 1 – 1, Rudiger Helm, Germany, 1:56.06. 2, Zoltan Sztanity, Hungary, 1:57.12. Also: 6, Henry Krawczyk, New York, 2 04.64. First Repechage – 1, Ladislay Soucek, Czech Republic, 1:53.20. 2, Hans Eich, Germany, 1:54.23.

—

Gymnastics:

Parallel Bars – 1, Joe Smith, Houston, 9.675 points. 2, Ed Jones, Albany, N.Y., 9.54. 3, Andy Brown, Los Angeles, 9.4.

—

ATHENS, Greece (AP) – Final results Saturday of the weightlifting event from the Summer Olympics:

Men's 85kg

1. Juan Jose Madrigal, Costa Rica, 472.5 kg.

2. Rampa Mosweu, Botswana, 470.0.

Additional examples are provided in the entries for several of the sports that are reported in this format.

For international events in which U.S. competitors are not among the leaders, add them in a separate paragraph as follows:

Also: 14, Dick Green, New York, 6.8.

In events where points, rather than time or distance, are recorded as performances, mention the word points on the first usage only:

1. Jim Benson, Springfield, N.J., 150 points. 2. Jerry Green, Canada, 149.

basketball The spellings of some frequently used words and phrases:

alley-oop	half-court pass
backboard	hook shot
foul line	jump ball
foul shot	jump shot
free throw	layup
free-throw line	man-to-man
frontcourt	pivotman
full-court press	tip off (v.)
goaltending	tipoff (n., adj.)

NUMBERS: Some sample uses of numbers: *in the first quarter, a second-quarter lead, nine field goals, a 3-pointer, 3-point play, 10 field goals, the 6-foot-5 forward, the 6-10 center. He is 6 feet 10 inches tall.*

LEAGUE: *National Basketball Association or NBA.*

For subdivisions: *the Atlantic Division of the Eastern Conference, the Pacific Division of the Western Conference,* etc. On second reference: *the NBA East, the division, the conference,* etc.

PLAYOFFS: In the NBA, *Eastern Conference first round, Western Conference semifinals, Eastern Conference finals, Western Conference finals, NBA Finals.*

NCAA Tournament It is acceptable to refer to the regional semifinals as the *Sweet 16*, the regional finals as the *Elite Eight* and the national semifinals as the *Final Four*.

BOX SCORE: A sample follows. The visiting team always is listed first.

In listing the players, begin with the five starters — two forwards, center, two guards — and follow with all substitutes who played.

Figures after each player's last name denote field goals made and attempted, free throws made and attempted and total points.

Example:

Hornets-Bulls, Box

NEW ORLEANS (95)

Ariza 7-12 0-0 16, Ayon 2-6 1-2 5, Kaman 7-18 3-4 17, Vasquez 4-10 4-4 12, Belinelli 3-7 0-0 6, Jones 4-10 2-2 10, Aminu 0-4 2-2 2, Jack 4-9 0-0 10, Henry 3-10 6-7 12, Thomas 2-3 1-1 5. Totals 36-89 19-22 95.

CHICAGO (99)

Deng 6-16 1-2 14, Boozer 7-14 0-0 14, Noah 7-12 1-3 15, Rose 11-24 9-11 32, Hamilton 2-5 1-1 5, Brewer 3-6 0-0 6, Gibson 2-4 1-2 5, Watson 0-2 0-0 0, Korver 2-6 0-0 5, Asik 1-1 1-1 3. Totals 41-90 14-20 99.

New Orleans 26·24·20·25_95

Chicago   30·17·29·23_99

3-Point Goals_New Orleans 4-9 (Jack 2-2, Ariza 2-2, Henry 0-1, Vasquez 0-1, Belinelli 0-3), Chicago 3-18 (Korver 1-5, Deng 1-5, Rose 1-5, Brewer 0-1, Hamilton 0-1, Watson 0-1). Fouled Out_None. Rebounds_New Orleans 55 (Kaman 11), Chicago 56 (Noah 16). Assists_New Orleans 22 (Kaman 5), Chicago 25 (Rose 9). Total Fouls_New Orleans 18, Chicago 16. Technicals_Boozer, Noah. A_21,919 (20,917).

An expanded box example:

BC-BKN--Lakers-Nuggets, Long Box

NUGGETS 119, LAKERS 108

L.A. LAKERS	Min	FG M-A	FT M-A	Reb O-T	A	PF	PTS
World Peace	30:53	6-11	1-2	2-2	0	3	15
Clark	22:40	4-9	0-2	0-1	0	2	8
Howard	38:20	6-8	3-14	4-14	1	2	15
Nash	34:03	6-8	4-5	0-3	5	3	16
Bryant	38:44	12-23	5-6	0-6	9	3	29
Jamison	24:15	5-12	1-2	0-3	1	0	14
Meeks	31:34	3-5	0-0	2-5	1	3	8
Blake	19:31	1-2	0-0	0-2	4	1	3
Totals	240:00	43-78	14-31	8-36	21	17	108

Percentages: FG .551, FT .452.

3-Point Goals: 8-19, .421 (Jamison 3-4, Meeks 2-4, World Peace 2-5, Blake 1-2, Bryant 0-1, Nash 0-1, Clark 0-2).

Team Rebounds: 13. Team Turnovers: 15 (22 PTS).

Blocked Shots: 5 (Howard 4, Clark).

Turnovers: 15 (Nash 6, Bryant 4, World Peace 2, Blake, Howard, Meeks).

Steals: 6 (World Peace 3, Clark, Jamison, Meeks).

Technical Fouls: World Peace, 11:37 first; Defensive three second, 10:02 first; Bryant, 12:00 third.

DENVER	Min	FG M-A	FT M-A	Reb O-T	A	PF	PTS
Chandler	25:24	10-18	0-0	2-4	1	3	23
Faried	31:48	6-10	0-0	4-10	0	5	12
Koufos	14:24	3-4	2-4	3-5	0	5	8
Lawson	40:30	8-19	5-7	0-4	8	3	22
Iguodala	36:45	6-9	2-5	0-4	12	0	14
Brewer	25:40	6-15	3-5	0-2	3	3	16
McGee	23:19	3-4	1-2	2-7	0	3	7
AMiller	27:41	3-4	3-4	0-3	5	0	9
Randolph	6:18	3-3	0-0	2-4	0	1	6
Hamilton	4:15	0-1	0-0	0-1	1	0	0
Mozgov	3:56	1-1	0-0	0-0	0	2	2
Totals	240:00	49-88	16-27	13-44	30	25	119

Percentages: FG .557, FT .593.

3-Point Goals: 5-18, .278 (Chandler 3-5, Brewer 1-5, Lawson 1-6, Iguodala 0-1, A.Miller 0-1).

Team Rebounds: 9. Team Turnovers: 10 (16 PTS).

Blocked Shots: 7 (McGee 4, Faried 2, Iguodala).

Turnovers: 9 (Lawson 4, Iguodala 2, Brewer, Faried, McGee).

Steals: 13 (Faried 3, McGee 2, A.Miller 2, Brewer, Chandler, Iguodala, Koufos, Lawson, Randolph).

Technical Fouls: Coach Karl, 7:27 first; Defensive three second, 3:56 second; Defensive three second, 4:17 third.

L.A. Lakers 29 25 29 25_108

Denver 35 32 28 24_119

A_19,155 (19,155). T_2:14.

Officials_Joe Crawford, David Guthrie, Josh Tiven.

STANDINGS: The format for professional standings:

Eastern Conference

Atlantic Division

	W	L	Pct.	GB
Boston	43	22	.662	–
Philadelphia	40	30	.571	5 1/2

In college boxes, the score by periods is omitted because the games are divided only into halves.

No. 19 CONNECTICUT 74, No. 8 SYRACUSE 66

CONNECTICUT (15-5)

Villanueva 9-13 3-7 21, Boone 2-4 3-5 7, Brown 0-2 5-6 5, Williams 3-11 1-2 9, Gay 6-13 4-4 18, Armstrong 2-2 2-2 6, Kellogg 0-0 0-0 0, Anderson 1-4 2-3 4, Nelson 1-1 2-3 4. Totals 24-50 22-32 74.

SYRACUSE (21-3)

Warrick 6-13 4-7 16, Pace 7-9 0-0 14, Forth 0-1 0-0 0, McNamara 4-18 0-0 9, McCroskey 2-5 0-0 4, Watkins 2-2 0-0 4, Edelin 3-8 1-2 7, Roberts 4-10 4-5 12. Totals 28-66 9-14 66.

Halftime_Connecticut 37-36. 3-Point Goals_Connecticut 4-14 (Gay 2-5, Williams 2-5, Brown 0-2, Anderson 0-2), Syracuse 1-9 (McNamara 1-9). Fouled Out_Roberts. Rebounds_Connecticut 36 (Villanueva 10), Syracuse 34 (Warrick 7). Assists_

Connecticut 14 (Williams 6), Syracuse 17 (Edelin, McNamara 6). Total Fouls_Connecticut 15, Syracuse 24. A_27,651.

The format for college conference standings:

	Conference			All Games		
	W	L	Pct.	W	L	Pct.
Missouri	12	2	.857	24	4	.857

betting odds Use figures and a hyphen: *The odds were 5-4, he won despite 3-2 odds against him.*

The word *to* seldom is necessary, but when it appears it should be hyphenated in all constructions: *3-to-2 odds, odds of 3-to-2, the odds were 3-to-2.*

bettor A person who bets.

billiards Use a **match summary**.

bobsledding, luge Scoring is in minutes, seconds and tenths of a second. Extend to hundredths if available.

Identify events as *two-man, four-man, men's luge, women's luge.* In Olympics, *women's bob, two-man bob, four-man bob, men's luge, women's luge.*

Use a **basic summary**. Example:

Women

1. Kaillie Humphries and Jennifer Ciochetti, Canada, 3 minutes, 48.57 seconds (57.10- 57.07-57.22-57.18).

2. Sandra Kiriasis and Petra Lammert, Germany, 3:48.90 (57.30-57.28-57.21-57.11).

3. Elana Meyers and Katie Eberling, United States, 3:49.57 (57.22-57.45-57.41-57.49).

bowl games Capitalize them: *Cotton Bowl, Orange Bowl, Rose Bowl,* etc.

bowling Scoring systems use both total points and won-lost records.

Use the **basic summary** format in paragraph form. Note that a comma is used in giving pinfalls of more than 999.

Examples:

ST. LOUIS (AP) – Second-round leaders and their total pinfalls in the $100,000 Professional Bowlers Association tournament:

1. Bill Spigner, Hamden, Conn., 2,820.

2. Gary Dickinson, Fort Worth, Texas, 2,759.

ALAMEDA, Calif. (AP) – The 24 match play finalists with their won-lost records and total pinfall Thursday night after four rounds – 26 games – of the $65,000 Alameda Open bowling tournament:

1. Jay Robinson, Los Angeles, 5-3, 5,937.

2. Butch Soper, Huntington Beach, Calif., 3-5, 5,932.

boxing The four major sanctioning bodies for professional boxing are the World Boxing Association, the World Boxing Council, the World Boxing Organization and the International Boxing Federation.

Weight classes and titles by organization:

105 pounds – Mini Flyweight, WBF, IBF, WBO; Strawweight, WBC

108 pounds – Light Flyweight, WBA, WBC; Junior Flyweight, IBF, WBO

112 pounds – Flyweight, WBA, WBC, IBF, WBO

115 pounds – Super Flyweight, WBA, WBC; Junior Bantamweight, IBF, WBO

118 pounds – Bantamweight, WBA, WBC, IBF, WBO

122 pounds – Super Bantamweight, WBA, WBC; Junior Featherweight, IBF, WBO

126 pounds – Featherweight, WBA, WBC, IBF, WBO

130 pounds – Super Featherweight, WBA, WBC; Junior Lightweight, IBF, WBO

135 pounds – Lightweight, WBA, WBC, IBF, WBO

140 pounds – Super Lightweight, WBA, WBC; Junior Welterweight, IBF, WBO

147 pounds – Welterweight, WBA, WBC, WBO, IBF

154 pounds – Super Welterweight, WBA, WBC; Junior Middleweight, IBF, WBO

160 pounds – Middleweight, WBA, WBC, IBF, WBO

168 pounds – Super Middleweight, WBA, WBC, IBF, WBO

175 pounds – Light Heavyweight, WBA, WBC, IBF, WBO

190 pounds – Cruiserweight, WBA, WBC, IBF, WBO

More than 200 pounds – Heavyweight, WBA, WBC, IBF, WBO

Some other terms:

kidney punch A punch to an opponent's kidney when the puncher has only one hand free. It is illegal. If the puncher has both hands free, it is legal.

knockout (n. and adj.) **knock out** (v.) A fighter is knocked out if he takes a 10-count.

If a match ends early because one fighter is unable to continue, say that the winner stopped the loser. In most boxing jurisdictions there is no such thing as a technical knockout.

outpointed Not *outdecisioned*.

rabbit punch A punch behind an opponent's neck. It is illegal.

box office (n.) **box-office** (adj.)

bullfight, bullfighter, bullfighting

C

canoeing Scoring is in minutes, seconds and tenths of a second. Extend to hundredths if available.

In Olympics, slalom and sprint events for both men and women. See **basic summary**.

cliches A team losing a game is not a "disaster." *Home runs* are *homers*, not "dingers," "jacks" or "bombs." A player scored 10 *straight points*, not 10 "unanswered" points. If a football team scores two touchdowns and the opponent doesn't come back, say it "never trailed" rather than "never looked back." In short, avoid hackneyed words and phrases, redundancies and exaggerations.

coach See **titles** entry in sports guidelines.

collective nouns Nouns that denote a unit take singular verbs and pronouns: *class, committee, crowd, family, group, herd, jury, orchestra, team.*

However, team names such as *the Jazz, the Magic, the Avalanche* and *the Thunder* take plural verbs.

Many singular names take singular verbs: *Boston is favored in the playoffs. Stanford is in the NCAA Tournament.*

conferences Major college basketball and football conferences are listed on the following pages.

cross-country Note hyphen, which is an exception to the practices of U.S. and international governing bodies for the sport.

Scoring for this track event is in minutes, seconds and tenths of a second. Extended to hundredths if available.

National AAU Championship

Cross-Country

Frank Shorter, Miami, 5:25.67; 2. Tom Coster, Los Angeles, 5:30.72

Adapt the **basic summary** to paragraph form under a dateline for a field of more than 10 competitors.

See **auto racing** and **bowling** for examples.

cross-country skiing Events include freestyle sprint, classical-style event; 10-kilometer race, also abbreviated 10km or 10K.

cycling Use the **basic summary** format.

D

day to day Hyphenate only as a compound modifier preceding a noun: *Aaron Rodgers will be evaluated on a day-to-day basis.* Otherwise, no hyphen: *LeBron James was day to day with an injured right ankle.*

decathlon Summaries include time or distance performance, points earned in that event and the cumulative total of points earned in previous events.

Contestants are listed in the order of their overall point totals. First name and hometown (or nation) are included only on the first and last events on the first day of competition; on the last day, first names are included only in the first event and in the summary denoting final placings.

Use the **basic summary** format. Include all entrants in summaries of each of the 10 events.

An example for individual events:

Decathlon

(Group A)

100 – 1, Fred Dixon, Los Angeles, 10.8 seconds, 854 points. 2, Bruce Jenner, San Jose State, 11.09, 783.

Long jump – 1, Dixon 14-7 (7.34m), 889, 1,743. 2, Jenner, 23-6 (7.17m), 855, 1,638.

Decathlon final – Bruce Jenner, San Jose State, 8,524 points. 2, Fred Dixon, Los Angeles, 8,277.

discus The disc thrown in track and field events.

diving Use a **basic summary**.

E

event names See **sports sponsorships**.

Major College Basketball Conferences

AMERICA EAST CONFERENCE – Albany (N.Y.); Binghamton; Hartford; Maine; Mass.-Lowell; New Hampshire; Stony Brook; UMBC (Maryland-Baltimore County); Vermont.

AMERICAN ATHLETIC CONFERENCE – Cincinnati; ECU (East Carolina); Houston; Memphis; SMU; South Florida; Temple; Tulane; UCF (Central Florida); UConn; Tulsa.

ATLANTIC 10 CONFERENCE – Davidson; Dayton; Duquesne; George Mason; Fordham; George Washington; LaSalle; Richmond; St. Bonaventure; Saint Joseph's; Saint Louis; Rhode Island; UMass; VCU (Virginia Commonwealth).

ATLANTIC COAST CONFERENCE – Boston College; Clemson; Duke; Florida State; Georgia Tech; Louisville; Miami; North Carolina; North Carolina State; Notre Dame; Pittsburgh; Syracuse; Virginia; Virginia Tech; Wake Forest.

ATLANTIC SUN CONFERENCE – Florida Gulf Coast; Jacksonville; Kennesaw St.; Lipscomb; North Florida; Northern Kentucky; S.C. Upstate; Stetson.

BIG 12 CONFERENCE – Baylor; Iowa State; Kansas; Kansas State; Oklahoma; Oklahoma State; Texas; TCU; Texas Tech; West Virginia.

BIG EAST CONFERENCE – Butler; Creighton; DePaul; Georgetown; Marquette; Providence; St. John's; Seton Hall; Villanova; Xavier.

BIG SKY CONFERENCE – Eastern Washington; Idaho; Idaho State; Montana; Montana State; North Dakota; Northern Arizona; Northern Colorado; Portland State; Sacramento State; Southern Utah; Weber State.

BIG SOUTH CONFERENCE – North Division: Campbell; High Point; Liberty; Longwood; Radford. South Division: Charleston Southern; Coastal Carolina; Gardner-Webb; Presbyterian; UNC-Asheville; Winthrop.

BIG TEN CONFERENCE – Illinois; Indiana; Iowa; Maryland; Michigan; Michigan State; Minnesota; Nebraska; Northwestern; Ohio State; Penn State; Purdue; Rutgers; Wisconsin.

BIG WEST CONFERENCE – Cal Poly; Cal State Fullerton; CS Northridge; Hawaii; Long Beach State; UC Davis; UC Irvine; UC Riverside; UC Santa Barbara.

COLONIAL ATHLETIC ASSOCIATION – College of Charleston; Delaware; Drexel; Elon; Hofstra; James Madison; Northeastern; Towson; UNC-Wilmington; William & Mary.

CONFERENCE USA – Charlotte; East Carolina; FAU (Florida Atlantic); FIU (Florida International); Louisiana Tech; Marshall; Middle Tennessee; North Texas; Old Dominion; Rice; Southern Mississippi; Tulane; Tulsa; UAB (Alabama-Birmingham); UTEP; UTSA (Texas-San Antonio); Western Kentucky.

HORIZON LEAGUE – Cleveland State; Detroit; Green Bay; Illinois-Chicago; Milwaukee; Oakland; Valparaiso; Wright State; Youngstown State.

IVY LEAGUE – Brown; Columbia; Cornell; Dartmouth; Harvard; Pennsylvania; Princeton; Yale.

METRO ATLANTIC ATHLETIC CONFERENCE – Canisius; Fairfield; Iona; Manhattan; Marist; Monmouth (N.J.); Niagara; Quinnipiac; Rider; St. Peter's; Siena.

MID-AMERICAN CONFERENCE – East Division: Akron; Bowling Green; Buffalo; Kent State; Miami (Ohio); Ohio. West Division: Ball State; Central Michigan; Eastern Michigan; Northern Illinois; Toledo; Western Michigan.

MID-EASTERN ATHLETIC CONFERENCE – Bethune-Cookman; Coppin State; Delaware State; Florida A&M; Hampton; Howard; Maryland-Eastern Shore; Morgan State; Norfolk State; N.C. A&T; N.C. Central; Savannah State; S.C. State.

MISSOURI VALLEY CONFERENCE – Bradley; Drake; Evansville; Illinois State; Indiana State; Loyola of Chicago; Missouri State; Northern Iowa; Southern Illinois; Wichita State.

MOUNTAIN WEST CONFERENCE – Air Force; Boise State; Colorado State; Fresno State; Nevada; New Mexico; San Diego State; San Jose State; UNLV; Utah State; Wyoming.

NORTHEAST CONFERENCE – Bryant; CCSU (Central Connecticut State); Fairleigh Dickinson; LIU Brooklyn; Mount St. Mary's (Md.); Robert Morris; Sacred Heart; St. Francis (NY); St. Francis (Pa.); Wagner.

OHIO VALLEY CONFERENCE – East Division: Belmont; Eastern Kentucky; Jacksonville State; Morehead State; Tennessee State; Tennessee Tech. West Divsion: Austin Peay; Eastern Illinois; Murray State; SIU-Edwardsville; Southeast Missouri State; UT-Martin.

PACIFIC-12 CONFERENCE – Arizona; Arizona State; California; Colorado; Oregon; Oregon State; Southern California; Stanford; UCLA; Utah; Washington; Washington State.

PATRIOT LEAGUE – American U.; Army; Boston U.; Bucknell; Colgate; Holy Cross; Lafayette; Lehigh; Loyola (Md.); Navy.

SOUTHEASTERN CONFERENCE – Alabama; Arkansas; Auburn; Florida; Georgia; Kentucky; LSU; Mississippi; Mississippi State; Missouri; South Carolina; Tennessee; Texas A&M; Vanderbilt.

SOUTHERN CONFERENCE – Chattanooga; ETSU (Eastern Tennessee State); Furman; Mercer; Samford; UNC Greensboro; Western Carolina; The Citadel; VMI; Wofford.

SOUTHLAND CONFERENCE – Abilene Christian; Central Arkansas; Houston Baptist; Incarnate Word; Lamar; McNeese State; New Orleans; Nicholls State; Northwestern State; Oral Roberts; Sam Houston State; Southeastern Louisiana; Stephen F. Austin; Texas A&M-Corpus Christi.

SOUTHWESTERN ATHLETIC CONFERENCE – Alabama A&M; Alabama State; Alcorn State; Arkansas-Pine Bluff; Grambling State; Jackson State; MVSU (Mississippi Valley State); Prairie View; Southern U.; Texas Southern.

SUMMIT LEAGUE – Denver; IPFW (Indiana-Purdue-Fort Wayne); IUPUI (Indiana-Purdue-Indianapolis); Nebraska-Omaha; North Dakota State; Oral Roberts; South Dakota; South Dakota State; Western Illinois.

SUN BELT CONFERENCE – Appalachian State; Arkansas State; Georgia State; Georgia Southern; Louisiana-Lafayette; Louisiana-Monroe; South Alabama; Texas-Arlington; Texas State; Troy; UALR (Arkansas-Little Rock).

WEST COAST CONFERENCE – BYU; Gonzaga; Loyola Marymount; Pacific; Pepperdine; Portland; Saint Mary's (Calif.); San Diego; San Francisco; Santa Clara.

WESTERN ATHLETIC CONFERENCE – CS Bakersfield; Chicago State; Grand Canyon; New Mexico State; Seattle; Texas-Pan American; UMKC (Missouri-Kansas City); Utah Valley.

INDEPENDENTS – NJIT.

Major College Football Conferences

AMERICAN ATHLETIC CONFERENCE – Cincinnati; East Carolina; Houston; Memphis; South Florida; SMU; Temple; Tulane; Tulsa; UCF (Central Florida); UConn.

ATLANTIC COAST CONFERENCE – Atlantic Division: Boston College; Clemson; Florida State; Louisville; NC State; Syracuse; Wake Forest. Coastal Division: Duke; Georgia Tech; Miami; North Carolina; Pittsburgh; Virginia; Virginia Tech.

BIG 12 CONFERENCE – Baylor; Iowa State; Kansas; Kansas State; Oklahoma; Oklahoma State; Texas; TCU; Texas Tech; West Virginia.

BIG TEN CONFERENCE – East Division: Indiana; Maryland; Michigan; Michigan State; Ohio State; Penn State; Rutgers. West Division: Illinois; Iowa; Minnesota; Nebraska; Northwestern; Purdue; Wisconsin.

CONFERENCE USA – East Division: Florida Atlantic; Florida International; Marshall; Middle Tennessee; Old Dominion (FCS); Western Kentucky. West Division: Louisiana Tech; North Texas; Rice; Southern Mississippi; UTEP; UTSA.

MID-AMERICAN CONFERENCE – East Division: Akron; Bowling Green; Buffalo; Kent State; Massachusetts; Miami (Ohio); Ohio. West Division: Ball State; Central Michigan; Eastern Michigan; Northern Illinois; Toledo; Western Michigan.

MOUNTAIN WEST CONFERENCE – Mountain Division: Air Force; Boise State; Colorado State; New Mexico; Utah State; Wyoming. West Division: Fresno State; Hawaii; Nevada; San Diego State; San Jose State; UNLV.

PACIFIC-12 CONFERENCE – North Division: California; Oregon; Oregon State; Stanford; Washington; Washington State. South Division: Arizona; Arizona State; Colorado; Southern California; UCLA; Utah.

SOUTHEASTERN CONFERENCE – East Division: Florida; Georgia; Kentucky; Missouri; South Carolina; Tennessee; Vanderbilt. West Division: Alabama; Arkansas; Auburn; LSU; Mississippi; Mississippi State; Texas A&M.

SUN BELT CONFERENCE – Appalachian State; Arkansas State; Georgia Southern; Georgia State; Idaho; Louisiana-Lafayette; Louisiana-Monroe; New Mexico State; South Alabama; Texas State; Troy.

INDEPENDENTS – Army; BYU; Navy; Notre Dame.

Football Championship Subdivision

BIG SKY CONFERENCE – Cal Poly; Eastern Washington; Idaho State; Montana; Montana State; North Dakota; Northern Arizona; Northern Colorado; Portland State; Sacramento State; Southern Utah; UC Davis; Weber State.

BIG SOUTH CONFERENCE – Charleston Southern; Coastal Carolina; Gardner-Webb; Liberty; Monmouth (N.J.); Presbyterian.

COLONIAL ATHLETIC ASSOCIATION – Albany (N.Y.); Delaware; Elon; James Madison; Maine; New Hampshire; Rhode Island; Richmond; Stony Brook; Towson; Villanova; William & Mary.

IVY LEAGUE – Brown; Columbia; Cornell; Dartmouth; Harvard; Pennsylvania; Princeton; Yale.

MID-EASTERN ATHLETIC CONFERENCE – Bethune-Cookman; Delaware State; Florida A&M; Hampton; Howard; Morgan State; Norfolk State; North Carolina A&T; N.C. Central; Savannah State; South Carolina State.

MISSOURI VALLEY CONFERENCE – Illinois State; Indiana State; Missouri State; North Dakota State; Northern Iowa; South Dakota; South Dakota State; Southern Illinois; Western Illinois; Youngstown State.

NORTHEAST CONFERENCE – Bryant; CCSU (Central Connecticut State); Duquesne; Robert Morris; Sacred Heart; St. Francis (Pa.); Wagner.

OHIO VALLEY CONFERENCE – Austin Peay; Eastern Illinois; Eastern Kentucky; Jacksonville State; Murray State; Southeast Missouri State; Tennessee State; Tennessee Tech; UT-Martin.

PATRIOT LEAGUE – Bucknell; Colgate; Fordham; Georgetown; Holy Cross; Lafayette; Lehigh.

PIONEER LEAGUE – Butler; Campbell; Davidson; Dayton; Drake; Jacksonville; Marist; Morehead State; San Diego; Stetson; Valparaiso.

SOUTHERN CONFERENCE – Chattanooga; ETSU (East Tennessee State); Furman; Mercer; Samford; The Citadel; Western Carolina; Wofford; VMI.

SOUTHLAND CONFERENCE – Abilene Christian; Central Arkansas; Houston Baptist; Incarnate Word; Lamar; McNeese State; Nicholls State; Northwestern State; Sam Houston State; Southeastern Louisiana; Stephen F. Austin.

SOUTHWESTERN ATHLETIC CONFERENCE – East Division: Alabama A&M; Alabama State; Alcorn State; Jackson State; MVSU. West Division: Arkansas-Pine Bluff; Grambling State; Prairie View; Southern U.; Texas Southern.

INDEPENDENTS – Charlotte.

F

fast break

FBS Abbreviation for *Football Bowl Subdivision*. The higher level of NCAA Division I football. Formerly known as the I-A Division. *FBS* is used on second reference.

FBS (Football Bowl Subdivision) conferences: Atlantic Coast, Big 12, Big East, Big Ten, Conference USA, Mid-American, Mountain West, Pacific-12, Southeastern, Sun Belt, Western Athletic, Independents (Army, Navy, Notre Dame)

FCS Abbreviation for *Football Championship Subdivision*. The lower level of NCAA Division I football. Formerly known as the I-AA Division. *FCS* is used on second reference.

FCS (Football Championship Subdivision) conferences: Big Sky, Big South, Colonial Athletic Association, Great West, Ivy League, Mid-Eastern Athletic, Missouri Valley, Northeast, Ohio Valley, Patriot League, Pioneer League, Southern, Southland, Southwestern Athletic, Independents (North Carolina Central, Old Dominion, Savannah St.)

field goal

fencing Identify epee, foil and saber classes as: *men's individual foil, women's team foil*, etc.

Use **match summary** for early rounds of major events, for lesser dual meets and for tournaments.

Use **basic summary** for final results of major championships.

For major events, where competitors meet in a round-robin and are divided into pools, use this form:

Epee, first round (four qualify for semi-finals) Pool 1 – Joe Smith, Springfield, Mass., 4-1. Enrique Lopez, Chile, 3-2.

figure skating All jumps, spins and other moves are lowercase even if named after someone: *double axel, triple flip-triple toe loop, triple lutz, triple salchow, sit spin, camel spin, death spiral.* Use a **basic summary**.

football The spellings of some frequently used words and phrases:

blitz (n., v.)	out of bounds (adv.)
cornerback	out-of-bounds (adj.)
end line	pitchout (n.)
end zone	place kick
fair catch	place-kicker
fourth-and-1 (adj.)	play off (v.)
fullback	playoff (n., adj.)
goal line	quarterback
goal-line stand	runback (n.)
halfback	running back
handoff	split end
kick off (v.)	tailback
kickoff (n., adj.)	tight end
left guard	touchback
linebacker	touchdown
lineman	wideout
line of scrimmage	wide receiver
onside kick	X's and O's

NUMBERS: Use figures for yardage: *The 5-yard line, the 10-yard line, a 5-yard pass play, he plunged in from the 2, he ran 6 yards, a 7-yard gain; a fourth-and-2 play.*

Some other uses of numbers: *The final score was 21-14. The team won its fourth game in 10 starts. The team record is 4-5-1.*

PLAYOFFS: *wild-card round, wild card, divisional round, NFC championship game, AFC championship game.*

SUPER BOWL: Refer to the Super Bowl by the year of the game, not by Roman numeral unless using as a literary device: *1969 Super Bowl*, rather than *Super Bowl III*

LEAGUE: *National Football League*, or *NFL*.

TD Acceptable in all references to touchdown.

O-line, D-line Acceptable abbreviations for offensive line, defensive line.

STATISTICS: All football games, whether using the one- or two-point conversion, use the same summary style.

The visiting team always is listed first.

Field goals are measured from the point where the ball was kicked — not the line of scrimmage. The goal posts are 10 yards behind the goal lines. Include that distance.

Abbreviate team names to four letters or fewer on the scoring and statistical lines as illustrated.

The passing line shows, in order: completions-attempts-interceptions.

A sample agate package:

Jets-Giants Stats

N.Y. Jets	7	10	7	0_24
N.Y. Giants	0	7	14	14_35

First Quarter
NYJ_Rhodes 11 fumble return (Nugent kick), 8:36.
Second Quarter
NYG_Ward 8 run (Tynes kick), 10:54.
NYJ_B.Smith 16 pass from Pennington (Nugent kick), :33.
NYJ_FG Nugent 47, :00.
Third Quarter
NYG_Jacobs 19 run (Tynes kick), 11:17.
NYJ_L.Washington 98 kickoff return (Nugent kick), 11:03.
NYG_Shockey 13 pass from Manning (Tynes kick), :33.
Fourth Quarter
NYG_Burress 53 pass from Manning (Tynes kick), 7:52.
NYG_Ross 43 interception return (Tynes kick), 3:15.
A_78,809

	NYJ	NYG
First downs	16	21
Total Net Yards	277	374
Rushes-yards	22-55	39-188
Passing	222	186
Punt Returns	2-20	2-16
Kickoff Returns	5-200	3-62
Interceptions Ret.	1-1	3-68
Comp-Att-Int	21-36-3	13-25-1
Sacked-Yards Lost	1-7	0-0
Punts	4-45.3	5-46.8
Fumbles-Lost	0-0	1-1
Penalties-Yards	6-40	3-37
Time of Possession	26:15	33:45

INDIVIDUAL STATISTICS

RUSHING_N.Y. Jets, T.Jones 13-36, L.Washington 9-13, Pennington 2-6, B.Smith 1-0. N.Y. Giants, Jacobs 20-100, Ward 13-56, Manning 4-17, Droughns 2-15.

PASSING_N.Y. Jets, Pennington 21-36-3-229. N.Y. Giants, Manning 13-25-1-186.

RECEIVING_N.Y. Jets, Coles 8-89, Cotchery 4-31, Baker 3-52, B.Smith 3-44, T.Jones 2-14, L.Washington 1-(minus 1). N.Y. Giants, Burress 5-124, Ward 3-8, Shockey 2-33, Moss 1-10, Matthews 1-6, Hedgecock 1-5.

MISSED FIELD GOAL_N.Y. Jets, Nugent 42 (WL).

The rushing and receiving paragraph for individual leaders shows attempts and yardage gained. The passing paragraph shows completions, attempts, interceptions and total yards gained.

STANDINGS: The form for **professional standings**:

American Conference
East

	W	L	T	Pct.	PF	PA
y-New England	12	3	0	.800	464	321
N.Y. Jets	8	7	0	.533	360	344
Buffalo	6	9	0	.400	351	385

y-clinched division

The form for college **conference standings**:

Atlantic Coast Conference
Atlantic Division

	Conference				All games			
	W	L	PF	PA	W	L	PF	PA
Wake Forest	6	2	175	145	11	2	289	191
Boston College	5	3	189	133	9	3	313	180

In college conference standings, limit team names to nine letters or fewer. Abbreviate as necessary.

fractions In general, follow **fractions** entry in the Stylebook's main section, writing fractions with two numerals separated by a forward slash: 1/2, 2/3 or 3/4. Do not use single fractional characters, which do not appear properly for some computer systems. For mixed numbers, separate the whole integer from the fraction with a space: *J.J. Watt had 2 1/2 sacks, Matt Cain pitched 7 2/3 innings.* In baseball, avoid using fractions to describe outings of less than an inning. Simply write: *Craig Kimbrel got the last two outs for the save.*

free agent, free agent signing

freestyle skiing Events are *halfpipe, moguls, aerials.*

G

game plan

golf Some frequently used terms and some definitions:

birdie, birdies, birdied One stroke under par.

bogey, bogeys One stroke over par. The past tense is *bogeyed.*

caddie

eagle, eagled Two strokes under par.

fairway

green fee A fee paid to play on a golf course. Not *greens fee. Green* refers to all parts of a golf course, not just the putting green.

hole-in-one

Masters, Masters Tournament No possessive. Use *the Masters* on second reference.

tee, tee off

NUMBERS: Some sample uses of numbers:

Use figures for handicaps: *He has a 3 handicap; a 3-handicap golfer, a handicap of 3 strokes; a 3-stroke handicap.*

Use figures for par listings: *He had a par 5 to finish 2-up for the round, a par-4 hole; a 7-under-par 64, the par-3 seventh hole.*

Use figures for club ratings: *a 5-iron, a 7-iron shot, a 4-wood, 3-hybrid.*

Miscellaneous: *the first hole, a nine-hole course, the 10th hole, the back nine, the final 18, the third round. He won 3 and 2.*

ASSOCIATIONS: *Professional Golfers' Association of America* (note the apostrophe) or *PGA.* Headquarters is in Palm Beach Gardens, Florida. Members teach golf at golf shops and teaching facilities across the country.

The *PGA Tour* is a separate organization made up of competing professional golfers. Use *tour* (lowercase) on second reference.

The PGA conducts the PGA Championship, the Senior PGA Championship, and the Ryder Cup as well as other golf championships not associated with the PGA Tour.

The *United States Golf Association* or *USGA* is headquartered in Far Hills, New Jersey. It conducts the United States' national championships. These include the U.S. Open, the U.S. Women's Open, the U.S. Senior Open, 10 national amateur championships and the State Team Championships.

SUMMARIES — Stroke (Medal) Play: List scores in ascending order. Ties are listed in the order in which they were played. Use a dash before the final figure, hyphens between others.

On the first day, use the player's score for the first nine holes, a hyphen, the player's score for the second nine holes, a dash and the player's total for the day:

First round:

Lorena Ochoa	35-34 – 69	
Se Ri Pak	36-33 – 69	

On subsequent days, give the player's scores for each day, then the total for all rounds completed:

Second round:

Rory McIlroy	66-69 – 135	
Tiger Woods	65-71 – 136	

Final round, professional tournaments, including prize money:

Final Round:
(FedExCup points in parentheses)
J.B. Holmes (4,500), $1,080,000 68-65-66-70 – 269
Phil Mickelson (2,700), $648,000 68-68-67-67 – 270

Use hometowns only on national championship amateur tournaments. For tournaments including both amateurs and professionals, indicate amateurs with an "a-" before the name:

a-Stacey Lewis, The Woodlands, Texas 70-69 – 139

The form for cards:

Par out	444 343 544-35
Watson out	454 333 435-34
Nicklaus out	434 243 544-33
Par in	434 443 454-35 – 70
Watson in	434 342 443-31 – 65
Nicklaus in	433 443 453-33 – 66

SUMMARIES — Match Play: In the first example that follows, "and 2" means that the 17th and 18th hole were skipped because Rose had a three-hole lead with two to play. In the second, the match went 18 holes. In the third, a 19th and 20th hole were played because the golfers were tied after 18.

Justin Rose def. Charles Howell III, 3 and 2.

Paul Casey def. Shaun Micheel, 2 up.

Nick O'Hern def. Tiger Woods, 20 holes.

Grey Cup The Canadian Football League's championship game.

Gulfstream Park The racetrack.

gymnastics Scoring is by points. Identify events by name: Men: *floor exercise, vault, pommel horse, still rings, horizontal bar* (or *high bar*), *parallel bars.* Women: *floor exercise, vault, balance beam, uneven bars.*

Use a **basic summary**. Example:

Parallel Bars – 1, Joe Smith, Houston, 9.675 points. 2, Ed Jones, Albany, N.Y., 9.54. 3, Andy Brown, Los Angeles, 9.4.

H

halftime

handball Use a **match summary**.

heatstroke

hit-and-run (n. and adj.) **hit and run** (v.) *The coach told him to hit and run. He scored on a hit-and-run.*

hockey The spellings of some frequently used words:

blue line	penalty box
crease	power play
face off (v.)	power-play goal
faceoff (n., adj.)	red line
goalie	short-handed
goal line	slap shot
goal post	two-on-one break

hat trick Three goals in one game. *Natural hat trick* means three goals scored consecutively by one player in a game or period. *Gordie Howe hat trick* refers to a goal, an assist and a fight by one player. Use sparingly and with explanation.

Stanley Cup The trophy awarded to the NHL champion, the Cup on second reference. It is a traveling trophy awarded to the league champion for one year and then passed to the next winner. Accordingly, it should never be plural: *Mark Messier won six Stanley Cup titles.*

LEAGUE: *National Hockey League* or *NHL.*

For NHL subdivisions: *the Central Division of the Western Conference, the division, the conference,* etc.

SCORING: A player's points total is equal to the sum of his goals and assists. The format G-A--P may be used on second reference and in notes. *Anze Kopitar led the Kings in scoring (29-41--70) en route to the team's 2014 Stanley Cup championship.*

RECORDS: In the NHL, a team's record is expressed in the Win-Loss-Overtime Loss format in which a win is worth 2 points, an overtime loss is worth 1 point and a loss is zero. In college and international play, records are written in the Win-

Loss-Tie format. Unless there is a likelihood of confusion, no further explanation is necessary. *The Bruins went 54-19-9 last season to finish with 117 points, the most in the league. Rick DiPietro had an 18-5-5 record in college before going 130-138-28 with eight ties in his NHL career.*

PLAYOFFS: *Stanley Cup* or *NHL playoffs* until the final round, then *Stanley Cup Final.* Note singular *Final.* But *final* or *finals,* lowercase, when used alone.

SUMMARIES: The visiting team always is listed first in the score by periods.

Note that each goal is numbered according to its sequence in the game.

The figure after the name of a scoring player shows his total goals for the season.

Names in parentheses are players credited with an assist on a goal.

The final figure in the listing of each goal is the number of minutes elapsed in the period when the goal was scored.

Senators-Flyers, Sums

Ottawa	111_3
Philadelphia	311_5

First Period_1, Ottawa, Neil 8 (Simpson, Havlat), 4:07. 2, Philadelphia, Lapointe 4 (Somik, Slaney), 10:41. 3, Philadelphia, Recchi 25 (LeClair, Handzus), 11:11. 4, Philadelphia, Markov 6 (Handzus, LeClair), 16:10. Penalty_Amonte, Phi (ob.-holding), 5:17.

Second Period_5, Philadelphia, Johnsson 9 (Zhamnov, Slaney), 5:22 (pp). 6, Ottawa, Chara 15 (Spezza, Schaefer), 14:32 (pp). Penalties_Fisher, Ott (tripping), 3:57; Simpson, Ott (holding), 6:06; Somik, Phi (slashing), 13:08; Fisher, Ott (highsticking), 17:07.

Third Period_7, Philadelphia, Zhamnov 10 (Gagne, Amonte), 6:54. 8, Ottawa, Bondra 23 (Alfredsson, Schaefer), 19:47 (pp). Penalties_Alfredsson, Ott (rough) 9:03; Zhamnov, Phi (roughing), 9:03; Smolinski, Ott (roughing), 12:18; Sharp, Phi (roughing), 12:18; Simpson, Ott (slashing), 14:21; Philadelphia bench, served by Sharp (too many men), 15:57; Van Allen, Ott, major-double game misconduct (fighting), 18:15; Ray, Ott, major (fighting), 18:15; Lalime, Ott, minor-major-game misconduct (leaving the crease, fighting), 18:15; Simpson, Ott, major-game misconduct (fighting), 18:15 Brashear, Phi, double minor-double major-misconduct-game misconduct; (instigator, roughing, fighting), 18:15; Radivojevic, Phi, major-double game misconduct (fighting), 18:15; Esche, Phi, minor-major-double game misconduct (leaving the crease, fighting), 18:15; Markov, Phi, major-game misconduct (fighting), 18:15; Chara, Ott, minor-major-misconduct-game misconduct (instigator, fighting), 18:18; Neil, Ott, major (fighting), 18:18; Somik, Phi, major (fighting) 18:18; Timander, Phi, major (fighting), 18:18.

Shots on goal_Ottawa 7-9-10_26. Philadelphia 13-11-6_30.

Power-play Opportunities_Ottawa 2 of 6; Philadelphia 1 of 4.

Goalies_Ottawa, Lalime 22-19-7 (30 shots-25 saves), Prusek (18:15 third, 0-0). Philadelphia, Esche 18-7-5 (22-20), Burke (18:15 third, 4-3).

A_19,539 (19,519). T_2:39.

Referees_Marc Joannette, Dan Marouelli. Linesmen_Jonny Murray, Tim Nowak.

STANDINGS: The form:

Eastern Conference
Atlantic Division

	GP	W	L	OT	Pts.	GF	GA
Philadelphia	71	47	10	14	108	314	184
NY Islanders	71	45	17	9	99	310	192

home field (n.) **home-field** (adj.)

horse races Capitalize their formal names: *Kentucky Derby, Preakness, Belmont Stakes,* etc.

horse racing Some frequently used terms and their definitions:

across the board A bet on a horse to win, place and show. If the horse wins, the player collects three ways; if second, two ways; if third, one way.

also-ran Fails to finish in the money: first, second or third.

backstretch Straight portion of the far side of the racing surface between the turns.

Belmont Stakes First run in 1867, the Belmont is three weeks after the Preakness at Belmont Park on Long Island. The distance is 1 1/2 miles on a dirt track.

broodmare A female horse used for breeding.

bug boy An apprentice jockey, so-called because of the asterisk beside the individual's name in a program. It means that the jockey's mount gets a weight allowance.

colt A male thoroughbred horse 4 years old and under, or a standard-bred 3 years of age.

daily double Wager calling for the selection of winners of two consecutive races, usually the first and second.

entry Two or more horses owned by same owner running as a single betting interest. In some states two or more horses trained by same person but having different owners also are coupled in betting.

exacta Wager in which the first two finishers in a race, in exact order of finish, must be picked.

filly A female horse under the age of 5.

furlong One-eighth of a mile. Race distances are given in furlongs up through seven furlongs (spell out the number), after that in miles, as in *one-mile, 1/1-16 miles.*

gelding A castrated male horse.

graded stakes A thoroughbred race that derives its name from the stake, or entry fee, that owners must pay. There are three levels, assigned by the American Graded Stakes Committee. *Grade 1* is the highest level, the most prestigious, based partly on purse but also on such considerations as previous winners and race history. The other levels are *Grade 2* and *Grade 3*. Do not use Roman numerals. *Grade 2*, not *Grade II*.

half-mile pole The pole on a race-track that marks one-half mile from the finish. All distances are measured from the finish line, meaning that when a horse reaches the quarter pole, he is one-quarter mile from the finish.

horse A male horse over 4 years old.

Kentucky Derby Dating from 1875, the "Run for the Roses" is held on the first Saturday in May at Churchill Downs. The race distance is 1 1/4 miles on a dirt track.

length A measurement approximating the length of a horse, used to denote distance between horses in a race.

long shot (two words)

maiden A horse that has not won a race.

mare A female horse 5 years and older.

margin of victory Expressed in lengths of a horse, or other part of the horse's anatomy at the finish line: by a nose, by a neck, or in a photo finish: *Seattle Slew won by three lengths.*

mutuel field Not *mutual field.* Two or more horses, long shots, that have different owners and trainers. They are coupled as a single betting interest to give the field not more than 12 wagering interests. There cannot be more than 12 betting interests in a race. The bettor wins if either horse finishes in the money.

odds-on For a strong favorite to win, odds of less than even money: *Overanalyze was sent off as the 4-5 favorite.*

Preakness Stakes First run in 1873, the Preakness is two weeks after the Derby at Pimlico Race Course in Maryland. The distance is 1 3/16 miles on a dirt track.

race distances Under a mile expressed in furlongs: six furlongs (3/4ths of a mile); more than a mile in figures: 1 1/4 miles, 1 3/16 miles.

stallion A male horse used for breeding.

trifecta A wager picking the first three finishers in exact order.

Triple Crown Annual series of races for 3-year-old horses: the Kentucky Derby, the Preakness Stakes and Belmont Stakes.

winning times Expressed In minutes, seconds and hundredths of a second: *I'll Have Another's winning time in the Derby was 2:01.83.*

wire-to-wire A horse leading a race from start to finish.

horses' names Capitalize. See **animals** in main section.

I

IC4A Abbreviation for *Intercollegiate Association of Amateur Athletes of America*. In general, spell out on first reference. A phrase such as *IC4A tournament* may be used on first reference, however, to avoid a cumbersome lead. If this is done, provide the full name later in the story.

indoor (adj.) **indoors** (adv.) *He plays indoor tennis. He went indoors.*

injuries Be precise in describing injuries. Instead of knee injury describe how a player hurt his or her left knee, right knee or both knees. Avoid medical jargon as much as possible and try to define injuries as simply as information allows without just parroting team or league language if vague.

J

judo Use the **basic summary** format by weight divisions for major tournaments; use the **match summary** for dual and lesser meets.

K

Kentucky Derby *The Derby* on second reference. An exception to normal second-reference practice. Plural is *Derbys* — an exception to Webster's New World College Dictionary.

See **capitalization** in main section.

knuckleball One word is an exception to Webster's New World College Dictionary.

L

lacrosse Scoring in goals, worth one point each.

The playing field is 110 yards long. The goals are 80 yards apart, with 15 yards of playing area behind each goal.

A match consists of four 15-minute periods. Overtimes of varying lengths may be played to break a tie.

Adapt the summary format in **hockey**.

Ladies Professional Golf Association No apostrophe after *Ladies*. Use *LPGA Tour* in all references.

left hand (n.) **left-handed** (adj.) **left-hander** (n.)

M

marathon Use the formats illustrated in the **cross-country** and **track and field** entries.

match summary This format for summarizing sports events applies to individual contests such as tennis, match play golf, etc.

Give a competitor's name, followed either by a hometown or by a college or club affiliation. For competitors from outside the United States, a country name alone is sufficient in summaries sent for U.S. domestic use.

Rafael Nadal, Spain, def. Jarkko Nieminen, Finland, 7-5, 6-3, 6-1.

Serena Williams, United States, def. Nicole Vaidisova, Czech Republic, 6-3, 6-4.

Some other examples:

Billiards

Minnesota Fats, St. Paul, Minn., def. Pool Hall Duke, 150-141.

Handball

Bob Richards, Yale, def. Paul Johnson, Dartmouth, 21-18, 21-19.

Tom Brenna, Massachusetts, def. Bill Stevens, Michigan, 21-19, 17-21, 21-20.

MCL When describing injuries, acceptable in all references to the *medial cruciate ligament*.

midcourt, midfield

minicamp

mixed martial arts *MMA* acceptable in all references.

motor sports Two words unless different in the official name of an event.

motorboat racing Scoring may be posted in miles per hour, points or laps, depending on the competition.

In general, use the **basic summary** format. For some major events, adapt the basic summary to paragraph form under a dateline. See **auto racing** for an example.

motorcycle racing Follow the formats shown under **auto racing**.

MVP Acceptable in all references for most valuable player.

N

NASCAR Acceptable in all references for National Association for Stock Car Auto Racing.

NCAA Acceptable in all references for National Collegiate Athletic Association.

nonconference No hyphen.

numerals In general, follow numerals entry in main section, spelling out one through nine in most uses and using figures for 10 or above. Use figures whenever preceding a unit of measure or points, as well as for team records or game numbers. Some sample uses of numbers: *first place; second quarter; 10th inning; a 3-pointer with 0.2 seconds left; 3-of-8 shooting; he made 3 of 4; the 6-foot-5 player; the 6-5 tight end; the 5-yard line; Game 6; The final score was 21-14. The team won its fourth game in 10 days. The team's record is 4-5-1. Johnson had seven catches for 188 yards. Stafford was 8 for 18 for 200 yards and two touchdowns.* See entries for individual sports for specialized uses, as well as entries for **fractions** and **time**.

O

offseason No hyphen.

Olympics, Olympic, Olympic Games, Olympian Always capitalized: *Winter Olympics* and *Summer Olympics*. Each is staged every four years, but two years apart. The next Summer Games is 2016 in Rio de Janeiro. Capitalize games when attached to the host city or year: *the Rio de Janeiro Games* and *the 2016 Games*. When standing alone, spell games lowercase: *The games open Aug. 5, 2016.*

Names and acronyms:

IOC International Olympic Committee. Either is OK on first reference, but use full title in the story. *IOC President Thomas Bach*; the title is capitalized.

International sports federations. All Olympic sports are run by international federations. Avoid abbreviation *IF*; use *international federation* or *governing body*.

National Olympic committee. In news stories, avoid *NOC* and use *national Olympic committees* or *national bodies*. Abbreviations for U.S. Olympic Committee (USOC) and British Olympic Association (BOA) acceptable on second reference.

Sports in the 2016 Summer Olympics in Rio de Janeiro, Aug. 5-21: archery, badminton, basketball, beach volleyball, boxing, canoe/kayak, cycling, diving, equestrian, fencing, soccer, golf, gymnastics, handball, field hockey, judo, modern pentathlon, rowing, rugby, sailing, shooting, swimming, synchronized swimming, table tennis, taekwondo, tennis, track and field, triathlon, volleyball, water polo, weightlifting, wrestling.

Sports in the 2018 Winter Olympics in Pyeongchang, South Korea, Feb. 9-25: biathlon, bobsled, curling, hockey, luge, figure skating, speedskating, short track speedskating, Alpine skiing, cross-country skiing, Nordic combined, freestyle skiing, ski jumping, skeleton, snowboarding.

Sports in the 2020 Summer Olympics in Tokyo, July 24-Aug. 9: archery, badminton, basketball, beach volleyball, boxing, canoe/kayak, cycling, diving, equestrian, fencing, golf, gymnastics, handball, hockey, judo, pentathlon, rowing, rugby, sailing, shooting, soccer, swimming, synchronized swimming, table tennis, taekwondo, tennis, trampoline, triathlon, volleyball (indoor), water polo, weightlifting, wrestling.

overtime, double overtime, triple overtime

P

pari-mutuel

performance-enhancing drugs Avoid using abbreviations *PEDs*, *PED* in stories and headlines unless in direct quotes. Whenever possible, be more specific in describing drugs considered performance-enhancing, including anabolic steroids, stimulants and human growth hormone.

play Use names for set plays or packages but do not automatically capitalize. Instead use standard AP style for the descriptive word: *wildcat package*, *West Coast offense*, *triangle offense*.

playoff (n.) **play off** (v.)

possessives See **apostrophes** in Punctuation Guide.

postgame, pregame

postseason, preseason No hyphen.

R

racket Not *racquet*, for the light bat used in tennis and badminton.

racquetball Amateur games are played to 15 points in a best-of-three match. Professional matches are played to 11 points, unless it is necessary to continue until one player has a two-point spread. Most matches go to the winner of three of five games.

Use a **match summary**.

record Avoid the redundant *new record.*

right hand (n.) **right-hander** (n.) **right-handed** (adj.)

rodeo Use the **basic summary** format by classes, listing points.

Roman numerals Except in formal reference as a literary device, pro football Super Bowls should be identified by the year — not the season — played, rather than the Roman numerals: *1969 Super Bowl,* not *Super Bowl III.*

rowing Scoring is in minutes, seconds and tenths of a second. Extend to hundredths if available.
Use a **basic summary**. An example, for a major event where qualifying heats are required:
Single Sculls Heats (first two in each heat qualify for Monday's quarterfinals, losers go to repechage Friday): Heat 1 – 1, Peter Smith, Australia, 4:24.7. 2. Etc. Heat 2 – 1, John Jones, Canada, 4:26.3. 72

runner-up, runners-up

S

scores Use figures exclusively, placing a hyphen between the totals of the winning and losing teams: *The Reds defeated the Red Sox 4-3, the Giants scored a 12-6 football victory over the Cardinals, the golfer had a 5 on the first hole but finished with a 2-under-par score.*
Use a comma in this format: *Boston 6, Baltimore 5.*
See individual listings for each sport for further details.

series Best-of-seven series, best of seven. Hyphenate when used as a modifier with the number spelled out: *best-of-seven matchup.* On its

own, no hyphens in the term: *The Red Sox and Phillies meet in a best of seven.*

shoestring catch

short-handed

skiing Identify events as: *men's downhill, women's slalom,* cross-country (note hyphen), etc. In ski jumping, note style where two jumps and points are posted.
Use a **basic summary**. Example:
90-meter special jumping – 1, Karl Schnabel, Austria, 320 and 318 feet, 234.8 points. 2, Toni Innauer, Austria, 377-299, 232.9. 3, Etc. Also; 27, Bob Smith, Hanover, N.H., 312-280, 201. 29

ski, skis, skier, skied, skiing
Also: *ski jump, ski jumping.*

soccer Soccer is the preferred term in the United States, but around the world the sport is referred to as football.
The spellings of some frequently used words and phrases:
AFC Asian Football Confederation.
backpass A pass that a player makes back toward his own goal, to the goalkeeper on his team. The goalkeeper is unable to pick up the ball if the pass comes from the player's foot.
Bundesliga German League first division.
CAF Confederation Africaine de Football. Refer to it as the governing body of African soccer rather than spelling out French acronym.
Champions League
coach Also known as *manager* on British teams and *technical director* on some Latin American teams.
CONCACAF The Confederation of North, Central American and Caribbean Association Football.
Conference National Fifth-highest division of English soccer.

Conference North, Conference South Sixth-highest division of English soccer.

CONMEBOL Confederacion Sudamerica de Futbol. Refer to it as South America's governing body rather than spelling out Spanish acronym.

Copa America South American national team championship. Use the Spanish name, not *America Cup*.

Copa Libertadores South American club championship. Use the Spanish name, not *Liberators Cup*.

corner A kick taken from the corner of the field by an attacking player. Awarded when the ball has passed over the goal line after last touching a defensive player. The shot is taken from the corner nearest to where the ball went out.

defender Do not use *defenseman*.

Eredivisie Netherlands first division.

FA Cup Acceptable on first reference for The Football Association Cup.

false nine A forward player who appears to be playing as a team's main attacker but who drops back, closer to the midfield. It leaves the defense of the opposing team with no one to mark.

FIFA Federation International de Football Association. *FIFA* acceptable on first reference. Refer to it as the international soccer governing body rather than spelling out French acronym.

forward or **striker**

4-2-3-1 formation The typical lineup of a modern-day soccer team, with four defenders, two deep midfielders, three attacking midfielders and a lone forward.

free kick A kick awarded to a team if its player is fouled by an opponent anywhere on the field except for the two penalty areas near the goals. The kick can either be direct (able to shoot straight into the net) or indirect (cannot shoot into the net).

friendly An exhibition game.

goalkeeper *Goalie* is acceptable. Do not use *goaltender*.

hand ball A foul awarded when a player deliberately touches the ball with his hand or any part of his arm.

La Liga Spanish first division.

League Championship Second-highest division of English soccer.

League Cup The No. 2 cup competition in England. Do not refer to as *Carling Cup*.

League One Third-highest division of English soccer.

League Two Fourth-highest division of English soccer.

Ligue 1 French first division.

midfielder

MLS Major League Soccer. *MLS* acceptable on first reference.

OFC Oceania Football Confederation.

offside Offside occurs when a player is nearer to his opponent's goal line than the second-to-last opponent when a ball is passed to him by a teammate. It does not apply if the player is in his half of the field. A free kick is awarded to the opposing team at the place where the offside happened.

one-two When a player passes the ball to a teammate, who then returns it to the same player with his first touch. A move usually done on the run, making it hard to defend against.

parking the bus A phrase used to describe how a team packs its defense to protect a lead or a draw.

penalty A refereeing decision awarded if a player from the defensive team fouls a player from the attacking team inside the penalty area. The attacking team chooses a player to have a free shot at goal from the penalty spot, 12 yards from the goal line.

penalty area Sometimes referred to as *penalty box*. Do not refer to solely as *box* on U.S. wires.

Premier League Top league in England. Also the name of the top league in Scotland. Note that England, Scotland, Wales and Northern Ireland have separate national teams. Do not refer to *Premiership* or *Barclay's Premier League*.

red card Issued to a player who commits a serious foul or who has been issued with two yellow cards in the same game. The player must leave the field and cannot be replaced.

Serie A Italian League first division.

sideline *Touchline* for international wires.

throw-in When a player restarts play by throwing the ball back onto the pitch from its perimeter. The player must keep both feet on the ground and have both hands behind his head as he throws the ball.

"tiki-taka" A system of intricate, one-touch and rapid passing artistry developed by Spanish club Barcelona and eventually adopted by Spain's national soccer team.

total football The label given to a tactical theory, pioneered in international soccer by the Netherlands in the 1974 World Cup, in which any outfield player can take over the role of any of his teammates.

UEFA Union of European Football Associations.

wall A line of defensive players that protects the team's goalkeeper at a free kick.

World Cup Not *World Cup Finals*.

zonal marking A system of defending at corners where players from the defensive team mark areas rather than opposition players. An alternative to man-to-man marking.

In summaries and key lines for international wires, the home team is listed first; on U.S. wires, the visiting team is listed first.

SUMMARY:

At Saint-Denis, France

Italy 0 2 – 2

France 2 0 – 2

(France won 4-3 on penalty kicks)

First half – 1, France, Zidane 4 (Djorkaeff), 12th minute. 2, France, Deschamps (penalty kick), 45th minute.

Second half – 3, Italy, own goal, 88th minute. 4, Italy, R. Baggio 6 (D. Baggio), 90th minute.

First overtime – None.

Second overtime – None.

Penalty kicks – France 4 (Zidane G, Lizarazu NG, Trezeguet G, Henry G, Blanc G); Italy 3 (Baggio G, Albertini NG, Costacurta G, Vieri G, Di Biagio NG).

Yellow Cards – Italy, Del Piero, 26th minute; Bergomi, 28th; Rostacurta, 113th. France, Guivarc'h, 53rd minute; Deschamps, 63rd.

Referee – Dallas (Scotland). Linesmen – Grigorescu (Romania),

Warren (England).

A –77,000

Lineups

Italy – Gianluca Pagliuca; Giuseppe Bergomi, Fabio Cannavaro, Alessandro Costacurta, Paolo Maldini; Francesco Moriero, Dino Baggio (Demetrio Albertini, 52nd), Luigi Di Biagio, Gianluca Pessotto (Angelo Di Livio, 90th); Christian Vieri, Alessandro Del Piero (Roberto Baggio, 67th).

France – Fabien Barthez; Lilian Thuram, Laurent Blanc, Marcel Desailly, Bixente Lizarazu; Didier Deschamps, Emmanuel Petit, Zinedine Zidane, Christian Karembeu (Thierry Henry, 65th); Stephane Guivarc'h (David Trezeguet, 65th), Youri Djorkaeff.

Lineup order is goalkeepers, defenders, midfielders, forwards.

Separate the different positions with semicolons and the players within a position with commas.

STANDINGS:

Scores and standings move in separate files.

Schedule on world wires has times GMT instead of EST or EDT.

Schedule lists home teams first.

Sunday, Jan. 31

Bari vs. Lazio of Rome, 0130

Cagliari vs. Juventus of Turin, 0130

Fiorentina vs. Vicenza, 0130

Standings for international leagues have a different style: GP (games played), W (wins), D (draws), L (losses), GF (goals for),

GA (goals against) and *Pts* (points). Standings for Major League Soccer follow the same style as National Football League: *W* (wins), *L* (losses), *T* (ties), *Pts* (points), *GF* (goals for) and *GA* (goals against).

Spanish Soccer
At A Glance

By The Associated Press

La Liga

Team	GP	W	D	L	GF	GA	Pts
Real Madrid	25	8	2	5	54	21	56
Barcelona	25	16	6	3	49	17	54
Villarreal	25	14	4	7	43	35	46

Major League Soccer

By The Associated Press

EASTERN CONFERENCE

	W	L	T	Pts	GF	GA
D.C. United	16	7	7	55	56	34
New England	14	8	8	50	51	43
New York	12	11	7	43	47	45

speedskating Scoring is in minutes, seconds and tenths of a second. Extend to hundredths if available.

Use a **basic summary**.

sports editor Capitalize as a formal title before a name. See **titles** in main section.

sports sponsorship If the sponsor's name is part of the event name, such as Buick Open, use the name in the title. If there is a previously established name commonly accepted for the event — *Orange Bowl, Sugar Bowl* — use that name even if there currently is a corporate sponsor. *Orange Bowl*, not *Discover Orange Bowl*. However, mention the sponsor somewhere in the story or in a self-contained paragraph after a 3-em dash at the bottom of the story.

sports writer Two words. An exception to Webster's New World College Dictionary.

stadium, stadiums Capitalize only when part of a proper name: *Yankee Stadium*.

swimming Scoring is in minutes, if appropriate, seconds and tenths of a second. Extend to hundredths if available.

Most events are measured in metric units.

Identify events as *men's 4x100 relay, women's 100 backstroke*, etc.

See **track and field** for the style on relay teams and events where a record is broken

Use a **basic summary**. Examples, where qualifying heats are required:

100 Butterfly

Final

1, Michael Phelps, United States, 50.77. 2, Ian Crocker, United States, 50.82. 3, Albert Subirats, Venezuela, 51.82.

T

table tennis Do not use the synonym *pingpong* to refer to the sport. The trademark name is *Ping-Pong*.

tennis Some commonly used terms: *double-fault, double-faulted. Love, 15, 30, 40, deuce, advantage, tiebreaker*. Report set scores thusly: *Serena Williams defeated Madison Keys 7-6 (5), 6-2*. Indicate tiebreakers in parentheses after the set score, using only the loser's total points in the tiebreaker.

time Follow advice in **time sequences** and **times** entries in Stylebook's main section. Use common descriptions for time frames in sports events unless the exact time is truly relevant: *Midway through the second quarter rather than 6:28 into the second quarter*. Precise times down to the second are usually reserved for the final minute or two minutes of each period, depending on the sport.

titles Capitalize or use lowercase according to guidelines in **titles** in Stylebook's main section. Job descriptions, field positions and informal titles are lowercase: *coach John Calipari*; *outfielder Bryce Harper*; *general manager John Elway*. Some other informal titles commonly used in sports include *general manager, trainer, team doctor, manager, captain*.

Tommy John surgery Acceptable when referring to *ulnar collateral ligament reconstruction surgery* in the elbow, more commonly referred to as *surgery to repair a torn ligament in the elbow*.

track and field Scoring is in distance, time or height, depending on the event.

Most events are measured in metric units. For those meets that include feet, make sure the measurement is clearly stated, as in *men's 100-meter, women's 880-yard run*, etc.

For time events, spell out *minutes* and *seconds* on first reference, as in *3 minutes, 26.1 seconds*. Subsequent times in stories and all times in agate require a colon and decimal point: *3:26.1*. For a marathon, it would be *2 hours, 11 minutes, 5.01 seconds* on first reference then the form *2:11:5.01* for later listings.

In running events, the first event should be spelled out, as in *men's 100-meter*. Later references can be condensed to phrases such as *the 200, the 400*, etc.

For hurdle and relay events, the progression can be: *100-meter hurdles, 400 hurdles*, etc.

For field events — those that do not involve running — use these forms: *26 1/2 for 26 feet, one-half inch*; *25-10 1/2 for 25 feet, 10 1/2 inches*, etc.

In general, use a **basic summary**.

For the style when a record is broken, note the mile event in the example below. For the style in listing relay teams, note 4x400 meter relay.

60-yard dash – 1, Steve Williams, Florida TC, 6.0. 2, Hasley Crawford, Philadelphia Pioneer, 6.2. 3, Mike McFarland, Chicago TC, 6.23.

100 – 1, Steve Williams, Florida TC, 10.1. 2.

Mile – 1, Filbert Bayi, Tanzania, 3:55.1, meet record, old record 3:59, Jim Beatty, Los Angeles TC, Feb. 27, 1963. 2, Paul Cummings, Beverly Hills TC, 3:56.1.

Women's 880 – 1, Johanna Forman, Falmouth TC, 2:07.9.

4x400 relay – 1, St. John's (John Kennedy, Doug Johnson, Gary Gordon, Ordner Emanuel), 3:21.9. 2, Brown, 3:23.5. 3, Fordham, 3:24.1.

Team scoring – Chicago TC 32, Philadelphia Pioneer 29.

Where qualifying heats are required:

Men's 100-meter heats (first two in each heat qualify for Friday's semifinals): Heat 1 – 1, Steve Williams, Florida TC, 10.1.

U

Ultimate fighting *UFC* acceptable in all references.

up-tempo

USGA Acceptable in all references for the *United States Golf Association*.

V

volleyball In all indoor international, U.S. college and USA Volleyball games, each of the first four sets is won by the first team to score 25 points. If the match is tied in sets after the first four sets, a deciding fifth set will be played to 15 points. In all five sets, teams must win by two points without a cap on points.

Use a **match summary**. Example:

U.S.-Women def. Korea 21-25, 25-16, 29-27, 16-25, 15-12.

volley, volleys

W

warmup (n.) **warm up** (v.)

water polo Scoring is by goals. List team scores. Example:

World Water Polo Championship
First Round

    United States 7, Canada 1

    Britain 5, France 3

water skiing Scoring is in points. Use a **basic summary**. Example:

World Water Skiing Championships
Men

    Overall – 1, George Jones, Canada, 1,987 points. 2, Phil Brown, Britain, 1,756.

    Slalom – 1, George Jones, Canada, 73 buoys (two rounds).

water sports

weight In agate listings, use abbreviations for some sports, such as *lbs.* for pounds and *kg.* for kilograms.

weightlifting Use a **basic summary**. Example:

    ATHENS, Greece (AP) – Final results Saturday of the weightlifting event from the Summer Olympics:

Men's 85kg

    1. Juan Jose Madrigal, Costa Rica, 472.5 kg.

    2. Rampa Mosweu, Botswana, 470.0.

wild card (n.) **wild-card** (adj.)

World Series Or *the Series* on second reference. A rare exception to the general principles under **capitalization**.

wrestling Identify events by weight division.

Y

yachting Use a **basic summary**, identifying events by classes.

yard Equal to 3 feet. The metric equivalent is approximately 0.91 meter.

To convert to meters, multiply by 0.91 (5 yards x 0.91 = 4.55 meters). See **foot**; **meter**; and **distances**.

yard lines Use figures to indicate the dividing lines on a football field and distance traveled: *40-yard line, he plunged in from the 2, he ran 6 yards, a 7-yard gain.*

yearling An animal 1 year old or in its second year. The birthdays of all horses arbitrarily are set at Jan. 1. On that date, any foal born in the preceding year is considered 1 year old.

Z

zone, zone defense

FOOD GUIDELINES

Common Culinary Conversions
1 tablespoon = 3 teaspoons
2 tablespoons = 1 fluid ounce
1 cup = 16 tablespoons = 8 fluid ounces
1 pint = 2 cups = 16 fluid ounces
1 quart = 4 cups = 32 fluid ounces
1 pound = 16 ounces
1 stick butter = ½ cup = 8 tablespoons = 4 ounces

AP Recipe Style
Recipe guidelines. Always use figures. See **fractions.**

Break out recipes in list and instruction format. Do not write as regular text. Use figures for all quantities in recipes. Do not use abbreviations. Spell out *teaspoon, tablespoon*, etc.

Following is the format for recipes:
— The title of the recipe is capitalized.
— Start to finish time goes below the title, noting estimate for active time in parentheses if hands-off cooking time is significantly longer than active prep time.
— Savory recipes that call for measured amounts of salt should always refer to kosher salt, 1 1/2 *teaspoons kosher salt.* Recipes for baked goods should call for table salt, 2 *teaspoons salt,* as table salt is the preferred ingredient for baking. Recipes that do not specify volume can simply call for salt, *salt and ground black pepper.*
— The number of servings appears next.
— List ingredients in the order used and spell out all measurements. When appropriate, unusual ingredients can be clarified within the list, *ghee (clarified butter).*
— Use numerals for all measurements, times and oven settings. Exception: When two numbers follow one another, write out the first for clarity, *two 12-ounce cans.*
— Instructions for making the recipe follow, and should be written in short, easy-to-digest paragraphs.
— When an oven is used, *Heat the oven to 350 F,* should be the first line of the method (unless the oven is not used until more than 30 minutes after the start of the recipe).
— Begin sentences with equipment and technique, rather than ingredients. *In a medium saucepan over low heat, whisk together the butter and sugar.*
— Nutrition information, if available, follows the method.
— If the recipe source is not the bylined writer of the story, the source should appear at the bottom in parentheses:
(*Recipe from John Smith's "Book of Recipes," Recipe Publishers, 2007.*)
(*Recipe from January 2007 issue of Gourmet.*)

(Recipe from epicurious.com.)
(Recipe from the January issue of Gourmet, as listed at epicurious.com.)
(Recipe from AP Food Editor J.M. Hirsch)
(Recipe adapted from John Smith's "Book of Recipes," Recipe Publishers, 2007)

PIZZA WITH RAINBOW CHARD, GOAT CHEESE AND EGG
Start to finish: 30 minutes
Servings: 4
1 tablespoon olive oil
1 bunch rainbow chard, chopped
1 medium yellow onion, diced
1/4 teaspoon red pepper flakes
2 cloves garlic, minced
20-ounce ball prepared pizza dough, room temperature
4 ounces (about 8 slices) prosciutto, finely chopped
8-ounce log chevre (fresh goat cheese)
4 large eggs
Heat the oven to 400 F. Lightly spritz 2 baking sheets with cooking spray.

In a large skillet over medium-high, heat the oil. Add the chard, onion, red pepper flakes and garlic. Saute until the chard is wilted, about 8 minutes. Set aside.

Divide the dough into 4 pieces. On a lightly floured surface, roll out each to the size of a dinner plate. Place 2 rounds of dough on each baking sheet. Top each piece of dough with a quarter of the chard mixture, spreading it evenly.

Top with the prosciutto, then crumble goat cheese over each pizza.

Bake for 12 minutes, or until the crust is lightly puffed, but not browned. Crack an egg into the center of each pizza, then bake for another 12 minutes, or until the whites are cooked but the yolks are still runny. Serve immediately.

Nutrition information per serving (values are rounded to the nearest whole number): 651 calories; 254 calories from fat; 28 g fat (11 g saturated; 0 g trans fats); 228 mg cholesterol; 70 g carbohydrate; 36 g protein; 4 g fiber; 1,668 mg sodium.

(Recipe from AP Food Editor J.M. Hirsch)

See the **food** entry in the main section for guidelines on when to capitalize the names of foods.

A

absinthe A bitter green liqueur made from wormwood.

adobo sauce A spicy red sauce made from chilies, herbs and vinegar that is common to Mexican cooking.

agave A honeylike syrup made from succulent plants.

aioli A garlic mayonnaise, an emulsification of olive oil, egg yolks and lemon juice.

a la carte A restaurant menu in which each item is individually priced.

a la king A chopped meat dish, often chicken or turkey, served in a cream sauce.

a la mode In the U.S., a dessert served with ice cream, often pies or cakes.

al dente Italian for *to the tooth*, refers to pasta cooked until tender, but slightly firm.

Alfredo A creamy Italian sauce made with butter and Parmesan cheese; *fettuccine Alfredo*.

alfresco A meal eaten outside.

all-purpose flour Preferred term for *white wheat flour*.

amaretti An Italian macaroon made with almonds rather than coconut.

amaretto Almond liqueur.

amuse-bouche French, a bite-sized dish served at restaurants before the meal, usually free.

andouille sausage

angel food cake

angel hair pasta A thin pasta resembling spaghetti.

angostura bitters A cocktail flavoring made from the bark of a South American tree.

Angus Angus cattle comprises two breeds of hornless cattle from the original Scottish Aberdeen stock, Black Angus and Red Angus. Black is the predominant color. Black Angus is the most popular breed for beef in the U.S.

antipasto Italian for *hors d'oeuvre* or *appetizer*.

apples Most varieties are capitalized, including *Cortland, Golden Delicious, Granny Smith, Honeycrisp* and *McIntosh*. An exception: *crabapple*.

applesauce

arborio rice A short-grain, starchy Italian variety of white rice, used in risotto.

artisanal Foods and drinks produced in small batches often using traditional techniques and local ingredients.

Asiago cheese A sharp, aged cow's milk cheese from Italy's Veneto region.

B

baba ghanoush A Middle Eastern dish of pureed roasted eggplant with tahini, lemon juice and garlic.

baby back ribs

Baileys A brand name cream-based liqueur.

baked Alaska A cake topped with ice cream and meringue that is briefly baked.

baker's dozen 13, not 12.

baking sheet Preferred to *cookie sheet*.

baklava A Middle Eastern pastry of layered phyllo dough, honey and chopped nuts.

bananas Foster A dessert of sautéed bananas served with rum and vanilla ice cream. Created during the 1950s at Brennan's Restaurant in New Orleans. Named for a customer.

banh mi Both Vietnamese bread and, in the U.S., a Vietnamese-style sandwich.

barbecue The verb refers to the cooking of foods (usually meat) over flame or hot coals. As a noun, can be both the meat cooked in this manner or the fire pit (grill). Not *barbeque*, *Bar-B-Q* or *BBQ*.

basmati rice A long-grain aromatic rice.

bearnaise sauce A French sauce made from reduced wine, vinegar, tarragon, shallots, egg yolks and butter.

Beaujolais A fruity wine from France. *Beaujolais Nouveau* is a young version.

bechamel French milk-based savory sauce.

beef stroganoff

beef Wellington A fillet of beef wrapped and roasted in pastry.

Bellini A cocktail made from sparkling wine and peach juice.

Benedictine French liqueur made with herbs and spices.

bialy, bialys A Jewish-American yeast roll that is large, round and chewy, topped with onions.

bibb lettuce A variety of butter lettuce.

Bing cherries A variety of sweet cherries.

bisque A rich, thick soup often made from seafood and cream.

black-eyed pea A small beige bean with a black dot.

Black Forest cake A German layered chocolate cake with cherries and whipped cream.

blanch To briefly cook by submerging in boiling water, then cooling in cold water.

blind bake To bake the crust of a pie or a tart before filling it.

bloody mary A cocktail of tomato juice, vodka, Worcestershire sauce and hot sauce.

BLT Acceptable on first reference for a *bacon, lettuce and tomato sandwich*.

blue cheese Not *bleu*.

bok choy A leafy vegetable, also called *pak choi* or *Chinese white cabbage*.

bologna The lunch meat.

Bolognese A thick Italian meat sauce made from beef or veal and vegetables, often served over pasta, also called *ragu*.

bonbon A filled chocolate candy.

Bordeaux Red or white wines made in France's Bordeaux region.

borscht A Russian or Polish soup made from beets.

Boston brown bread A steamed bread made from rye and wheat flours, cornmeal and molasses.

Boston cream pie Not a pie, two layers of spongecake with custard filling, usually dusted with powdered sugar or chocolate glaze.

Boston lettuce

bouillabaisse French seafood stew.

bourbon An American whiskey named for Kentucky's Bourbon County.

bow tie pasta Also called *farfalle*.

brandy A spirit distilled from wine or fermented fruit.

Brazil nut

bread-and-butter pickles

breadbox

breadcrumb

breadstick

brie A soft, mold-ripened cow's milk cheese.

brioche A rich French yeast bread made with butter and eggs.

broccoli

broccoli raab

Broccolini A trademark for a broccoli hybrid.

Brussels sprouts

Buffalo wings Also *Buffalo sauce*.

bulgur wheat A wheat that has been steamed, dried and crushed.

bulkie roll Bulkie roll, also called kaiser roll, Vienna roll or a hard roll, is popular in the United States and Canada. Often used as a bun for sandwiches. *Bulkie roll* is used in New England.

Bundt pan A trademark for a fluted cake pan, also called a *tube pan*.

Burgundy Red or white wines, typically dry, produce in France's Burgundy region.

burrito, burritos A Mexican dish in which a flour tortilla is wrapped around meat, vegetables, cheese or a combination of ingredients, then heated.

busboy

buttercream A variety of frosting.

butterfat The fatty part of milk, from which butter is made.

C

cabernet sauvignon A grape variety used to produce many of the top red wines in California and Bordeaux. The wines tend to be full-bodied, fruity and boldly flavored.

cactus pear A pear-shaped fruit of a cactus, also *prickly pear*.

Caesar salad A salad of greens, cheese, croutons and anchovies.

caipirinha A Brazilian cocktail.

calamari Italian for *squid*.

California roll An American variety of rolled sushi (called *maki*), now popular worldwide. Generally contains avocado, crab and vegetables.

Calvados A French brandy made from apple cider.

Camembert A soft, creamy, partly ripened cheese.

Campari A bitter Italian liqueur.

Canadian bacon A lean smoked pork, called *back bacon* in Canada.

canape, canapes Hors d'oeuvres made from small pieces of bread or crackers topped with cheese, meat or vegetables.

cannellini A white bean common in Italian dishes.

cannelloni A large tubular pasta, often stuffed and baked.

cannoli A tube-shaped Italian pastry fried and filled with sweetened ricotta cheese and other fillings.

cantaloupe

cappuccino An espresso topped with the foam from steamed milk.

carnaroli rice An Italian variety of rice similar to arborio, often used in risotto.

cast-iron (adj.) **cast iron** (n.) A *cast-iron pot*, but the pot is made from *cast iron*.

catfish

cava A Spanish sparkling wine.

ceviche Seafood marinated in an acidic liquid.

challah Jewish braided bread.

Champagne A sparkling wine from the Champagne region of France. If made elsewhere, call it *sparkling wine*.

chardonnay A grape variety used in white wines such as Champagne and white Burgundy. Chardonnays tend to be dry with buttery, creamy notes.

cheddar

cheesecloth

cheesemaker

chevre A soft goat cheese.

Chianti A bold, dry red wine made in the Chianti region of Italy.

chicken cordon bleu

chicken-fried steak

chicken Kiev A dish in which boneless, flattened chicken breasts are rolled, breaded and fried.

chiffonade To slice vegetables very thinly.

chili, chilies Refers generally to spicy peppers, as well as the meat- or sometimes bean-based dish. Exception is the *Hatch chile* produced in Hatch, New Mexico.

china The tableware.

chipotle A dried, smoked jalapeno pepper, often packed in adobo sauce.

chocolate Bittersweet, dark, milk, semisweet, white.

chopsticks

ciabatta A long, wide loaf of Italian bread.

Cobb salad Made famous by Hollywood's Brown Derby Restaurant in the 1920s. It typically consists of finely chopped chicken or turkey, bacon, hard-cooked eggs, tomatoes, avocado, scallions, watercress, cheddar cheese and lettuce tossed with a vinaigrette dressing and topped with a large portion of crumbled Roquefort or other blue cheese.

Coca-Cola, Coke, Coca-Cola Co.

coffeecake

cognac A variety of French brandy.

Cointreau A sweet, orange-flavored liqueur.

colander *Strainer* is preferred.

colby cheese A cow's milk cheese similar to cheddar.

Collins glass

cooking spray Use for nonstick cooking spray.

corkscrew

corn dog

corn flour

Cornish hen

corn on the cob

cornbread

cornflakes

cornmeal

cornstarch

couscous A North African dish made from crushed semolina.

cow's milk cheese

crabcake

crabmeat

cracklings The crisped skin from cooked pork.

craft brewery A small, independent beer producer. Preferred term for *microbrewery*.

creme brulee A custard served topped with a crust of caramelized sugar.

creme fraiche A thickened cream similar in texture to Greek yogurt.

Crisco A trademark for a brand of vegetable shortening.

cupful, cupfuls

Crock-Pot A brand name, not to be used unless referencing that brand, otherwise *slow cooker*.

D

Danish pastry A flaky pastry, usually filled with fruit or cheese.

deep-fry, deep-fried *Deep-fried pickles*.

demi-glace A rich, beef stock-based sauce seasoned with Madeira or sherry.

Dijon mustard

dimensions Pan dimensions are expressed as: *a 9-by-12-inch pan*.

dolmades Stuffed grape leaves.

double boiler A pair of sauce-pans, one filled with water and heated, the other set above it for gentle cooking.

doughnut

draft beer Not draught.

Drambuie A trademark for a brand of Scottish liqueur.

dredge A cooking technique in which food is lightly coated with flour or another ingredient before frying.

drive-thru

Dr Pepper No period after *Dr*

dry-roasted

dulce de leche A blend of cooked milk and sugar resembling caramel.

Dungeness crab A Pacific coast crab found from Alaska to Mexico.

Dutch oven A large, lidded heavy pot.

E

edamame Soybeans, often served steamed in the pod.

eggs Benedict A poached egg served with ham over an English muffin with hollandaise sauce. In eggs Florentine, spinach is substituted for the ham.

Emmenthal Also *Emmenthaler*. A mild, hard Swiss cheese.

enchilada, enchiladas A Mexican dish in which a soft corn tortilla is wrapped around meat or other fillings. Served hot and topped with salsa and cheese.

endive A bitter green. Two most common varieties are Belgian, which resembles small, oval cabbages, and curly, which has frilly, loose leaves.

English muffin

entree

escargot French for *snail*. Generally refers to the dish of cooked snails served with melted butter.

escarole A variety of endive with a mild flavor.

espresso The coffee is *espresso*, not *expresso*.

extra-virgin olive oil

F

fair trade

fajita, fajitas A Mexican dish in which warm flour tortillas are wrapped around strips of marinated and grilled meat.

falafel A Middle Eastern fritter made from ground chickpeas.

farmers market No apostrophe.

farmstead Generally used to describe a cheese produced solely from the milk of one farm.

farm-to-table A popular restaurant trend in which ingredients are sourced locally.

fettuccine A wide, flat pasta. Often confused with *linguine*, which is narrower.

filet mignon An extremely tender boneless cut of beef from the tenderloin. Usually cut 1 to 2 inches thick and cooked by searing briefly on the stove and finished in the oven or under a broiler.

Filet-O-Fish The fish sandwich served at McDonald's.

fillet As a noun, a boneless cut of fish or meat. As a verb, to cut or prepare as a fillet.

five-spice powder A Chinese spice blend.

flatbread

flat iron steak

flaxseed

Fluffernutter A trademarked name for a sandwich made with peanut butter and Marshmallow Fluff.

focaccia A flat Italian yeast bread drizzled with olive oil and salt, sometimes rosemary.

foie gras The fatty liver of a force-fed goose or duck, often made into pate.

foil Use for *tin foil* or *aluminum foil*.

fontina cheese Also called fontina Val d'Aosta after the Italian valley from which it originated. It is a semi-firm and creamy cow's milk cheese. It has a mild, nutty flavor.

foodie Slang for a person with a strong interest in good food.

foodways Refers to a set of food traditions.

fra diavolo An Italian dish with a spicy tomato sauce.

frankfurter

free-range (adj.)

french To trim the meat from the end of a bone, or to cut thin strips (often string beans).

French bread

French dressing

french fries Lowercase *french* because it refers to the style of cut, not the nation.

French toast

frisee A small, bitter salad green.

fruitcake

G

ganache A rich filling or icing made from chocolate and heavy cream.

garam masala Indian spice blend.

garbanzo bean *Chickpea* is preferred.

gazpacho Chilled vegetable soup.

gelato An Italian ice cream made from whole milk. Generally denser than American ice cream.

General Tso's chicken

ghee A clarified butter used in Indian cooking.

ginger Distinguish ground (dry) or fresh (usually grated or minced).

gingerbread

gingersnap cookie

gluten A protein found in wheat and some other grains; lends structure to bread and other baked goods. Also, *gluten-free.*

GMO Genetically modified organism. *GMO* is acceptable on second reference. Refers to food grown from seeds that are genetically engineered in a laboratory.

gnocchi Italian dumpling, often made with potatoes.

Gorgonzola cheese An Italian blue cheese.

Gouda A Dutch cow's milk cheese.

gourmand, gourmet A *gourmand* is a person who likes good food and tends to eat to excess; a *glutton.* A *gourmet* is a person who likes fine food and is an excellent judge of food and drink.

graham crackers Crackers made from a finely ground whole-wheat flour named for Sylvester Graham, a U.S. dietary reformer.

grand cru wines Wines produced from a specialized group of high-end French vineyards.

Grand Marnier An orange liqueur.

Grape-Nuts

grapeseed oil

grits Ground hominy, eaten as a porridge. The word normally takes plural verbs and pronouns.

Gruyere cheese A rich Swiss cheese.

H

half-and-half A blend of equal parts cream and milk.

hard-boil (v.) **hard-boiled** (adj.)

harissa North African red pepper sauce.

Hass avocado Dominant avocado sold in the U.S.

havarti cheese A semisoft Danish cheese.

hazelnut Preferred to *filbert.*

heatproof

herbes de Provence An herb blend from southern France.

Hereford A breed of hardy red-coated beef cattle of English origin with white faces and markings. Also raised in North and South America, Australia and New Zealand.

hibachi

hoisin sauce A dark, savory Chinese sauce.

hollandaise A creamy sauce made from butter, egg yolks and lemon juice.

hors d'oeuvre, hors d'oeuvres

horseradish

hot dog

hot plate

hot sauce A generic term for hot pepper-based sauces, such as *Tabasco*.

huitlacoche Also called *corn smut*. A fungus that grows on corn. Considered a delicacy of Mexican cuisine, it has a smoky-sweet flavor.

hummus

I

icebox pie Pie with a filling that is chilled or frozen, rather than baked.

icing Use to describe sugar decorations applied to cookies; use *frosting* for cupcakes and cakes. Both cookies and cakes can be *glazed* (drizzled with a thin sugar mixture).

IHOP Restaurants franchised and run by International House of Pancakes LLC and its affiliates. International House of Pancakes LLC is a subsidiary of DineEquity Inc.

India pale ale

Irish coffee A coffee blended with Irish whiskey and topped with whipped cream.

J

Jamaica rum Not *Jamaican rum*.

Jarlsberg cheese A buttery cheese from Norway.

jasmine rice An aromatic rice from Thailand, similar to basmati.

Jell-O

jellyroll

jigger Also called a shot or shot glass, about 1 ½ fluid ounces.

johnnycake Dating to the early 1700s, the johnnycake is a flat griddlecake made of cornmeal, salt and either boiling water or cold milk. Today's johnnycakes often have eggs, oil or melted butter and baking powder.

K

kaiser roll A large round roll with a hard crust.

Kalamata olive A black Greek olive.

kamut Considered an "ancient grain," *kamut* is an older, high-protein variety of wheat.

kebabs

ketchup Not catchup or catsup.

Key lime

kielbasa A smoked Polish sausage.

kimchee Korean pickled vegetables.

kitchen parchment Preferred term for *parchment paper* or *baking paper*.

Kobe beef An exclusive grade of beef from cattle raised in Kobe, Japan. The cattle are massaged with sake and fed a special diet that includes beer, resulting in a very tender and full-flavored beef. Extremely expensive.

Kool-Aid

kosher food Food that has been produced or prepared according to Jewish dietary laws.

kosher salt A coarse, additive-free salt. 1 ¼ teaspoons kosher salt = 1 teaspoon table salt.

L

ladyfinger A finger-shaped cookie. Can be spongy or crisp.

lager A beer aged at a low temperature after brewing.

latke Fried pancake, often made of potatoes.

latte An espresso mixed with steamed milk.

leavener An ingredient, such as baking powder, that causes baked goods to rise or have a lighter texture.

lemon grass A Thai herb.

Limburger cheese

liqueur A sweetened, flavored spirit.

liquor An alcoholic drink, usually distilled.

locavore The preferred term for a person who strives to eat locally produced foods.

London broil A boneless beef steak that is marinated, broiled, then served thinly sliced.

low-fat

M

M&M's

macaron A French, often brightly colored sandwich cookie made from egg whites, sugar and almond powder, typically filled with jam or ganache.

macaroon A soft, chewy cookie typically made from coconut, egg whites and sugar, often confused with the *macaron*.

Madeira A fortified wine.

madeleine A small, shell-shaped French cake.

manchego cheese A Spanish sheep's milk cheese.

mandarin orange

mandoline A vegetable slicer.

Manhattan cocktail A classic cocktail made from rye whiskey or bourbon.

Manhattan clam chowder A tomato-based soup of clams.

maraschino cherries

Marsala An Italian fortified wine.

Marshmallow Fluff A trademark. Use *marshmallow spread* unless specifically referring to the *Marshmallow Fluff* brand.

mascarpone cheese A thick spreadable cream from Italy, similar to clotted cream.

matzo Unleavened Jewish bread.

McDonald's Corp.

meatball

meatloaf

medium-rare

melon baller

meringue A dessert made from egg whites and sugar beaten until stiff, then usually baked.

merlot A grape variety and a wine. The wines are similar to cabernet sauvignon, but milder.

mesclun A popular salad greens mix.

Meyer lemon

meze Middle Eastern appetizers.

milkshake

mise en place A French term for having ingredients prepared before making a recipe.

mixologist A person who specializes in making high-end cocktails.

mole Mexican sauce.

molecular gastronomy An often deconstructive approach to cooking in which science and laboratory approaches and equipment are used in the kitchen. Also known as *modernist cuisine.*

Monterey Jack cheese A mild semisoft cheese, also called jack cheese.

Mornay sauce A *bechamel* to which cheese has been added.

MSG Acceptable on first reference for *monosodium glutamate.*

Muenster cheese A mild semisoft cheese.

mushrooms Generally not capitalized, as in *button, chanterelle, cremini, morel, porcini, portobello* and *shiitake.*

mustard Use for the condiment. Use *dry mustard* for powdered form.

N

nan An Indian flatbread.

napa cabbage

napoleon A dessert made with crisp layers of puff pastry spread with pastry creme and either glazed with a thin icing or dusted with powdered sugar.

navel orange A seedless orange so named because it has a small depression, like a navel.

Negroni Cocktail of gin, Campari and sweet vermouth.

Neufchatel cheese A soft cow's milk cheese, similar to cream cheese.

New England clam chowder A dairy-based soup of clams.

nonstick

O

omelet

onions *Spanish onion*, also called *yellow onion*; *red onion*, also called *Italian onion*; *Vidalia onion*.

open-faced sandwich

orecchiette A small pasta shaped like a disk.

Oreo A trademark for a brand of chocolate sandwich cookie held together by a white filling.

ovenproof Also *oven-safe*.

P

pad thai A Thai noodle dish.

paella Spanish rice dish.

palate, palette A *palate* refers to the roof of the mouth and the sense of taste (*to have a sophisticated palate*); *palette* is the term for an artist's paint board.

pan-fry

panko Coarse Japanese-style breadcrumbs.

parboil To partially cook in boiling water.

parkerhouse roll

Parmesan A hard, sharp cow's milk cheese style after Italy's Parmigiano-Reggiano.

Parmigiano-Reggiano An Italian Parmesan cheese, only used with cheese made in specific regions of Italy.

parsley Common varieties are *flat-leaf* (Italian) and *curly-leaf*.

passion fruit

pasteurize

pears In general, capitalize most varieties, including *Anjou*, *Asian* (also called *apple pear*), *Bosc* and *Bartlett*.

pecorino An Italian sheep's milk cheese.

peperonata An Italian blend of sweet peppers and vegetables.

pepitas Hulled pumpkin seeds popular in Mexican cuisine.

Peppadew A brand name for jarred red pepper from South Africa.

pepper jack cheese

Pepsi, Pepsi-Cola, PepsiCo Inc.

petit four, petits fours Bite-sized cakes.

Philly cheesesteak Also called *Philadelphia cheesesteak* or *cheesesteak*.

phyllo A paper-thin pastry dough common to Mediterranean cooking.

piccata A classic Italian dish using very thin, flattened slices of meat, such as veal or chicken, sauteed and served in a sauce of pan drippings, lemon, butter and white wine. Capers, chopped Italian parsley, shallots and garlic are common additions.

Pilsner A pale lager.

pimento A tree and berry.

pimiento A sweet, mild pepper.

pine nut Term is preferred to *pignoli*.

pinot grigio A light, dry white wine that originated in Italy.

pinot noir A grape and wine. The wines tend to be spicy and complex.

pitmaster

Pizza Hut

plonk A slang term for low-quality wine.

po'boy No space, classic New Orleans sandwich.

pomegranate

Popsicle A trademark for a brand of flavored ice on a stick. Use *ice pop* or *frozen pop* as the generic.

port A sweet, fortified Portuguese wine.

porterhouse A beef steak cut from the loin.

pot sticker A small Asian-style dumpling.

potatoes Varieties are written *fingerling, new, red bliss, russet, Yukon Gold*.

potluck

potpie

pound cake

powdered sugar Not *confectioner's sugar*.

precooked

preheat Avoid use of the term: *Preheat the oven to 350 F.* Use instead: *Heat the oven to 350 F.*

prix fixe A menu for which a set price is charged for all courses of the meal.

profiterole Small cream puff.

prosciutto A salt-cured Italian ham, served thinly sliced.

prosecco An Italian sparkling wine.

provolone A tangy cow's milk cheese, originally from Italy.

puff pastry Flaky pastry made from numerous thin layers.

puree (v.) to grind until smooth (n.) food reduced to a smooth liquid or paste.

Pyrex A trademark for a brand of oven-safe glassware.

Q

quinoa A high-protein seed originally from the Andes. It is cooked similar to rice and resembles couscous. It has a nutty flavor and a lightly crunchy texture.

R

ranch dressing A creamy salad dressing containing buttermilk.

ratatouille A popular vegetable dish from France's Provence region.

refried beans

restaurateur

Reuben sandwich The classic corned beef sandwich.

rib-eye steak

Rice Krispies The cereal. Also *Rice Krispies Treats.*

rickey Usually a cocktail with lime juice, soda water and liquor. Also a nonalcoholic drink, often made of seltzer water, lime juice and flavored syrups.

riesling A white wine that can range from quite sweet to dry.

rocky road ice cream

romaine lettuce

Romano Sharp, hard Italian cheese.

Roquefort cheese A strong blue cheese from France.

root beer

roux (singular and plural) A cooked blend of fat and flour, usually used to thicken sauces.

ruby red grapefruit

rugelach Jewish filled pastry.

Russian dressing A mayonnaise- and chili sauce-based dressing.

S

salade nicoise

Salisbury steak

salmon Types are *king, coho* and *sockeye.*

saltine cracker

sandwich

sashimi A Japanese dish of thinly sliced raw seafood.

saute, sauteed, sauteing To cook with fat on the stovetop.

saute pan A wide, shallow pan with straight sides.

sauvignon blanc A grape and a wine. Wines are white and tend to be dry.

savoy cabbage

scallions The preferred term for *green onions*.

scotch Capitalize *Scotch* and use the spelling *whisky* only when the two words are used together.

scotch barley, scotch broth, scotch salmon, scotch sour

Scotch whisky A type of whiskey distilled in Scotland from malted barley. The malt is dried over a peat fire.

seasonings In recipes, note whether herbs are fresh or dried: *1 teaspoon fresh oregano* or *1/2 teaspoon dried thyme*. For spices and other seasonings, when appropriate note whether ground or whole: *1 teaspoon ground black pepper* or *1 teaspoon whole cardamom pods*.

seltzer water Carbonated water. Differs from *soda water* (also called *club soda*), which contains sodium bicarbonate.

serrano chili A small, hot chili.

serrano ham Dry-cured Spanish ham.

7-Eleven Trademark for stores operated and licensed by 7-Eleven Inc., a subsidiary of Seven-Eleven Japan Co. Ltd.

7UP Trademark for a brand of soft drink.

shepherd's pie A baked dish that consists of layers of ground meat and mashed potatoes.

sherbet A frozen dessert similar to ice cream but made from sweetened fruit juice and water.

sherry A Spanish fortified wine.

shiraz A grape and a red wine, known as *syrah* in France. The wine tends to be bold and spicy.

Sichuan The preferred spelling, *Sichuan peppercorns* (not *Szechwan*).

skillet A long-handled shallow pan with gently sloping sides. Also called a *frying pan*, though *skillet* is preferred.

sloppy Joes

slow cooker

Smithfield Ham A trademark for a ham dry-cured, smoked and aged in Smithfield, Virginia.

s'more A campfire dessert of toasted marshmallow and chocolate between graham crackers.

soft serve ice cream

soppressata A variety of cured Italian salami.

sous vide A method of cooking in which food is vacuum sealed in plastic bags, then slowly cooked in water at low temperatures.

Spam

spareribs

spongecake

springform pan A baking pan with removable sides.

Sriracha sauce A Thai hot chili sauce.

stand mixer The preferred term for a stationary kitchen mixer. Use *electric mixer* for a hand-held mixer.

Stilton An English blue cheese.

stir-fry (n. and v.)

stockpot

sun-dried tomatoes

sugar Common varieties include *brown*, *granulated* (*white*), *powdered* (preferred to *confectioner's*), *superfine* and *turbinado* (a raw sugar). In recipes, if only granulated sugar is called for, *sugar* can be used alone.

sugarplums

sushi A Japanese dish of cooked, seasoned and cooled rice served topped with or wrapped around seafood, vegetables or egg.

sweet-and-sour sauce

Swiss chard

Swiss cheese

T

Tabasco A trademark for a brand of hot pepper sauce.

tabbouleh A Middle Eastern salad made from bulgur, vegetables, herbs, olive oil and lemon juice.

tacos

tahini

takeout

tamale, tamales A Mexican dish, usually wrapped and cooked in corn husks.

tapas The small plates of food usually served in bars in Spain.

tapenade A spread of black olives, capers and anchovies from France's Provence region.

taproom

Tater Tots

T-bone steak

temperatures In recipes written as *450 F* or *232 C*.

Tex-Mex Characterized by elements of Texas and Mexico, such as *Tex-Mex cooking*.

Thai chilies, Thai chili sauce

Thai red curry paste

thermos

Thousand Island dressing

Tiki bar

Toll House cookie

tomatoes Varieties are capitalized, as in *Brandywine*.

tonic water A carbonated water flavored with sugar and quinine.

triple sec A generic name for a clear orange liqueur.

tsimmes Jewish sweet stew often made from carrots and dried fruit.

tureen A large, deep serving dish with a lid, usually used for soups and stews. *Terrine* refers to a pate, as well as the dish it is made in.

Turkish delight A soft, gelatinous candy popular in the Middle East.

tzatziki A Greek yogurt sauce.

U

umami A Japanese term roughly translated as *savory*, the suspected fifth taste (in addition to sweet, salty, sour and bitter).

upside-down cake

V

vegan A person who abstains from eating animal products, such as meat, dairy, eggs and seafood. Some also avoid honey.

vegetarian Generally understood as a person who abstains from eating meat but does eat dairy. There are many variations of vegetarian, including some who eat seafood or poultry.

vinaigrette A blend of oil and vinegar, usually used as salad dressing.

vitamin Lowercase *vitamin C.*

W

wagyu Wagyu refers to several beef breeds of cattle, such as *Japanese Black*, *Japanese Brown*, *Japanese Polled* and *Japanese Shorthorn*, which are genetically bred to produce intense marbling. Wagyu beef is very expensive. Wagyu is also known as *Kobe-style beef*, although only beef raised in the Kobe prefecture of Japan can be called *Kobe*, a branded name. See **Kobe beef.**

Waldorf salad

waxed paper

wheat germ

wheatgrass

whiskey, whiskeys Use the spelling *whisky* only in conjunction with *Scotch whisky* and *Canadian whisky.*

whole wheat (n.) **whole-wheat** (adj.) *Whole-wheat bread.*

whole-grain (adj.) *Whole-grain bread, whole-grain mustard.*

whoopie pie

wineglass

winemaker

wines Wine names for grape varietals, such as *chardonnay* and *shiraz*, are not capitalized. Wines named for regions, such as *Champagne* or *Chianti*, are capitalized.

Wonder bread

wonton

Worcestershire sauce A condiment originally made by the English in India.

Y

yam Botanically, yams and sweet potatoes are not related, although several varieties of moist-fleshed sweet potatoes are popularly called *yams* in some parts of the United States.

yogurt Also, *Greek yogurt.*

York peppermint patties

Z

zest As a noun, the thin, colorful outer skin of citrus, not the white pith beneath it. As a verb, to remove the thin outer skin of citrus, usually with a grater or zester.

zip-close bag Not *Ziploc* (a brand name).

FASHION GUIDELINES

A

A-line Skirt that is narrow at the waist, then flares out along a straight line to the hem like a triangle or an A.

anorak Hooded jacket, often a pullover silhouette.

applique Decoration fastened to a larger piece of material.

argyle Geometric pattern on knitted garments of colored diamonds on plain background.

Armani, Giorgio (1934 -) Italian-born designer who started his label in 1975, making his mark with tailored suits. He also forged an early relationship with Hollywood, both on screen and on red carpets.

atelier A designer's workshop or studio.

B

babydoll

back-to-school clothing

Balenciaga, Cristobal (1895 - 1972) Spanish-born designer moved to Paris during the Spanish Civil War, where he solidified his reputation as a fine couturier. The house's current creative chief is Alexander Wang.

ballgown

Barneys New York New York-based department store. No apostrophe.

batik Method of making colored designs on textiles using wax to resist the dye. Originated in Indonesia.

bespoke Custom-made item.

bias cut Fabric cut on an approximately 45-degree angle to create a clingy, draped effect. French designer Madeleine Vionnet introduced it in the 1920s.

Blahnik, Manolo (1942 -) Spanish high-end shoe designer often mentioned by Carrie Bradshaw on the television series "Sex and the City."

Bloomingdale's Upscale U.S. department stores, owned by Macy's Inc. Flagship store is at 59th Street and Lexington Avenue in Manhattan.

boatneck, bateau Neckline named for its similarity in shape to a skimmer boat. It has a narrow opening that extends almost shoulder to shoulder.

bodysuit

boho Style that draws on bohemian influences.

boucle Curly yarn that gives fabric a tufted or knotted texture.

bra Acceptable in all references for *brassiere*.

brogue Lace-up shoe with perforations in the leather.

brooch

buffalo check Checkered pattern with bold, well-defined squares.

bustier Formfitting, corset-style garment shaped around the bustline and bodice that cinches the waist. Originally worn as an underpinning, it has been adapted to street clothes and, particularly, eveningwear.

button-down

C

camisole, cami Thin-strapped, sleeveless top for women.

capelet Short cape.

chambray Lightweight fabric woven with colored and white yarns.

Chanel Gabrielle Bonheur "Coco" Chanel (1883 – 1971) French designer, one of most famous names in modern fashion. Her skirt suits, with collarless jackets and braided chain hardware, are often imitated. German designer Karl Lagerfeld has been at helm of company since 1983.

chichi Ostentatiously stylish; deliberately chic.

citrine Lemon-colored.

cloche Close-fitting hat. Takes its name from French for bell.

closed-toe shoes

collections

colorblocking Garments with geometric chunks of bright colors, fashion staples since French designer Yves Saint Laurent's 1965

collection inspired by Dutch painter Piet Mondrian.

compliment, complement *Complement* is a noun and a verb denoting completeness or the process of supplementing something: *The ship has a complement of 200 sailors and 20 officers. The tie complements his suit.*
Compliment is a noun or a verb that denotes praise or the expression of courtesy: *The captain complimented the sailors. She was flattered by the compliments on her project.*

couture, couturier *Couture* refers to the design and manufacture of fashionable clothing, usually custom made. *Couturier* is someone who makes and sells couture clothes. See **haute couture**.

cowl Draped, loose neckline with a cascading effect; also used as back of dress.

crinoline Stiff cloth used as a lining for stiffening garments.

culottes

D

Dacron A trademark for a brand of polyester fiber.

de la Renta, Oscar (1932 - 2014) Dominican-born fashion designer. After stints in Europe with the houses of Balenciaga and Lanvin, he opened his own label in New York in 1965. His specialties were elaborate eveningwear and dressed-up daywear with a refined uptown aesthetic. The label continues after de la Renta's death with Peter Copping as its executive director.

decolletage, decollete A low neckline on a dress or top.

deconstructed Look implies edginess with exposed seams, fraying fabric edges and distressed finishes.

Dior, Christian (1905 – 1957) French designer who dominated post-World War II fashion with his hourglass-shaped New Look, which debuted in 1947. Pierre Cardin and Yves Saint Laurent both served as his assistants before starting their own houses.

dirndl Dress style that features a tightly fitted bodice, a low neck and a gathered skirt. Also used to describe full skirts with tightly fitted waistbands.

Dolce & Gabbana Italian fashion house started by designers Domenico Dolce (1958 -) and Stefano Gabbana (1962-). Note ampersand in name.

dolman sleeve Sleeve that is wide at the armhole and narrows toward the wrist, often creates the effect of a dropped shoulder.

d'Orsay Shoe style resembling pumps, but with high vamp on the front of the foot and cutout sides, exposing arch of foot.

double-breasted

double-faced

duchesse Soft, heavy type of satin.

dyeing Refers to changing colors.

E

Elizabethan Characteristic of the time when Queen Elizabeth I ruled England in the 16th century. Her ornate neck ruffs, cloaks and jewels helped shape the royal look.

embellishment Decoration on articles of clothing and accessories.

empire waist Waistline hits above the natural waist, sometimes right under the bust. Popular for babydoll tops, evening gowns and maternity clothes.

epaulet Fabric tab that sits on the shoulder, often found on military uniforms and military-inspired fashion.

F

faille Soft fabric with ribbed texture.

Fair Isle sweater Multicolored geometric design in woolen sweaters, originating in the Shetland Islands, off Scotland.

fascinator Headpiece often anchored by a flower or feather, often called a *cocktail hat*.

fashion-forward label

fashion week Capitalize in an official name, such as *New York Fashion Week* or *London Fashion Week*.

Ferragamo, Salvatore (1898 - 1960) Italian shoe designer. Family-owned company, which now includes larger collections of clothing and accessories, continues to operate under his name.

fishnet Fabric often used in lingerie or hosiery, with an open-mesh weave resembling a fishing net.

flair, flare *Flair* is conspicuous talent or style. *Flare* is a curving or spreading outward, as in a skirt.

flannel Soft, brushed-finish fabric, typically made of cotton or wool.

Ford, Tom (1961 -) Former Gucci and Yves Saint Laurent creative director who launched his own fashion, beauty and accessories line in 2006. Also directed the 2006 film "A Single Man."

formfitting

froufrou Fussy or showy dress or ornamentations.

G

Gap Inc. U.S. clothing retailer. Do not use *The Gap*.

gauchos Midcalf length pants with wide legs fashioned after South American cowboys.

Gaultier, Jean Paul (1952 -) French fashion designer and former creative director of Hermes who created costumes for singer Madonna.

gazar Silk organza.

Gibson Girl Illustrator Charles Dana Gibson depicted in his work in the late 1800s and early 1900s the ideal fashionable young American woman.

girlie Connotes young, feminine, flirty.

Givenchy French fashion, beauty and accessories label founded in 1952 and owned by LVMH Moet Hennessy Louis Vuitton SA.

Goth A dark, medieval-inspired style that also borrows elements from Victoriana, mourning clothes and the punk music scene.

gray

Gres, Madame Germaine Emilie Krebs (1903-1993) Parisian couturier who used the name *Madame Gres*. She was considered master of the bias cut and credited with adapting the modern goddess gown. Gres was based on an anagram of her artist husband's first name, Serge. He signed his work Gres.

guayabera Lightweight sport shirt, usually short-sleeved, designed to be worn untucked.

Gucci Italian fashion and leather goods company founded by Guccio Gucci in 1921.

H

Halston Roy Halston Frowick (1932 – 1990) American designer who started as a milliner, famously designing the pillbox hat Jacqueline Kennedy wore on Inauguration Day in 1961. Halston's clothing, though, is more closely associated with the disco era, especially his jersey dresses.

haute couture French term refers to one-of-a-kind clothing produced by design houses that meet criteria established by French

Ministry of Industry. A protected appellation. Used informally to mean fancy, expensive fashion.

headscarf, headscarves

henley Pullover shirt that is collarless, split with a short row of vertical buttons.

high-waisted

hoodie Short for hooded sweatshirt.

houndstooth Large dog-tooth pattern.

I

ikat Printed fabric based on a weaving technique originated in Uzbekistan; pattern created from tie-dyed thread.

indigo Blue dye originally derived from plants in the pea family, often used to color denim. Used to describe deep blue colors with purple overtones.

inverted pleats Pleats are folds of fabric. This style is a stacked box pleat on the inside of a garment so it lies flatter.

J

jabot Ruffled, sometimes-detachable collar on front of a shirt or blouse.

Jacobs, Marc (1963 -) New York-born designer has his own collections and is creative director for French fashion house Louis Vuitton. He is considered an industry showman, staging elaborate runway productions.

Jacquard Fabric with woven pattern, sometimes an elaborate one. In 1801, Joseph Marie Jacquard invented the loom that could control the pattern sequence using punch cards.

K

Karan, Donna (1948 -) New York-born designer who first served as head designer of Anne Klein before launching her own label in 1984. She routinely cites working women and her hometown as her inspirations.

keyhole Peek-a-boo opening used on neckline, front or back of garment. Oblong shape like a keyhole.

kimono Japanese wrap-style robe with wide sleeves and tied with a wide sash, or *obi*.

Klein, Calvin (1942 -) New York-born designer who made as much of a splash with his provocative advertising as his sexy, minimal styles. In 2003, he gave up his role in the company he co-founded in 1968 after a corporate sale to Phillips-Van Heusen Corp.

knife pleat Fold in fabric that creates a fanlike effect. Knife pleats are basic pleating technique.

L

Lagerfeld, Karl (1933 or 1938 -) German-born designer who moved to Paris in his teens. He is best known as the longtime creative director at Chanel but also designs for Fendi and under his own name. Also a photographer, he often shoots his own ad campaigns.

Lauren, Ralph (1939 -) New York-born designer known for polo pony logo and elegant sportswear. He has created a huge public company that has expanded to categories that range from home goods to uniforms for the U.S. Olympic teams.

Le Smoking Menswear-inspired outfit for women created by French designer Yves Saint Laurent. Tuxedo silhouette marked the beginning of an era of sexy, androgynous clothes.

Louboutin, Christian (1963 -) French footwear designer whose trademark is shiny red-lacquered soles.

luxe Luxury.

LVMH Moet Hennessy Louis Vuitton SA. Leading luxury goods conglomerate based in Paris. Parent company of fashion houses Louis Vuitton, Celine, Donna Karan, Givenchy, Marc Jacobs, Fendi and Christian Dior.

Lycra Unless referring to the trademark fiber or fabric, use a generic term such as *spandex* or *elastic* or *stretch fabric*.

M

Macy's Inc. Top U.S. department store chain, with about 850 stores under the Macy's and Bloomingdale's names. Macy's flagship store in Manhattan's Herald Square is the world's largest. The Macy's Thanksgiving Day Parade began in 1924. Formerly Federated Department Stores.

madras Lightweight cotton cloth, usually striped or plaid, originating in India.

maillot One-piece swimming suit or bodysuit.

makeup

mannequin

McQueen, Alexander (1969-2010) British designer who was considered one of the industry's most creative and skillful designers. After his 2010 suicide, his label was taken over by assistant Sarah Burton.

menswear Not men's wear.

miniskirt

monokini Topless swimsuit introduced by Austrian designer Rudi Gernreich in 1964. Term has evolved to describe one-piece swimsuits with deep cutouts.

mousseline Semi-opaque fabric.

N

negligee Light, filmy dressing gown.

Nehru jacket Fitted, single-breasted jacket with standup Mandarin or band collar. Named after late Indian Prime Minister Jawaharlal Nehru.

Neiman Marcus Inc. Dallas-based high-fashion retail stores.

neoprene A synthetic rubber, originally used for gloves and wetsuits, incorporated into figure-hugging apparel.

New Look 1947 silhouette by French designer Christian Dior, with a nipped waist and full skirt that ushered in a different post-World War II style.

notched lapel Flap on front of a jacket that is common to business suits and tuxedos.

nude Avoid as a description of a color. Use more specific terms, such as *champagne* and *sand*.

nylon Not a trademark.

O

ombre Effect created by dip dyeing fabric with various gradations. Sometimes called *degrade*. Color appears lighter in some spots and darker in others. It can be done with more than one color, but shading a single color is more common.

opera gloves Over-the-elbow gloves, known in French as *mousquetaire gloves*, inspired by the gauntlets worn by musketeers in the 19th century.

organza Sheer and delicate, yet stiff, fabric.

Orlon Trademark for a form of acrylic fiber, similar to nylon.

overlay Outer layer of a garment.

P

paillette Flat sequin.

palette Color range.

pantsuit

passe

peacoat Double-breasted, hip-length coat with slash pockets and notched lapels, often made of heavy wool.

peplum Flounce of fabric that juts out just above the hips, typically on a fitted fabric or dress.

plait Braiding of hair.

pleat Fold in fabric.

plus-size clothing But *plus size* when used alone.

polka dot (n.) **polka-dot** (adj.)

pompom Ornamental ball or tuft on clothing; also crepe paper ball waved by cheerleaders.

portrait collar Open neckline that is wider than it is deep. It provides both a frame and blank space around the face, drawing the eye upward.

pouf, poufy, pouffed Any part of a garment with excess, gathered fabric.

Prada, Miuccia (1949 -) Italian designer whose usually minimalist designs largely set broader fashion trends. Prada, the brand, was founded in 1913 by her grandfather, Mario, as a leather company.

Proenza Schouler American designers Jack McCollough and Lazaro Hernandez founded their company — named after their mothers' maiden names — in 2002, after selling their final project for Parsons School of Design to Barneys New York.

pret-a-porter line Designer clothing sold ready-to-wear.

Q

Quant, Mary (1934 -) British designer whose miniskirts — a silhouette some credit her with inventing — epitomized Swinging London in the 1960s.

queens *Elizabethan* and *Victorian* refer to Britain's Queen Elizabeth I, who ruled in the 16th century, and Queen Victoria, 19th-century ruler. Elizabeth's ornate neck ruffs, cloaks and jewels helped shape the royal look. Queen Victoria moved from oversized crinoline-cage garments with high collars to a sleeker, elongated shape with a lower neckline.

quilting Sewing technique, initially used for bedding, now part of popular fashion. Quilted garments have three layers, two pieces of fabric as well as insular batting, sewn together with visible, often artful, stitching.

R

rayon Not a trademark.

riding pants Pants with roomy hips and tight-fitting legs started for equestrians. Modern fashion has interpreted them with an exaggerated shape. Also *jodhpurs*.

Reard, Louis (1897-1984) French creator of the bikini was, by trade, an auto engineer.

Rodarte California-based clothing company founded by sisters Kate and Laura Mulleavy.

ruching Detail of gathered fabric, often at a seam and, in particular, on the sides of the bodice.

S

Saint Laurent, Yves (1936 – 2008) Algerian-born designer who popularized many silhouettes that have since become fashion classics, including menswear for women, trapeze dresses, safari jackets and peasant skirts. He opened his own house in Paris in 1962 after years as Christian Dior's assistant and then hand-picked successor. When Hedi Slimane took over as creative director in 2012, the name for collections and garments changed to Saint Laurent Paris.

Saks Fifth Avenue Inc. Upscale retail store owned by Hudson's Bay Co. Flagship store is on Fifth Avenue in Manhattan. No apostrophe.

Savile Row Shopping street in London known for its bespoke tailoring.

serape Shawl or blanket worn as a cloak in Latin America.

shapewear Undergarments that mold the body's appearance; the 2000s brought a surge in popularity with improved shaping fabrics.

sheath Dress silhouette that is long and lean with a nipped waist, usually without a waistband, to create an hourglass shape.

shirtdress

shirt sleeve, shirt sleeves (n.) **shirt-sleeve** (adj.)

sizes Use figures: *a size 8 dress, size 40 long, 10 1/2B shoes, a 34 1/2 sleeve.*

sleeve (n.) That part of a garment that covers an arm or part of an arm.

sleeved (adj.) Fitted with sleeves, often in hyphenated compounds: *short-sleeved.*

soigne Elegant, well-groomed.

soiree Party or gathering in the evening.

spandex See **Lycra**.

spectator Style of two-tone shoes. Men's are typically wing-tips and women's are pumps with wing tip-style perforation and details.

super-skinny

supermodel

sweatpants, sweatshirt, sweatsuit

T

tie-dye

Tiffany & Co. New York-based jewelry stores. No apostrophe.

trapeze Short dress style with narrow shoulders and a bodice that flares out in a trapezoid shape.

trenchcoat

T-shirt Acceptable to use *tee* on subsequent references.

tulip skirt Skirt shape that mimics an upside-down tulip; waist and hemline are similar widths.

tulle Fine net material used to make veils and dresses.

twin set Pairing of cardigan and crewneck sweaters.

U

underlay Underneath layer of a garment, often under a sheer fabric.

unitard Tight-fitting body stocking covering legs, torso and usually arms.

utilitarian Inspired by practical clothing. Cargo pants, ripstop nylon and hoodies have become fashionable details.

V

valise Small travel case with handles.

Velcro Trademark for a nylon material that can be pressed together or pulled apart for easy fastening and unfastening. Use a generic term such as *fabric fastener.*

Versace Fashion house based in Milan, Italy, known for super sexy styles. Founded in 1978 by Gianni

Versace; his younger sister Donatella took over as creative director when he was murdered in 1997.

Victorian Characteristic of the reign of England's Queen Victoria from 1837 to 1901. Victoria moved from oversized crinoline-cage garments with high collars to a sleeker, elongated shape with a lower neckline.

Victoria's Secret American retailer of lingerie founded in 1977.

vintage Term to describe clothes from another era. Antique clothes need to be more than 100 years old; vintage clothes are generally assumed to be newer but older than the most recent decade.

V-neck (n. and adj.)

von Furstenberg, Diane (1946 -) Belgian-born American fashion designer known for the wrap dress.

Vuitton, Louis French fashion house founded in 1854, known for its monogrammed products that include shoes, leather goods, clothing and trunks. Owned by LVMH Moet Hennessy Louis Vuitton SA.

W

Wang, Alexander (1983 -) American fashion designer and creative director for Balenciaga.

wash and wear Clothes that can be cleaned with soap and water, dried and worn without ironing.

-wear *Activewear, daywear, eveningwear, eyewear, headwear, menswear, outerwear, sportswear, swimwear, womenswear.*

windbreaker

Wintour, Anna (1949 -) British-born editor-in-chief of American Vogue magazine since 1988. Widely considered the most powerful person in fashion, making or breaking trends and careers.

womenswear Not *women's wear*.

wool

Wu, Jason (1982 -) Taiwanese-born, New York-based designer launched his first collection in 2006. Rose to stardom when first lady Michelle Obama wore a one-shoulder white gown designed by him to presidential inaugural balls in 2009.

Y

Yamamoto, Yohji (1943 -) Japanese designer whose signature style is skewed proportions. He was introduced to the mainstream via his Y-3 collaboration with German sportswear maker Adidas AG.

yoke Line across the shoulders or hips that creates a more fitted shape.

Z

zebra print Print that mimics the black-and-white stripes of a zebra. Zebra, cheetah and leopard prints became trends in the 1960s and are now considered classics.

zigzag

zoot suit Exaggerated style of long jackets and full, high-waisted

pants worn mostly by young black
and Latino men in the 1940s.

RELIGION GUIDELINES

A

abaya Robe-like outer garment worn by Muslim women.

Advent Period including the four Sundays preceding Christmas.

Adventist See **Seventh-day Adventist Church**.

agnostic, atheist An *agnostic* is a person who believes it is impossible to know whether there is a God.

An *atheist* is a person who believes there is no God.

Al-Aqsa The mosque completed in the eighth century atop the Haram al-Sharif, or *Noble Sanctuary*, in the Old City of Jerusalem; Arabs also use *Al-Aqsa* to refer to the whole area, which houses the Dome of the Rock shrine, too. To Jews the area is known as the *Temple Mount*, the site of the ancient Jewish temples.

Allah The Arabic word for God. The word *God* should be used, unless the Arabic name is used in a quote written or spoken in English.

Allahu akbar The Arabic phrase for *God is great*.

altar, alter An *altar* is a tablelike platform used in a religious service.
To alter is to change.

Anglican Communion The name for the worldwide association of national Anglican churches.

Each national church is independent. A special position of honor is accorded to the archbishop of Canterbury, as the pre-eminent officer in the original Anglican body, the Church of England.

The test of membership in the Anglican Communion traditionally has been whether a church has been in communion with the See of Canterbury. No legislative or juridical ties exist, however.

BELIEFS: Anglicans believe in the Trinity, the humanity and divinity of Christ, the virginity of Mary, salvation through Christ, and everlasting heaven and hell.

A principal difference between Roman Catholics and Anglicans is still the dispute that led to the formation of the Church of England — refusal to acknowledge that the pope, as bishop of Rome, has ruling authority over other bishops. See **catholic, catholicism**.

ANGLICAN CHURCHES: Members of the Anglican Communion, in addition to the Church of England, include the Scottish Episcopal Church, the Anglican Church of Canada, and, in the United States, the Episcopal Church.
See **Episcopal Church**.

Antichrist, anti-Christ
Antichrist is the proper name for the individual the Bible says will challenge Christ.

The adjective *anti-Christ* would be applied to someone or something opposed to Christ.

Antiochian Orthodox Christian Archdiocese of North America Formed in 1975 by the merger of the Antiochian Orthodox Christian Archdiocese of New York and All North America and the Archdiocese of Toledo, Ohio, and Dependencies in North America. It is under the jurisdiction of the patriarch of Antioch.

See **Eastern Orthodox churches**.

apostolic delegate, papal nuncio An *apostolic delegate* is a Roman Catholic diplomat chosen by the pope to be his envoy to the church in a nation that does not have formal diplomatic relations with the Vatican.

A *papal nuncio* is the pope's envoy to a nation with which the Vatican has diplomatic relations.

archbishop See **Episcopal Church**; **Roman Catholic Church**; and **religious titles**.

archbishop of Canterbury In general, lowercase *archbishop* unless it is used before the name of the individual who holds the office.

Capitalize *Archbishop of Canterbury* standing alone only when it is used in a story that also refers to members of Britain's nobility. See **nobility** in the A-Z section for the relevant guidelines.

archdiocese Capitalize as part of a proper name: *the Archdiocese of Chicago, the Chicago Archdiocese.* Lowercase when it stands alone.

See the entry for the particular denomination in question.

Armenian Church of America The term encompasses two independent dioceses that cooperate in some activities. The Eastern Diocese of the Armenian Church of America serves much of the U.S., while the Western Diocese of the Armenian Church of America serves California, Washington, Nevada, New Mexico, Utah and Arizona.

Ashoura The Shiite Muslim commemoration marking the death of Hussein, the grandson of the Prophet Muhammad, at the Battle of Karbala in present-day Iraq in the seventh century.

Ash Wednesday The first day of Lent, 46 days before Easter. See **Easter** and **Lent**.

B

Baha'i A monotheistic religion founded in the 1860s by Baha'u'llah, a Persian nobleman considered a prophet by the Baha'is. Baha'u'llah taught that all religions represent progressive stages in the revelation of God's will, leading to the unity of all people and faiths. The Baha'is have no clergy; they are governed by local, national and international elected councils. The international governing body, the Universal House of Justice, is based in Haifa, Israel. Its U.S. offices are in Evanston, Illinois.

baptism See **sacraments**.

Baptist churches It is incorrect to apply the term church to any Baptist unit except the local church.

There are a wide range of Baptist bodies in the U.S. with varied beliefs and practices.

The largest is the Southern Baptist Convention; most of its members are in the South, although it has churches nationwide. The largest predominantly Northern body is American Baptist Churches in the U.S.A.

Three other large Baptist bodies are predominantly African-American: the National Baptist Convention of America, the National Baptist Convention U.S.A. Inc., and the Progressive National Baptist Convention Inc.

Other Baptist groups include the Cooperative Baptist Fellowship, formed in the 1990s by Southern Baptists who disagreed with the denomination's conservative direction, and the Baptist World Alliance, an international voluntary association for Baptists located in the Washington, D.C. area.

CLERGY: All members of the Baptist clergy may be referred to as *ministers*. *Pastor* applies if a minister leads a congregation.

On first reference, use *the Rev.* before the name of a man or woman. On second reference, use only the last name.

See **religious titles**.

See **religious movements** for definitions of some descriptive terms that often apply to Baptists but are not limited to them.

bar mitzvah The Jewish rite of passage and family celebration that marks a boy's 13th birthday. A similar ceremony for girls is held at age 12 and called the *bat mitzvah* or *bas mitzvah*. Many, but not all, branches of Judaism, hold the ceremony for girls. Judaism regards the age as a benchmark of religious maturity. Bar mitzvah translates as "one who is responsible for the Commandments."

Bible Capitalize, without quotation marks, when referring to the Scriptures in the Old Testament or the New Testament. Capitalize also related terms such as the *Gospels, Gospel of St. Mark, the Scriptures, the Holy Scriptures*.

Lowercase *biblical* in all uses.

Lowercase *bible* as a nonreligious term: *My dictionary is my bible.*

Do not abbreviate individual books of the Bible.

Old Testament is a Christian designation; Hebrew Bible or Jewish Bible is the appropriate term for stories dealing with Judaism alone.

The standard names and order of Old Testament books as they appear

in Protestant Bibles are: Genesis, Exodus, Leviticus, Numbers, Deuteronomy, Joshua, Judges, Ruth, 1 Samuel, 2 Samuel, 1 Kings, 2 Kings, 1 Chronicles, 2 Chronicles, Ezra, Nehemiah, Esther, Job, Psalms, Proverbs, Ecclesiastes, Song of Solomon, Isaiah, Jeremiah, Lamentations, Ezekiel, Daniel, Hosea, Joel, Amos, Obadiah, Jonah, Micah, Nahum, Habakkuk, Zephaniah, Haggai, Zechariah, Malachi.

Jewish Bibles contain the same 39 books, in different order. Roman Catholic Bibles follow a different order, usually use some different names and include the seven Deuterocanonical books (called the Apocrypha by Protestants): Tobit, Judith, 1 Maccabees, 2 Maccabees, Wisdom, Sirach, Baruch.

The books of the New Testament, in order: Matthew, Mark, Luke, John, Acts, Romans, 1 Corinthians, 2 Corinthians, Galatians, Ephesians, Philippians, Colossians, 1 Thessalonians, 2 Thessalonians, 1 Timothy, 2 Timothy, Titus, Philemon, Hebrews, James, 1 Peter, 2 Peter, 1 John, 2 John, 3 John, Jude, Revelation.

Citation listing the number of chapter and verse(s) use this form: *Matthew 3:16, Luke 21:1-13, 1 Peter 2:1.*

Bible-believing Do not use the term to distinguish one faction from another, because all Christians believe in the Bible. The differences are over interpretations.

Bible Belt Those sections of the United States, especially in the South and Middle West, where strictly conservative Christian beliefs prevail. The term was believed to be coined by H.L. Mencken as a derisive commentary on fundamentalism. The term should be used with care, because in certain contexts it can give offense.

bishop See **religious titles** and the entry for the denomination in question.

Blessed Sacrament, Blessed Virgin

B'nai B'rith See **fraternal organizations and service clubs** in the A-Z section.

Brahman, Brahmin

Brahman applies to the priestly Hindu caste and a breed of cattle.

Brahmin applies to aristocracy in general: *Boston Brahmin*.

See **Hindu, Hinduism.**

Buddha, Buddhism

The religion founded in India around 500 B.C. based on the teachings of Siddhartha Gautama, who was called Buddha, or enlightened one, by his followers.

Buddhism is considered the world's fourth-largest religious tradition. The overwhelming majority of Buddhists live in the Asia-Pacific region. About half live in China.

Countries with Buddhist majorities include Thailand, Cambodia and Myanmar. Small communities of Buddhists can be found in North America and Europe.

Buddhists believe that right, or virtuous, thinking and behavior can liberate people from suffering. Nirvana is the state of ultimate enlightenment and peace. Until nirvana is reached, believers cannot be freed from the cycle of death and rebirth.

There are many variants of Buddhist practice and teaching, but scholars generally categorize the streams as:

—Mahayana Buddhism. Prevalent in China, Japan, South Korea and Vietnam. Stresses enlightenment is possible for all.

—Theravada Buddhism. Found in countries such as Thailand, Myanmar and Sri Lanka. Stresses monastic discipline and meditation.

—Vajrayana Buddhism. Concentrated in Tibet, Nepal and Mongolia. Sometimes called Tibetan Buddhism.

burqa The all-covering dress worn by some Muslim women.

C

cantor See **Jewish congregations.**

cardinal See **Roman Catholic Church.**

Catholic, Catholicism

Use *Roman Catholic Church, Roman Catholic* or *Roman Catholicism* in the first references to those who believe that the pope, as bishop of Rome, has the ultimate authority in administering an earthly organization founded by Jesus Christ.

Most subsequent references may be condensed to *Catholic Church, Catholic* or *Catholicism. Roman Catholic* should continue to be used, however, if the context requires a distinction between Roman Catholics and members of other denominations who often describe themselves as Catholic. They include some high church Episcopalians (who often call themselves *Anglo-Catholics*), members of Eastern Orthodox churches, and members of some national Catholic churches that have broken with Rome. Included in this last category is the Polish National Catholic Church.

Lowercase *catholic* where used in its generic sense of general or universal, meanings derived from a similar word in Greek.

Those who use *Catholic* in a religious sense are indicating their belief that they are members of a universal church that Jesus Christ left on Earth.

See **Roman Catholic Church**.

celebrant, celebrator Reserve *celebrant* for someone who conducts a religious rite: *He was the celebrant of the Mass.*

Use *celebrator* for someone having a good time: *The celebrators kept the party going until 3 a.m.*

Central Conference of American Rabbis See **Jewish congregations**.

charismatic groups See **religious movements**.

Christian Church (Disciples of Christ) The parentheses and the words they surround are part of the formal name.

The body owes its origins to an early-19th-century frontier movement to unify Christians.

The Disciples, led by Alexander Campbell in western Pennsylvania, and the Christians, led by Barton W. Stone in Kentucky, merged in 1832.

The local church is the basic organizational unit.

National policies are developed by the General Assembly, made up of representatives chosen by local churches and regional organizations.

All members of the clergy may be referred to as *ministers*. *Pastor* applies if a minister leads a congregation.

On first reference, use *the Rev.* before the name of a man or woman. On second reference, use only the last name.

Christian Science Church See **Church of Christ, Scientist**.

Christmas, Christmas Day Dec. 25. The federal legal holiday is observed on Friday if Dec. 25 falls on a Saturday, on Monday if it falls on a Sunday.

Never abbreviate *Christmas* to *Xmas* or any other form.

Christmastime One word.

Christmas tree Lowercase *tree* and other seasonal terms with *Christmas*: *card, wreath, carol*, etc. Exception: *National Christmas Tree*.

church Capitalize as part of the formal name of a building, a congregation or a denomination; lowercase in other uses: *St. Mary's Church, the Roman Catholic Church, the Catholic and Episcopal churches, a Roman Catholic church, a church.*

Lowercase in phrases where the church is used in an institutional sense: *She believes in the separation of church and state. The pope said the church opposes abortion.*

See **religious titles** and the entry for the denomination in question.

Churches of Christ Thousands of independent U.S. congregations cooperate under this name. Each local church is autonomous and operates under a governing board of elders. The minister is an *evangelist*, addressed by members as *Brother*. The ministers do not use clergy titles. Do not precede their names by a title.

The churches do not regard themselves as a denomination. Rather, they stress a nondenominational effort to preach what they consider basic Bible teachings and they restrict worship activities to those they've identified in the New Testament. For this reason, they generally exclude instrumental music from worship. The churches also teach that baptism by immersion is essential for salvation.

Within the U.S., the churches are concentrated in the South and

Southwest. But many of the churches are located overseas, in countries such as India.

See **religious movements**.

churchgoer

Church of Christ, Scientist

This denomination was founded in 1879 by Mary Baker Eddy. Her teachings are contained in "Science and Health with Key to the Scriptures," which, along with the Bible, she ordained as the "dual and impersonal pastor" of the church.

The Mother Church in Boston is the international headquarters. Its government provides for a board of directors, which transacts the business of the Mother Church.

A branch church, governed by its own democratically chosen board, is named First Church of Christ, Scientist, or Second Church, etc., according to the order of its establishment in a community.

The terms *Christian Science Church* or *Churches of Christ, Scientist*, are acceptable in all references to the denomination.

The word *Christian* is used because its teachings are based on the word and works of Jesus Christ. The word *Science* is used to reflect the concept that the laws of God are replicable and can be proved in healing sickness and sin.

The church is composed entirely of lay members and does not have clergy in the usual sense. Both men and women may serve as *readers*, *practitioners*, or *lecturers*.

The preferred form for these titles is to use a construction that sets them off from a name with commas. Capitalize them only when used as a formal title immediately before a name. Do not continue use of the title in subsequent references.

The terms *reverend* and *minister* are not applicable. Do not use *the Rev.* in any references.

See **religious titles**.

Church of England See Anglican Communion.

Church of Jesus Christ of Latter-day Saints, The

Note the capitalization and punctuation of *Latter-day*. *Mormon church*, *LDS church* or the *Latter-day Saints* can be used, but the official name is preferred in first reference in a story dealing primarily with church activities.

Members are referred to as *Latter-day Saints* or *Mormons*, the latter based on the church's sacred Book of Mormon.

The church is based on revelations that Joseph Smith said were brought to him in the 1820s by heavenly messengers.

The headquarters is in Salt Lake City, but millions of its members live outside the U.S.

Church hierarchy is composed of men known as general authorities. Among them, the policymaking body is the First Presidency, made up of a president and two or more counselors. It has final authority in all church matters.

CLERGY: All worthy young men over the age of 12 are members of the priesthood. They can be ordained elders after age 18, usually after graduating from high school and before serving as missionaries. They may later become high priests, or bishops.

The only formal titles are *president* (for members of the First Presidency), *bishop* (for members of the Presiding Bishopric and for local bishops) and *elder* (for other general authorities and church missionaries). Capitalize these formal titles before a name on first reference; use only the last name on second reference.

The terms *minister* or *the Rev.* are not used.

See **religious titles**.

SPLINTER GROUPS: The term Mormon is not properly applied to the other Latter Day Saints churches that resulted from the split after Smith's death.

This includes polygamous groups. The LDS church renounced polygamy in 1890.

One splinter group is the Community of Christ, headquartered in Independence, Missouri. From 1860 to 2001, it was called the Reorganized Church of Jesus Christ of Latter Day Saints (note the lack of a hyphen and the capitalized Day).

College of Cardinals See **Roman Catholic Church**.

conclave A private or secret meeting. In the Roman Catholic Church it describes the private meeting of cardinals to elect a pope.

confirmation See **sacraments**.

Conservative Judaism See **Jewish congregations**.

Coptic Christian The Coptic Orthodox Church traces its origins to the Apostle Mark in first century Alexandria. The word Copt is derived from the Greek word for Egypt. Coptic Christians generally share the beliefs of other Orthodox churches, but have some distinct teachings, mainly concerning Christology, or the nature of Christ. There are no definitive statistics for the Coptic Christian population, but they are considered to be the largest Christian community in the Mideast. Scholars estimate that Copts comprise 10 percent of the Egyptian population, or 8.5 million

people. Significant diaspora Coptic Christian communities can be found in the United States, Canada and Australia.

curate See **religious titles**.

Curia See **Roman Catholic Church**.

D

dalai lama The traditional high priest of Tibetan Buddhism. *Dalai lama* is a title rather than a name, but it is all that is used when referring to the man. Capitalize *Dalai Lama* in references to the holder of the title, in keeping with the principles outlined in the **nobility** entry. The title is lowercase in generic references to the religion and history.

deacon See the entry for the individual's denomination.

deity Lowercase. See **gods** and **religious references**.

devil But capitalize *Satan*.

diocese Capitalize as part of a proper name: *the Diocese of Rochester*, *the Rochester Diocese*, *the diocese*.

See **Episcopal Church** and **Roman Catholic Church**.

Druze A tradition that developed from a medieval sect of Shiite Islam. The religion draws from Christian, Muslim and Jewish beliefs and was influenced by gnosticism, with believers divided into two main classes: the "initiated" who have studied the faith's sacred writings and serve as authorities, and the "uninitiated" who comprise the majority of Druze.

The Druze call themselves the "People of Unity." The exact number of Druze is not known, but they are concentrated in Syria, Lebanon and Israel, with diaspora populations in Europe, North America, Australia and elsewhere.

E

Easter Christian holy day commemorating the resurrection of Jesus Christ. Christians believe Jesus was raised from the dead three days after his crucifixion.

Western Christian churches and most Orthodox Christian churches follow different calendars and observe Easter on different dates.

Eastern Orthodox churches

The term applies to a group of churches that have roots in the earliest days of Christianity and do not recognize papal authority over their activities.

Churches in this tradition were part of the undivided Christendom that existed until the Great Schism of 1054. At that time, many of the churches in the western half of the old Roman Empire accorded the bishop of Rome supremacy over other bishops. The result was a split between eastern and western churches.

The autonomous churches that constitute Eastern Orthodoxy are organized along mostly national lines. They recognize the patriarch of Constantinople (modern-day Istanbul) as their leader. He convenes councils, but his authority is otherwise that of a "first among equals."

Eastern orthodox churches include the Greek Orthodox Church and the Russian Orthodox Church.

In the United States, organizational lines are rooted in the national backgrounds of various ethnic groups, such as the Greek Orthodox Archdiocese of America, and the Orthodox Church in America, which includes people of Bulgarian, Romanian, Russian and Syrian descent.

The churches have their own disciplines on matters such as married clergy — a married man may be ordained, but a priest may not marry after ordination.

Some of these churches call the archbishop who leads them a *metropolitan*; others use the term *patriarch*. He normally heads the principal archdiocese within a nation. Working with him are other archbishops, bishops, priests and deacons.

Archbishops and bishops frequently follow a monastic tradition in which they are known only by a first name. When no last name is used, repeat the title before the sole name in subsequent references.

Some forms: *Metropolitan Tikhon, archbishop of Washington and metropolitan of America and Canada*. On second reference: *Metropolitan Tikhon. Archbishop* may be replaced by *the Most Rev.* on first reference. *Bishop* may be replaced by *the Rt. Rev.* on first reference.

Use *the Rev.* before the name of a priest on first reference.

See **religious titles**.

Eastern rite churches

The term applies to a group of Catholic churches that had been organized along ethnic lines traceable to the churches established during the earliest days of Christianity.

These churches accept the authority of the pope, but they have considerable autonomy in ritual and questions of discipline such as married clergy — a married man may be ordained, but marriage is not permitted after ordination.

Among the churches of the Eastern rite are the Antiochean-Maronite, Armenian Catholic, Byzantine-Byelorussian, Byzantine-Russian, Byzantine-Ruthenian, Byzantine-Ukrainian and Chaldean Catholic.

Eid al-Adha Meaning "Feast of Sacrifice," this most important Islamic holiday marks the willingness of the Prophet Ibrahim (Abraham to Christians and Jews) to sacrifice his son. During the holiday, which in most places lasts four days, Muslims slaughter sheep or cattle, distribute part of the meat to the poor and eat the rest. The holiday begins on the 10th day of the Islamic lunar month of Dhul-Hijja, during the annual hajj pilgrimage to Mecca.

Eid al-Fitr A three-day holiday marking the end of Ramadan, Islam's holy month of fasting.

elder For its use in religious contexts, see the entry for an individual's denomination.

Episcopal Church Acceptable in all references for *the Episcopal Church*, the U.S. national church that is a member of the Anglican Communion.

The church is governed nationally by two bodies — the permanent Executive Council and the General Convention, which meets every three years.

After the council, the principal organizational units are, in descending order of size, provinces, dioceses or missionary districts, local parishes and local missions.

The Executive Council is composed of bishops, priests, laymen and laywomen. One bishop is designated leader of the church and holds the formal title of presiding bishop.

The General Convention has final authority in matters of policy and doctrine. All acts must pass both of its houses — the House of Bishops and the House of Deputies. The latter is composed of an equal number of clergy and lay delegates from each diocese.

A province is composed of several dioceses. Each has a provincial synod made up of a house of bishops and a house of deputies. The synod's primary duty is to coordinate the work of the church in its area.

Within a diocese, a bishop is the principal official. He is helped by the Diocesan Convention, which consists of all the clergy in the diocese and lay representatives from each parish.

The parish or local church is governed by a vestry, composed of the pastor and lay members elected by the congregation.

The clergy consists of bishops, priests, deacons and brothers. A priest who heads a parish is described as a *rector* rather than a pastor.

For first reference to bishops, use *Bishop* before the individual's name: *Bishop Rob Wright*. An acceptable alternative in referring to U.S. bishops is *the Rt. Rev.* The designation *the Most Rev.* is used before the names of the archbishops of Canterbury and York.

For first references, use *the Rev.* before the name of a priest, *Deacon* before the name of a deacon.

See **Anglican Communion** and **religious titles**.

Episcopal, Episcopalian *Episcopal* is the adjective form; use *Episcopalian* only as a noun referring to a member of the Episcopal Church: *She is an Episcopalian*. But: *She is an Episcopal priest*.

Capitalize *Episcopal* when referring to the Episcopal Church. Use lowercase when the reference is simply to a body governed by bishops.

evangelical See **religious movements**.

Evangelical Friends Alliance See **Quakers**.

evangelism See **religious movements**.

evangelist Capitalize only in reference to the men credited with writing the Gospels: *The four Evangelists were Matthew, Mark, Luke and John.*

In lowercase, it means a preacher who makes a profession of seeking conversions. Often confused with the term *evangelical*. See **evangelical**.

exorcise, exorcism

F

father Use *the Rev.* in first reference before the names of Episcopal, Orthodox and Roman Catholic priests. Use *Father* before a name only in direct quotations.

See **religious titles**.

fundamentalist See **religious movements**.

G

gentile Generally, any person not Jewish; often, specifically a Christian. But to Mormons it is anyone not a Mormon.

gods and goddesses Capitalize *God* in references to the deity of all monotheistic religions. Capitalize all noun references to the deity: *God the Father, Holy Ghost, Holy Spirit, Allah,* etc. Lowercase personal pronouns: *he, him, thee, thou.*

Lowercase *gods* and *goddesses* in references to the deities of polytheistic religions.

Lowercase *god, gods* and *goddesses* in references to false gods: *He made money his god.*

See **religious references**.

Good Friday The Friday before Easter.

Gospel(s), gospel Capitalize when referring to any or all of the first four books of the New Testament: *the Gospel of St. John, the Gospels.*

Lowercase in other references: *She is a famous gospel singer.*

Greek Orthodox Church See **Eastern Orthodox churches**.

gurdwara A house of worship in the Sikh religion where the faith's scriptures are stored.

H

Hades But lowercase *hell.*

hajj The pilgrimage to Mecca required of every Muslim who can afford it and is physically able to make it. The person making the *hajj* is a *hajji.*

halal Arabic for *permitted* or *lawful.* The word is used to describe foods allowed under Islamic dietary laws. Always lowercase.

hallelujah Lowercase the biblical praise to God, but capitalize in composition titles: Handel's "Hallelujah" chorus.

Hanukkah The Jewish Festival of Lights, an eight-day commemoration of rededication of the Temple by the Maccabees after their victory over the Syrians.

Usually occurs in December but sometimes falls in late November.

Haram al-Sharif Arabic for *Noble Sanctuary*, the Muslim name for the walled, elevated area in Jerusalem's Old City that was the site of the ancient Jewish temples. Better known as the *Temple Mount*, the area now houses the centuries-old Dome of the Rock shrine and Al-Aqsa mosque. Muslims believe Prophet Muhammad made his night journey to heaven from the site.

heaven

hell But capitalize *Hades*.

hijab The headscarf worn by some Muslim women.

Hindu, Hinduism The dominant religion of India and the world's third-largest religion, after Christianity and Islam.

Nearly all the world's 1.1 billion Hindus live in India, Nepal, Bangladesh, Indonesia, Malaysia and the United States. They are a majority in India, Nepal and Mauritius. The original Hindu scriptures are called the Vedas.

Hindus believe the soul never dies, but is reborn — in either human or animal form — each time the body dies. Under the Hindu rule of karma, a person's every action and thought will affect how the soul is reborn. The cycle of death and rebirth continues until a soul reaches spiritual perfection, and can then be united in total enlightenment and peace, known as nirvana, with the supreme being, ending the cycle.

Hindus believe in one supreme being who is represented in different gods and goddesses. The primary gods are Brahma, the creator; Vishnu, the preserver; and Siva, the destroyer. Vishnu has had important human incarnations such as Krishna and Rama.

The primary goddess is Devi, who has several manifestations including Durga, Kali, Sarasvati and Lakshmi. She represents in her forms either motherhood and good fortune or destruction. There are thousands of other deities and saints that also may receive prayers and offerings.

Hindus also believe that animals have souls and many are worshipped as manifestations of god.

There are thousands of sects. There is no formal clergy.

holidays and holy days Capitalize them: *New Year's Eve, New Year's Day, Groundhog Day, Easter, Hanukkah*, etc.

The federal legal holidays are New Year's, Martin Luther King Jr. Day, Washington's Birthday, Memorial Day, Independence Day, Labor Day, Columbus Day, Veterans Day, Thanksgiving and Christmas. See individual entries for the official dates and when they are observed if they fall on a weekend.

The designation of a day as a federal legal holiday means that federal employees receive the day off or are paid overtime if they must work. Other requirements that may apply to holidays generally are left to the states. Many follow the federal lead in designating a holiday, but they are not required to do so.

Holy Communion See **sacraments**.

Holy Father The preferred form is to use *the pope* or *the pontiff*, or to give the individual's name.

Use *Holy Father* in direct quotations or special contexts where a particular literary effect is desired.

Holy Land Capitalize the biblical region.

holy orders See **sacraments**.

Holy See The headquarters of the Roman Catholic Church in Vatican City.

Holy Spirit Preferred over *Holy Ghost* in most usage.

I

iftar The breaking of the daily fast during the holy Islamic month of Ramadan.

imam Lowercase when describing the leader of a prayer in a Muslim mosque. Capitalize before a name when used as the formal title for a Muslim leader or ruler.
See **religious titles**.

Inner Light See **Quakers**.

Islam Followers are called Muslims. Their holy book is the Quran, which according to Islamic belief was revealed by Allah (God) to the Prophet Muhammad in the seventh century in Mecca and Medina. The place of worship is a mosque. The weekly holy day is Friday.

It is the religion of more than 1 billion people in the world, making it the world's second-largest faith, after Christianity. Although Arabic is the language of the Quran and Muslim prayers, not all Arabs are Muslims and not all Muslims are Arabs. Most of the world's Muslims live in a wide belt that stretches halfway around the world: across West Africa and North Africa, through the Arab countries of the Middle East and on to Turkey, Iran, Afghanistan, Pakistan and other Asian countries, parts of the former Soviet Union and western China, to Indonesia and the southern Philippines.

There are two major divisions in Islam:

—*Sunni* The biggest single sect in Islam, comprising about 85 percent of all Muslims. Nations with Sunni majorities include Egypt, Saudi Arabia and most other Arab nations, as well as non-Arab Turkey and Afghanistan. Most Palestinian Muslims and most West African Muslims are Sunnis.

The Saudis sometimes are referred to as Wahhabi Muslims. This is a subgroup within the Sunni branch of Islam.

—*Shiite* The second-largest sect. Iran is the only nation with an overwhelming Shiite majority. Iraq, Lebanon and Bahrain have large Shiite communities, in proportion to their overall populations.

(The schism between Sunni and Shiite stems from the early days of Islam and arguments over Muhammad's successors as caliph, the spiritual and temporal leader of Muslims during that period. The Shiites wanted the caliphate to descend through Ali, Muhammad's son-in-law. Ali eventually became the fourth caliph, but he was murdered; Ali's son al-Hussein was massacred with his fighters at Karbala, in what is now Iraq. Shiites considered the later caliphs to be usurpers. The Sunnis no longer have a caliph.)

Titles for the clergy vary from sect to sect and from country to country, but these are the most common:

Grand Mufti — The highest authority in Quranic law and interpretation, a title used mostly by Sunnis.

Sheikh — Used by most clergymen in the same manner that the Rev. is used as a Christian clerical title, especially common among Sunnis. (Not all sheikhs are clergymen. *Sheikh* can also be a secular title of respect or nobility.)

Ayatollah — Used by Shiites, especially in Iran, to denote senior clergymen, such as *Ayatollah Ruhollah Khomeini.*

Hojatoleslam — A rank below ayatollah.

Mullah — Lower-level clergy.

Imam — Used by some sects as a title for the prayer leader at a mosque. Among the Shiites, it usually has a more exalted connotation.

The adjective is *Islamic. Islamist* is an advocate of political Islam, the philosophy that the Quran should rule all aspects of life — religious, political and personal. *Islamic fundamentalist* should not be used as a synonym for *Islamic militant* or *radical.*

Islamic holy days See **Ashoura**, **Eid al-Adha**, **Eid al-Fitr** and **Ramadan**. Because the Muslim faith operates on the lunar calendar, these commemorations fall on different days each year on the Western calendar.

Islamist An advocate or supporter of a political movement that favors reordering government and society in accordance with laws prescribed by Islam. Do not use as a synonym for *Islamic fighters, militants, extremists* or *radicals,* who may or may not be Islamists. Where possible, be specific and use the name of militant affiliations: *al-Qaida-linked, Hezbollah, Taliban,* etc. Those who view the Quran as a political model encompass a wide range of Muslims, from mainstream politicians to militants known as jihadis.

J

Jehovah's Witnesses The denomination was founded in Pittsburgh in 1872 by Charles Taze Russell, a former Congregationalist layman.

Witnesses do most of their work through three legal corporations: the Watch Tower Bible and Tract Society of Pennsylvania, the Watchtower Bible and Tract Society of New York Inc., and, in England, the International Bible Students Association. A governing body consisting largely of the principal officers of the corporations oversees the denomination.

Jehovah's Witnesses believe that they adhere to the oldest religion on Earth, the worship of Almighty God revealed in the Bible as Jehovah.

They regard civil authority as necessary and obey it "as long as its laws do not contradict God's law." Witnesses refuse to bear arms, salute the flag or participate in secular government.

They refuse blood transfusions as being against the Bible, citing the section of Leviticus that reads: "Whatsoever man ... eats any manner of blood, I will cut him off from among his people."

There are no formal titles, but there are three levels of ministry: *publishers* (baptized members who do evangelistic work), *regular pioneers,* who devote greater time to activities, and *special pioneers* (full-time workers).

Jesus The central figure of Christianity, he also may be called *Jesus Christ* or *Christ.*

Personal pronouns referring to him are lowercase as is *savior.*

Jewish congregations A Jewish congregation is autonomous. No synods, assemblies or hierarchies control the activities of an individual synagogue.

Among the major expressions of Judaism in North America are:

1. Orthodox Judaism. The Orthodox Union is the umbrella organization for modern or centrist Orthodox congregations whose rabbis are represented by the Rabbinical Council of America. Many additional Orthodox congregations and rabbis in North America are part of strictly observant ultra-Orthodox communities.

2. Reform Judaism. Congregations are represented by the Union for Reform Judaism, and clergy by the Central Conference of American Rabbis.

3. Conservative Judaism. Congregations are represented by the United Synagogue of Conservative Judaism, and clergy are represented by the Rabbinical Assembly.

Reform is the largest organized movement in Judaism, while Orthodoxy is the fastest-growing.

Jews generally believe that a divine kingdom will be established on Earth, opening a messianic era that will be marked by peace and bliss. They also believe that they have a mandate from God to work toward this kingdom.

The spiritual leader of congregation is called a *rabbi*, while the individual who leads the congregation in song is called a *cantor*. Capitalize these titles before an individual's full name on first reference. On second reference, use only the last name.

See **religious titles** and **Zionism**.

Jewish holy days See separate listings for **Hanukkah, Passover, Purim, Rosh Hashana, Shavuot, Sukkot** and **Yom Kippur**.

The High Holy Days are Rosh Hashana and Yom Kippur. All Jewish holy days and the Jewish Sabbath start at sunset before the day marked on most calendars.

jihad Arabic noun used to refer to the Islamic concept of the struggle to do good. In particular situations, that can include holy war, the meaning extremist Muslims commonly use. Use *jihadi* and *jihadis*. Do not use *jihadist*.

K

Koran Use *Quran* in all references except when preferred by an organization or in a specific title or name. See **Quran**.

Kwanzaa A seven-day celebration, based on African festivals, from Dec. 26 through Jan. 1.

L

Last Supper

Latin Rite See **Roman Catholic Church**.

Latter Day Saints, Latter-day Saints See **Church of Jesus Christ of Latter-day Saints**.

lecturer A formal title in the Christian Science Church. An occupational description in other uses.

Lent The period from Ash Wednesday through Holy Saturday, the day before Easter. The 40-day Lenten period for penance, suggested by Christ's 40 days in the desert, does not include the six Sundays between Ash Wednesday and Easter.

Lord's Supper See **sacraments**.

Lutheran churches The basic unit of government in Lutheran practice is the congregation. It normally is administered by a council, headed either by the senior pastor or a lay person elected from the membership of the council. The council customarily consists of a congregation's clergy and elected lay people.

The Evangelical Lutheran Church in America is the largest Lutheran group in the U.S.

The Lutheran Church-Missouri Synod, founded in 1847, is a separate and distinct body.

Lutheran teachings go back to Martin Luther, a 16th-century Roman Catholic priest whose objections to elements of Roman Catholic practice began the movement known as the Protestant Reformation.

Members of the clergy are known as *ministers*. *Pastor* applies if a minister leads a congregation.

On first reference, use *the Rev.* before the name of a man or woman. On second reference, use only the last name.

See **religious titles**.

M

Magi Wise men who brought gifts to the infant Jesus at Epiphany, celebrated Jan. 6.

Mass It is *celebrated*, not *said*. Always capitalize when referring to the ceremony, but lowercase any preceding adjectives: *high Mass, low Mass, requiem Mass*.

In Eastern Orthodox churches the correct term is *Divine Liturgy*.

See **Roman Catholic Church**.

matrimony See **sacraments**.

megachurch Generally used to describe a Protestant church with an average of 2,000 or more attendees at weekly worship services.

Melkite Church See **Eastern Rite churches**.

menorah The seven-branch candelabrum from the ancient temple in Jerusalem. Also the popular term for the nine-branch candelabrum, or hanukkiah, used on the Jewish holiday of Hanukkah.

messiah Capitalize in religious uses, such as references to the promised deliverer of the Jews or to Jesus in Christianity. Lowercase when referring to the liberator of a people or country.

Methodist churches The term *Methodist* originated as a nickname applied to a group of 18th-century Oxford University students known for their methodical application to Scripture study and prayer.

The principal Methodist body in the United States is the United Methodist Church, which also has member conferences in other countries.

The General Conference, which meets every four years, has final authority in all matters.

A Methodist bishop presides over a "church area," which may embrace one or more annual conferences. Bishops have extensive administrative powers, including the authority to place, transfer and remove local church pastors, usually in consultation with district superintendents.

Districts in each conference are responsible for promotion of mission work, support of colleges, hospitals and publications, and examination of candidates for the ministry.

Methodism in the United States also includes three major black denominations: the African Methodist Episcopal Church, the African Methodist Episcopal Zion Church and the Christian Methodist Episcopal Church.

Methodists believe in the Trinity and the humanity and divinity of Christ. There are two sacraments, baptism and the Lord's Supper.

Ordained individuals are known as *bishops* and *ministers*. *Pastor* applies if a minister leads a congregation.

For first references to bishops use the word: *Bishop W. Kenneth Goodson* of Richmond, Virginia.

For first reference to ministers, use *the Rev.* before the name of a man or woman. On second reference, use only the last name.

See **religious titles**.

minister It is not a formal title in most religions, with exceptions such as the Nation of Islam, and is not capitalized. Where it is a formal title, it should be capitalized before the name: *Minister John Jones*.

See **religious titles** and the entry for an individual's denomination.

monsignor See **Roman Catholic Church**.

Mormon church Acceptable in references to *The Church of Jesus Christ of Latter-day Saints*, but the official name is preferred in first reference in a story dealing primarily with church activities.

See **Church of Jesus Christ of Latter-day Saints, The**.

Muhammad The chief prophet and central figure of the Islamic religion, *Prophet Muhammad*. Use other spellings only if preferred by a specific person for his own name or in a title or the name of an organization. Capitalize *Prophet* before a name.

mullah An Islamic leader or teacher, often a general title of respect for a learned man.

Muslims The preferred term to describe adherents of Islam. The term *Black Muslim* has been used in the past to describe members of predominantly African-American Islamic sects that originated in the United States. However, the term is considered derogatory.

N

National Baptist Convention of America See **Baptist churches**.

National Baptist Convention U.S.A. Inc. See **Baptist churches**.

National Council of the Churches of Christ in the U.S.A. This interdenominational, cooperative body includes most major Protestant and Eastern Orthodox denominations in the United States.

The shortened form *National Council of Churches* is acceptable in all references.

Headquarters is in Washington. See **World Council of Churches**.

Nation of Islam The nationalist religious movement traces its origins in 1930 to W.D. Fard, also known as Wali Fard, who called for racial separation. Elijah Muhammad took over the leadership in 1934, holding the post until his death in 1975. A son, Warith (Wallace) Dean Muhammad, succeeded to the leadership and pointed the movement toward integration and traditional Islam. Louis Farrakhan led a militant faction into a separatist movement in 1976.

The Nation of Islam does not release membership figures.

Use the title *minister* on first reference to clergymen: *Minister Louis Farrakhan.*

Nativity scene Only the first word is capitalized.

New Testament See **Bible**.

niqab The veil worn by the most conservative Muslim women, in which, at most, only the eyes show.

nondenominational Term used by Protestants to describe churches or ministries that are not affiliated with a specific denomination. *Independent* is also acceptable. Always lowercase.

O

Old Testament See **Bible**.

orthodox Capitalize when referring to membership in or the activities of an Eastern Orthodox church. See **Eastern Orthodox Churches**.

Capitalize also in phrases such as *Orthodox Judaism* or *Orthodox Jew*. See **Jewish congregations**.

Do not describe a member of an Eastern Orthodox church as a *Protestant*. Use a phrase such as *Orthodox Christian* instead.

Lowercase *orthodox* in nonreligious uses: *an orthodox procedure.*

Orthodox Church in America See **Eastern Orthodox churches**.

P

papal nuncio Do not confuse with an *apostolic delegate*. See **apostolic delegate, papal nuncio**.

parish Capitalize as part of the formal name for a church congregation or a governmental jurisdiction: *St. John's Parish, Jefferson Parish.*

Lowercase standing alone or in plural combinations: *the parish, St. John's and St. Mary's parishes, Jefferson and Plaquemines parishes.*

parishioner Note this spelling for the member of a parish, an administrative district of various churches, particularly Roman Catholic and Anglican. Do not use for Judaism or non-hierarchal Protestant denominations.

Passover The weeklong Jewish commemoration of the deliverance of the ancient Hebrews from slavery in Egypt. Occurs in March or April.

Capitalize *Seder* in references to the *Passover* feast commemorating the exodus.

pastor See **religious titles** and the entry for the individual's denomination.

patriarch Lowercase when describing someone of great age and dignity.

Capitalize as a formal title before a name in some religious uses. See **Eastern Orthodox churches; religious titles;** and **Roman Catholic Church.**

Pentecost The seventh Sunday after Easter.

Pentecostalism See **religious movements**.

pontiff Not a formal title. Always lowercase.

pope Capitalize when used as a formal title before a name; lowercase in all other uses: *Pope Francis spoke to the crowd. At the close of his address, the pope gave his blessing. Pope Emeritus Benedict XVI* or *Benedict XVI, the pope emeritus. Benedict* alone on second reference.

Use *St. John Paul II* and *St. John XXIII* on first reference for the canonized popes. On second reference *John Paul* and *John.* Make clear in the body of a story they were popes.

See **Roman Catholic Church** and **religious titles**.

practitioner See **Church of Christ, Scientist**.

preacher A job description, not a formal religious title. Do not capitalize.

See **titles** and **religious titles**.

Presbyterian churches Presbyterian churches in the U.S. have roots in Calvinism and in churches in Scotland and England, and are distinguished in part by how they govern their church. They typically have four levels of authority — individual congregations, presbyteries, synods and a general assembly.

Congregations are led by a pastor and a session comprised of ruling elders who represent congregants on matters of government and discipline.

Presbyteries, composed of a district's ministers and ruling elders, form a synod, which generally meets once a year to decide matters not related to doctrine or the church constitution.

A general assembly, composed of delegations of pastors and ruling elders from each presbytery, meets every two years to decide issues of doctrine and discipline.

The northern and southern branches of Presbyterianism merged in 1983 to become the Presbyterian Church (U.S.A.).

There are also several distinctly conservative Presbyterian denominations, such as the Presbyterian Church in America. Be careful to specify the denomination being written about.

Presbyterians believe in the Trinity and the humanity and divinity of Christ. Baptism, which may be administered to children, and the Lord's Supper are the only sacraments.

All Presbyterian clergymen may be described as *ministers*. Pastor applies if a minister leads a congregation.

On first reference, use *the Rev.* before the name of a man or woman. On second reference, use only the last name.

See **religious titles**.

priest A vocational description, not a formal title. Do not capitalize.

See **religious titles** and the entries for the **Roman Catholic Church** and **Episcopal Church**.

Protestant Episcopal Church
See **Episcopal Church**.

Protestant, Protestantism
Capitalize these words when they refer either to denominations formed as a result of the break from the Roman Catholic Church in the 16th century or to the members of these denominations.

Church groups covered by the term include Anglican, Baptist, Congregational, Methodist, Lutheran, Presbyterian and Quaker denominations. See separate entries for each.

Protestant is not applied to Christian Scientists, Jehovah's Witnesses or Mormons.

Do not use *Protestant* to describe a member of an Eastern Orthodox church. Use a phrase such as *Orthodox Christian* instead.

See **religious movements**.

Purim The Jewish Feast of Lots, commemorating Esther's deliverance of the Jews in Persia from a massacre plotted by Haman. Occurs in February or March.

Q

Quakers This informal name may be used in all references to members of the *Religious Society of Friends*, but always include the full name in a story dealing primarily with Quaker activities.

The denomination originated with George Fox, an Englishman who objected to Anglican emphasis on ceremony. In the 1640s, he said he heard a voice that opened the way for him to develop a personal relationship with Christ, described as the Inner Light, a term based on the Gospel description of Christ as the "true light."

Brought to court for opposing the established church, Fox tangled with a judge who derided him as a "quaker" in reference to his agitation over religious matters.

The basic unit of Quaker organization is the weekly meeting, which corresponds to the congregation in other churches. Quaker practices and beliefs vary from a more Bible-centered Christianity with pastors as worship leaders to a more liberal approach with less structured worship and a wide range of teachings.

Quaker associations include the Friends United Meeting, which has a global membership focused on evangelism, communications and other projects; Evangelical Friends Church International and the more liberal Friends General Conference.

Fox taught that the Inner Light emancipates a person from adherence to any creed, ecclesiastical authority or ritual forms.

There is no recognized ranking of clergy over lay people. However, there are meeting officers, called *elders* or *ministers*. Quaker ministers sometimes use *the Rev.* before their names and describe themselves as *pastors*.

Capitalize *elder*, *minister* or *pastor* when used as a formal title before a name. Use *the Rev.* before a name on first reference if it is a minister's practice. On second reference, use only the last name.

See **religious titles**.

Quran The preferred spelling for the Muslim holy book. Use the spelling *Koran* only if preferred by a specific organization or in a specific title or name.

R

rabbi See **Jewish congregations**.

Rabbinical Assembly See **Jewish congregations**.

Rabbinical Council of America See **Jewish congregations**.

Ramadan The Muslim holy month, marked by daily fasting from dawn to sunset, ending with the Islamic holiday of Eid al-Fitr. Avoid using *holiday* on second reference.

rector See **religious titles**.

Reform Judaism See **Jewish congregations**.

religious affiliations Capitalize the names and the related terms applied to members of the orders: *He is a member of the Society of Jesus. He is a Jesuit.*

religious movements The terms that follow have been grouped under a single entry because they are interrelated and frequently cross denominational lines.

evangelical Historically, *evangelical* was used as an adjective describing Protestant dedication to conveying the message of Christ. Today it also is used as a noun, referring to a category of doctrinally conservative Protestants. They emphasize the need for a definite, adult commitment or conversion to faith in Christ and the duty of all believers to persuade others to accept Christ.

Evangelicals make up some conservative denominations and are numerous in broader denominations. Evangelicals stress both doctrinal absolutes and vigorous efforts to win others to belief.

The National Association of Evangelicals is an interdenominational, cooperative body of relatively small, conservative Protestant denominations.

evangelism The word refers to activity directed outside the church fold to influence others to commit themselves to faith in Christ, to his work of serving others and to infuse his principles into society's conduct.

Styles of evangelism vary from direct preaching appeals at large public meetings to practical deeds of carrying the name of Christ, indirectly conveying the same call to allegiance to him.

The word *evangelism* is derived from the Greek *evangelion*, which means the gospel or good news of Christ's saving action on behalf of humanity.

fundamentalist The word gained usage in an early-20th century fundamentalist-modernist controversy within Protestantism. In recent years, however, *fundamentalist* has to a large extent taken on pejorative connotations except when applied to groups that stress strict, literal interpretations of Scripture and separation from other Christians.

In general, do not use *fundamentalist* unless a group applies the word to itself.

neo-Pentecostal, charismatic These terms apply to a movement that has developed within mainline Protestant and Roman Catholic denominations since the mid-20th century. It is distinguished by its emotional expressiveness, spontaneity in worship, speaking or praying in "unknown tongues" and healing. Participants often characterize themselves as "spirit-filled" Christians.

Unlike the earlier Pentecostal movement, which led to separate denominations, this movement has swelled within major churches.

Pentecostalism A movement that arose in the early 20th century and separated from historic Protestant denominations. It is distinguished by the belief in tangible manifestations of the Holy Spirit, often in demonstrative, emotional ways such as speaking in "unknown tongues" and healing.

Pentecostal denominations include the Assemblies of God, the Pentecostal Holiness Church, the United Pentecostal Church Inc. and the International Church of the Foursquare Gospel founded by Aimee Semple McPherson.

religious references The basic guidelines:

DEITIES: Capitalize the proper names of monotheistic deities: *God, Allah, the Father, the Son, Jesus Christ, the Son of God, the Redeemer, the Holy Spirit,* etc.

Lowercase pronouns referring to the deity: *he, him, his, thee, thou, who, whose, thy,* etc.

Lowercase *gods* in referring to the deities of polytheistic religions.

Capitalize the proper names of pagan and mythological gods and goddesses: *Neptune, Thor, Venus,* etc.

Lowercase such words as *god-awful, goddamn, godlike, godliness, godsend.*

LIFE OF CHRIST: Capitalize the names of major events in the life of Jesus Christ in references that do not use his name: *The doctrines of the Last Supper, the Crucifixion, the Resurrection and the Ascension are central to Christian belief.*

But use lowercase when the words are used with his name: *The ascension of Jesus into heaven took place 40 days after his resurrection from the dead.*

Apply the principle also to events in the life of his mother: *He cited the doctrines of the Immaculate Conception and the Assumption.* But: *She referred to the assumption of Mary into heaven.*

RITES: Capitalize proper names for rites that commemorate the Last Supper or signify a belief in Christ's presence: *the Lord's Supper, Holy Communion, Holy Eucharist.*

Lowercase the names of other sacraments. See **sacraments**.

Capitalize *Benediction* and *Mass.* But: *a high Mass, a low Mass, a requiem Mass.*

HOLY DAYS: Capitalize the names of holy days. See **holidays and holy days** and separate entries for major Christian, Jewish and Muslim feasts.

OTHER WORDS: Lowercase *heaven, hell, devil, angel, cherub, an apostle, a priest,* etc.

Capitalize *Hades* and *Satan.*

For additional details, see **Bible**, entries for frequently used religious terms, the entries for major denominations, the entries for **religious movements** and **religious titles**.

Religious Society of Friends
See **Quakers**.

religious titles The first reference to a clergyman or clergywoman normally should include a capitalized title before the individual's name.

In many cases, *the Rev.* is the designation that applies before a name on first reference. Use *the Rev. Dr.* only if the individual has an earned doctoral degree (doctor of divinity degrees frequently are honorary) and reference to the degree is relevant.

On second reference to members of the clergy, use only a last name: *the Rev. Billy Graham* on first reference, *Graham* on second. If known only by a religious name, repeat the title: *Pope John XXIII* on first reference, *John, the pope* or *the pontiff* on second; *Pope Emeritus Benedict XVI* or *Benedict XVI, the pope emeritus. Benedict* alone on second reference. *Metropolitan Herman* on first reference, *Metropolitan Herman* or *the metropolitan* on second.

Detailed guidance on specific titles and descriptive words such as *priest* and *minister* is provided in the entries for major denominations. In general, however:

CARDINALS, ARCHBISHOPS, BISHOPS: The preferred form for first reference is to use *Cardinal, Archbishop* or *Bishop* before the individual's name: *Cardinal Daniel DiNardo, archbishop of Galveston-Houston.* On second reference: *DiNardo* or *the cardinal.*

Substitute *the Most Rev.* if applicable and appropriate in the context:

He spoke to the Most Rev. Jose Gomez, archbishop of Los Angeles. On second reference: *Gomez* or *the archbishop*.

Entries for individual denominations tell when *the Most Rev.*, *the Very Rev.*, etc., are applicable.

MINISTERS AND PRIESTS: Use *the Rev.* before a name on first reference.

Substitute *Monsignor* before the name of a Roman Catholic priest who has received this honor.

Do not routinely use *curate, father, pastor* and similar words before an individual's name. If they appear before a name in a quotation, capitalize them.

RABBIS: Use *Rabbi* before a name on first reference. On second reference, use only the last name.

NUNS: Always use *Sister*, or *Mother* if applicable, before a name: *Sister Agnes Rita* in all references if the nun uses only a religious name; *Sister Mary Ann Walsh* on first reference if she uses a surname. *Walsh* on subsequent references.

OFFICEHOLDERS: The preferred first-reference form for those who hold church office but are not ordained clergy in the usual sense is to use a construction that sets the title apart from the name by commas. Capitalize the formal title of an office, however, if it is used directly before an individual's name.

Reorganized Church of Jesus Christ of Latter Day Saints
Now called *the Community of Christ*. Not properly described as a *Mormon church*. See the explanation under **Church of Jesus Christ of Latter-day Saints**.

Rev.
When this description is used before an individual's name, precede it with the word *"the"* because, unlike the case with *Mr.* and *Mrs.*, the abbreviation *Rev.* does not stand for a noun.

If an individual also has a secular title such as *Rep.*, use whichever is appropriate to the context. See **religious titles**.

Roman Catholic Church
The church teaches that its bishops have been established as the successors of the apostles through generations of ceremonies in which authority was passed down by a laying-on of hands.

Responsibility for teaching the faithful and administering the church rests with the bishops. However, the church holds that the pope has final authority over their actions because he is the bishop of Rome, the office it teaches was held by the Apostle Peter at his death.

The Curia serves as a form of governmental cabinet. Its members, appointed by the pope, handle both administrative and judicial functions.

The pope also chooses members of the College of Cardinals, who serve as his principal counselors. When a new pope must be chosen, they meet in a conclave to select a new pope by majority vote. In practice, cardinals are mostly bishops, but there is no requirement that a cardinal be a bishop.

In the United States, the church's principal organizational units are archdioceses and dioceses. They are headed, respectively, by archbishops and bishops, who have final responsibility for many activities within their jurisdictions and report directly to Rome.

The church counts more than 1 billion members worldwide. In the United States it has more than 66 million members, making it the largest single body of Christians in the nation.

Roman Catholics believe in the Trinity — that there is one God who exists as three divine persons — the

Father, the Son and the Holy Spirit. They believe that the Son became man as Jesus Christ.

In addition to the Holy Eucharist, there are six other sacraments — baptism, confirmation, penance (often called the sacrament of reconciliation), matrimony, holy orders, and the sacrament of the sick (formerly extreme unction).

The clergy below pope are, in descending order, cardinal, archbishop, bishop, monsignor, priest and deacon. In religious orders, some men who are not priests have the title *brother*.

Capitalize *pope* when used as a title before a name: *Pope John XXIII, Pope Francis*. Lowercase in all other uses. See **religious titles**.

The first-reference forms for other titles follow. Use only last names on second reference.

Cardinals: *Cardinal Daniel DiNardo*. The usage *Daniel Cardinal DiNardo*, a practice traceable to the nobility's custom of identifications such as *William, Duke of Norfolk*, is still used in formal documents but otherwise is considered archaic.

Archbishops: *Archbishop Gregory Aymond*, or *the Most Rev. Gregory Aymond, archbishop of New Orleans*.

Bishops: *Bishop Thomas Paprocki*, or *the Most Rev. Thomas Paprocki, bishop of Springfield, Illinois*.

Monsignors: *Monsignor Martin Krebs*. Do not use the abbreviation *Msgr*. Do not use *the Rt. Rev.* or *the Very Rev.* — this distinction between types of monsignors no longer is made.

Priests: *the Rev. James Martin*. See **religious titles**.

rosary It is *recited* or *said*, never *read*. Always lowercase.

Rosh Hashana The Jewish new year. Occurs in September or October.

Russian Orthodox Church See **Eastern Orthodox churches**.

S

Sabbath Capitalize in religious references.

sacraments Capitalize the proper names used for a sacramental rite that commemorates the life of Jesus Christ or signifies a belief in his presence: *the Lord's Supper, Holy Communion, Holy Eucharist*.

Lowercase the names of other sacraments: *baptism, confirmation, penance* (now often called the *sacrament of reconciliation*), *matrimony, holy orders*, and *the sacrament of anointing the sick* (formerly *extreme unction*).

See entries for the major religious denominations and **religious references**.

sacrilegious

Satan But lowercase *devil* and *satanic*.

savior Use this spelling for all senses, rather than the alternate form, *saviour*.

Seventh-day Adventist Church The denomination is traceable to the preaching of William Miller of New Hampton, New York, a Baptist layman who said his study of the Book of Daniel showed that the end of the world would come in the mid-1840s.

When the prediction did not come true, the Millerites split into smaller groups. One, influenced by visions described by Ellen Harmon, later the wife of James White, is the precursor of the Seventh-day Adventist practice today.

The church has four constituent levels: 1. Local churches. 2. Local conferences of churches for a state or part of a state. 3. Union conferences of a number of local conferences. 4. The General Conference.

The General Conference in Session and the General Conference Executive Committee are the highest administrative authorities.

The headquarters is in Silver Spring, Maryland.

The description *adventist* is based on the belief that a second coming of Christ is near. *Seventh-day* derives from the contention that the Bible requires observing the seventh day of the week as the Sabbath.

Baptism, by immersion, is reserved for those old enough to understand its meaning. Baptism and the Lord's Supper are the only sacraments.

The head of the General Conference holds the formal title of *president*. The formal titles for ministers are *pastor* or *elder*. Capitalize them when used immediately before a name on first reference. On second reference, use only the last name.

The designation *the Rev.* is not used.

See **religious titles**.

Shariah Islamic law.

Shavuot The Jewish Feast of Weeks, commemorating the receiving of the Ten Commandments. Occurs in May or June.

Shiite The spelling for this branch of Islam. Plural is *Shiites*. The alternate spelling *Shia* is acceptable in quotes. See **Islam**.

sister Capitalize in all references before the names of nuns.

If no surname is given, the name is the same in all references: *Sister Agnes Rita*.

If a surname is used in first reference, drop the given name and sister on second reference: *Sister Mary Ann Walsh* on first reference, *Walsh* in subsequent references.

Use *Mother* the same way when referring to a woman who heads a group of nuns.

See **religious titles**.

Society of Friends See **Quakers**.

Sukkot The Jewish Feast of Tabernacles, celebrating the fall harvest and commemorating the desert wandering of the Jews during the Exodus. Occurs in September or October.

synagogue Capitalize only when part of a formal name.

synod A council of churches or church officials. See the entry for the denomination in question.

T

Talmud The collection of writings that constitute the Jewish civil and religious law.

Temple Mount The walled, elevated area in Jerusalem's Old City that was the site of the ancient Jewish temples. It now houses the centuries-old Dome of the Rock shrine and Al-Aqsa mosque and is known to Muslims as the *Haram al-Sharif*, or *Noble Sanctuary*. Muslims believe the Prophet Muhammad made his night journey to heaven from the site.

Ten Commandments Do not abbreviate or use figures.

Twelve Apostles The disciples of Jesus. An exception to the normal practice of using figures for 10 and above.

U

Ukrainian Catholic Church
See **Eastern Rite churches**.

United Church of Christ
The Evangelical and Reformed Church merged with the Congregational Christian Churches in 1957 to form the United Church of Christ.

The word *church* is correctly applied only to an individual local church. Each such church is responsible for the doctrine, ministry and ritual of its congregation.

A small body of churches that did not enter the United Church of Christ is known as the National Association of Congregational Churches.

Jesus is regarded as man's savior, but no subscription to a set creed is required for membership.

Members of the clergy are known as *ministers*. *Pastor* applies if a minister leads a congregation.

On first reference, use *the Rev.* before the name of a man or woman. On second reference, use only the last name.

See **religious titles**.

United Methodist Church
See **Methodist churches**.

United States Conference of Catholic Bishops
Formerly the National Conference of Catholic Bishops, it is the national organization of Roman Catholic bishops.

United Synagogue of Conservative Judaism
Not *synagogues*. See **Jewish congregations**.

V

Vatican City
Stands alone in datelines.

Very Rev.
See **Episcopal Church**; **religious titles**; and **Roman Catholic Church**.

Voodoo
Capitalize when referring specifically to the religion, practiced primarily in Haiti and parts of Africa. Lowercase in other uses, especially when ascribing magical solutions to problems, as in *voodoo economics*.

W

Wahhabi
Follower of a strict Muslim sect that adheres closely to the Quran; it's most powerful in Saudi Arabia.

Wicca
Religion shaped by pagan beliefs and practices. The term encompasses a wide range of traditions generally organized around seasonal festivals, and can include ritual magic, a belief in both female and male deities, and the formation of covens led by priestesses and priests. *Wiccan* is both an adjective and a noun. Uppercase in all uses.

World Council of Churches
An international, interdenominational cooperative body of Anglican, Eastern Orthodox, Protestant and old or national Catholic churches.

The Roman Catholic Church is not a member but cooperates with the council in various programs.

Headquarters is in Geneva.

worship, worshipped, worshipper

Y

Yom Kippur The Jewish Day of Atonement. Occurs in September or October.

Z

Zionism The effort of Jews to regain and retain their biblical homeland. It is based on the promise of God in the book of Genesis that Israel would forever belong to Abraham and his descendants as a nation.

The term is named for Mount Zion, the site of the ancient temple in Jerusalem.

BUSINESS GUIDELINES

Our market is the individual consumer of business news. We must write in a lively, clear and accessible style that provides explanation and content for people who may not have a deep knowledge of business and finance. We must avoid insider jargon and present complex issues in an understandable, straightforward manner. No story is too small or routine to meet this standard: Each has meaning for readers and viewers. They may own a stock we are writing about, live in a community where a company is based, use a product or service or have some other connection to the news we are providing. We must keep in mind that we are writing on a global scale and make sure that our reporting reflects that and think about creative ways to tell stories.

AP business journalists must be careful with numbers; quickly grasp what those numbers mean and turn those numbers into real stories, not just about companies or profits but about people's lives.

When stories break, or when you set out to break a story yourself, you need experts or insiders who can help. And you need to know where you can find all the facts you need: in SEC filings, court documents, lists of shareholders and creditors, company histories, etc.

COVERING CORPORATE EARNINGS REPORTS

U.S. federal law requires corporations whose stock is publicly traded to report revenue and profit or losses every three months. This is what business is all about, whether a corporation made money or lost it, and why. These statements are usually released on the major public relations wire services during "earnings season," a three- or four-week period that begins roughly two weeks after the end of each quarter.

Before each quarterly reporting period begins, AP business editors and reporters determine which companies will receive expanded coverage based on reader interest, corporate developments, legal or regulatory issues, and influence on financial markets and consumers. When these companies report earnings, AP typically will publish a several-hundred word report and, in some cases, additional elements such as video and graphics.

The AP automates the writing of thousands of quarterly earnings stories using software. These stories average about 200 words and provide customers with the basics: the net income and revenue that the company reported for the quarter — and year — when applicable. An algorithm that creates the stories also is designed to report if the company beat the expectations of Wall Street analysts that cover the company and to include forward-looking guidance when that information is available. The standard style for slugs is BC-US--Earns-Company Name.

While AP is automating many earnings reports, there are times when reporters can and should write original earnings stories or add to automated earnings reports. The decision to add original reporting depends on many factors including the stock activity following an earnings announcement.

Many of the following principles should be followed whether a reporter writes an earnings story from the beginning or adds to one that was automatically generated.

- We should tell the reader what the company does and give the increase or decline of net income either in percentage or absolute terms, along with the reason. Net income is synonymous with profit or earnings. The story should also include the company's revenue, which is sometimes called sales. In AP copy, however, this should always be referred to as revenue.
- Comparisons of profits or losses and revenues/sales should be made with the same period a year earlier, expressed both as a total and as earnings-per-share, which is simply the profit divided by the number of shares of stock outstanding. Company statements sometimes express this figure as fully diluted. Many company statements also include basic earnings-per-share, but AP uses fully diluted as a more meaningful figure.
- Use active verbs — rose, fell and the like — not passive constructions like were up/down. And to calculate the percentage change in profit, use the year-over-year change in net income, not the earnings-per-share numbers. The number of shares outstanding can, and often does, change year to year, which doesn't make it a clear apples-to-apples comparison.
- Include comments on the corporation's performance from the chief executive or outside analysts, and any background that puts the performance in perspective.
- Be alert to announcements of job cuts, executive resignations, acquisitions, changes in strategy, data about key products, warnings of a reduction of future earnings or upward revisions of earnings forecasts.

Why net income is important

Net income truly is the bottom line and the benchmark for companies' performance over time. It's what they are required to report to the SEC in accordance with generally accepted accounting principles, and it gives us a standard reporting format that brings a consistency to our news report.

In the rare cases where companies don't provide the net income number in their news release, we need to press their representatives for those numbers. And if they are not immediately available, we need to be as transparent as possible in explaining to readers why we are providing pro forma or some other adjusted or non-GAAP representation of the company's results instead of the net income figures, which were not disclosed.

Wall Street analysts have been much more concerned in recent years with operating earnings per share, which are calculated by excluding one-time "extraordinary" gains or charges, and revenue totals. Operating earnings may exclude the costs of a big reorganization, such as severance payments to laid-off workers or penalties for breaking leases on factories that are closed. If a company has no extraordinary events, operating earnings and net earnings can be identical.

In the days and weeks before earnings reports, analysts issue EPS predictions, and these predictions are compiled into a "consensus" figure by research companies such as FactSet and Zacks Investment Research.

On the day of the report, investors compare the consensus prediction for operating earnings per share with the actual number and the stock price often moves up or down based on whether the company falls short of, meets or exceeds expectations. When AP says in a story "Company X's performance beat Wall Street analysts' predictions," this is the number we're referring to. In most stories we explain how the adjusted number was calculated and immediately compare the adjusted earnings per share to the consensus, or average, analyst forecast.

It's worth noting that the analysts' forecast for earnings and revenue in a quarter often reflects the guidance provided by companies about what they expect their earnings and sales will be. That's why it's important to not only review what the analysts' consensus forecast is, but to determine whether a company has made a public forecast. When earnings or revenue disappoint, it's a much more powerful statement for us to say the company's earnings fell short of its own forecast, as well as analysts' expectations — assuming those facts are obtainable.

"Operating earnings" is sometimes confused with "earnings from continuing operations." Continuing operations is a subset of operations. It refers to business units that existed in the past and will exist in the future. It excludes "discontinued operations" which represent businesses that have been sold or shut down in the past year. Companies often downplay earnings of these operations since they are no longer relevant to future profits.

Importance of the conference call

Stocks often move within seconds of an unexpected pronouncement by the CEO or CFO on the analyst conference call after the earnings are released. It could come from their response to a question about a big contract, the reason for a revised sales or earnings forecast, or any number of other reasons. That's information we obviously will want in a quick writethru of the story. But even if there are no dramatic announcements, it's important to listen to the call to gain a more complete understanding of how the company is positioning itself going forward. And it may provide a colorful key quote from a top company executive.

Make the company come to life

Earnings are the report cards for top corporate executives. The results, more often than not, are a consequence of decisions they made — acquisitions they engineered, factories they convinced their boards of directors to build or shutter, advertising campaigns they approved. Including detail about the decisions corporate executives have made helps us show that companies are made up of people who win or lose based on the decisions they make.

How to assemble a wrap story

When two or more companies in the same industry report earnings on the same day, we often want an earnings wrap story after the separate earnings stories are out and updated with details from the conference calls. These should read like a seamless narrative with one or more thematic elements holding them together. And in almost every case, a wrap should have a forward-looking element that gives readers a sense of whether the good or bad earnings are likely to get better or worse in future quarters, and why.

The basis for the thematic element may come from one or more of the conference calls that company executives hold after releasing earnings. Or there may be cases where your reporting will take you in a different direction in identifying the unifying theme. Talk to money managers who own the stock, competitors and others who you think can provide insight into what is going on. There also may be cases where the earnings are so divergent that the theme could be that the industry appears to be in disarray. But in all cases, our aim should be to convey to readers who is winning, who is losing and why. That often means that the wrap story may have a more complete explanation of how specific decisions made by executives impacted the earnings.

It also isn't necessary to repeat in the wrap version every number that is in the separate earnings stories. Instead, you should use a common sense approach that asks the question: Is this number necessary to convey the main points we are trying to make? They don't have to be lengthy expositions; if you can tell the tale in 400 or 500 words, all the better.

INTERNATIONAL BUREAUS

Currency Conversions

Currency conversions are necessary in stories that use foreign currency to make clear for readers how a number translates into dollars. But conversions should be used sparingly and preferably not in the lead unless it's a significant part of a story. A conversion is generally needed only the first time a currency is mentioned. The reader can make the necessary conversions after that.

Do not convert amounts that are not current because exchange rates change over time. If necessary for clarity in the story, specify that the conversion is at current exchange rates.

When conversions are needed, use the $ sign to report U.S. dollar amounts and write euros in the form *100 euros*. Do not use the euro symbol (€). Examples:

AMSTERDAM (AP) — Anheuser-Busch InBev, the world's largest brewer, says its third-quarter profits rose as the takeover of new brands and higher selling prices offset the impact of lower sales volumes.

The company, based in Leuven, Belgium, said Thursday that net profit was up 31 percent to $2.37 billion (1.73 billion euros), from $1.81 billion in the same period a year earlier.

The gain largely reflects the company's $20 billion purchase in June of the 50 percent of Mexico's Grupo Modelo it didn't already own.

PARIS (AP) — French cosmetics giant L'Oreal says sales of its Maybelline makeup, Garnier shampoo and other beauty aids helped lift earnings to a new record in 2013.

The company behind Lancome cosmetics and the Body Shop retail chain reported net profit of 2.96 billion euros ($4 billion) last year, up 3.2 percent from 2.87 billion in 2012.

For all other currencies, following the amount, spell out the name of the currency followed in parentheses by the equivalent in U.S. dollars. *Japan approved a 1.8 trillion yen ($18 billion) extra budget to partially finance an economic stimulus package.*

When dealing with a dollar currency of a country other than the United States, use the following abbreviations before the amount on second and subsequent references:

AU$ Australian dollars
CA$ Canadian dollars
SG$ Singapore dollars
NZ$ New Zealand dollars

HK$ Hong Kong dollars
NT$ New Taiwan dollars
ZW$ Zimbabwe dollars

Treasurer Wayne Swan approved a 16 billion Australian dollar ($10.74 billion) deal. Swan said AU$8 billion would be reserved for capital expenditure.

Different Accounting Rules

In some countries, companies don't report every quarter. The reports may come out every six months or even annually. Many foreign companies don't report "net income" or "earnings per share." Some report "earnings before taxes." If that's all they report, call them to see if they will give you net income. If they won't, use whatever number seems closest.

For the companies that report only half-year and full-year results, add a line saying, "The company did not break out quarterly results," so it's clear why we're not using them. Similarly, when reporting sales results for French companies, note that they often report sales a week or two before profit.

Foreign companies that sell shares in the United States (called American depositary receipts) often issue a separate earnings statement using American accounting standards. Use this when you can.

BANKRUPTCY

Bankruptcy categories – personal and business

Federal courts have exclusive jurisdiction over bankruptcy cases, and each of the 94 federal judicial districts handles bankruptcy matters. The primary purposes of the federal bankruptcy laws are to give an honest debtor a "fresh start" in life by relieving the debtor of most debts, and to repay creditors in an orderly manner to the extent that the debtor has property available for payment. Bankruptcies can also be **voluntary** or **involuntary**.

Chapter 7 of the Bankruptcy Code is available to both individual and business debtors. Its purpose is to achieve a fair distribution to creditors of the debtor's available non-exempt property. It provides a fresh financial start for individuals, although not all debt is wiped away; debts for certain taxes, fraudulently incurred credit card debt, family support obligations — including child support and alimony — and most student loans must still be repaid. And the new bankruptcy law that took effect in October 2005 limits Chapter 7 as an option for many Americans: Those deemed by a **"means test"** to have at least $100 a month left over after paying certain debts and expenses will have to file a 5-year repayment plan under the more restrictive Chapter 13 instead. **When a company files for Chapter 7, it usually leads to liquidation.** But a company in Chapter 7 proceedings can continue to operate under the direction of a court trustee until the matter is settled, and if it can settle with creditors in the interim, it may not have to be liquidated.

Chapter 11 of the Bankruptcy Code is available for both business and consumer debtors. Its purpose is to rehabilitate a business as a going concern or reorganize an individual's finances through a **court-approved reorganization plan**. When we refer to such a filing, we should say the company is **seeking Chapter 11 protection**. This action frees a company from the threat of creditors' lawsuits while it reorganizes its finances. The debtor's reorganization plan must be accepted by a majority of its creditors. Unless the court rules otherwise, the debtor remains in control of the business and its assets.

Chapter 12 of the Bankruptcy Code is designed to give special debt relief to a family farmer with regular income from farming.

Chapter 13 of the Bankruptcy Code is likely to be required for an increasing percentage of individuals seeking to wipe the slate clean. As mentioned above, those deemed by a "means test" to have at least $100 a month left over after paying certain debts and expenses will have to file a 5-year repayment plan under Chapter 13 that allows **unsecured creditors to recover part or all of what they are owed**. Supporters believe the changes will help rein in consumers who pile up credit card debt only to wipe it out with a Chapter 7 filing. Opponents say the law will hurt those who incur debt unexpectedly such as with health problems or lost jobs.

Chapter 15 of the Bankruptcy Code is a new section added in the 2005 reforms that deals with foreign bankruptcies. It is a way for companies with U.S. assets that are organized or nominally headquartered overseas to file bankruptcy in that foreign jurisdiction and in the U.S. as well, and have the U.S. court recognize the foreign bankruptcy as the primary one. The chapter is based on a model law developed by the United Nations in 1997. It has thus far been relatively uncommon, but **may be used more in the future, particularly by hedge funds that are organized overseas but operate in the U.S.**

How to prepare if a big corporate bankruptcy filing seems imminent

Burdensome debt and the refusal of lenders to extend new loans are the common denominators for most companies seeking bankruptcy court protection. Those tend not to crop up suddenly, which means you should be able to judge the likelihood that one of your companies may be filing. That's why we encourage all reporters to set up **SEC filing alerts** for key companies using their own user name and password on the Morningstar Document Research service. Bankruptcy should be one of the keywords you choose because outside auditors often force companies to tip their hands by flagging to investors the possibility of a bankruptcy filing. One expression you'll want to add to your company alert setup is **"going concern."** That's the term companies use when they note that their outside auditors are questioning their ability to remain in business.

Beyond that, you need to have a good understanding of the **balance sheet** and the **income statement** of the major companies you cover to answer these questions: How much debt do they have and how much of it must be repaid or refinanced in this quarter or the quarters to come? Have they demonstrated an inability to raise fresh cash through the sale of stock or debt financing? Has cash flow gone negative?

After a company seeks Chapter 11 protection, **holders of the company's debt** are often the best source of information about the status of bankruptcy negotiations since they often stand to gain control of the company in the reorganization process.

Few companies will be chatty about bankruptcy filings ahead of time, but it's still a good idea to plant the seed with company spokesmen that you want to be alerted as soon as a filing is made, that you want to know in which court it will come (more and more of the big ones seem to be ending up in the Southern District of New York in Manhattan), and that you would like a full set of documents if possible.

Another question to ask is: What will happen to the company's employees? When a company seeks bankruptcy protection, it often pushes for job cuts, pay cuts and reductions in benefits. If any workers are represented by unions, those unions will likely fight those cuts. A company seeking Chapter 11 protection will sometimes try to use bankruptcy court to achieve concessions if it can't reach an agreement on its own with unions. So stay in contact with union representatives to keep up with out-of-court negotiations, and check docket reports on Pacer for requests for permission to impose wage concessions, to reject union contracts or anything similar.

Also, companies seeking bankruptcy protection often turn over their pension plans to the Pension Benefit Guaranty Corporation, the federal pension insurance agency (http://www.pbgc.gov). But eliminating pension plans altogether is also common — United Airlines, US Airways, TWA and Pan Am, among others, all canceled their pension plans in bankruptcy.

And a reminder on tracking a company's stock after it files for bankruptcy: Companies are usually **delisted** by the New York Stock Exchange and the Nasdaq stock market after they seek bankruptcy court protection. That means they usually begin trading on the over-the-counter market known as the **Pink Sheets**. The **letter Q** at the end of a ticker signifies that the company is operating under bankruptcy protection and **PK** means it trades on the Pink Sheets. (Example: Delphi Corp. went from DPH on the New York Stock Exchange to DPHIQ.PK — four letters required in the ticker symbol for bankrupt companies — on the Pink Sheets.)

Is it a reorganization or a liquidation?

Knowing the answer to this question is key to how we describe the filing in our story. If it's a Chapter 11 filing and the company hopes to stay in business, don't say "Company XX filed for bankruptcy on DATE TK ..." Instead, we should say "Company XX **sought bankruptcy court protection** on DATE TK ..."

If a company closes its doors, says it's unable to raise new cash and is **going out of business** via a Chapter 7 filing, spell that out in the lead.

Secured and unsecured creditors

When you borrow money to buy a car, the lender is a **secured creditor**; they get to reclaim the car if you stop making payments. Similarly, companies usually have to pledge some kind of **collateral** when they sell bonds or otherwise borrow money. There can be several levels or rankings of security pledged for various categories of a company's debt. For our purposes, we need to know which creditor stands first, second and so on in line for repayment if a company files for bankruptcy because their claims and desires often conflict with what management wants to happen.

In a bankruptcy reorganization, secured lenders and debt holders obviously want to be repaid 100 cents on the dollar. Management often is against that idea, because they need whatever money they still have to continue operating the company. What often happens is that after extensive negotiations (and big lawyer bills) secured debt holders agree to **exchange their securities for new shares of stock** (i.e., equity) in the post-bankruptcy company, which emerges as a consequence with a much-reduced debt load.

So what happens to **existing shareholders**? In most cases, **their shares become worthless**. But every so often, secured debt holders' claims can be satisfied in a way that leaves some residual equity value in the company. But even then, existing shareholders' ownership stake in the company is often **severely diluted** by the issuance of new shares to former debt holders. That's why the stocks of companies seeking bankruptcy protection often continue to trade at a few dollars a share. It's mostly a fool's game, but something we need to be able to explain as part of our reporting and writing.

Prepackaged bankruptcies and DIP financing

Companies heading toward bankruptcy sometimes start negotiations with major secured creditors on what is known as a **prepackaged bankruptcy** filing. If a company can reach agreement on key details before the bankruptcy court supervision begins, it can speed its eventual reorganization and exit from bankruptcy. Known as an out-of-court restructuring plan, it is filed simultaneously with a Chapter 11 petition. But such plans require the approval of at least two-thirds in amount and more than one-half in the number of allowed claims held by creditors.

One study makes the case that the prepackaged bankruptcy approach is taken most often by companies that had a higher ratio of operating income to total debt in the years before financial stress set in, and when long-term debt represents a larger percentage of total debt (which makes sense because there typically would be fewer debt holders to negotiate with).

These prepackaged plans, as well as regular Chapter 11 reorganizations, often are accompanied by what is known as **debtor-in-possession financing**. This is a term for new money extended by a lender in Chapter 11 cases. Investopedia.com describes DIP financing as being unique from other financing methods in that it usually has priority over existing debt, equity and other claims.

Why should we care about DIP financing? It's a profitable line of business for banks. And companies' ability to obtain it often is a critical factor in whether they continue to operate or have to shut down.

Emerging from bankruptcy

When the reorganization is completed and a company emerges from bankruptcy, we should be able to spell out how much of the company's debt has been wiped away. If debt holders swap their holdings for shares of the reorganized company, spell that out and explain what role they will play. Also include whether the company attracted new equity holders as part of the reorganization.

MERGERS AND ACQUISITIONS

Is it a merger or a takeover?

Few business combinations are truly a merger of equals, so we need to be precise and sparing in the use of the word "merger." It is **not a synonym for an acquisition or takeover**, which should be the preferred descriptive used in most of our stories. But how do we first decide whether or not it's a merger, and if the answer is not, what are the rules that should guide us in concluding who's buying whom?

The AP M&A Checklist:

1. Is one of the companies' stock being used as the currency? If the answer is yes, that's usually a good sign that company is the acquirer and it is not a merger.

2. What is the message from the exchange ratio in stock transactions? Typically when shareholders of Company A are offered new shares in a combined company at a 1-for-1 ratio, and Company B shares are exchanged at something less or more (i.e., each Company B share will be exchanged for 0.47 percent of a share of the new company), it's an indication that Company A's stock is being used as the basis for the transaction. But it also could be a sign that the companies' boards have agreed to a merger that uses a formula to compensate for the differing market value (total number of shares multiplied by the closing stock price the day before the announcement) of the two companies to come up with an exchange ratio for stock in the new company.

3. What is the message from the stock movements after the announcement? Shares of companies being acquired typically rise and shares of the acquirer often fall after the announcement. Not always, of course, but that's usually the case because most bidders **pay a premium**, or an above-market price, for the shares of the company being acquired, and investors often are worried about the amount of debt the acquirer is taking on to complete the transaction.

4. Whose cash is being used to fund the cash portion of a transaction? If the announcement says Company A's cash will be used or that its existing lines of credit will be tapped to pay for Company B's shares, that's a pretty strong indication that Company A is the acquirer.

5. Which company's executives are filling most of the top management roles? The key distinction usually is who gets the CEO slot. But if one of the two CEOs is named to head the company for a limited period (say two years or less) before his fellow CEO takes over, that's a good sign of a political compromise to paper over the fact that the second CEO's company is going to be in charge long-term.

6. Which company will end up with the majority of the seats on the new board of directors? This is often a key tiebreaker. It's a good indication of which outfit is going to be in charge if one ends up with 60 percent of the board and the other gets 40 percent. Also, make sure to get not only the short-term makeup of the board of the combined company, but also whether there were any deals cut for some members to retire in short order.

7. Whose name will be on the big sign outside the headquarters? Usually an obvious tell, but not always. First Union clearly was the acquirer of Wachovia, but the board members decided for their own reasons to use the Wachovia name when the two North Carolina banks combined operations. It may have been a deal killer for some Wachovia board members if their name didn't survive, or it may have simply been a marketing decision by First Union's brass that the name Wachovia had a better chance of standing out in the crowded banking space. Wachovia, incidentally, was acquired by Wells Fargo in 2008.

8. Where will the company be headquartered? Since CEOs typically do the negotiating and they typically aren't anxious to move, this can be an informative tell.

How to value the transaction

Our basic rule is to **exclude the debt** of the acquired company when calculating the value of a takeover. If Company A has agreed to pay $50 a share in cash for all of the stock of Company B, you would multiply $50 times the fully diluted number of shares outstanding of Company B to come up with transaction's total value. Companies often include the debt in their news release, which places a higher total value on the transaction. In cases like that, if they spell out the debt total, back it out and fashion a lead something like this:

Company A, the world's largest TK, agreed Monday to pay $XX million to acquire Company B, whose product line XXX will do XXXX. The transaction, valued at $50 per share, or a X.X premium to Friday's closing price, includes the assumption of $XXX million of Company B's debt.

Unfortunately, news releases sometimes only provide the per-share number for the transaction. So in addition to calling the company to get the key numbers we need to value the transaction, we should backstop by reviewing the latest 10-Q filing of the acquired company to get the number of fully diluted shares outstanding so we can do the math ourselves. In some cases, companies only give the per-share number because they don't want to call attention to the fact that there are an enormous number of options of the acquired company that can be exercised as part of transaction.

When stock is the currency used in the transaction, or is part of a stock and cash offer, the valuation equation changes. If Company A offers 1 share of its stock for each share of Company B, for the NewsNow you would multiply the previous day's closing price of Company A by the number of fully diluted shares outstanding of Company B. When there is a cash component per share, or if the exchange ratio is greater or lesser than 1-for-1, the math gets a little more complicated, but it's also straightforward. First calculate the value of the stock portion (If Company A is offering 0.47 of a share of its stock that was trading at $50 yesterday, the stock portion is worth 50 x .47, or $23.50.) Then add whatever will be paid in cash per share (say $10) to give a total value of $33.50 per Company B share and multiply that times the total number of shares of Company B outstanding.

Any time stock of the acquirer is used as a currency in a takeover, the value of the transaction obviously can change throughout the day based on the stock movement of the acquirer. But for our purposes, on the day the takeover is announced, we should stay with our initial valuation (based on the closing price of the acquirer a day earlier) until the markets close.

Then we should redo the math based on that day's closing value of the acquirer's stock — and make it clear to readers why the total has changed from what they have been reading throughout the day.

What needs to be in the APNewsNow

Lead with the **full name of the buyer** and include a descriptive size and scope, **explain the terms** and **value of the deal** as simply as possible (all cash? cash and stock? all stock?) while adding the name of the company to be acquired, and **provide a reason why** the deal is happening — or, if the release is mum on that point, a description of what the combined company will look like or the capabilities it will have (making it the world's biggest maker of fish tacos).

If there are **job cuts** or other major corporate developments, including a warning that future earnings will be lower because of **earnings dilution**, aim to get those in the NewsNow. Dilution occurs when a stock-based transaction increases the number of shares of the acquirer without a near-term corresponding increase in earnings per share.

Specify where the two companies are **headquartered**. Also include **stock price history** and **premarket trading**, if it is available, for both the acquirer and the acquiree. And if it is easily obtainable, specify what the **premium** that the acquiring company is offering and whether it is a **hostile bid**.

As the urgent series continues, include any pertinent details about potential antitrust issues, contingencies like the need for board approval, government approval, shareholder approval, court approval, break-up fees, **due diligence** (the review by the acquirer of a target company's internal books and operations), and **nondisclosure/confidentiality agreements**.

Also specify the **stage of the transaction** — letter of intent, definitive agreement, closing, etc. And if not added already, provide details about how the acquirer will finance the takeover, what the seller's plans are for the proceeds it will be receiving, the projected effect on future sales/earnings, other details on how the companies will change as a result of the deal (layoffs, management changes, etc.), and when the deal is expected to close.

Add historical perspective. A news story showed a good example: In early 2003, Overture bought Altavista from CMGI for $140 million in cash and stock. That didn't look like much of a deal until they added the needed perspective that CMGI bought Altavista from Compaq only four years earlier for $2.3 billion.

What is the stock reaction telling us?

If Company A offers $50 in cash for Company B and the share price of Company B rises to $55 or $60, that's a pretty strong indication that some investors are betting at least one **competing bid** will emerge. Alternatively, if Company B's shares trade way below $50, we need to find out why investors are skittish about the deal closing.

It also should be standard practice to keep track of the stock prices of both the acquirer and the target in the days and weeks after the initial announcement. Depending on how they perform, you may want to write additional stories about whether investors are betting the deal is on track or in trouble. And when stock is used as part or all of the currency for a proposed takeover, it's a good idea to build the formula into a spreadsheet and track it daily to see whether the spread between the market price is narrowing or widening from the offer's valuation.

Some investors make and lose millions on these bets, so be careful when you interview them about these deals — and make sure to explain what they have at stake if we quote them either speaking in support of or objecting to the transaction.

Assessing the deal's chances for success

Besides the market implications about whether a deal will close or not, we should also from the first day be sharpening our analysis about whether the proposal makes business sense. There are several ways to approach this. Are the promised cost cuts doable, and what will they cost in human terms (jobs lost) and the effects on local economies? Will it deliver the higher profits the acquirer is promising? Will it position the acquirer's stock for future market gains? We should be asking these questions as part of our first-day coverage and come back as often as needed for deals both pending and completed.

BROADCAST GUIDELINES

"Barack Obama has been elected president of the United States."
"Osama bin Laden is dead."
"The Dow Jones industrial average has reached 13,000."

These sentences illustrate AP's broadcast news writing style. They are easily understood, but intelligent; conversational, but not stiff. Many broadcast stories can be effectively told using such straightforward writing and this simple structure:

Lead —> Backup —> Details —> Background

For example:

A huge wildfire in eastern Arizona is expected to spread to New Mexico. Both wind and dry lightning are forecast over the next two days.
Arizona fire officials say more than 1,000 firefighters are working the blaze. There have been no serious injuries, but hundreds of people have been evacuated, and 11 buildings have been destroyed.
The fire has burned more than 350 square miles. It's the third-largest wildfire in Arizona's history.

Lead. The first sentence in this story reports the essential facts that are the news:
A huge wildfire [*the subject of the story*] in eastern Arizona [*location*] is expected to spread to New Mexico [*the story's latest development*].
Backup. The second sentence "backs up" the lead:
Both wind and dry lightning are forecast over the next two days [*answers the implied question "Why is the fire expected to spread?"*].
Details. These next sentences report additional important facts — mainly, the extent to which people are injured or at risk.
Arizona fire officials [*the story's sources*] say more than 1,000 firefighters are working the blaze [*these lives are potentially at risk*]. There have been no serious injuries, but hundreds of people have been evacuated [*impact of the fire on people*], and 11 buildings have been destroyed [*impact on property*].
Background. The story ends by putting the fire into current and historical perspective:
The fire has burned more than 350 square miles. It's the third-largest wildfire in Arizona's history.

The fire story follows principles used by AP's broadcast writers:

1. Lead with the news. The story first reports its latest newsworthy development. If the latest development had been evacuations, the lead would have been: "Hundreds of people are being evacuated because of a huge wildfire in eastern Arizona."

2. In leads, use forms of the present or future verb tenses. "The fire is expected to spread," not "The fire was expected to spread today." But don't write in the simple present tense "headline" style: "Twelve buildings are destroyed in a wildfire." Present perfect tense sounds more natural: "A wildfire has destroyed 12 buildings."

3. Keep leads short and to the point. It's easy for listeners and viewers to miss details. Use the lead to introduce a story, and save details for subsequent sentences.

4. Favor the active voice. "Firefighters are working the blaze," not "the blaze is being worked by firefighters."

5. Attribute at the beginning of sentences. "Fire officials say...," not "...said fire officials."

6. Identify newsmakers before naming them. Write: "Fire information officer Ed Toby," not "Ed Toby, the fire information officer, says..." (Unless a name is essential to the story, it can generally be left out.)

7. Omit needless words. "It's the third largest fire in Arizona's history," not "This particular blaze is the third-largest in the history of the state of Arizona."

8. Prefer the simple to the complex. "Fire" or "blaze" but not "conflagration."

9. Don't strain for synonyms. "Arizona," not "the state." Someone who hears "...in the state's history" might not have heard the rest of the story.

10. Use direct quotes only when a paraphrase doesn't work better. In most cases, it does. "There have been no serious injuries," not, "Toby says, 'Two people reported bruises and five others pulled muscles carrying heavy suitcases while being evacuated, but otherwise no one was hurt.'"

11. Simplify numbers. "More than 350 square miles," not "352.67 square miles."

12. Use a variety of sentence lengths, but keep most of them short. The sentences in the fire story are 8, 9, 12, 13, 13 and 19 words long – and that's counting every word, including "a."

A radio story on the fire could include recorded sound of a newsmaker talking:

(*Reporter*) A huge wildfire in eastern Arizona is expected to spread to New Mexico. Both wind and dry lightning are forecast over the next two days.

Arizona fire officials say more than 1,000 firefighters are working the blaze. Fire information officer Ed Toby says still more may be needed:

(*Newsmaker*) *"We already have firefighters from New York, Colorado and Texas helping us. We might bring some more in from California."*

(*Reporter*) There have been no serious injuries, but hundreds of people have been evacuated, and 11 buildings have been destroyed.

The fire has burned more than 350 square miles. It's the third-largest wildfire in Arizona's history.

Always identify newsmakers before their voices are heard. Give a general sense of the subject of the upcoming sound bite, but don't "parrot." Write: "Toby says still more may be needed," not "Toby says firefighters from New York, Colorado and Texas are already helping."

A television story might incorporate not only sound and video, but also locator maps and graphics:

(*Reporter reading over animated map showing fire's location*) A huge wildfire in eastern Arizona is expected to spread to New Mexico. (*Over video of fire*) Both wind and dry lightning are forecast over the next two days.

(*Over video of firefighters working*) Arizona fire officials say more than 1,000 firefighters are working the blaze. Still more may be needed:

(*On-screen identification, seen over shot of newsmaker talking*)
Ed Toby
Fire Information Officer

"*We already have firefighters from New York, Colorado and Texas helping us. We might bring some more in from California.*"

(*Reporter reading over shots of people evacuating; then shots of destroyed buildings*) There have been no serious injuries, but hundreds of people have been evacuated, and 11 buildings have been destroyed.

(*Reporter on-camera, with fire burning in distance*) The fire has burned more than 350 square miles. It's the third-largest wildfire in Arizona's history.

A grasp of these basic concepts will help you go on to create more complicated stories, whether for wires, radio, TV or new media.

Corrections, correctives, clarifications

Factual errors in AP video stories need to be immediately repaired with either a CORRECTION if the story is in that six-hour news cycle, or a CORRECTIVE if the time from the error having occurred to setting the record straight extends beyond six hours.

Both a CORRECTION and a CORRECTIVE must begin with an Editors' Note citing the date of the story's original publication, the original story keyword (or slug) and the specifics of the error. If the error being corrected is of a serious enough nature to materially change the original item, a story KILL should be immediately sent stating: Please KILL the story filed from Switzerland on World Peace on January 31, 2013, titled SWIWORLDPEACE20133101. A replacement item, correcting a material error, will run shortly.

In a CORRECTION, write a brief description of what has gone wrong and how it has been changed. For example: Editors' Note: Please replace the shotlist and storyline in SYRIA FIGHTING first transmitted today Jan. 31 at 1038GMT and slugged SYR FIGHTING 20130131 . This version corrects that the fighting took place in a southern suburb of Idlib and not in the heart of the city as was initially reported.

In a CORRECTIVE where the error is being fixed in a subsequent news cycle — beyond six hours — a similar approach should be taken but a more detailed explanation may be needed depending on the nature of the mistake. For example: Editors' Note: On Jan. 31, 2013, The Associated Press published a story from Switzerland titled SWI WORLD PEACE 20130131 which incorrectly named Fred

Smith as chairman of the Committee for World Peace and described the comments he made as the official view of the organization. Smith in fact held no formal office within the organization, having resigned his position at an earlier meeting. He was participating in the gathering in support of the organization's ideals, but his comments were his personal view and not made formally as a spokesman of, or office bearer on, the committee.

In the case of a CORRECTION, it shall be at the discretion of the senior manager in charge of video production whether the video itself needs to be retransmitted to customers. Updating the script and shotlist may be sufficient. In the case of a CORRECTIVE where changes were necessary to the video or the script/shotlist, all stories must be retransmitted.

In circumstances where a clarification is required but no inaccuracy needs correcting, issue an Editor's Note slugged with the term CLARIFICATION. A rewritten script and shot list should be sent specifying what is clarified in the updated version. So, for example, we might say: "This version clarifies the people seen in shot 7 were villagers heading from the conflict who were given food by an aid agency rather than locals who lived near the aid agency feeding station, as originally stated based on initial information."

Correctives, corrections and clarifications need to be published and posted.

actuality In radio, the sound of a newsmaker talking. Generally, an actuality should be 10 to 20 seconds long. Don't use an actuality just to have newsmaker sound in a story. Use an actuality only if it makes sense, can be clearly understood and contributes something of substance to the story, such as the newsmaker's point of view or the unique way the newsmaker said something. If you, as a reporter or an anchor, can say something more effectively than the newsmaker, write the story without actuality.

b-roll In a video story, the supporting shots and scenes used to provide context and continuity for the main story. B-roll can be file or stock tape containing background or historical information. It is sometimes provided by sources outside the news organization, as when newsmakers provide personal videos.

cut In radio, a piece of audio, whether the sound of a newsmaker talking, a reporter's narrative or natural sound.

fade In radio, a gradual increase (fade-up) or decrease (fade-down) in sound. In video, a gradual increase (fade-in) or decrease (fade-out) in the appearance of video and, usually, in the volume of accompanying sound.

fast file Video segment with in and out points, but no additional edited-in content.

first person In a video piece, a newsmaker's description of a news event or subject matter, presented as one long sound bite.

incue, inq, in-point The first two or three seconds of sound signaling the start of a segment of audio or video. An incue can consist of any man-made or natural sound, including words, music or ambient noise.

live shot Broadcast report delivered in real time from the scene of a news event or a studio or newsroom.

lockout Words used by a reporter to end a radio story. A common format is name and location: *Sagar Meghani, Washington.* See **sigout**.

LSR Live Special Report. Short or long-form live program covering breaking news or a special event. Reports may be anchored from a studio or an outside location.

MOS Man on the street. Sound of randomly chosen people, traditionally walking on a city sidewalk, commenting on a news event. Also known as *vox pops*, shortened form of *vox populi* or *voice of the people*.

natural sound or **NATS** Nonverbal sound of a news event. Natural sound can include ambient sound, such as trucks rumbling or background cheers. It can also be the dominant sound of a news event, such as a band playing or a chainsaw cutting up debris from a storm. For AP Radio, a piece of natural sound should run 30 to 40 seconds, with fades at the beginning and end. Generally, the fade-up is fast (about four seconds) and the fade-down is slow (about eight seconds). If you're writing natural sound into a story for AP, begin with sound up and let it play long enough for the audience to recognize it, then fade down low enough to talk over it.

nonlinear editing Digital video and audio systems that allow editors to swiftly copy video sequences and sound bites in any order onto a new timeline, without altering the original file (recording).

outcue, outq, out-point The final two or three seconds of sound signaling the end of a segment of audio or video. An outcue can consist of any man-made or natural sound, including words, music and/or ambient noise.

package For video, an umbrella term for fully edited stories with sound, fonts and possibly on-camera appearances by reporters. For audio, an umbrella term for fully edited stories with a reporter's voice and possibly newsmaker actuality. An audio package often includes a wrap or voicer and several individual sound bites. See **wrap** and **voicer**.

Q-and-A In radio, a sound bite of a correspondent taken from a question-and-answer session with another colleague. Q-and-A cuts run from 10 to 20 seconds and provide the reporter with a format in which a brief aspect of the story is reported. The rules of balance, objectivity and attribution all apply. A reporter should never express views or draw conclusions. There is no lockout. Reporters and their locations are identified in the anchors' lead-ins. In AP's online video products, Q-and-A pieces show a reporter or newsmaker answering questions posed in writing displayed on a graphic.

raw edit or **rough cut** Video and sound loosely edited together without voice track, reporter presence or font. This allows broadcast customers to have their own newspeople narrate a video package and gives them editing flexibility.

rough cut See **raw edit**.

scener In radio, a report from the actual scene of an event, with the sound of the event in the background. Whether live or taped, a scener must be done while the sounds in the background actually are taking place. The idea is to use words and background sound to create a picture of what's happening in the listener's mind. If you play back tape of an event behind your voice in a studio, that is not a scener – it's a voicer. AP Radio sceners run 35 seconds maximum.

sigout Words used to end a video story. A common format is name and location: *Haven Daley, San Francisco*. See **lockout**.

sound bite Snippet of sound of someone talking.

standup A portion of a video story in which a reporter faces the camera and addresses the audience directly. When a standup appears at the end of a story, it contains a sigout. When a standup appears between two pieces of video in the same story, it is referred to as a bridge. A hand-held standup is when a reporter holds a camera at arm's length and focuses on his or her own face. This allows the reporter to react to and narrate from the scene of a breaking news story.

UGC User-generated content. Information in the form of text, photos, video or audio supplied by users of a product which then becomes part of that product. Websites and, increasingly, TV news broadcasts, often contain UGC.

voice-over or **VO** Sound of a reporter's voice narrating a story as videotape plays. In radio, reporters may also speak over a music or natural sound track.

voice track or **track** Narration of an audio or video piece. In video, it may occur along with a voice-over or standup.

voicer Self-contained radio correspondent report. All the listener hears from beginning to end is the sound of a reporter talking. AP Radio voicers run no more than 35 seconds and end in a lockout: *Sandy Kozel, Washington.* Many voicers are done in-studio. Compare to scener, which has no lockout and must be created at the scene of a news event, with natural sound in the background. See **scener**.

vox pops See **MOS**.

wall-to-wall coverage Continuous broadcast reporting, with few or no interruptions, of a single news story. Generally reserved for transcendent stories, such as the 9/11 terrorist attacks, the outbreak of war or the results of a U.S. presidential election.

wrap A radio voice report that includes both the correspondent and a newsmaker actuality. AP Radio wrap runs no more than 40 seconds and ends in a lockout: *Jerry Bodlander, Capitol Hill.* The newsmaker actuality generally should be no shorter than 10 seconds and no longer than 15 seconds.

PHOTO CAPTIONS

Nearly all AP captions follow a simple formula:

The first sentence of the caption should:

- Describe who is in the photograph and what is going on within the photo in the present tense.

- Name the city and state (or country, if it was made outside the United States) where the image was made, following AP style for the city and state as appropriate.

- Provide the date the photo was made, including the day of the week if the photo was made within the past two weeks, and preceded by a comma. (e.g., Tuesday, Jan. 27, 2015).

These three elements are MANDATORY and no caption is complete without all of them. Names should always be listed in order, left to right, unless it is impossible for the caption to read normally otherwise. With multiple people identified within the caption, enough representations to placement are necessary so there is no confusion as to each subject's identity.

Captions must give attribution for action not seen (e.g., the scene of accident where more than 10 died, according to police).

The second sentence of the caption is used to give context to the news event or describe why the photo is significant. While a second sentence can be illuminating, it also has the potential to create problems and is often where errors can be found. A photo caption's second sentence should be carefully crafted to include information from the text wire story when appropriate or additional relevant observations from the photographer on scene. There may be some instances when a second sentence is not needed. Many sports photos taken during a game or match, for example, do not require a second sentence; nor do photos from some ongoing news events. Most daily pictures of the president do not need a second sentence either.

Most captions should be no more than two concise sentences, while including the relevant information. Try to anticipate what information the reader will need.

THIS IS AN EXAMPLE OF THE STANDARD AP CAPTION:

German Chancellor Angela Merkel addresses the media during a joint news conference with Turkish Prime Minister Ahmet Davutoglu after a meeting at the chancellery in Berlin, Monday, Jan. 12, 2015. (AP Photo/Michael Sohn)

FOR HANDOUT PHOTOS (provided by governments, armies, companies or other official sources):

In this Monday, Feb. 24, 2014, photo provided by the Bureau of Alcohol, Tobacco and Firearms, officials examine the scene of a blast at the Kilgore Flares factory in Toone, Tenn. Hardeman County Sheriff John Doolen told WMC-TV on Monday night that Michael Chism, who was burned over 90 percent of his body in Saturday's blast, has died. (Bureau of Alcohol, Tobacco and Firearms via AP)

The caption should begin with *In this photo released by (or provided by)*, followed by the name of the providing body.

The name of the releasing body is then repeated in the photo credit: The name of the releasing person or organization should be translated according to AP style, where applicable.

We do not use the word "handout" in the caption or photo credit.

ALL handout images from ANY source MUST, as a final step, be examined carefully in Photoshop by at least two editors on the handling regional photo desk. If there is any doubt about the integrity of a handout image, it should not be transmitted.

DO NOT use DESCRIPTIVE OVERLINES such as:

1. SAFE AT SECOND-For a baseball play at second base, or PRESIDENT ADDRESSES WOMEN-For a presidential speech to a women's group. Regular captions have NO overlines.

INSTRUCTIVE OVERLINES will be used in the following cases:

1. For FILE PHOTOS the word FILE will be the OVERLINE.

Example: FILE - In this Jan. 14, 2015, file photo, Russian opposition activist and anti-corruption crusader Alexei Navalny, center, is detained by police officers in Moscow after defying his house arrest to speak on Radio Echo Moskvy. Moscow police detained Navalny on Sunday, Feb. 15, 2015, as he and supporters were handing out leaflets in the subway. (AP Photo/Pavel Golovkin, File)

2. For ADVANCES the OVERLINE is the word ADVANCE and the RELEASE DATE. Do not use story slugs or writer's name in the OVERLINE.

Example: ADVANCE FOR WEEKEND EDITIONS, NOV. 8-9 - In this Oct. 28, 2014, photo, California's Penina Davidson plays during a practice in Berkeley, Calif. Davidson has found a home at Cal after an unusual collaboration between the two coaches for the longtime rival schools. (AP Photo/Ben Margot)

3. For EMBARGOED photos the OVERLINE should be the word EMBARGOED with the RELEASE TIME and DATE. Also, add HFR (Hold for Release) in the SUPPLEMENTAL CATEGORY field of the NAA/IPTC header for embargoed photos for same day release.

Example: EMBARGOED UNTIL 5 A.M. EST, FRIDAY, FEB. 13, 2015 - This undated photo provided by Sotheby's shows a white diamond before being crafted into an emerald-cut diamond, which Sotheby's will auction in New York on April 21. The 100-carat emerald-cut diamond, which Sotheby's says is internally flawless, was mined in South Africa and weighed over 200 carats in the rough. (Sotheby's via AP)

If the date when the photo was made is unknown, state "undated photo" in the body of the caption and in the INSTRUCTIONS field of the NAA/IPTC header.

CAPTION SIGNOFFS:

The caption SIGNOFF for a photo by an AP staff or freelance photographer is, in parentheses, AP Photo followed by a slash and the name of the photographer. Don't use str or stf. Example: (AP Photo/Rick Bowmer). If the name of the photographer is not known or needs to be withheld, the signoff is: (AP Photo).

The SIGNOFF for all other photos (i.e. photos NOT owned by AP) is, in parentheses, the photographer's name followed by a slash, then the source followed by "via AP."

MEMBER PHOTO SIGNOFF: (Anne Ryan/USA Today via AP)

HANDOUT PHOTO SIGNOFF: (General Motors via AP). If photographer is known: (John Smith/General Motors via AP).

TV FRAMEGRAB PHOTO SIGNOFF: (KABC-TV via AP)

FILE PHOTO SIGNOFF: File photos have a comma and space followed by File at the end of the signoff inside the parentheses. Example: (AP Photo/Lenny Ignelzi, File). If the name of the photographer who shot the file photo is not known, the signoff should be: (AP Photo/File)

POOL PHOTO SIGNOFF: Pool photos shot by staff photographers, freelancers and members have a comma and space followed by Pool at the end of the signoff inside the parentheses. For example (AP Photo/Richard Drew, Pool) or (Mark Henle/The Arizona Republic via AP, Pool). For pool photos from another agency, we name the photographer who shot the pool photo, but do not name the agency that the photographer was working for. In this case, the signoff is written like this: (Photographer/Pool Photo via AP). In all cases, put the name of the organization that shot the pool in the SOURCE field after the word Pool, for example, Pool AP. The BYLINE TITLE field of the NAA/IPTC header should contain the word POOL. The Instructions field should also say POOL PHOTO.

HANDOUT PHOTOS:

The use of handout photos requires the written permission of the copyright owner whenever possible. When it is not possible to contact the copyright owner, we may get written permission from the copyright owner's authorized agent, such as a family spokesperson. The AP has two categories of handout photos, with byline titles **HOGP** and **HONS**.

HOGP: These are handout photos produced by a government body, such as NASA, the Department of Defense, a state or local police department, etc. When it is determined that a photo fits this category, it should be given HOGP as a byline title, and the following HOGP language should be added to the INSTRUCTIONS field:
AP provides access to this publicly distributed handout photo provided by [source goes here]. Mandatory credit.

HONS: These are handout photos obtained for approved, story-specific use only. This includes family photos, as well as editorial publicity photos that are provided to the AP to accompany stories about products, movies, books, etc. When it has been determined that a photo fits this category, it should be given HONS as a byline title, and the following HONS language should be added to the INSTRUCTIONS field:

AP provides access to this handout photo to be used solely to illustrate news reporting or commentary on the facts or events depicted in this image. This image may only be used for 14 days from the time of transmission; No Archiving; No Licensing. Mandatory credit.

CAPTION CORRECTIONS, ADDITIONS, PHOTO KILLS

An AP caption **CORRECTION** is moved when a simple and nonlibelous error occurs in a caption. Examples would be a misspelled name, wrong hometown, sports score or date. The procedure AP uses to file a caption correction is to point out the information that is being corrected in an overline at the start of the caption and to write a corrected caption in publishable form following. The word **CORRECTION** is added to the **OBJECT NAME** field in the NAA/IPTC header.

Example of a caption CORRECTION:

CORRECTS TO HOUSTON ASTROS OUTFIELDERS, NOT ATLANTA BRAVES OUTFIELDERS – Houston Astros outfielders, from left, J.D. Martinez, Delino DeShields and George Springer celebrate after a spring exhibition baseball game against the Atlanta Braves, Friday, Feb. 28, 2014, in Kissimmee, Fla. The Astros won 7-5. (AP Photo/John Doe)

An AP caption **ADDITION** is moved when the original caption is incomplete but otherwise accurate. An AP caption **ADDITION** may add the name of someone in the photo or other important background information. The same procedure is followed for an AP caption **ADDITION** as for a caption **CORRECTION**.

Example of a caption ADDITION:

ADDS NAME OF ATHLETE – Biathlete Mykhaylo Tkachenko, representing Ukraine, enters the arena during the opening ceremony of the 2014 Winter Paralympics at the Fisht Olympic stadium in Sochi, Russia, Friday, March 7, 2014. (AP Photo/John Doe)

An AP PHOTO **KILL** is issued when there are problems with a photo's integrity or authenticity, questions about a photo's copyright ownership or other potential legal problems, or when the caption misrepresents the photo in some way. When this occurs, an AP PHOTO **KILL** form is moved alerting members and subscribers, illustrating the image with a circle and line through the image. The first sentence of the caption is clear directive to remove the photo from any archives and a description of the image, including the transref number, slug and date it was transmitted. The second sentence provides a clear and simple reason why the photo is being killed. An optional third sentence provides information about whether another photo will be moved to replace the killed image.

Example of a photo KILL:
EDITORS AND LIBRARIANS: KILL FROM YOUR SYSTEMS AND ARCHIVES PHOTO CAET683 OF JAN. 9, 2014, SLUGGED US MUSIC-FORUM-THE EAGLES. THE PHOTO WAS RETOUCHED AT THE SOURCE. A NEW VERSION OF THE PHOTO, WITH THE RETOUCHED PORTION CROPPED OUT OF THE IMAGE, WILL MOVE AS CAET701. (AP PHOTO)

NAA/IPTC HEADER FIELDS

Byline: The Byline field lists the name of the person who made the photo.

Byline Title: The Byline Title field lists the title of the person who made the photo, or in the case of a handout, indicates the photo is provided by a third party. This typically comes from a controlled list, with acceptable values of STF, STR, FRE, HOGP, HONS, CTR, MBR, MBO, MBI, POOL and SUB.

Caption: The Caption field is the text that accompanies the photo, containing the information of who, what, where and when, plus additional information, if necessary, to provide context in describing the photograph.

Caption Writer: The Caption Writer field lists the initials of all the people who wrote or edited the caption, header fields or image file. This includes toning and pixel editing.

Category: The Category field lists codes that aid in a more detailed search. (See category definitions in this section.)

City: The City field lists where the photo was originally made. For file photos, do not use the transmission point's city.

Country: The Country field lists the ISO Alpha-3 code where the photo was originally made. For file photos, do not put the transmission point's country.

Create Date Time: The Create Date Time field is the date the photo was originally made. For file photos, use the date the photo was originally made, if known. Vague dates (using zeros where exact dates are unknown) can be used in this field.

Credit: The Credit field is the name of the service transmitting the photo.

Headline: The Headline field primarily contains the names of those represented within the image delimited by a comma.

Instructions: The Instructions field lists special notations that apply uniquely to a photo, such as if the photo is from files, a correction or advance. This field may also contain restrictions on the use or outs.

Object Name: The Object Name field lists the story slug associated with a photo. For photos without a story, Associated Press photographers or photo editors will make up a logical slug to aid in a search. If a related story moves on DataStream, the photo should be retransmitted with the appropriate OBJECT NAME to match the story. This field should not contain punctuation marks, such as apostrophes, ampersands, currency symbols, asterisks and most others. Exceptions to this are the underscore (_) and the hyphen (-).

Source: The Source field lists who is the original provider of a photo, typically the owner of the image. Such as: AP, an AP member, pool photo provider or handout photo provider.

State: The State field lists the state where the photo was originally made. Use U.S. postal code abbreviations. For file photos, do not use the transmission point's state.

Supp Categories: The Supplemental Categories field lists codes that aid in a more detailed search for a photo. (See supplemental categories definitions in this section.)

Trans Reference: The Trans Reference field lists a call letter/number combination associated with a photo. It may include an originating transmit point's call letters and picture number from that point's sequence of offerings for a given day. Example: NY105. Most likely it will contain the postal state code from where the image was transmitted, combined with two character initials of the person transmitting the image. This should NOT include an extension for the file type, such as .JPG.

SUPPLEMENTAL CATEGORIES

GENERAL:
ADV Advance
APN APNewsfeatures
ENT Entertainment, celebrities (don't use the word people)
FEA Feature pictures of a non-news nature
FILE File photo
HFR Hold for Release (embargoed photos for same day release)
MAP Map or graphic
NAT National Geographic package
SPF Special Features package
SPCL Special
WEA Weather

NEWS EVENTS:
CVN National political conventions
ELN For election cycles only
XGR State legislatures

SPORTS: (See full list in Sports Guidelines.)
ATH Athletics (Track & Field)
BAD Badminton
BBA Professional Baseball (American League)
BBC College Baseball Men
BBH High School Baseball
BBI International Baseball
BBM Minor League Baseball
BBN Professional Baseball (National League)
BBO Professional Baseball (Other)
BBW Baseball Women
BBY Youth Baseball (Little League)
BIA Biathalon
BKC College Basketball Men
BKH High School Basketball
BKL Basketball-Women's Pro (WNBA)
BKN NBA Basketball
BKO Basketball (Other)
BKW Basketball-Women's College
BOB Bobsledding

BOX Boxing
CAR Auto Racing
CER Olympic Ceremony
CRI Cricket
CYC Bicycle Racing
DIV Diving
EQU Equestrian
FBC College Football
FBH High School Football
FBN NFL Football
FBO Football (other)
FIG Figure Skating
GLF Golf
GYM Gymnastics
HKC College Hockey
HKN NHL Hockey
HKO Hockey (Other)
JUD Judo
JUM Ski Jumping
LUG Luge
OLY Olympics
RAC Racing (animals)
RUG Rugby
SHO Skeet Shooting
SKI Alpine Skiing
SOC Soccer
SOF Softball
SPE Speed Skating
SWM Swimming
SYN Synchronized Swimming
TEN Tennis
TTN Table Tennis
VBB Beach Volleyball
VBL Volleyball
WRE Wrestling
WTL Weightlifting
WTP Water Polo
YAT Yachting

AP Caption and NAA/IPTC Header
Quick Reference Guide

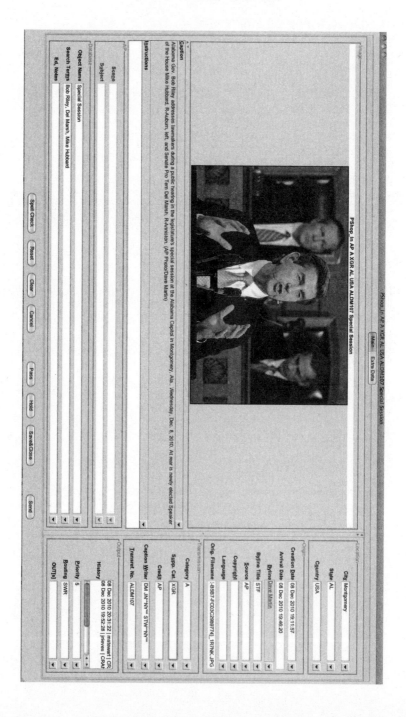

EDITING MARKS

¶ ATLANTA (AP)—The organization	indent for paragraph
said Thursday. It was the first	paragraph
the last attempts.	no paragraph
With this the president tried	
the Jones Smith company is not	transpose
over a period of sixty or more years	use figures
there were 9 in the group.	spell it out
Ada, Oklahoma is the hometown	abbreviate
The Ga man was the guest of	don't abbreviate
prince edward said it was his	uppercase
as a result This will be	lowercase
the ac cuser pointed to them	remove space
In these times it is necessary	insert space
the order for the later devices	retain
The ruling a fine example	insert word
according to the this source	delete
BF ⊐ By DONALD AMES ⊏	boldface, center
J.R. Thomas⌉	flush right
⌈J.R. Thomas	flush left
⌃	insert comma
⌄	insert apostrophe
⌄ ⌄	insert quotation marks
⊗ or ⊙	insert period
=	hyphen
⊢—⊣	dash

BIBLIOGRAPHY

The following are standard references for the AP Stylebook and for material not covered by the Stylebook.

First reference for spelling, style, usage and foreign geographic names:
Webster's New World College Dictionary, Fifth Edition, Houghton Mifflin Harcourt, Boston and New York, 2014.

Other references for spelling, style, usage and foreign geographic names:
The American Heritage Dictionary of the English Language, Fifth Edition, Houghton Mifflin Harcourt, Boston and New York, 2011.
http://www.ahdictionary.com/
Concise Oxford English Dictionary, Twelfth Edition, Oxford University Press, Oxford, 2011.
Webster's Third New International Dictionary of the English Language, unabridged, Merriam-Webster, Springfield, Mass., 1993.
National Geographic Atlas of the World, 10th Edition, 2014. National Geographic Society, Washington, D.C.
http://maps.nationalgeographic.com/maps

For aircraft names:
IHS Jane's All the World's Aircraft, IHS, Englewood, Colo.

For military ships:
IHS Jane's Fighting Ships, IHS, Englewood, Colo.

For nonmilitary ships:
Lloyd's Register of Ships, IHS, Englewood, Colo.

For railroads:
Official Railway Guide — Freight Service Edition; JOC Group Inc., Newark, N.J.

For federal government questions:
Congressional Directory; U.S. Government Printing Office, Washington, D.C. This link allows searching of the directory for the 104th Congress (1995-1996) through the 113th Congress (2013-2014).
http://www.gpo.gov/fdsys/browse/collection.action?collectionCode=CDIR

For foreign government questions:
Political Handbook of the World, 2014; CQ Press, an imprint of SAGE Publications, Washington, D.C.

For a company's formal name:
Consult the national stock exchanges: the New York Stock Exchange, http://www.nyse.com, or Nasdaq, http://www.nasdaq.com.

For religion questions:
Handbook of Denominations in the United States, 13th Edition, 2010; Abingdon Press, Nashville, Tenn., and New York.
World Christian Encyclopedia; Second Edition, 2001; Oxford University Press, New York, N.Y. http://worldchristiandatabase.org
Yearbook of American and Canadian Churches, 2012; Abingdon Press, Nashville, Tenn., and New York, for the National Council of Churches of Christ in the U.S.A., N.Y.

For medical questions:
Centers for Disease Control and Prevention: http://www.cdc.gov/
The Merck Manuals Online Medical Library: http://www.merck.com/mmpe/index.html
U.S. National Library of Medicine and the National Institutes of Health, MedlinePlus: http://www.nlm.nih.gov/medlineplus/

Other references and writing guides consulted in the preparation of the AP Stylebook:
Bernstein, Theodore M. *The Careful Writer: A Modern Guide to English Usage.* Free Press, Second Edition, 1995.
Bernstein, Theodore M. *More Language That Needs Watching.* Channel Press, 1962.
Bernstein, Theodore M. *Watch Your Language.* Channel Press, 1958.
Cappon, Rene J. *The Word.* The Associated Press, 1982; Second Edition, 1991.
Follett, Wilson. *Modern American Usage: A Guide.* lst rev. ed. Revised by Erik Wensberg. New York: Hill and Wang, 1998.
Fowler, H.W. *A Dictionary of Modern English Usage*, Second Edition, Rev., Oxford University Press, 1965.
Fowler, H.W. and R.W. Burchfield. *Fowler's Modern English Usage*, Rev. Third Edition. Oxford University Press, 2004.
The Chicago Manual of Style, 16th Edition. University of Chicago Press, 2010.
Morris, William and Morris, Mary. *Harper Dictionary of Contemporary Usage.* Harper & Row, 1975; Second Edition, 1985.
Newton, Harry, *Newton's Telecom Dictionary*, 28th Updated & Expanded Edition. Harry Newton Publishing. 2014.
Shaw, Harry. *Dictionary of Problem Words & Expressions.* McGraw Hill Book Co., 1975; Revised Edition, 1987.
Skillin, Marjorie E. and Gay, Robert M. *Words into Type*, Third Edition. Prentice-Hall Inc., 1974.
Strunk, William Jr. and White, E.B. *The Elements of Style*, Second Edition. The Macmillan Co., 1972. New Edition: 4th Edition. Longman 1999.

ABOUT THE AP

Since 1846, The Associated Press has been on the scene wherever news is breaking. AP is a not-for-profit newsgathering cooperative whose content — across subjects, formats and continents — is seen by half of the world's population every day. Our unmatched expertise in global newsgathering, distribution and service makes AP the most trusted, definitive source for news.

The AP's mission is to get it first but first get it right, and to be the first choice for news, by providing the fastest, most accurate reporting from every corner of the globe across all media types and platforms.

Headquartered in New York, AP delivers coverage of news, sports, business, weather, entertainment, politics, lifestyles and technology in text, audio, video, graphics, photos and interactives. AP is also a leader in developing and marketing innovative newsroom technology and newsgathering services.

AP does what it takes to get the story, even in the world's most dangerous and challenging places. Our global network of journalists work in more than 280 locations in 110 countries worldwide. Journalists staff every statehouse in the United States, providing unrivaled access to more sources of information and newsmakers.

The extensive network that is the AP grew from a single notion more than a century and a half ago: that cooperation can help authoritative news reach readers faster.

In late 1846, hostilities began in what would become the Mexican War. American newspapers, most based in the Northeast at the time, faced huge obstacles in reporting the conflict.

War reports for the New York Sun were sent from Mexico to Mobile, Alabama, by boat, rushed by special pony express to Montgomery and then 700 miles by U.S. Mail stagecoach to the southern terminus of the newly invented — and costly — telegraph near Richmond, Virginia. That express gave the Sun an edge of 24 hours or more on papers using regular mail.

But Moses Yale Beach, the Sun's publisher, relinquished that advantage by inviting other New York publishers to join a cooperative venture. Five newspapers signed on: the Sun, the Journal of Commerce, the Courier and Enquirer, the Herald and the Express. It was the beginning of the AP.

AP assumed its modern legal form in 1900 when it incorporated as a not-for-profit cooperative under the Membership Corporation Law of New York state. Today, the AP membership elects the board of directors, the cooperative's governing body.

AP staffers are governed by a comprehensive ethics statement, available for viewing at http://www.ap.org/company/news-values.

Nearly 170 years since its inception, AP remains the undisputed source for news, delivering fast, unbiased news globally to all media platforms and formats.

HEADQUARTERS
The Associated Press
450 W. 33rd St.
New York, NY 10001
212-621-1500

Order an AP Stylebook product

You can learn more about all of our AP Stylebook products and place your order on our secure website: **apstylebook.com**.

You can pay by credit card or you can place your order and create a PDF invoice to mail in a check, if you prefer.

The mailing address for Stylebook check payments is:
The Associated Press
P.O. Box 415458
Boston, MA 02241-5458

Product and rate details for the spiral-bound AP Stylebook, AP Stylebook Online, AP Stylebook & Webster's New World Online, AP Style Quizzes, AP Stylebook Mobile, AP Lingofy and AP StyleGuard are available on **apstylebook.com**.

Order Form

Qty	Item	Del	Unit Price	Total
	choose a product	✖	0.00	$0.00
	choose a product	✖	0.00	$0.00
	choose a product	✖	0.00	$0.00
	choose a product	✖	0.00	$0.00
	choose a product	✖	0.00	$0.00
	choose a product	✖	0.00	$0.00
	choose a product	✖	0.00	$0.00
			Subtotal	$0.00
			Tax	$0.00
			Shipping	$0.00
			Total Due	**$0.00**
			Total Due at Checkout	**$0.00**

AP does not accept returns. If you are ordering books, please order only the exact number you need.

Stylebook offers 24/7 support

Whether you have a question about when you can get the next edition of the spiral-bound Stylebook, how to reset your Stylebook Online password or how to pay for an order by check, AP Stylebook can help. We have answers to many of the most common questions listed on our self-service help center: **apstylebook.com/help**.

You can browse by topic to find what you need or search the help center to get an answer. If you don't find the answer to your question, we offer a toll-free number to call and a form to request help via email, so you can get a personal response 24 / 7.

We value your business. We want to make it easy for you to get answers any time of day or night.

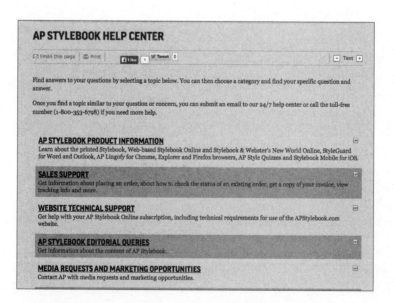

AP Stylebook Online

AP Stylebook Online is a fully searchable version of the AP Stylebook, complete with interactive features, links and customization options. This Web-based reference guide includes all the content you love about the Stylebook and adds online-only features:

– Submit questions via "Ask the Editor" and search thousands of previously answered questions in the archive.

– Look up phonetic spellings of hundreds of words and hear audio files as well in our Pronunciation Guide.

– Stylebook Online is updated throughout the year as AP's editors add or change style guidance. Users can get email updates whenever a change is made.

The website is mobile optimized and your subscription now also includes AP Stylebook Mobile, an iOS app that syncs with your account. We also offer a Microsoft Office app so you can use your subscription to search or browse Stylebook Online entries within Microsoft Word at no additional charge.

Rates are based on the number of users, and for many organizations, it is more affordable than hard-copy books.

Learn more at **apstylebook.com/web**.

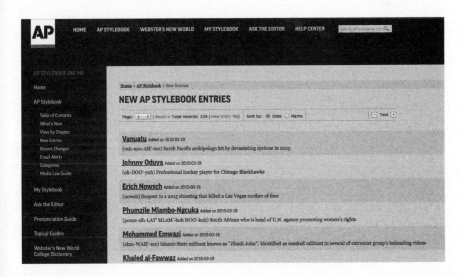

AP Stylebook & Webster's New World Online

Webster's New World College Dictionary has been AP Stylebook's first reference for spelling, style, usage and foreign geographic names for decades.

Now AP is collaborating with Houghton Mifflin Harcourt to include 185,000 definitions from the fifth edition of Webster's New World College Dictionary together in a subscription service: AP Stylebook & Webster's New World Online.

With Stylebook & Webster's New World Online, a single search delivers results from both your trusted journalist's resource and our primary dictionary and clearly identifies the source of each entry.

Learn more at **apstylebook.com/websters**.

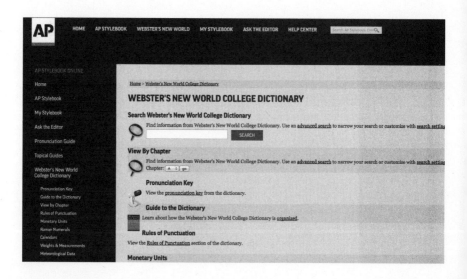

AP StyleGuard

AP StyleGuard, powered by Equiom Linguistic Labs, is a powerful yet easy solution that integrates with Microsoft Word and Outlook, providing automatic checking of your text for AP style while you are writing or editing.

Using defined structure and rules similar to Word's spelling and grammar checking, AP StyleGuard helps ensure the consistency of your writing style. It saves you the time of manually referring to the AP Stylebook and offers recommendations on items you might not have realized are covered by AP style.

AP StyleGuard helps you stay on top of all of the current spelling, grammar, punctuation and usage guidelines from the journalist's bible. StyleGuard includes the latest AP Stylebook guidance, with rules updated throughout the year to keep your writing covered by the newest additions and changes responding to news events and the evolution of the language.

StyleGuard for Word operates on Windows XP and higher and on Microsoft Office 2007 and higher. A Mac-compatible version operates on Mac OS X 10.6 through 10.9 running Office for Mac 2011 and Safari 5.17 or above. StyleGuard for Outlook runs on Microsoft Outlook 2007, 2010 and 2013 on PCs.

Learn more at **apstylebook.com/styleguard**.

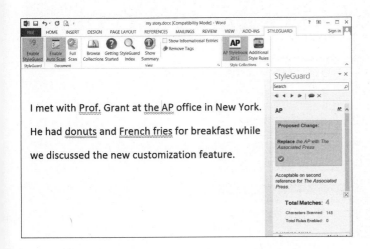

AP Lingofy

AP Lingofy proofs the content you create in Web browsers, helping find errors in spelling, usage and AP style as you post to WordPress, Blogger, Twitter, Tumblr, Facebook and more.

AP Lingofy is a Web browser plug-in powered by Tansa Systems's advanced proofing engine, providing automated style checking directly in the most popular browsers, including Mozilla Firefox, Internet Explorer and Google's Chrome. Unlike traditional spellcheckers, Lingofy is a server-based solution that parses text in phrases, applying advanced algorithms, which allows greater precision in flagging errors in spelling, AP style and usage.

The Lingofy dictionaries are highly customizable and provide a personal dictionary in which you can enter and maintain your own terms, such as:

– Proper names of people, places and products

– Common typos

– Pet peeves

– Warning words, such as vulgarities, cliches and jargon

Learn more at **apstylebook.com/lingofy**.

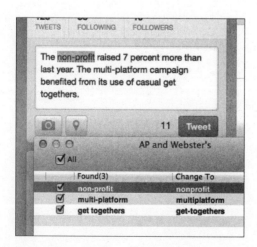

AP Style Quizzes

Test your knowledge of AP style and usage with online quizzes from AP Stylebook. As a quiz subscriber you will have access to about 60 multiple-choice quizzes compiled by David Minthorn, one of the editors of the AP Stylebook.

Choose your answers, click to submit and get your results showing which answers were right or wrong, along with the corresponding style rule to explain why each right answer is correct.

Take each quiz as many times as you like, in whatever order you like. AP Style Quizzes keep track of your results so you can see which quizzes you have not yet taken or which topics you might want to review.

If you want to brag about your score to your friends, we make it easy to share your results on Facebook and Twitter.

Quiz topics include apostrophes, plurals, travel, science, sports, religion, fashion and military.

Learn more at **apstylebook.com/quizzes**.

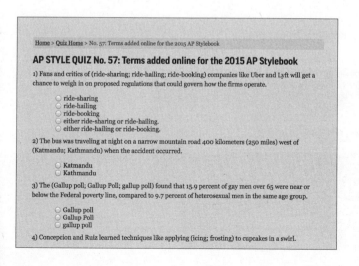

AP STYLE QUIZ No. 57: Terms added online for the 2015 AP Stylebook

1) Fans and critics of (ride-sharing; ride-hailing; ride-booking) companies like Uber and Lyft will get a chance to weigh in on proposed regulations that could govern how the firms operate.

○ ride-sharing
○ ride-hailing
○ ride-booking
○ either ride-sharing or ride-hailing.
○ either ride-hailing or ride-booking.

2) The bus was traveling at night on a narrow mountain road 400 kilometers (250 miles) west of (Katmandu; Kathmandu) when the accident occurred.

○ Katmandu
○ Kathmandu

3) The (Gallup poll; Gallup Poll; gallup poll) found that 15.9 percent of gay men over 65 were near or below the Federal poverty line, compared to 9.7 percent of heterosexual men in the same age group.

○ Gallup poll
○ Gallup Poll
○ gallup poll

4) Concepcion and Ruiz learned techniques like applying (icing; frosting) to cupcakes in a swirl.

Manual de Estilo Online de la AP

The Associated Press offers a Spanish-language Stylebook for publishers, broadcasters and readers from all Spanish-speaking countries, with an emphasis on Latin America and the United States.

Manual de Estilo Online de la AP is a Web-based, searchable, customizable stylebook with a comprehensive list of thousands of the most common standardized Spanish terms, some translated from the English AP Stylebook and the majority written especially for Spanish writers and editors.

This style guide includes extensive chapters on sports and entertainment vocabulary, as well as a pronunciation guide with audio files of hundreds of place names and terms.

The section on Social Media Guidelines lays out AP standards for tweeting, retweeting others' tweets and sourcing and attribution from social media. It also includes frequently used Internet terms and social media language used by the AP such as blog, hashtag, emoticon, metadata and tuitear (tweet).

AP updates Manual de Estilo throughout the year, adding new entries and modifying existing entries.

Rates are based on the number of users, and the website is mobile optimized so you can use it on your desktop, laptop, smartphone or tablet.

Learn more at **manualdeestiloap.com.**

AP Mobile

The Associated Press' fast, accurate and trusted news is available on your smartphone and tablet device through the AP Mobile application. AP Mobile is your first choice for global and local news on the go.

Get breaking U.S. and international news from the world's most trusted news source, plus local stories from regional news sources. Choose to see the content that interests you most, whether it's the latest sports updates, entertainment highlights, global news or the latest from your hometown. Access the best of the AP's award-winning photography, watch videos and check out rich multimedia news coverage.

Let AP Mobile be your first choice for accurate global and local news every day. The latest version of AP Mobile is now available through iTunes, Google Play and Amazon app stores.

Get more information and download the AP Mobile app at **ap.org/apmobile**.

AP Planner

The AP Planner provides journalists with a rolling calendar of important events to support their research and planning. The interactive database contains over 140,000 calendar entries organized in more than 100 categories. Topics include major international news events, political activities, news conferences, court cases, awareness days, legislative activities, key financial and economic announcements, trade and consumer conferences, and other events around news, politics, entertainment and finance.

For more information or to request a trial of AP Planner, visit **applanner.com**.

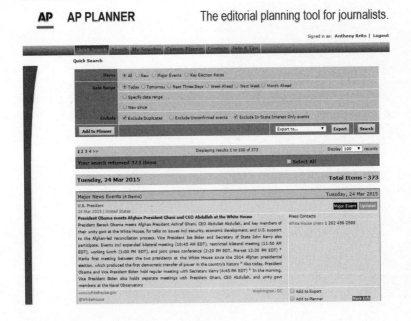